Volume 27

DIRECTORY OF WORLD CINEMA SCOTLAND

Edited by Bob Nowlan and Zach Finch

intellect Bristol, UK / Chicago, USA

First published in the UK in 2015 by
Intellect Books, The Mill, Parnall Road, Fishponds, Bristol, BS16 3JG, UK

First published in the USA in 2015 by Intellect Books, The University of Chicago Press,
1427 E. 60th Street, Chicago, IL 60637, USA

A catalogue record for this book is available from the British Library.

Publisher: May Yao
Publishing Managers: Jelena Stanovnik and Heather Gibson

Cover photograph: *Trainspotting*, courtesy of the British Film Institute.
Cover designer: Holly Rose
Copy-editor: Emma Rhys
Typesetter: John Teehan

Directory of World Cinema ISSN 2040-7971
Directory of World Cinema eISSN 2040-798X

Directory of World Cinema: Scotland ISBN 978-1-78320-394-9
Directory of World Cinema: Scotland eISBN 978-1-78320-395-6

Printed and bound by Short Run Press, UK.

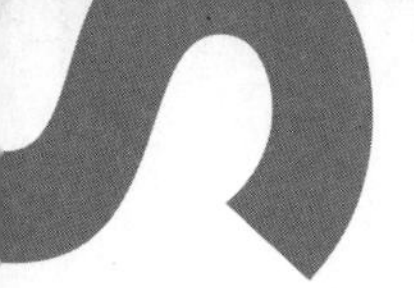

DIRECTORY OF WORLD CINEMA

SCOTLAND

Acknowledgements 5

Introduction by the Editors 6

Industry Spotlight 11
Production

Marketing Mix 19
Finance

Location 25
Gaelic Film-making In Scotland

Cultural Crossover 31
Radical and Engaged Cinema

Directors 46
Bill Douglas
Bill Forsyth
Murray Grigor
Ken Loach
David Mackenzie
Peter Mullan
Lynne Ramsay
Margaret Tait

Mythic Visions: Critique and Counter-Critique 90
Essay
Reviews

From Social Realism To Social Art Cinema and Beyond 180
Essay
Reviews

Comedy, Fantasy and Horror 266
Essay
Reviews

Documentary 322
Essay
Reviews

Recommended Reading 346

Scottish Cinema Online 354

Test Your Knowledge 360

Notes On Contributors 363

Filmography 368

ACKNOWLEDGEMENTS

We thank all of our fellow contributors for their dedication, patience and insight. We thank Stephanie Turner for alerting us to the opportunity to propose editing and writing this book, as well as for bringing us to the attention of Intellect. At Intellect, we thank Amy Damutz, May Yao, Melanie Marshall, Jelena Stanovnik and Heather Gibson for their indispensable support and assistance in making this book possible. We thank Janet McBain, retired curator with the Scottish Screen Archive, for her early encouragement and help in initially contacting potential contributors. We thank Tony Dykes of the British Film Institute and Jennifer Armitage of Creative Scotland for their help in providing us images. And, for painstaking assistance in formatting and typescript preparation, we thank Alex Long and David Hammersborg. We also thank Emma Rhys for her meticulous and thorough work in copy-editing.

Bob thanks the staff of the Scottish Screen Archive for their generosity during his visit to screen and take notes on films during July 2012. He also acknowledges the invaluable assistance provided by the University of Wisconsin-Eau Claire first through a university research and creative activity grant in the spring semester of 2013 and second by way of sabbatical throughout the 2013–14 academic year. Bob thanks his colleagues in the English Department at the University of Wisconsin-Eau Claire for their interest and support, as well as the students in his Fall 2010 and Fall 2012 Scottish Cinema classes, and in his Spring 2011 Scottish Crime Fiction class, for the same. He thanks, in addition, all the indie rock, pop, folk, folk rock and folktronica musicians from Scotland he has featured on his weekly radio show, *Insurgence*, for many years, and who continually reinforce his strongly felt sense of connection with Scotland. And, above all else, he thanks his co-editor Zach Finch, and his partner and husband Andy Swanson, both of whom have given far more than can possibly be recounted in this short space to make this book a reality.

Zach thanks his co-editor, Bob Nowlan, for his patience, guidance, friendship and much more; his partner and wife, Dana Bertelsen, for her steadfast support; his parents, Don and Connie Finch; William H Phillips; the University of Wisconsin-Eau Claire English Faculty; the North Carolina State University Film Studies Faculty; and the University of Wisconsin-Milwaukee English and Film Studies Faculty for everything they have done to help him in his work on this book.

INTRODUCTION BY THE EDITORS

Scotland is a small nation, and, as of the present writing, yet still part of the United Kingdom of Great Britain and Northern Ireland, where Scotland is a nation within a kingdom comprised of the four nations of England, Scotland, Wales and Northern Ireland. Within the United Kingdom as a whole, approximately 83.5 per cent of the population lives in England, approximately 8.5 per cent lives in Scotland, approximately 5 per cent lives in Wales and approximately 3 per cent lives in Northern Ireland. Even so, Scotland comprises approximately one-third of the physical territory comprising the United Kingdom, while England comprises a little over one-half. Nevertheless, England has long occupied a multiply privileged position within the United Kingdom as a whole, leading many foreigners, especially in the United States, often enough to use 'England', 'Britain' and 'the United Kingdom' interchangeably, and even to refer to Scots as English – much to the justified annoyance of Scots themselves.

Scots have exerted an enormous impact on world history (with Scots' contributions as scientific inventors and to the philosophical legacy of the European Enlightenment serving as merely two of the most famous examples of this impact). In addition, Scotland and Scottishness have long exercised a considerable global fascination and appeal (Scotland continues to attract a significantly higher level of tourism, given its share of the population, than the rest of the United Kingdom, while serving as a seemingly endlessly protean stimulus for romance and myth). What's more, even over the course of the now over 300-plus years since the Act of Union in 1707 that effectively eliminated Scotland as an independently sovereign nation-state, Scotland has retained a highly distinct national culture as well as many highly distinct – and highly influential – social institutions (including in areas, for example, of law, education, religion and the provision of social welfare). 'Scots' is itself today widely recognized by many linguistics scholars as a full-fledged language in its own right, not simply a dialect of English, while Scottish English is full of words and phrases, as well as marked by accents and pronunciations, that diverge considerably from what is commonplace in much of England. At the same time, as surveys of public opinion in recent decades repeatedly attest, Scots today identify as Scottish in much higher proportions than they do as British. In addition, since 1999, with the re-establishment of the Scottish parliament and the devolution of significant self-governing authority – and national autonomy – to a Scottish government elected by the Scottish people, Scottish distinctiveness is now routinely manifest and widely acknowledged, even by staunch Unionists (i.e. by those who oppose full Scottish independence, and who instead support the continuation of Scotland within the United Kingdom, and the continued ultimate subordination of the Scottish government in Edinburgh to the United Kingdom government in Westminster).

One striking recent illustration of Scotland's distinctiveness showed up in the results of the May 2010 UK parliament election, where the Labour Party comfortably won the largest number of votes across Scotland, while the Conservative Party comfortably won the largest number of votes across much of England. Post-election-results maps of the United Kingdom often depicted Scotland as overwhelmingly red, for Labour, and England as overwhelmingly blue, for Conservative. Indeed, Scotland has maintained – post-Thatcher, post-New Labour, and throughout the late twentieth century and early twenty-first century epoch of neo-liberal economic orthodoxy broadly uniting the politically centre-left with the politically centre-right – significantly stronger support for a continuing social democratic form of welfare state capitalist society (as well as for a culture that privileges communal social bonds and the virtues of class-based collective solidarity over individualism and privatization) than in much of England (even though, as many on the broad left have extensively argued and thoroughly documented, Scotland remains, in practice, far from a substantially egalitarian society). Another, more recent, illustration of the sharp political difference between Scotland and England occurred in the May 2011 Scottish parliamentary election, where the Scottish National Party, which only operates in Scotland, won a majority of seats in the Scottish parliament to continue another four years in charge of the Scottish government. This election result is all the more remarkable because the system of election to the Scottish parliament is deliberately designed to make it much more difficult than in the case of the UK parliament for a single party to win an outright majority. Finally, and potentially far more significant than either of the two preceding examples, a nationwide referendum on Scottish independence is due to take place in September of 2014. Even if this referendum fails to win a majority, Scots today overwhelmingly support devolution of yet further governmental powers to the Scottish parliament from the UK Parliament such that, whatever the result of the vote come September of 2014, Scotland is almost certain to become steadily more distinct within, and steadily more autonomous versus, the rest of the United Kingdom. In addition, as many scholars have compellingly argued, Scotland has achieved an extent of cultural devolution over the course of the past thirty years that has, if anything, exceeded that of political devolution.

Yet what it means to be Scottish, and what is conceived to be distinctive about Scotland and Scottishness – past and present – continue to function as sites of intense contestation, especially among Scots themselves. Scotland, in fact, encompasses 'many Scotlands' with their own considerably distinct characteristics in turn – and these 'Scotlands' can be distinguished along lines of region, locale, class, ethnicity, gender, sexuality, generation, subcultural affiliation, political identification, language, religion, and yet many more lines of demarcation. At the same time, the history of modern Scotland has been obsessed with *imagined* Scotlands and *imagined* Scottishnesses, as well as with *myths* of Scotland, and *myths* of Scottishness. These are neither simple falsehoods, nor illusions (let alone delusions), not by any means. These are, instead, ways people have represented to themselves and to others what they conceive Scotland and Scottishness to be – and to mean. These representations include images people conjure up in thinking, talking and writing of Scotland and Scottishness, as well as stories people tell about how they conceive of Scotland and Scottishness. And these images and stories in turn exert immense impact – and exercise immense power. Imaginations of Scotland and Scottishness exercise enormous, real effects, over what people think, feel, believe and do in 'real life'. The same is true of myths – *these are myths people live by*, and which they continually turn to and draw upon in seeking to make sense of their own experience, and that of others both (seemingly) similar to and different from themselves, both (seemingly) close to and distant from themselves, and both (seemingly) related to and unrelated to themselves.

Scottish cinema (along with Scottish literature and other influential kinds of artistic, media and cultural production) represents a pre-eminent site through which the dissemination of diverse, contesting imaginations – and myths – of Scotland and of Scottishness takes place. Yet the question of what constitutes 'Scottish cinema' is complicated. Operating out of a small nation, Scots have long struggled to find adequate means to produce, distribute and exhibit films. They have likewise often struggled to secure adequate training, as well as adequate means of sustaining a livelihood through film-making such that they could concentrate considerable time and energy to film-making. At the same time, Scottish film-makers have had to deal not only with the global hegemony of Hollywood, but also the considerable weight of continental European national cinemas, and the prioritization of the interests of English film-making (and of English film-makers) within British national cinema. Nevertheless, Scots have often demonstrated considerable ingenuity in finding ways to make many impressive films, including films with distinctively Scottish accents, emphases, styles and flavours.

Throughout the history of film-making in Scotland, government support – on the United Kingdom level, on the Scottish national level and on regional and local levels within Scotland – has often proven vital in enabling Scottish films to be produced, distributed and exhibited. However, the forms by which this support has been made available, as well as the structures under which and the strictures according to which it has been allocated have repeatedly shifted, often considerably, as have the amounts available for the kinds of film-making projects Scottish film-makers have been most interested in pursuing. The 1990s, and especially the latter half of that decade, represented a breakthrough period for Scottish cinema, which some even dubbed a 'renaissance', but Scottish film-makers today maintain considerable uncertainty, as well as anxiety, about what the future of government support will be like. Film-makers worry about actual and potential reductions in state support for art and culture as well as about lack of support for films of artistic and cultural merit that are at the same time unlikely to generate substantial commercial revenue, especially films that are critical, questioning, provocative and transgressive. Yet Scottish film-makers have long made films dependent upon the support of, and involvement from, many people outside of Scotland, not relying solely on British or Scottish government support, and Scottish film-makers will likely do so far into the foreseeable future. What's more, many films focused on Scottish characters and Scottish stories have been made and continue to be made in Scotland by people who are not Scottish citizens, and many films whose stories are set in Scotland, and which feature Scottish characters, are – and long have been – filmed outside of Scotland. Work in Scottish cinema studies today encompasses the critical examination of a broad range of films, including films (past and present) that are not made by Scots, and not made in Scotland, but that nevertheless relate stories set in Scotland and feature Scottish characters. In this context, 'Scottish cinema' thereby includes multiply diverse and contesting ways film-makers and film audiences imagine Scotland, and imagine Scottishness. This means, in turn, that 'Scottish cinema' includes multiply diverse and contesting myths of Scotland and Scottishness that disparate film-makers – and film audiences – find compelling and appealing. The independence debate provides an exciting opportunity for Scots to re-imagine, and prospectively re-invent, what Scotland is to mean and to be, including by taking into account visions of a future Scotland that move in far more radically innovative and transformative directions than those promoted within 'official' narratives propounded by representatives of the social and political establishment. Scottish films and film-makers, as well as scholarly interpretation and discussion of Scottish films and film-makers, collectively maintain the potential to contribute powerfully toward re-imagining and re-inventing what Scotland is and will be about, including how Scotland conceives and represents itself, at a time in which such work of national re-imagination and re-invention has become immediately relevant, and even urgent, throughout Scotland.

As First Minister Alex Salmond writes in the 'Preface' to *Scotland's Future: Your Guide to an Independent Scotland*, the late-2013 book-length publication of the Scottish government's 'white paper' on Scottish independence,

> Scotland is an ancient nation, renowned for the ingenuity and creativity of our people, the breathtaking beauty of our land and the brilliance of our scholars. Our national story has been shaped down the generations by values of compassion, equality, an unrivalled commitment to the empowerment of education, and passion and curiosity for invention that has helped to shape the world around us. Scots have been at the forefront of the great moral, political and economic debates of our times as humanity has searched for progress in the modern age. It is in that spirit of progress that you will be asked on 18 September 2014, 'Should Scotland be an independent country'? The answer to that question will determine how we can shape our nation for the future. The year ahead should be a national celebration of who we are and what we could be. The debate we are engaged in as a nation is about the future of all of us lucky enough to live in this diverse and vibrant country. It is a rare and precious moment in the history of Scotland – a once in a generation opportunity to chart a better way. (The Scottish Government 2013: viii)

Although Salmond and the Scottish National Party-led Scottish government firmly support independence, the energy currently focused upon critically inquiring into Scotland's past and present in the interest of creatively re-imagining and re-inventing Scotland's future will continue regardless of how this referendum vote turns out. What is more, *Scotland's Future* argues in support of increasing production of broadcasting content in Scotland, as well as in developing more distinctly Scottish avenues for disseminating this content, and, even more importantly, declares that 'distinct from Westminster' the Scottish government recognizes 'the intrinsic value of culture and heritage, and do not value them for their economic benefit, substantial though that is' and that culture and heritage are 'fundamental to our wellbeing and quality of life' (19). While the Scottish government likewise 'does not measure the worth of culture and heritage solely in [terms of] money – we value culture and heritage precisely because they embody our heart and soul, and our essence' (309) and the Scottish government knows 'that public funding of the arts is a fundamental good' (313). Certainly, many Scottish writers and artists are understandably sceptical of what these sentiments are likely to result in, in practice, noting that, as *Scotland's Future* also indicates, 'culture and heritage are already the responsibility of the Scottish Parliament' (309). Yet these kinds of statements, however vaguely posed and readily elusive, nevertheless provide a potentially useful starting point for continuing to press forward arguments on behalf of not only maintaining but also strengthening public investment in, and support of, the arts, including film-making and cinema culture, in line with a conception of value that surpasses narrowly defined notions of economic profitability.

Directory of World Cinema: Scotland is a contribution to this ongoing discussion and debate and, we hope also, to this current process of re-imagination and re-invention. This book represents a diversity of perspectives on issues subject to contestation in Scottish cinema and cultural studies (no single overriding consensus of thinking predominates, and attentive readers will note well multiple areas where contributors disagree). *Directory of World Cinema: Scotland* provides an introductory overview of major lines of scholarly thinking, writing and talking, past and present, about Scottish films, Scottish film-makers and themes and issues concerning Scottish films and film-makers – while also offering a number of new takes, new points of emphasis, new frames for interpretation and evaluation, new sets of references and new series of connections. Our aim is to provide a valuable resource for people beginning to explore interests in Scottish cinema, as well as for those who have been pursuing such interests for some time. Readers maintaining little or no familiarity with Scottish cinema might approach this book with the same questions in mind that some of our friends and colleagues have asked us over the course of the three years we have worked on this project: 'is there a Scottish cinema?' and 'what does Scottish cinema include beyond *Brigadoon* (Vincente Minnelli, 1954), *Braveheart* (Mel Gibson, 1995) and *Trainspotting* (Danny Boyle, 1996)?' We are confident that this book provides a decisively affirmative response to the first question and a compellingly elaborate response to the second. Indeed, we have been highly selective in this first volume, as we could readily imagine including more than twice as many reviews of noteworthy individual films along with more than twice as many profiles of accomplished individual film-makers, while we could at the same time readily imagine including essays addressing a host of additional themes and issues. And we have barely begun to engage with major areas of film-making and cinema culture that have been highly significant in Scotland, including silent film, short film, educational film, animation film, experimental film, independent and amateur film, and exhibition and movie-going. We are excitedly looking forward to work on *Directory of World Cinema: Scotland 2*, in which we will address those kinds of films and issues as well as review many additional individual Scottish films and profile multiple additional individual Scottish film-makers. Yet this first volume provides the solid basis for such further work, as it covers a wide territory, including the history of production and of finance of film-making in Scotland; the history of Gaelic film-making and of documentary and of radical and engaged film-making in Scotland; a thorough introductory account of the discussions and debates concerning myths of Scottishness and Scottish cinema as well as of the movement in recent Scottish cinema from social realism to social art cinema and beyond; a critical reflection on significant patterns of work done across the three principal popular genres of comedy, horror and fantasy; extended profiles of eight directors and considered reviews of 82 films; and the further resources available via our closing Filmography, Scottish Cinema Online, Recommended Reading and Test Your Knowledge quiz sections. We conceive of this book as complementing a history of book-length scholarly projects focused on Scottish cinema running from *Scotch Reels: Scotland in Cinema and Television* (Colin McArthur [ed.], 1982), through *Scotland in Film* (Forsyth Hardy, 1990), *From Limelight to Satellite: A Scottish Film Book* (Eddie Dick [ed.], 1990), *Scotland: The Movie* (David Bruce, 1996), *Screening Scotland* (Duncan Petrie, 2000), *Scottish Cinema Now* (Jonathan Murray, Fidelma Farley and Rod Stoneman [editors], 2009), *Scotland: Global Cinema – Genres, Modes and Identities* (David Martin-Jones, 2009), and *The New Scottish Cinema* (Jonathan Murray, forthcoming). We have benefitted greatly from the work of these and many other prior and current writers on Scottish cinema and culture, and we hope this book will spur yet more scholarly writing, and even greater scholarly interest in the same direction. We also hope that this book will spur further interest in, and greater support for, the work of current and future Scottish film-makers, and for the continued and enhanced health and vitality of Scottish cinema culture. For us, as editors, work on this book has been richly rewarding, even when arduous and exhausting, and it reflects our genuinely, sincerely passionate enthusiasm for the subject. We hope that what you read in this book will prove usefully enabling to you, and that it will spark at least the beginning of a similar degree of interest and enthusiasm for you concerning Scottish films, Scottish film-makers, and issues in Scottish cinema and culture.

Bob Nowlan and Zach Finch

Reference

The Scottish Government (2013) *Scotland's Future: Your Guide to an Independent Scotland*, Edinburgh: Scottish Government/APS Group Scotland.

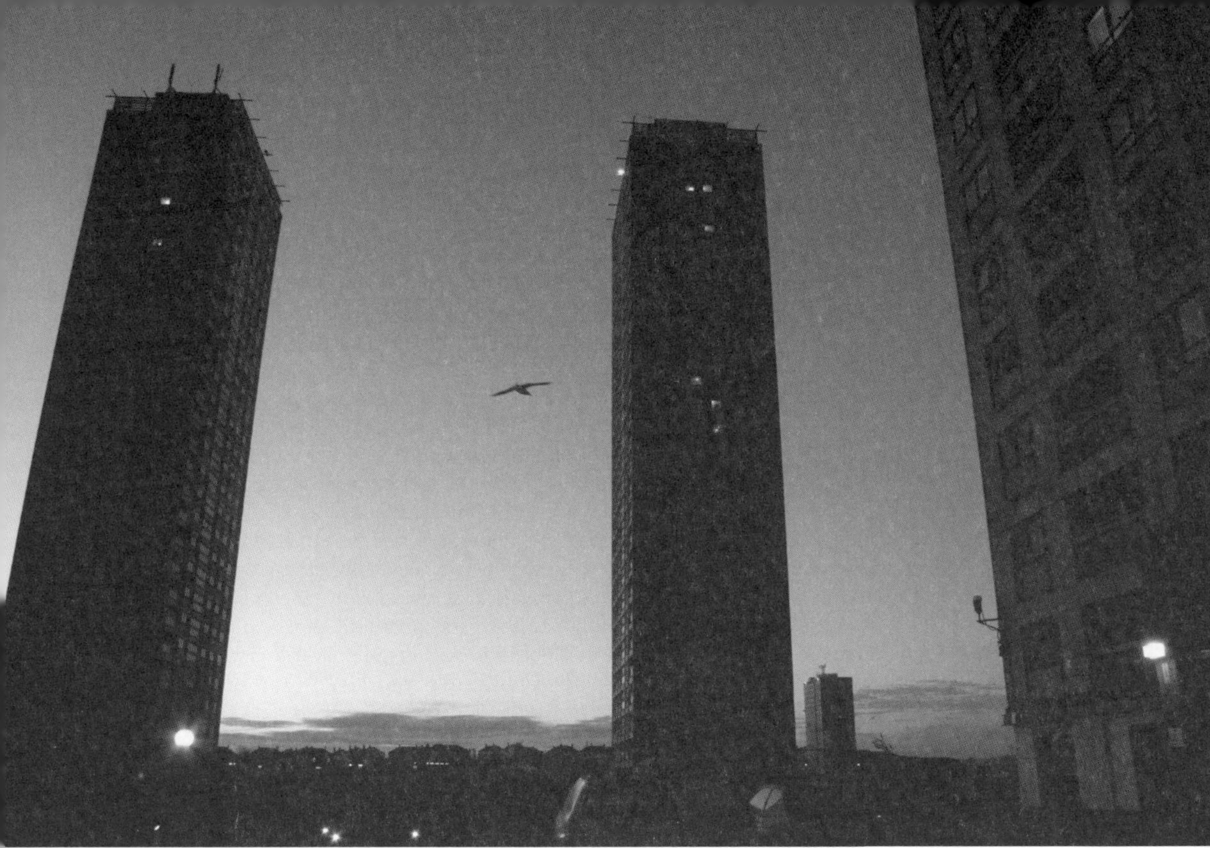

Red Road (2006),
British Film Institute Collection

INDUSTRY SPOTLIGHT
PRODUCTION

> The past twenty years have witnessed an unprecedented flourishing of cultural activity and expression in Scotland, embracing a wide range of artistic forms from literature and painting to cinema and theatre.
>
> (Duncan Petrie 2004: 1)

Scotland has been a site of cinematic interest since the very beginnings of film-making. Many early practitioners sought to create and capture Scottish scenery and way of life. As the cinema boomed in the early twentieth century, film-makers from England travelled to Scotland in hopes of capturing its culture on celluloid. Producers from England and abroad instigated many productions, often as a way of testing new film stocks, such as the Kinemacolor two-strip colour celluloid, and were able to capture Scottish locations and culture. Early experimentation in colour celluloid can be found depicting Scottish culture as a means for tourism for those who could not afford to travel. Even today, Scotland relies heavily on film-makers from outside its borders for production. Film-makers like Ken Loach and Danny Boyle identify strongly with Scotland and have built strong relationships with Scottish talent, such as Robert Carlyle and Ewan McGregor, as well as with Scottish writers Paul Laverty and John Hodge, which, as a consequence, attracts Scottish funding. Hollywood has also made many attempts to capture Scotland, such as early adaptations of Sir Walter Scott's novels, including *Heart of Midlothian*, which became *A Woman's Triumph* (J Searle Dawley, 1914). After World War II, Hollywood produced many more populist films set in Scotland, such as the musical *Brigadoon* (Vincente Minnelli, 1954) and *Greyfriars Bobby: The True Story of a Dog* (Don Chaffey, 1961), which was remade in 2005, and *Loch Ness* (John Henderson, 1996). Big-budget Hollywood efforts such as *Braveheart* (Mel Gibson, 1995) present, some would argue, a highly distorted version of Scottish history. These films prompted a sharply divided response amongst Scots: 'From the moment of its announcement as a possible project to its delirious European premiere in Stirling and beyond, it has convulsed Scottish society, seen by some as manna from heaven and by others as an unmitigated curse' (McArthur 2003: 123).

Although the history of production in Scotland is heavily associated with documentary, particularly the works of John Grierson, identified often as 'godfather' of the genre, recent Scottish productions are heavily associated with 'social realism', a form that tends to depict urban, working-class social issues with gritty characters and downbeat imagery. Film-makers, such as Ken Loach, who pioneered this approach south of the border in England with films like *Kes* (1969), have developed a body of films reflecting contemporary social issues, such as *Carla's Song* (1997) and *My Name is Joe* (1998), sympathetically representing the conditions and advocating on behalf of the interests of the socially marginalized. Loach's critical and, to some extent, commercial success has encouraged many film-makers in Scotland to adopt this approach to develop personal stories within constricted budgets. Social realism has become a staple genre of British film, and of Scottish cinema in particular. The genre proceeds from a long tradition rooted in television drama: from Ken Loach and Tony Garnett in the 1960s in England through Peter McDougall and John Mackenzie in Scotland in the 1970s and 1980s. From a less commercial perspective, Bill Douglas's work has had a heavy influence on Scottish social realism, particularly the trilogy of films he created focusing on his childhood, which itself was inspired by 1940s Italian neo-realism. Social realism in Scotland blends into 'art cinema' with Douglas, and with contemporary film-makers such as Lynne Ramsay and Peter Mullan, who have used the traditional urban working-class themes and settings of social realism to experiment with and create stylistically diverse dramas such as *Ratcatcher* (1999) and *Orphans* (1998) respectively. Both films deploy socially grounded poetic and magic realisms.

In terms of cinematic output, Scotland sees a relatively small number of indigenous films produced and released annually, especially counting films pitched outside of a relatively small, niche market. Yet, independent producers have, in the early twenty-first century, nonetheless taken it on themselves to establish Scotland as a site of new film-making, working to create films in diverse forms and styles to help establish a viable Scottish cinema. Despite an under-developed film industry, producers, such as Gillian Berrie, have been successful in establishing relationships with film-makers from other nations, particularly Denmark. Lars von Trier's and Peter Aalbæk Jensen's company, Zentropa, has been co-producing with the Glasgow-based company, Sigma, since early in the new century, instigating a kind of cinematic presence within Scotland. Their Advance Party Initiative, in which they co-finance projects using the same cast and crew for different films, has led to successful films such as Andrea Arnold's *Red Road* (2006). This approach aids in establishing the beginnings of a significant transnational cinema that may signal an opportunity for long-term sustainable growth.

Scotland's film industry is typically evaluated as part of Britain as a whole. This poses a problem for a developing Scottish 'national cinema', in terms of both its production and its reception:

> For many small national cinemas it can be unclear whether films that are successful on the festival circuit present a 'national' viewpoint and can even be seen as representative of a country like Scotland, or whether they are appreciated internationally because they conform to preconceived notions of how 'Scotland' should appear in cinema. (Martin-Jones 2009: 220)

Where Scotland is identifiable through its history of literature, this can overshadow its cinematic output. As a national cinema, it is relatively small and thus is overlooked in comparison with literature and theatre:

> Scotland [...] with its long history of literary output in both the elevated and public domains, its own long-standing press and theatre, and even its own small-scale cinematic and televisual output, has at its disposal a range of discourses of national identity stretching back well over two centuries. (Castelló, Dobson and O'Donnell 2009: 470)

Scotland has been depicted in small- to large-scale productions and, recently, used as a key location for large-scale films including *World War Z* (Marc Forster, 2013) and *The Dark Knight Rises* (Christopher Nolan, 2012). However, Scotland has made very little contribution to these large-scale productions other than providing some locations and some crew. Most prominent cinematic depictions of Scotland within larger-scale productions are from Hollywood:

> Since the very beginnings of the cinema a great many films have been made which feature Scottish subject-matter [...] But practically all of these have, by and large, been initiated, developed, financed and produced by individuals and companies based either in London or Los Angeles. (Petrie 2000: 15)
>
> Yet it can be argued that Scotland is working slowly toward establishing its own film production to represent its own identity: 'After a century of (almost all) cinematic representations of Scotland and the Scots having been produced furth of Scotland, mainly in Hollywood and the Home Countries of England, indigenous film production structures have emerged. (McArthur 2003: 6)

In the early years of cinema, we can locate multiple examples of film's engagement with Scottish culture. Documentary was one of the first cinematic forms to attract a significant audience, as the idea of capturing reality, including as it is experienced in different cultures, was a way to provide cheap tourism. Many films of the 1900s tried to capture traditional images commonly associated with different nations, including Scotland, such as Highland landscapes, tartan patterns, bagpipes and whisky. Early experimentation with colour can also be placed in contact with Scottish culture. Film-maker GA Smith, an Englishman, conducted significant early experiments with the new Kinemacolor film stock. Considering one of Scotland's most iconic images is the tartan, it is unsurprising that Smith tested Kinemacolor on different tartan cloths. *Tartans of Scottish Clans* (1906) was an experiment to see how the new stock would work: '*Tartans of Scottish Clans* was one of Smith's Kinemacolor experiments, a very simple idea (essentially, a sequence of Scottish tartan cloths, each appropriately labelled) which nonetheless demanded colour in order to convey the necessary information'

(Brooke n.d.). In 1908 Smith developed his experiments further with tartan in *Woman Draped in Patterned Handkerchiefs*, one of the first two-strip colour British films. Again, its simplistic approach was merely to test the new form of colour stock.

John Grierson first became prominent in the 1920s by producing and directing documentaries. His legacy is significant to this day: 'The British documentary film movement, and Grierson in particular, had a considerable impact on film culture and theory in Britain and abroad in the 1920s to the present day' (Aitken 1990: 4). Documentary, moreover, plays an important part in Scottish film history: 'The documentary occupies a position of particular significance in the historical relationship between Scotland and the cinema, particularly in terms of sustenance of indigenous film production' (Petrie 2000: 97). Grierson's methods, and his innovative conception of, and approach to, documentary remain pertinent: 'The use of institutional sponsorship, public and private, to pay for his kind of film-making, rather than dependence returns on box office, was one key Grierson innovation' (Ellis 2002: 363). By maintaining his Scottish identity, Grierson was instrumental in maintaining a film industry within Scotland and Britain: 'Despite his association with the nurturing and projection of a British national culture, Grierson nevertheless retained a strong attachment to the land of his birth and to his own identity as a Scot' (Petrie 2000: 97).

Gradually, documentary practices began to exert an impact on fictional films, especially of a social realist vein. Scottish cinema, particularly contemporary productions, has come to be identified with social realist subject matter, with gritty, urban Scottish landscapes and working-class protagonists. However, how do we identify social realism?

> The term social realism is one which is often used uncritically and indiscriminately in popular film criticism. It is something of a catch-all term which conveys an idea of a text's content, its concerns, and its visual style. Social realist texts are described as "gritty" and "raw", offering a "slice of life" or a view of "life" as it *really* is. (Lay 2002: 5)

When we consider social realism we associate the term with everyday life rather than life perceived in escapist cinema:

> Social realism in films is representative of real life, with all its difficulties. The stories and people portrayed are everyday characters, usually from working class backgrounds. Typically, films within the social realist canon are gritty, urban dramas about the struggle to survive the daily grind' (Strozykowski 2008)

As social realism focuses, typically, on the working class, it is then practical to cast unknown actors, at times non-professional actors, in the key roles, adding further 'realistic' performances to the film, clearly suggestive of a kinship with documentary coverage of 'the real' 'as it is' and 'as it happens'. Many productions eschew the use of named stars which could weaken a film's overall examination of working-class, urban life: 'Social realist films [...] do not use international stars, which would undermine the film's ability to focus on the social conditions and milieu they evoke' (Lay 2002: 34).
Ken Loach is an English social realist film-maker working within Scotland who can be accepted as a representative of a transnational form of film-making, or he can be considered a British film-maker working in northern Britain: 'Such visiting film-makers have made good use of Scottish material and talent and have expanded cinematic representations of Scotland. However, their very success helps to obscure the underlying fragility of Scotland's indigenous industry' (MacPherson 2012: 226). Loach's relationship with writer Paul Laverty has created many features that focus on social issues confronting troubled working-class characters. As Loach is an established film-maker, this helps Scotland break through barriers, not just in the United Kingdom but internationally:

> Scottish cinema has been, and can in some respects still be, regarded as part of a larger British national cinema which itself struggled to survive in the face of the apparently unassailable dominance of Hollywood at the British box office. (Petrie 2000: 153)

However, film-makers such as Loach, who at first embraced the notion of social realism, have grown weary of the label: "the words 'social-realism" [...] and the adjective "gritty" is one that's worn out, I think' (Maytum 2012).

Where Loach has been able to make critically acclaimed social realist films, Scottish film-makers such as Bill Forsyth have been able to infuse naturalistic scenes with humour. Forsyth's *Gregory's Girl* (1981) and *Local Hero* (1983) are his most well-known films, with small-town Scottish settings, focusing on comically desperate groups of characters: 'Audiences and critics often associate Scottish film-maker Bill Forsyth with a whimsical and absurdist sense of humour' (Lay 2001: 97). Forsyth's magic realism contrasts with the typically stark, downbeat narratives of Loach's cinema.

Audiences for Scottish films are then limited as many productions are made on low budgets, mainly financed by funding bodies such as Creative Scotland, the British Film Institute and, at times, through the MEDIA initiative. Compared to major studio releases with massive budgets capable of pursuing extensive marketing campaigns, social realist films – and, in general, low-budget independent films – suffer as they cannot afford that same kind of publicity. It is then up to niche markets to fill the gap; these typically consist of audiences who frequent independent, arthouse cinemas where most social realist films are shown before given a life on the DVD market:

> Film-makers who make social realist texts, to varying degrees eschew mainstream audiences but run the risk of being accused of "preaching to the converted." Or worse, of making films from a liberal middle class perspective for liberal thinking middle class audiences *about* (but not *for*) the working classes.' (Lay 2002: 34)

Yet Britain, certainly including Scotland, cannot afford to compete with Hollywood. As British films, particularly those that are created with a social realistic aesthetic, reach smaller audiences, British cinema struggles as a consequence. Social realism attempts to replicate the real and not romanticize locations, characters or themes. But this runs directly counter to mainstream Hollywood cinema norms: 'the position of social realism in British cinema has been portrayed as characteristically anti-Hollywood and this was [...] deemed to be enough to be "typically British"' (Lay 2002: 102). Lynne Ramsay's debut, *Ratcatcher*, set during the 1973 dustbin worker strikes, is at first glance a social realist film, with the expected urban setting and working-class environment. However, Ramsay departs from tropes common to the form by exploring the lead character's dreamlike existence, and by eschewing reliance on gritty, urban, masculine figures rife within preceding Scottish social realist films:

> Though set in the bleakest of urban landscapes [...] Ramsay's film still manages to find hope through the impulse of her central character to dream beyond his surroundings and though the startling images that she makes of the details of the lives that are also not sentimentalized. (Blandford 2007: 78–79)

This subversion of the social realist form offers promise of a kind of Scottish cinema. Ramsay has, moreover, been able to cross national borders, creating projects in the United States, while maintaining a strong connection with her national identity as a Scot. Contemporary Scottish cinema can, in a sense, be regarded as increasingly transnational as influential film-makers, such as Peter Mullan as well as Lynne Ramsay, have worked internationally yet maintained their Scottish identity: 'The contemporary Scottish cinema [...] is one defined by international migration and exploration on the part of local artists' (Murray 2012: 401).

Recent developments in working to create an indigenous film industry in Scotland are exemplified in the working relationship between the Scottish Sigma Films and the Danish Zentropa. This partnership establishes Scotland as a transnational collaborator and practitioner, forging a viable cinema that strives to break boundaries, in terms of form and style as well as in terms of content and theme:

> A still ongoing process of collaboration between individuals and institutions working within the Scottish and Danish production sectors represents perhaps the most visible example of contemporary Scottish cinema's systematic move beyond a single set of national borders in both industrial and representational terms. (Murray 2012: 403)

Sigma's Gillian Berrie has become a pivotal figure within Scottish film production:

> Gillian's contribution to the indigenous screen industries, in terms of both advocating an infrastructure for film production in Scotland, and her artistic contributions to Scottish film, has been instrumental in establishing Scotland as an increasingly thriving and viable production base. (Film City Glasgow 2014)

The success of establishing Sigma Films has allowed productions to be created under the 'Advanced Party' initiative:

> The Scottish-Danish Advance Party project has become well-known in Scotland in recent years. A projected trilogy, the series began with the release of Andrea Arnold's Dogme 95 style *Red Road*, which blended Danish film-making zeitgeist with gritty Glasgow locations. The project aims for every film to be made by a first-time director, filmed and set in Scotland, using the same characters and cast. (Balkind 2011)

Collaborating this way allows Scottish film-makers not just to create projects that reflect their own national identity; it creates opportunities to produce internationally, becoming a key part of a film network within Europe:

> Scandinavian involvement within 2000s Scottish cinema also exerted a marked degree of influence over representational trends during the period. Locally set co-productions with Nordic partners contributed substantially to a wider contemporary qualification or circumnavigation of national identity's traditional pre-eminence within Scottish film-making. (Murray 2012: 405)

This opportunity creates a Scottish cinema that moves away from social realism and the notion of deliberately creating narrowly intra-national representations through cinema. Essentially, what is enabled is not one form of cinema but many: 'The collaboration with Scandinavian counterparts was of pronounced significance for Scottish cinema during the 2000s which, as the decade wore on, increasingly transcended nationally exclusive or essentialist concerns, both industrial and representational' (Murray 2012: 409).

Scotland is thus a paradox in terms of its contemporary indigenous production and its history. The ground for experimentation seen in the early films of GA

Smith was at the behest of an American producer, who came to Britain to push the potential of a film industry. The outside forces that came to Scotland established an outsider view on Scottish life. The documentary boom in the early history of film-making, led by a Scotsman, made a massive impact on British cinema as a whole. Social realism has exerted, in turn, a substantial impact on film-making, including as an affordable pursuit for those film-makers working, of necessity, with low budgets, especially with the advent of digital technology for shooting and editing. Aspiring film-makers in the United Kingdom can work with this form even as a lack of funding inhibits any studio form of production. The creation of such a genre is rooted in the documentary movement of the 1950s from which future fictional film-makers learned to adopt a documentary-style approach to present working-class issues fictionally yet simultaneously as truthfully as possible. Film-makers such as Bill Douglas and Ken Loach have affected a lasting influence within this genre whereas more recent film-makers such as Lynne Ramsay and Andrea Arnold have innovated within and beyond social realism to appeal to twenty-first century audiences.

Scottish cinematic production is in a constant flux; it is unable to produce a sufficient amount of home-grown films to consistently attract large-scale audiences. Also, it has to co-produce with a larger European neighbour, further emphasizing Scotland's lack of a national cinema – in a conventional sense. Scotland's film industry relies heavily upon its interaction with other nations. It is here where production companies such as Sigma will remain important. Their work in collaboration with the likes of Zentropa maintains the small but significant Scottish presence within European and international film-making. Though Scotland still relies on outside sources to help fund productions, contemporary Scottish cinema continues to grow, especially as a co-producer. In doing so, it contributes to compelling varieties of formal innovation, within and beyond traditional social realism.

Kyle Barrett

References

Aitken, Ian (1990) *Film and Reform: John Grierson and the Documentary Film Movement*, London: Routledge.

Balkind, Nikola (2011) '15 Years of Sigma Film', http://www.unculturedcritic.com/2011/02/15-years-of-sigma-film.html. Accessed 11 November 2012.

Blandford, Steven (2007) *Film, Drama and the Break-Up of Britain*, Bristol: Intellect.

Brooke, Michael (n.d.) 'Tartans of Scottish Clans (1906)', http://www.screenonline.org.uk/film/id/726114/index.html. Accessed 9 November 2012.

Castelló, Enric, Dobson, Nichola and O'Donnell, Hugh (2009) 'Telling it like it is? Social and linguistic realism in Scottish and Catalan soaps', *Media Culture & Society*, 31: 3, pp. 467–84.

Dupin, Christophe (n.d.) 'Free Cinema', http://www.screenonline.org.uk/film/id/444789/index.html. Accessed 17 August 2012.

Ellis, John (2002) *John Grierson: Life, Contributions, Influence*, Illinois: Southern Illinois University Press.

Film City Glasgow (2014) 'Inspiration', http://www.filmcityglasgow.com/inspiration. Accessed 20 January 2014.

Hallam, Julia and Marshment, Margaret (2000) *Realism and Popular Cinema*, Manchester: MUP.

Lay, Samantha (2001) 'Bill Forsyth', in Yoram Allon, Dell Cullen and Hannah Patterson (eds), *Contemporary British and Irish Film Directors: A Wallflower Critical Guide*, London: Wallflower.

__________ (2002) *British Social Realism: From Documentary to Brit Grit*, London: Wallflower.

Low, Rachel and Manvell, Roger (1948) *The History of British Film: Volume I: The History of British Film 1896–1906*, London: Routledge.

MacPherson, Robin (2012) 'Scotland', in Emma Bell and Neil Mitchell (eds), *Directory of World Cinema: Britain*, Bristol: Intellect.

Martin-Jones, David (2009) *Scotland: Global Cinema – Genres, Modes and Identities*, Edinburgh: EUP.

Maytum, Matt (2012) 'Ken Loach and Paul Laverty on *The Angel's Share*: Interview', http://www.totalfilm.com/news/ken-loach-and-paul-laverty-on-the-angels-share-interview. Accessed 9 November 2012.

McArthur, Colin (2003) *Brigadoon, Braveheart and the Scots: Distortions of Scotland in Hollywood Cinema*, London: IB Tauris & Co. Ltd.

McIntyre, Steve (1984) 'New Images of Scotland', *Screen*, 25: 1, pp. 53–60.

Murray, Jonathan (2012) 'Blurring Borders: Scottish Cinema in the Twenty-First Century', in *Journal of British Cinema and Television*, 9, pp. 400–18.

Petrie, Duncan (2000) *Screening Scotland*, London: BFI.

__________ (2004) *Contemporary Scottish Fictions: Film, Television and the Novel*, Edinburgh: EUP.

Street, Sarah (1997) *British National Cinema*, London: Routledge.

Strozykowski, Michelle (2008) 'Social Realism in British Film', https://suite.io/michelle-strozykowski/hr02rk. Accessed 14 April 2014.

MARKETING MIX
FINANCE

Financing films made in and/or about Scotland has never been easy, although the situation has been transformed in recent times.

Before the 1980s such fiction films as appeared would, almost without exception, have been funded by English or American studios. *Whisky Galore!* (1949) and *The Maggie* (1954), both directed by Alexander Mackendrick, were Ealing Studios productions, while Disney was responsible for the 1953 version of *Rob Roy*, directed by Harold French, and Twentieth Century Fox for *The Prime of Miss Jean Brodie* (Ronald Neame, 1969).

At this time, films were being made in Scotland with Scottish finance but these were documentaries, as often as not under the aegis of Films of Scotland, a body which operated during the period 1954–82 (an earlier organization with the same name had been set up with private finance specifically to make short films to be shown at the 1938 Empire Exhibition in Glasgow). Films of Scotland was government-encouraged but not government-funded. The money for productions came from the films' sponsors – industry associations, local authorities, tourist organizations and the like – and that inevitably acted as a constraint on content: a commercial organization is unlikely to be willing to

My Ain Folk (1973), British Film Institute Collection

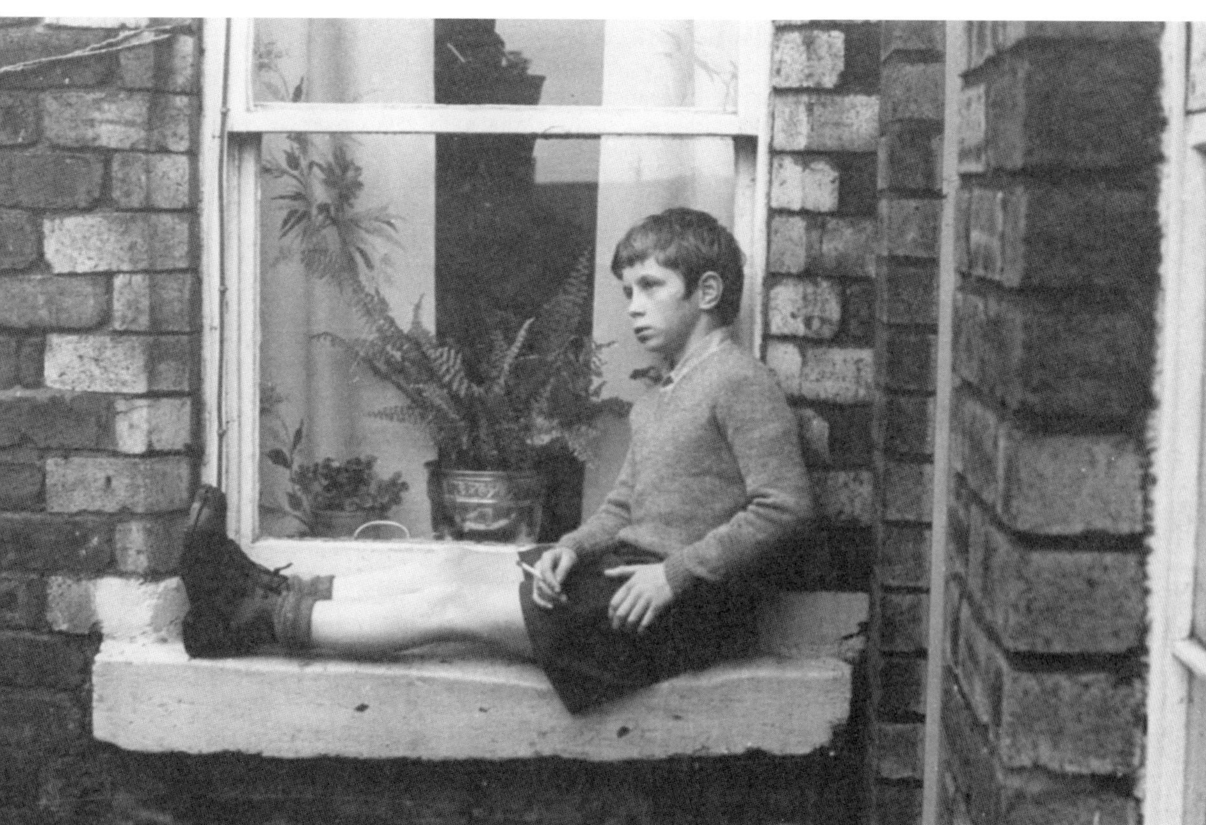

pay for a representation of its activities which is less than complimentary. However, some interesting films were produced – for example *Seawards the Great Ships* (Hilary Harris, 1961), which won a best short film Oscar – and in the small number of companies which eked out a living from Films of Scotland, broadcast and other commissions, several people were given the opportunity to develop skills which were subsequently put to good use when feature films began to be made in Scotland on a regular basis, Bill Forsyth being the most conspicuous example (Hardy 1990:174).

It is worth noting here, to provide context for this discussion, that the United States is probably the only western country where there is no significant public funding available towards the cost of feature film production; the contrast with its neighbour to the north is striking. There both the National Film Board and Telefilm Canada invest significant amounts of taxpayers' dollars in television productions, feature films and documentaries. In recent years Telefilm Canada has had government funding of around $100 million CAN annually, and the National Film Board around $70 million CAN, although both organizations had their budgets cut by 10 per cent in 2012. The population of Canada is six times that of Scotland; if similar bodies existed in Scotland, the proportionate level of annual support would therefore be around £17 million.

In the United Kingdom, in the period after World War II, both the National Film Finance Corporation (1949–85) and the production board of the British Film Institute (1933–), acted in a funding support capacity, albeit on a relatively modest scale. Some money from the former found its way into the budget of *The Brave Don't Cry* (1952), and the latter financed Bill Douglas's low-budget autobiographical trilogy, *My Childhood* (1972), *My Ain Folk* (1973) and *My Way Home* (1978).

North of the border, the Scottish Film Production Fund was established in 1982 under the auspices of the state-financed Scottish Film Council, an organization whose remit also included exhibition (it could claim much credit for the establishment of a network of arthouse cinemas in the country), archiving and media education. The initial sum available was £80,000 per year, which even in a world of small-scale non-extravagant production, bordered on the laughable. However, over the next few years as the BBC, Scottish Television (the major commercial television company in Scotland), Channel 4 and Comataidh Telebhisein Gàidhlig (the government-financed Gaelic Television Committee) became involved, the Fund increased, so that by the mid-1990s almost three quarters of a million pounds was available annually. Partial funding was provided for the development and/or production of a number of notable features including *Silent Scream* (David Hayman,1990), *Shallow Grave* (Danny Boyle, 1994) and the 1995 version of *Rob Roy* by Michael Caton-Jones (Bruce 1996: 138 ff.; Petrie 2000: 174 ff.).

When Channel 4 went on air across the United Kingdom in 1982, it did so with a substantial commitment to its Film on Four strand, feature films produced for both the television and cinema markets. Among the Scottish titles that emerged were *Ill Fares the Land* (1982), *Another Time, Another Place* (1983) and *Heavenly Pursuits* (1986). Not many of the Film on Four productions returned profits for the company and the emphasis shifted from being funder to part funder; *Shallow Grave* and *Trainspotting* (Danny Boyle, 1996) were among the films which subsequently appeared with Channel 4 backing.

No doubt stimulated by the Film on Four initiative, the BBC began to be involved in feature film production. The Corporation might well wish to argue that within its strand of original dramas transmitted in the Wednesday Play (1964–70) and Play for Today (1970–84) slots – the loss of which has been a serious blow to the cause of stimulating and socially critical drama on British television – it had commissioned and screened several productions which were made on film and were as cinematic as anything appearing in movie houses. Peter McDougall's *Just Another Saturday* (1975) and *Just a Boys' Game* (1979) are obvious Scottish examples. Among the films which now emerged to be shown on air and in cinemas were *Mrs Brown* (John Madden, 1997), *Ratcatcher* (Lynne Ramsay, 1999), *Sweet Sixteen* (Ken Loach, 2002) and *Morvern Callar* (Lynne Ramsay, 2002). These were BBC films but co-finance from other sources and countries was involved.

Glasgow, for much of the nineteenth and twentieth centuries, was not only Scotland's pre-eminent industrial city, it was one of the biggest centres of manufacturing in the world. Although some ships – usually naval vessels – are still built there and a few other engineering companies remain, it is a pale shadow of its former self. However, in the last thirty years it has sought to re-invent itself – 'Glasgow's Miles Better' has been the advertising slogan – as a centre of financial services and tourism, and of the so-called creative industries. It was not really surprising therefore when in 1995 the Glasgow Film Fund was established with local authority and other public-sector backing, including, for a few years, some EU funding. As with the Scottish Film Production Fund, the initial resources were modest, some £160,000 per year, but within a few years it was able to offer that level of funding to several projects and, on occasion, to offer more. The Glasgow Film Fund was an investor in *Shallow Grave*, which, for all the funders involved, proved a very shrewd judgment, since the film, which cost £1 million, took £5 million at the UK box office alone. Among other films which secured funding from the Glasgow Film Fund were *My Name is Joe* (Ken Loach, 1998) and *Orphans* (Peter Mullan, 1998), both of which were critical and ultimately financial successes. There have also, and inevitably, been failures: the most glaring example is perhaps John Byrne's *The Slab Boys* (1997) which the author, who also adapted it from his highly successful stage play and directed it, ruefully claimed had fewer people paying to see it at the box office than any previous British film. The Glasgow Film Fund discontinued in 2003, but a Film Office survives as a locations promoter and facilitator in the city.

The most abiding legacy of Conservative Prime Minister John Major's Westminster administration (1992–97) is probably the establishment of the National Lottery, some of the revenue from which was allocated to a variety of good causes including the arts. Film's share of this largesse has meant that in Scotland funding of around £5 million per year has become available. Initially disbursed by the Scottish Arts Council, then by Scottish Screen (the successor body to the Scottish Film Council which was established in 1997), it is now the responsibility of Creative Scotland, which was formed when the Scottish Arts Council and Scottish Screen were merged in 2010. Initially the Scottish Film Production Fund administered the Lottery income on behalf of the Scottish Arts Council and used the management fee paid by the Council to enhance the total available. Thereafter Scottish Screen took on the responsibility of administering the Lottery Fund, which it augmented on occasion with money from its grant in aid. The Scottish Film Production Fund was then retired as a source for funding films.

Producers were able to apply to both the Glasgow Film Fund and the Lottery Fund: *My Name is Joe*, for example, obtained £100,000 from the former and £500,000 from the latter, while the ill-fated *The Slab Boys* notched up £170,000 and £550,000. The figures for *Orphans* were £250,000 and £900,000 (Petrie 2000: 227–28). By Hollywood standards these are relatively small sums, but in a country where it is possible to make a non-blockbuster movie for two or three million pounds, they are substantial percentages of production budgets. *Hallam Foe* (David Mackenzie, 2007), *Red Road* (Andrea Arnold, 2006) and *Neds* (Peter Mullan, 2010) are more recent beneficiaries of Lottery funding

It would appear that funding from that source for film production in Scotland will continue at around the £5 million-per-year level, although it was announced that in

2012–13 £1 million of it would be allocated to television projects. At the beginning of 2012 it was also reported that Creative Scotland was entering into a partnership with commercial funders, under the rubric of the Mackendrick Film Fund, and was seeking to support movies with budgets between £3 million and £6 million. One of the participating organizations was Aegis Film Fund which was the largest backer of *The King's Speech* (Tom Hooper, 2010), which grossed £266 million worldwide. A figure of £35 million being available in the new Scottish fund was mentioned, although as more of an aspiration than a concrete reality at that time.

Producers will continue to trawl widely for funds in Scotland, Britain and Europe, where the MEDIA Programme of the European Union has been another source of money. To judge from the credits at the end of many non-Hollywood films, and their attendant publicity material, the process of putting together funding packages is both complicated and potentially exhausting. The poster for *Morvern Callar* informs readers that, in addition to finance from the BBC, Scottish Screen and the Glasgow Film Fund, the Canadian production company, Alliance Atlantis, put money into the film, while the poster for *My Name is Joe* describes it as 'a co-production between Britain, Germany and Spain'. Scotland is not very different in this respect from many other countries, but its film producers are probably only part way up the learning curve and remain constrained by the relatively modest sums available in their home base.

However, very substantial progress has been made since the 1980s, as can be illustrated by looking at the career of Bill Forsyth. Forsyth, as noted earlier, had worked in the documentary sector in Scotland, and in 1979 on the basis of a few thousand pounds borrowed from friends, he directed on 16 mm *That Sinking Feeling* (1980) using actors from the non-professional Scottish Youth Theatre. Its success at the Edinburgh Film Festival enabled Forsyth to obtain the still very modest sum of £250,000 from the National Film Finance Corporation and Scottish Television to make *Gregory's Girl* (1981). His whimsical style now clearly bankable, with the support of producer David Puttnam and the UK-based Goldcrest, he moved on to *Local Hero* (1983) budgeted at £3 million, and starring Burt Lancaster alongside a largely Scottish cast. Forsyth soon found himself in Hollywood. His work there included *Housekeeping* (1987) and *Breaking In* (1989) but his career took a downward turn when the $30 million Warners-financed *Being Human* (1993) proved a critical and box office disaster. Forsyth's trajectory need not have stalled like this – some might argue that his penchant for writing his own scripts is a fatal flaw – and his career does demonstrate that it is possible now to be a Scottish-based film-maker and to work internationally, as the career of Lynne Ramsay, for example, has subsequently shown.

The fact that contemporary Scottish film-makers have access to funding levels which simply were not available thirty years ago is a matter for celebration, as is the wider range of features which has been produced in recent times (Martin-Jones 2010: *passim*). But it would be foolish to pretend that there have not been difficulties along the way. It is also the case that there has been ongoing discussion about what kinds of films should be made in Scotland with the – still limited – resources available. The kinds of films which feature in this discussion, it should be emphasized, are those which purport to be Scottish in content and/or orientation, not those like, for example, the Brad Pitt film *World War Z* (Marc Forster, 2013) which used Glasgow as a stand-in for Philadelphia in its location shooting in 2011. 'Offshore' productions of that kind are welcomed as sources of local employment – film and non-film related – but they do not usually count as part of the corpus of Scottish film.

Scotland is a small country with a population of only five million. Its film and broadcasting community is not large, and the people who are part of it know each other well, and often find themselves working with each other at different stages in their careers. If public funding is to be allocated judiciously – something it is very hard to do in the movie business, where it is never easy to predict what will succeed and what fail – then it is important that the expertise available within the production community can be drawn on. But immediately a problem arises: some of the people on the bodies allocating funds might wish to – legitimately – access these funds for themselves, or may be associated with individuals or companies who are seeking to do so. In such a situation accusations of partiality are almost inevitable, and the early days of the Lottery Panel were marred by controversies deriving from such accusations. It is difficult to see how, in a country where there will never be enough work, such controversy can be avoided (Petrie 2000: 177).

Then there is the question of the success or failure of particular projects. There was a time in the Scottish theatre several decades ago when so few indigenous plays were being produced that any new script which was presented found itself having to bear an enormous weight of expectations, which no one play could hope to meet. Something similar used to be the case with Scottish films, as so few of them were being made. At the present time, it is still rare for the annual output to get very far into double figures so the problem has not really disappeared. And if there are spectacular failures, such as *The Slab Boys*, criticism of the funding bodies can be intense. The argument that in the movie business worldwide many films lose money, and only a few are really successful, is hard to deploy when public money from a very limited source is lost. It would be a different matter if the investment, or most of it, had come from private individuals or commercial organizations. Nor is it the wisest of rhetorical strategies to draw attention to the number of European films, partially funded by the EU taxpayer, which do very poorly or never secure any kind of release, theatrical or non-theatrical.

All funding bodies, particularly in recessionary times, are bound to be sensitive to accusations of improvidence, and are anxious that there are real returns on projects that can then be re-invested in other ventures. The danger for film is that, as a defensive strategy, investment policy might become excessively cautious, with risk confined to the relatively modest sums made available for short films, which can be justified in terms of talent development, whether there is any return on the investment or not.

With the changes in the funding of Scottish film previously described, an ongoing critical controversy has emerged over the kinds of cinematic representations/constructions of Scotland that should be encouraged. Colin McArthur has argued forcibly that a 'poor cinema' might be a better option for Scotland, that is to say a cinema which does not seek to create pale imitations of mainstream commercial movies but looks to alternative aesthetic strategies and to engagement with the specifics of the society and national culture in which it is situated (McArthur 1994: 124). In order to encourage such an approach, McArthur suggests budgets should be limited to £300,000 per film (he was writing in the early 1990s).

McArthur's recommendations did not arouse much enthusiasm within what might be described as the embryonic film establishment in Scotland, where there was, and continues to be, a strong desire to make films which are successful in Scotland and beyond the country's borders, not least on the international festival circuit. A fair number of films which have succeeded in that aim in recent years – for example, *My Name is Joe*, *Orphans*, *Sweet Sixteen* and *Neds* – could be seen as owing something to the so-called discourse of Clydesidism (concerned with traditional urban, industrial Scottish working-class life, located along the River Clyde) which, in a seminal essay published in 1982, McArthur argued was at least potentially more progressive than the discourses conventionally characterized as Tartanry and Kailyard (McArthur 1982: 40 ff.). In that sense there has indeed been an engagement with aspects of national identity, though it is a partial engagement. It may be that some Scottish producers and funders have become inadvertently committed to rather limited representations and constructions of Scotland – working class, macho, violent, grim, even hopeless – which are seen as authentic and, crucially, marketable. There has at times seemed to be a near invisibility of the Scottish bourgeoisie, except in walk-on, often unsympathetic, roles – and of the country beyond the central belt. The same criticism can be levelled to some degree at television drama output; the reader will recall that a fair number of Scottish films now have money from television companies invested in them (Hutchison 2005: 197 ff.).

It is important for the development of a vibrant and challenging Scottish cinema that, even with limited resources, a wide range of representations and constructions of Scotland appear on-screen. It is also crucial that many people see them at home and abroad. Allan Shiach, when chair of the Scottish Film Council, remarked that there was no point in making films nobody went to see. It is an obvious but fundamental point, and all the stronger for coming from Shiach who, as Allan Scott, has a very successful career as a scriptwriter in the United States and Britain behind him.

Scottish film funders will be obliged to wrestle with the art/commerce dilemma for the foreseeable future and they will do so in a country which has attained more political autonomy than it has had for the last three hundred years, and may indeed be moving, if not to complete independence, to a constitutional status like that enjoyed by the states in the United States or the provinces in Canada. The Scottish government has until now been content to allow the funding agencies to do their job without overt political direction; broadcasting has excited far more debate and controversy. Even so, Alex Salmond, the Scottish National Party leader, who has been First Minister of the Holyrood parliament since 2007, was very happy to associate himself with any favourable publicity accruing to his country from the Pixar production of *Brave* (Mark Andrews, Brenda Chapman and Steve Purcell) in 2012. However, that association was not so much aesthetic as commercial since, like the national tourist agency, VisitScotland, Mr Salmond envisaged foreign visitors descending on the Highlands after seeing the film, and spending money accordingly.

No sensible observer would argue that more political direction of film production is needed from the Scottish government but, as the comparison with Canada made earlier suggests, rather more public money might usefully be found to enhance current funding sources. If the example of a country of comparable population size is wanted, then Denmark might be cited: in the period 2011–14 the Danish government offered £50 million annually to support film production. The Scottish government in 2010 committed itself to the establishment of a new television channel in Scotland which is budgeted at around £70 million per year, although it is far from clear where that money is to come from. It might be argued that a more modest sum made available by the Scottish government in Holyrood could put Scottish feature film production on a more secure base than it has enjoyed to date.

David Hutchison

References

Bruce, David (1996) *Scotland the Movie*, Edinburgh: Polygon.
Hardy, Forsyth (1990) *Scotland in Film*, Edinburgh: EUP.
Hutchison, David (2005) 'Representing Glasgow on Television', in Bill Marshall (ed.), *Montreal-Glasgow*, Glasgow: University of Glasgow, pp. 197–206.
McArthur, Colin (1982) 'Scotland and Cinema: The Iniquity of the Fathers', in Colin McArthur (ed.), *Scotch Reels*, London: BFI, pp. 40–69.
__________ (1994) 'The cultural necessity of a Poor Celtic Cinema', in Paul Hainsworth, John Hill and Martin McLoone (eds), *Border Crossing: Film in Ireland, Britain and Europe*, Belfast: Institute of Irish Studies, pp. 112–25.
Martin-Jones, David (2009) *Scotland: Global Cinema – Genres, Modes and Identities*, Edinburgh: EUP.
Petrie, Duncan (2000) *Screening Scotland*, London: BFI.

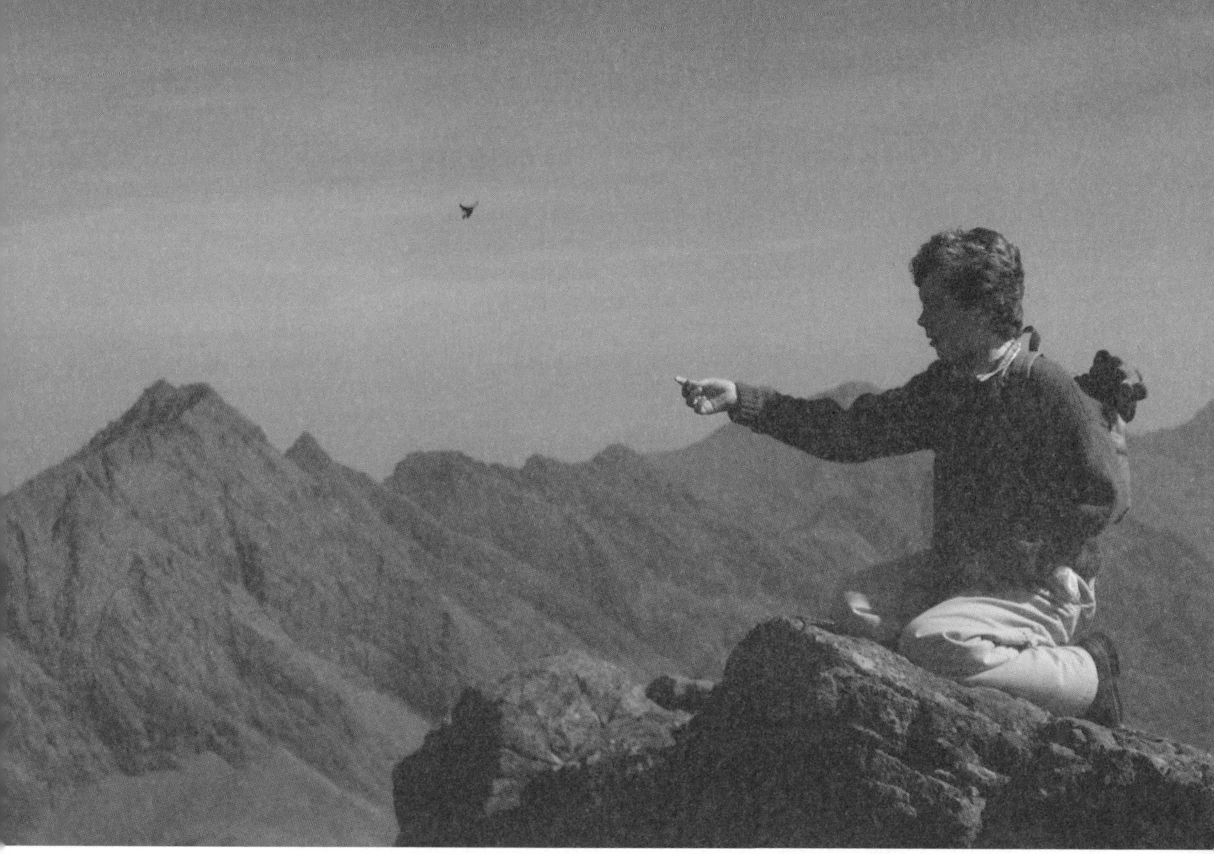

Seachd: The Inaccessible Pinnacle (2007),
Courtesy of Creative Scotland

LOCATION
GAELIC FILM-MAKING IN SCOTLAND

Gaelic film-making in Scotland exists as a sporadic but gradually growing, sub-national or regional film culture. Gaelic film-making emerged in the 1980s, and like much film-making in Scotland might never have existed were it not for finance from television. At present it would be inaccurate to discuss a Gaelic film industry, or Gaelic cinema. However, Gaelic film-making does exist, and should be understood in relation to the history of the Gàidhealtachd (Gaeldom). The Gàidhealtachd is, broadly speaking, in geographical terms the Highlands and Islands of Scotland, but in particular the Western Isles where around 60 per cent of the population speak Gaelic. Gaelic film-making reflects upon the region's history and identity. It is often a very youthful phenomenon, which attempts to depict visually an oral history passed down through a language nearing threat of extinction, in relation to a distinctive landscape that is imagined by film-makers to be alive with mythical stories and legends.

To understand Gaelic films we must first know something of the history of the Gàidhealtachd, and of the recent emergence of Gaelic media. First, the Gàidhealtachd. The nation now known as Scotland has a long and complex history that, at different points, variously intertwines different heritages – Pict, Gael, Scots, Norse, Anglo-Saxon and Briton. The history of the Gàidhealtachd is similarly long and complex, a history of both a region of what is now Scotland, and also of the Gaelic language and culture. At certain points in the past Gaelic was spoken throughout large parts of what is now known as Scotland. It is from the Gaelic word Alba that the term Scotland originates. The consolidation of Scotland as a nation is integrally bound up with the gradual decline of Gaelic language and culture, especially after the Statutes of Iona in 1609, and a 1616 agreement signed at an annual meeting of the Highland clan chiefs in Edinburgh. The Statutes of Iona required, amongst their nine clauses, that the eldest sons of clan chiefs be educated in the Lowlands, in English. This was one measure amongst several taken during the rule of James VI to enable greater control over the Highlands and Islands.

The historical decline in Gaelic language and culture was exacerbated in the eighteenth and nineteenth centuries. This included measures taken against the military culture of the Highland clans after the defeat of the Jacobite uprising at Culloden in 1746, and the Highland Clearances which depopulated large parts of the Highlands to make way for extensive sheep farming, and hunting and fishing resorts for the upper classes. The population of the Gàidhealtachd also declined due to mass emigration from Scotland, in particular to Canada, the United States, New Zealand and Australia during this period, although this did create a diaspora in which many aspects of Gaelic culture were preserved.

As a result of this long history of marginalization of a once dominant culture in the region, a census in 2001 identified that there were at that time less than 60,000 Gaelic speakers in Scotland, mostly concentrated in the Western Highlands and Islands, and in and around Glasgow. This was around 1.2 per cent of the 5 million people of Scotland.

In order to stem the decline of the Gaelic language, a range of initiatives has been implemented by governments in Scotland. State support for the Gaelic language has been increasing since the 1960s, including several important measures passed in the 1980s, such as the Education (Scotland) Act of 1980, which recognized the need for Gaelic to be taught in schools in Gaelic-speaking areas. With devolution, a Minister for Gaelic was appointed to the Scottish Executive (now the Scottish government) in 1997. Perhaps most significantly the Gaelic Language (Scotland) Act 2005 constituted the Bórd na Gàidhlig, a body with several functions with respect of the promotion of Gaelic, both as a culture and as a language of equal status to English in Scotland. This is evident in everyday life in Scotland, in dual language signs at airports, railway stations and on road signs, but more importantly the promotion of Gaelic-language education – for example through the establishing of Gaelic-medium schools in Glasgow, Inverness and Edinburgh.

Where does Gaelic media fit into this picture? Since the 1990s, dedicated funding has been set aside for the promotion of Gaelic media, including radio and television. In 2008 a dedicated Gaelic television channel was launched, BBC ALBA. This was the culmination of a process that began in 2003, when the Serbheis Nam Meadhanan Gàidhlig (Gaelic Media Service) (GMS), was charged with establishing a Gaelic television channel. GMS traces its origins back to the Broadcasting Acts of 1990 and 1996, which provided state support for Gaelic broadcasting in Scotland, including £9.5 million of annual funding for Gaelic Television. The Comataidh Telebhisein Gàidhlig (Gaelic Television Committee) (CTG), began broadcasting Gaelic television in 1993, radio was added to the fund's remit in 1996 (although without additional funding), and in 1997 the Committee's name was changed to Comataidh Craolaidh Gàidhlig (The Gaelic Broadcasting Committee) (CCG). CCG became GMS in 2003, and was granted an additional £3 million annually by the Scottish Executive. Bringing this discussion to the present, MG ALBA (Meadhanan Gàidhlig ALBA [Gaelic Media Scotland]), who work in partnership with BBC ALBA, are the latest manifestation of the Committee that has transformed from CTG through CCG and GMS to MG ALBA. In its many forms, this committee has been responsible for providing a great deal of the financial support for the initial shoots of Gaelic film-making, along with BBC Scotland, Channel 4 and the Scottish Film Production Fund (later part of Scottish Screen, now Creative Scotland).

The Gaelic films made during this period include the first Gaelic feature, *Hero* (Barney Platts-Mills, 1982) – its status as a Gaelic film often being disputed because the young cast were not native Gaelic speakers, even though they speak Gaelic in the film – and the first short, *Sealladh/The Vision* (Douglas Mackinnon, 1992), which starred a young Peter Mullan. These first films were funded by Channel 4 (*Hero*), and CTG and Channel 4 (*Sealladh*) respectively. *Play Me Something* (Timothy Neat, 1989), which starred a young Tilda Swinton, whilst predominantly in English, contained some Gaelic dialogue and songs. It was funded by the British Film Institute, Film 4, Grampian Television and the Scottish Film Production Fund. In the mid-1990s, CTG/CCG, along with the Scottish Film Production Fund and BBC Scotland, co-funded a series of Gaelic short films entitled Geur Gheàrr. These were *Roimh Ghaoth A'Gheamhraidh/Before Winter Winds* (Bill MacLeod, 1996), *An Iobairt/The Sacrifice* (Gerda Stevenson, 1996), *Ag Iasgach/Fishing* (Roddy Cunningham, 1997), *A'Bhean Eudach/The Jealous Sister* (Domhnall Ruadh, 1997), *Dathan/Colours* (Iain F MacLeod, 1998), *Keino* (Iseabil Maciver, 1998) and *Mac* (Alasdair Maclean, 1998).

Two other feature-length films also require mention, *As An Eilean/From the Island* (Mike Alexander, 1995), which was funded by CTG, Grampian Television and Channel 4, and *Seachd: The Inaccessible Pinnacle* (Simon Miller, 2007), which was a developed remake of the Gaelic short *Foighidinn: The Crimson Snowdrop/Patience* (Simon Miller, 2005). *Seachd*, released in the United States as *Seachd: The Crimson Snowdrop*, was funded by GMS, BBC Scotland and Scottish Screen.

Due to the amount of funding put into Gaelic film-making by television production companies, this is not a movement that can yet be thought of in terms of a Gaelic cinema. However, *Seachd* became the first Gaelic feature to achieve theatrical release in the United Kingdom through Soda Pictures, and US distribution through Altadena, who are part of Hollywood Classics. This was a remarkable achievement for a film which began life as a short, *Foighidinn* (which was made on the unused remains of film reels used on movies like *Wimbledon* [Richard Loncraine, 2004] and *Bridget Jones: The Edge of Reason* [Beeban Kidron, 2004] donated to director Simon Miller by Working Title in London) and whose budget was a miniscule £680,000, around one-quarter to one-sixth of the cost of a typical Scottish art film.

These Gaelic films, then, can be considered together as an expression of a broader renaissance in Gaelic culture, which can be contextualized in relation to the Gàidhealtachd, although it can also be seen in terms of the transformation of the cultural landscape that Scotland has experienced since the 1980s, or more broadly still in relation to the rise of ethnonationalism in various regions of the world such as Cornwall in the south of England, or Catalonia or the Basque Country in Spain.

The specificities of media production in the Gàidhealtachd are of great importance for the continuation of Gaelic media. The funded infrastructure provided by MG ALBA, the distribution outlet of BBC ALBA (which is able to screen the Gaelic films listed above, that would otherwise be consigned to silence in the Scottish Screen archive), along with educational opportunities such as the Diploma in Gaelic Media at Sabhal Mòr Ostaig (the Gaelic College on Skye, established in 1973 and now a part of the University of the Highlands and Islands), and the relocation of Chris Young's production company Young Films to Skye (Young Films produced *Seachd*), suggest that Gaelic film-making will continue to develop in the future. For example, in 2009 MG ALBA launched the annual FilmG ALBA competition, which not only awards prizes for three- to five-minute Gaelic shorts in a range of categories (Best Drama Short, Best Factual Short, Best Community

Short, etc.), but also offers workshops to train aspiring Gaelic film-makers. The winner of the first competition was *Siubhlachan/The Traveller* (Uisdean Murray, 2009), a short film about a little girl, Seonag (Cassandra MacLean), who discovers that her deceased grandfather's pocket watch enables her to travel back in time. It was later made into a 30-minute television pilot *Siubhlachan: Mòr Mineag* and screened on BBC ALBA in 2010. Whilst far from financially well-endowed, competitions like FilmG at least offer opportunities to gain experience, some degree of training, and potentially even television air time for aspiring Gaelic film-makers.

Based on the existing available body of films, four interlinked features can be isolated that characterize much of the Gaelic film-making to emerge thus far.

First, Gaelic film-making is clearly engaged with the continuation of the oral culture of the Gàidhealtachd, and especially the role of storytelling in maintaining the region's history. For centuries Gaelic history has been preserved in oral form, in stories and songs. The importance of the bard as repository of Gaelic cultural history is evident in the manner in which the Statutes of Iona singled out and banned bards in the Gàidhealtachd. What jumps out at the viewer when screening many Gaelic films is their engagement with this preserved oral history, which is evident if we look both in front of and behind the camera.

Hero's opening intertitle proclaims it to be based on 'the story of Dermid and Grannia, gathered from the oral tradition in the West Coast of Scotland'. It also features a bard who engages the characters in a discussion of their lives, as though commenting on the narrative itself. Many other films are stories about stories being told, including *Play Me Something*, *Foighidinn* and *Seachd*. The idea for the latter two was initially conceived by its director (Englishman Simon Miller) to capture the electric experience of being in the presence of a Gaelic storyteller. We might add to this the mythical or fairy-tale register of *A'Bhean Eudach*, the parable-like *Sealladh* and *An Iobairt*, and the almost magic realist fantasy of *Mac*.

The clearest foregrounding of the importance of storytelling to the maintenance of Gaelic culture occurs in *Seachd*. The focal point of the story is the struggle between a grandfather and his adult grandson, both called Aonghas, over the importance of stories in their lives. At the close of the film, the young man Aonghas inherits his grandfather's book of stories. This book has featured prominently in his life, being present whenever his grandfather told a story. However, after his grandfather's death the young Aonghas opens the book only to find its pages blank. In this moment, Aonghas finally accepts his role as the next in line to carry on the role of storytelling. Thus, *Seachd* points to the importance of the maintenance of an oral history of the Gàidhealtachd.

In front of the camera, several of these films feature Gaelic poets or bards. *Play Me Something* includes Hamish Henderson, the Highland folklorist and poet, whose mother was a singer of Gaelic songs. In *Seachd*, Aonghas the grandfather is played by Gaelic novelist and bard Aonghas Padraig Caimbeul. *An Iobairt* features Margaret Bennett, a folklorist and Gaelic signer, who plays a forensic archaeologist, pictured excavating the earth of the Gàidhealtachd in order to better understand its past history. These casting decisions provide knowing nods for Gaelic audiences familiar with these bards, to emphasize the role that film can play as another means for maintaining Gaelic history, akin to the oral histories kept alive by bards in the absence of written history.

Behind the camera, although many of the films mentioned above are directed by people who may well not claim to be Gaelic, but rather Scottish and in some cases English, the most influential figure is the Gaelic poet Aonghas MacNeacail, who has been involved in the scripts for *Hero*, *An Iobairt*, *Foighidinn* and *Seachd*.

The second identifiable characteristic is the youthfulness of many of the projects, in terms of their casts and crews. There is a clear sense that we are watching young people encountering old myths and legends, and interpreting them for themselves. This contrast of youth with ancient cultural history emphasizes the importance of engaging young people with their cultural history if they are to maintain it into the future.

For this reason, many films feature small children at the heart of their narratives, including *Sealladh*, *Mac*, *Foighidinn*, *Seachd* and *Siubhlachan*. Many others focus on teenagers, including *Hero*, *Play Me Something*, *As An Eilean* and *Ag Iasgach*, often making reference to the contrary pulls of the Gàidhealtachd and the larger cities of Scotland or North America for the life prospects of those born in the Gàidhealtachd (in terms of education and employment). This also features as a concern for the adult Aonghas in *Seachd*, and is seen to directly impact upon the lives of children in *Sealladh*, *Mac* and *Seachd*.

It is fair to say that some of this youthful Gaelic film-making does not always produce a polished aesthetic. There are moments in certain films during which a rather raw production quality is evident (be it in terms of elements of *mise-en-scène*, like costumes, or acting styles), even if this is often balanced on other occasions by, for example, some beautiful cinematographic renderings of the landscape of the Gàidhealtachd. *Hero* is the standout instance of this youthful aesthetic, with comical fights and deaths by swords clearly tucked under armpits. Yet the appearance of the 'Young Bucks' teenage gang from Drumchapel in Glasgow was important because of the opportunity it gave to several young men, already set into lives of petty crime, to work on a creative project that connected them to traditional forms of rural labour – they rebuilt the ruined stone and thatch village of Barnakil which features in the film before shooting commenced – as well as a mythical sense of Scotland's past. This is the case even if the focus on youth is arguably of greater importance for films like *As An Eilean* and *Seachd*, films made in the Gàidhealtachd by Gaelic film-makers and starring native Gaelic speakers.

Third, perhaps the most dominant feature of all is the prominence of the Gàidhealtachd's distinctive rural landscape in locating the stories and legends through which Gaelic culture is explored. *A'Bhean Eudach* is a dark fairy tale set by the sea. The liminal space of the coast, between sea and land, plays a key role in this story of jealousy in which a mute young woman murders her sister by platting her hair into seaweed so that she is trapped and dies by the sea (perhaps of exposure, perhaps drowning). Human life on the coast is thus shown to be intricately bound to the sea, as a life-giving force (the jealous sister commits the murder after an ambiguously sexual brush with something scaly in the sea, and inherits her murdered sister's family as a result) and indeed, as a potentially deadly context in which to live and make a living. In this way, the Gàidhealtachd's centuries of dependence on the sea is rendered in a story of people tied, almost literally, to the landscape.

Hero also integrates its characters into the landscape in several ways. It uses long shots that dwarf characters against mountain ranges; contains animation sequences showing the superhuman skipping of a boulder across the sea and the amazing killing of a distant flying bird by bow and arrow (both of which bring characters and location closer than is humanly possible, as in the distortion of strength typical of legend); and even features supernatural transformations that see, for example, a fish plucked from the river metamorphose into a character who then joins the narrative.

Foighidinn and *Seachd*, for their part, focus on the impressive Cuillin mountain range on the Isle of Skye. One mountain in particular, Sgurr Dearg (Inaccessible Pinnacle) is a focal point for this narrative, a location in which mythical narratives of heroic deeds from the past mingle with present-day reality. In both films, storytelling blurs the distinction between fantasy and fact in order to keep alive the history of the Gàidhealtachd, and maintain the continuity of cultural identity through identification with place. *Seachd* even contains a standout moment in which all the stories told by the adult Aonghas's grandfather appear before his eyes, as a series of fantastic figures in the landscape. At this moment his grandfather suddenly materializes in the back seat of his car (whether he is alive or dead is unclear) in order to pass on his storytelling legacy to Aonghas by taking him to Sgurr Dearg. The coincidence of these events stresses the role of the landscape as repository of stories, as though locations contain the 'ghosts' of the past, as stories, in a way that can inform the present.

Perhaps the clearest example of the importance of landscape, however, is the film *An Iobairt*, in which two peat diggers uncover a corpse of a ritual sacrifice from the pre-Christian past, whose ghost then appears. *An Iobairt* draws parallels between a story set on the Isle of Skye in the present and the events that led up to the sacrifice of the man whose corpse is uncovered. In this way it foregrounds the possibility of maintaining, or unearthing, links to the region's past by considering the landscape as a repository of history, a location that is imbued with the memories of the Gàidhealtachd. In all these films, tapping into this very physical terrain, this earthy, watery, rocky mountainous databank, is shown to be akin to listening to a story or song, or, watching a film.

Fourth and finally, many Gaelic films engage with the idea that the passing of time is experienced differently (or at least can be allegorically understood to be passing differently) in the Gàidhealtachd to Scotland, Europe or the world at large; this is due to the way in which Gaelic culture has been marginalized by the progressive teleology of modern history. This final characteristic ties together the former three, as Gaelic film-makers consider the Gàidhealtachd in terms of its history and its place in the world using mythical stories that connect people to place in (or rather, through) time. Of the Gaelic films to self-consciously play with time, *Foighidinn* and *Seachd* go to the greatest lengths to suggest that time can be imagined to be passing more slowly in the Gàidhealtachd, through the fantastical story (told, noticeably, to little children) of a man who has lived for hundreds of years because his heart only beats once for every ten beats of a normal human heart. This story is not intended to suggest that the region is 'backward' in relation to the modern world, however, but rather to point to the manner in which its history requires patience (the meaning of the Gaelic word *foighidinn*) for its preservation through the telling of stories that are far older than individual human lives. These are collective stories through which the culture is preserved for hundreds of years, and accordingly they exist in a timescape akin to that of legend.

This is a theme that works extremely well with child characters in *Mac* and *Siubhlachan*. As the grandfather says in *Siubhlachan*:

> Remember Seonag. We all exist in time. Even when our days are over there is a small fragment in time where we still live. Don't think of me as gone forever, but instead just think of me as being somewhere else.

As his granddaughter, Seonag, turns the winder on her deceased grandfather's pocket watch, the clouds move quickly across the coastal landscape, the sun and moon rising and setting unnaturally fast, whilst a single shaft of sunlight sweeps swiftly over the empty window of a ruined house, evoking the transience of human lives amidst the ancient history of the location. In this one image the four characteristics are perfectly encapsulated. The passing of time around this young girl time traveller, then, is shown to be tied to the history of the region, which is itself to be found in the landscape of the Gàidhealtachd as it appears in Gaelic stories, songs and films.

David Martin-Jones

CULTURAL CROSSOVER RADICAL AND ENGAGED CINEMA

Introduction: Periodization

For film-makers, politicians and social campaigners in Scotland, cinema's potential to provoke debate and, in the right circumstances, encourage action on social and political issues, became apparent, just as elsewhere, early in the medium's history, and in the Scottish context from at least 1917. In the decades following, developments in the technology, art and consumption of cinema served to confirm both to those in possession of, and those in pursuit of, power or influence that cinema had the capacity to engage audiences on a scale and with more immediacy and visual impact than any other medium, at least until the invention of television. Even now in the Internet age, engaged cinema continues to play a significant part in documenting or dramatizing political conflict, social change and the myriad challenges humanity faces.

Although Scots were as early as the 1920s (and indeed still are) amongst the most avid cinemagoers in Britain, it is one of Scotland's many paradoxes that it has produced relatively few films in comparison to similar-sized countries elsewhere in Europe (Hutchinson 1990: 32). In that context the number which have approached the world with an explicit or at least a substantial, implicit social or political purpose are few in absolute terms but nonetheless significant. Equally, given a history that has not lacked significant social change or political conflict, it is perhaps surprising that there has not been greater use of the medium as a tool for liberation or at least a mining of that history for subject matter. This essay sets out to document the key moments in the history of 'radical and engaged' Scottish film-making and to examine both what has impelled and what has impeded the harnessing of film to movements for social change.

Cinema and the progressive movement in Scotland between the wars

There is evidence of the employment of film in support of radical (for the time) causes from at least 1917 when Suffragists screened footage of Scottish Women's field hospitals in war-torn France in support of 'votes for women' (Hutchinson 1990: 37). Following its first extensive use as a government propaganda tool during World War II, film became recognized across the political spectrum as a potentially important tool of persuasion (Hollins 1981). In 1920 the British Labour Party published a pamphlet on the uses of cinema as propaganda, and a film of famine victims in war-torn central Europe was screened at public meetings to bolster support for those calling on the British government to help restore free trade and provide credit to Germany. However, it was the growing circulation of Soviet cinema, following the Bolsheviks' 1922 victory in the Russian Civil War, that provided both film-

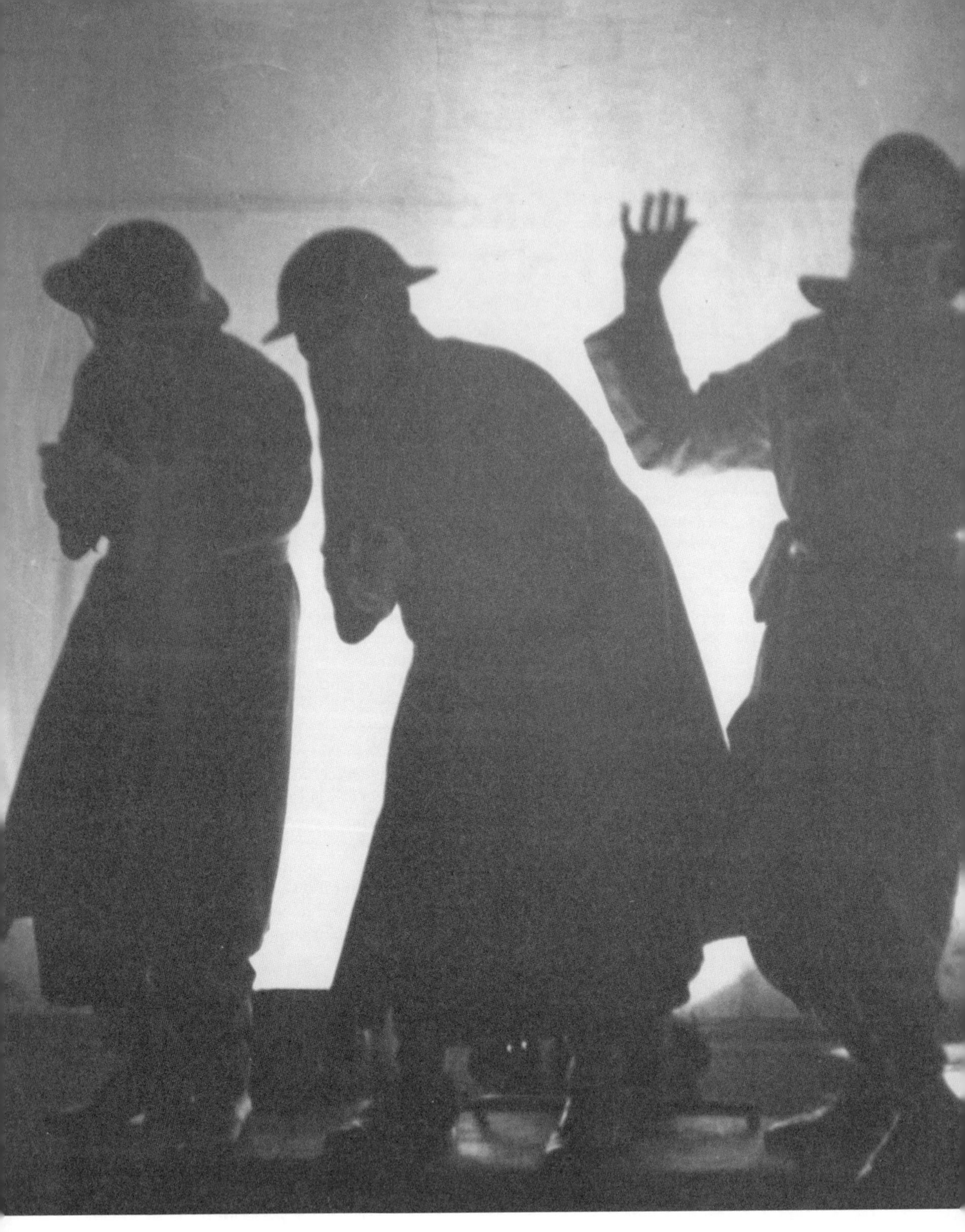

Hell Unlimited (1936), British Film Institute Collection

makers and social activists with a powerful new source of artistic and political inspiration, at a time when art and left-wing politics were becoming increasingly intertwined (Hogenkamp 1986: 13). In 1922 the Scottish communist activist John MacLean, a leading figure on Glasgow's 'Red Clydeside' and the Bolshevik government's official representative in Scotland, led calls for the establishment of 'municipal cinemas' (Hogenkamp 1986: 20), an instance perhaps of Lenin's reported view that '*of all the arts, for us* [communists] *cinema is the most important*' (Scottish Communists n.d., emphasis added). From 1925, when films such as Eisenstein's *Battleship Potemkin* began to circulate through the growing network of film societies (despite considerable opposition and attempted censorship by the British authorities) the power of explicitly political cinema to engage audiences with the issues of the day began to take hold (MacPherson 1980).

One of the first commentators to advocate on behalf of both Soviet cinema and the establishment of 'Workers' Film Societies', where ordinary people could be inspired by the achievements of their fellow workers in the pre-Stalinist Soviet Union, was the London-based Scottish novelist and champion of the artistic avant-garde, Kenneth MacPherson. The founding editor of the film journal *Close Up*, established in 1927 and one of the very first dedicated to the art and indeed politics of film, MacPherson exemplified the conjunction of progressive politics and modernist aesthetics that reached something of a highpoint in the interwar period. MacPherson and Ralph Bond (who later became a protégé of John Grierson) campaigned in *Close Up* for the establishment of workers' film societies to screen the work of Soviet and other progressive film-makers (Donald, Friedberg and Marcus 1999). Labour movement activists in Scotland were amongst the first to hear their call and, encouraged by screenings of Pudovkin's *Mother* (1926) and *The End of St. Petersburg* (1927), by 1930 workers' film societies had been established in Glasgow, Edinburgh and elsewhere (Hogenkamp 1986: 52). As private clubs, these societies were usually, though not always, able to circumvent the censorship that regularly prevented Soviet films such as Pudovkin's *Storm Over Asia* (1928) from being screened publicly.

Mirroring the movement elsewhere in the United Kingdom to take the logical next step into the production of films highlighting domestic political issues, Scottish socialist film-making groups soon followed. The first, the 'Glasgow Kino Group', was established in 1935, the eve of the Spanish Civil War which, following its outbreak in July 1936, greatly enlarged the audience for the anti-fascist cause and the public appetite for news from Spain in particular (Allen 1982). Exposure to the films of Eisenstein, Pudovkin, Dovshenko and others proved to be a pivotal influence on an emerging generation of Scottish artists and intellectuals, amongst whom were Norman McLaren and Helen Biggar, graduates of the Glasgow School of Art and early members of the Glasgow Kino Group. Following an unsuccessful attempt to make a film about health and the environment, their first collaboration while at the Art School, came McLaren's and Biggar's anti-arms trade short *Hell Unlimited* (1936) 'addressed to all who are made to pay each day for their own and other people's destruction'. This early example of agitprop combined animation, archival footage and dramatic vignettes with innovative techniques such as scratching the film emulsion.

Helen Biggar, a Communist Party member and daughter of a prominent Independent Labour Party leader and Lord Provost of the City, remained in Glasgow where she helped produce Glasgow Kino's first film, *Challenge To Fascism* (1938), which documents a May Day Parade in solidarity with the republican cause in the Spanish Civil War (Hogenkamp 1986 and Scullion 1990: 50–52). Sadly, most of the group's output documenting the activities of the labour movement – marches, demonstrations, sit-ins and strikes – has not survived. However ample evidence remains of the group's activities, which included touring programs of films to other parts of Scotland. McLaren's extraordinary inventiveness brought him an invitation to join Scots documentary pioneer John

Grierson's GPO (General Post Office) Film Unit, which in the 1930s nurtured many of Britain's brightest film talents, including fellow Scot Harry Watt, co-director of *Night Mail* (1936), as well as pioneering Scotswoman documentary film-maker Jenny Gilbertson. In 1941, two years after Grierson had moved to Canada to establish its National Film Board, he invited McLaren to join him and establish the National Film Board's first animation unit.

After the war: Documentary, avant-garde and the beginnings of Scottish feature film

The outbreak of World War II brought organized radical film-making in the United Kingdom to a virtual stop as most on the left subordinated campaigning politics to support for the war effort. Following the war, with the election of a Labour government in 1945 and the Communist Party of Great Britain's move towards parliamentarianism, anti-establishment or 'oppositional' film-making appeared to lose much of its *raison d'être*. A core of film activists based mainly in London continued to document social causes such as the squatters' movement, but almost no such political film-making activity appears to have taken place in Scotland in the 1940s. One rare example of an early post-war film touching directly on politics in Scotland is *The Glen is Ours* (Henry Cass, 1946). It dramatizes a demobilized soldier's fight to prevent the glen he grew up in from being sold, by standing for and winning a seat on the local council. The film was produced by a London company and sponsored by the government's Central Office of Information to encourage participation in local government.

This post-war dearth of engaged film-making stands in marked contrast to the resilience of politically engaged theatre and the continued vitality of a broad range of other left cultural activity in Scotland during the 1940s (Scullion 2002). Indeed it was the left-wing theatre company Glasgow Unity Theatre to which, following her brief film-making career, Helen Biggar devoted her energies and it was one of that company's most successful plays which provided the basis for one of the few instances of cinema engaging directly with Scottish social or political themes in the 1950s.

The Gorbals Story (David MacKane, 1950) was originally produced for the stage in 1946 and the play was described in the press at the time as 'a grim study of conditions in a city slum' (Anon. 1946). At its Glasgow theatre premiere, a squatters' movement leader was invited to address the audience. In 1948 the company re-staged the play in London, attracting the attention of two film producers who engaged expatriate Scot David MacKane to direct it for the screen. Despite or perhaps because it was in some respects ahead of its time in its frank portrayal of the Scottish working class, it failed to generate either critical or commercial success (Hill 1982). Two years later, however, the harsh conditions experienced by Scotland's industrial working class made another and more successful appearance in *The Brave Don't Cry* (1952), a production of John Grierson's 'Group 3' offshoot from the government-backed National Film Finance Corporation.

The Brave Don't Cry's dramatization of a real mining disaster dealt with experiences that resonated deeply with Grierson's early personal experience of deprived mining communities (Caughie and McArthur 1982). Like *The Gorbals Story*, it drew on the resources of a progressive Scottish theatre company, the Glasgow Citizens Theatre, for much of its cast and faced hostility from parts of the cinema industry that allegedly attempted to block its being chosen to open the 1952 Edinburgh Film Festival (Caughie and McArthur 1982). Despite their efforts, *The Brave Don't Cry* proved to be a critical and commercial success. However, for the remainder of the decade feature film representations of Scotland steered clear of such stark social subjects, though rural deprivation provided the background to the comedy *Laxdale Hall* (John Eldridge, 1953) and the exploration of the question of landlordism in *Trouble in the Glen* (Herbert Wilcox, 1954).

Not until the 1960s would self-consciously political film practice in the United Kingdom re-emerge, and when it did, as in other aspects of cinema, Scotland was not in a position to be a part of it. Such film-making in Scotland as then was taking place (and there was not a great deal) was almost exclusively confined to the sponsored documentary.

In 1946 an (unsuccessful) attempt had been made to establish a Scottish film studio in Glasgow, an initiative partly driven by a democratic imperative inasmuch as its leading lights were motivated by progressive and nationalist political objectives (Bruce 1996). Indeed, amongst the erstwhile studio's unrealized projects was a biography of a pioneering Scottish woman trade unionist, while the project as a whole attracted the support of cooperative societies along with other elements of the labour movement (Bruce 1990).

However, it was the documentary movement, which John Grierson had inspired and nurtured through his leading role in successive government and private initiatives, from the GPO Film Unit and Film Centre to Group 3 and the National Film Finance Corporation, that offered the best, if still limited, chance of generating critical cinematic perspectives on British society. This was a reflection of leading documentarians' concern in the immediate post-war period to use the medium of film to expose persistent social ills such as poor housing and ill-health as well as to promote initiatives to remedy them.

In Scotland, the epicentre of documentary film-making was a public body, 'Films of Scotland', originally established at Grierson's suggestion in 1938 by the government in Scotland. Films of Scotland had been tasked with the production of films celebrating the country's achievements, to be screened at the 1938 Empire Exhibition in Glasgow and then promoted internationally (Caughie and McArthur 1982). Though disbanded in 1939, its job apparently done, a successor body of the same name was established in 1954 with the aim of using film to promote Scotland as a place to live, work and trade with the rest of the United Kingdom – and internationally. Films of Scotland thus provided the main avenue for aspirant Scottish film-makers to gain employment and experience, albeit in the production of sponsored promotional films extolling the virtues, for example, of the country's public utilities, natural assets or major infrastructure works. Despite some of the film-makers' best efforts to stretch the creative boundaries of these sponsored films, and the social concerns evident in films such as *Glasgow: 1980* (Dawn Cine Group, 1971), the Films of Scotland documentaries were, by their very nature as promotional tools, very constrained in their capacity to offer any searching critique of society or public policy.

Beyond the sponsored documentary, Scottish film-making from the late 1950s to the mid-1970s remained largely the preserve of three groups: enthusiastic amateurs; a tiny clutch of artists using film as their primary medium; and a few determined professionals endeavouring, through the occasional self-financed short film or via more adventurous narrative elements smuggled into documentaries, to escape the bounds of sponsorship and graduate to the feature film. Indeed, the Dawn Cine Group, comprised of Communist Party activists, stands out precisely because it appears to be the only example of radical activist film-making in the period. Echoing their Kino Cinema forbearers from the 1930s, the Dawn group set out to document social conditions such as slum housing and promote causes ranging from the anti-nuclear movement to reversing rural depopulation. In one case, *Let Glasgow Flourish* (1952/56), a 15-minutes-long short on slum conditions and a campaign for new social housing, the film-makers use a mix of documentary and reconstructed scenes in a conscious attempt to counter the rose-tinted view of civic progress propounded by the local authority's own promotional documentaries (Stewart n.d.).

In 1950s and 1960s Scotland the absence of a feature film industry – i.e. no local control or source of support for finance, distribution or exhibition – meant that film-makers, with or without social or political agendas, could not effectively reach a cinema audience in Scotland or further afield. Until the advent of (even then very limited) Scottish public funding for film production in the early 1980s, Scots could only pursue a film-making career or any kind of formal training in England or overseas – and this was the route taken by the first generation of Scottish feature film-makers (Scott 2009). Television, however, in this period presented more opportunities to the engaged film-maker, despite public service and commercial broadcasters' general aversion to controversial subjects.

Although its characterization as the 'golden age' of British television drama is problematic (Caughie 2000), the 1960s did see a sustained and influential (particularly given the three-channel system then in place) output of often very socially engaged drama, especially but not only in the form closest to cinema, the feature-length 'single play'. Mainly evident on the BBC, notably the Wednesday Play (1964–70) and Play for Today (1970–84) strands but also with Granada TV in Manchester – a key force in the commercial ITV's dramatic output – these television plays were in many cases written, produced or directed by political radicals such as Ken Loach, director of one of the first and best-known examples, *Cathy Come Home* (1966). Standing at the centre of this so-called 'golden age' of British television drama are two Scots, James McTaggart, who produced the Wednesday Play from 1964–70, and Troy Kennedy Martin, a writer who joined the BBC as a script editor and who in 1962 created, with John McGrath, the groundbreaking, gritty realist police series *Z-Cars* (1962–78). McTaggart's reputation had been established through his direction of the first Scottish television play, *Three Ring Circus* (1960) produced by BBC Scotland for Network transmission and now considered a key influence in the development of modern British television drama (Cook 2009). McTaggart and those around him were, like their theatre counterparts, influenced by the New Left politics of the Cold War period and were operating under a mandate from the BBC's then Head of Drama, Sidney Newman, '*to concentrate on the turning points in English society*' (Gardner and Wyver 1983: 116, emphasis added).

Amongst the members of this group, several of whom later played a leading role in shaking up British cinema, were key figures in the emergence of Scotland on the screen. These included writer, producer and director John McGrath (like Ken Loach he was not a Scot but nonetheless a vocal champion of Scotland and socialist politics), expatriate Scottish director John Mackenzie and writer Peter McDougall. Although figures like McGrath had played an important role in the creative and political modernization of British television drama in the 1960s, it was not until the 1970s that Scotland itself featured in this progressive drama. One notable exception however is Peter Watkins's ground-breaking dramatized documentary *Culloden* (1964), arguably the first example of a Scottish subject examined through a radical television lens, although Watkins himself was neither Scottish nor based in Scotland. By no means for the last time it took an outsider to bring a fresh and politicized angle to the representation of Scotland.

Like world cinema (MacPherson 2012), television in the 1960s treated Scotland largely as a source of safe historical stories, with television drama departments mining its extensive literary heritage for material (Cook 2008). Only in the 1970s did the realities of modern Scottish life begin to feature in the schedules, to begin with largely in serial soap opera form. However, in 1974 the BBC broadcasted *The Cheviot, the Stag and the Black Black Oil* (John McGrath and John Mackenzie), a feature-length and unapologetically political view of Scotland past and present, transmitted in the high-rating network Play for Today slot which, despite its name, included single-camera film work. It presaged a string of increasingly cinematic dramas dealing directly with some of the uncomfortable realities of Scottish life – from sectarianism to drug abuse. Adapted from the successful touring stage play by radical theatre Company 7:84, *The Cheviot* was written by John McGrath, the company's founder, as well as directed by another, John Mackenzie, both key figures in British TV Drama (Moat n.d.). Mackenzie then collaborated with Scottish screenwriter Peter MacDougall on *Just Another Saturday* (John Mackenzie, 1975), a Prix Italia-winning Play for Today, which broke new ground in tackling Glasgow's religious sectarianism and associated violence (though McDougall had written an earlier Play for Today, *Just Your Luck* [1972] which dealt with similar themes), at a time when 'the Troubles' in Northern Ireland were at their height (Davidson n.d.). McDougall and Mackenzie went on to make another two BBC Plays for Today, *The Elephants' Graveyard* (1976) and *Just a Boys' Game* (1979), works which have come to be seen as cinematic in all but their financing and distribution, recognized in a retrospective at the 2009 Edinburgh International Film Festival (Fulton, 2011). The partnership of McDougall and Mackenzie finally reached the cinema screen with *A Sense of Freedom* (1979), their adaptation of the autobiography of convicted but reformed murderer-turned-artist and prison-reform-campaigner Jimmy Boyle.

Amidst the otherwise arid conditions of film-making in Scotland in the 1950s and 1960s a few alternative film-makers did manage to blossom, although they did so in the context of an independent practice outside of recognized professional film-making in a way which has comparatively recently been valued or indeed recognized as such (Neely 2009: 301). The first is Margaret Tait, a poet and truly independent film-maker in the sense that, largely failing to secure external finance from arts or other public bodies, she was obliged to fund almost all of her thirty or so experimental short films between 1951 and 1981 from her professional earnings as a doctor (Neely 2008). A graduate of the Centro Sperimentale di Cinematografia in Rome, Tait has in recent years been rediscovered – and, in particular, reclaimed by feminist scholarship (Neely 2008). The difficulties Tait faced in securing support for her work, despite being one of the few 'artist film-makers' in Scotland in a period when film as art was actively promoted by the major arts funding bodies, are now seen by some as evidence of both institutional marginalization and sexism (Loukopoulou 2007). Her smaller-scale work, much of it made around her home in the Orkney Islands, is often concerned with a poetic rendition of everyday life although some films, such as *Caora Mor the Big Sheep* (1966), touch on larger-scale political themes, in this case the historical scar of the Highland Clearances. After many years of attempting to secure funding and having secured this, at age 74 Tait finally reached a wider audience with her first (and only) feature film *Blue Black Permanent* (1992), a semi-autobiographical and unconventional narrative of three generations of an Orcadian family.

Even less well-known than Tait is the equally independent Enrico Cocozza, the son of Italian immigrants to Scotland, who, having worked in Rome with King Vidor and Jean Cocteau, produced more than sixty short films from his home in Wishaw near Glasgow. As with Tait, Cocozza's film-making was supported by his day job, in his case as a university lecturer in Italian and, like Tait's work, Cocozza's can best be seen as engaging with the experimental or avant-garde strand of 1950s and 1960s European cinema (Neely and Riach 2009). Nonetheless, several of the subjects he chose to address were politically charged, in both the personal and more public senses. His work ranged from the ambition of what we would now call a 'micro-budget' half-hour melodrama, *Chick's Day* (1950), a self-styled 'fiction documentary' which deals with parental neglect, alcoholism, unemployment and the social causes of crime, to the more experimental *Bongo Erotico* (1959) which, for its time and national context, dealt in quite a forthright way with bisexuality. Although an amateur film-maker, Cocozza's work stands out for its singular aesthetic ambition and in a number of instances prefigures the work of established film-makers: his *Porphyra* (1959), for example, foreshadows Michael Powell's *Peeping Tom* (1960) in its depiction of murderous scopophilia.

Concern with illuminating the realities of industrial working-class life evident in Cocozza's *Chick's Day* anticipates the first films of both Bill Douglas and Bill Forsyth, the two figures most identified with the birth of modern Scottish cinema in the 1970s. The same austere landscape of a coal-mining community presented in Douglas's celebrated *My Childhood* (1972) is evident in *Chick's Day*, while Cocozza's portrayal of under-employed 1950s youth drawn into criminality pre-figures *That Sinking Feeling* (1980), Bill Forsyth's debut film, a gentle comedy satirizing the effects of de-industrialization on a group of unemployed youths.

However, we should not overstate the case – in the 1960s and 1970s most Scottish film-makers, amateurs and professionals alike, were primarily concerned to express themselves creatively to a mainstream cinema or television audience rather than use film in pursuit of social or political change. In Scotland no equivalent developed to the Independent Film-makers Association established in England in 1974 (MacPherson 1990). As in other aspects of Scotland's audio-visual landscape it once again fell to outsiders to engage directly with the issues of the day. Thus, for example, it was the pioneering London-based activist film-making group Cinema Action who in *UCS1* (1971) and *Class Struggle: Film from the Clyde* (1977) documented, in depth, the historic 'work-in' by Glasgow shipworkers in the Upper Clyde Shipyard (Fraser and Webb n.d.).

One of the contradictions of Scottish film culture is that while, for example, in 1975 the Edinburgh Film Festival was pioneering new critical approaches to cinema (as it had pioneered the documentary in the immediate post-war years) and championing alternative film-makers such as Laura Mulvey and Peter Wollen, most Scottish film-makers, even when sympathetic to left-wing politics, largely shunned these radical critiques of film form and style as an inherently ideological practice, in contrast with a perspective increasingly influential amongst the independent film sector in England (Dickinson 1999). This gap between the theoretically informed radical film-making practice in England and the more pragmatic concerns of the majority of the Scottish film-making community continued through the 1980s. During the 1970s Scotland's professional film-makers became increasingly vocal and politically organized around a quasi-nationalist agenda expressed at events such as *Film Bang* (1976) and *Cinema and the Small Country* (1977). These semi-campaigning conferences articulated aims such as the establishment of a Scottish film production fund but beyond a desire for more autonomous resources they avoided adopting a manifesto of film-making aesthetics or politics – though film-maker Murray Grigor's exhibition and film *Scotch Myths* (1981) suggested what they should avoid. At the same time, those local advocates of a politicized film practice, given their mainly academic background, were more concerned (and more equipped) to deconstruct cinematic stereotypes of Scotland and Scottishness than to articulate a strategy for countering them. To the extent that the latter had a program for how more progressive films could be made, it centred on community-based initiatives and the potential role of film and video workshops.

With the exception of the 1974 BBC TV production of 7:84 Theatre's overtly political play *The Cheviot, the Stag and the Black Black Oil* (see above), the first shoots of an explicitly socially engaged film practice in late 1970s and early 1980s Scotland appeared elsewhere, amongst community activists and academics, with the support of only a tiny handful of professional film-makers. This grouping was sympathetic to the growing critique of conventional cinema and television amplified by the newly emerging academic discipline of film studies. At the same time, the recent arrival of portable video technology, combined with examples such as Canada's 'Challenge for Change' programme (Warren 1973) (which itself owed much to the influence of John Grierson, although he stopped short of endorsing its concern to empower ordinary people as film-makers) and other social film initiatives, offered both means and methods of addressing social issues and community concerns through the moving image (Glassman 2010).

Dark days and video: The rise of community media and cinema under Thatcherism

The film and video workshop movement (Dickinson, Cottringer and Petley 1993), which had sprung out of the mix of alternative film practices centred on London from the 1970s onwards, took root in Scotland with the founding of the Edinburgh Film Workshop Trust (EFWT) in 1977; two more Edinburgh organizations, Red Star Cinema in 1980 and Video in Pilton (VIP) in 1981; and Glasgow Film and Video Workshop (GFVW) in 1983 (Rushton 2003). Two rurally based workshops, one in the central Scotland town of Alva and the other, Fradharc Ur on the Hebridean Island of Lewis, and a number of less well-resourced community-based groups in areas such as Glasgow's Drumchapel and Cranhill, meant at its height the sector boasted in excess of a dozen organizations. In distinct but overlapping ways these groups endeavoured to bring professional expertise and production values to a socialized conception of film-making practice and, in the case of GFVW, one which aimed to be informed by then current debates in critical film theory. The majority of their output was documentary-based and mainly destined for non-broadcast distribution. However, first EFWT and then VIP secured television broadcast via a unique and pioneering funding arrangement, 'The Workshop Declaration', negotiated in 1982 by the film technicians union Association of Cinemagraph Television and Allied Technicians (ACTT) with the British Film Institute and the newly launched Channel 4 Television (Roberts n.d.). Despite tensions around the erosion of traditional union demarcation boundaries, the workshops and other ACTT members joined together during the 1984–85 miners' strike to produce and distribute alternatives to manifestly hostile mainstream media coverage of a bitter and era-defining industrial dispute which devastated whole communities.

Nevertheless, the emergence of a community media movement outside of mainstream television made little initial impact on Scottish cinema per se; it was a movement primarily concerned with empowering local communities through the use of video (and occasionally film), often for directly didactic campaigning purposes – for example the anti-nuclear documentary *On Site Torness* (Alistair Scott and Mike Sharples,1979) or community development *Clyde Film* (Ian Venart, Charlie Tracy, Ian Miller, Mandy Merrick, Alistair McCallum, and Ken Currie,1985).

The 1980s also a new generation of women film-makers emerge, several of whom were concerned, such as Rosie Gibson and Penny Thompson in the documentary *The Work They Say is Mine* (Rosie Gibson,1986), to address the under-representation of women's experiences on the screen. Though in the familiar pattern of external eyes being quicker to the scene it was a workshop group from Sheffield in England who were first to document radical Scottish women's history in *Red Skirts on Clydeside* (1984), which narrated the rent strikes and women activists of Glasgow in 1915 (Hedditch n.d.). Meanwhile, Edinburgh Film Workshop Trust's 'Women's Unit' played a significant role in encouraging women documentary film-makers such as Sarah Noble, who made *Site One: Holy Loch* (1985) on the US nuclear presence on the Clyde and Cassandra McGrogan's films *Your Health's Your Wealth* (1990) on the politics of health and *Behind Closed Doors* (1991) on the issue of domestic violence against women.

Although issue-based documentary was their preferred mode of film-making, some of those active in the community and workshop sector developed aspirations to produce fiction. However, it would take ten years from the 'New Wave' Scottish features of the early 1980s for the workshops to reach the stage where they could mount full-scale drama productions. Video in Pilton were the first, with their video feature, *The Priest and the Pirate* (1994) followed by Edinburgh Film Workshop Trust's *The Butterfly Man* (1996) a half-hour film drama which, like David Leland's 1990 adaptation of William McIvanney's novel *The Big Man*, drew on the human cost of the 1984–85 miners' strike.

In 1990 two film-makers who had made a trilogy of documentaries on the issue of homelessness for Channel 4 Television as well as a two-part documentary on the revolution in Nicaragua (*Into Nicaragua* [1988]) began making what is arguably the first self-consciously political feature film in Scotland, *Tickets for the Zoo* (1991). Director Brian Crumlish and Producer Christeen Winford's first and only feature film, partly financed by Channel 4, dramatized the issue of youth homelessness in Edinburgh and screened at the Edinburgh Film Festival.

Three years later, in a technological first for Scotland, Video in Pilton, based in an amenity-deprived peripheral housing estate on the outskirts of Edinburgh, used video to shoot their first feature-length micro-budget drama, *The Priest and the Pirate*. Funded and subsequently broadcast by BBC Scotland, it portrays a near-future Scotland in which political independence is a hot topic and pirate television operators are challenging the mainstream media's coverage of events – although it failed to secure a cinema release. Both films were part-financed by Channel 4, which, particularly in the 1980s and early 1990s, had an explicit policy of supporting alternative voices (e.g. through the funding of film and video workshops) and addressing social and political themes in its commissioned output. The 1990s were a period of considerable dynamism in Scottish cinema as a whole, with the success of films such as Danny Boyle's *Shallow Grave* (1994) and *Trainspotting* (1996), Michael Caton-Jones's *Rob Roy* (1995) and Lynne Ramsay's *Ratcatcher* (1999) attracting international audiences, awards and industry attention to Scottish talent and fuelling a sense of optimism about the future prospects for a sustainable Scottish industry. Social and political themes were touched on in several of these films with even big-budget and studio-backed historical dramas *Rob Roy* and *Braveheart* (Mel Gibson, 1995) resonating with a resurgent Scottish national identity, partly associated with the revival of nationalist politics but more broadly reflecting widespread discontent with the democratic deficit which had seen Scotland endure four successive Conservative governments which it had rejected electorally. That resentment was fleetingly portrayed in *Trainspotting* (adapted from the novel by Irvine Welsh), which viscerally highlighted the legacy of neo-liberalist economic policies in the drug-infested squalor of Edinburgh's high-unemployment, low-hope peripheral housing estates. Two years later, Lynne Ramsay, only the second woman director of a Scottish feature, set her debut feature film *Ratcatcher* amongst the industrial strife of the early 1970s, a period of energy shortages, frequent strikes and political crises. The narrative, however, is more a personal and poetic working-class coming-of-age story told by a film-maker who explicitly eschewed obvious political messages (Bond 1999).

Once again it would take an outsider, the veteran activist director Ken Loach, together with producer Sally Hibben (who also produced Kenny Glenaan's *Yasmin* [2004] – see below), to more directly address contemporary political concerns. Collaborating with first-time Scottish screenwriter Paul Laverty – a former lawyer and human rights activist who had worked in Sandinista-era Nicaragua – in *Carla's Song* (1997), Loach applied his trademark naturalistic style and concern for issues of class politics to the story of a Glaswegian bus driver who becomes involved with an exiled Nicaraguan and travels with her back to her homeland during the Reagan-backed Contra insurgency (Cranston n.d.). Laverty, Loach and Hibben went on to make *My Name is Joe* (1998), starring Peter Mullan as a recovering alcoholic in a drama/romance again set against the backdrop of urban decay in Glasgow, and *Sweet Sixteen* (2002), the story of a teenage boy from a deprived background drawn into drug dealing.

Indigenous feature film-makers meanwhile were apt to deal more obliquely with social or political controversy. Gillies MacKinnon's *Small Faces* (1996), written with his brother Billy, deals with much the same milieu as *Sweet Sixteen* but from a historical angle, drawing on their experiences growing up amidst the gang-culture of late 1960s Glasgow. London-based director Coky Giedroyc's *Stella Does Tricks* (1996), from a script by Scottish novelist AL Kennedy, deals with a Glaswegian prostitute in London, attempting to escape the cycle of abuse. Edinburgh's gang-culture in the 1980s was the backdrop to Richard Jobson's *16 Years of Alcohol* (2003) while in *Neds* (2010) Peter Mullan also dealt with gang violence, but in 1970s-era Glasgow.

Although these and other Scottish films of the 1990s and 2000s depict urban communities scarred by poverty, drugs and violence, they steer clear of the more direct political messages to be found in the work of Laverty and Loach, portraying people who find respite or escape through individual creativity, friendship or romance rather than through political consciousness or collective action. The latter, combined with a recurring concern for international issues, remains more visible in the hands of Scottish documentarians such as Lucinda Broadbent's *Sex and the Sandinistas* (1991), one of the first films from a liberal perspective to question the Nicaraguan Revolution's sexual politics, and *Macho* (Lucinda Broadbent, 2000) which documented a men-against-violence group (Women Make Movies). Closer to home, Doug Aubrey's *Victim of Geography* (1999) explored in road movie style the ramifications of the late 1990s Balkan conflict.

The 1990s also saw something of a revived debate in the Scottish arts, though discussion of cinema, Scottish or otherwise, appeared to have declined dramatically since the political period of the Edinburgh International Film Festival from the late 1970s to the mid-1980s or the public debate in the press that followed the establishment of the Scottish Film Production Fund in 1982 (Lloyd 2011). Such dissident or avant-garde voices as there were found a platform in the critical art journal *Variant* (est. 1984, relaunched in 1996) and Scottish Film and Visual Arts (1992–93), where both the history of moving image practice and the possibilities of video technology in the hands of visual artists were debated.

Although the eve of the twenty-first century witnessed the return to power of a Labour government in London and ushered in a devolution referendum leading to the opening in 1999 of the first Scottish parliament in 300 years, political themes remained virtually absent from Scottish cinema or television drama, unlike theatre and the visual arts which remained more actively engaged with questions of personal as well as large-scale politics (Fisher 2002). Amongst an increased annual output of feature films a handful of engaged voices stand out. May Miles Thomas, who had pioneered low-budget digital film-making with her debut feature *One Life Stand* (2000), made a very personal and political film about the lasting impact of asbestosis on Glasgow shipyard workers and their families. It drew on her father's experience of being unjustly denied compensation for his illness. *Gas Attack* (2001) by Kenny Glenaan was set in Glasgow and dealt with the plight of Kurdish refugees seeking political asylum in the United Kingdom through the device of an anthrax attack unleashed by an ultra-rightist terrorist. Produced shortly before the 9/11 attacks, this film anticipated the climate of fear and Islamophobia that dominated the years following and informed Glenaan's second film *Yasmin* (2004).

In the first decade or so of the new millennium the continuing small number of Scottish features – four to six indigenous films a year – means the likelihood of a challenging film-maker breaking through remains very low. On the other hand, more financeable 'proven talents' such as Peter Mullan with *Neds* and the fifth Laverty/Loach pairing, *The Angels' Share* (2012), maintain a concern for the so-called underclass. *The Angels' Share* revisits the excluded youth of Glasgow's peripheral housing estates in a bittersweet comedy that recalls Bill Forsyth's *That Sinking Feeling* of some thirty years earlier.

The radical and collectivist documentary tradition established by Glasgow Kino in the 1930s and reprised in the 1980s by the Film and Video Workshops and groups such as Red Star Cinema, is visible once again in groups such as the not-for-profit collective 'Camcorder Guerrillas,' who since 2003 have set out to give 'voice to the voiceless' and 'Media Co-op', whose members produce work for voluntary sector organizations and campaign groups but also more 'authored' work Media Co-ops' films include *Red Oil* (2008), a profile of Venezuela's socialist leader Hugo Chavez, and the observational documentary on gender identity *Man for a Day* (2012). Other Scottish-based film-makers who, in recent years, have engaged directly with sociopolitical issues include Desmond Bell in his feature-length drama documentary *Rebel Frontier* (2004) which reveals the repression of radicalized Finnish and Irish miners in Montana's copper mines before World War I and Anthony Baxter's *You've Been Trumped* (2011) which documents US tycoon Donald Trump's determination to ride roughshod over local residents and environmentalists' objections in order to build a golf course on an environmentally sensitive site on the north-east coast of Scotland.

Many of the films and film-makers associated with the Scottish Documentary Institute (SDI), which since 2004 has played a pivotal role in fostering and promoting new documentary talent not just from or indeed in Scotland but internationally, have been concerned with social and political themes. In many respects, the Scottish Documentary

Institute's cosmopolitanism reflects a more mobile and globally connected generation for whom the issues and stories which inspire them and their film-making collaborators are as likely to be found on another continent as they are in their own milieu. Working with film-makers in Bangladesh, Palestine, Libya and elsewhere, SDI has fostered a network of creative and in many instances activist documentarians whose collective output and impact has been substantial (Scottish Documentary Institute n.d.).

The global–local connection allied to a collectivist ethos also provided the means by which Theatre Workshop, a community-based organization committed to promoting social inclusivity, made the transition from stage to screen with their debut narrative feature film *Trouble Sleeping* (2008) (Theatre Workshop Scotland n.d.). Dramatizing the experiences of asylum seekers in Scotland, it built on the company's tradition of mixing professional and amateur performers and, just as Video in Pilton had done in 1994 with *The Priest and the Pirate*, engaged the local community in the production of their work which featured refugees both as writers and members of the cast (Byrne and Dickson 1998). Their second film, *The Happy Lands* (2012), was similarly co-created, this time with a mining community in the Fife coalfields, historically a highly politicized region that in 1935 elected one of only two communist MPs to the British parliament in London.

The limited extent of socially engaged film-making in Scotland has, allowing for the cyclical pattern of ups and downs that characterizes Scottish film production as a whole, remained fairly constant over the past couple of decades. However, over the same period the availability and consumption of engaged cinema has reached the point where it is arguably higher than at any time since the 1930s. A revived distribution chain (aided by the reduction in cost and complexity brought about by the widespread availability of digital production and distribution tools), the emergence of specialist film festivals and the much improved availability of films on DVD and online has helped to attract a new audience to work which might otherwise struggle to secure screen time. Festivals such as the Document International Human Rights Festival (est. 2003), Scottish Mental Health Arts and Film Festival (est. 2007) and Take One Action Film Festival (est. 2008) have revived a tradition of socially and politically engaged curation which was last clearly visible in the late 1980s in, for example, the Fringe Film Festival (est. 1984, from 1991 the Fringe Film and Video Festival) (Russell 1991) and the 'Questions of Third Cinema' event at the 1986 Edinburgh International Film Festival (Cooper 1989). The reach of these new festivals goes well beyond that which their predecessors could achieve however, with extensive programs of outreach to schools and community groups, touring packages to other cities and rural communities and an increasing emphasis on year-round programming. The breadth and depth of audience engagement achieved by this new breed of socially and politically motivated festivals in Scotland is, together with the much wider availability of related films on DVD and online, the realization of an aspiration first pursued in Scotland in the 1930s by labour movement and other activists inspired by the power of consciously political cinema. It was an objective taken up by the independent-, community- and workshop-sector film-makers who, in the late 1970s and 1980s, advocated an integrated practice in which production, distribution, exhibition and education would be linked in order to challenge the hegemony of conventional, commercial cinema. Since the 1990s that radical and often (though not always) collectivist ethos has given way, in the main, to a less consciously political culture in which, particularly in narrative fiction, film-making with an agenda has become unfashionable. The would-be engaged film-maker in Scotland today faces considerable resistance on many fronts, perhaps not the least of which may be an internalized anxiety or doubt over the place of politics and social issues in the cinema of the twenty-first century. That this is less of an obstacle to film-makers in other parts of the world where social and political questions seem to press more keenly on creative practitioners of all kinds, is no doubt a reflection of the appearance of relative stability and security in modern Scottish life.

However, appearances can be and often are deceptive. The possibility remains of more radical and engaged cinematic voices emerging in Scotland, perhaps from amongst those minority communities whose concerns and experiences have had little representation on the screen thus far, or if in the future the social and political context inspires a new generation of film-makers to embrace radical and engaged cinema.

Robin MacPherson

References

Anon. (1920) '"A cinematograph of misery": Starvation and chaos in central Europe', *The Scotsman*, 5 February, http://search.proquest.com/hnpscotsman/docview/482999571/138CE85BA783D15210F/4?accountid=12801. Accessed 27 August 2013.

__________ (1946) 'The Gorbals Story', *The Scotsman*, 3 September, http://search.proquest.com/hnpscotsman/ docview/490324443/ 139016888962110A993/22?accountid=12801. Accessed 6 September 2013.

Allen, Douglas (1982) 'Workers' Films: Scotland's Hidden Film Culture', in Colin McArthur (ed.), *Scotch Reels*, London: BFI, pp. 93–99.

Bond, Paul (1999) 'Paul Bond reviews *Ratcatcher*: A film by Lynne Ramsay', *World Socialist Web Site*, 27 November, http://www.wsws.org/en/articles/1999/11/rat-n27.html?view=print. Accessed 30 August 2013.

Bruce, David (1990) 'Hollywood Comes to the Highlands', in Eddie Dick (ed.), *From Limelight to Satellite: A Scottish Film Book*, London: BFI, 71-82.

__________ (1996) *Scotland the Movie*, Edinburgh: Polygon.

Byrne, Chris and Dickson, Malcolm (1998) 'Moving History', *Variant* 6, http://www.variant.org. uk/6texts/Moving_History.html. Accessed 1 September 2013.

Caughie, John (2000) *Television Drama: Realism, Modernism and British Culture*, Oxford: OUP.

Caughie, John and McArthur, Colin (1982) 'An Interview With Forsyth Hardy', in Colin McArthur (ed.), *Scotch Reels*, London: BFI, pp. 73–92.

Cook, John (2008) 'Three Ring Circus: Television Drama about, by and for Scotland', in Neil Blain and David Hutchinson (eds), *The Media in Scotland*, Edinburgh: EUP, 107-122.

Cook, Lez (2009) 'Three Ring Circus: The ur-text of modernist television drama', *Screen*, 50: 4, pp. 428–38.

Cooper, Scott (1989) 'The study of Third Cinema in the United States: A reaffirmation', in Jim Pines and Paul Willemen (eds), *Questions of Third Cinema*, London: BFI, 218-222.

Cranston, Ros (n.d.) 'Carla's Song (1996)', *BFI Screenonline*, http://www.screenonline.org.uk/f ilm/id/557052/. Accessed 29 August 2013.

Davidson, Ewan (n.d.) 'Just Another Saturday (1975)', *BFI Screenonline*, http://www.screenonline .org.uk/tv/id/442522/index.html. Accessed 31 August 2013.

Dickinson, Margaret, Cottringer, Ann and Petley, Julian (1993) 'Workshops: A dossier', *Vertigo*, Spring, pp. 16–20.

Dickinson, Margaret (ed.) (1999) *Rogue Reels: Oppositional Filmmaking in Britain, 1945–1990*, London: BFI.

Donald, James, Friedberg, Anne and Marcus, Laura (eds) (1999) *Close Up 1927–1933*, Princeton: PUP.

Fisher, Mark (2002) 'The plurality of Scottish theatre', *International Journal of Scottish Theatre*, 3: 1, http://journals.qmu.ac.uk/index.php/IJoST/article/view/91/html, Accessed 14 April 2014.

Fulton, Niall (2011) 'John Mackenzie', *Edinburgh International Film Festival*, 10 June, http://www.edfilmfest.org.uk/news/2011/06/john-mackenzie., Accessed 14 April 2014.

Fraser, Alice and Webb, Kieron (n.d.) 'Cinema Action', *BFI Screenonline*, http://www.screenonline .org.uk/people/id/529319/index.html. Accessed 31 August 2013.

Gardner, Carl and Wyver, John (1983) 'The Single Play: From Reithan Reverence to Cost Accounting and Censorship', *Screen*, 24: 4–5, p. 116.

Glassman, Marc (2010) 'Documentary Activism: Empowering Communities Through the Media', *International Documentary Association*, http://www.documentary.org/magazine/documentary-activism-empowering-communities-through-media. Accessed 28 August 2013.

Hedditch, Emma (n.d.) 'Red Skirts on Clydeside (1984)', *BFI Screenonline*, http://www.screenonline.org.uk/film/id/890164/. Accessed 1 September 2013.

Hill, John (1982) 'Scotland doesna mean much tae Glesca: Some notes on *The Gorbals Story*', in Colin McArthur (ed.), *Scotch Reels*, London: BFI, pp. 100–11.

Hutchinson, David (1990) 'Flickering Light: Some Scottish silent films', in Eddie Dick (ed.), *From Limelight to Satellite: A Scottish Film Book*, London: BFI, 31-40.

Hogenkamp, Bert (1986) *Deadly Parallels: Film and the Left in Britain, 1929–1939*, London: Lawrence and Wishart.

Hollins, TJ (1981) 'The Conservative Party and Film Policy Between the Wars', *English Historical Review*, 95, pp. 359–69.

Lloyd, Matthew (2011) *How the Movie Brats Took Over Edinburgh: The Impact of Cinephilia on the Edinburgh Film Festival, 1968–1980*, Edinburgh: St. Andrews Film Studies.

Loukopoulou, Katerina (2007) '"Films Bring Art to the People": The Art Film Tour in Britain (1950–1980)', *Film History*, 19: 4, pp. 414–22.

MacPherson, Don (ed.) (1980) *Traditions of Independence: British Cinema in the Thirties*, London: BFI.

MacPherson, Robin (1990) 'Declarations of Independence', in Eddie Dick (ed.), *From Limelight to Satellite: A Scottish Film Book*, London: BFI, 207-220.

__________ (2012) 'Scottish cinema: Myth and reality from Hollywood to Holyrood', in Emma Bell and Neil Mitchell (eds), *Directory of World Cinema: Britain*, Bristol: Intellect, pp. 225–27.

Moat, Janet (n.d.) 'McGrath, John (1935–2002)', *BFI Screenonline*, http://www.screenonline.org.uk /people/id/472530/index.html. Accessed 31 August 2013.

Neely, Sarah (2008) 'Contemporary Scottish cinema', in Neil Blain and David Hutchinson (eds), *The Media in Scotland*, Edinburgh: EUP, pp. 151–65.

__________ (2009) '"Ploughing a Lonely Furrow": Margaret Tait and Professional Filmmaking Practices in 1950s Scotland', in Ian Craven (ed.), *Movies on Home Ground: Explorations in Amateur Cinema*, Newcastle upon Tyne: Cambridge Scholars Publishing, pp. 301–26.

Neely, Sarah and Alan Riach (2009) 'Demons in the Machine: Experimental Film, Poetry and Modernism in Twentieth-Century Scotland', in Jonathan Murray, Fidelma Farley and Rod Stoneman (eds), *Scottish Cinema Now*, Newcastle upon Tyne: Cambridge Scholars Publishing, pp. 1–19.

Roberts, Tom (n.d.) '1982', *LUXOnline Histories*, http://www.luxonline.org.uk/history/1980-1989/actt_declaration.html. Accessed 28 August 2012.

Rushton, Dave (2003) 'Community Television: a brief perspective', *2.4TV*, http://freespace.virgin.net/ local.tv/Community%20TV%20History.html. Accessed 1 September 2013.

Russell, William (1991) 'Film Showcase', *The Herald*, 5 November, http://www.heraldscotland.com/ sport/spl/aberdeen/film-showcase-1.814504. Accessed 9 August 2013.

Scullion, Adrienne (1990) 'Screening the Heyday: Scottish Cinema in the 1930s', in Eddie Dick (ed.), *From Limelight to Satellite: A Scottish Film Book*, London: BFI, pp. 41–52.

__________ (2002) 'Glasgow Unity Theatre: The Necessary Contradictions of Scottish Political Theatre', in *Twentieth Century British History*, 13: 3, pp. 215–52.

Scott, Alistair (2009) 'What's the Point of Film School, or, What did Beaconsfield Studios ever do for the Scottish film industry?', in Jonathan Murray, Fidelma Marley and Rod Stoneman (eds), *Scottish Cinema Now*, Newcastle upon Tyne: Cambridge Scholars Publishing.

Scottish Communists (n.d.) 'Videos', http://www.scottishcommunists.org.uk/videos/. Accessed 3 September 2012.

Scottish Documentary Institute (n.d.) http://www.scottishdocinstitute.com/. Accessed 1 September 2013.

Stewart, Melissa (n.d.) 'Biography of dawn "Cine-Group"', *Scottish Screen Archive*, http://ssa.nls.uk/ biography.cfm?bid=10035. Accessed 31 August 2013.

Theatre Workshop Scotland (n.d.) http://www.theatre-workshop.com/. Accessed 1 September 2013.

Warren, J (1973) 'Community video, its Canadian roots and beginnings in Scotland', *Scottish International*, December, pp. 15–17.

Webb, Kieron (n.d.) 'Class struggle: Films from the Clyde (1977)', *BFI Screenonline*, http://www.screenonline.org.uk/film/id/1084218/. Accessed 30 August 2013.

Women Make Movies (n.d.) 'Sex and the Sandinistas', http://www.wmm.com/filmcatalog/pages/c27.shtml. Accessed 1 September 2013.

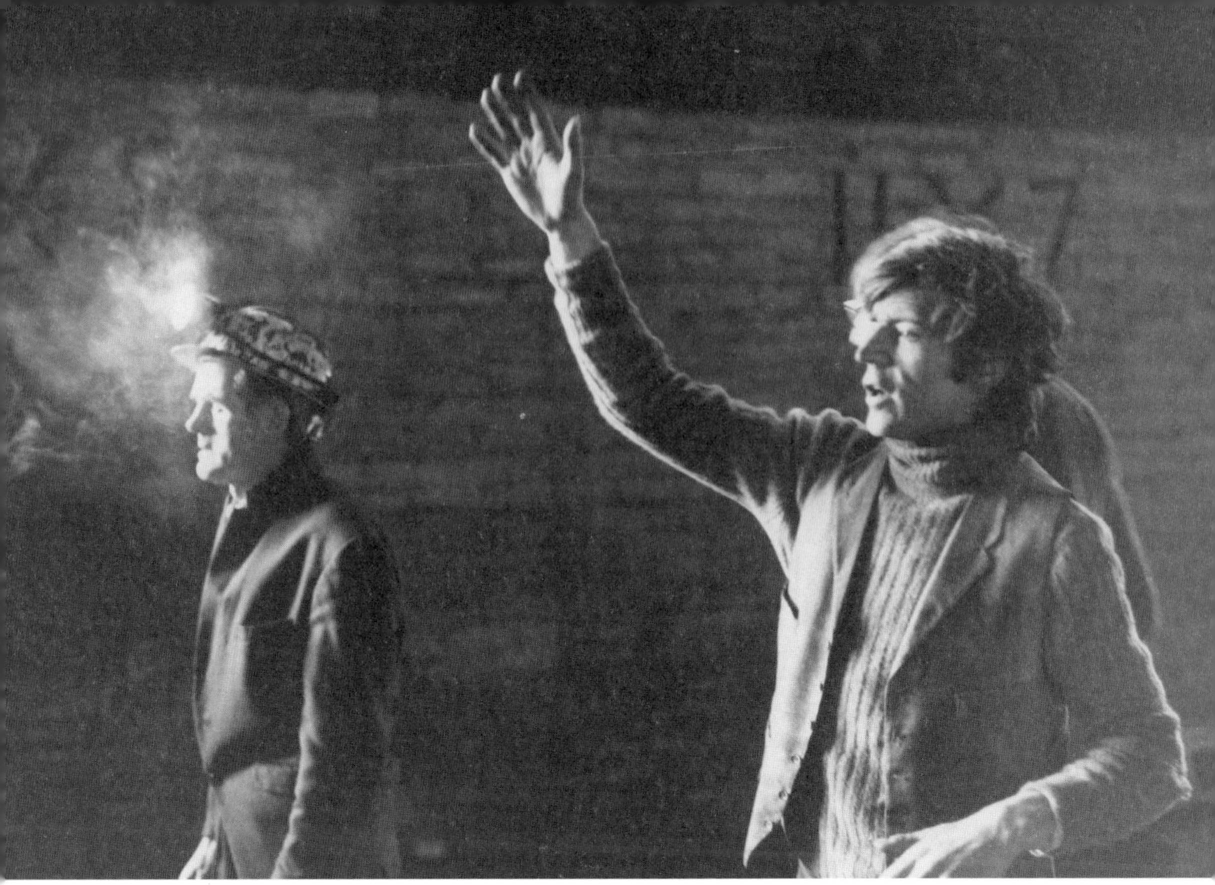

Bill Douglas, British Film Institute Collection

DIRECTORS

BILL DOUGLAS

On the basis of four remarkable films, Bill Douglas is widely acclaimed as the greatest art film-maker in the history of Scottish cinema to date, as well as a major figure within mid- to late-twentieth-century European art cinema. William Gerald Forbes (Bill) Douglas was born 17 April 1934 in the small coal-mining village of Newcraighall, just five miles south-east of Edinburgh city centre. Douglas was born out of wedlock, and his mother was shortly thereafter committed to a mental asylum. Douglas initially lived with his maternal grandmother, yet she died when he was a young boy; Douglas then transferred to live with his paternal grandmother. The former household was desolately poor, while the latter was cruelly abusive. Douglas experienced extreme alienation not only from family and relatives but also from the prevailing local culture within Newcraighall, especially versus what was then conventionally a 'normal' life direction for a working-class male in the community – one organized around the pit, the pitch, the pub and the betting shop. Douglas turned his attention toward improvised theatrical games, and, especially, attending the local cinema, often sneaking in without paying when he could not manage to find jam jars to trade for the price of a ticket. Bill's national service with the Royal Air Force in the Suez Canal Zone in 1955 proved liberating, and it is during this period of time that he met his great friend, and lifelong companion, Peter Jewell, an Englishman from Devon who supported and encouraged Douglas's intellectual and artistic interests. Upon completion of his national service Douglas soon moved to London, sharing a flat with Jewell, and shortly thereafter joined Joan Littlewood's Theatre Workshop Company at the Stratford East, concentrating his energy on acting and writing, including performing as a member of the cast of the Granada Television series, *The Younger Generation*, in 1961, and gaining production of a musical he wrote, *Solo*, at Cheltenham, in 1962. Fulfilling a long-term dream, Douglas earned admission to the London Film School in 1968; he graduated in 1969 with first-class honours after completing three student films. One of these films, '*Come Dancing*', caught the attention of the new head of production with the British Film Institute, Mamoun Hassan, encouraging Hassan to provide financial support for the production of *My Childhood*, the first film in what has subsequently come to be known as *The Bill Douglas Trilogy*. *My Childhood* was completed and released in 1972, to be followed by *My Ain Folk* in 1973 and by *My Way Home* in 1978. Over the course of eight years of hard work and difficult struggle, Douglas subsequently completed *Comrades: A Lanternist's Account of the Tolpuddle Martyrs and What Became of Them* (1986), the fourth and last film he was able to finish writing and directing before his death. Douglas also taught film – first, after the completion of the *Trilogy*, at the National Film and Television School in Beaconsfield, and second, after the completion of *Comrades*, as Carnegie Visiting Fellow with Strathclyde's Department of English Studies in Glasgow. Douglas died of cancer in 1991, leaving behind a significant collection of unpublished writings, including the screenplays *Justified Sinner*, a cinematic adaptation of James Hogg's classic *The Private Memoirs and Confessions of a Justified Sinner*, frequently touted as one of the most extraordinary as well as most important works in the history of Scottish literature, along with *Flying Horse*, based on the life of Eadweard Muybridge, a pioneering figure in the pre-cinematic rendering of the moving image. Another posthumous Douglas script, *Ring of Truth*, was produced in 1996, with sponsorship from the Scottish Arts Council, the Scottish Film Production Fund, BBC Scotland and Channel 4 – this production was dedicated to the memory of Bill Douglas. Douglas is buried in Devon, England, and on his tombstone is inscribed: 'Bill Douglas … Film Maker … Friend … Died 18th June 1991 … *We only have to love one another to know what we must do*' (the last sentence is a key line from early in *Comrades*). Douglas and Jewell were passionate collectors of books, memorabilia, and artefacts representative of the history and prehistory of cinema; their personal collection provides the foundation of the Bill Douglas Centre for the History of Cinema and Popular Culture, located at the University of Exeter. The Centre opened in 1997 as a public museum and academic research centre; it includes the largest library collection in the United Kingdom of books concerned with the history and culture of the moving image.

The Bill Douglas Trilogy draws heavily upon Douglas's own experience and strongly reflects his recollection of the impact of this experience upon him, but the films are more than mere autobiography. These films represent an artistic response to life experience, which is filtered through the mediation not only of personal memory but also of poetic re-invention. Jamie, the protagonist of the *Trilogy*, is not simply identical with Bill Douglas, as a child and a young adult, but rather is a complex, dynamic, fictional character maintaining his own distinct integrity. Douglas did not shirk from drawing courageously upon harrowing experiences and relationships from his childhood and youth – and he deliberately filmed in Newcraighall, as well as in Egypt, at, or as close as possible to, the precise locations where he encountered much the same kinds of challenges Jamie does in the course of the three films. Douglas, moreover, insisted on meticulous precision in relation to minute details of what should appear, and how so, in preparing locations for shooting, as well as in the positioning and movement of both the actors and the cinematographic apparatus during shooting. Yet the intensity of Douglas's drive in making these films, and in seeking to make them conform as precisely as possible to his vision, emanated not as much from the ferocity of his personal experience as it did from the ferocity of his commitment toward realizing that vision. As Andrew Noble (2008: 11) shares, 'Bill was insistent [...]. . . that he was involved in art, not personal catharsis' ('Bill Douglas's Trilogy' 11).' Beyond the fact that Douglas had personally experienced much of what his trilogy of films depicts, 'What also was terrifying was that Bill was tapping into a primary, universal childhood terror of abandonment and exclusion [...] . . . a dark line of imminent suicide runs through it' (10). Over the course of these three films Jamie is repeatedly pushed to the verge of giving it all up, not only in response to persistent isolation, loneliness, indifference, and abandonment, but also on account of rampant cruelty, abuse, deprivation, and scorn, most disturbingly perpetrated by his paternal grandmother. Jamie is voiceless throughout much of the first two films, with the magical escape provided by means of the world of cinema offering one of the very few, limited and temporary, means of solace, and compensation, for what he otherwise all too routinely suffers. In Egypt, however, aided by his new friend Robert, Jamie finds his voice, an incipient self-confidence, and an embryonic focus for his intellectual capacity and creative imagination. Most of all, he finds, for the first time in his life, a 'way home'.

For Douglas himself, as he writes in 'Palace of Dreams: The Making of a Filmmaker', from an early age the cinema was his one true 'home':

> For as long as I can remember I always liked the pictures. As a boy I spent so much time in cinemas, a friend suggested I take my bed with me. I would have, had it been possible. That was my first real home, my happiest place when I was lucky enough to be there. Outside, whether in the village or the city, whether I was seven or seventeen, it always seemed to be raining or grey and my heart would sink to despairing depths. I hated reality. (Douglas 2008: 4)

Eventually, as Douglas further recounts, he received the opportunity to make the world of cinema his reality:

> Then an incredible thing happened. A friend gave me an enormous Christmas gift. Inside the crate lay all the 8 mm equipment any film-maker could wish for. There was a camera, film, projector, editor, splicer, titler – everything. I wandered the streets filming everything I could set my eyes on, zooming, tilting, panning, whizzing, rarely static, learning from my mistakes. (Douglas 2008: 6)

As his learning progressed, Douglas wrote a screenplay, made costumes and built sets as well as did a great deal of other writing (including novels, stories, plays and poems). Upon graduating from the London Film School, he was confronted with the question of what kind of film, and about what, to make as one now committed toward living the life of a film-maker. He decided he needed to make a film about a subject that he knew well, which he could succeed in realizing, and which he knew and could realize better than anyone else. But making a film focused on his childhood would be a far more complex process than many might estimate, because

> There had to be a distance. I had to be objective so that the characters could come to life, so that the work could have shape. Good work cannot succeed unless the creator feels compassion. He can only begin when the self is put into perspective, when he has a fixed point of view. Chekhov put it better than I: "I can write only from memory. I never write directly from life. The subject must pass through the sieve of my memory so that alone what is typical or important remains there as on a filter". It is as simple as that. (Douglas 2008: 7)

Conceiving of the *Trilogy* as a dramatic account filtered through the mediation of memory (rather than a documentary-style depiction drawn directly from life, as it happens) enhances understanding of and appreciation for the many impressively poetic features of Douglas's film-making. Consider the use of austere black-and-white film stock; the substantial emphasis on the power of silence and stillness, including striking instances in which the actors and the action freeze in visual tableaux; the sparse dialogue and often flat enunciation combined with the absence of non-diegetic music, and the resultant eerie amplification of other ordinary, everyday sounds; the frequent narrative ellipses, the often forcefully contrapuntal imagery and the persistent investment of motifs with symbolic resonance; the precisely focused and carefully prolonged extent of deliberately defamiliarizing attention to minute details of expression, gesture, movement, posture, arrangement and action; the sudden, even occasionally frenetic, disruptions of silence and stillness, as well as the similar impact generated through surprising camera distances, heights and angles along with surprising outcomes or shifts in the trajectory of how characters relate to each other and to familiar objects within their immediate physical environments; and the selection and arrangement of images across time in dialectical patterns not only of repetition and variation, parallelism and antithesis, and echo and reverberation, but also of intersection, interaction, collision and unity of opposing forces and tendencies. And this preceding enumeration cannot begin to do justice to the distinctive qualities of each of the films of the *Trilogy*; as Douglas himself indicated, he deliberately worked with different crews for the three films because he conceived of each one as maintaining its own precise look and feel, such that even as the films comprise a series each stands independently on its own. Yet, perhaps above all else, it is worth noting that Douglas maintained an extraordinarily keen eye for composition, well aware of exactly how to organize and frame a shot – including the crucial importance of determining what to exclude along with what to include.

Douglas's film-making has prompted comparisons with many famous European art film-makers, including Robert Bresson, Andrei Tarkovsky, Jean Vigo, Jean Renoir, Alexander Dovzhenko, and Carl Theodore Dreyer. Duncan Petrie has suggested, in 'The Lanternist Revisited: The Making of *"Comrades"*' (1993: 193), that Douglas maintains a clear kinship with the aesthetic theory famously championed by French theorist André Bazin, with its emphasis on a sustained scrutiny of objective reality so as to 'reveal the reality of the world' (193), and as exemplified by Dreyer, F.W. Murnau, Erich von Stroheim, Robert Flaherty, and Italian Neo-Realism. Noteworthy in this connection are Douglas's frequent use of relatively long takes and his preference for a fixed-position as opposed to a moving camera. But, at the same time, as Petrie adds, Douglas maintains a clear kinship as well with Soviet montage, as exemplified by the likes of Sergei Eisenstein, Dziga Vertov and Vsevolod Pudovkin. Especially relevant here is Douglas's emphasis on composing his films akin to a classical musical composition, especially a fugue, dependent upon a complicated patterning of internal connections and intra-textual references both forwards and backwards in time. Many commentators, including Douglas himself, have compared Douglas's film-making, especially in the case of the *Trilogy*, with silent cinema. This is apt given Douglas's insistence upon the primacy of the visual image over speech as privileged means and medium of cinematic communication. Douglas believed that cinema was, first and last, a visual medium, and that it was his responsibility always to find a visual means of conveying meaning and exerting impact, as opposed to relying on words to do so. Douglas resolutely refused to spell out what could be suggested and what should be inferred, challenging his audience to use its intelligence and its imagination; as Mamoun Hassan has written, Douglas aimed, deliberately, at 'keeping the audience held and stretched. He was determined not to insult or bore' (2003: 227). As Noble adds,

> in an extraordinary binary manner we see Jamie from within and without. The brilliance of the narrative structure is that at no point are we more aware than Jamie of the menacingly convoluted world that surrounds him. We the audience, are consequently involved in a simultaneous, anguished act of interpretation. (Noble 1993: 12)

Douglas related to his cast, and his crew, much the same as to his audience, refusing to allow them protectively to distance themselves from a riveted attention to, and concentrated engagement with, what each moment in the process required, not providing them with copies of the script, and not spelling out ahead of time every detail of where the film was headed – or every detail concerning what their specific role would be, and how this should change. Throughout his career as a director, especially memorably in the case of Stephen Archibald performing as Jamie, Douglas often found himself at greater ease working with non-professional actors, or with relatively inexperienced or unknown actors, who more readily trusted and intuited what he sought to achieve. In relation to the casting of Archibald as Jamie, Noble writes,

> In the most brilliant of his many hunches and against all advice, Bill intuitively understood the potential emotional intelligence of this deprived, dyslexic, near illiterate child. Stephen, in his symbiotic creative relationship with Bill, triumphantly overcame every obstacle, even his own physical immaturity, for the Egyptian section. His is one of the greatest performances in the history of cinema. (Noble 1993: 13–14)

Testifying to the pedagogical impact Douglas's approach to film-making continues to exert with receptive audiences that include future film-makers, Andy Kimpton-Nye, who has, since 1994, produced and directed hundreds of documentary films, recounts how

> Bill Douglas taught me that the camera could linger long and hard on a character's face, going right down into the depths of the actor's soul – without any sign-posted performance or over-acting. He taught me that story-telling doesn't have to be crudely coercive, but instead he invited me, as a member of the audience, to work out for myself the connection between one scene, or sequence, and another. And he taught me if a film-maker had a clear vision of what he or she wants to say, then this is worth a 100, even a 1000, others who simply direct by numbers – which is the failing of so much commercial cinema. His Trilogy is a too-often overlooked masterpiece, combining the expressiveness of silent cinema (Bill was a big, big fan of Charlie Chaplin – who also experienced an appallingly deprived childhood) and the poetic qualities of Humphrey Jennings' documentaries. (Kimpton-Nye 2008: 16–17)

As many commentators have observed, the *Trilogy* offers an insightful critique of romantic myths of Scotland and Scottishness that effectively deny, conceal and even justify inequality, deprivation and oppression. The fact that Jamie needs to leave Scotland behind to 'find his way home' is indictment enough, but so is the close proximity of the devastating poverty, neglect and abuse he suffers to the architectural grandeur, the monuments to great historic and cultural achievement, and the economic wealth and social power concentrated in centre city Edinburgh. The *Trilogy* incisively demonstrates, in repeated striking juxtapositions within and across individual shots, that people live in effectively different worlds, even when living in close proximity, according to differences in social class. The *Trilogy* likewise underscores how people living lives defined by repression and deprivation can and do end up behaving in callous and cruel ways with others, notably their children and grandchildren. As Joyce McMillan has written, Douglas's depiction of Jamie's two grandmothers is extraordinarily powerful because Douglas depicts them as two *real* women, who cannot be made sense of in terms of a familiar madonna–whore dichotomy, and whose anguish, frustration and rage is as convincing as it is chilling. As McMillan elaborates, not only does Douglas 'confront one of the deepest taboos of this or any other culture, namely its capacity for neglecting and abusing its own children, its occasional complete failures of nurturing' (1993: 219), but also, and especially stunning, is the 'counterblast' his *Trilogy* offers to the romantic image of 'the sacred mother' (220) – the perpetually self-sacrificing, endlessly resilient, unfailingly nurturing caretaker of hearth and home, to whom the child can always turn for strength and support as well as love and kindness, even when the mother herself is in the most desperate of straits. The *Trilogy* demonstrates it is necessary to attend to the material conditions of possibility of human warmth, kindness, love, affection, nurturance, support and generous fellow feeling – that, contrary to common presumption, these do not and cannot persist, let alone flourish, independent of a concrete material basis – in particular, a substantial and sustainable social infrastructure.

Comrades complicates this argument by portraying a community of farm labourers and skilled craftsmen who demonstrate not only tremendous courage, conviction and commitment, but also an equally powerful warmth of loving care, mutual support and generous regard for the greater well-being of people maintaining the same class position. The film is a paean to the goodness of character, rightness of action, capacity for principled sacrifice and struggle, talent and skill, and imagination and ingenuity of so-called 'ordinary' peasant, worker, and poor people. *Comrades* is steadfastly aligned with the Tolpuddle Martyrs, their families, their friends, their fellow workers and their supporters. The film makes clear the historically indispensable necessity as well as the historically transformative value of labour unions, of strength achieved through combination and unity, and of principled, committed, active solidarity. The film is movingly inspirational, notably in repeatedly invoking the ideal of comradeship and dramatizing the determination of the Tolpuddle Martyrs to be free. A number of commentators have mentioned that it is 'ironic' Douglas began work on this film in 1979, the year Margaret Thatcher first was elected prime minister, and also 'ironic' that the film was finally released in 1986, at the height of Thatcher's power, and well after the severely reactionary impact of Thatcherism, in particular in relation to organized labour and the post-World War II social-democratic welfare state, had become abundantly evident. Yet this is not so much an 'irony', as it is a testimony to the urgency of what Douglas, cast and crew provide with *Comrades* – an urgency that, if anything, has grown all the graver since that time, with the continued acceleration of efforts, in Britain and throughout comparable so-called 'First World' societies, to undermine the social power of organized labour, as well as to inculcate a widespread indifference to, forgetfulness concerning and even outright denial of the historic importance of unions, collective resistance to common exploitation and active solidarity along lines of common class interest. Jeremy Isaacs of Channel 4 recognized the political importance of *Comrades*, in 1983 investing £1 million to support the making of the film, the largest single investment Channel 4 had made in a film up to that point in time, because 'I thought that the values the Trade Union movement had stood for at its best and noblest, the values that informed a more humane and just society than Margaret Thatcher stood for, were the values we should espouse in our films' (quoted in Petrie 1993: 177). The British Film Institute recognized the same significance, reissuing the film in 2011 to coincide with the 175th anniversary of the trial of the Tolpuddle Martyrs.

The film maintains many impressive formal and stylistic features. Undoubtedly the most readily striking is the way *Comrades* interweaves its depiction of the Tolpuddle labourers, first among their families and community in Dorset, and then in a series of individual adventures in Australia, with the figure of the lanternist, and references to multiple means of producing and sharing moving images, prior to the development of motion picture photography. The same actor, Alex Norton, performs fourteen different roles, including eleven different kinds of conveyors of pre-cinematic illusion. The film itself is ostensibly 'a lanternist's account' of the story of the Tolpuddle Martyrs. It opens and closes with the same bookend image of the oval of light cast by the magic lantern's projection. And the film directly credits the lanternist for his pivotal role in telling the story at the scene of the triumphant reception for the Martyrs upon their return to Tolpuddle. Critics have offered many interpretations of the lanternist's role in this film. For example: he maintains a common class position and therefore a strong empathetic identification with the position and interest of the Tolpuddle farm labourers, as a poor itinerant entertainer who travels by foot from community to community with his apparatus strapped to his back; the frequent references in the film to illusion and mediation demonstrate a critical self-reflexivity on Douglas's part, a ready acknowledgment that his film is a creative work of artistic imagination and invention, representative of an interested vantage point and perspective, and that it is by means, paradoxically, of the virtually magical power of cinematic, pre-cinematic and post-cinematic illusion that we come to recognize, understand and appreciate aesthetic, moral, existential and social-historical truths; and what the magic lantern, and other pre-cinematic devices, do, akin to that of cinema, is provide 'illumination' so that audiences can 'see' what they otherwise would not, or at least far from well, including struggles for social justice and human freedom. Certainly, frequent attention within the film to the captivating power of the moving image attests to the importance of what cinema can and does do for audiences, including by enabling people to become passionately interested in and engaged with historical events, as well as to recognize their indebtedness to what people suffered and struggled to achieve in the past along with their responsibility to carry on these same kinds of commitments, to support these same kinds of values, and to strive for these same kinds of ends in the present – and in the future.

What Douglas and his collaborators have fashioned with *Comrades* is a film of extraordinary beauty as well as considerable social relevance. In striking contrast with the black and white of the *Trilogy*, *Comrades* includes a rich range of crisp, vivid colours, often with a select range of hues predominating within a particular shot or sequence of shots, along with frequently ample brightness; scenes set in the morning, afternoon, evening and night, as well as at dusk and dawn, and during spring, summer, winter and autumn; and a concentrated focus upon landscape and geography, and flora and fauna, in both England and Australia. The film takes its time to establish the visual flavour of its locations, and to establish not only an incisive portrait of characters' relations with each other and with their social and natural environs but also of the rhythms of the lives they lead in these locations. The film makes apt use of correspondingly wide shots, periodically composed as visual tableaux suggestive of a painting, as well as of close-ups and medium close-ups when characters are speaking, including on more than one occasion directly to the camera. In characteristic Douglas fashion, *Comrades* respects the evocative possibilities of silence and stillness, while working with carefully minimal use of sound, such that, for instance, non-diegetic accompaniment only appears once the story arrives in Australia. As is likewise typical with Douglas, fixed as opposed to moving camera predominates while variations in camera distance, height and angle not only aid in the elaboration of the narrative but also reinforce theme and add symbolic resonance. To accentuate the film's depiction of the stark difference between members of opposing social classes, Douglas cast lesser-known actors to play the Tolpuddle farm labourers, craftsmen and their families, while casting well-known actors to play aristocrats and professionals. This decision succeeds impressively, and many of the lesser-known actors offer especially affecting performances. And, once more, as with the *Trilogy*, the structure of the film Douglas conceives akin to that of a musical score, encompassing thoughtful patterns of repetition and variation, parallelism and antithesis, converging and diverging lines of movement and a finely textured arrangement among moments, emphasizing each of the following predominant elements: lightness, humour, intimacy, fellowship, camaraderie, wonder, fear, isolation, sanctimony, hypocrisy, arrogance, ignorance, absurdity, pain, gravity, intensity, hardship, brutality, resilience and hope.

In 'Bill Douglas, 1934–1991: A Memoir' (1993), Andrew Noble recalls that Douglas had declared, regarding his conception and practice of film-making, 'every shot is a sentence' (24), while, as Noble recounts in his essay 'The Making of the Trilogy' (1993), Douglas also used to say 'every shot is a verb' (127). In 'The Making of the Trilogy' Noble also cites Mamoun Hassan identifying Douglas as a rare film-maker who conceived the shots in his films such that they 'cannot be taken from any other angle' (127). In his own essay, 'Working with Bill' (1993), Hassan refutes the notion that Douglas refused to explain what he had in mind, and how and why he wanted this filmed as he did; on the contrary, Hassan recounts, he would not hesitate to do so, and in fact what many have come to identify as 'the difficulty working with Bill Douglas in making a film' had to do with Douglas's insistence, as he explained to his students, that film-makers need to 'be true to what you see inside your head' and 'reject what is not essential' in striving to realize this same truth (Hassan 1993: 229). In a most interesting set of interviews included with the 2011, two-DVD British Film Institute edition of *Comrades*, Douglas likewise makes clear his appreciation for film-making as a highly collaborative process but also suggests many of his students, and, by implication, also a number of those he collaborated with in making his films, found it hard to think cinematically, to think in elaborately detailed images and patterns of moving images, especially without relying upon words to provide a ground or a bridge where thinking in such cinematic terms alone could not be easily sustained. It remains a tragic loss to world cinema that Douglas was unable to bring more of his ideas for films to completion, yet the *Trilogy* and *Comrades* nonetheless testify to what an extraordinarily visionary film-maker he was.

Bob Nowlan

References

Dick, Eddie, Noble, Andrew and Petrie, Duncan (eds) (1993) *Bill Douglas: A Lanternist's Account*, London: BFI (in association with the Scottish Film Council).

Doll, Susan (ed.) (2008) *Bill Douglas: Bitter Memories, Brutal Realism*, Facets Cine-Notes, Chicago: Facets Multi-Media.

Douglas, Bill (2008 [1978]) 'Palace of Dreams: The Making of a Filmmaker', *Bill Douglas: Bitter Memories, Brutal Realism*, Facets Cine-Notes, Chicago: Facets Multi-Media, pp. 4–7.

_________ (2011) 'Bill Douglas Interviews 1978' [Bill Douglas interviewed by Charles Rees and Mamoun Hassan, as filmed by Gale Tattershall and Peter Harvey and recorded by Roger Ollerhead], in Bill Douglas, dir. (1986), *Comrades* [2-DVD set], BFI.

Hassan, Mamoun (1993) 'Working with Bill', in Eddie Dick, Andrew Noble and Duncan Petrie (eds), *Bill Douglas: A Lanternist's Account*, London: BFI (in association with the Scottish Film Council), pp. 227–31.

Kimpton-Nye, Andy (2008) 'Making the Documentary *Bill Douglas: Intent on Getting the Image*', *Bill Douglas: Bitter Memories, Brutal Realism*, Facets Cine-Notes, Chicago: Facets Multi-Media, pp. 16–17.

McMillan, Joyce (1993) 'Women in the Bill Douglas Trilogy', in Eddie Dick, Andrew Noble and Duncan Petrie (eds), *Bill Douglas: A Lanternist's Account*, London: BFI (in association with the Scottish Film Council), pp. 219–26.

Noble, Andrew (1993) 'Bill Douglas, 1934–1991: A Memoir', in Eddie Dick, Andrew Noble and Duncan Petrie (eds), *Bill Douglas: A Lanternist's Account*, London: BFI (in association with the Scottish Film Council), pp. 13–27.

_________ (2008) 'Bill Douglas's Trilogy', *Bill Douglas: Bitter Memories, Brutal Realism*, Facets Cine-Notes, Chicago: Facets Multi-Media, pp. 8–14.

_________ (1993) 'The Making of the Trilogy', in Eddie Dick, Andrew Noble and Duncan Petrie (ed.), *Bill Douglas: A Lanternist's Account*, London: BFI (in association with the Scottish Film Council), pp. 117–72.

Petrie, Duncan (1993) 'The Lanternist Revisited: The Making of *Comrades*', in Eddie Dick, Andrew Noble and Duncan Petrie (eds), *Bill Douglas: A Lanternist's Account*, London: BFI (in association with the Scottish Film Council), pp. 173–96.

BILL FORSYTH

Bill Forsyth is the single most important indigenous film-maker in the history of Scottish cinema, and it would not be overstating the case to argue that many of the achievements of the so-called 'new Scottish cinema' would have been inconceivable without his pioneering work in the late 1970s and early 1980s. Forsyth's career as a film-maker, if we are to believe his own accounts, began as virtual happenstance. More or less on a whim, a teenage Forsyth answered an advertisement in his local newspaper seeking assistants to work at a local production company. Being a naive adolescent, Forsyth assumed there was a lot of money in film-making and so applied for the position. In an interview that sounds like a scene from one of his films, he was then given the job when he assured the head of the company that he could indeed lift the heavy equipment used for film shoots (Brown 1983: 157). From this humble beginning, Forsyth moved into the business of making documentaries and corporate videos before transitioning into feature films.

Forsyth's reputation in Scottish film history rests on the five feature films he made in the country, four of which were made in the early 1980s. His work at this time was in many ways trailblazing for Scottish film-makers. Before making his first feature in 1979, Forsyth was a regular on the local film-making scene and particularly active in advocating on behalf of the local industry. Around this time, he took part in seminal events such as Film Bang and Cinema in a Small Nation, events which would help agitate for the establishment of the Scottish Film Production Fund (SFPF) in the early 1980s. These events took place against a backdrop of calls for Scottish devolution from Great Britain and though the 1979 Scottish referendum on the

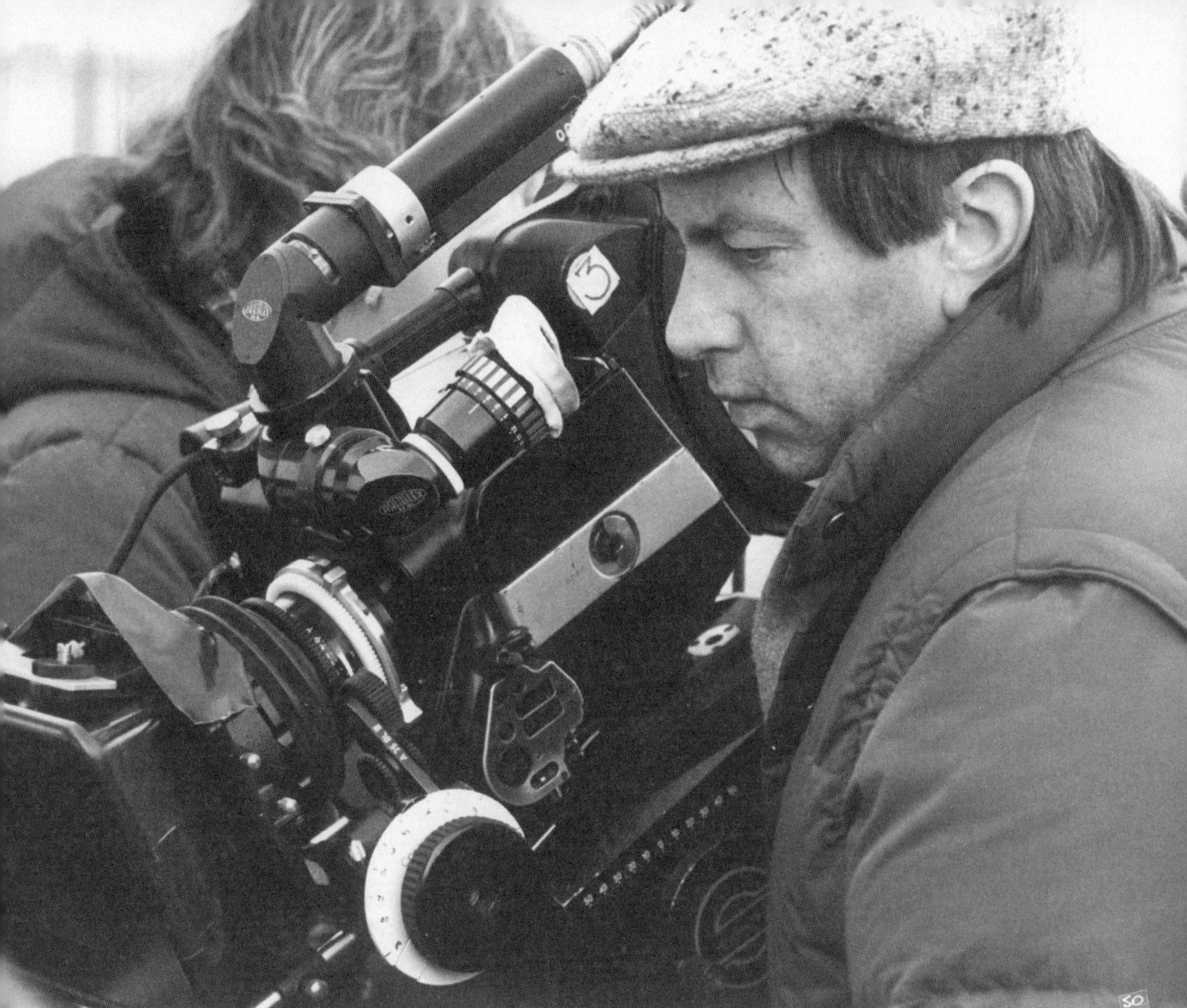

Bill Forsyth, British Film Institute Collection

subject failed on a dubious technicality, the central government in London was still keen on pacifying malcontents in Scotland and acceded to the devolved cultural structure that would henceforth be a key driver in Scottish cinema.

Unwilling to wait for government support for his own transition into feature film-making, Forsyth did what many penniless but talented film-makers have done before and since: he set out to make a no-budget DIY film in spite of the many challenges that would surely ensue. To this end, he enlisted the help of the Glasgow Youth Theatre to provide actors and set about making *That Sinking Feeling* (1980). The film, which was a topical satire dealing with unemployed youth turning (comically) to crime to make ends meet, would prove to be a landmark in Scottish cinema. The film debuted at the Edinburgh International Film Festival in 1979 and was very popular with Scottish audiences. Forsyth then followed this up with *Gregory's Girl* (1981), a film made in collaboration with STV, a partnership that afforded Forsyth a relatively comfortable budget and a wider range of distribution options. The film, a teenage romantic comedy set in a suburban secondary school and again starring members of the Glasgow Youth Theatre, took Forsyth to a new level of popularity, becoming a big hit throughout the

United Kingdom and eventually touring as part of a double bill with *Chariots of Fire* (Hugh Hudson, 1981).

The momentum Forsyth had built up in the early 1980s culminated in the making of *Local Hero* (1983). For this film, Forsyth partnered with producer David Puttnam – who was then at the pinnacle of his career having won an Oscar for *Chariots* – and Goldcrest Pictures to make a film that was inspired by Ealing films such as *Whisky Galore!* (Alexander Mackendrick, 1949). The film was in many ways an international affair, involving as it did English capital, an English producer and American stars in the form of Burt Lancaster and Peter Riegert. But it also featured Scottish talents such as Fulton McKay and, in his debut role, Peter Capaldi, who would go on to a long and storied career as an actor and writer/director. The film would prove to be a big commercial success and the artistic high point of Forsyth's career as a whole, but it also drew the enmity of the Scottish critical establishment, who resented Forsyth's usage of Tartanry and Kailyardism, usage that they mistook as a straightforward rehashing of the regressive discourses for the film's international consumption. As many later critics (e.g. Meir 2004; Murray 2011) have since argued, however, the film was anything but straightforward with these conventional ways of seeing Scotland, and the critical backlash at the time is perhaps better seen now as a document of Scottish critical attitudes in the early 1980s than a fair assessment of Forsyth's film.

Forsyth would follow up *Local Hero* with *Comfort and Joy* (1984), a film concerned with the attempts of middle-class Glaswegian disc jockey Alan 'Dicky' Bird to intervene in a turf war between rival ice-cream vendors. The film was based on a real (and violent) gangland feud between organized crime syndicates who controlled, amongst other things, the city's ice-cream trade. Forsyth wove together this true-life crime story with Dicky's tale of loneliness and alienation to forge a film that enjoys something of a cult following to this day.

Comfort and Joy would prove to be Forsyth's last Scottish film for fifteen years as, like many successful British and European directors before and since, he set sail for America and there made three feature films. While *Housekeeping* (1987) and *Breaking In* (1989) were gems in their own right, Forsyth's sojourn in Hollywood is now best remembered for the debacle that was *Being Human* (1994). The film, which starred Robin Williams and was in some ways a magnum opus of Forsyth's in terms of realizing his preferred themes of existential alienation, was also an unmitigated commercial disaster. Its production was beset by innumerable problems and ran well over budget. Unhappy with what they saw of Forsyth's initial cut, the studio (Warner Brothers) then forced the film-maker to re-edit the film, rendering it neither the art film that Forsyth was seeking nor the crowd pleaser the studio wanted. The end result was a project that went straight to video in Europe and which had only a short theatrical run in the United States. The fallout from the making of the film ended Forsyth's career in Hollywood and left him embittered about film-making generally.

Forsyth did not give up on the cinema after the experience of *Being Human*. Instead, his last film would see him return to Scotland for the making of a sequel to his breakthrough film *Gregory's Girl*. The aptly named *Gregory's Two Girls* (1998) allowed Forsyth to benefit from the institutions that he helped inspire, including the Scottish Arts Council Lottery Fund, a descendent of the SFPF. It also allowed Forsyth the opportunity to take part in the *annus mirabilis* for Scottish film-making that was 1999, the year that also saw the establishment of a devolved Scottish parliament. While the film itself was a bit of a disappointment artistically, it nonetheless continued Forsyth's exploration of the modern male psyche and explored some of the ways in which Scotland was implicated in human rights atrocities that are seemingly far removed from the nation.

As Jonathan Murray has demonstrated in great detail, there is a clear auteurist sensibility visible across Forsyth's oeuvre wherever the individual films may be set. Primary amongst Forsyth's auteur signatures is his sense of humour, which has consistently been wry and seemingly gentle, while always containing a darker edge. This trademark sense of humour is beloved by Forsyth's fans but, as Murray has argued, its gentle tone, along with Forsyth's self-deprecating media persona, has also led many critics to underestimate the director and his satirical vision (2011: 3). Also uniting Forsyth's oeuvre are existential themes of loneliness and alienation. While his earliest films were dark comedies, such themes are especially apparent from *Local Hero* onward, permeating films that were ostensibly concerned with disparate topics such as environmentalism, underworld conflict and house burglars. This thematic preoccupation, as Murray has shown, ties Forsyth, despite the apparently genial tone of his films, to the traditions of European art cinema.

Despite his importance to the establishment of a Scottish film industry and substantial achievements as a film-maker, Forsyth's critical reputation within Scottish cinema has been a checkered one. Though initially enamoured with *That Sinking Feeling* and *Gregory's Girl*, the critics of the *Scotch Reels* movement in the early 1980s cast a suspicious eye on the film-maker's attempt to make the internationally oriented *Local Hero*. They then pilloried the film itself as a case of a local artist losing his way when tempted by foreign money. Duncan Petrie, Scottish cinema's leading historian, continued this ambivalent line on Forsyth, praising works such as *Gregory's Girl* and *Comfort and Joy*, while maintaining the disdain for *Local Hero* that his predecessors held. A new generation of critics, however, has sought to restore Forsyth's reputation as Scotland's leading indigenous film-maker. David Martin-Jones (2009), myself (in press) and, above all, Jonathan Murray in his encyclopedic study of the director (2011) have led the rethinking of this vital and unfairly maligned figure.

Christopher Meir

References

Brown, John (1983) 'A Suitable Job for a Scot', *Sight and Sound*, 52: 3, pp. 157–62.

Martin-Jones, David (2009) *Scotland: Global Cinema – Genres, Modes and Identities*, Edinburgh: EUP.

Meir, Christopher (2004) 'Bill Forsyth', *Senses of Cinema*, Issue Number 33, http://sensesofcinema.com/2004/great-directors/forsyth/, Accessed 14 April 2014.

__________ (in press) *Scottish Cinema: Texts and Contexts*, Manchester: MUP (Accepted for publication).

Murray, Jonathan (2011) *Discomfort and Joy: The Cinema of Bill Forsyth*, Berlin: Peter Lang.

MURRAY GRIGOR

> He soon discovered that the reputation he had acquired abroad made not the slightest difference to his status in Glasgow and the applause […] had no effect whatever on the stolid, unimaginative men-of-the-world with whom he had to do business.
>
> (Howarth 1952: 193)

This was written not about Murray Grigor but about Charles Rennie Mackintosh, whose career bears an uncanny resemblance to Grigor's. It is not that the latter is wholly unknown in Scotland. He has collaborated with prominent Scots in mounting exhibitions and sociocultural public advocacy campaigns. Nor has the Scottish press been uniformly hostile to his work. The run-of-the-mill press often responded warmly, if somewhat bemusedly, and more politically and culturally alert commentators were positively enthusiastic. In Grigor's case, the equivalent of the 'stolid, unimaginative men-of-the-world' who had thwarted Mackintosh were the uncomprehending apparatchiks in certain Scottish arts, broadcasting and film institutions.

Murray Grigor's take on the lachrymose Scottish narrative of the Massacre of Glencoe (Courtesy of Murray Grigor)

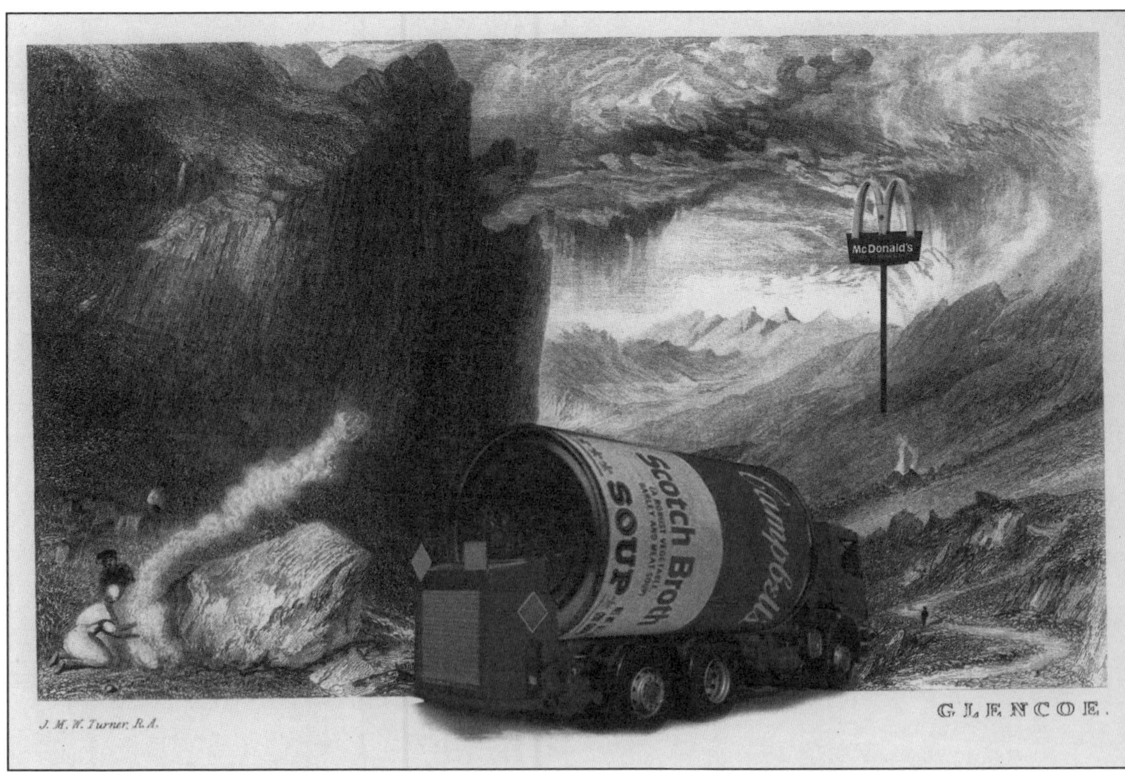

The title of this piece describes Grigor as 'auteur', a term formulated within French film criticism (particularly *Cahiers du Cinéma*) to describe the kind of film director whose stylistic and thematic identity is discernible across the whole range of his work. This essay retains the 'auteur' idea of identity and coherence, but – while being centrally concerned with Grigor's films – extends it to include his journalism, public advocacy, graphic art and association with the Edinburgh International Film Festival. His directorship of the latter (1967–73) coincided with the importation into the United Kingdom of the cinephilia that had reanimated post-war French film culture. At that time ideas of authorship and *mise-en-scène* were taken up and applied by younger British critics primarily associated with the journal *Movie* and the British Film Institute Education Department. Inheriting a festival that was well established and thoroughly respectable, but cripplingly marked by the realist- and documentary-focused aesthetic of its co-founder and Grierson biographer, Forsyth Hardy, Grigor entered into alliance with the *Movie*/British Film Institute Education initiative and brought into the festival younger figures like Lynda Myles and David Will. The result was a dazzling series of auteurist retrospectives, on Samuel Fuller and Douglas Sirk among others, each accompanied by a book of essays. By the time (the early 1970s) that the auteurist interest had mutated into engagement with theoretical issues such as ideology and psychoanalysis, Grigor had handed the festival over to his younger colleagues.

Grigor meanwhile was embarking on his own film-making career, the subject of his first two 'documentary' films in 1968 and 1970 being, appropriately, Charles Rennie Mackintosh. Today the phenomenon of Mackintosh (or, as Grigor derisively calls it, 'Mockintosh') is so omnipresent in Scotland that it requires an effort of historical will to recall that serious appreciation of his work had to be laboriously constructed. Grigor's films were part of that process. At the time, the only funding mechanisms available in Scotland, apart from the broadcasters, were those specializing in sponsored documentaries, such as Films of Scotland and the Highlands and Islands Development Board. Grigor worked with them, his early films like *Travelpass* (1973) and *Suilven* (1975) employing young Scots actors such as Bill Paterson, John Bett and Alex Norton. (*Travelpass* looks like a characteristic Scottish travelogue except that the soundtrack disdains the usual plaintive *clarsach* or fiddle music, opting for modern music in the folk tradition, and aiming for the 'folkish' not the '*volkisch*').

Scots film-makers had access to two other funding mechanisms, the Scottish Arts Council and the Arts Council of Great Britain, both of which maintained film sections. It was here that Grigor's modernism and, in a non-pejorative sense, formalism, were allowed freer rein, as in his *Blast* (1975), about Wyndham Lewis and Vorticism. His modernism would elicit the most immediate appreciation and reward, though mainly outside Scotland, with *Blast* receiving awards at festivals in Melbourne, Tampere and Sydney. I have described elsewhere (McArthur 2009) much of Grigor's work as 'ludic modernism', the ludic element deriving from the surrealists, Samuel Beckett and, above all, James Joyce. This strain appeared early in two films he made with the Scots comedian Billy Connolly: *Clydescope* (1974) and *Big Banana Feet* (1975). The latter was a record of Connolly's recent Irish tour and, aesthetically very much resembles the film of Bob Dylan's 1965 British tour, *Don't Look Back* (DA Pennebaker, 1967). However, *Clydescope* is much more interesting. With few exceptions, Scottish travelogues tended towards the po-faced and reverent, often drawing on regressive discourses about Scotland such as Tartanry and Kailyardism. In *Clydescope* Grigor upends this tradition. Funded by the Clyde Tourist Board, it follows Connolly down the Clyde from its source. One could imagine such a project in other hands being constructed on the pattern of the Ur-Tartan Documentary with vistas of hills and lochs and a reverent commentary stressing the timelessness of the river and the 'proud and independent' people who inhabit its banks (see the Stakhanovite *Seawards the Great Ships* [Hilary Harris, 1961], for example).

Instead of dwelling on 'views' of the Clyde, Grigor opts for a photographic studio and the complex Edwardian glasswork on the roof of Wemyss Bay railway station – a Scotland of culture rather than nature. Loch Lomond is a central trope in Tartanry, views of it being endlessly recycled and celebrated in popular song. Grigor demurs, drawing attention to a bear-garden on its shore and, against the image of the stately *Maid of the Loch* cruising into frame, Grigor adds the tune 'Loch Lomond', but on a ship's siren.

Grigor's work is unremittingly political. His early project on the Scots poet Hugh Macdiarmid, *The Hammer and the Thistle* (1977), most explicitly unites politics and culture. The apparent anomaly of its being funded by a north of England broadcasting company, Granada Television, is explained by the presence, at a senior level in Granada, of Gus Macdonald, a Scot with *gauchiste* sympathies. This is the first of several instances in which Grigor's career was advanced by powerful émigré Scots. In 1977/78 Grigor himself lived in the United States on a UK/US Bicentennial Fellowship in the Arts, awarded to allow him to research a film on the American architect Frank Lloyd Wright. This experience would have a profound effect on his later career. His return to Scottish film-making was quite a low-key affair, *Sean Connery's Edinburgh* (1981), funded by the City of Edinburgh and 'starring' the Hollywood actor himself. Less obviously political than many of Grigor's other projects, it nevertheless is less than reverent to certain venerable Scots institutions. A memorable moment has Connery driving off on a golf course followed by a golf ball striking the head of the statue of John Knox, the historical lynchpin of Scottish Calvinism.

As has been previously indicated, Grigor is active across a range of practices outside cinema. In this context, it is appropriate to consider his graphic work that invariably gives a humorous twist to phenomena often treated solemnly in Scottish writing. In Scottish culture, as in Irish culture, a strong vein of victimhood has long persisted, a pleasurable scab-scratching attended by lachrymose nostalgia. One such generative event is the Massacre of Glencoe (1692), at which members of the Clan Campbell, on the orders of the British government, murdered several of the Clan Macdonald. While mainline Scottish culture wrung its hands and wiped the tears from its eyes on the 300th anniversary of that event, Grigor's take on it was to construct a montage of Glencoe with on one side a Campbell's soup tin and on the other the logo of the fast-food giant McDonald's. On a postcard of Holyrood House, Scottish residence of the monarch, Grigor added to the background hills, in the style of the famous Los Angeles sign, the word 'Holyrood'.

The melding of the ludic and the political is at the heart of what, in the Scottish context, is arguably Grigor's most important work – *Scotch Myths* (1981). In 1979 a nationwide referendum took place on whether a devolved Scottish governing assembly would be set up in Edinburgh. Widely seen to have been gerrymandered, the referendum returned a negative vote, but the paradoxical outcome was that the subsequent energy that might have flowed into overtly political activity was channelled instead into culture. Grigor and other Scots intellectuals were familiar with Tom Nairn's 'Old and New Scottish Nationalism' (Nairn 1977), which offered a scathing account of Scottish (popular) culture for not having been mobilized in the formation of the nation, as had been the case with other European nation-states. To oversimplify somewhat, the dominant cultural discourses that emerged in Scotland under the sign of Romanticism were Tartanry and Kailyardism. *Scotch Myths* simply took these discourses apart. The project began in St Andrews in 1981, co-mounted by Grigor and his wife Barbara who, until her tragically early death in 1994, was a central organizing and stabilizing force on his work. The exhibition *Scotch Myths* enacted was primarily a delirious kaleidoscope of artefacts incarnating the dominant Romantic discourses: postcards, tea towels, shortbread tins, whisky labels, souvenirs and popular songs. The Grigors identified, and implicated, the key historical figures that gave these discourses life: James 'Ossian' Macpherson, Sir Walter Scott, Felix Mendelssohn, Queen Victoria and Prince Albert, and Harry Lauder.

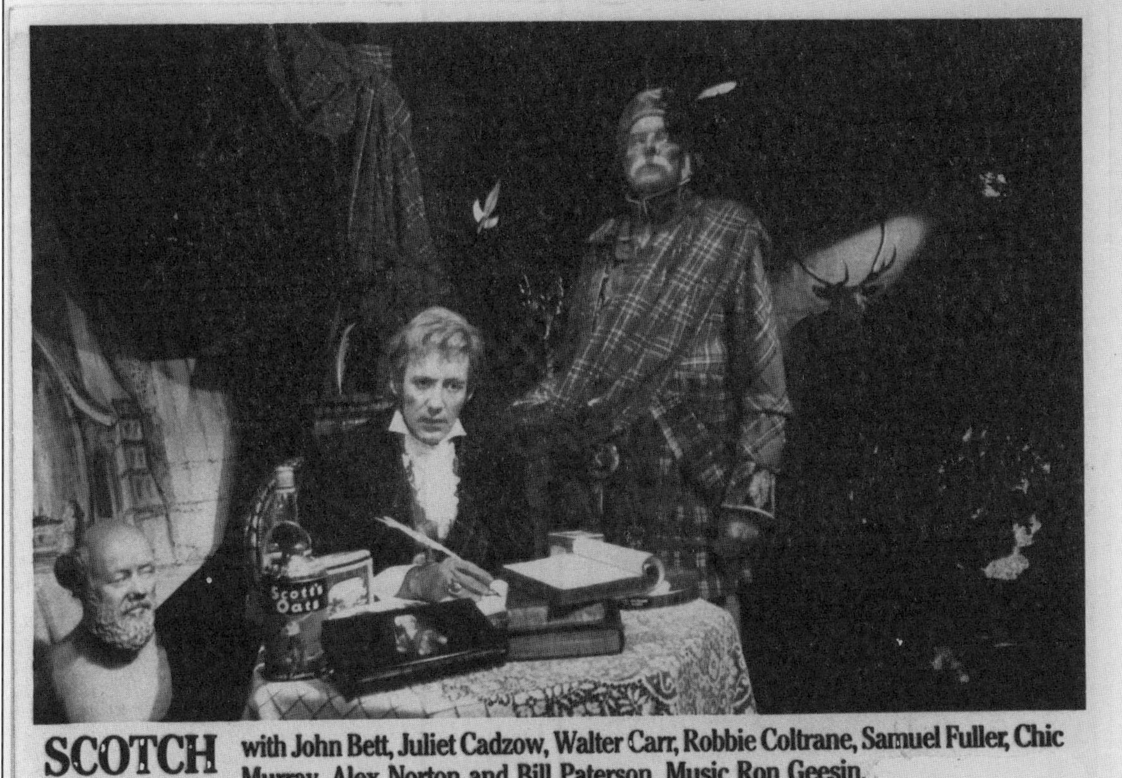

Murray Grigor deconstructs the Tartanry discourse: Sir Walter Scott (John Bett) and his servant (Chic Murray) 'invent' the diverse Scottish tartans (Courtesy of Murray Grigor)

It is significant that *Scotch Myths* transmogrified into film less through the institutions of Scottish moving image culture than through yet another key Scots émigré in UK-wide broadcasting, Jeremy Isaacs, CEO of Channel 4. The film, taking advantage of a special deal between the channel and the broadcast unions, was made for just £100,000, a perfect example of the kind of 'poor cinema' (McArthur 1993) the emergent Scottish film-funding institutions might have encouraged, had their priorities not lain elsewhere. The film's scheduling was itself a political act. Programmed around midnight on 31 December 1982 (Hogmanay, a key Scottish festival), it was in deliberate competition and contrast with BBC Scotland and Scottish Television, both of which in this slot traditionally ran programmes constructed wholly within the discourses of Tartanry and Kailyardism.

Classical narrative realism is of tangential interest to Grigor, who is much more concerned with ideas, style, wit and texture. Such is the hegemony, however, of the classical, Hollywood-based model that Grigor has made minimal gestures to it in order to enable projects to get off the ground. And this is true even in the case of *Scotch Myths*, at least at first. The ostensible story of *Scotch Myths* concerns a group of tourists lost on a Scottish moor that turns out to be Culloden Moor, site of the battle in 1746, which ended the pretensions of the House of Stuart to the British crown. By foregrounding this icon of romantic Tartanry, Grigor signals the seriousness of his project. The tourists are sidetracked to Castle Dundreich to partake of 'the Dundreich Experience', Grigor's swipe at what may now be called the 'Braveheartization' of Scotland, the impulse to render Scottish history as theme park. A separate, equally tangential, narrative strand emerges wherein the famous Hollywood film director Samuel Fuller, 'as himself', upbraids his assistant for being unable to find Castle Dundreich on the map. This represents another key side of Grigor the film-maker: his cinephilia. And yet an additional allusion to film history occurs in this scene. Anyone familiar with discussion of cinema in relation to Scotland would recognize that two figures lost in a mist-shrouded Scottish landscape could refer only to *Brigadoon* (Vincente Minnelli, 1954). Grigor is telling us that his film will be about not only Scottish history, but also how Scottish history is represented in discourse, cinematic and otherwise.

Within the diverse historical charades of 'the Dundreich Experience', Grigor also jettisons the classical narrative convention of the individual actor embodying a single character. Not only do most of the actors playing the diverse historical personages we meet in *Scotch Myths* cover more than one role (Alex Norton as James Boswell, Robert Burns, Napoleon, Felix Mendelssohn, Prince Albert and John Brown; John Bett as James Macpherson, Ossian, Sir Walter Scott and Lord Byron; Bill Paterson as Samuel Johnson and Harry Lauder, etc.) but they adopt a declamatory style of delivery quite at odds with a naturalistic mode of acting. Its ludic elements apart, *Scotch Myths* is reminiscent of another great modernist, anti-naturalistic film: Hans-Jürgen Syberberg's *Ludwig: Requiem für einen jungfräulichen König/Ludwig: Requiem for a Virgin King* (1972). Like another non-naturalistic project nearer home, John McGrath's and John Mackenzie's *The Cheviot, the Stag and the Black Black Oil* (1974), *Scotch Myths* is also Brechtian in punctuating events with songs and is multi-discursive in accommodating naturalistic action, stylized performance and animation. The latter figures in one of the most accomplished sequences in which Sir Walter Scott, with his faithful retainer (played by the Keaton-faced Scots comic, Chic Murray), 'tartans the kingdom', an imaginative rendering of the key role Scott played in what has been described as 'the invention of tradition' (Hobsbawm and Ranger 1983).

I have described elsewhere (McArthur 2009), without too much exaggeration, the 'suppression' of *Scotch Myths* within Scotland, the officers of the Scottish Film Council dismissing it as irrelevant and banning its acquisition to their own film library and to the Scottish Film Archive. A print of *Scotch Myths* would eventually find its way into the latter, not through the support of any of the indigenous film institutions, but by donation from Grigor himself. Yet, if *Scotch Myths* represents Grigor's engagement with the great internationally known discursive figures of Scottish (cultural) history, *Budgies Repaired Saturdays: A Wake for Bud Neill* (1993) marks his encounter with the most local and parochial of Scots artists. Bud Neill ran a comic strip in the *Glasgow Evening Times* from 1949–55 entitled *Lobey Dosser*, the implicit readers of which were working-class Glaswegians. Lobey Dosser (a Glasgow term for a rough sleeper who dossed rent-free in tenement lobbies) was the sheriff of Calton Creek, a mythical town ostensibly in the American west but whose denizens speak in the Glasgow idiom. Like so much else of Grigor's work, *Budgies* is a multi-discourse film made up of vox pop interviews, contemporary newsreels and animations of some of the strips and extracts from feature films (e.g. those of William S Hart) that Neill revered. It is a standing indictment of the view that Scots cinema has to be 'toned down' for international audiences and that this must go hand in hand with larger budgets and 'production values', the emergent orthodoxy in Scotland at the time.

Some of Grigor's films (e.g. *Clydescope* and *Scotch Myths*) have been given their due in that most even-handed account of Scottish cinema, Duncan Petrie's *Screening*

Scotland (Petrie 2000). The latter also moves deftly through the kaleidoscopic changes from the early 1980s to 2000 in the institutions supporting film-making in Scotland with a list of the feature films and shorts funded by them over this period and an indication of the personnel involved. Grigor's name does not figure in this list. Part of the explanation is that he worked in the United States over the period 1983–86 on an individual film on Frank Lloyd Wright and on the ambitious series of eight 57-minute films on American architecture, *Pride of Place (*1986), both of which considerably enhanced his reputation in architectural circles. However, during the period covered by Petrie's list Grigor worked on many projects in the United Kingdom, but instead of the indigenous Scottish film institutions backing these projects, the funders which recur most frequently are Channel 4 (*E.P. Sculptor* [1987]; *The Demarco Dimension* [1989]; *The Great Wall of China* [1989]; *Irony Curtain: Art and Politics Between USA and USSR* [1990]; *The Why's Man* [1990]; *Distilling Whisky Galore* [1991]; and *Carlo Scarpa* [1995]) and Scottish Television (*The Why's Man, The Fall and Rise of Mackintosh* [both 1991]); *Top Casting* [1993]; *Budgies*

Murray Grigor's engagement with contemporary Scottish culture showing the Royal Bank of Scotland (founded in 1727), a casualty of the recent United Kingdom banking scandal, disappearing beneath the waves (Courtesy of Murray Grigor)

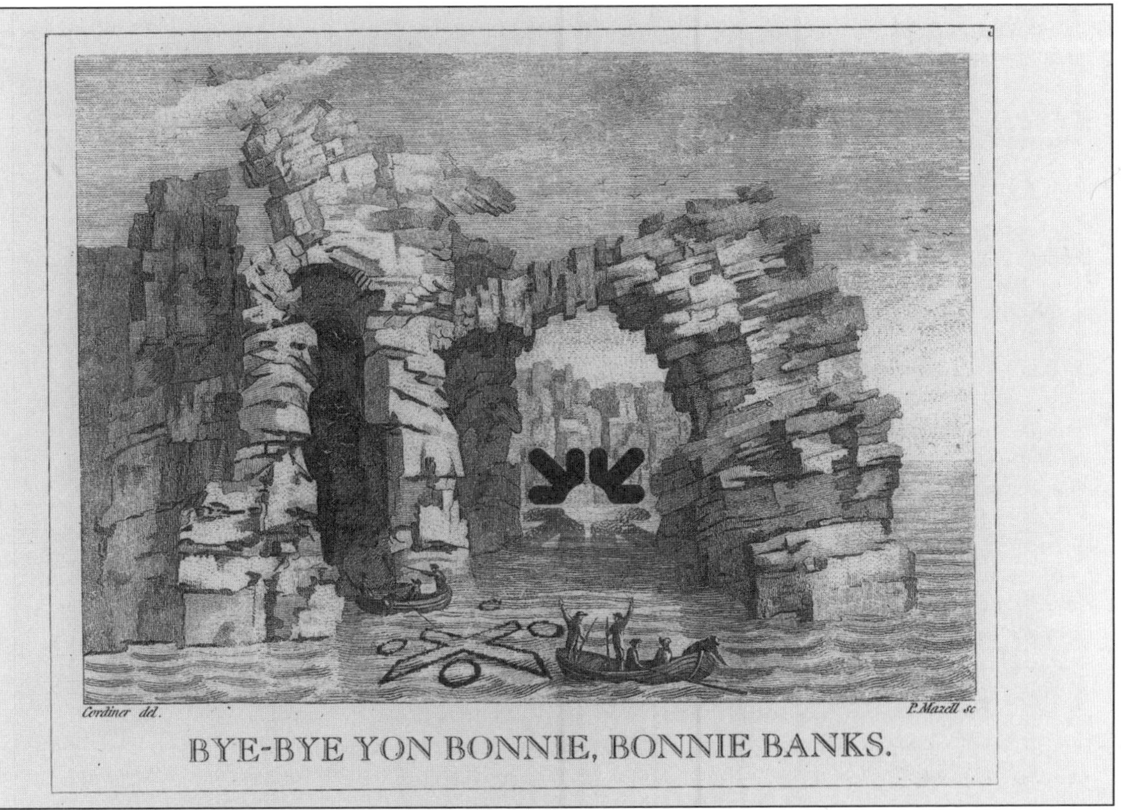

Repaired Saturdays: A Wake for Bud Neill,[1993]; *Fakelore: The Cultural Set-Aside [Scotland]Act* [1994]). A key element in Channel 4's and Scottish Television's support for Grigor's work at this time is the presence at senior levels in these organizations of figures who admired and understood that work, unlike analogous figures in the indigenous film-making and broadcasting institutions. For example, Jeremy Isaacs remained as CEO of Channel 4 throughout much of this period and Gus Macdonald moved from Granada to Scottish Television, first as Director of Programmes then as CEO.

Throughout Grigor's CV there are only two mentions of the Scottish Film Production Fund. One involves its input to Margaret Tait's feature film *Blue Black Permanent* (1992), produced by Barbara Grigor, and the other its modest input to *The Why's Man*. He also received small script-development grants for *Green Fire*, about the 'Celtic Revival' Scottish writer William Sharp and his curious literary doppelgänger Fiona Macleod, and for another script titled *Scotch Gothic*, but neither received production funding. It is doubtful whether there was ever a high level of understanding, far less support, for his work in this milieu, but it would be mistaken to see his virtual exclusion as simply a matter of personal prejudice. The explanation is much more likely to have been structural. Duncan Petrie, in a later essay (Petrie 2009), traces the dialectic between culture and commerce within the Scottish film-making institutions, culminating in the triumph of the commercial. Petrie, like many of the best people associated with public (part-)funding of national cinemas, remains cautiously optimistic that the culture/commerce dialectic can produce good results. The kind of films Petrie offers as examples are Peter Mullan's *Orphans* (1998) and Lynne Ramsay's *Ratcatcher* (1999). However, and here the argument reconnects with the question of Grigor's exclusion, both films subscribe in essential respects to the classical Hollywood-style narrative realist norm. That implicit commitment to this and only this kind of film-making is written across every policy initiative taken by the Scottish Film Production Fund and its successors: the setting-up of a script development fund; the drafting in of whisky magnate/Hollywood screenwriter Allan Schiach to serve in senior roles; the setting up of Movie Makars, kicked off with an address by Hollywood screenwriter William Goldman; and the creation of short-film mechanisms like Tartan Shorts to bring young film-makers up in the faith, so to speak. Is it any wonder that the policy has been dubbed 'Hollywood on the Clyde'!

Scottish cinema's Gadarene rush to an economically industrial and aesthetically Hollywoodean narrative model was not simply an aberration peculiar to Scotland. The process is discernible across the cultures of all the developed countries stemming, on the one hand, from the adoption of neo-liberal economic policies within which every feature of society, including culture, must give 'value for money' and, on the other hand, the amoeba-like spread of what might be called 'story-structure discourse'. The latter, emanating initially from the do-it-yourself screenwriting manuals and courses of Syd Field, Robert McKee and others, fetishizes the 90–120-minute Hollywood feature film, asserting that its characteristic structure (set-up, development and resolution; goal-driven protagonists and antagonists; plots and (often several) subplots; action arcs and false endings) constitute a veritable definition of the essence of cinema. To opt for this structure carries discernible ideological costs, as Jonathan Murray demonstrates (Murray in press) in his analysis of, among other films, *Rob Roy* (Michael Caton-Jones, 1995). It is hardly surprising that some cinephiles, sated with the structured procrastination of this kind of cinema, should look to the cinemas of cultures (e.g. Senegal, Iran) insulated from Hollywood's economic and aesthetic determinants.

Cold-shouldered by Scottish film-making institutions, Grigor continued his cultural activism mounting an exhibition entitled *Seeds of Change* (1992), timed to coincide with the European Economic Community summit in Edinburgh and (ironically) celebrating Scottish innovation and invention. His film *Nineveh on the Clyde: The Architecture of Alexander 'Greek' Thomson* (1999–2000) did for its subject what Grigor's earliest films had done for Mackintosh and, like them, helped mobilize public opinion in support of threatened Thomson buildings in Scotland. Alongside these indigenous projects, he embarked on a series of films on modernist architects mostly funded outwith Scotland. Yet, as was suggested at the outset, it would be wrong to suggest that Grigor has been wholly ignored in Scotland. On the one hand, he can be seen as a well-connected member of the Scottish arts establishment: not just Director but later Chair of the Edinburgh International Film Festival, a member of the board of Channel 4 from 1995–1999, appointed to the Scottish Broadcasting Commission in 2007, Fellow of the Royal Society of the Arts, Honorary Fellow of the Royal Incorporation of Architects in Scotland and the Royal Institution of British Architects, recipient of the Royal Television Society's Reith Award and, the final establishment cachet, awarded the Order of the British Empire in 2012 'for services to architecture and the film industry'. Set against all of these accomplishments, however, is his relative absence from the funding rosters of the successive Scottish film institutions. These remain monstrously culpable in not providing production funding for Grigor's work. In particular they missed the opportunity to develop with Grigor a progressive take on Scottish history, a gap filled by aesthetically and politically execrable films such as *Braveheart* (Mel Gibson, 1995). Germany has its Sÿberberg, Italy its Visconti, Hungary its Jansco, and Greece its Angelopoulos. But for the purblindness of successive indigenous film institutions, Grigor might have filled what remains the most egregious lacuna in Scottish cinema.

Colin McArthur

References

Hobsbawm, Eric J and Ranger, Terence O (eds) (1983) *The Invention of Tradition*, Cambridge, CUP.

Howarth, Thomas (1952) *Charles Rennie Mackintosh and the Modern Movement*, London, Routledge and Kegan Paul.

McArthur, Colin (1993) 'In Praise of a Poor Cinema', *Sight and Sound*, 3: 8, pp. 30–32.

_________ (2009) 'Scotch Myths, Scottish Film Culture and the Suppression of Ludic Modernism', in Jonathan Murray et al. (eds), *Scottish Cinema Now*, Newcastle upon Tyne: Cambridge Scholars Publishing, pp. 39–55.

Murray, Jonathan (in press) *The New Scottish Cinema*, London: IB Tauris.

Nairn, Tom (1977) *The Break-up of Britain: Crisis and Neo-Nationalism*, London: New Left Books.

Petrie, Duncan (2000) *Screening Scotland*, London: BFI.

_________ (2009) 'Cinema and the Economics of Representation: Public Funding of Film in Scotland', in Berthold Schoene (ed.), *Contemporary Scottish Literature*, Edinburgh: EUP, pp. 362–70.

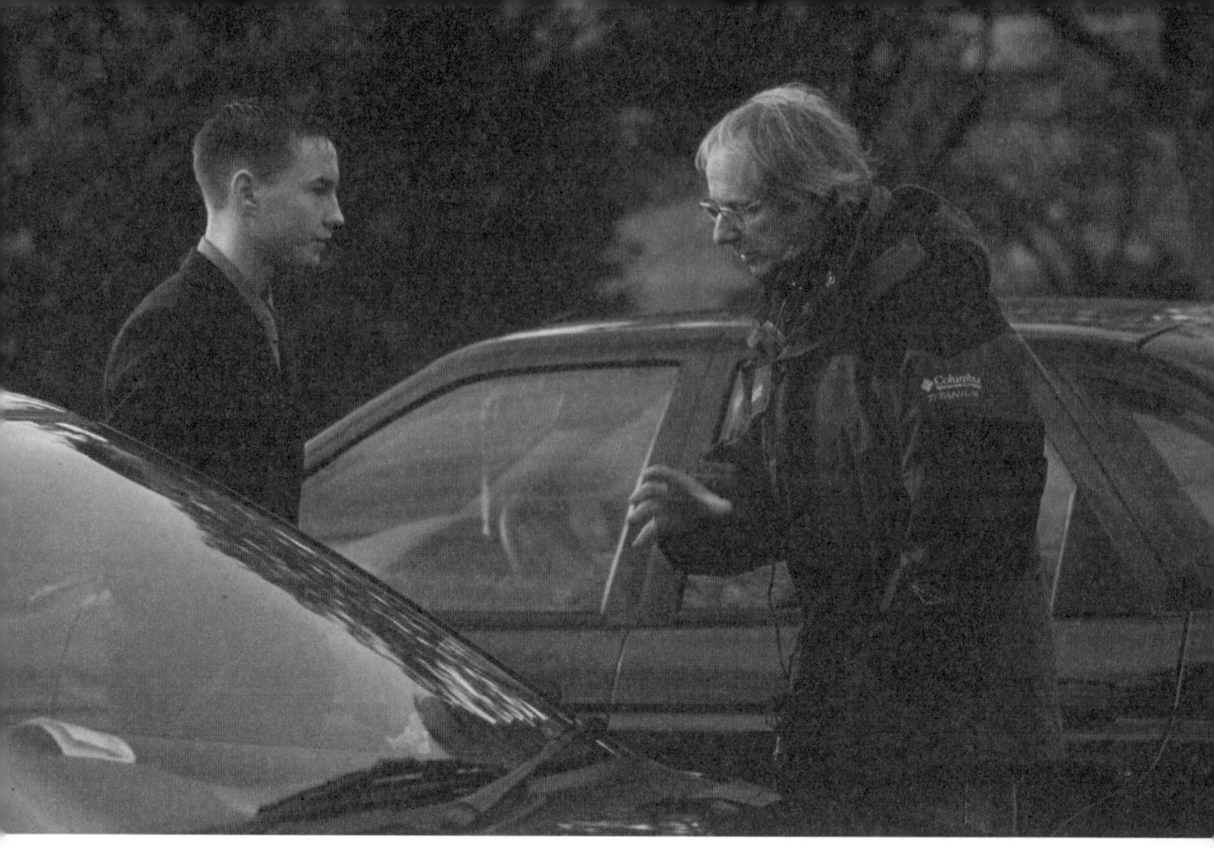

Ken Loach, British Film Institute Collection

KEN LOACH

Widely renowned as one of the most important auteur directors in contemporary European and British cinema, Ken Loach has had an enormous impact on Scottish cinema. To date, Loach has made five feature films in Scotland, along with a memorable Scottish-themed contribution to the portmanteau film *Tickets* (Ermanno Olmi, Abbas Kiarostami and Ken Loach, 2005), making him more prolific in terms of making Scottish-themed feature films than Lynne Ramsay and Peter Mullan combined. Loach's Scottish films have been very high-profile affairs, with critical plaudits greeting each to varying degrees and an admirable box office track record, particularly in Western European markets. Somewhat paradoxically, despite being an Englishman, one could thus make the case that Loach is the single most important director working in contemporary Scottish cinema. Loach's 'Scottish turn' began in 1997 with *Carla's Song* and has continued up to the 2012 release *The Angels' Share*. The reasons for this turn are multiple and include creative as well as economic and political factors.

The primary creative context for Loach looking to Scotland has been his partnership with Glaswegian screenwriter Paul Laverty. As John Hill has shown (2011: 182–83), Loach's collaborations with screenwriters have been crucial to his work as a director and Laverty has proven to be the longest running and most fruitful partnership of the director's career to date. Laverty has penned the script for every Loach project since *Carla's Song*, including non-Scottish hits such as *The Wind that Shakes the Barley* (2006) and *Looking for Eric* (2009) as well as all of Loach's Scottish films. Laverty's personal interests and background have had a big impact on the projects that the duo has collaborated on. It was his experience as a human rights lawyer investigating CIA-backed atrocities in Nicaragua in the 1980s that led directly to his interest in writing the screenplay for *Carla's Song*. Similarly, his familiarity with working-class Glaswegian life has helped to inspire the so-called 'west Scotland trilogy' of *My Name is Joe* (1998), *Sweet Sixteen* (2002) and *Ae Fond Kiss* (2004) as well as the duo's contribution to *Tickets*, which tells the story of three young supporters of Celtic football club (Laverty's own favourite club) as they travel across Europe to see a Champion's League fixture.

Another important Scottish collaborator for Loach has been producer Rebecca O'Brien. O'Brien has been working with the director since the making of *Hidden Agenda* (1990) and has been, along with fellow producer Sally Hibbin, instrumental in putting Loach on the solid financial footing that has allowed for his resurgence as a creative force after a lost decade of sorts in the 1980s (Hill 2011: 158). O'Brien helped to build a network of distributors across Western Europe who are now the reliable supporters of Loach's films, helping them not only to find audiences but also regularly providing production funding to get the films made in the first place. She has also been very adept at working with British subsidy bodies, particularly Scottish Screen and the UK Film Council (for whom she worked for a time), as well as British broadcasters. With such an infrastructure in place for production and distribution, Loach has been able to simply make films, rather than having to worry about finding financial backing for each of his projects. This infrastructure has meant that, since 1995, when O'Brien became the director's exclusive producer, Loach has been able to make twelve features and numerous shorts and documentary segments, a rate of productivity that is unprecedented for the director and is the envy of many other independent film-makers.

O'Brien's work with financiers, particularly public bodies, brings us to another important context for Loach's work in Scotland, that being the availability of public funding for film-making in Scotland. Scottish Screen has provided subsidies for *Sweet Sixteen* and *Ae Fond Kiss*, while the Scottish Arts Council supported *My Name is Joe*. Similarly, the Glasgow Film Fund supported *Carla's Song* and *My Name is Joe*. While none of these investments on the part of public funders were enough to single-handedly get the films made, they were important to assuring other investors as to the viability of the projects, thereby playing an important role within the funding packages of the individual films. The availability of this funding has been cited by some historians as well as Loach himself as one of the primary reasons for setting his films in Scotland, when the scripts in question could have easily been adapted to settings in England (Hill 2011: 188).

Formally speaking, Loach's Scottish films have, like all of his larger oeuvre, focused on political themes. Multicultural tensions within Scotland and the neo-imperial activities of the US government in Nicaragua are readily apparent in the agendas of *Ae Fond Kiss* and *Carla's Song* respectively, but even films without clear 'issues' – such as *Sweet Sixteen* and *My Name is Joe* –still focus on class and inequality in the nation. Although resolutely political at a thematic level, Loach's Scottish films, like many of his films generally since the early 1990s, also attempt to balance political didacticism with audience engagement via the usage of popular generic modes (Hill 2011: 169). So it is that many of the Scottish films have been dubbed melodramas by critics while *The Angels' Share* in part recalls Ealing comedies such as *Whisky Galore!* (Alexander Mackendrick, 1949). This shift on Loach's part, from modernist film-making and documentary, has been motivated by a desire to get his films (and thematic messages) out to the largest possible audience while sacrificing as little of the films' political content as possible. The balancing act here between political and commercial concerns is in some respects typical of Scottish and British cinema during the so-called 'cultural industries' era and has forced the director to think more and more carefully about target audiences. This balance is not always struck successfully – *Carla's Song* and parts of *Ae Fond Kiss* are particularly guilty of off-putting didacticism – but the films have nevertheless been very successful in attracting significant audiences outside of Scotland, even if local consumption has been less forthcoming.

In terms of Scottish cinema as a whole, during the so-called 'new Scottish cinema' period from the late 1980s onward, Loach's films have garnered nearly universal respect from critics and historians. Duncan Petrie has praised the film-maker for depicting an urban Scotland – as opposed to the traditions of Tartanry and Kailyardism which picture the nation in bucolic terms – and for engaging with the real social problems which plague the nation (2000: 200–03; 2004: 170–3), points echoed by Hill (2009, 2011). Hill has also argued that Loach has made films which uniquely speak to the political inclinations of Scotland, which have tended to be more left-wing than England's (2011: 183). David Martin-Jones has praised the film-maker for utilizing popular genre conventions to productively open up questions of Scottish identity in transnational contexts (2009: 53–63 and 175–87).

In addition to his impact on Scottish film history, Loach has also made a substantial impact on the Scottish film industry. This impact goes beyond the obvious internal investment created by his (relatively) prolific Scottish output over the last sixteen years. Loach has also helped to shape the careers of a number of Scottish artists in addition to Laverty and O'Brien. This can be seen most vividly in the cases of his actors. As has been his preferred working method for much of his career, Loach has largely chosen lesser-known or non-professional actors to star in his Scottish films. This practice has now led to breakthrough roles for numerous actors. These include Robert Carlyle, who had his first major part in the director's London-set film *Riff-Raff* (1991), followed by his lead role in *Carla's Song*. Peter Mullan was an established character before his starring role in *My Name is Joe* but that performance won him the Best Actor Award at the Cannes Film Festival. Debut roles in *Sweet Sixteen* turned into established careers for Martin Compston and William Ruane, while *Ae Fond Kiss* stars Atta Yaqub and Eva Birthistle have also seen their careers transformed by their casting in Loach's film. Loach's style and film-making techniques have, furthermore, influenced a new generation of Scottish directors, with Ramsay and Mullan in particular adopting some of Loach's characteristic artistic practices and thematic concerns.

Loach has thus made a multifaceted contribution to Scottish cinema and can count this as one of his many achievements in a long and distinguished career in British cinema. With the success of *The Angels' Share* at Cannes, where it won the Jury Prize, it would seem that Loach, along with Laverty and O'Brien, will continue making important and popular films about contemporary Scottish life for a while to come.

Christopher Meir

References

Hill, John (2009) '"Bonnie Scotland, eh?": Scottish Cinema, the Working Class and the Films of Ken Loach', in Jonathan Murray, Fidelma Farley and Rod Stoneman (eds), *Scottish Cinema Now*, Newcastle: Cambridge Scholars Publishing, pp. 88–104.

__________ (2011) *Ken Loach: The Politics of Film and Television*, London: BFI.

Martin-Jones, David (2009) *Scotland: Global Cinema – Genres, Modes and Identities*, Edinburgh: EUP.

Petrie, Duncan (2000) *Screening Scotland*, London: BFI.

__________ (2004) *Contemporary Scottish Fictions: Film, Television and the Novel*, Edinburgh: EUP.

DAVID MACKENZIE

Scholars and critics regularly identify David Mackenzie as a leading figure among the cadre of film-makers responsible for the 'New Scottish Cinema' of the late 1990s and early 2000s. Mackenzie is frequently cited along with Lynne Ramsay and Peter Mullan as one of Scottish cinema's most recent homegrown auteurs. Mackenzie has in fact been the most prolific, but he does not have a resounding critical or commercial success to date. It is more productive, though, to think of Mackenzie as a transnational film-maker whose best work explores broad themes while situated within Scottish settings and milieus. In particular, as Bob Nowlan writes in this volume, films such as Mackenzie's 'engage the intersection of the universal and particular, while exploring local, regional, national *and* international resonances of contemporary lived experiences' (2014).

Born on 10 May 1966, David Mackenzie's skills as a director were forged by creating short films, including a Tartan Short (a film-making programme and collaboration between the Scottish Film Production Fund and BBC Scotland), 'Marcie's Dowry', which won an Audience Award at the 1999 Best European Short Film Festival. In 1996, Mackenzie co-founded a production company, Sigma Films, with Gillian Berrie, who has produced nearly all of the director's short and feature-length films to date. In addition, Mackenzie's short

David Mackenzie, British Film Institute Collection

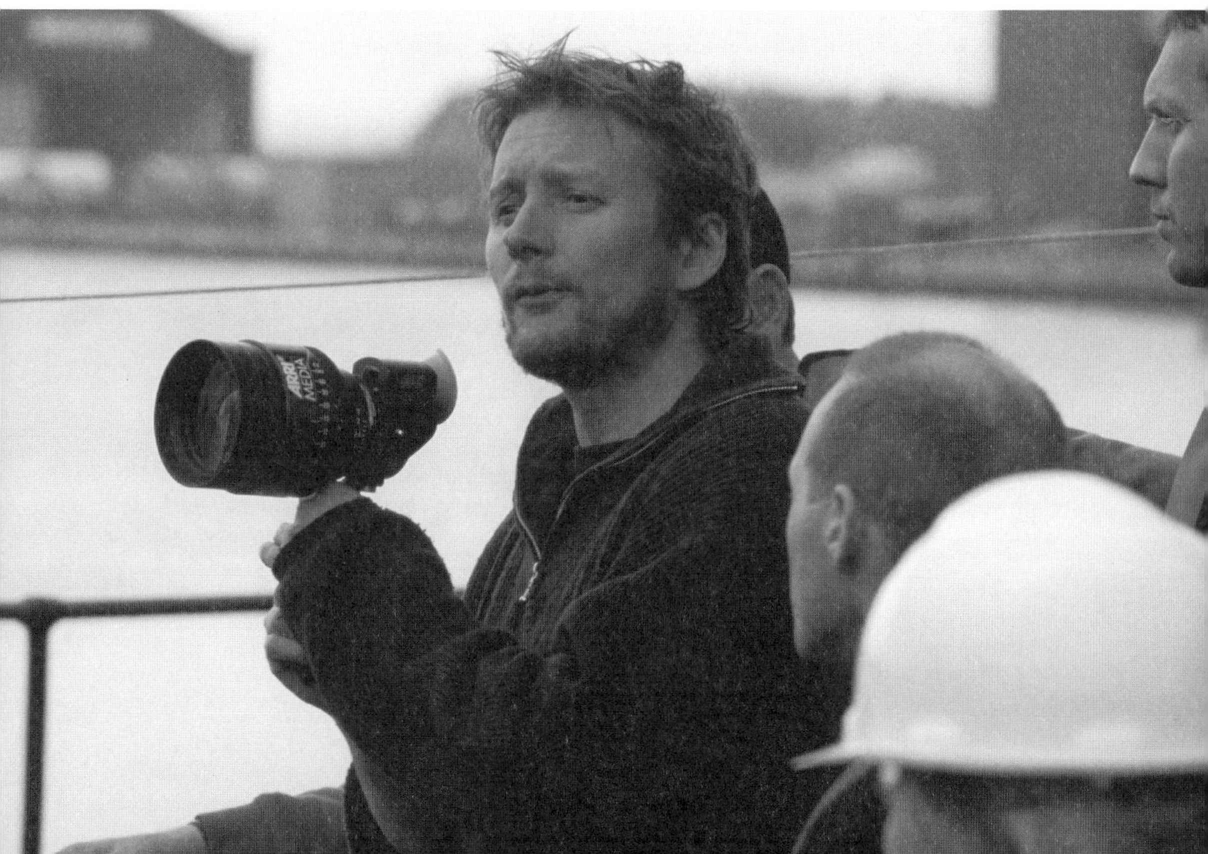

films *California Sunshine* (1997) and *Somersault* (1999) also won awards and helped to propel his career into feature films. Short films, and in particular those made under the auspices of the Tartan Shorts scheme, were vital to the early directing careers of many of the New Scottish Cinema's most promising directors, including Mackenzie.

With a foundation in successful short films, and teamed with producer Gillian Berrie, Mackenzie's first feature film, *The Last Great Wilderness*, was released in 2002. Shot on digital video and starring brother Alastair Mackenzie, *The Last Great Wilderness* begins with a premise typical of horror films – two lost souls on the run are stuck roadside and take shelter in an isolated country lodge – and defies those generic expectations by focusing more on the emotionally damaged principal characters, eschewing chainsaws and werewolves. In this first, feature effort, Mackenzie establishes some of the principal characteristics of his films: Scotland as a setting in which to explore broad themes, including but not limited to, fate, personal responsibility, psychological trauma and transgression. Additionally, the film's defiance of easy generic conventions (a fairly bold and independent-minded move for a first-time feature writer-director) also foreshadows Mackenzie's later work and willingness to take on difficult issues and questions, perhaps at the expense of commercial success. In an interview with *indieLondon*, in which he speaks about his later film, *Hallam Foe* (2007), Mackenzie states that 'I think I probably gravitate towards a slightly more European, auteur model rather than the studio thing [...] I want the stories to have loose ends and to pose some questions – or even say things that aren't too comfortable.' These sensibilities were evident in *The Last Great Wilderness*, and they were used to promote his next film, the much anticipated adaptation of the notorious Alexander Trocchi novel, *Young Adam* (2002).

As several scholars have written, including in this volume, *Young Adam* was conceived of, and marketed as, a European art film. The positioning of the film was limited in its success, as Christopher Meir points out:

> *Young Adam* was presented from the very start as a complex, challenging and important art cinema work. At the same time, however, the film was also presented in terms which would appeal to mass audiences: a noirish erotic thriller with transgressive sexual content. (2009: 200)

Though the film straddles and conflates several conventional genres, its promoters attempted to, somewhat unsuccessfully, peg it to a simpler series of discrete categories with the goal of generating commercial success. As Meir attests: 'Those marketing *Young Adam* felt the need to play up the generic, sensationalist aspects of that film' (2009: 202). Those promoting *Young Adam* attempted to classify it as a European art film and a 'noirish erotic thriller' in an attempt to win both critical and popular praise. The film is generally perceived as uneven yet revealing of Mackenzie's potential, but part of its perceived unevenness may be due to *Young Adam*'s defiance of conventional generic categorization.

Young Adam also attempted to negotiate a balance between 'European-ness' and Scottishness. As David Martin-Jones writes, 'Scottish art cinema treads a wary path between establishing a unique national identity and simultaneously erasing anything too off-puttingly Scottish' (2009: 223). Martin-Jones concludes that perhaps *Young Adam* failed to strongly connect with the European art film circuit because, unlike *Red Road* (Andrea Arnold, 2006), it was 'too Scottish' (2009: 228–29). This argument is bolstered by the highly visible and specific setting of the film: the river Clyde near Glasgow, in the 1950s. As a result, we are able to see the tensions at play in Mackenzie's first two films that, in part, will come to characterize his feature-length filmography: the tension between auteur-driven, European art cinema versus marketing for a wider, popular audience; and the tension over how 'Scottish' a film can or should be when positioned as a transnational work.

As previously mentioned, Mackenzie co-founded Sigma Films with Gillian Berrie, which, along with Danish production company, Zentropa (founded by Lars von Trier and Peter Aalbaek Jensen), collaborated to form the Advance Party Initiative. Though Mackenzie was not directly involved in the production of the Advance Party films, his producing partner, Gillian Berrie, has been instrumental to the Advance Party scheme. Conceived as an artistic, creative and financial co-production between Scandinavian and Scottish film-makers, the Advance Party's goal was to produce three films by first-time directors and producers, two of which have received some acclaim – *Red Road* (Andrea Arnold, 2006) and *Donkeys* (Morag McKinnon, 2010) – with the same characters and a common Glasgow setting. The Advance Party Initiative is one example of transnational collaboration that many feel is a promising direction for 'Scottish film-making', given the difficulties involved in sustaining an indigenous Scottish film industry, particularly in relation to uncertain levels of public funding support.

Mackenzie has repeatedly stated that he sees himself as both a Scottish and an international, European film-maker. In a 2007 article in *The Guardian* discussing the release of *Hallam Foe*, Patrick Barkham writes:

> Mackenzie rejects the idea that he makes distinctively Scottish films. He was attracted to *Young Adam*, he says, by the internationalism of Alexander Trocchi, the drug-addicted Scottish beat author who wrote the original novel. 'I'm an international director. I felt that the more internationalist the Scottish perspective was, the better. I'm definitely going to continue to make films in Scotland but that doesn't mean it will be exclusively there and I don't have any particular need to wave a flag.'

Hallam Foe is set in Scotland, and unmistakably so, given the extensive location shooting in Edinburgh Old Town, but the film does not foreground exclusively 'Scottish' issues or identities. Rather, the film deals with broadly common issues like growing up, illicit sexual attraction and the effects of psychological trauma and grief.

The period of time during and shortly after the production of *Spread* (2009) was a turning point in Mackenzie's career. This turn has taken him from Hollywood back to his home in Glasgow, and, with that, a return to film-making based in Scotland, yet he continues to focus on issues of manifestly international resonance. Mackenzie's Hollywood project was a box office flop panned by most critics. However, *Spread* offers an incisive critique of the upper class of Los Angeles and its culture of shallow consumption and exploitation. Ashton Kutcher plays Nikki, a drifter who fancies himself a gigolo to the wealthy and lonely women of Beverly Hills. After securing Samantha (Anne Heche) as a long-term client, things seem to be going well for Nikki, until he falls for the younger Heather (Margarita Levieva), whom he discovers is in the pleasure business herself. This unexpected romantic attachment between the two eventually ruins his relationship with Samantha, who, because of feelings of betrayal, fires him. Also, Heather ultimately rejects Nikki in favour of a financially secure relationship. The film ends with Nikki alone and working as a delivery boy, having quit his sexual profession, though he is perhaps a bit wiser. *Spread*, in line with other films directed by Mackenzie, does not avoid difficult issues or wrap up loose ends in classic Hollywood 'feel good' fashion. There is no 'happily ever after' for Nikki, just an uncertain future in a low-paying job.

In an August 2011 interview with the Scottish magazine, *The List*, Mackenzie states that during the production of *Spread* he and his family moved to Los Angeles and were set to live there permanently. However, on a brief trip back to Glasgow to deal with renting out his flat, he had a change of heart:

> I thought staying was a no-brainer: my family are [*sic*] out there, they make films out there, I now have friends out there, the weather's good. Came back to Glasgow at the beginning of October 2009 and there was coal and wood smoke in the air, and

> a nip, which you don't ever get in LA, and the will to leave Glasgow instantaneously evaporated. The big bubble of the illusion of Hollywood just popped. (Fielder 2011)

One version of the Hollywood 'bubble of illusion' is precisely the subject of *Spread*. Hollywood's 'glamour' is reserved only for the wealthy able to conspicuously consume. For the rarely seen working class of LA, unsteady employment and menial labour are the ordinary state of things, as exemplified by Nikki's tenuous work as a gigolo and, at the end, as a delivery boy. The rich are not represented as happy or emotionally and spiritually fulfilled, while the poor struggle to feed themselves. All of this, the film argues, occurs just beneath the gilded veneer of glamorous lifestyles and endless sunshine. Of the several factors that led to *Spread*'s perceived failure, which may have included genre and marketing confusion (the film was labelled as a 'sex comedy'), it is perhaps this unflinching look at the ugly side of Hollywood and its vast class separations, its relatively unhappy ending and the portrayal of unfulfilling lifestyles that made the film difficult for audiences to like. In spite of the film's poor reception and the move back to Glasgow, Mackenzie is not opposed to making another film in Hollywood if the project is attractive:

> If an opportunity came up to do one of our films there, or the opportunity to do something over there that felt like the right fit, then sure. A larger-scale, bigger-budget movie with a bigger train set to play with is always going to appeal to a director, but there are all sorts of compromises and extra things you have to deal with that may or may not be pleasant. It's about increasing the range of your experience. (Anon. 2011)

For now, though, Mackenzie is a Scotland-based film-maker once again.

After returning home, Mackenzie reunited with Gillian Berrie and Sigma Films for *Perfect Sense* (2011) and *Tonight You're Mine* (originally entitled *You Instead*) (2011). In both films, Scotland is the setting for narratives that explore 'universal' experiences and problems. These films are also a return for Mackenzie to international co-productions, as Jonathan Murray points out in this volume's review of *Perfect Sense*. *Perfect Sense* is, in some ways, Mackenzie's bleakest, most beautiful, and most thought-provoking film. Two independent but psychologically scarred individuals, Michael (Ewan MacGregor) and Susan (Eva Green) find each other, and love, amidst a global plague that robs humanity of its senses, one at a time. Unfortunately, many popular reviewers were unable to see past the unlikely premise (and images of Ewan MacGregor shoving a stick of butter into his mouth) to note that the film is meant to be metaphorically poetic. It is a meditation on mortality, human sustainability in an era of ecological crisis and how we cling to some essential residue of humanity as our senses are taken from us. As he articulates in a March 2012 video interview with the French film publication, *Cinecdoche* (Cinecdoche 2012), Mackenzie is more interested in an 'ideas sci-fi' as opposed to an 'effects sci-fi'. He cites Chris Marker's *La Jetée* (1962) and Francois Truffaut's *Fahrenheit 451* (1966) as chief influences on *Perfect Sense*. With that in mind, it is easy to see how audiences expecting a more mainstream, action-filled tale focusing on the outbreak of apocalyptic doom may have been disappointed by the film's far-fetched disease and the ending in which there is no 'post-' to this apocalyptic tale. What matters, however, to *Perfect Sense*, is not how realistic the premise is, or if the protagonists are able to survive and find a cure for the plague. It is our confrontation with our own mortality that matters, for as we all age we, too, gradually lose our senses, leading up to the point at which the lights go out.

Tonight You're Mine is a meditation on interconnectedness, but this time the plot device to frame that theme is the old 'feuding couple handcuffed together' gag. The film is part comedy, part rock and roll musical, part romance and part drama, and it is as light as *Perfect Sense* is heavy. Its handheld, grainy cinematography recalls the rock documentary, as well as *A Hard Day's Night* (Richard Lester, 1964). The film tells the story of two rock and roll musicians handcuffed together by a preacher-like figure at a music festival. As expected, their relationship transforms from mutual disdain to mutual attraction and romance. Though the plot is pleasant enough, the setting and guerilla-style production of *Tonight You're Mine* are its most exciting aspects. *Tonight You're Mine* received funding from the BBC and Creative Scotland. Budgeted at about £1 million, the film was shot on location during Scotland's largest music festival, T in the Park, located in Kinross-shire. In just five days in July 2010, the film was shot and partially edited on site due to the fact that nothing could be re-shot after the festival ended. The fast and loose pace of the production appealed to Mackenzie. Citing something of a creative reinvigoration, Mackenzie said: 'Generally, I like to have the possibility of the unexpected rather than everything being pre-visualised and the entire shoot was like that. This film feels like modern film making in so many ways and I found it an incredibly refreshing experience' (Creative Scotland 2011). Though the focus of the film is the relationship between Lucie (Rebecca Benson) and Adam (Luke Treadaway), the setting provides a Scottish texture upon which to explore issues of love and relationships. Scottish music, weather and youth culture are brought to the forefront in a film whose setting is in many ways the visual and cultural antithesis of *Spread*'s LA.

Mackenzie's latest work as of this writing is *Starred Up* (2013), a film about a violent teenager transferred to adult prison where he begins to form a relationship with his father, who is also an inmate. Starring Rupert Friend and Jack O'Connell, the early reviews have been some of the most favourable of all of Mackenzie's films thus far. The film is slated for a release in the United Kingdom in March 2014, and presumably an international one later in the year.

In sum, David Mackenzie is often considered to be a transnational and international film-maker because of the co-productions between his own Sigma Films and Scandinavian production companies. His films are also often aimed at the international festival circuit more than a home UK audience or the United States, aspiring to bridge that gap by attaining the extent of critical praise and a level of indie and international popularity that *Trainspotting* (Danny Boyle, 1996) famously succeeded in accomplishing. Mackenzie is also on record as a director who dislikes straight genre films, as he finds them constricting and uncreative (Cinecdoche 2012). This preference is evident because his films fuse genres or defy generic classification. *Hallam Foe*, for instance, combines a coming-of-age tale with elements of the thriller and comedy, but it is not firmly aligned with only one or two genres. In addition to this independent and international focus, Mackenzie is at the same time a Scottish film-maker, choosing to regularly base his productions in Scotland, and using Scottish settings and characters. Doing so has proven productive in exploring revenge (*The Last Great Wilderness*), guilt and personal responsibility (*Young Adam*), sexual transgression (virtually all of his films) and human mortality (*Perfect Sense*) – to name only a few of his films' principal focuses of interest and concern. Since 2002, Mackenzie has proven to be one of Scotland's most prolific feature film-makers, whose commitment to making challenging films indicates that his best work may yet be ahead of him.

Zach Finch

References

Anon. (2011) 'Interview: David Mackenzie on the joys of guerilla film making at T in the Park', *The Scotsman*, http://www.scotsman.com/news/interview_david_mackenzie_on_the_joys_of_guerilla_film_making_at_t_in_the_park_1_1494328. Accessed 14 November 2011.

Barkham, Patrick (2007) 'I've Done Sex. Now I'm Doing Money', http://www.guardian.co.uk/film/2007/aug/29/1/print. Accessed 12 November 2011.

Cinedoche (2012) 'Interview de David Mackenzie pour "Perfect Sense"' [online video], http://vimeo.com/39269158. Accessed 11 August 2013.

Creative Scotland (2011) 'You Instead', http://www.creativescotland.com/showcase/filming-in-scotland/you-instead. Accessed 11 August 2013.

Fielder, Miles (2011) 'Director returns from Hollywood to Glasgow to make two films back-to-back', http://film.list.co.uk/article/37047-interview-david-mackenzie-on-perfect-sense-and-you-instead/. Accessed 10 August 2013.

Foley, Jack (2008) 'Hallam Foe – David Mackenzie interview', http://www.indielondon.co.uk/Film-Review/hallam-foe-david-mackenzie-interview. Accessed 12 November 2011.

Martin-Jones, David (2009) *Scotland: Global Cinema – Genres, Modes and Identities*, Edinburgh: EUP.

Meir, Christopher (2009) 'Chasing Crossover: Selling Scottish Cinema Abroad', in Jonathan Murray, Fidelma Farley, and Rod Stoneman (ed.), *Scottish Cinema Now*, Newcastle upon Tyne: Cambridge Scholars Publishing, pp. 188–205.

Petrie, Duncan (2000) *Screening Scotland*, London: BFI.

PETER MULLAN

Although he has written and directed only three feature films to date – *Orphans* (1998), *The Magdalene Sisters* (2002) and *Neds* (2010) – a strong case can be made for Peter Mullan as the most prominent and provocative figure within contemporary Scottish cinema. Mullan's visibility stems in significant part from his identity as a creative polymath, an artist widely acclaimed both for his work behind the camera as writer/director and his activities in front of it as an actor. He has won no fewer than 21 major international awards (including the European MEDIA Prize and the Venice Film Festival Golden Lion)

Peter Mullan, British Film Institute Collection

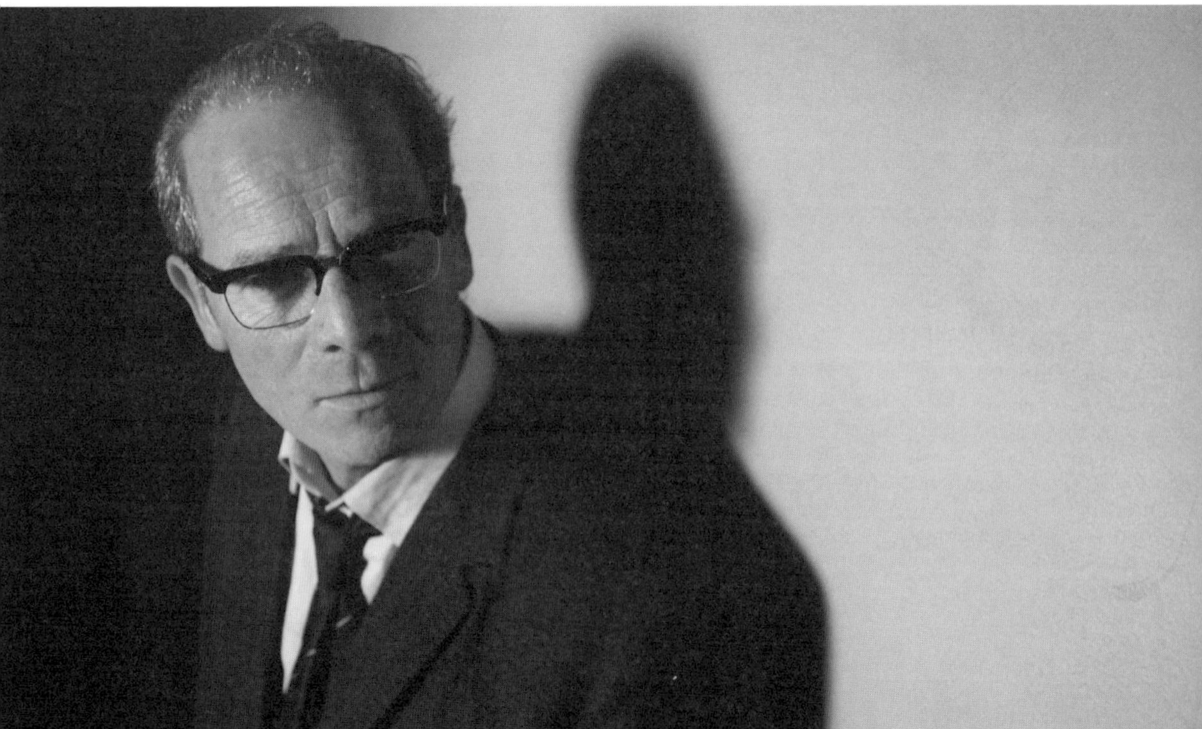

in the former capacity and eight (including Best Actor at the Cannes Film Festival and the Special Jury Prize at Sundance) in the latter. The provocative nature of his small but distinguished directorial oeuvre is similarly multi-stranded. On one hand, we might point to the challenging nature of many recurring themes within Mullan's movies: dispossessed, damaged and borderline psychotic masculine identities and the moral corruption and hypocrisy of socially respected institutions, to name but two. But on the other, the works in question are also markedly (and deliberately) confrontational at aesthetic and tonal levels, delighting as they do in an unlikely and exuberantly imaginative fusion of social realist film-making traditions with surrealist and blackly comic counterparts. Nearly a quarter of a century on from his silver-screen debut in *The Big Man* (David Leland, 1990), Mullan's position within his native film culture is contradictory and central in equal measure: he somehow manages to be Scottish cinema's *éminence grise* and its *enfant terrible* at one and the same time.

Orphans is the story of four Glasgow siblings who endure a long dark night of the soul, both literally and figuratively speaking, during the hours before their recently deceased mother's funeral. It represented a remarkably ambitious and assured feature debut, one that quickly established a range of key aesthetic characteristics and thematic concerns also discernible within its maker's subsequent work. To take one representative example of this, *Orphans* instantiates a notably emotional and quasi-autobiographical form of film-making: Mullan spoke at the time of the film's British theatrical release of the project's roots in his own experience of overwhelming grief after his own mother's death. Autobiographical or testimonial sources proved similarly important to the development of both *The Magdalene Sisters* and *Neds*. Their writer/director conducted extensive interview fieldwork with surviving victims of the Magdalene laundry system in mid-twentieth-century Ireland when researching the former, and drew extensively upon his memories of growing up as a working-class teenager in gang-ridden early-1970s Glasgow while writing the latter. Yet despite the intensely personal nature of the individual human stories at the heart of all three films, Mullan goes to conspicuous lengths to frame those narratives in ways that consistently stress their wider sociopolitical resonance. The bereaved family of *Orphans* represent an entire social class within contemporary urban Scotland, one profoundly disorientated by the loss of individual and collective certainties embodied within a range of increasingly defunct and disregarded public institutions. The latter include the post-1945 British Welfare State, the Roman Catholic Church and the heavy industries that once dominated the social and economic life of cities like Glasgow. The four abused young women who are the central protagonists of *The Magdalene Sisters* speak not only for thousands of their forgotten or ignored real-life counterparts, but also of the conspiratorial corruption between Church and State that influenced many aspects of Irish life during the twentieth century's middle decades. Rather than simply telling the story of one good boy gone bad, *Neds* highlights the extent to which individual access to educational and emotional opportunity within the Scotland of recent decades was – and, perhaps, continues to be – inequitably determined by considerations of socio-economic class.

Pronounced aesthetic and tonal affinities also link *Orphans*, *The Magdalene Sisters* and *Neds*, with the earliest of those films again setting a precedent for those that came after. *Orphans*'s highly distinctive treatment of its main characters' bewildered and bewildering emotional responses to the experience of bereavement leaves viewers uncomfortably caught between solicitous empathy with and scathing laughter at those they see on-screen. Religiose eldest sibling Thomas does not allow his self-important nocturnal vigil over his mother's coffin and cadaver to be interrupted by the small matter of a storm that tears the roof from the church within which dead parent and devout child await the former's interment. Meanwhile, Thomas's brother Michael nearly kills himself in the course of a pathetically inept attempt to fake a workplace injury in order to claim financial compensation. He succeeds only in loading physical anguish on top of an already-existing psychological equivalent. A comparable authorial impulse to treat socially and emotional serious narrative material in blackly comic and surreal ways also manifests itself in both *The Magdalene Sisters* and *Neds*. The former reaches a scabrous satirical peak when the imprisoned female inmates of a brutal Magdalene laundry are forced, as an ostensible respite from their endless backbreaking physical labours, to sit through a screening of the black-and-white Hollywood movie *The Bells of St Mary's* (Leo McCarey, 1945). The ironic contrast between a beatific American fiction of Catholic institutional charity and a horrific Irish real-life experience of the same phenomenon is so savagely underscored that the viewer hardly knows whether to laugh, cry or engage in both at once. *Neds* possesses a range of similarly surreal set-piece scenes: in one of these, central protagonist John's anger-and-angst-filled alienation becomes intense enough to goad a graven image of Christ down from its Cross in order to engage in a no-holds-barred knife fight.

Much else can and should be said within any remotely comprehensive textual analysis of a directorial oeuvre as audacious and ambitious as Peter Mullan's. But the remainder of this essay attempts another way of approaching its subject's film-making career to date. While it would be perverse not to acknowledge the unusual aesthetic, emotional and intellectual complexity of his three movies as writer/director, there is a critical danger inherent in fixating exclusively upon those works and their distinguished qualities. Clearly, Mullan is an unusually talented artist, internationally acclaimed to a degree that the vast majority of his local contemporaries can only envy. But still, we ought to resist the critical temptation to set his work definitively above (and thus, apart from) the wider body of late-twentieth- and early-twenty-first-century Scottish film-making. The development of Mullan's career specifically illuminates much about the contemporaneous evolution of Scottish cinema more generally: both phenomena have been comparably defined and directed by a complex amalgam of obstacles and opportunities. First, as an actor Mullan was associated with several of the mid- to late-1990s features that initially brought Scottish film-making to sustained critical and commercial prominence in an international context. Eye-catching early cameos in *Braveheart* (Mel Gibson, 1995) and *Trainspotting* (Danny Boyle, 1996) were swiftly followed by his breakthrough lead role in Ken Loach and Paul Laverty's *My Name is Joe* (1998). Second, we might note the publicly funded hothousing of Mullan's fledgling directorial career through a trilogy of subsidized short films – *Close* (1993), *Fridge* (1995) and *Good Day for the Bad Guys* (1995) – that preceded his feature debut with *Orphans*. This early trajectory mirrors that taken by his best-known contemporaries, David Mackenzie and Lynne Ramsay, who both worked on a range of subsidized short projects before making their own acclaimed first features, *Ratcatcher* (1999) and *The Last Great Wilderness* (2002) respectively. Granted, some of the precise institutional structures and circumstances that facilitated the beginning of careers such as Mullan's, Ramsay's and Mackenzie's during the late 1990s no longer apply in the early 2010s. But a historically informed appreciation of such figures' early film-making activities underscores the persistence of a central question that still confronts Scottish film culture today, namely, how best to support and develop new creative talent within local industrial structures that remain comparatively under-developed when considered in relation to many (if not most) European and anglophone counterparts.

It is certainly the case, for instance, that other aspects of Mullan's career path to date demonstrate many of the difficulties that have confronted numerous Scottish film-makers during the last two decades. The double-edged nature of enhanced collective access to, but enforced dependence on, external sources of production finance bedevilled the theatrical release of *Orphans*. Although shot in early 1997, the movie did not reach British cinema screens until May 1999, a delay that Mullan publicly blamed on the breakdown of working relations with his major production funder, the London-based broadcaster Channel 4. Mullan claimed that the inability of film-maker and financier to settle upon a mutually acceptable final cut stemmed from the latter's culturally insensitive determination to force the late-1990s Scottish feature projects it supported to conform to a supposedly lucrative and modish national stereotype established by the global box office success of

Trainspotting. This complaint was one echoed by several local contemporaries who also worked with Channel 4 after 1996, including John Byrne and (ironically enough) Irvine Welsh. Several years later, the production financing problems faced by Mullan's second feature, *The Magdalene Sisters*, illustrated the materially parlous state of existence that routinely faces those attempting to work as independent producers from a Scottish base. The film's main local producer, Antonine Films, went bankrupt in April 2001, while in the same month producer Frances Higson announced that the project would probably be forced to shoot in Ireland, not Scotland, because of a shortfall in envisaged production finance and the lure of Irish government-sponsored tax breaks. Only the last-minute intervention of an extraordinary coalition of public funders allowed *The Magdalene Sisters* shoot to proceed. Lastly in this regard, we might also note that the enduring difficulty of financing feature film work from a Scottish base is also suggested by the near-decade-long interval between Mullan's second feature and his third, *Neds*, not to mention the fact that the latter film was made largely with the support of French and Italian financiers.

The final major way in which the story of Peter Mullan's film-making career is closely intertwined with that of Scottish cinema more generally relates to his remarkable energy and generosity as an actor. Of the 68 on-screen credits on Mullan's CV at time of writing in early 2014, seven (not including cameo roles in his own movies) are Scottish features that he supported in the years after *My Name is Joe* cemented his international reputation as a screen performer. Moreover, despite playing a range of notably desperate and/or dangerous male characters in several of the films in question – see, for example, *Blinded* (Eleanor Yule, 2003), *On a Clear Day* (Gaby Dellal, 2004), *Cargo* (Clive Gordon, 2006), *True North* (Steve Hudson, 2006) – it would be emphatically untrue to say that Mullan has used his local acting activities as a platform from which to reiterate the same authorial ideas and interests important to him as a writer/director. Rather, his local film-making choices as an actor have exemplified his above-noted determination that Scottish cinema transcend a narrow and received range of aesthetic modes, artistic voices and images of national culture and identity. Mullan's Scottish feature work as an actor spans markedly different film genres and traditions, from European art cinema – *Young Adam* (David Mackenzie, 2002) – through melodrama – *Blinded* – to jukebox musical – *Sunshine on Leith* (Dexter Fletcher, 2013). Moreover, of the seven movies in question, three – *Blinded*, *On a Clear Day*, *True North* – were fiction feature debuts for their respective writer/directors. While Mullan's own films have undoubtedly established him as one of Scottish cinema's most distinctive, distinguished and non-conformist artistic voices, that fact should not distract attention from his wider collaborative achievements as a figurehead who has driven the ongoing expansion and diversification of the nation's film industry and culture in multiple ways.

Jonathan Murray

LYNNE RAMSAY

Cinephiles began heralding Lynne Ramsay (born in Glasgow on 5 December 1969) as one of Scottish cinema's most radiant visionaries when her short, coming-of-age film *Small Deaths* received the Prix de Jury at Cannes in 1996. The film, Ramsay's final project for the United Kingdom's National Film and Television School, established the elements that have remained central to her *oeuvre* up through *We Need to Talk About Kevin* (2011): a thematic fixation on the disconnect between children and adults, and a gaze finely attuned to the subtleties of texture, shade, movement and composition.

Despite her obvious affinity for children and young adults, Ramsay's work studiously avoids the clichés of childhood innocence. Her youthful characters are wracked with guilt, prone to violence, sexually curious and confused, and at the same time they are quite capable of profound acts of tenderness. Even her music video for the Doves's 'Black and White Town' (2005) uses images of children roughhousing and sulking to complement the song's moody angst. In the two films where Ramsay shifts to the adult perspective – *Kill the Day* (1996) and We *Need to Talk About Kevin* – her interest remains on the tormented relationship between children and their parents, and the challenges of growing from youth to adulthood. Though *Kill the Day* (also a recipient of Cannes's Jury Prize) focuses on the day-to-day struggles of junkie James Gallagher, this short character study culminates in the revelation (via flashback) that his heroin addiction is the by-product of lingering guilt over a childhood prank turned deadly. In *We Need to Talk About Kevin*, the focal point is the fraught bond between Eva Khatchadourian and her son, who eventually enacts a Columbine-style slaughter of his classmates.

Beyond her steadfast refusal to idealize childhood or reduce it to the overwrought tragedy of Dickensian melodrama, Ramsay's films stand out because of her eye's knack for establishing mood through minutiae and her ability to capture even the most delicate body language. Before going to film school to study cinematography, Ramsay pursued photography at Napier College in Edinburgh, and she singles out post-punk photographer Nan Goldin, visual autobiographer Richard Billingham and William Eggleston (famous for helping to legitimize colour photography) as being pivotal influences on her work (O'Hagan 2009). Ramsay's background in photography is most evident in the way she uses layered and fragmented portraiture to capture the disquiet of children and their disappointed yearning for emotional connections that never come to pass. Most obviously, her reliance on shallow and rack focus underscores the tension between individuals and their environment. Similarly, extreme close-ups of faces and bodies suggest how her characters repress emotion; on the surface they remain affectless, but inwardly their feelings roil with intensity, which often manifests itself in subtle but obsessive physical gestures: Morvern Callar digs her fingers into the soil and watches as ants scurry over her hands; Eva slowly pulls the shards of egg shells from her mouth that had been stirred into her scrambled eggs and meticulously lines them up along the rim of her plate. Ramsay's films are very tactile and sensual precisely because interacting with objects seems to be the only emotional outlet available to her characters.

While critics inevitably link Ramsay's status as an auteur to her interest in children, one rarely remarked-upon aspect of her *oeuvre* is its emphasis on obstructed mobility. Ramsay's first film, *Small Deaths*, opens with the image of Anne Marie riding her tricycle in circles around the flat. She asks her parents if she can go outside to play, but her request is denied. Meanwhile, Da states resolutely that he's going out to the pub, leaving Ma and Anne Marie behind. This brief episode establishes a recurring pattern in Ramsay's films: characters fantasize about movement and escape, but inevitably find themselves trapped in or

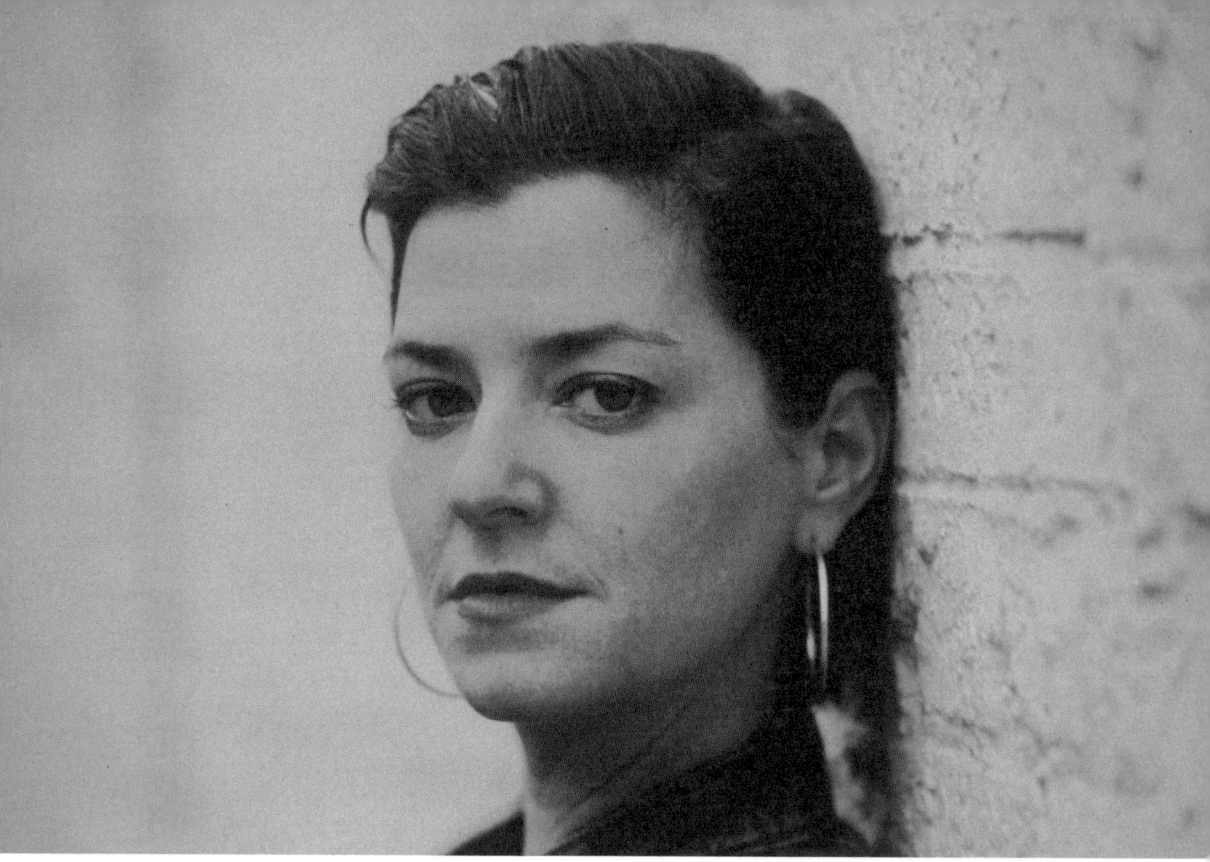

Lynne Ramsay, British Film Institute Collection

returning to the status quo. Mobility is generally reserved for adult males. In other words, the circularity of Anne Marie's play is a veritable metaphor for *all* of Ramsay's central characters. In Ramsay's next short, *Gasman* (1998), little girl Lynne prepares to accompany her father and brother on a walk to the pub for a Christmas party. As she dresses, she clicks her heels and proclaims, 'There's no place like home. There's no place like home'. The blatant reference to *The Wizard of Oz* (Victor Fleming, 1939) draws attention to the narrative structure both films share: a girl's departure from and ultimate return to home. But if Dorothy returns to Kansas with a restored sense of place and family, Lynne's sense of familial solidarity is shattered by the revelation that she has a half brother and sister. Too young to comprehend that the myth of the nuclear family is sometimes maintained via duplicity, Lynne discovers that merely chanting a wish for the perfect home guarantees nothing about place or family.

At the time of their release, these short films' emphasis on circularity linked Ramsay specifically to British cinema's tradition of social realism, with its attendant focus on individuals trapped by social circumstance. Ramsay is most frequently compared to Ken Loach and Bill Douglas. With *Ratcatcher* (1999), Ramsay fleshed out a plot scenario introduced in *Kill the Day* and the end result wowed critics and won a host of awards at international festivals, including a British Academy of Film and Television Awards prize for Most Promising Newcomer, the New Director's Award at Edinburgh and a Silver Hugo at Chicago International Film Festival. Like her short films, *Ratcatcher* relies on images of stifled mobility and circularity to symbolize the effects of social alienation and poverty in Glasgow. Ramsay's representation of the stagnant canals that circumscribe James

Gillespie's community upsets the usual literary associations of water with flow, momentum and transport; her imagery is the antithesis of that American ode to mobility, *Huckleberry Finn*. More obviously, James's physical and emotional containment is visible in the way Ramsay repeatedly frames him against barricades: the heaps of trash piling up in the streets (because of the sanitation workers' strike), walls and stairwells.

The film counters its own images of children ensnared by the canals and walled in behind mounds of refuse with occasional images of flight. In the most poignant, James spends all his change on a bus ride, going nowhere in particular. The bus reaches the end of its line, and James finds himself in an ethereal pastoral setting. Ramsay self-consciously resists the usual associations of the Scottish landscape with the majestic valleys and lochs of the Highlands. Instead, she evokes the boy's sense of wonder by drawing on the fantasy of endless possibility typically linked to America's capacious landscape: '[This] is […] probably the first time he's seen a field, so I wanted to give this field a wide-open, almost Midwestern American feel' (Ramsay, quoted in Murray 2005: 223). James spends a blissful day exploring the quiet, vacant spaces of a nearby construction site, and later running carefree through the grasses. Crucially, this image of escape is marked as fantasy. James's visit to the development mirrors Anne Marie's elliptical tricycle ride and Lynne's journey to the party: ultimately, it gets him nowhere, and he must complete the circular route and return home. When his troubles escalate, James tries to recapture the experience, only to find the doors to the half-finished housing development locked and the weather dismal. His only option is to return once more to his home, and ultimately, to the deadly canals.

James's story is a road movie caught within a domestic melodrama, and in the end domestic strife stifles the boy's hopes for transcendence through motion. Ramsay's subsequent feature, more obviously a road movie, expands on her interest in characters' quests for mobility. Unlike James, Morvern Callar is a self-sufficient young adult whose working-class life has settled into a fairly dull routine. 'Excitement' for Morvern seems limited to hazy weekend raves. As Ewa Mazierska and Laura Rascaroli observe, when Morvern sells her dead boyfriend's book as her own and uses the proceeds to journey to Spain, she is allowing herself the opportunity to try on new identities. Travelling offers Morvern a means of re-inventing herself with each new stop, rather than settling into the one role her small town allows her to play (2006: 194). As Morvern's travels take her into more remote areas of Spain, she moves further and further away from the stable identity she's trying to shirk.

Like Anne Marie, Lynne and James, however, Morvern's trek is circular. She returns home and tries to convince her friend Lanna to join her on a never-ending journey of self-discovery, but Lanna fails to comprehend Morvern's restlessness: 'There's nothing wrong with here. It is just the same crap as everywhere else'. The film concludes with Morvern once again raving, her disengagement with the environment around her made obvious by the fact that she's listening to her own music on headphones. At the end of *Ratcatcher*, James throws his body into the canal's murky waters; Morvern throws hers into the music club. Though her mind wanders, she seems to accept her position at home with weary resignation.

If the bulk of Ramsay's canon follows the same pattern of stagnation, escape and return, *We Need to Talk About Kevin* focuses its attention on what happens after the return. The film begins by establishing Eva Khatchadourian's backstory as a celebrity travel writer using a cryptic flashback that shows her ecstatically writhing around in tomato pulp at Spain's Tomatina festival. In sharp contrast, the next scene situates the audience in Eva's present tense, alone and miserable in American suburbia. The oozing tomato flesh and the primal liberation it represents have been replaced by red paint, which hostile neighbours have flung on her property in retaliation for her son Kevin's murderous rampage. The film then unfolds in a series of flashbacks, which trace Eva's gradual enslavement to familial obligation. First she sacrifices her career, and ultimately she chooses a life of maternal martyrdom. Refusing to leave the town Kevin terrorized, her transformation from the perpetual quester to the damned domestic homemaker is complete.

Ramsay seems to encourage audiences to read her first three features as a triptych of sorts. In spirit, if not literally in terms of plot, each film continues where the previous had left off. Morvern's dead lover shares James Gillespie's name, visible on the electronic manuscript she calls her own; *Ratcatcher* ends with James's suicide, and *Morvern Callar* begins with James having committed suicide. Morvern travels Spain's byways and returns home, and Eva sits at home reminiscing about her days as a cultural adventurer in Spain. Taken together, these films map out the familiar motif of circularity.

On one hand, these three films follow life's trajectory from childhood to parenthood. But their thematic arc also enacts the tension between Ramsay's position as a representative of a Scottish national cinema and the halting momentum of her career as an international auteur. Released in 1999, *Ratcatcher* closed out a productive decade in which Scottish film garnered widening international recognition, which many heralded as a Scottish cinematic renaissance. Generally speaking, the films of the decade – including Danny Boyle's *Shallow Grave* (1994) and *Trainspotting* (1996) and Ken Loach's *My Name is Joe* (1998), to name a few – redirected the cultural imagination away from the age-old colonialist representations of Scotland (the fact that Boyle and Loach are English demonstrates how the Scottish renaissance was in part defined by a readjustment of the outsiders' gaze). The decade's emphasis on urban drama avoided altogether the rural Tartanry and Kailyard mythologies, which painted Scotland 'as a lost, pre-industrial idyll, a fictional place for the film viewer to visit for a brief wallow in nostalgia' (Martin-Jones 2009: 5). But at the same time, these films complicated the conventional representation of Scotland's urban experience, which typically relied on either a 'Gothic vision of Edinburgh where under the surface of bourgeois respectability there lurks a dark and macabre world of terror and criminality' (Petrie 2000: 74) or the 'Clydesidist' myth of male industrial labour, which celebrated '"the real Glasgow" beneath the yuppie surface of shopping malls and Garden Festival and City of Culture' (Caughie 1990: 16). Duncan Petrie argues that *Ratcatcher* and the other urban films of the decade reflect the political urgency of Scotland's bid for devolution; film-makers – supported by national film funds and showcased at Edinburgh and other international film festivals – could establish 'a distinctive, a vibrant and an increasingly visible Scottish national cinema distinct from an increasingly redundant all-encompassing notion of British cinema' (Petrie 2006: 133). The vibrancy of the movement speaks to an invigorated nationalist sentiment. Just as Scotland was on the verge of liberating itself politically via a referendum that established an independent parliament, Ramsay and her peers were expanding Scottish cinema's capacity for producing and promoting independent Celtic voices.

At the same time, the marketability of an 'indigenous voice' trades on its accessibility to a global audience. As John Caughie explained at the beginning of the decade,

> there is still an expectation of what a 'Scottish film' can be about [...]. Scotland is still more readily imagined, and the imaginings are more easily sold, along the predictable lines of the scenery, the small community, and the post-industrial male angst. Most debilitating of all, loss still pervades Scottish feature films, still appearing as the characteristic mark of really serious Scottishness. (Caughie 1990: 25)

This overly familiar narrative of [male] loss is at the heart of *Ratcatcher*, and Ramsay herself chafed at the idea of her art being defined by national allegiance or gender: 'I don't want to become the person who makes films about "gritty Glasgow". I don't want to be called the next Scottish film-maker or the next woman film-maker' (quoted in Spencer 1999: 19).

Seemingly in response to this anxiety, Ramsay literally left Scotland behind with her subsequent film. If James Gillespie is the prototypical suffering Scot, his 'death' at the beginning of *Morvern Callar* liberates Morvern/Ramsay to explore the world beyond the British isle. To begin, Ramsay saw the film as an opportunity to escape the tradition of kitchen-sink realism:

> 'I started getting compared with Ken Loach,' she says. 'Oh, she's working-class, her films are too slow and too dark. I think *Morvern Callar* put paid to those early comparisons but they still linger because I don't like using jump cuts and I always want to try something new. That's why I'm a film-maker, to keep testing the form, and myself.' (Ramsay, quoted in O'Hagan 2011)

Robert Morace argues that this ambition to broaden her scope is apparent in the ways Ramsay de-emphasizes the 'Scottishness' so central to Alan Warner's original novel. For example, Ramsay's direction makes no attempt to mask Samantha Morton's Nottingham accent, rendering the issue of nationality virtually irrelevant (Morace 2012: 118). Similarly, Ramsay minimizes the importance of setting: '[T]here were parts of the book that I was less interested in, like the crazy Oban culture, which I felt was quite parochial. I wanted to make it more generic' (Ramsay, quoted in Morace 2012: 120). Moreover, the film's resolution, unlike the novel's, does not specify that Morvern returns to Scotland pregnant and ready to settle. For Mazierska and Rascaroli, 'Ramsay's unfaithfulness to the novel in this respect [...] reflects her unwillingness to constrain her heroine by domesticity' (2006: 198) or, one might add, nationality. Morace concludes that Ramsay's strategies link her to a post-devolutionary Scottish artistic consciousness, liberated from the responsibility of representing Scotland (2012: 121–22). For John Caughie, Ramsay's adaptation 'confound[s] the received notion of national cinemas and confuse[s] the desire for a national identity expressed through cinema' (2007: 105), and this refusal is why the film failed to garner critical raves (111).

If *Morvern Callar* marked Ramsay's bid to establish herself as a true auteur, freed from cultural and national obligations, subsequent events illuminated the difficulties of actually following through on these ambitions. After completing her second feature, Ramsay began adapting another novel, this one American, potentially allowing Ramsay the opportunity to move further afield from her native Scotland: Alice Sebold's *The Lovely Bones*. British production company Film4 had acquired production rights and hired Ramsay to adapt the novel while it was still a work in progress, but *The Lovely Bones*'s subsequent year-long ride on the *New York Times* hardcover bestseller list made the novel a hot commodity, attracting the attention of director/producer Peter Jackson. Eventually Hollywood studio DreamWorks signed on to co-produce the film, Peter Jackson was hired to direct, and Ramsay's screenplay was abandoned. Distraught, Ramsay put her career on hiatus for a decade: 'I think my confidence took a wee bit of a kicking. If you feel you have made a great piece of work, which the script for *The Lovely Bones* was, and that it suddenly means nothing, it's like being in the land of the lost' (quoted in O'Hagan 2011).

Given the immense popularity of the novel, completing *The Lovely Bones* would have given her an opportunity to work with a major international studio (DreamWorks) and catapulted Ramsay's career into the international arena, perhaps bringing her the unique combination of popularity and critical appeal enjoyed by Danny Boyle. But the collapse of the project points to the difficulties of shaking off the creative restrictions and cultural assumptions imposed on film-makers from 'peripheral' nations. Crucially, Ramsay attributed the loss of *The Lovely Bones* to the combination of her gender and her Glaswegian background: '[T]he film industry is completely sexist and completely class-biased. [...] Plus, I have the Glasgow thing as well. I always feel as soon as they hear a Scottish accent, they're backing away' (quoted in O'Hagan 2011). Tied to her satellite status as a Scot and as a woman, her career's forward momentum stalled. She found herself, in a word, stuck at home.

Perhaps not coincidentally, then, *We Need to Talk About Kevin*'s production and its plot both enact the fear of female entrapment. At the point at which she was poised to enjoy international fame and a broad general audience, Ramsay found herself restricted to the insular realm of small-budget art cinema. Despite the fact that the film combines American and Scottish talent and was filmed on location in Connecticut, its miniscule budget ($7 million) and tight shooting schedule (30 days) were a far cry from the support Jackson received for *The Lovely Bones* ($65 million). Furthermore, the film revisits the familial theme Ramsay had left behind after *Ratcatcher*. With Eva Khatchadourian, the wandering spirit embodied by Morvern Callar becomes domesticated, transformed into an American version of *Ratcatcher*'s Ma Gillespie.

While most of the critical discussion of the film has centred on the debate over the source of Kevin's violence (bad seed or poor parenting?), Ramsay is actually more concerned with the woman whose professional and personal ambitions lose out in the competition with male prerogative. In this light, it's difficult not to see parallels between Eva and Ramsay herself. Eva, stuck in suburban mediocrity and condemned for Kevin's behaviour, watches as her son becomes a media sensation. Whereas the novel's unreliable narration is perhaps more ambivalent about Eva's fears that her husband is unresponsive and her son psychopathic, the film's sympathies are clearly aligned with the adventurer who succumbs to her prescribed gender role. Like Eva, Lynne Ramsay found her career stuck in the realm of domestic melodrama (with a touch of horror) at a time when she clearly had ambitions to explore other genres.

London's 2012 Olympics extravaganza confirmed Ramsay's standing as one of Britain's most poetic voices. Her film *The Swimmer* was one of four shorts commissioned to contribute to a nationalist fervour designed to market the image of a culturally diverse Britain abroad. Again, Ramsay returned to images of mobility, though with a decidedly more optimistic spin: the poetic meditation on national splendour follows a swimmer through British streams and lakes, and up its coast, a celebratory evocation of national pride that stands in sharp contrast to *Ratcatcher*'s stagnant canals. Ramsay's participation in the proceedings illuminated her status as a national treasure. But her stated ambition to shoot an adaptation of *Moby Dick* set in outer space reiterated her determination to avoid being labelled as *just* a Scottish director or *just* a director of women's films.

Tom Wallis

References

Caughie, John (2007) '*Morvern Callar*, Art Cinema and the "Monstrous Archive"', *Scottish Studies Review*, 8: 1, pp. 101–15.

__________ (1990) 'Representing Scotland: New Questions for Scottish Cinema', in Eddie Dick (ed.), *From Limelight to Satellite*, London: BFI, pp. 13–30.

O'Hagan, Sean (2011) 'Lynne Ramsay: "Just Talk to Me Straight"', *The Observer*, 2 October, http://www.guardian.co.uk/film/2011/oct/02/lynne-ramsay-interview-about-kevin. Accessed 13 March 2013.

Martin-Jones, David (2009) *Scotland: Global Cinema – Genres, Modes and Identities*, Edinburgh: EUP.

Mazierska, Ewa and Rascaroli, Laura (2006) *Crossing New Europe: Postmodern Travel and the European Road Movie*, London: Wallflower.

Morace, Robert (2012) 'The Devolutionary Jekyll and Post-Devolutionary Hyde of the Two *Morvern Callars*', *Critique: Studies in Contemporary Fiction*, 53: 2, pp. 115–23.

Murray, Jonathan (2005) 'Kids in America?: Narratives of Transatlantic Influence in 1990s Scottish Cinema', *Screen*, 46: 2, pp. 217–25.

Petrie, Duncan (2006) 'National Cinema as Cultural Exchange', in Sylvia Harvey (ed.), *Trading Culture: Global Traffic and Local Cultures in Film and Television*, London: John Libbey, pp. 133–44.

__________ (2000) *Screening Scotland*, London: BFI.

Spencer, Liese (1999) 'What Are You Looking At?', *Sight and Sound*, 9: 10, pp. 16–19.

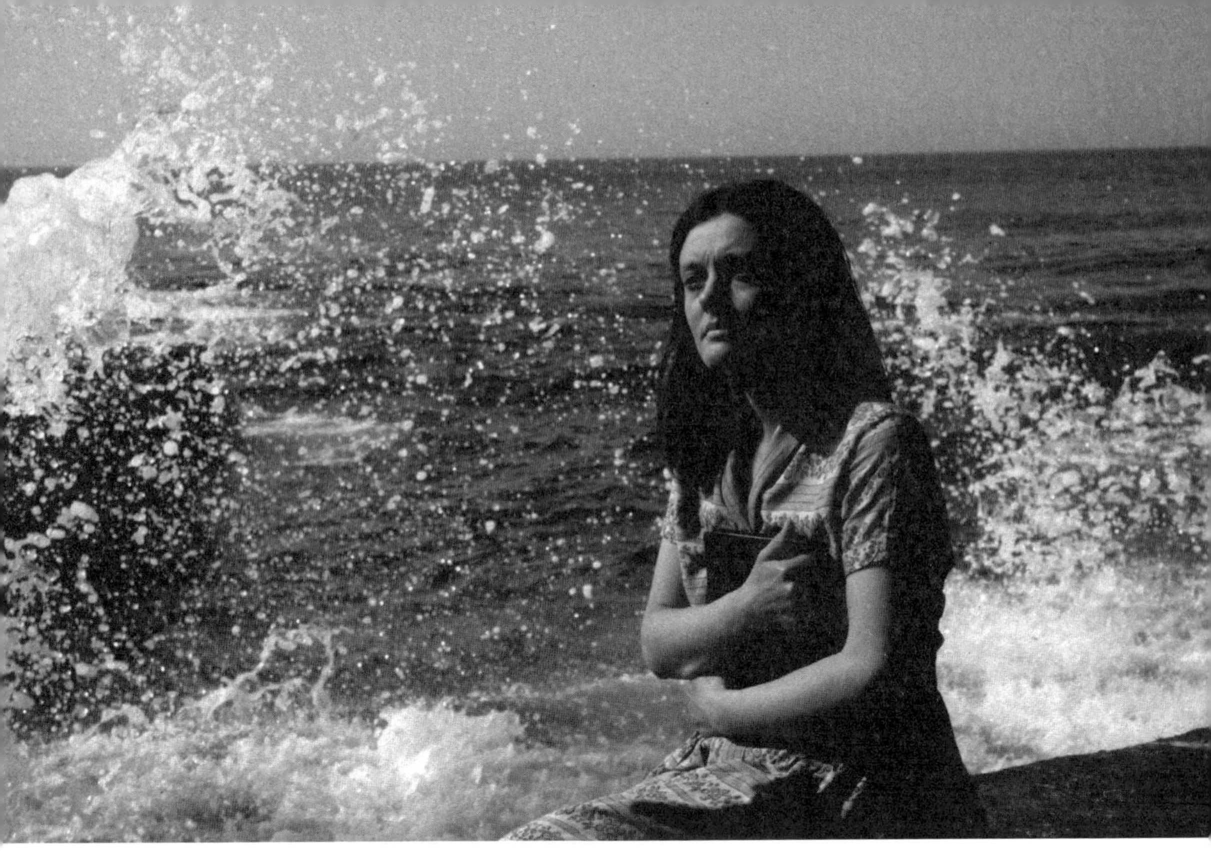

Blue Black Permanent (1992), directed by Margaret Tait, British Film Institute Collection

MARGARET TAIT

Margaret Tait is one of the most important and fascinating figures in Scottish cinema history. Her biography, artistic productions and boundary-defying modes of film-making left behind a legacy that challenges the border between the amateur and the professional, and provides inspiration for film-makers of all persuasions. Thanks to a number of film critics and historians, Margaret Tait and her work have also become important to the history of previously neglected women film-makers. Scholars such as Sarah Neely have used Tait's work to contest and complicate narratives of film production and scholarship that are all too often male-centric. Tait's life and work have been recently re-discovered, to the benefit of Scottish film culture.

Margaret Caroline Tait was born on 11 November 1918 in Kirkwall, Orkney. According to her obituary in *The Independent*, 'her family sprang from a long line of seafaring merchants' (Grigor 1999). Tait did not grow up to become a seafaring merchant, but, like her films, she travelled the world. She attended and graduated from the University of Edinburgh, where she received training in medicine (McBain n.d.). Tait was a General Medical Practitioner, often using her earnings to fund her film-making and other artistic endeavours. From 1943–46, she served in the Royal Army Medical Corps. She was stationed in Jhansi, India, a city 'that served as a recuperation point for troops returning from Burma' (Neely 2009: 304). During this time, she developed an interest in photography and writing stories about her experiences in World War II. After she returned to Scotland, she enrolled in the Edinburgh College of Art and wrote a number of pieces, including a novel manuscript entitled, 'The Lilywhite Boys', which was rejected by publishers. After moving to London for a time, Tait relocated to Rome and attended the Centro Sperimentale di Cinematographia from 1950–52 (Neely 2009: 304). While living in Italy, she fell in love with Italian neo-realist films and the country's rich film culture. Tait learned how to make films at the Centro, and she also forged important friendships with fellow students and film-makers, Peter Hollander and Fernando Birri (Neely 2009: 305). Tait returned to Scotland and formed her production company, Ancona Films, in Edinburgh on Rose Street with Peter Hollander. The street itself became the title for, and the subject of, her 1956 short film (McBain n.d.). This was a prolific era of artistic production for Tait, who, in addition to making 33 films, was a painter and wrote a prodigious amount of poetry, prose and correspondence. During the 1950s and 1960s, she remained mostly uninterested in the traditional sponsored documentary, which was the most prevalent film made in Scotland until the 1970s (Grigor 1999). This, in part, contributed to her difficulty in securing funding for her films, as her productions were far different from the 'professional' documentaries of that era. Tait's inspirations often came from her everyday surroundings, Orcadian geography and culture, and her own experiences and memories. This 'personal' kind of work seemed to serve little-to-no commercial purpose, at least in terms of the sponsored documentary mode of film-making, thus distancing her from the mainstream form of film production in Scotland at the time. In 1968 she married writer Alex Pirie, and their marriage lasted until her death in 1999. A 1970 retrospective screening of her films at the Edinburgh Film Festival led to wider recognition of her talent (Neely 1999: 322). In spite of her popularity in some circles during the 1970s and 1980s, Tait directed only one feature-length film, *Blue Black Permanent* (1992). This film was based on a screenplay she had written in the 1940s, and it tells the story of three generations of women who struggle to balance domestic and artistic aspects of their lives, while the deadly lure of the sea seems to transcend the generations (McBain n.d.). It opened the Edinburgh Film Festival, and when Sam Fuller saw the film 'he called it a poem' (Grigor 1999). Her final film, *Garden Pieces*, was completed in 1998. She died on 16 April 1999. In a culture noted for its independent-mindedness, Murray Grigor eulogized Tait, calling her 'Scotland's most independent film-maker' (1999).

Access to Margaret Tait's films has eased considerably since her passing. Though, as Sarah Neely points out, Tait was uninterested in the preservation of her work, her husband consented to donate many of her films to the Scottish Screen Archive in Glasgow after her death (2008: 221). This led to a second period of re-discovery of Tait's work in the early 2000s. Ryan Shand states in a 2007 volume of *The Moving Image*:

> Ironically for an artist who spent most of her days on the island of Orkney (north of the Scottish mainland), she had a loyal following not in Glasgow or Edinburgh but in London. There she was embraced by figures from the avant-garde film community, who saw in her a kindred spirit. The efforts of these London filmmakers, programmers, and critics led to the 2004 retrospective and subsequent touring program around Britain and beyond that the films eventually came to light. (Shand 2007: 108)

The 2004 retrospective screenings in Edinburgh and elsewhere inspired the 2006 book published by Wallflower, *Subjects and Sequences: A Margaret Tait Reader*, the first volume devoted solely to Tait and her work, edited by Peter Todd and Benjamin Cook. Additionally, the Scottish Screen Archive and LUX (formerly the London Filmmaker's Cooperative) restored her films and made them more accessible than ever before (Neely

2009: 317–18). Several of Tait's films are available to view online, including *A Portrait of Ga* (1952), *Rose Street* (1956), *Where I Am Is Here* (1964), *Calypso* (1955), *Hugh MacDiarmid: A Portrait* (1964) and others at the Scottish Screen Archive website. Other examples and samples of her work may also be found online, though her complete filmography is only accessible through the Scottish Screen Archive. Unfortunately, *Blue Black Permanent* has not been released on DVD at the time of this writing, and access to Tait's only feature film remains limited. Tait struggled throughout her life to screen and distribute her films, and it is only within the last decade that several of them are available for a much wider audience. This is largely thanks to online technologies and the work of critics, scholars, archivists and film-makers who have raised awareness of her films.

Margaret Tait's film-making practices challenged the (so-called) boundaries between amateur and professional film-making. For most of her life, Tait was a 'one woman film industry', as she was referred to during a 1979 screening of her work at Calton Studios in Edinburgh (Neely 2009: 301). She shot her films with her own 16 mm Bolex camera that she purchased while studying in Rome, edited her own work, and drew and painted her own animation sequences by hand (Neely and Riach 2009: 4). Her work as a General Practitioner funded her film-making projects, and only three of her films received outside sources of financing. This is not to say, however, that she was a recluse or a 'pure' artist who shunned external funding for fear of a compromised final work. Rather, she occupied a space between the amateur and the professional and, perhaps, because of that, sources of money to make films often eluded her. For example, Sarah Neely relates an anecdote about a time when

> the Guinness Company [...] wrote to Tait in her capacity as a General Practitioner about the health-benefits of their product, Tait wrote back immediately, suggesting the possibility that she produce a film, similar to *Orquil Burn*, about the organization of the hops harvest. (Neely 2009: 319)

Nothing came of her proposal, probably, as Neely goes on to say, because 'her work was perceived to be *outside* the mainstream by the commercial film industry in Scotland and England' (2009: 320). One glaring example of this perception was revealed when John Grierson himself attended Tait's 1954 Rose Street Film Festival (an event organized by Tait and others to showcase her work and the work of her classmates from the Centro) and praised her films. However, this was not parlayed into future financing or distribution. When she attempted to get her film, *Hugh MacDiarmid: A Portrait*, screened on Grierson's documentary television series, *This Wonderful Life* (1957–66), she was told that 'the film was felt to be unsuitable for transmission' (Neely 2009: 319). Largely ignored by the dominant film-making industry, Tait had almost as little luck within the realm of funding for the arts. A 1957 application to the Carnegie Trust was 'rejected on the grounds that the trustees did not support filmmaking conducted for profit', as were several appeals to the Scottish Film Council (Neely 2009: 320). Presumably, Tait's efforts at attaining funding from other sources, including private businesses, such as the Guinness example mentioned above, did not ingratiate her to those who disperse funding for the arts. Attempts at raising money and securing wide distribution were usually unsuccessful, and, as a necessity, her methods of production and distribution fell under what is commonly considered to be self-financed, amateur film-making. Most of Tait's films were shot on 16 mm, a cheaper gauge popular with amateur and experimental film-makers, yet in personal correspondence she expressed her eagerness to work with 35 mm film, a far more expensive and 'professional' film stock (Neely 2009: 321). Further correspondence suggests that she enjoyed working on a much larger scale on *Blue Black Permanent*, and that she likely would have continued to make feature films with larger budgets if the opportunities had presented themselves (Neely 2009: 321). Tait was also savvy at distributing her films in guerilla-fashion, succeeding in doing so in diverse ways and, in some cases, internationally. This is impressive when one considers that the era she worked in was mostly before home video and the Internet. Though she rarely made enough money to cover costs of production, Tait sold prints to a variety of organizations, sent her films on international tours and organized her own screenings locally and regionally, including in her own home and village halls (Neely 2009: 318). These varied production, distribution and exhibition strategies contribute to what could be considered a 'fusion' of amateur and professional film-making methods (Neely 2009: 319).

In addition to blending amateur and professional modes of production, fundraising, exhibition and distribution, Tait's films incorporate animation, documentary, experimental and home movie aesthetics. This hybrid quality makes her work often difficult to place within established film-making traditions. It seems Tait herself cared little for distinctions between genres and modes of film-making, preferring to call her work 'film poems' (LUX Online). As several writers have pointed out, her films often foreground the minutiae of everyday life, the details of specific places and, in her more documentary-like works, such as *Hugh MacDiarmid: A Portrait*, the candid rather than the didactic. This attention to the small things, the seemingly innocuous elements of life and experience, is typical of her work. For example, in *A Portrait of Ga*, Tait films her mother doing everyday activities, such as gardening and smoking. Just over two-and-a-half minutes into the film, Tait's camera lingers on her mother carefully unwrapping and eating a piece of candy. The close-up of her hands as she delicately unfolds the wrapper without touching the candy at once memorializes a very specific detail about Ga (the way she eats candy) and provides a momentary and fragmentary experience of the subject, much like a memory. *A Portrait of Ga* is at once a home movie because Tait films her mother in her home environment; it is a documentary because it is a portrait of an elderly woman and her life on the Islands in the 1950s; and it is an experimental film, or art film, in part because it eschews classical Hollywood narrative, causality and closure.

Critical analyses of Tait's films have been a major factor in the renewed appreciation for, and recognition of, her work. Several scholars have brought attention to her films for their importance to Scottish cinema and women's film-making history (see Ian Goode, Sarah Neely, and Peter Todd and Benjamin Cooke). Unfortunately, due to space limitations, this essay cannot engage in a detailed analysis of all, or even very many, of Tait's works. However, it is worth looking closer at two films that exemplify Tait's style and themes of concern suggested in the preceding discussion. The following brief analyses of *Three Portrait Sketches* (1951) and *These Walls* (1974) focus on films from two different periods of Tait's film-making career. In the first, we see Tait's work as a young student film-maker, experimenting and learning. In the second, Tait is preparing to move out of her Rose Street studio and back to Orkney, marking the end of a near-twenty-year period in that location. Both films offer insights into Tait's artistic concerns and working methods during each period.

Three Portrait Sketches was made during the time Tait was a student at the Centro. According to the Scottish Screen Archive, this film was a team effort between Tait, who directed, edited and wrote the film, and her classmates and friends Peter Hollander and Fernando Birri. Hollander operated the camera and also edited; Birri is the subject of one of the portraits and also served as an editor. This 7-minute and 44-second, black-and-white silent film is not a documentary featuring three figures, as its title might suggest, but an experimental film featuring three characters: a young girl named Claudia, Fernando Birri and Saulat Rahman. All three perform in various ways for the camera, providing brief 'sketches' and displaying their personalities. Claudia smiles, laughs and picks grass off the ground in a series of medium close-ups; Birri laughs, gesticulates and mock-imitates the pose of a Roman statue, revealing a humorous and playful demeanour; Rahman picks flowers and places them in her hair, and she poses with other forms of plant life, indicating a quiet and perhaps shy demeanour. Most of the shots take place in exterior locations, and they foreshadow some of Tait's future motifs. This film features shots of fountains, waterfalls and streams, and it has been noted that Tait's films often prominently feature images of water, which is perhaps unsurprising for a native of Orkney. Tait's interest in animation is apparent in this film, too. A brief, stop-motion animated sequence begins just over two minutes into the film. In this sequence, a group of bricks appears to assemble into a simple 'log cabin' structure, and this structure is topped off with a roof of growing grass. Here we can see Margaret Tait beginning to learn her film-making craft, playing with film-making techniques and establishing some of the major visual motifs of her overall body of work: images of water, close-ups of people, shots of the natural environment, and simply animated sequences.

These Walls is a good example of the in-between-ness of Tait's films discussed earlier in this profile. The Scottish Screen Archive website states that the subject of this 1974 film is the interior of Tait's studio located on Rose Street in Edinburgh. The author also speculates that the film was shot just as Tait was about to move out of the studio. With that context in mind, it is clear that the film records images of a significant place in the life of the film-maker. It is also something of a documentary about film-making because it gives insight into Tait's working processes, as well as the place in which she made films. And, finally, the film is experimental in some ways, with its repeated shots and poetic intertitle insertions ('Ah-These Walls!' becomes 'Ah-Those Walls!' and back again to 'These Walls'), suggesting themes broader than the documentation of a place or a memorial keepsake. This colour, silent film depicts Tait's studio interior in 6-minutes and 16-seconds, composed primarily of close-ups and panning shots of the walls. Artwork, photos, clippings and images fill the walls of Tait's studio. Early in the film, several close-ups of a collage of mostly black-and-white photos and pictures on the wall are followed by a striking cut to the same wall, only this time it is bare (presumably because the images were taken down or discarded). The bareness of the space after the images have been removed is jarring. There is no gradual takedown, but rather a sudden sparseness. However, this transition from a space-in-use to an empty studio is complicated by the editing. Shots of the same walls filled with art and images from earlier in the film are repeated in the latter scenes among shots of the studio nearly cleared out. This editing technique suggests the fleetingness of art, and perhaps of time (Tait spent nearly twenty years in the same studio), but also its capacity to return, or live on, in memory or in another context. The text that appears four-and-a-half minutes into the film: 'But that was long ago', seems to support the theme of the passage of time and the possible ephemerality of art. It is worth noting how small and simply furnished Tait's studio is shown to be, as well. A single chair and table (cluttered with items such as tape and pieces of celluloid) served as a writing desk, an animation studio and an editing table. Even by today's DIY film-making standards, in which a feature film can supposedly be shot and edited on a phone, Tait's set-up was remarkably minimalist. *These Walls* is a great example of a film-maker turning the camera upon her working methods, her position as a film-maker and reflecting upon her history of film-making. Though this film appears to depict the end of a film-making career, it was really more of the end of an era. Sarah Neely and Alan Riach point out that Tait moved her operations from Rose Street to Orkney, where she set up in an old kirk (2009: 4). Tait made films for over twenty years after the completion of *These Walls.*

Both of these films demonstrate many of Tait's film-making characteristics. In these and other films, we see Tait 'engaged with the local and the specific', such as the shots looking out of her studio window onto Rose Street and observing construction happening across the way in *These Walls* (Neely and Riach 2009: 16). We also see a vision of Rome at the time Tait was a student there in *Three Portrait Sketches*. As Neely and Riach write, Tait's film-making 'reflects her belief in the innate, lyrical qualities of everyday life' (2009: 10).

The long project to re-discover and appreciate Tait's work has been successful in many ways, but it is also important to remember why such a project was necessary in the first place. The systemic marginalization of women film-makers throughout much of film history (though not just in Scotland, of course) has prompted a need to uncover 'lost' or 'neglected' works. Compounding the patriarchal leanings of film-making practice for much of the twentieth century were the specific circumstances of film-making in Scotland that made it extremely difficult for anyone to make a film and get it seen if it was not a sponsored documentary, a London-centred British or a Hollywood production. Thus, female voices like Tait's, and alternative representations that focus on the intimate, the feminine and the everyday, have only recently received in-depth analysis. Tait, in her own ways, was able to overcome a near-total lack of external funding, geographical distance from London and Hollywood and very little infrastructure for the distribution and exhibition of her films. In spite of those difficulties, Tait's films did find an audience, mostly outside of the mainstream film-going public, and that audience has in turn made her work more accessible. For both film-makers and audiences, Tait inspires for overcoming many of those obstacles, while remaining true to her visions of what she wanted her films to be, and to be about. Yet, the difficulty of her circumstances should also serve as a reminder of the challenges many women and independent film-makers have had and continue to face, and that those challenges could be, and can be, alleviated by institutional and cultural changes. Difficulties in the arenas of (especially) distribution and exhibition still exist in spite of new technologies such as YouTube and the proliferation of film festivals. It can be hoped that Tait and her work may inspire not only film-making, but also reforms in distribution and exhibition practices that would allow for a wider range of artistic visions.

Zach Finch

References

Goode, Ian (2005) 'Scottish cinema and Scottish imaginings: *Blue Black Permanent* and *Stella Does Tricks*', *Screen*, 36: 2, pp. 235–39.

Grigor, Murray (1999) 'Obituary: Margaret Tait', *The Independent*, 12 May, http://www.independent.co.uk/arts-entertainment/obituary-margaret-tait-1093051. Accessed 10 October 2013.

LUXOnline (n.d.) 'Margaret Tait', http://www.luxonline.org.uk/artists/margaret_tait/. Accessed 10 October 2013.

McBain, Janet (n.d.) 'Biography of TAIT, Margaret', *Scottish Screen Archive*, http://ssa.nls.uk/biography/10032. Accessed 17 September 2013.

Neely, Sarah (2009) '"Ploughing a lonely furrow": Margaret Tait and Professional Filmmaking Practices in 1950s Scotland', in I Craven (ed.), *Movies on Home Ground: Explorations in Amateur Cinema*, Newcastle upon Tyne: Cambridge Scholars Publishing, pp. 301–26.

__________ (2008) 'Stalking the image: Margaret Tait and intimate filmmaking practices', *Screen*, 49: 2, pp. 216–21.

Neely, Sarah and Riach, Alan (2009) 'Demons in the Machine: Experimental Film, Poetry and Modernism in Twentieth-Century Scotland', in Jonathan Murray, Fidelma Farley and Rod Stoneman (eds), *Scottish Cinema Now*, Newcastle upon Tyne: Cambridge Scholars Publishing, pp. 1–19.

Shand, Ryan (2007) 'Subjects and Sequences: A Margaret Tait reader (review)', *The Moving Image*, 7: 1, pp. 107–10.

MYTHIC VISIONS

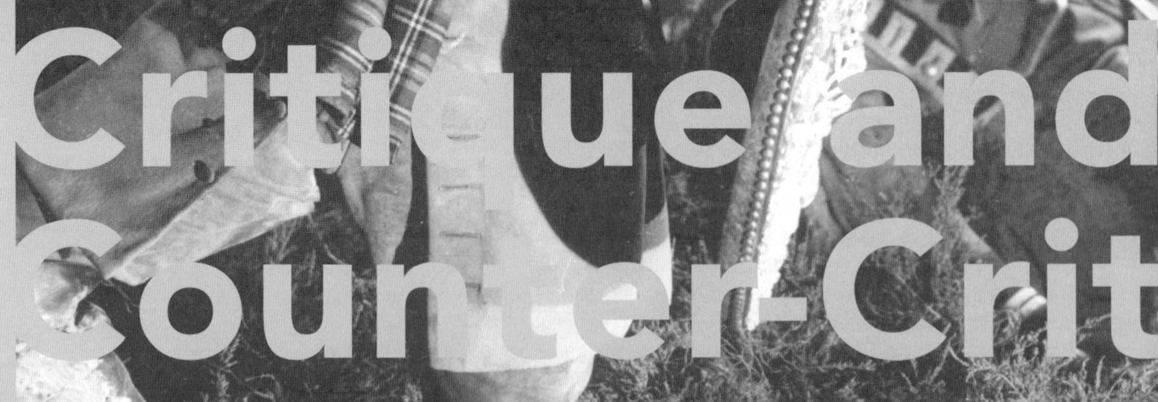

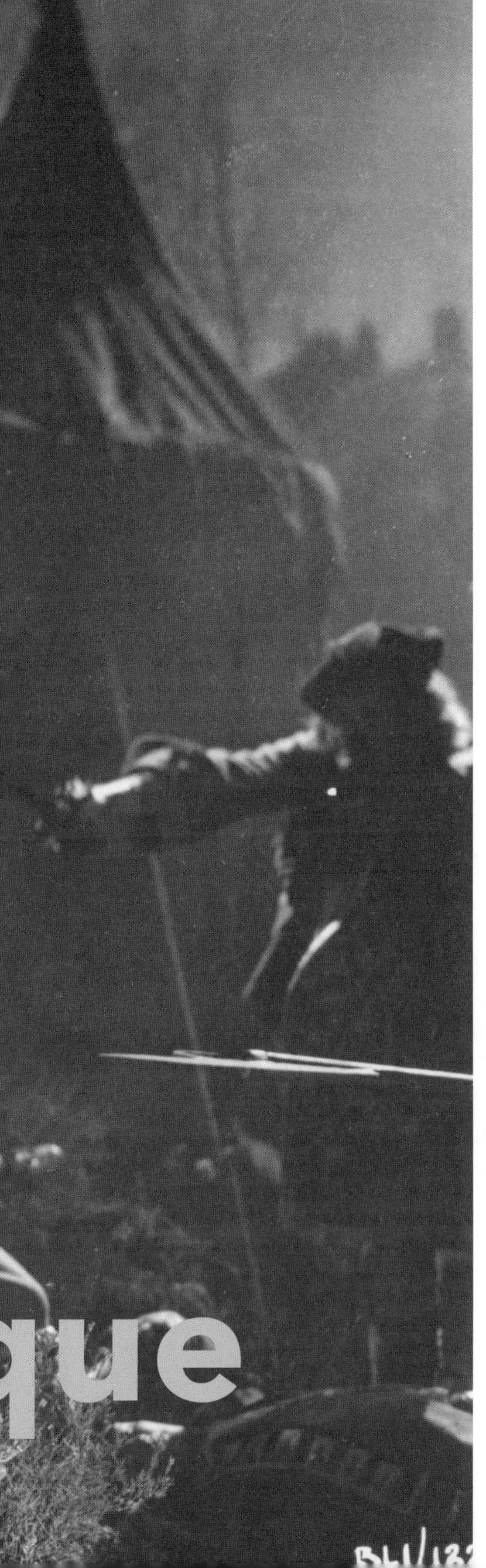

Bonnie Prince Charlie (1948), British Film Institute Collection

Scottish cinema-studies scholars have frequently focused on predominant 'myths' animating, and circulated by, cinematic representations of Scotland, Scots and Scottishness. Among some of the most historically prominent of these myths are the following: (1) the Scottish Highlands and Islands as remote, primitive, exotic, isolated and pristine locations overpoweringly suggestive of a pre-modern wilderness and sublimely resonant with the force of the supernatural; (2) rural Scots as canny and wily yet also simple and childlike, or, alternately, as simultaneously noble yet savage; (3) Scots – especially Scottish Highlanders – as an historical race replete with idealistic, romantic and courageous rebels and freedom fighters; (4) Scots as people with pronounced tendencies toward exceptionally strong interest in – and, especially, exceptionally strong attraction to – the mysterious, the macabre, the morbid, the gothic fantastical, the bizarrely horrific and the surreally miserablist; (5) Scots as tending likewise toward intense fascination with – and, indeed, as strongly convinced of the ineradicable – duality and division of identity, with doubles and doppelgängers, as well as with continuous internal tensions along with continuous external struggles between light and dark, good and evil, and the elect and the damned; (6) middle class Scots as inclined toward a dour, distrustful and overtly prickly outward demeanour combined with a strong proclivity toward frugality and asceticism; (7) Scots as highly argumentative, restless, dissatisfied and even hyper-critical while at the same time stridently anti-sentimental yet quickly inclined toward and readily indulgent in sentimentality; (8) urban working-class Scottish males as tough, hard men, with a penchant for drinking, fighting, criminal gangs and other forms of violent masculine excess which they will revel in when and if not otherwise adequately employed in productive physical wage-labour, or the equivalent (such as sport); and (9) Scottish urban working-class communities – especially in 'post-industrial' times – as poor and often struggling desperately to hold themselves together yet, at the same time, functioning either as sites of persistently resilient social solidarity or as sites of edgy, perversely attractive collective pursuits of alternative lifestyles.

Scotch Reels: Scotland in Cinema and Television, edited by Colin McArthur, and published in 1982 (following an earlier three-day 'event' of the same name at the 1982 Edinburgh International Film Festival), to this day epitomizes the position that staunchly critiques cinematic representations of these same Scottish myths – and others like them – as stereotypes, i.e. as reductive and denigrative mis-representations of what Scotland, Scots and Scottishness have been and are actually like. At its most extreme, this line of criticism, David Stenhouse suggests, finds these mythic representations 'inauthentic', indeed 'debased, deformed, and pathological', traceable to a cultural-imperialist imposition by privileged American or English 'outsiders' who do not know what Scotland, Scots and Scottishness 'really are like' (Stenhouse 2009: 179). Over the course of the last three decades, however, this (*Scotch Reels*) line of criticism has receded in popularity, with most scholars today interpreting common mythic representations of Scotland and Scottishness in more positive (or at least ambiguous) terms. As Stenhouse proposes, 'many of these cultural manifestations of interest in Scotland are playful, celebratory, and exploratory rather than reductive or definitive statements about Scottish identity' (2009: 182). Likewise, critics such as Jane Sillars (2009) argue that even long reviled traditions of sentimental popular representation, such as of the small-town, rural Scottish 'Kailyard' (or 'cabbage patch') are more contradictory and open to positive re-appropriation than previously recognized. As Duncan Petrie writes, 'cinema's engagement with Scottish history [...] constitutes a full-blown celebration of myth, fantasy and overt display, rather than any concerted effort to resurrect or engage with historical reality' and 'these mythical constructions of Scotland [...] directly engage a wide range of audience pleasures, emotions and fantasies' (2000: 72). Moreover, as Adrienne Scullion argues,

> the role of mythology, legend and fable, the Gothic, the supernatural and the unconscious within the development of the Scottish imagination is not a symptom of psychosis but a sophisticated engagement with the fantastic that other cultures might celebrate as magic realism. (Scullion 1995: 201)

In addition, as a number of contemporary scholars have further noted, the *Scotch Reels* line of criticism has tended to marginalize and dismiss not only the fantastical but also the feminine, while arguing that only a highly masculinist (Brechtian) high modernism (or, at least, a rigorously Zola-esque naturalism) offers an 'authentic' cinematic representation of Scotland and of Scottishness.

Nevertheless, *Scotch Reels* continues, over thirty years later, to stand as a signal contribution – and a watershed moment – in the history of scholarly engagement with Scottish moving image culture. *Scotch Reels* deliberately aimed to make a decisive intervention, by mounting a polemical critique versus the overwhelmingly predominant influence of ostensibly reactionary discourses of 'Tartanry' and 'Kailyard' (what McArthur later identifies as the twin pillars of 'The Scottish Discursive Unconscious') throughout the prior history of cinematic (and televisual) representation of Scotland, Scots and Scottishness. And *Scotch Reels* aimed to do the same versus supposedly 'alternative' discourses such as 'Scotland on the Move' and 'Clydesidism' which, McArthur and fellow *Scotch Reels* contributors claimed, likewise failed to do justice to the complexity and the contradictoriness of modern Scottish life. *Scotch Reels* contributor John Caughie, writing eight years later, in 'Representing Scotland: New Questions for Scottish Cinema' (1990), explains that '"Tartanry" takes [the devastating defeat of "Bonnie Prince Charlie" and his supporters at] Culloden [in 1746] as its privileged moment: a moment recast as an epic of tragic loss and triumphal defeat' and

> is tied to the Romanticism which sought wildness in the now empty landscapes of one of the last 'wildernesses' of Europe, emptied by Cumberland and the Clearances, and filled, by Scott and MacPherson, with wild, charismatic men and fey, elusive women. (Caughie 1990: 15)

Continuing, Caughie explains that 'The privileged moment of the "kailyard" mythology is probably the Great Disruption of the Church of Scotland in 1843' (when over one-third of the ministers and elders left to form the Free Church of Scotland in a struggle over parishioner versus patron control of the appointment of ministers, and of local congregation versus central government and aristocratic control of the Kirk) (1990: 15). As Caughie elaborates, 'the imagery and imaginary of the kailyard is domesticated and social, concerned with a real disturbance, but moderated by the couthy and benign view from the manse window' (16). Kailyard involves a fragmentation of Scottish culture into the shards of what transpires within the highly limited confines of small, insular, self-protective local communities. Kailyard, as Caughie suggests, is famously associated with both the music hall comic performances of the internationally renowned Harry Lauder as well as the novels, short stories and popular lectures of JM Barrie. Next, as Caughie states, '"Clydesidism" is the mythology of the Scottish twentieth century, the discourse which seems currently most potent, and not yet universally acknowledged as mythology' (16). This myth focuses on 'the gritty hardness of urban life', offers 'a modernised myth of male industrial labour', and 'when masculinity can no longer define itself as "hard work" it increasingly identifies itself with the "hard man" whose anguish, cynicism and violence are the only ways to recover the lost dignity of labour' (16). Scotland on the Move, in turn, represents a prominent tendency that *Scotch Reels* contributors and other critics perceived within the documentary films produced by both the first and the second Films of Scotland Committees. In sum, the discourse of Scotland on the Move depicts an energetic, dynamic, productive Scotland where Scots, through their exemplary strength of character, diligence and determination, persistently triumph in industry, agriculture, engineering, science, technology and yet more areas, while likewise making steadily impressive gains in terms of institutional modernization, standards of living, opportunities for education and leisure and quality of everyday life. Scotland on the Move films tended to be relentlessly positive in tone and to depict Scots as maintaining an overriding commonality of interest across class lines, and across other lines of actual social division. Critics of the impact of the Scotland on the Move discourse within these documentary films interpreted this influence as a result of the fact that Films of Scotland Committee documentaries were, of necessity, sponsored – paid for – by the very organizations and enterprises they depicted, resulting in a tendency for the films to resemble advertisements, and even propaganda, on behalf of their sponsors. And as Colin McArthur argues, in *Scotch Reels*, these films often show strong effects of Tartanry and Kailyard in how they depict Scottish locations and enterprises, emphasizing familiar motifs of 'beauty, sadness, dignity, loss' (McArthur 1982: 59).

Scotch Reels critiqued Tartanry and Kailyard in particular, but also Scotland on the Move and Clydesidism as well, for supporting aristocratic landowner, industrial and financial capitalist, and managerial, professional and commercial middle-class interests in the reproduction and maintenance of the socio-economic and sociopolitical status quo versus the interests of the working class and the poor in the substantial reformation and especially the revolutionary transformation of the same. Taken as a whole, these dominant discourses, so the argument goes, represented Scotland – and Scots – as wild and primitive, backward-looking and nostalgic, insular and parochial, self-trivializing and self-denigrating, officious and conformist, and corporatist and consensualist. *Scotch Reels* advocated a decisive break with the entire array of images, stories and formal as well as stylistic modes long most familiarly associated with Scotland, Scots and Scottishness – not only in film and television, but also across all major media conventionally conceived to be constitutive of 'popular' culture (what *Scotch Reels* suggested actually amounted to a 'mass culture' responsible for inculcation of ideological 'false consciousness'). Ultimately, creators of Scottish film and television needed, *Scotch Reels* asserted, to embrace discourses of Marxism and modernism, or, at the least, Marxism and progressive forms of naturalism, such as those naturalisms recently adopted by radical Third World – including revolutionary 'Third Cinema' – film-makers.

Early critics of *Scotch Reels* argued that McArthur and his co-writers focused too narrowly on what they found problematic about pre-existing work in Scottish cinema without offering concrete ideas concerning how to realize progressive alternatives. According to Forsyth Hardy, for instance, not only was *Scotch Reels*'s polemic misdirected, as it should have targeted outsiders, especially based in Hollywood or London, as primarily responsible for generating the most egregiously inauthentic cinematic images of Scotland, but also *Scotch Reels* was far more frustrating than it was helpful to Scottish film-makers, because *Scotch Reels* failed to address the key challenge facing the latter, and that was the long-standing lack of financial support in Scotland sufficient to enable Scottish film-makers to make the kinds of films they aspired to make. Subsequently, McArthur advocated a 'poor Scottish cinema', with all films to be made on budgets of 300,000 pounds or less; this would be a cinema 'poor in resources' yet 'rich in imagination' (McArthur 2009: 41). And it would be an artistically avant-garde as well as a politically critical-oppositional Scottish cinema. Focusing on this kind of cinema, McArthur argued, would be economically sustainable, and it would facilitate a collectivist approach toward making films, involving a pooling of resources as well as extensive collaboration among Scottish film-makers and Scottish film institutions. It would reject the model of 'Hollywood on the Clyde' (attempting to make a limited number of Hollywood-style films with dicey support from scarce Scottish resources), and instead offer a fresh, distinct alternative to Hollywood-style film-making. Most respondents to McArthur have contended, however, that Scotland should support the production of a range of different kinds of films, at a mix of budget levels, and that a critical-oppositional Scottish cinema needs something to critically oppose.

Another frequent criticism of *Scotch Reels* charges McArthur and his fellow contributors with ignoring work that did not fit the terms of their analysis, especially those representative of a rich 'anti-Kailyard' vein of Scottish literary and cultural production, most notably the pre-eminently anti-Kailyard films of Bill Douglas. Likewise, critics of *Scotch Reels* have argued that Scottish film-makers can and do make artistically and politically 'progressive' films without necessarily privileging, or foregrounding, the particular blend of Marxism and modernism that *Scotch Reels* championed. Yet the most sustained response to

Scotch Reels has taken the form of a vigorous defense of Scottish popular culture, including of the two dimensions of this culture most denigrated by *Scotch Reels*, Tartanry and Kailyard.

From Tartan to Tartanry: Scottish Culture, History and Myth, edited by Ian Brown, and published in 2010, is exemplary of the line of argument I have just introduced. According to Brown, 'both tartan and tartanry [...] are polysemic and multivalent, embodying meanings that cannot be contained in any single discourse' (2010b: 2). What's more, tartan's long and complex etymological history consistently foregrounds qualities of 'hybridity or crossing, even contrariness' (3), while tartan has maintained a long-standing 'potentially anarchic, influence' – a potential for the 'comedic and subversive' – which famous comic performers have actualized in donning tartan as playful 'masquerade' (4). Donning tartan costumes is not necessarily complicit with demeaning (self-)caricature, because this process can 'equally – or perhaps even more – be seen as celebratory, joyously conspiratorial with the audience and full of ebullient life' (4). Tartan maintains the potential 'to represent an alterity that supports the unbuttoned, emotionally spirited and carnivalesque' (6). Contrary to McArthur and *Scotch Reels*, and contrary to Tom Nairn (2003 [1977]) in 'Old and New Scottish Nationalism' (a major influence upon *Scotch Reels*), as well as versus Hugh Trevor-Roper (1983) in 'The Invention of Tradition: The Highland Tradition of Scotland' (offering substantial support for *Scotch Reels*'s critique), Brown and other contributors to *From Tartan to Tartanry* argue that tartan imagery and iconography are not artificial inventions of the late eighteenth century, imposed upon the Scottish nation and its people by the likes of Sir Walter Scott and James MacPherson, but rather maintain deep roots in Scottish cultural life, including across Lowland as well as Highland Scotland, dating as far back as the eleventh century. What's more, the nineteenth-century rehabilitation of and enthusiasm for tartan, these writers contend, represented not a 'duping' of Scots, or a 'regression' via identification with a mystical illusion, but rather a means by which Scots manifested their continuing pride in the distinctiveness of Scottish history, culture and society, while simultaneously loyally supporting the Union.

According to Brown, it is the critics of tartan and Tartanry who have been responsible for turning it into a reactionary dead weight: 'tartan and tartanry contain [...] countervailing traditions within their own discourses and those are much richer and more immanent than regressive critics like Nairn and McArthur seem to allow' (Brown 2010c: 111). As Ian Maitland Hume adds,

> there is a growing awareness that tartan is endowed with a large range of complex meanings, depending on its use and the circumstances in which it is found. Likewise, tartanry itself, rather than just representing a romantic, kitsch interpretation of the past, now embraces whole spectrums of different meanings beyond relatively simple publicity often associated with the tourist industry. (Hume 2010: 82)

According to Hume, tartan has become a significant dimension of contemporary Scottish identity and material culture. As Hume elaborates, most Scottish men who wear kilts today do so to *celebrate* Scottish identity or heritage, and as kilt-wearing has become much more widespread and commonplace, across socio-economic and local/regional lines, far less attention is paid to who can or should wear kilts with particular patterns, let alone when and where so, allowing ample room for the signification of new meanings through kilt-wearing, and by means of likewise adapting other familiar tartan tropes and artefacts. David Goldie supports this position by proposing that Scots who deliberately associate themselves with tartan and Tartanry today 'are not mere victims of Scottish representational tradition but its masters', and, what's more, 'in actively consuming and replicating tartanry in this way popular culture did not yield but effectively took ownership of it' (2010: 244). Margaret Munro (2010) likewise argues that too many critics have missed the irony in Scots comics' use of tartan and in their playful engagement with Tartanry, as these comics have often used, for instance, the kilt to establish a ready connection with Scotland and Scottishness, while at the same time playfully subverting these iconic associations. Munro claims tartan can be readily used to suggest excess and transgression versus conventional societal norms – including those of sexuality and gender. Murray Pittock endorses this position, observing that 'kilts can now be as much for looking up, having fall off, suggest cross-dressing or celebrating gender ambiguity as they are symbols of Scottish manhood in the older sense' (2010:192). In *The Road to Independence? Scotland Since the Sixties* (2008), Pittock finds 'the supreme irony' affecting the 'demythologizing moment' in Scottish cultural studies was

> that just as academics and cultural commentators lamented the meretriciousness of tartan and shortbread images of their country, the kilt and all its associated furniture of stereotype were being increasingly adopted by young people as a mark of vibrant, modern Scotland. (Pittock 2008: 123)

Indeed, as Pittock suggests, wearing a kilt has become so commonplace on all kinds of formal occasions that it is now widely accepted as 'simply the visible performance of being a Scot' (123). As Pittock and a number of other contributors to *From Tartan to Tartanry* recount, tendencies toward ironic, playful, subversive and dynamically re-inventive ways of making use of tartan and Tartanry are especially notable in rock, pop and especially punk scenes and subcultures, as well as in the so-called 'Tartan Army' of Scottish national football team supporters. In sum, as Goldie puts it, citing Bollywood to make his case, 'all cultures have their Kitsch, but most are more relaxed in their attitudes towards it' (2010: 241). Pittock, in *The Road to Independence?* endorses the same position: 'We all have our myths, and it turned out that "Scotch myths" are no worse than anyone else's' (2008: 123). According to this position, then, Tartanry does not simply interpellate subjects into passive conformity with fixed discursive positions, but rather is a site that allows for potential agency, including to modify the nature of the position, and to redefine the terms of the discourse. Tartanry, these critics propose, is not simply passively consumed, but also actively engaged, as it is meshes with other discourses, and as it is modified, resignified and redeployed in the course of so doing.

Arguing along parallel lines with the contributors to *From Tartan to Tartanry*, Jane Sillars (2009) urges re-evaluation of Kailyard. Drawing upon an argument she credits to Cairns Craig, Sillars suggests that 'terror of the parochial' reflects 'hatred of the intellectuals for the culture they inhabited' and their 'profound embarrassment' over popular cultural representations of Scottishness (2009: 127). Sillars suggests that intellectual critics of Kailyard fear that 'its smallness and softness might collapse a national identity shored up around ideas of masculinity and hardness' (127). Sillars notes persistent strains of misogyny in anti-Kailyard discourses, and that in these kinds of works symbolic representatives of the national mother are often shown 'to be broken or marginal, or the agent of a repressive culture' (128). In response, Sillars declares that 'Kailyard's stress on the feminine and domestic should not necessitate its treatment with contempt' (129) while also observing how most critical accounts of Kailyard literature ignore the prolific involvement of women as writers of classic Kailyard fiction, as well as the considerable popularity of this same fiction among women readers. Sillars proposes moving beyond condemning the Kailyard toward reassessing and reunderstanding it – toward examining precisely and concretely how and why it did appeal, and in particular how and why it did speak 'to an experience of change, migration and trauma' at the time it emerged and became popular (129). What's more, again in line with Goldie and Pittock, Sillars points out that many cultures have their own Kailyard fictions, and this means Kailyard is not simply a Scottish phenomenon.

In a contribution to the same volume (Murray, Farley and Stoneman 2009), Cairns Craig charges critics of Scottish popular culture, and especially of its supposedly pronounced orientation towards nostalgia, with 'nostophobia'. According to Craig, Scottish 'nostophobes' have long derided Scottish popular cultural nostalgia for a romantic pre-modern past richly resonant with the infusion of the sacred within the profane that in turn offers virtually magical avenues for personal fulfilment and/or redemption, and which, at the same time, valorizes ideals of organic community and communal belonging. Craig contends nostophobes fail adequately to appreciate that this nostalgia is representative of the potentially progressive appeal of 'a simpler but more humane way of life' (2009: 57). Nostophobes instead aim to dispel the illusion and replace fanciful indulgence in 'romance' with a clear-eyed and hard-edged commitment to 'realism.' As Craig elaborates,

> The nostophobe always presents his or her realization of the bleak reality of that culture as a radical breakthrough, as the recovery of sanity in a world of pathological illusion. Nostophobes never acknowledge, however, that their own responses are the expression of a pattern just as powerful – and just as baleful – as the one they want to overthrow. If, as is claimed, nineteenth-century Scotland was the country of nostalgia, then twentieth-century Scotland has been the century of nostophobia. Far from being the minority opposition in modern Scottish culture, nostophobia has been, in fact, the ideology of the cultural establishment. (Murray, Farley and Stoneman 2009: 64–65)

What's more, Craig elaborates, the roots of more recent nostophobia, such as that found in *Scotch Reels*, are traceable at least as far back as 'the Scottish Renaissance' movement in (literature and the arts in) the early twentieth century. From Craig's vantage point, anti-Kailyard representations of Scotland as, in essence, a place of exploitation, suffering and repression, are just as selectively (un)realistic, and just as dependent on mythic forms of thinking, as what they imagine they have displaced and superseded. Craig's re-evaluation of nostalgia here echoes that of Pam Cook, who likewise argues that 'rather than a refusal of nostalgia, it seems more pertinent to investigate the powerful emotional appeal of reliving the past and the part it plays in popular imaginings of community and resistance at specific, historical moments' (Cook 1996: 26).

Craig's critiques of the 'demythologizing tendency' in 1960s through 1980s Scottish cultural (including cinema) studies are especially interesting, not only because of Craig's considerable intellectual stature and influence within Scottish Studies but also because he was a contributor to *Scotch Reels*. In his contribution to *Scotch Reels*, 'Myths Against History: Tartanry and Kailyard in 19th-Century Scottish Literature' (1982), Craig argued, quite forcefully, that Tartanry and Kailyard were guilty of 'hollowness', defeatism, 'caricature, simplification and condescension', reflecting a national culture whose identity 'had been swamped by its incorporation into the United Kingdom' and which was 'lost and irrecoverable', now functioning, in residual form, to 'contain' 'any social or political conflict' and to rob contemporary Scots of 'the power to *imagine* the future and so take control of it' (Craig 1982: 7–15). In other words, the influence of Tartanry and Kailyard has proven so thoroughly destructive that 'there are no tools which the artist can inherit from the past which are not tainted, warped or blunted by the uses to which they have been put' (1982: 14–15). But Craig has changed his position since *Scotch Reels* and his critiques of his former position have proven influential with many subsequent scholars writing about issues in Scottish cinema studies. As Craig suggests in his 1996 book *Out of History: Narrative Paradigms in Scottish and English Culture*, Tartanry and Kailyard cannot be dismissed through sheer act of will, on account of aesthetic distaste or political disidentification, because these discourses and all they entail remain 'part of *our* past, and a real part of our past because the community of which we are a part has lived through those images and symbols, lived with them' and, in doing so, invested them with meanings and significances that have not remained fixed and frozen (1996: 111). In his book *Intending Scotland: Explorations in Scottish Culture Since the Enlightenment* (2009) Craig critiques a common notion that Scottish culture, and Scottish intellectual life, experienced a sharp decline after the Scottish Enlightenment, proceeding through a lengthy period devoid of substantial productivity and collective vitality. *Intending Scotland* argues, to the contrary, that many Scottish intellectuals, working within and across a wide array of fields of study, made powerful, substantial and distinct contributions that maintained strong connections with the work of Scottish Enlightenment thinkers, while extending considerably beyond the limits of what these predecessors had achieved, all the while being very much indebted to and inspired by their Scottish cultural backgrounds and experiences as well as the Scottish intellectual milieus in and from which they carried out their work. In revisiting post-Enlightenment Scottish intellectual and cultural life, Craig thus finds ample reason to revise his earlier stance versus the supposedly entirely reactionary and thoroughly stunting effects of Tartanry and Kailyard. In *Screening Scotland* (2000) Duncan Petrie credits Craig with a compelling defense of Sir Walter Scott's 'romanticization' of Scottish history; through this means Scott is able, in Petrie's words, to found a 'counter-historical tradition' focused on 'the absences and blind spots of historical consciousness', with representation of Scotland as a wilderness allowing for 'the imagination of alternative worlds, emotions and possibilities' (2000: 54). Likewise, in *Scotland: Global Cinema – Genres, Modes and Identities* (2009) David Martin-Jones credits Craig with demonstrating 'that myths like Tartanry could be seen in a more positive light if considered as ways of remythologizing a Scottish past which had been deliberately excluded from official, English versions of British history' (2009: 6). Later on in this same book Martin-Jones builds upon Craig's proposition that it is possible to recognize 'the positive power of myths like Tartanry' by reading these myths as remythologizing 'the past that had been excluded from an official, predominantly English history of Britain', and by countering a prospective erasure of Scottish identity with a remythologization 'of the roots of an independent Scottish identity' (114). As Martin-Jones elaborates, 'rather than a nostalgic escape from official history, then, Tartanry can be seen as an attempt to counter the linear history of Britain' (115). Working with this idea, Martin-Jones interprets recent horror films set in the Highlands and Islands of Scotland, such as *Dog Soldiers* (Neil Marshall, 2002), which work with idea of the Scotsman as '*essentially* embodying an ancient, Celtic masculine myth' (120), to be suggesting that this pre-modern Celtic masculinity can provide the source of an answer to a contemporary crisis of masculinity. These kinds of films, Martin-Jones proposes, question the complacency of English film-makers in imagining an altogether 'tamed' Highlands, now little more than a largely depopulated region, the chief function of which is to serve as a scenic tourist destination. *Dog Soldiers* thus dramatically enacts a return of the repressed – the repressed history of Scotland, including that of the (Lowland and Highland) Clearances. By conjuring the power of ancient myths, films like *Dog Soldiers* raise questions concerning the viability of alternatives to official histories, and of what has been buried as well as why so in privileging the latter accounts over the former possibilities. Werewolves here 'represent the lost history of Scotland' (Martin-Jones 2009: 125): 'through the figure of the werewolf, then, the wild, hairy, "homo celticus" stereotype so often applied to representations of Scotland is cleverly deconstructed' (126), and this, once again, reflects 'the subversive power of this excluded history to reemerge and "queer" the progression of legitimate history' (127).

Martin-Jones continues this line of argument in support of reconsidering the value of the genre of heritage costume drama, noting the pleasures this kind of film can provide, via the spectacle so foregrounded, especially to women and/or gay audiences. Martin-Jones notes furthermore that female characters have become the central focus of a number of more recent costume dramas in Scotland, such as in the case of *The Governess* (Sandra Goldbacher, 1998). As Martin-Jones argues, historical spectacle can enable contemporary audiences to rethink their own social identities, reconsidering the historical roots of the same, and genres such as the Gothic, while superficially maintaining seemingly little to do with any conventionally 'realistic' account of historical situations and events, can in fact contribute toward usefully interrogating and countering official histories. Films like *The Governess* deploy alternative heritages that have been marginalized by official history, and in doing so contribute to the possibility of forging new kinds and varieties of national identities derived from a complex of contesting sources and influences. Duncan Petrie has offered a similar reconsideration, in *Screening Scotland* (2000), of the appeal of the kind of historical fiction most often condemned as epitomizing the worst proclivities of Tartanry: 'Despite the greater emphasis on men rather than women, the Jacobite romance can also be coded as feminine, with the flamboyant kilted male heroes constructed in terms of overt spectacle and display' (Petrie 2000: 67). Petrie here draws upon the work of Pam Cook (1996) in proposing that 'inauthenticity' is intrinsic to 'costume melodrama and the emphasis it places on masquerade, facilitating a productive exploration of identity precisely through the crossing of boundaries that dressing-up entails', and he likewise draws upon Cook in suggesting that 'the pleasures and meanings attached to the act of dressing-up are far too rich and complex to be reduced to some reactionary acquiescence in the perpetuation of a pernicious myth' (Petrie 2000: 67). Petrie further claims that the associations these kinds of pleasures provide with escapism, the popular and the domain of the feminine constitute an alternative aesthetic to that epitomized by the documentary-realist tradition in which Scottish identity is rooted in a masculine realm of industrial labour. The Jacobite romance, Petrie adds, has long retained a significant political resonance for many, preserving a kernel of radical opposition to full-fledged Unionist incorporation. Petrie refers readers here to Craig Beveridge and Ronald Turnbull: 'In the survival of Jacobitism was sustained a powerful expression of Scottish identity, a symbol of ideas and aspirations which though once defeated, cannot be forgotten or erased' (Beveridge and Turnbull 1989: 34). And Alan Riach has likewise supported a reconsideration of the political meaning and value of pleasures that common mythic representations of Scotland and Scottishness, frequently criticized as reactionary stereotypes and clichés, in fact often can and do provide. For example, Riach cites the nostalgic appeal of Tartanry and Kailyard as compellingly critical of trends, in contemporary urban social life, that involve 'destroying the value of kinship, hospitality and familial support' while replacing this with 'rapacious mendacity' (Riach 2010: 121).

TM Devine, in his epic history of modern Scotland, *The Scottish Nation: A Modern History* (2012) adds useful perspective on these matters. According to Devine, late-eighteenth and early-nineteenth-century adoption of Highland emblems, costumes and associations as representative of the nation was 'curious but not entirely incomprehensible' (2012: 244). Scotland now depended on close ties with England to sustain its rapidly rising economic prosperity but Scots were also anxious about being assimilated into a mere province of a Greater England. At the same time, nineteenth-century European Romanticism as well as simultaneous emerging new nationalisms, across the continent, significantly impacted Scotland as well. Highlandism offered a safe avenue in which to maintain a distinctive Scottish national identity without compromising support for the Union, especially as the Highland regiments within the British Army demonstrated that Scottish patriotism and unflinching service to the Union could readily work hand in hand. Highlandism, in other words, provided 'an alluring myth for a society searching for an identity amid unprecedented economic and social change and under the threat of cultural conquest by a much more powerful neighbour' (Devine 2012: 245). Devine proceeds further to contest influential accounts, offered by the likes of Tom Nairn and George Davies, that the age of Liberal dominance in Scotland between 1832 and 1914 was one of profound crisis for Scottish nationhood, where the middle classes in effective charge of Scottish home affairs were, supposedly, so complaisantly anglicizing and assimilating that Scots were becoming invisible as a distinctive people, and where a loss of confidence in, as well as orientation towards, their own Scottishness led to a cultural collapse, leaving, in its void, a degenerative clinging to Kailyard and Tartanry. According to recent historical scholarship, Devine writes,

> Scottish national identity did not vanish but rather adapted itself to new circumstances [...] this was also a period of the reinvention of Scotland, when new or refurbished icons continued to provide the nation with crucial symbols of identity and distinctiveness within the union. (Devine 2012: 285)

Continuing, Devine declares

> it does not follow that, because the basis for a strong *political nationalism* did not exist in the Victorian era, Scottish national identity was therefore in itself inevitably emasculated. On the contrary, the economic success which helped to remove the basis of nationalist discontent was itself a tremendous source of national pride and self-congratulation' (Devine 2012: 289)

Scots saw themselves, and with good reason, as equal partners in the Union, in the successes of Britain and the British Empire – commonly presuming, for that matter, that the Empire would not have been possible except for this very union of the *two nations* of England and Scotland, with these successes dependent upon the combined contributions and achievements of both. Also, despite divisions within the Kirk at home, Scottish Presbyterianism was rapidly disseminating its influence across the world via Scottish missionaries, and 'Empire building was depicted as something peculiarly Scottish and as the fulfillment of a national destiny' (Devine 2012: 290). What's more, the 'Great Disruption' within Scottish Presbyterianism can be interpreted as a religious form of quasi-nationalism, involving a rejection of the right of authorities closely tied to the government in London to decide how Scottish religious affairs would be conducted at the local level. And 'it was the Presbyterian inheritance that shaped the values of thrift, independence, sobriety, the work ethic and education, which were the very foundations of the middle- and "respectable" working-class culture' for which Scots were well-known then, and have been since (Devine 2012: 291). At the same time, Devine suggests, it is important not to underestimate the considerable appeal of a literature that hearkened backward to a distinctive national past, prior to modern industrialization. The cult of national heroes represents a significant dimension of nineteenth-century Scottish national culture as well: Robert Burns was the archetypal 'lad o' pairts', and also appreciated for his links to the seventeenth-century Covenanters, widely regarded as martyrs, as well as for his preservation of the ancient vernacular language, while the cult of William Wallace suggested to Scots that they had never been conquered, and that Scotland had freely entered into the Union to work together as an equal partner with England. In addition, as Cairns Craig (2009) has also documented, throughout the years ranging from 1832 to 1914 Scots made considerable contributions in the fields of engineering, natural science, medicine, technology, philosophy and anthropology, while 'in literature and the arts, the descent of Scottish culture into the abyss of the sentimental parochialism of the Kailyard has been grossly exaggerated by modern critics' (Devine 2012: 296). Kailyard writers, Devine acknowledges, have been 'mercilessly attacked' for their 'bad art, cultural degeneracy and sloppy sentimentality', as well as for committing 'the unforgivable sin of becoming hugely successful' (Devine 2012: 297), yet a great deal of Scottish literature from this period was not representative of, or even at all akin to that produced by, the so-called 'Kailyard school', and, in fact, the historical record reveals a 'rich diversity in Scottish art' at the time (Devine 2012: 298).

Scotch Reels and similar critics have often suggested that Scots long suffered from 'inferiorisation', worrying that their Scottishness put them at a disadvantage versus a contrasting Englishness that functioned, by default, as what was culturally normative within the United Kingdom. However, critics of the *Scotch Reels* line of argument suggest this take on Scottish popular culture itself displays clear signs of 'inferiorisation'. In 'Nairn's Nationalism' (1994), Ronald Turnbull cites Tom Nairn as arguing that modern Scottish cultural history is virtually entirely reducible to sentimental Kailyard and romanticized Highland nostalgia (i.e. Tartanry), and, in Turnbull's words, that this state of affairs in effect 'made cringing subservience the dominant national psychological trait' (Turnbull 1994: 37). However, in noting the ferocity of the terms used by Nairn to characterize Scottish (popular) culture, especially terms derived from psychopathology, Turnbull argues that Nairn himself exemplifies 'inferiorism', as his critique represents an extreme, or *reductio ad absurdum*, version 'of generally accepted beliefs and assumptions about the Scottish past' (Turnbull 1994: 38) – generally accepted, that is, among many Scottish intellectuals, past and present, who have been and continue to be embarrassed by what they perceive as the relative backwardness of their country and its people. Turnbull and Craig Beveridge had already made this same point all the more directly in their earlier book *The Eclipse of Scottish Culture: Inferiorism and the Intellectuals* (1989):

> The view that popular consciousness is dominated by tartanry, that the populace is sunk in ignorance and irrationality, accords perfectly with the governing image of Scotland as a dark and backward culture. This reflection allows us to locate the real significance of the discussion on tartanry, namely as another instance of the Scottish intelligentsia's readiness to embrace damning conceptions of national culture – in other words as an expression of inferiorism. (Beveridge and Turnbull 1989: 14)

Alternately, in contrast with the charge of 'inferiorisation', David Goldie (2010) accuses *Scotch Reels* of an elitist arrogance in 'confidently separating out the Scottish workerist sheep from the tartan goats' while too often indulging in a 'supercilious tone', as well as a tendency to rely on 'crude value judgment' and even 'straightforward snobbery'

(239). Goldie finds 'the argument, that two popular cultural modes can effectively corner a national market and make alternative forms of expression impossible, is in itself extremely limiting and, to this reader at least, quite unpersuasive. Not only does it fail to account for the fact that a book like *Scotch Reels* has appeared out of that culture, but it is an argument that also immediately places itself outside or above that culture' (Goldie 2010: 239). *Scotch Reels* failed, Goldie contends, to grasp the powerful and continuing appeal of the popular cultural discourses these critics found so thoroughly reactionary. Similar to Goldie, Scott L Malcolmson (1985) finds Tartanry and Kailyard too simple and too convenient a set of terms – i.e. reductive and contrived – and is suspicious of the implicit idea that intellectuals must form the vanguard, in place of the working class, in leading the way forward toward progressive social transformation; again, as with Goldie, Malcolmson contends *Scotch Reels* fails to do justice to the wide appeal of Tartanry and Kailyard among their supposed 'victims', while also ignoring selective, ironic and critically appreciative responses to the appeal of these discourses.

Although certainly at the least skeptical of, and at the most unconvinced by, many of these critical responses to the overall argument *Scotch Reels* had advanced, Colin McArthur does subsequently admit *Scotch Reels*'s claim that popular iconography of Scottishness had been 'irreversibly tarnished', 'may indeed have been too rigid and this same iconography is more malleable than was supposed' (*Brigadoon, Braveheart, and the Scots* 2003: 135). As McArthur explains, further,

> The anti-Tartanry/Kailyard position became, in the 1980s and the 1990s and at least as far as the Scottish intelligentsia is concerned, *hegemonic*. Every hegemony is, by definition, fragile and contested and the anti-Tartanry/Kailyard position is no exception, having been attacked in its turn [...] principally for seeking to replace one essentialist national identity with another at a moment when (national) identity needed to be theorised as open, complex and hybrid, an identity constantly being remade rather than fixed. (McArthur 2003: 113)

McArthur is unlikely to agree with Ian Brown that 'if the Scottish national identity can be said to have a core at all, it is hybridity and migration' (Brown 2010c: 99), but he does here acknowledge the credibility of a critique of *Scotch Reels* advanced by David McCrone, in that latter's book *Understanding Scotland: The Sociology of a Stateless Nation* (1992), where McCrone contends that it is critics, like those contributing to *Scotch Reels*, who have effectively reduced Scottish national identity to Tartanry, Kailyard and Clydesidism, and it is these critics themselves who exclude Scots who cannot readily find representation in any of these discourses. McCrone argues that Scottish national identity has always been multiple and complex, and, in fact, over the course of the twentieth century it has become steadily more so. National identities, including Scottish national identities, are not, McCrone adds, created in isolation or separation from, but rather through interaction and exchange with, what develops and what is happening within other nations. 'Scotch myths' do not prevent Scots from accessing their 'true national identity', because no such singular identity ever actually exists: 'the question to ask is not how best do cultural forms reflect an essential national identity, but how do cultural forms actually help to construct and shape identity, or rather, identities' (McCrone 1992: 195).

A major theoretical issue at stake in the division between *Scotch Reels* and its critics is how to conceive of 'myth'. For *Scotch Reels* 'myth' connotes falsity. More precisely, this is 'falsity' in the sense of a distortion and mystification of social reality, both historical and contemporary, involving a conversion of what is isolated within and withdrawn from reality and then reworked and transformed in the process of this withdrawal such that it becomes the stuff and substance of 'ideology'. Ideology here entails 'false consciousness', and, more precisely, elision and erasure of the determinate impact of concrete material forces and relations of production grounding the formation and the constitution of particular structures and patterns of social organization, consciousness, interaction and engagement (with the latter array including the dominant discourses rendering sociality intelligible along with the dominant institutions rendering sociality practical). Most significantly, ideology as false consciousness elides and erases the real class divisions, and real class interests, at stake in the construction and re-construction of society along particular lines (according to particular configurations). 'Scotch myths' ultimately serve the interests of dominant social classes in maintaining their dominance over dominated classes, especially by encouraging the latter to long for a return to an idyllic past or for an escape to an equally 'unreal' haven from the pressures of modern life – or to mis-recognize their social positionings such that these seem inevitable and unalterable, even naturally and eternally so, possibly entirely satisfying and fulfilling, and, even more broadly, right and good, as well as desirable and appealing. What's more, ready opportunities for at least temporary 'escape' into wondrous 'imaginary worlds' can effectively 'compensate' for what is otherwise lacking in ordinary, everyday (working, family and community) life. In turn, the exploited and oppressed thereby continue to consent and conform to the conditions of their own exploitation and oppression (especially passively, and even contentedly, so).

Yet critics of *Scotch Reels* tend to conceive of 'myth' – and of 'Scotch myths' – quite differently. For example, Alan Riach argues that

> The myths of Scottishness are not merely the masks which divert attention from underlying conditions of economic and class oppression. They are masks which actually speak of those conditions. Crucial to this way of reading is the proposition that Scotland has traditionally been seen as 'an imaginary space' where fantasies, desires and anxieties have been projected. (Riach 2005: 198)

As Riach elaborates upon this proposition, phenomena such as Tartanry, Kailyard and Clydesidism 'are both mythologies and enormously potent ways by which people make sense of their own reality' (2005: 199). In 'Tartanry and its Discontents: The Idea of Popular Scottishness' (2010) Riach proposes that it is especially important to grasp the utopian dimension of myth (recalling Fredric Jameson's similar argument concerning 'ideology and utopia' in his book *The Political Unconscious: Narrative as a Socially Symbolic Act* [1981], where Jameson likewise reads 'myth' in dialectical terms). Following Claude Lévi-Strauss, Riach declares 'myths embody necessary contradictions. Myths are always part of the human fabric and we are richer for them' (2010: 119). From this perspective, Riach suggests the tartan myth may not, as has commonly been claimed, have been overused and exhausted; on the contrary, this myth might not yet have been fully exploited for its potential advantages. Like Riach, Ian Brown recommends Lévi-Strauss's theory of myth, which he cites near the very beginning of his essay by way of Mary Douglas's summary, in her book *Implicit Meanings* (1975):

> the function of myth is to portray the contradictions in the basic premises of the culture. The same goes for the relation of the myth to social reality. The myth is a contemplation of the unsatisfactory compromises which, after all, compose social life' (Lévi-Strauss, quoted in Brown 2010c: 92)

Riach also endorses Roland Barthes's conception of myths as, in Brown's words, 'embodiments of often rich contradictions' (2010: 92). In *Screening Scotland* (2000) Duncan Petrie likewise writes in favour of a Nietzschean conception of myth, which he credits to Cairns Craig; according to this approach, limited and problematic myths are not best opposed by un-masking, de-mystification and de-mythologization, but rather by challenging old myths with new myths, or by intervening within existing myths to reconceive and rearticulate their meanings. In other words, respond to the problems and limitations of Tartanry, Kailyard and Clydesidism not by showing how these are myths, and thereby 'false', but rather by generating new myths to compete with, and potentially displace, those myths – or, by intervening to reconceive and rearticulate what Tartanry, Kailyard and Clydesidism can and will mean. In this direction, Petrie, and Craig, recall an argument advanced on a number of occasions by Laurence Coupe (for example, in his book *Myth*, published in 1997 as part of Routledge's New Idiom series) in support of 'radical typology' versus 'allegory' as the more productive – and more progressive – mode of 'mythic reading'.

What I propose needs to be recognized here is that *people live by myths; myths are the stories we tell that give meaning, value and significance to our lives*; and myths can be understood, and made use of, in multiple, and indeed multiply opposing, ways. *Myths cannot be easily reduced to a question of whether they are simply 'true or false'; people identify with myths as a matter of belief and of faith.* A better set of questions to ask, in critically examining a myth, is as follows: for whom, when and where, do people identify with this myth *as if it is true*; what in particular about it do they so identify with and why so; and what are the consequences that follow for how these people live out their lives, as they are influenced and impacted in doing so by their identification with this myth? *Cultural myths operate like religions*: people readily identify with and follow cultural myths without requiring anything approaching absolute logical proof or incontrovertible scientific evidence of their 'truth'; the 'truth' people find in cultural myths, just as is the case with religions, is of a fundamentally different order. With myths of Scotland and of Scottishness we therefore need to focus on *what it means to identify with these myths, to believe in them, to find them compelling and useful.* We need to focus on how they influence and impact people who identify with them, who respond positively to them, in any way and to any degree. And we need to focus on *the multiple and contesting ways that people make sense and make use of these myths*, as well as on *how these myths vary from one place where they show up to another and how they change from one period of time to another.* As just one illustration, many Scots (and many people of Scottish ethnic descent outside of Scotland maintaining romantic associations with an 'ancestral Scottish homeland') have found ingenious ways to positively, albeit often playfully, embrace the popular cultural myth that critics have denigrated as Tartanry (i.e. identification with a mythical Highland inheritance, made visible in kilts and other kinds of 'Highland wear', bagpipes, 'Highland games', and the like). What's crucial, in sum, in assessing mythic representations of Scotland and Scottishness, is what ideas they embody and circulate, and how these representations are interpreted and put to use, for what ends and in whose interests. All of this can be multiple and contradictory as well as subject to variation and change. Individual films may well embody and circulate multiple and contradictory ideas about Scotland and Scottishness; these films may invite multiple and contradictory interpretations of what they are expressing and communicating in relation to Scotland and Scottishness; and the ways audiences make sense of, as well as respond to, the representations of Scotland and Scottishness these films maintain will vary depending on who makes up the audience as well as change over time. It is this kind of argument that Alan Riach advances in *Representing Scotland in Literature, Popular Culture and Iconography* (2005) and that he and his fellow contributors to do in *From Tartan to Tartanry* (Brown 2010a): familiar images and icons of Scotland and Scottishness need not be dismissed or denied, nor so the pleasures they entail, but rather made subject to concrete inquiry and careful scrutiny, sensitive to the variability as well as the durability, and to the complexity and contradictoriness as well as the perniciousness and offensiveness, that their mythic articulations, including in Scottish films/films of Scotland, can and do entail.

In *Contemporary Scottish Fictions: Film, Television and the Novel* (2004), Duncan Petrie illustrates, notably in his discussion of Clydesidism, that such an approach does not mean tempering criticism of reactionary elements in how dominant myths of Scotland and Scottishness are employed. As Petrie recounts, Clydesidism emerged as a recognizable alternative to the discourses of Tartanry and Kailyard, emphasizing areas of Scotland and kinds of Scots absent from the latter – Clydesidism's focus is urban, industrial, working class and male. Ironically, however, this discourse and fictional representatives of it only garnered significant attention, as Clydesidism, at a time in which the way of life the discourse valorized was declining and passing away. As a result, Clydesidism was all the more readily 'rendered "mythic" in association with the loss of a particular kind of "authentic" Scottish community and way of life, and consequently became no less elegiac or nostalgic than tartanry or Kailyard' (Petrie 2004: 18). What's more, in exclusively privileging an 'overtly masculine and heterosexual concept of native virtue', Clydesidism exercises a 'regressive and pernicious' impact (2004: 19). In short, Clydesidism emphasizes hard, tough, aggressive and violent men, often to the virtual exclusion (and even, at times, to the outright denigration and scapegoating) of women. The 'hard man' in Clydesidist discourse can, as such, be interpreted as another expression of 'inferiorism' – of erstwhile urban industrial working-class masculine heterosexual males' anxiety over the loss of a previously securely satisfying social position. At the same time, Petrie entertains the notion that Clydesidism represents a direct reaction versus Kailyardism, with the latter epitomizing a seemingly ultra-feminized social world, versus the former epitomizing a seemingly ultra-masculinized one. As a result, 'the tropes of Clydesidism', Petrie writes, are 'rooted in male comradeship, the football match, the pub and an exaggerated use of Scots vernacular, emphasising a no-nonsense and vigorous masculine attitude to which women have no legitimate recourse' (2004: 65). Again, Petrie suggests, 'inferiorisation' might account for this, with Scots here over-investing in a masculine version of Scottish national identity as compensation for their experience of subordination within the Union, and in opposition to a popular 'feminized' conception of 'Englishness'. My point, however, is not to reiterate the details of Petrie's discussion of Clydesidism, but rather to point out that he situates his interpretation of what Clydesidism means in precise relation to concrete historical and cultural developments, discusses how Clydesidism changes in relation to larger changes in economics and politics, and addresses how Clydesidism is taken up and engaged with differently across a range of novels, films and television shows from the late 1960s through the early 1990s.

Brigadoon (Vincente Minnelli, 1954), Colin McArthur writes, in *Scotch Reels* (1982), marks 'the apotheosis' of the cinematic tradition of blending, and foregrounding, Tartanry and Kailyard in representing Scotland (47). According to Forsyth Hardy, it is 'the archetypal film of bogus Scotland' (1990: 1). Indeed many critics and commentators have long excoriated *Brigadoon* as, again in McArthur's words, 'the very nadir of mawkish Tartanry and Kailyard' and 'as shorthand for all that is twee and regressive' (McArthur 2003: 3). Yet McArthur also acknowledges the film's 'charm' and 'its far from negligible aesthetic qualities' while, nonetheless, 'still finding its representation of Scotland and the Scots problematic' (2003: 5). McArthur and many other scholars have suggested it is important to take into account the manifestly 'unreal' quality of the fantastical cinematic world *Brigadoon* conjures up, and to recognize that the film is highly self-reflexive about its own artificiality (and its own constructedness). As early as *Scotch Reels* McArthur argued that 'No British feature film has the progressive force of *Brigadoon*' (1982: 47), and this is so because *Brigadoon* provides an at least partial deconstruction of the all-too-familiar discourses concerning Scotland and Scottishness that it once again accentuates. As McArthur later summarizes, '*Brigadoon*, through the force of its *mise-en-scène*, demonstrates the artificial construction of Scotland in discourse' (2003: 115). What's more, as McArthur explains within the first half of *Brigadoon, Braveheart and the Scots* (2003), *Brigadoon* in fact engages with topical American rather than Scottish issues, not only the longing to escape the hustle and bustle of modern urban American life, as well as the alienation and emptiness that this can readily entail, but also 'conformity and the deadly consequences of failing to conform' (2003: 8), in so doing alluding to McCarthyism, the blacklists and the anti-Communist witch hunts in 1950s United States (and, especially, to the impact of these pressures within and upon Hollywood). McArthur nevertheless agrees with Richard Zumkhawala-Cook, who writes that *Brigadoon* offers an 'American fantasy of Scottish culture' which 'was not interested in speaking *to*, *with*, or *for* Scots' (Zumkhawala-Cook 2008: 22), and, unfortunately, 'Scots now economically depend on the international proliferation of a *Brigadoon* version of Scottish society' (2008: 23). Yet, as David Bruce writes, in reference to *Brigadoon* and other 'outsider' cinematic visions of Scotland like *Brigadoon*,

> It is a test of our maturity as a nation, not to mention our sense of humour, to be able to cope with the fact that our strongly identifiable culture can lay us open to such a variety of fascinating, charming, alarming, degrading, ludicrous, insulting, patronising and flattering versions of ourselves. At least it is better than being ignored. (Bruce 1996: 178)

Bonnie Prince Charlie (Anthony Kimmins, 1948) also well exemplifies a familiar, oversized, outsiders' revelling in Tartanry. The film has long been widely condemned as a colossal failure, but at the least it well attests to the romantic appeal of Bonnie Prince Charlie and 'the 45' within Jacobite discourse, including how much this discourse is consumed with nostalgia and loss. *Rob Roy: The Highland Rogue* (Harold French, 1953) offers yet another notable example of post-World War II Hollywood Tartanry, while likely the two most famous recent examples of Hollywood-style 'epic Tartanry', *Rob Roy* (Michael Caton-Jones, 1995) and *Braveheart* (Mel Gibson, 1995), maintain considerable continuity with the earlier films I just mentioned, albeit updating production values and linking up with more recent political issues. Writers such as David Bruce point out that *Rob Roy*, although financed by Hollywood, 'was essentially a home-grown product, the first ever multi-million dollar film on a Scottish subject originated and actually shot in Scotland' (1996: 15) and in *Screening Scotland* (2000) Duncan Petrie also notes the appeal of an overt emphasis on 'masculine display' in *Rob Roy: The Highland Rogue* as well as the later *Rob Roy* and *Braveheart*. As Petrie further comments, 'while *Braveheart's* representation of Scottish history at times verges on the ludicrous […] *Rob Roy* situates its action within a more complex and subtle acknowledgment of the political power structures of eighteenth-century Scotland' (2000: 211).

Braveheart in particular has attracted enormous attention, sharply dividing Scots between those finding the film moving and inspiring, praising the film as contributing significantly to national pride and increased support for national self-determination, versus critics who have condemned the film not only as egregiously historically inaccurate but also for offering powerful support to far-right politics. For example, McArthur identifies *Braveheart* as 'the modern "Ur-Fascist" text *par excellence*' and 'a godsend to the proto-fascist psyche' (2003). As Zumkhawala-Cook adds,

> in many ways, *Braveheart* functions almost as an allegory for the mainstream conservative politics of the United States and, even further, those of most Western nations. What they share is support for local private control of social and cultural matters, Christian piety, government deregulation of daily affairs, including the right of individuals to arm themselves, the vilification of homosexuals, and the glorification of battlefield diplomacy. The same can be said about *Rob Roy*'s politics and its romanticized 'honor', which is portrayed as a universally appropriate but individually experienced ethos of a social order that punishes its transgressors with swordplay and the swift and satisfying justice of bloody duels. (Zumkhawala-Cook 2008: 161)

Zumkhawala-Cook further faults *Braveheart*, *Rob Roy* and *Trainspotting* (Danny Boyle, 1996) for marginalizing women, especially the first two films where women are depicted as only 'passive victims' (2008: 149). As Zumkhawala-Cook sees it, these kinds of hyper-masculinist films that are overwhelmingly focused on struggles among bands of male warriors 'reveal the contemporary anxieties of the most privileged members of society about the loss of economic movement, male control, and the cultural traditions of national "unity" that undergird their authority' (149). Continuing, Zumkhawala-Cook argues,

> Scotland may have 'gone global' in film, but as far as *Rob Roy* and *Braveheart* are concerned, it is only in the form of a reactionary, hard-boiled national home, reinforcing the internationally pervasive notion that significant historic social changes can only occur – and have only occurred – through the individual actions of uncompromisingly masculine, middle-class, heterosexual men. (Zumkhawala-Cook 2008: 162)

Smaller-budget films focused on parallel, or similar, historical personages and events, such as *Chasing the Deer* (Graham Holloway,1994), *The Bruce* (Bob Carruthers and David McWhinnie,1996) and *Donald of the Colours* (Ron Miller,1975) are far less widely known, and have received mixed reviews among scholars. *Culloden* (Peter Watkins, 1964), however, has received considerable attention and wide acclaim. *Culloden* marks a sharp contrast with conventional cinematic Tartanry, as not only a powerful anti-war film but also as an incisive contribution towards demythologization of Bonnie Prince Charlie, the Jacobite Rebellion of 1745–46, the traditional Highland clan system and the aftermath faced by the 'ordinary' peasant people of the Highlands in the wake of the devastating defeat of the Jacobite forces at Culloden. Yet, as a number of scholars, such as Duncan Petrie, remind us, Peter Watkins's film is just as much an interested construct as *Bonnie Prince Charlie*, and Watkins overtly foregrounds as much in offering us an interpretation and an argument rather than a simple revelation of 'the truth' of historical reality.

Within scholarly discussions of Scottish cinema, Alfred Hitchcock's *The 39 Steps* (1935) is often mentioned as an example of a film that exploits Scotland as little more than a convenient background for a suspenseful espionage thriller. Scotland does appear as a remote territory with plenty of sparsely populated, primarily 'wilderness' regions, as well as a collection of colourful local 'characters', yet according to Marilyn Reizbaum, in 'They Know Where They're Going: Landscape and Place in Scottish Cinema' (2009), *The 39 Steps* comments self-reflexively on the elements of Kailyard and Tartanry it employs, by archly, and playfully, reworking these, and thereby de-naturalizing common-sense conflation of discursive mediation with unmediated actuality. Michael Powell's *The Edge of the World* (1937) and *I Know Where I'm Going!* (With Emeric Pressburger, 1945) many scholars praise for taking seriously and treating respectfully the local histories and cultures of the Scottish Islands at the heart of these films. These two films, as well as *The Brothers* (David MacDonald, 1947), scholars often identify as films that focus on issues of concern, including of conflict, among people living within remote Scottish Island communities while *not* succumbing to the temptations of Kailyard. As Duncan Petrie suggests, in *Screening Scotland* (2000), *The Edge of the World* demonstrates a sensitive appreciation for the Islanders' mystical associations with landscape and traditional ways, while also posing a serious critique of how material concerns have taken precedence over spiritual ones in modern community and social life – a central issue yet again in *I Know Where I'm Going!* Both of these films as well as *The Brothers* explore the power of desire while *The Brothers* highlights dangerous desire and emphasizes 'the underlying cruelty of the islanders' existence' (Petrie 2000: 43) in a film that combines comic absurdity with sadomasochistic horror. Both *I Know Where I'm Going!* and *The Brothers* Petrie further praises for foregrounding consideration of women's agency, and, especially, of historical and cultural obstacles that prevent or forestall its effectiveness.

In relation to Clydesidism it is worthy of note that many members of initial audiences found early Clydesidist films such as *The Shipbuilders* (John Baxter, 1944), *Floodtide* (Frederick Wilson, 1949) and *The Gorbals Story* (David MacKane,1950) refreshing due to their emphasis on modern industry and on social life in modern urban Scotland. Scholars have also frequently praised the tightly conceived, tense and suspenseful use of (in Duncan Petrie's words) 'low-key naturalism' (2000: 89) in *The Brave Don't Cry* (Philip Leacock,1952). As Forsyth Hardy writes in praise of the same film, 'Its value for Scotland was that it broke entirely with traditional conceptions. It was as far away from the heather and the haggis as could be imagined' (1990: 88). Likewise, although noting what a selective and exaggerated portrait of Glasgow working-class life these films provided, emphasizing 'hard men' and gang violence, David Bruce notes that later Clydesidist films were not only 'about working class violent crime' but also about 'poverty, sectarianism and [a] stubborn refusal to be beaten by the system' (1996: 124). Bruce finds *A Sense of Freedom* (John Mackenzie,1979), *Silent Scream* (David Hayman,1989), *The Near Room* (David Hayman,1995) and *The Big Man* (David Leland, 1990) all exemplary of this kind of thematic range. Duncan Petrie praises Peter McDougall's screenplays as standouts among films made for TV at the time – 'hard-edged', eschewing sentimentality, using 'unadulterated west coast Scottish accents', shooting on 16 mm film rather than video, and following film production techniques such as 'single-camera shooting and film editing replacing multiple-camera set-ups and vision mixing' (2000: 134–35). Petrie notes the variety of camera angles and the handheld camera in *Just Another Saturday* (John Mackenzie, 1975), which he finds suggestive of *cinéma-vérité*. He likewise commends *Elephant's Graveyard* (John Mackenzie,1976) and *Just a Boys' Game* (John Mackenzie,1979) for compellingly conveying 'a profound ambivalence towards the world of work' (Petrie 2000: 137) – showing a social milieu in which a man's labour was no longer prized or celebrated but simply alienating and unsatisfying, and where working-class males urgently needed other outlets in order to pursue masculine desires and fulfil masculine needs. *A Sense of Freedom*, *Shoot for the Sun* (Ian Knox, 1987) and *Down Where the Buffalo Go* (Ian Knox, 1988), Petrie praises along similar lines. Ultimately, however, Petrie concludes, 'McDougall and Mackenzie [director John Mackenzie, McDougall's chief collaborator] create an alternative dark, urban world blighted by poverty, machismo and violence' but 'this vision is no more real than *Brigadoon*', and neither is it oriented toward a particular political agenda, but rather is 'mythic', 'enshrining the image of the working-class hard man as a contemporary "Wild West hero" or "gangster"' (Petrie 2000: 139). Doing so well befits films that, as Petrie recounts, in both *Screening Scotland* and *Contemporary Scottish Fictions* (2004), display the substantial influence of Hollywood Western, gangster and prison genres.

In *Contemporary Scottish Fictions* Petrie (2004) judges *Ill Fares the Land* (Bill Bryden, 1982) and *The Holy City* (Bill Bryden,1986) to be heavy-handed political elegies in Clydesidist mode, and, like with McDougall's films, finds women in these films depicted as either negative or insignificant influences, although other scholars have responded more sympathetically, especially to the former film (David Bruce, for example, praises *Ill Fares the Land* as 'moving' and 'fascinating' [1996: 20], and as displaying impressive attention to detail while being unfairly criticized for its insufficiently Hebridean cast). The television series *Blood Red Roses* (Freeway Films and Channel 4,1986) and *Tutti Frutti* (BBC Scotland,1987) Petrie (2004) prefers because he sees these productions as revising the already strongly mythic dimensions of Clydesidist discourse, which laments the loss of traditional place and stature for the urban working-class masculine heterosexual male, and sympathizes with his confusing and often anguished response to this loss. *Blood Red Roses* shifts the emphasis to a female protagonist and a resistant community of women, while engaging changes in the nature of working-class identity and experience as well as the intersection of issues of class and gender. *Tutti Frutti*, according to Petrie, marks a positive breakthrough by 'representing the extraordinary nature of the ordinary' (2004: 57) in urban working-class Scottish life. At the same time, *Tutti Frutti* works 'to bury the stereotype of the Scottish "hard man" once and for all' (57), while conveying 'a sense of a confident new Glasgow emerging' (61). As Petrie sees it, *Tutti Frutti* joins writers such as Alasdair Gray and James Kelman in offering a more honest and up-to-date engagement (than is found in late Clydesidist discourse) with the problematics of masculine male vulnerability as well as with forces at work in creatively re-imagining and re-inventing the twenty-first century Scottish city/twenty-first century Scottish urban life.

Among more recent films reflecting romantic visions of historic Scotland, *Mrs Brown* (John Madden,1997) is notable for recounting an historical episode, and in particular an historical relationship, otherwise not represented in film, and in recounting how a Scots ghillie played an important role in the private and public life of Queen Victoria. Yet critics such as Petrie (in *Screening Scotland* [2000]) evaluate the film as a typical example of British heritage cinema, involving a drama centred around the interpersonal relations of a small number of central characters that displaces careful attention to and consideration of the larger historical context in which this drama takes place. *The Last King of Scotland* (Kevin Macdonald, 2006) examines Scotland's complicity not simply with British imperialism at the height of the British Empire's success but also with Anglo-American neo-imperialism in the wake of ostensible de-colonization; Idi Amin's fascination with familiar myths and icons of an historically romantic Scottishness epitomizes the ways these same myths and icons can be appropriated in support of a brutal yet charismatic despotism. *Nina's Heavenly Delights* (Pratibha Parmar, 2006) overtly plays with familiar tropes of tartan and Tartanry, as part of a romantic story of 'coming out' and of 'coming together', in order ultimately to suggest these tropes have become fluid and flexible in terms of their range of possible meanings and uses. According to this film, contemporary urban Scotland is ready to support a smooth reconciliation between historical associations with Scottishness and contemporary multi-ethnic, multicultural, and multi-sexual forms of social identity. *Stone of Destiny* (Charles Martin Smith, 2008) offers a crowd-pleasing historical romance recounting a more recent deliberate effort at myth-making: the 'theft' by a small group of Scottish nationalist university students of the Stone of Scone from Westminster Abbey on Christmas Day, 1950, in an effort to spark a resurgence of nationalist sentiment across Scotland. Although the film struggles to successfully fuse elements drawn from Hollywood-style action-adventure, suspense thriller, farce and romance genres with serious political drama, the film at least focuses on a more recent historical event as its subject, and largely (although not entirely) avoids reliance upon the most clichéd elements of Tartanry, Kailyard and Clydesidism to articulate its predominant conception of Scottishness. *Brave* (Mark Andrews, Brenda

Chapman and Steve Purcell, 2013) returns to more familiar territory, albeit in animated form, drawing heavily on highly familiar elements of Tartanry – and Kailyard (much akin to what Duncan Petrie describes, discussing *Rob Roy: The Highland Rogue* in *Screening Scotland*, as a 'surfeit of Scotticisms' [2000: 64]), although it attempts to update attention to, and respect for, at least the possibility of female agency, and female self-determination, within an otherwise traditionally patriarchal social order.

Ronald Neame's *Tunes of Glory* (1960) and *The Prime of Miss Jean Brodie* (1969) are often overlooked in discussions of cinematic engagement with myths of Scotland and Scottishness, which is unfortunate, because both offer useful counters to trends that have served as the frequent source of considerable criticism. The former dramatizes an internal conflict within one of the classic mainstays of 'tartan tradition' – a Scottish military regiment – where kilt-wearing, pipes and drums, traditional Scottish folk music and dancing, whisky and more are all abundantly upon display. Yet this is a decamped regiment, away from the battlefield, where the problems and limits of fantasies of glory and of mythic continuity with heroic traditions, especially as these are conceived and employed in sharply contesting ways, ultimately lead to an explosive climax. *The Prime of Miss Jean Brodie* again depicts plenty of conventional trappings of Tartanry, including plaid skirts and romantic historical associations with Scotland (and especially Edinburgh), although these are backgrounded as the film focuses on its powerfully flawed protagonist, the charismatic yet deluded fascist-sympathizing schoolteacher, Miss Jean Brodie. The film, like the novel upon which it is based, examines the powerful appeal along with the considerable dangers of an overwhelmingly romantically mythic approach to making sense of, in Miss Brodie's words, 'goodness, truth and beauty', as well as aiming deliberately to transform one's life into a romantic myth. The at least partial and temporary success of Miss Brodie suggests the dangerous appeal of these very same tendencies within middle-class Scotland between the world wars.

Breaking the Waves (Lars von Trier, 1996) well illustrates how far familiar tropes of Kailyard can be stretched and revised; as Jane Sillars suggests, this film blends elements of Kailyard with elements of anti-Kailyard so as to effectively transcend their traditional antithesis (2009: 134–37). Among other issues, *Breaking the Waves* explores the multiple and contradictory ways that landscape and place can influence both individual character and the character of a community, especially in a relatively remote and isolated region, as well as the influence of individual character and the character of a community upon perceptions of and engagements with landscape and place. *Seachd: the Inaccessible Pinnacle* (Simon Miller, 2007) not only sensitively engages the continuing power of traditional Scottish Gaelic stories and storytelling but also equally sensitively dramatizes difficult struggles, as well as at least partial successes, in rendering Scottish Gaelic language and culture effectively meaningful and satisfyingly fulfilling to a younger generation restless with the tales told by their elders and with living as part of a culture and in a region that can all too readily seem overwhelmingly consumed with death and loss. The fraught but ultimately enduring bonds of family and community depicted in *Seachd* demonstrate little to none of the complacency, or even the insularity, commonly associated with Kailyard literature and film.

The Angels' Share (Ken Loach, 2012), strikingly for film-maker Ken Loach, commonly considered a paragon of social realist film-making, is also very much a romantic film as well. Not only does it recount the almost 'magical' success of an outlandish caper, but also the film is very much inspired by 'magical' associations with Scottish whisky and whisky-making, including the very notion of 'the angels' share', the 2 per cent of the spirit lost each year to evaporation from the cask during the time the whisky is maturing. *The Angels' Share* unabashedly celebrates the beauty of the Highland countryside its Glasgow-based protagonists encounter for the first time, as well as the possibility that sometimes those who are down and out, and who need help to gain another chance to move forward on a better path, will, almost 'miraculously', indeed find the help they need, as well as likewise virtually 'miraculously', find the means to work together with others from the same social position to help themselves. Although Colin McArthur has argued that whisky and tourism represent the 'two key sites of regressive discourse about Scotland' (2009: 42), Loach and company, in *The Angels' Share*, are willing to explore diametrically opposing possibilities in invoking both kinds of iconic associations with Scotland and Scottishness. *The Angels' Share* recalls *Whisky Galore!* (Alexander Mackendrick, 1949), which, as Duncan Petrie indicates, might at first glance seem sentimental and reactionary but in fact this is a misreading of the Islanders' ultimate triumph, by means of savvy determination: 'the islanders of Todday are not the backward-looking reactionaries of the Kailyard' (Petrie 2000: 43). *Whisky Galore!* critiques 'the arrogance of the white settler who makes no effort to understand the traditions and the language of the host community' (43), and also is notable for the extensive involvement of local residents of Barra in the making of the film, as well as for its playful send-up of the conventions of Griersonian documentary – in sum, this is a film conveying 'a mischievous celebration of life, ingenuity and wit' (44). *The Angels' Share* likewise is a product of Loach and company's characteristically meticulous research and extensive consultation with local experts, as well as characteristic casting of actors who can bring to bear an authentic connection between their own life-experience and that of the characters they will play, while the film likewise depicts its heroic gang succeeding at the expense of ultra-rich 'outsiders', whose immense fortune provides them privileged access to Scotland's 'national drink', which all too many working-class Scots cannot afford to access and enjoy.

In conclusion, much has changed since Colin McArthur and company wrote *Scotch Reels* (1982), and since Tom Nairn, even earlier, wrote 'Old and New Scottish Nationalism' (2003 [1977]) as a chapter in *The Break-Up of Britain*. According to many critics and commentators, and many direct participants and contributors as well, Scotland has experienced a remarkable period of cultural productivity, vitality and innovation over the course of the last 30 years, forging new, renewed, re-configured and transformed conceptions and articulations of what Scotland, as well as of what Scottishness can, does, has and might include. Many writers and artists have foregrounded a multiplicity of possibilities, as well as considerable emphasis on the complexity, contradiction, fluidity, mobility and hybridity concerning what forms and constitutes the nation of Scotland, and the character of its people. Many Scots have contended that Scotland has experienced a substantial movement of cultural nationalism during this period of time, in fact achieving a cultural devolution earlier and carrying this further than the political devolution that was realized with the restoration of the Scottish national parliament at the end of the twentieth century. With political devolution (and, in fact, preceding it), steadily more and more Scots have come to identify primarily, even exclusively, as Scottish (as opposed to British, or even Scottish and British), while steadily more and more Scots also support extended and enhanced devolution of greater authority to the Scottish parliament, if not outright independence from the United Kingdom. Certainly these trends have significantly affected work in Scottish cinema – both Scottish film production as well as Scottish film criticism. Film-makers today are far less constrained by, and film scholars today are far less worried about, Tartanry, Kailyard and Clydesidism. As Ken MacLeod writes, in *Unstated: Writers on Scottish Independence* (2012), even as the only one of the 27 writers contributing to the volume *not* supporting Scottish independence, the cultural deficiencies Tom Nairn railed against 37 years earlier have been almost entirely repaired, and Scotland today is a nation, on the contrary, in the midst of a virtually unprecedented 'artistic flourishing' (2012: 128). Writing in the same book, Margaret Elphinstone, while discussing her background as English and identifying herself, borrowing from Alasdair Gray, as 'Scottish by formation', argues the importance of recognizing, contrary to notions once prevalent of Scottish insularity and parochialism, that Scotland has never really been peripheral and isolated, but rather has long been extensively connected and engaged with other nations, while long witnessing an extensive movement of and interchange among people across national boundaries (MacLeod 2012: 71–76). Scotland today, in other words, is already in many if not most respects a self-confidently 'modern' and 'global' nation, and is on the verge of becoming fully so. Meaghan Delahunt (2012), who was born and lived for quite a while in Australia before moving to and settling in Scotland, echoes Elphinstone: 'The "cultural cringe" of a nation always stems from a sense of powerlessness, a lack of self-determination, a lack of true freedom' (2012: 57), but 'that is changing in Scotland just as it did earlier in Australia: change comes from progressive politics and from "artists and writers prepared to stick their necks out"' (58). And Magi Gibson (2012) recounts a progressive myth that Scots should not approach by merely 'exposing' how far it is and has been 'inaccurate' as a description of the 'reality' of Scottish social life, but rather use as a guide in envisioning what kind of (independent) nation Scotland should aspire to be, and how Scots (especially Scottish artists and writers) can usefully contribute toward bringing Scotland steadily closer to realizing this vision:

> I learned that to be Scottish meant to be part of a co-operative, caring community; to have a socialist mindset where hard work with either your hands or your brain was honorable and should be rewarded with decent wages; that everyone should have free healthcare and decent living conditions; that tolerance and acceptance of difference was a good thing. (Gibson 2012: 98)

As Gibson adds, 'Scotland will continue to have a crisis of identity until she stands on her own two feet and faces down the demons – many of them imaginary as demons so often are' (98).

Gibson's comments here suggest the importance, once again, of rethinking what 'myth' means. Paul Riceour (1986) famously argued that myth dramatizes the tension between the way things are and the way they can be, and that myth is not so much an explanation of the world as it is, or as it was, but rather an exploration of the world as it could or might be. Cinema, as a pre-eminent venue for creating richly enticing 'imaginary worlds', will continue to play a significant role in this work; Scottish film production and Scottish film criticism will continue to come to terms with and argue over the impact of past and present myths of Scotland and Scottishness while continuing to develop and disseminate new ones. In order to achieve the progressive political ends that *Scotch Reels* (1982) advocated, as well as additional progressive ends not envisioned or emphasized by those writers, Scottish film-makers and film scholars will need to continue to imagine what a progressive Scotland can and should be, how it might be possible to get there from here, what obstacles need to be confronted and overcome, and what elements from the present, and the past, can and should be preserved and brought forward versus what elements can and should be jettisoned and left behind. Richard Zumkhawala-Cook writes that, 'although myths are an important part of heritage', the problem comes when 'they are not presented as myths but [rather] as permanent conditions' (2008: 122). This in turn poses a daunting but nonetheless exciting challenge, which, as James Robertson discusses in 'The Curious Time-Piece of Scottish Identity' (2011), Sir Walter Scott astutely grasped back in 1826:

> People say that the whole human frame in all its parts and divisions is gradually in the act of decaying and renewing [...] What a curious time-piece it would be that could indicate to us the moment this gradual and insensible change had so completely taken place that no atom was left of the original person who had

> existed at a certain period but there existed in his stead another person having the same limbs, thewes and sinews, the same face and lineaments, the same consciousness – a new ship built on an old plank [...] Singular – to be at once another and the same. (quoted in Robertson 2011, 1)

As Robertson suggests, as with an individual human being, so with a nation as well. And to that, it is worth adding so also with a nation's culture and its predominant myths.

Bob Nowlan

References

Beattie, Bryan and Hassan, Gerry (ed.) (2011) *ImagiNation: Stories of Scotland's Future*, Drumderfit, Scotland: Big Sky Press.

Bell, Eleanor and Miller, Gavin (ed.) (1994) *Scotland in Theory: Reflections on Culture & Literature*, Scottish Cultural Review of Language and Literature, Volume 1, Amsterdam: Rodopi.

Beveridge, Craig and Turnbull, Ronald (1989) *The Eclipse of Scottish Culture: Inferiorism and the Intellectuals*, Edinburgh: Polygon.

Brown, Ian (ed.) (2010a) *From Tartan to Tartanry: Scottish Culture, History and Myth*, Edinburgh: EUP.

__________ (2010b) 'Introduction: Tartan, Tartanry and Hybridity' in Ian Brown (ed.), *From Tartan to Tartanry: Scottish Culture, History and Myth*, Edinburgh: EUP, pp. 1–12.

__________ (2010c) 'Myth, Political Caricature and Monstering the Tartan', in Ian Brown (ed.), *From Tartan to Tartanry: Scottish Culture, History and Myth*, Edinburgh: EUP, pp. 93–114.

Bruce, David (1996) *Scotland the Movie*, Edinburgh: Polygon.

Caughie, John (1990) 'Representing Scotland: New Questions for Scottish Cinema', in Eddie Dick (ed.), *From Limelight to Satellite: A Scottish Film Book*, Edinburgh: Scottish Film Council and British Film Institute.

Cook, Pam (1996) *Fashioning the Nation: Costuming and Identity in British Cinema*, London: BFI.

Coupe, Laurence (2009 [1997]) *Myth*, New Critical Idiom, 2nd edn, London: Routledge.

Craig, Cairns (2009) *Intending Scotland: Explorations in Scottish Culture Since the Enlightenment*, Edinburgh: EUP.

__________ (1982) 'Myths Against History: Tartanry and Kailyard in 19th-Century Scottish Literature', in Colin McArthur (ed.), *Scotch Reels: Scotland in Cinema and Television*, London: BFI, pp. 7–15.

__________ (2009) 'Nostophobia', in Jonathan Murray, Fidelma Farley and Rod Stoneman (eds), *Scottish Cinema Now*, Newcastle upon Tyne: Cambridge Scholars Publishing, pp. 56–71.

__________ (1996) *Out of History: Narrative Paradigms in Scottish and English Culture*, Edinburgh: Polygon.

Delahunt, Meaghan (2012) Untitled, in Scott Hames (ed.), *Unstated: Writers on Scottish Independence*, Edinburgh: Word Power Books, pp. 57–61.

Devine, T.M. (2012 [2006, 1999]) *The Scottish Nation: A Modern History*, London: Penguin.

Douglas, Mary (1975) *Implicit Meanings*, London: Routledge and Kegan Paul.

Elphinstone, Margaret (2012) Untitled, in Scott Hames (ed.), *Unstated: Writers on Scottish Independence*, Edinburgh: Word Power Books, pp. 71–76.

Gibson, Magi (2012) Untitled, in Scott Hames (ed.), *Unstated: Writers on Scottish Independence*, Edinburgh: Word Power Books, pp. 95–99.

Goldie, David (2010) 'Don't Take the High Road: Tartanry and its Critics', in Ian Brown (ed.), *From Tartan to Tartanry: Scottish Culture, History and Myth*, Edinburgh: EUP, pp. 232–45.
Hames, Scott (ed.) (2012) *Unstated: Writers on Scottish Independence*, Edinburgh: Word Power Books.
Hardy, Forsyth (1990) *Scotland in Film*, Edinburgh: EUP.
Hume, Ian Maitland (2010) 'Tartanry into Tartan: Heritage, Tourism and Material Culture', in Ian Brown (ed.), *From Tartan to Tartanry: Scottish Culture, History and Myth*, Edinburgh: EUP, pp. 82–92.
Jameson, Fredric (1981) *The Political Unconscious: Narrative as a Socially Symbolic Act*, Ithaca: Cornell University Press.
MacLeod, Ken (2012) Untitled, in Scott Hames (ed.), *Unstated: Writers on Scottish Independence*, Edinburgh: Word Power Books, pp. 128–32.
Malcolmson, Scott L (1985) 'Modernism Comes to the Cabbage Patch: Bill Forsyth and the "Scottish Cinema"', *Film Quarterly*, 38: 3, pp. 16–21.
Martin-Jones, David (2009) *Scotland: Global Cinema – Genres, Modes and Identities*, Edinburgh: EUP.
McArthur, Colin (2003) *Brigadoon, Braveheart, and the Scots: Distortions of Scotland in Hollywood Cinema*, London: IB Tauris.
_________ (1994) 'The Cultural Necessity of a Poor Celtic Cinema', in John Hill, Martin McLoone and Paul Hainsworth (eds), *Border Crossing: Film in Ireland, Britain and Europe*, Belfast: Institute of Irish Studies, Queens University, pp. 112–25.
_________ (1993) 'In Praise of a Poor Cinema', *Sight and Sound*, August, pp. 30–32.
_________ (1982) 'Scotland and Cinema: The Iniquity of the Fathers', in Colin McArthur (ed.), *Scotch Reels: Scotland in Cinema and Television*, London: BFI.
_________ (2009) '*Scotch Myths*, Scottish Film Culture and the Suppression of Ludic Modernism', in Jonathan Murray, Fidelma Farley and Rod Stoneman (eds), *Scottish Cinema Now*, Newcastle upon Tyne: Cambridge Scholars Publishing, pp. 39–55.
_________ (ed.) (1982) *Scotch Reels: Scotland in Cinema and Television*, London: BFI.
_________ (1996) 'The Scottish Discursive Unconscious', in Alasdair Cameron and Adrienne Scullion (eds), *Scottish Popular Theatre and Entertainment*, Glasgow: Glasgow University Library Studies, pp. 81–89.
McCrone, David (1992) *Understanding Scotland: The Sociology of a Stateless Nation*, London: Routledge.
Munro, Margaret (2010) 'Tartan Comics and Comic Tartanry', in Ian Brown (ed.), *From Tartan to Tartanry: Scottish Culture, History and Myth*, Edinburgh: EUP, pp. 180–94.
Murray, Jonathan, Farley, Fidelma and Stoneman, Rod (ed.) (2009) *Scottish Cinema Now*, Newcastle upon Tyne: Cambridge Scholars Publishing.
Nairn, Tom (2003 [1983, 1977]) 'Old and New Scottish Nationalism', *The Break-up of Britain: Crisis and Neo-Nationalism*, Edinburgh: Big Thinking, pp. 115–83.
Petrie, Duncan (2004) *Contemporary Scottish Fictions: Film, Television and the Novel*, Edinburgh: EUP.
_________ (2000) *Screening Scotland*, London: BFI.
Pittock, Murray (2010) 'Plaiding the Invention of Scotland', in Ian Brown (ed.), *From Tartan to Tartanry: Scottish Culture, History and Myth*, Edinburgh: EUP, pp. 32–47.
_________ (2008) *The Road to Independence? Scotland Since the Sixties*, Contemporary Worlds, London: Reaktion Books.
Reizbaum, Marilyn (2009) 'They Know Where They're Going: Landscape and place in Scottish Cinema', in Jonathan Murray, Fidelma Farley and Rod Stoneman (eds), *Scottish Cinema Now*, Newcastle upon Tyne: Cambridge Scholars Publishing, pp. 72–87.

Riach, Alan (2005) *Representing Scotland in Literature, Popular Culture and Iconography: The Masks of the Modern Nation*, Basingstoke: Palgrave Macmillan.

__________ (2010) 'Tartanry and its Discontents: The Idea of Popular Scottishness', in Ian Brown (ed.), *From Tartan to Tartanry: Scottish Culture, History and Myth*, Edinburgh: EUP, pp. 115–28.

Ricoeur, Paul (1986) *Lectures on Ideology and Utopia* (ed. George H Taylor), New York: Columbia University Press.

Robertson, James (2011) 'The Curious Time-Piece of Scottish Identity', in Bryan Beattie and Gerry Hassan (eds), *ImagiNation: Stories of Scotland's Future*, Drumderfit, Scotland: Big Sky Press, pp. 1–6.

Scullion, Adrienne (1995) 'Feminine Pleasures and Masculine Indignities: Gender and Community in Scottish Drama', in Christopher Whyte (ed.), *Gendering the Nation: Studies in Modern Scottish Literature*, Edinburgh: EUP, pp. 169–203.

Sillars, Jane (2009) 'Admitting the Kailyard', in Jonathan Murray, Fidelma Farley and Rod Stoneman (eds), *Scottish CPnema Now*, Newcastle upon Tyne: Cambridge Scholars Publishing, pp. 122–38.

Stenhouse, David (2009) 'Not Made in Scotland: Images of the Nation from Furth of the Forth', in Jonathan Murray, Fidelma Farley and Rod Stoneman (eds), *Scottish Cinema Now*, Newcastle upon Tyne: Cambridge Scholars Publishing, pp. 171–87.

Trevor-Roper, Hugh (1983) 'The Invention of Tradition: The Highland Tradition of Scotland', in Eric Hobsbawm and Terence Ranger (eds), *The Invention of Tradition*, Cambridge: CUP, pp. 15–41.

Turnbull, Ronald (1994) 'Nairn's Nationalism', in Eleanor Bell and Gavin Miller (eds), *Scotland in Theory: Reflections on Culture & Literature*, Scottish Cultural Review of Language and Literature Volume 1, Amsterdam: Rodopi, pp. 35–49.

Zumkhawala-Cook, Richard (2008) *Scotland as We Know It: Representations of National Identity in Literature, Film and Popular Culture*, Jefferson, NC: McFarland.

The 39 Steps

Country of Origin:

UK

Language:

English

Studio/Production Company:

Gaumont-British Picture Corporation

Director:

Alfred Hitchcock

Producers:

Michael Balcon
Ivor Montagu

Screenwriters:

Charles Bennett (screenplay)
Ian Hay (dialogue)
John Buchan (novel)

Cinematographer:

Bernard Knowles

Art Director:

Oscar Friedrich Werndorff

Editor:

Derek N Twist

Duration:

86 minutes

Genre:

Mystery
Suspense
Comedy
Caper

Cast:

Robert Donat
Madeleine Carroll
Lucie Mannheim
Godfrey Tearle

Year:

1935

Filming Locations:

Big Water of Fleet Viaduct, Scotland, UK
Edinburgh, Scotland, UK
Forth Bridge, Scotland, UK
Glen Coe, Scotland, UK
Lime Grove Studios, England, UK

Synopsis

When gunshots are fired in a London music hall, Canadian Richard Hannay offers shelter to a shaken young woman who claims she is being pursued by spies. Sceptical at first, Hannay's doubts are quickly dispelled when the girl is murdered during the night – but not before making reference to an enigmatic concept known only as 'the 39 steps'. Framed for the killing, Hannay soon finds himself in danger from police and villains alike. Following a map left by his dead acquaintance, he flees north to Scotland in a desperate attempt to solve the mystery and clear his name.

Critique

Although it was Alfred Hitchcock's 1927 silent cinema outing, *The Lodger*, that first saw him utilize the story of an innocent man on the run, it is *The 39 Steps* that is most often cited as the director's earliest signature film. Loosely adapted from John Buchan's 1915 novel of the same name, the plot as imagined by Hitchcock and screenwriter Charles Bennett contains a number of traits that would become hallmarks of the Master of Suspense's repertoire.

Indeed, between the perilous train journey that transports Hannay to Scotland, the doubled-up chase structure that sees our hero pursuing wrongdoers whilst being hunted as one himself, and the feisty blonde stranger he becomes entangled with along the way, the film almost serves as an exact prototype for Hitchcock's later classic, *North By Northwest* (1959). Even the film's mysterious title gets the director's trademark MacGuffin treatment, the secret behind the 39 steps serving as a plot device that drives Hannay's quest without ever becoming central to the audience's enjoyment. The 'steps' are, it is eventually revealed, a spy ring – one that seeks to steal vital secrets from the British military – though this is hardly important. The nature of these secrets and the ends they are intended to benefit are left entirely unexplained, with Hitchcock choosing to focus instead on excitement and suspense.

It is a decision he executes perfectly, with the absence of explanatory information doing nothing to detract from the film's tightly woven narrative, the concise yet effective nature of which is carefully crafted from the outset. Opening with a pan across the light bulb-lettered sign of a bustling Music Hall (a similar setting to where the plot will also reach its climax), Hitchcock instantly establishes London as a lively and vibrant city – a setting that will stand in stark contrast against the film's portrayal of rural Scotland when Hannay is forced to take flight. Yet even in these early surroundings, our sharp and dashing protagonist seems an immediately foreign presence, his immaculate overcoat and slicked-back hair marking him out as a notable minority amongst the flat-cap wearing working men's crowd. An expatriate Scot in Buchan's original novel, it is soon explained that – despite possessing actor Robert Donat's smooth and distinctly English vocal tones – this version of Hannay is 'a man from Canada'. The change cements an otherness about the character that pervades the film.

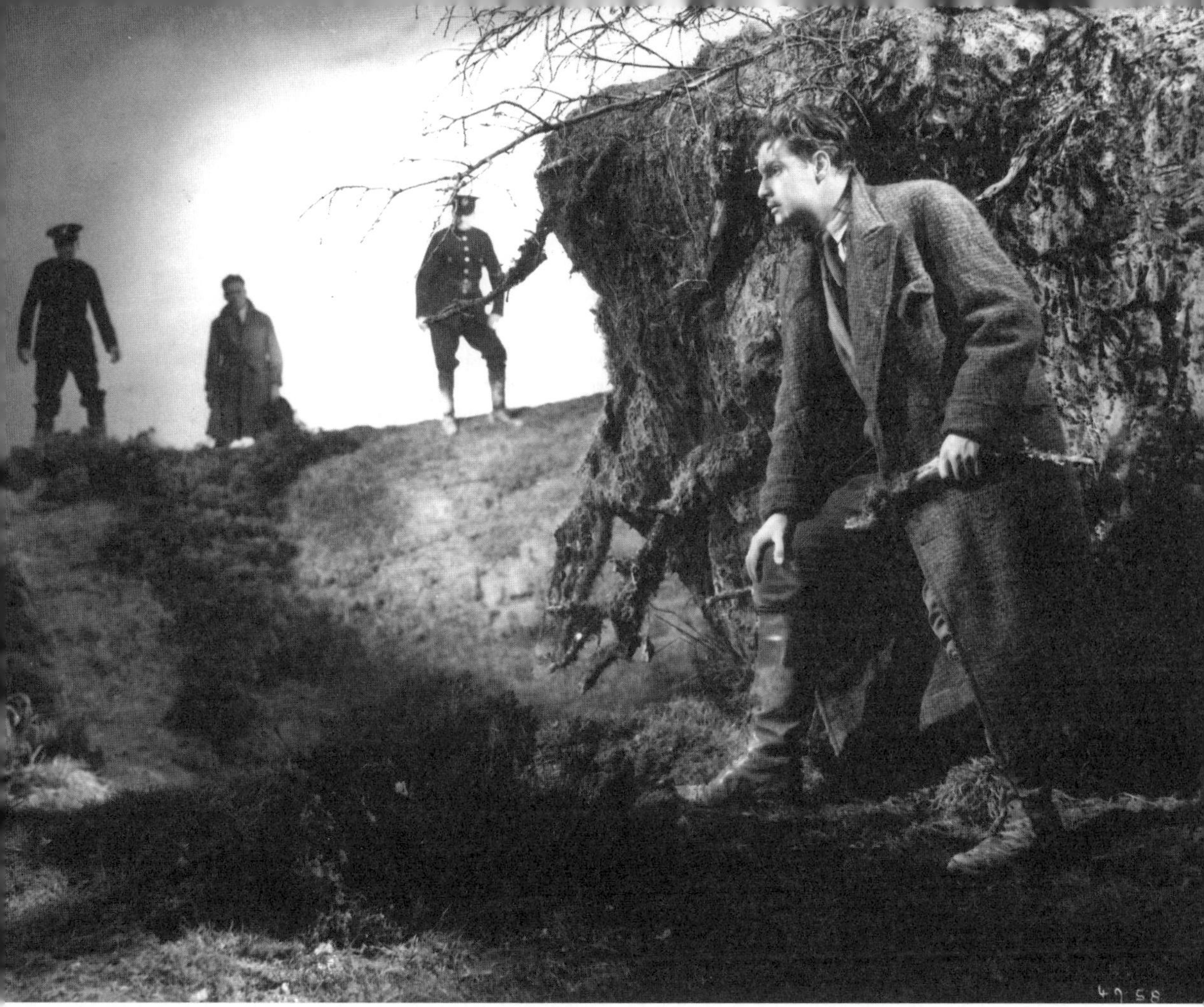

The 39 Steps (1935), British Film Institute Collection

Welwyn Studios, England, UK

Although such an outsider status is made somewhat inevitable by a plot that sees Hannay involuntarily transposed from city dweller to cross country escapee, the removal of his Scottish ties is in some ways vital. Indeed, though some of the locals seem to regard him with a pleasant sense of exoticism, he is in most cases greeted with an understandable suspicion, as a foreigner wandering the countryside in city clothes is bound to draw some attention, especially when he's wanted by the police. An entirely isolated figure, the Hannay of Hitchcock's film possesses no connection to the nation he is embroiled in trying to protect, thereby lessening any reason for people to believe his claims of conspiracy. Meanwhile, the story's true villain – a known and respected professor – is seen as the pinnacle of his village community, a man who could surely do no wrong. As the local police inspector responds when Hannay pleads his case: 'we're not so daft in Scotland as some smart Londoners may think'.

It is these moments that best capture the tone of *The 39 Steps*, showcasing it not only as a clever thriller, but also a consistently playful one. With the lighter moments often revolving around the charm that Donat brings to the lead role, it could again be suggested that this is the forerunner to Hitchcock's later work with Cary Grant. Though many of the people Hannay encounters are wary of the presence of strangers, in some cases he is able to turn this to his advantage. One memorable scene features a quick-thinking Hannay blend in at a political rally, delighting the crowd with a rousing speech that promises a fairer world. The film's best-known moments, however, come through Donat's interaction with Madeleine Carroll, cast as the alluring yet wilful Pamela. Thrown together when Hannay seeks shelter in her train compartment, Pamela twice attempts to turn him in to the police, an effort that, ironically, eventually finds the pair handcuffed together and forced to escape as a reluctant duo. With rumour suggesting Hitchcock used the same technique to bond the actors pre-filming, the resulting chemistry is undeniable. Buchan's novel has been adapted for the screen three times since, yet the provocative image of Carroll removing her stockings whilst still fastened to Donat remains unparalleled in its notoriety.

Patrick Harley

The Angels' Share

Country of Origin:
UK

Language:
English

Studio/Production Companies:
Sixteen Films
Why Not Productions
Wild Bunch

Director:
Ken Loach

Producer:
Rebecca O'Brien

Screenwriter:
Paul Laverty

Cinematographer:
Robbie Ryan

Production Designer:
Fergus Clegg

Synopsis

At the Glasgow Sheriff Court, Robbie, Mo, Rhino and Albert are all issued community payback sentences. For Robbie this sentence, the sheriff warns him, is his last chance, given his extensive prior criminal record, including previously serving time in the Polmont Young Offenders Institution. The sheriff offers him a last chance because Robbie has demonstrated energy and talent and because he is due to become a first-time father within days. Robbie and the others are fortunate to meet Harry, one of their community payback supervisors, who is kindly disposed to them, wants to help them get a break and is ready to be their friend. Harry accompanies Robbie to the hospital when they learn that Leonie, Robbie's partner, has gone into labour. Leonie's father, Matt, and two of Leonie's uncles prevent Robbie from seeing Leonie, pushing him into an emergency-exit stairwell and beating him up while Harry is forced to watch. Harry takes Robbie to his home afterward, helps Robbie attend to his wounds, and, toasts the birth of Robbie's son, Luke, with a glass of a 36-year-old Springbank whisky, the first single malt whisky Robbie has ever drunk. Harry also arranges with a friend at the hospital so Robbie can visit Leonie and Luke without her father or uncles intervening. Soon thereafter, at Leonie's urging, Robbie agrees to attend a 'Talk After Serious Crime' with the victim of the crime for which Robbie was sentenced to prison – Anthony – and Anthony's family. As Anthony describes what Robbie did to him, and as he and his mother describe the lasting consequences, a

Art Director:
Zoe Wright
Composer:
George Fenton
Editor:
Jonathan Morris
Duration:
97 minutes
Genre:
Social Drama
Comedy
Romance
Caper
Cast:
Paul Brannigan
Siobhan Reilly
John Henshaw

flashback shows Robbie, 'coked up to the eyeballs', pull Anthony out from his car and viciously beat him. Robbie's attack left Anthony with multiple broken fingers and a broken wrist, damage about the head requiring twelve stitches, a detached retina and permanent loss of eyesight in his left eye. Robbie is obviously deeply uncomfortable, ashamed and emotionally agitated, but is unable to say anything to Anthony or his family. Afterward he tells Leonie if anyone ever did what he did to Anthony to Luke he'd 'want the bastard hung', and promises Luke and Leonie he is done hurting people, although Leonie is skeptical that he will be able to carry through with this promise, given Robbie's long ongoing feud with Clancy. Shortly thereafter, Harry takes Robbie and the others to visit a distillery. The group participates in a guided tour where they learn about the process, and eventually enjoy a culminating sample tasting. Robbie is particularly interested, and, although initially angry at Mo for stealing a bunch of sample bottles from the distillery gift store, ends up using them to practice his nosing and tasting skills, after reading a number of books about whisky borrowed from a local library. As Mo, Robbie, Rhino and Albert are playing snooker, Clancy and friends enter. Robbie flees, to

The Angels' Share (2012), British Film Institute Collection

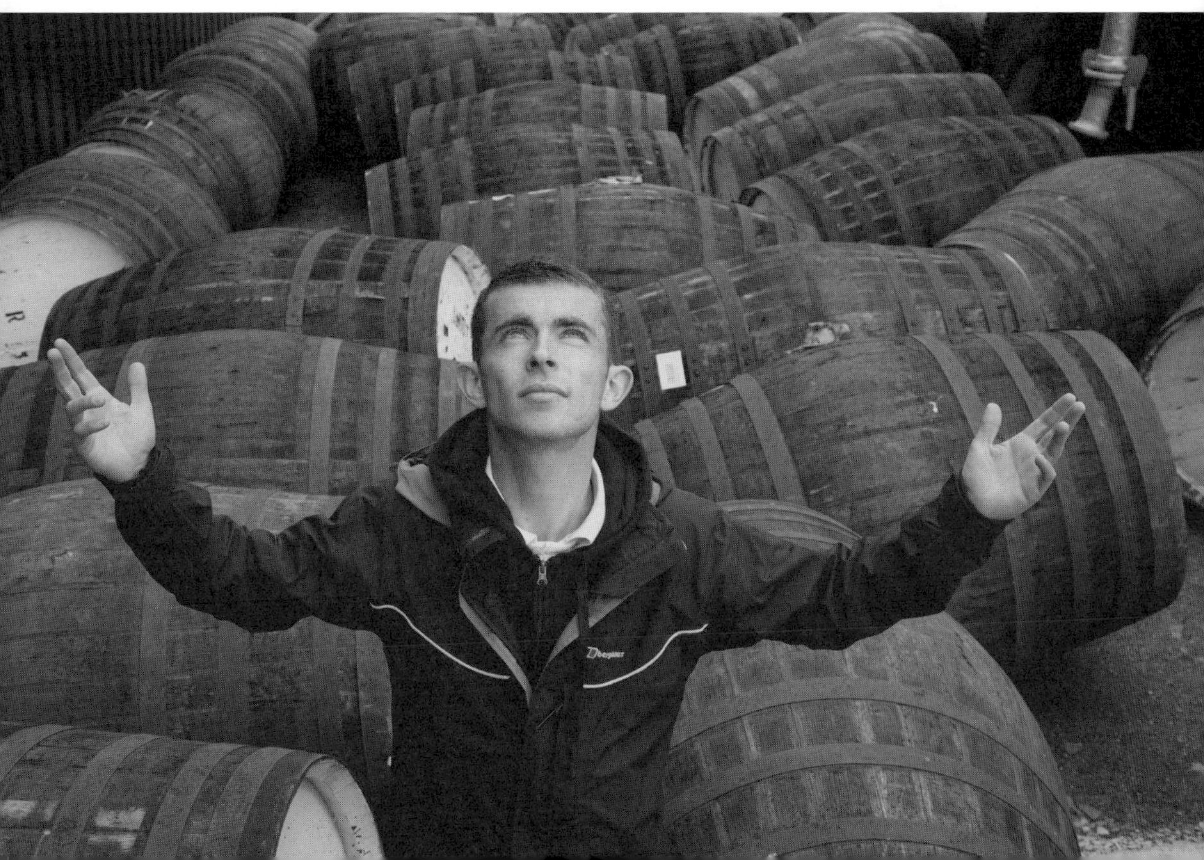

Gary Maitland
William Ruane
Jasmin Riggins
Roger Allam
Charles MacLean

Year:

2012

Filming Locations:

Glasgow, Scotland, UK
Edinburgh, Scotland, UK
Balblair, Scotland, UK
Deanston, Scotland, UK
Glengoyne, Scotland, UK

be rescued by Matt, who offers Robbie £5,000 if he will move to London and give up Leonie and Luke. Soon thereafter Harry invites Robbie, Mo, Rhino and Albert to a whisky tasting in Edinburgh. At this event, presided over by 'Grand Master of the Quaich' Rory McAllister, Robbie impresses 'whisky collector' Thaddeus in a blind tasting game, and Thaddeus gives Robbie his business card. The group also learns from McAllister about an upcoming auction of a 'Malt Mill', a rare single cask from a distillery that closed in the early 1960s. After Robbie discovers Clancy will always pursue him wherever he goes in Glasgow, Robbie decides he and his mates must pursue a daring caper to change their fortunes. Hitchhiking north to Balblair for the Malt Mill auction, dressed in kilts, as part of the 'Carntyne Malt Whisky Club', Robbie smooth talks his way into an invitation for the group to attend the auction, while gaining valuable information about the layout of the distillery. During a preliminary tasting, Robbie sneaks behind the casks, and later that night siphons off enough whisky from the Malt Mill to fill four Irn Bru bottles and a small tasting flask for himself. Robbie also overhears Thaddeus attempt to persuade the distillery manager to let him have three bottles of the Malt Mill without telling anyone, which the manager refuses. At the auction the next day, Thaddeus's client is outbid by an American, but Robbie tracks Thaddeus down to offer Thaddeus a cut-rate deal on the whisky he has taken. Thaddeus agrees to conclude the transaction back in Glasgow. Unfortunately, after being stopped by cops on arriving back in Glasgow, an outraged Albert accidentally smashes his bottle against Mo's, and only two are left. Yet Thaddeus agrees to buy a bottle from Robbie for his client, and to use his influence to get Robbie a job working for a distillery up north. Robbie leaves the last remaining bottle as a present for Harry in gratitude for Harry giving him a chance when no one else would.

Critique

As writer Paul Laverty has indicated, *The Angels' Share* is 'a little fable' concerned with 'wasted talent' and 'what happens when given a second chance in life' (2012: 7). Robbie, Mo, Rhino and Albert represent many like them at a time in which the number of unemployed young people in the United Kingdom exceeded 1 million and where, in director Ken Loach's words, among this generation of young people, 'a lot of whom face an empty future' because 'they can be pretty sure they won't get a job, a permanent job, a secure job' (quoted in Laverty 2012: 177). After making the exceedingly bleak *Route Irish* (2010), Laverty and Loach sought next to make a comedy, which, although persistently naturalistic, includes an element of the magical and conveys a climactic sense of hope. *The Angels' Share* thus recalls Loach's and Laverty's Manchester-based social realist melodrama meets comic fantasy, *Looking for Eric* (2009). For the characters in *The Angels' Share*, and for people like them in real life, humour serves not merely as a coping mechanism but also as a mode of resistance. Loach cites his deep appreciation for working-class Glaswegian sense of humour as one reason why he is as fond of Glasgow as he is, having now directed five fictional feature-length films set, at least in significant part, in Scotland's largest city (with *The Angels' Share* following *Carla's Song* [1997], *My Name is Joe* [1998], *Sweet Sixteen* [2002] and *Ae Fond Kiss* [2004]).

The making of *The Angels' Share* is characteristically 'Loachian'. The film is the product of extensive research not only concerning young, unemployed urban Scots struggling with the impact of drugs, alcohol, abuse, neglect, gangs, physical and emotional violence, and custodial as well as community payback sentences in response to conviction for miscellaneous criminal offenses – but also concerning the whisky business and whisky culture. Locations and props are selected and prepared with emphasis on accuracy and authenticity. Actors' lines are likewise written to convey credibility, while actors speak in accents that directly correspond to the local, regional and class backgrounds their characters represent. First-time actors, notably Paul Brannigan as the lead, and others with little to no previous professional experience, play prominent roles, for which they are recruited as the result of an exhaustive casting process, including elaborate auditions. Loach prizes novice actors able to draw upon background and experience closely akin to that of the characters they are chosen to play (Brannigan and Reilly, for instance, each have lived lives in many respects strikingly similar to the characters they play). The actors do not receive the entire screenplay ahead of shooting, as Loach distributes pieces of the script bit by bit, over the course of shooting, often providing actors only what is required for each scene they shoot as they shoot that scene, and often giving individual actors only their lines and not those of others working with them in the same scene. Nevertheless, the shooting closely follows the script even as actors are encouraged to introduce modifications they can make a case for, when these feel more 'natural'. Meticulous planning of precisely how the camera will be used in each scene precedes shooting, and Loach oversees an efficient, economical, fast process. Loach and crew shoot and edit on 35 mm film, using solely prime lenses, and often only a single camera, from heights, distances and angles approximating what a scene would look like to an unaided human eye. A respectfully observational distance is commonplace, with many medium long shots, and a preference for medium close-ups over close-ups in sit-down conversations. At the same time, the actors and their interactions serve as the central focus within framings; surrounding locations remain backgrounds. The camera is attached to a tripod except on rare occasions – such as running and fighting – where use of a handheld camera seems 'naturally' appropriate. Loach likewise prefers shooting with minimal additions to ambient lighting – preferring to work with lighting that is 'naturally' available at a location. Throughout the shoot Loach consistently maintains his position close to the actors, directly aside the camera operator, offering extensive hands-on direction before and after individual takes. The cinematography never calls attention to the camera as an independent presence within the film but rather strives for invisibility, so as to focus the audience's attention on the characters and the story, while editing likewise adheres to classic continuity conventions; for instance, even though cuts are used for transitions across time and space, these are always clearly aligned with transitions in actors' lines and actions. Music composed for the soundtrack is soft, minimal, almost always deeply backgrounded and frequently absent; the two points in the film incorporating The Proclaimers's 'I'm Gonna Be (500 Miles)' stand out all the more emphatically as a result.

What particularly distinguishes *The Angels' Share* from previous Loach – and Loach and Laverty – films is the emphasis on whisky. *The Angels' Share* respects the skill and talent involved in whisky making and in whisky nosing and tasting. The film also respects the many myths and legends long associated with making whisky, especially the element of the mysterious and the magical that whisky companies, and distillery tours, often do highlight in explaining the cumulative result of the successive stages in the process. The notion of 'the angels' share' – the 2 per cent of the spirit lost each year to evaporation from the cask during the period of time whisky matures – serves as an apt metaphor for the slight redistribution of wealth and opportunity enacted in the plot, a redistribution that doesn't really hurt anyone (Robbie, after all, only siphons off enough to fill a little more than four Irn Bru bottles, and he replaces what he has taken with an equal quantity of top mark whisky so the American buyer of the Malt Mill cask doesn't notice). Allusion to the magical further suggests that sometimes it is indeed possible, with the right assistance and support, at the right place and time, as well as by means of a little ingenuity and with a little luck, to break out of a desperate situation and obtain a chance at a much more fulfilling life. As Laverty indicates, the world of whisky maintains its fair share of snobbishness and phoniness, while also being priced and marketed such that it is effectively inaccessible to many, yet someone from Robbie's background is just as well equipped with what is required to become a whisky connoisseur as anyone. *The Angels' Share* argues that Scots like Robbie deserve the opportunity to enjoy what have long been widely celebrated as Scottish national treasures – including whisky, along with the fresh air and natural beauty of the Highlands. *The Angels' Share* argues Scottish working-class young people deserve not only 'bread' but also 'roses' too, echoing another earlier Loach and Laverty film, *Bread and Roses* (2000).

The Angels' Share was nominated for numerous awards; notable wins include the 2012 Cannes Jury Prize, the 2012 San Sebastián Audience Award and the 2012 British Academy of Film and Television Awards for Best Film Actor (Paul Brannigan) and Best Writer (Paul Laverty). The recognition that Brannigan received for his debut acting performance is especially noteworthy, launching a promising subsequent film-acting career. Indeed, what Laverty, Loach, O'Brien and company offered Brannigan parallels what Harry and eventually Thaddeus offer Robbie. Brannigan had lost his job as a community centre worker with at-risk youth at the time Laverty invited him to audition, and Brannigan turned down this invitation twice before Laverty pushed him hard enough to change his mind. As Laverty has commented, it was worth pushing because Brannigan impressed him from early on as bright, thoughtful, exerting of a charismatic presence among his peers and able compellingly to communicate both toughness and vulnerability. Brannigan thus exemplifies a key message of the film: unemployed working-class youth, including those with a criminal record and prison experience, don't deserve to be 'stereotyped as lazy, greedy, feckless' (Laverty 2012: 8) because they in fact maintain the potential to do and be much more and much better; what they need is opportunity and assistance. As Leonie's aunt's friend Grace explains why she is prepared to let Robbie, Leonie and Luke stay in her flat for free while she's away for three months in London, 'Someone gave me a chance once and it changed my life'.

Laverty and Loach don't pretend that Robbie has been innocent; as Laverty writes, the world distrusts him 'for good reason' (8). Inclusion of the scene where Robbie is confronted with the damage he caused to Anthony and his family underscores this point quite decisively. But Laverty and Loach propose Robbie is not reducible – and should not be treated as if he were reducible – to the crimes he has in the past committed, or to the deprived circumstances from which he comes. In this respect, Robbie, as Loach himself acknowledges, is a familiar type of character in a Loach film – a young working-class male intensely dedicated toward a project of his own, to which he brings to bear considerable industry, commitment and enthusiasm, yet in response to which most others around him are oblivious, indifferent, sceptical or outright hostile. Unlike, for example, Billy in *Kes* (1969), or Liam in *Sweet Sixteen* (2002), Robbie succeeds, and this has much to do not only with the friendship Harry offers him (Harry, significantly, loans Robbie the £500 Robbie needs to buy all the supplies required to carry out the caper) but also from Mo, Rhino and Albert. The value of friendship and the difference this can make in determining whether an individual succeeds or fails is certainly a major theme in *The Angels' Share*. This is an especially apt point of emphasis in the case of *The Angels' Share* because of the persistence in Glasgow, Loach finds, of 'a very collective, not an individualist culture' (quoted in Laverty 2012: 177). Producer Rebecca O'Brien declares, in the 'Making of' DVD extra, that she hopes *The Angels' Share* will be appreciated as 'a special Scottish film', given how clearly the film itself ultimately appreciates Scotland and Scottish culture, even as a site of contradiction. And, after all, as Charles MacLean has written in his *Malt Whisky* (1977), in reflecting on whisky and Scottishness, 'whisky epitomizes the inherent dichotomy of the Scottish psyche – at once passionate and rational, romantic and ironic, mystical and sceptical, heroic and craven, full of laughter and despair' (quoted in Laverty 2012: 237).

Bob Nowlan

References

McArdle, Liam (2012) 'Distilling *The Angels' Share*' ['Making of' DVD extra], in Ken Loach, dir. (2012), *The Angels' Share* [DVD], Entertainment One UK Limited.

Laverty, Paul et al. (2012) *The Angels' Share* [Screenplay with commentaries from Paul Laverty, Ken Loach, Rebecca O'Brien and others], Pontefract, UK: Route Publishing.

Bonnie Prince Charlie

Country of Origin:
UK
Language:
English
Studio/Production Company:
London Films
Directors:
Anthony Kimmins
Alexander Korda (uncredited)
Producers:
Edward Black
Alexander Korda
Screenwriter:
Clemence Dane
Cinematographer:
Robert Krasker
Art Directors:
Vincent Korda
W Shingleton
J Bato
Composer:
Ian Whyte
Editor:
Grace Garland
Duration:
118 minutes
Genre:
Historical Romance
Cast:
David Niven
Margaret Leighton
Year:
1948
Filming Location:
Shepperton Studios,

Synopsis

Charles Edward Stuart leads an uprising in order to restore his deposed Stuart line to the British throne. His arrival is met by Donald the shepherd who convenes the chieftains of the Highland clans. Charles and his men march against the British Royal Army under the Germanic Hanoverian monarchy. Early gains raise the specter of an imminent Jacobite victory. Charlie moves towards London until word of a gigantic English army forces the decision of a military retreat. All hope is lost at the catastrophic battle of Culloden. Charlie is urged to escape. Territory friendly to the prince is occupied by soldiers deployed for his capture. The Jacobite-sympathizing population is fined, penalized, harassed with curfews and dragged before summary interrogations. Charles must depend upon the loyalty of Donald, the assistance of Flora MacDonald and the sentiment of the native Highland Scots towards their ancestral king in order to complete his flight from Scottish territory and into the realms of Scottish myth.

Critique

Bonnie Prince Charlie offers itself as a biographical historical epic in the blood and thunder mode. The film proffers a sympathetic view of the Jacobite uprising of 1745 and a Great-Man-of-History attitude towards the title character. The opening sequence gives the impression that 'all of Scotland' is yearning for the return and restoration of the exiled Stuarts. The handsome prince takes the humble and courageous initiative in serving that purpose. The spectator is thus addressed as a Jacobite-sympathizing Scottish Highlander. The film makes significant use of several key supporting characters in order to so situate the viewer. Flora is the cultured and worldly daughter of the local governor. Donald is a rough-mannered but endearing peasant farmer. Blind Jamie 'always appears when there's a stir in the hills' with his harp and his 'true sight' focused somewhere beyond linear time. Charlie is depicted as a hero no matter his naive optimism concerning his political mission, while King George II and his even more terrible son the Duke of Cumberland are somatotypic villains. The royal court in London is composed of sharp-tongued, German-accented endomorphs in powdered wigs. The film relies upon strategies of representation and identification that function in a more or less reverse correlation with prior knowledge of Scottish, and British, history.

The film has gained a reputation as a colossal failure. Yet if the film fails it does so at the point of its narrative confrontation with its own predominantly animating myth. The film may be catastrophic in terms of representing the actual historical figure of Prince Charles Edward Stuart but it succeeds at the same time in highlighting

Shepperton, Surrey, England, UK
Eilean Donan Castle, Kyle of Lochalsh, Highland, Scotland, UK
Glen Coe, Highland, Scotland, UK
Glenfinnan, Highland, Scotland, UK
The Old Man of Storr, Skye, Highland, Scotland, UK

modes of identification long at work, beyond as well as within the film, in sustaining the mythos of the 'Bonnie Prince'.

The film anachronistically appropriates the Robert Burns 1794 poem 'For the Sake O' Somebody' as its lyrical theme and sentimental attitude. Charlie climbs a Scottish hill and presents himself to the first man he finds there as the 'certain Somebody' people are singing songs of. To Charlie, Scotland is the land that sings songs of him. His political ambitions are presented as ordained by a musically if not divinely predestined congruence between people and king. This demand is endorsed by good fortune, popular support and a messianic fervour for the return of the Stuart line. The struggle is thus one of symbolic hegemony more than territorial sovereignty. The film wants its audience to want Charlie to retake the throne as much as he does.

The placement of the catastrophic Battle of Culloden at the middle of the film deflates this hope but Bonnie Prince Charlie knows no sooner than Blind Jamie what the result of the battle will be. Military victory is no longer possible after a defeat of this scale but other modes of victory may yet be. The battlefront consequently makes a sudden shift from the socio-symbolic to the mytho-poetic. The prince is the 'one spark of liberty alive' for Scotland. He must 'keep it alight' by surviving. Charles Edward Stuart is transformed from an actual figurehead of a hopelessly lost cause to a purely symbolic icon of a free Scotland. The 'Bonnie Prince' becomes the mythical remainder of the really-existing Jacobite Rebellion. Representational legitimacy of a military cause gives way to a pure representation of its ideology – a Jacobitism of hearts and minds (Badiou 2007: 108–09).

The film posits the Stuart restoration as a prophecy which cannot succeed. The ruin of the Highland clans on the battlefield, however, marks their even greater spiritual victory. When a preordained event fails to occur in material reality the result is very often the belief that the event has actually taken place on another plane of existence (Melton 1985). Rather than the death-knell for Scottish aspirations, the film inflects Culloden as a rebirth of Scottish cultural subjectivity. Instead of destroying the Jacobite uprising, the battle ramifies Scottish patriotic sentiment. The Charlie who emerges victorious is not the future King of England and Scotland but the 'Bonnie Prince' of legend and song, a figurehead of a distinct national, cultural identity rather than of a territorial state. It is to this end that Charlie must disappear from the stage of history as a man and reappear in cultural mythology.

The unresolved tension around which the film falters is thus the same one it foregrounds. The second half of the film follows Charlie's trajectory into myth at the same time as it portrays him at his most human. This abyss between man and myth occasionally rises to nearly sublime heights of incongruity – the prince makes his dramatic escape by sea while disguised in a woman's dress and bonnet to a solemn choral rendition of 'The Skye Boat Song'. What must be distinguished here is the difference between identification with a hero and identification with a protagonist. While the hero of the film may be Charlie, the protagonist of the story is Scotland itself. The structure of the film confuses and conflates the two. What *Bonnie Prince Charlie* demands is thus an impossible direct identification with a legend. What this awkward double-bind brings into focus is the dynamic by which identification operates in a two-stage process. It is the formal quality of the idea-of-Charlie that allows the spectator to sing songs of 'Somebody' in solidarity with the Scotland of Flora, Donald and Jamie. It is Charlie qua 'spark of liberty' rather than the man himself who serves as the support of our empathy with the hopes and ambitions of the secondary characters (Lacan 1978: 267–68).

It may have been observed of *Bonnie Prince Charlie* that it works to make its 'Somebody' into a perfect nobody. On the contrary, the ostensible hero suffers a fate far worse. The physical manifestation of a Scottish Everybody is revealed to be not much more and not much different from anybody at all. The same qualities that perpetuate the Charlie of song and myth are precisely the ones that obstruct his cinematic cohesion into a sympathetic man of flesh and bone. One cannot occupy the roles of myth and mortal at the same time. No figure caught skulking as a spinning woman can command the charismatic fascination demanded of an 'Instrument of History'. Neither can a figure portrayed directly as the 'Embodiment of History' command the empathy and identification required of a true protagonist.

Alex F Brown

References

Badiou, Alain (2007) *The Century*, Cambridge/Malden: Polity.
Lacan, Jacques (1978) *The Four Fundamental Concepts of Psychoanalysis*, New York/London: WW Norton.
Melton, J Gordon (1985) 'Spiritualization and Reaffirmation: What Really Happens When Prophecy Fails', *American Studies*, 26: 2, pp. 17–29.

Brave

Country of Origin:

USA

Language:

English

Studio/Production Companies:

Walt Disney Pictures
Pixar Animation Studios

Directors:

Mark Andrews
Brenda Chapman
Steve Purcell

Synopsis

Set in a fantasy, medieval Highland realm, *Brave* is the story of Princess Merida, daughter of one-legged King Fergus (who lost the appendage in battle with the dreaded monster-bear, Mordu) and Queen Elinor. Much to her mother's disapproval, Merida's spirit is as free-flowing as her fire-red hair, but her horseback-riding and bow-and-arrow-shooting days are threatened when her politically mandated betrothal to one of the clan chieftain's sons looms. Rejecting all of the clans' potential suitors draws the ire of her mother, who wants her to conform to tradition. Merida flees to the forest to seek the aid of a witch, who gives her an enchanted tart that will 'change' her mother's mind, and her fate. When Merida tricks Elinor into eating the tart, the queen is transformed into a bear. Instantly regretting this choice, Merida must face its consequences. Mother and daughter embark on an imperiled

Producer:
Katherine Sarafian
Screenwriters:
Mark Andrews
Brenda Chapman
Irene Mecchi
Steve Purcell
Michael Arndt
Cinematographers:
Robert Anderson
Danielle Feinberg
Art Director:
Steve Pilcher
Composer:
Patrick Doyle
Editor:
Nicholas C Smith
Duration:
93 minutes
Genre:
Animation
Cast:
Kelly Macdonald
Billy Connolly
Emma Thompson
Julie Walters
Robbie Coltrane
Kevin McKidd
Craig Ferguson
Year:
2012
Filming Location:
Pixar Animation Studios
Award:
2013 Academy Award for Best Animated Feature
Box Office:
Worldwide US $535 million

quest to break the spell and heal their fractured relationship lest the transformation become permanent.

Critique

Director Mark Andrews's animated feature debut, *Brave*, proved to be one of the biggest hits with audiences and critics in 2012. The film grossed over $235 million in the United States and over $535 million worldwide, which continued Disney/Pixar's nearly two-decade streak of commercially successful animated features. *Brave* also won the Academy Award for Best Animated Feature in February 2013 (with Andrews sporting a kilt at the ceremony). The film is based on a story by Brenda Chapman and it took nearly six years to make, with Andrews replacing Chapman as principal director four years into the project. Andrews, a product of Pixar, has worked in a variety of capacities on several major animated films and television shows, including as the director of the Oscar-nominated short film, *One Man Band* (2006). He is joined by several Scottish and Scots American actors and musicians who lend their talents to the film, most notably Kelly Macdonald, Billy Connolly, Craig Ferguson and Kevin McKidd. With *Brave*, Andrews, Chapman, additional co-director Steve Purcell and co-screenwriter Irene Mecchi continue the evolution of the Disney princess within a fairy-tale Scotland.

Brave's Princess Merida is the latest in a long line of Disney princesses, and she continues Disney's revision of those princesses that began in the 1990s. The first generation of Disney princesses (Snow White, Cinderella and Sleeping Beauty among them) were notable for their beautiful singing voices and a proclivity to hope that 'someday my prince will come'. These princesses exhibited relatively little agency, and, in the cases of Snow White and Sleeping Beauty, were often comatose until the prince was able to save the day. In the early 1990s, princesses such as Ariel (*The Little Mermaid* [Ron Clements and John Musker, 1989]), Belle (*Beauty and the Beast* [Gary Trousdale and Kirk Wise, 1991]) and Jasmine (*Aladdin* [Ron Clements and John Musker, 1992]) were given more agency. These princesses were headstrong, active at times and even rebellious against the patriarchal order and authorities that held them in check, but, ultimately, they too searched for their princes to save the day and to live happily ever after. Merida is unique for a Disney princess in that her journey is one of reconciliation with her mother, and the love story of the film is between a mother and a daughter. The clans' potential mates for Merida are silly and incompetent, and Merida is intelligent enough to know that she is better off single, at least for now. Merida also pushes the independent character of the 1990s Disney princesses further. She is shown to be a better archer, rider, swordswoman and more intelligent than any of her potential suitors, yet she still remains coded as a feminine figure with her flowing locks and gowns.

The ending of the film is central to the continued revision of the Disney princess. *Brave* does not end with a new romantic coupling, but the reconstitution of an established, nuclear, royal family, with the question of succession seemingly put off for several more years. Because of Merida's actions, the clans have loosened their traditions somewhat in order to allow the young people to decide their marital futures. Everyone goes home happy due to Merida's semi-feminist reforms (the lads feel relief from the impending obligations of husband-hood, too). Merida lives happily ever after because she and her mother have repaired the split in the family – not because a prince saves the day. The youth are granted greater agency, yet the kingdom and the clans are fundamentally preserved.

A fairy-tale Scottish Highlands is the exotic yet familiar setting for this revision of the Disney princess. Part of this familiarity is due to the tropes of Tartanry that Disney and Hollywood have utilized before. In such films as *Brigadoon* (Vincente Minnelli, 1954), *Rob Roy: The Highland Rogue* (Harold French, 1953) and in *Braveheart* (Mel Gibson, 1995) as well, Scotland, and the Highlands in particular, are again portrayed as a place of magic, wonder and mythic timelessness. Producer Arthur Freed famously argued that Scotland did not look 'Scottish' enough, so it was built on a Hollywood soundstage for the production of *Brigadoon*. Seemingly the same problem has been solved by the animation studios of Pixar, and the result is a digital construction of a Hollywood Scotland. Like the Middle East in *Aladdin* and even North America circa 1607 in *Pocahontas* (Mike Gabriel and Mark Goldberg, 1995), the Scottish Highlands contain a cultural cache, at least for many US audiences, that evokes romance and mystery; the film's expressive lighting and computer-generated settings and effects underscore those feelings.

Brave employs a pastiche of gorgeously animated Scottish cultural artefacts, legends and other commonly used fairy-tale conventions in order to construct its mythic Scotland. In the DVD director commentary, Andrews states that much of the crew embarked on a research trip to Scotland, and they were impressed with the variety of local dialects, landscapes and cultures they encountered. In many respects, *Brave* reflects the directors' efforts to cram as many of their favourite aspects of a tourists' Scotland, its popular culture and its myths as they can into the film. Some of these include representations of Highland Games, bagpipes, standing stones, songs sung in Gaelic, a sinister-looking broch castle, will-o'-the-wisps and a variety of colourful characters (or caricatures based on a variety of Scottish stereotypes). Like most Disney/Pixar animated films, *Brave* is not overly concerned with cultural or historical accuracy.

Brave's chief objectives appear to be the reconciliation of certain feminist ideals of female empowerment with more conservative family values, along with a kind of 'full-blown celebration of myth, fantasy and overt display' Duncan Petrie describes in reference to many films that depict the Jacobite era (Petrie 2000: 70). In order to accomplish this, the film draws on stereotypes of Scottish independent-mindedness and a mythologized version of its medieval and clan histories. Those elements create a patriarchal order enforced by both the royal and clan structures. Merida's strong-headed rebellion against those structures is justified throughout the film, yet *Brave* argues compromises must be made and that the family unit, ultimately, must remain intact. While

Merida represents another step forward for the Disney princesses in 2012, the patriarchal structures in Disney films that limited Snow White to hope that her prince will come are preserved, if in a slightly reformed state.

Zach Finch

References

Box Office Mojo (2013) 'Brave', http://boxofficemojo.com/movies/?id=bearandthebow.htm. Accessed 1 April 2013.

Petrie, Duncan (2000) *Screening Scotland*, London: BFI.

Braveheart

Country of Origin:
USA

Languages:
English
French
Latin
Scottish Gaelic

Studio/Production Companies:
Icon Productions
The Ladd Company

Director:
Mel Gibson

Producers:
Mel Gibson
Alan Ladd, Jr
Bruce Davey
Stephen McEveety

Screenwriter:
Randall Wallace

Cinematographer:
John Toll

Art Directors:
Ken Court
Nathan Crowley
Daniel T Dorrance
John Lucas
Ned McLoughlin

Composer:
James Horner

Editor:
Steven Rosenblum

Synopsis

In the late thirteenth century, a young Scot named William Wallace witnesses the treachery and brutality of conquering English monarch, Edward I, when the King – having promised a truce – slays the inhabitants of a Scottish village and, shortly after, Wallace's family. Years later, having travelled to Europe and received an education, Wallace returns home to marry his childhood love, only to witness her assault, and then execution, by a group of English soldiers. Turning the village against her killers, Wallace sends a message to the King: Scotland is a free and independent country and shall be subjected to English rule no more. War between the two nations ensues and, eventually, Wallace is captured, but not before achieving vital military victories and setting in motion the claim of Scotland's right to independence.

Critique

Throughout his cinematic career, Mel Gibson has shown a notable interest in stories relating to oppression and rebellion. From *The Patriot* (2000) to *We Were Soldiers* (2002) and even his Biblical epic, *The Passion of The Christ* (2004), his work both as actor and director has suggested a significant attraction to those moments in history where the outcome could not be foreseen – where the ruling order was unexpectedly overturned. Yet no project illustrates this enthusiasm more clearly than his second directorial outing, *Braveheart*.

Assuming the film's lead role in addition to his duties behind camera, Gibson takes on the mantle of Scottish folk hero, William Wallace. Scripted by the warrior's namesake, Randall Wallace, the narrative has been criticized many times for a lack of historical accuracy, with complaints varying from details such as the costuming, to the title of the film itself – the 'brave heart' of Scottish lore being a title traditionally assigned to Robert the Bruce. Some of the changes are more provocative than others: the implication that Wallace may have fathered an heir (the future King Edward III) through an affair with Prince Edward's wife perhaps being the most spurious, not least because Princess Isabella would only have been an infant at the time. With some critics, such as Colin

Duration:

177 minutes

Genre:

Historical Romance

Cast:

Mel Gibson
Sophie Marceau
Patrick McGoohan
Angus Macfadyen
Brendan Gleeson
Catherine McCormack

Year:

1995

Filming Locations:

Aonach Eagach, Scotland, UK
Ardmore Studios, Ireland
Ballymore Eustace, Ireland
Bective Abbey, Ireland
Coronation Plantation, Ireland
Dunsany Castle, Ireland
Dunsoghly Castle, Ireland
Fort William, Scotland, UK
Glen Nevis, Scotland, UK
King John's Castle, Ireland
Loch Leven, Scotland, UK
Luggala Estate, Ireland
Sally's Gap, Ireland
St Margarets, Ireland
The Curragh, Ireland
Trim Castle, Ireland

McArthur (2003), identifying the film as a 'distortion', there is ground to suggest that *Braveheart* could readily be, and even has been, appropriated for the purposes of nationalistic propaganda. However, with Randall Wallace citing the embellished oral histories of poet Blind Harry as a major influence, and Gibson defending his choices as being more cinematically compelling, what matters most, at least as this reviewer sees it, is whether *Braveheart* succeeds as art.

With one of its earliest scenes depicting the corpses of Scots (including children) that have been hanged by King Edward's men, the film does not take long to establish the villains of its story. Although it is doubtful that any trustworthy historical record would portray the English ruler – often called The Hammer of The Scots – as anything resembling a sympathetic character, *Braveheart* is keen to ensure that the mistake will not be made in the case of this film. The monarch portrayed in the film is nothing short of a power-hungry sociopath – a mad man who is willing to order arrows fired upon his own men during battle, so long as Scots will be hit as well. With almost all of the Englishmen we see (save for the weak and ineffectual Prince Edward) being the King's loyal soldiers, it is hard to get a sense of them either as anything but villainous, especially when contrasted against the jovial scenes that introduce the Scottish leads. Yet, although some critics have claimed this is anglophobia, a reasonable suggestion is made in the film that personal gain – not nationality – spurs the plot's more despicable acts, with many Scottish noblemen choosing to betray their countrymen when the price is right.

Where *Braveheart* observes full equality, however, is in its depiction of violence. Whilst it is true we witness instances of Scottish japery even on the battlefield, such as the well-known mooning scene, these are soon cut short by the ferocity of the film's depiction of medieval warfare – one unfortunate Scotsman even taking an arrow before he can lower his kilt. Indeed, though much is made of Wallace's eye for military tactics, when physical conflict begins the film's battle scenes are kinetically fierce, and unrelentingly bloody. Sometimes the Scottish dominate, such as at the Battle of Stirling, while sometimes the English do. Where the key difference lies is in how each army responds to the bloodshed; the Scots seem to use injury as a motivational fuel, but the English find themselves wounded in pride as well as body.

Keeping the direction restrained (at least in comparison with other cinematic blockbusters), the film manages to maintain a feeling of intimacy not often found in the genre and, as the narrative reaches its conclusion, it is hard not to feel moved. With Wallace's execution being not only one of the most brutal scenes, but also one of the most accurate, his refusal to admit treachery, even in the midst of horrific torture, is poignant and his final cry of 'freedom' genuinely rousing. It is not surprising that, given its emotional power, *Braveheart* not only received a multitude of awards, but also provoked a renewed interest in Scottish history, both at home and abroad. Some cultural commentators have even suggested that this wave of enthusiasm may have been instrumental in mobilizing public support for the formation of Scotland's first parliament in 300 years, and, insofar as this is the case, the film may have helped change the political landscape of an entire nation. Wallace drove Scotland toward independence in the past and now, 700 years on, it is possible that he may do so again.

Patrick Harley

Reference

McArthur, Colin (2003) *Brigadoon, Braveheart and the Scots: Distortions of Scotland in Hollywood Cinema*, London: IB Tauris.

Breaking the Waves

Countries of Origin:

Denmark
Scotland

Language:

English

Studio/Production Company:

Zentropa Entertainments

Director:

Lars von Trier

Producers:

Vibeke Windeløv
Peter Aalbæk Jensen
Lars Jönsson

Screenwriters:

Lars von Trier
Peter Assmussen

Cinematographer:

Robby Müller

Art Director:

Karl Juliusson

Editor:

Anders Refn

Duration:

153 minutes

Genre:

Romance
Fantasy
Social/Psychological Drama

Synopsis

Set on the Isle of Skye in the 1970s, the pretty, young and innocent Bess McNeill lives in a small, patriarchically strict and religiously puritanical community. Simple, childlike and naive, Bess possesses a strong faith in her ability to communicate directly with God, who indeed answers Bess, using her voice. Against the reservations of her religious community she marries the older and more experienced oil rig worker Jan. At first sharing a happy and passionate marriage together, Bess becomes desperate about the frequent absences of her beloved who has to leave the village regularly due to nature of his work. Struggling with her feelings of loneliness and non-compliance versus prevailing social norms, Bess prays to God that Jan should come back. Jan does return home, yet as paralysed, after a tragic work accident. Realizing that he will never be able to maintain normal conjugal relations with Bess again, Jan asks her to take on lovers. Bess reacts hysterically, but Jan persuades her to save their relationship by telling him about these sexual adventures as if the two of them were sexually intimate. Feeling guilty, she agrees, believing these acts must be God's will. Bess's obsession with doing everything possible to save Jan drives her to her humiliating fate. Due to her inappropriate behaviour she is banned from her religious community. As Jan's health worsens, Bess makes a last attempt to save him through further sexual promiscuity. On a freighter, she is tortured, raped and finally dies in hospital. Jan recovers almost completely afterwards. While marked as a sinner and unable to obtain a proper funeral, Jan steals Bess's body and buries her at sea. The next morning huge church bells play in the sky right above the oil rig.

Critique

Together with the later *Idioterne/The Idiots* (1998) and *Dancer in the Dark* (2000), *Breaking the Waves* is part of Lars von Trier's so-called 'Golden Heart Trilogy'. Although set in slightly different contexts, all three films share the masochistic motif of female sacrifice for love while questioning conventional understandings of moral goodness. Based on two literary sources – the novel *Justine* by the Marquis de Sade (b.1740–d.1814) and a Danish children's

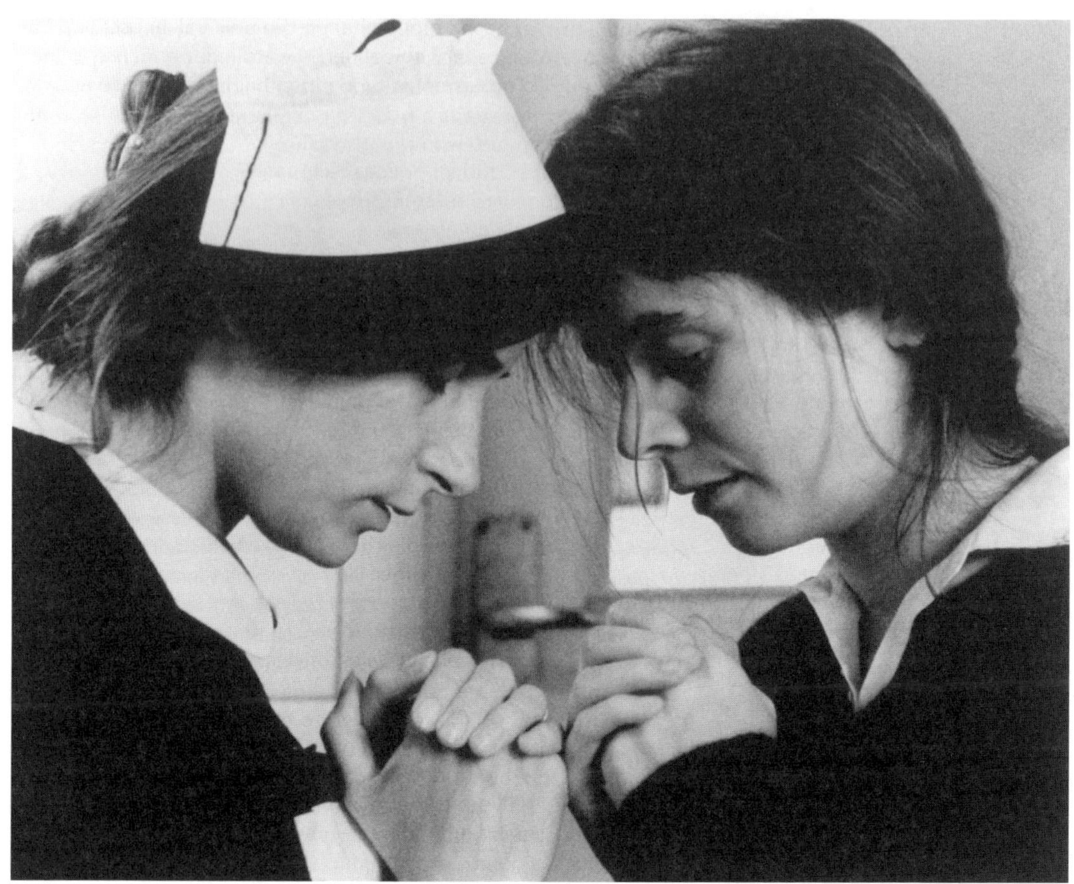

Breaking the Waves (1996), British Film Institute Collection

Social Art Cinema

Cast:

Emily Watson
Stellan Skarsgård
Katrin Cartlidge

Year:

1996

Filming Locations:

Isle of Skye, Scotland, UK
Mallaig, Scotland, UK
Lochailort, Scotland, UK
Copenhagen, Denmark
Lyngby, Denmark
Hellerup, Denmark
Det Danske Filmstudie,

picture book named *Guld Hjerte* – *Breaking the Waves* plays with tensions between religion, sexuality and obsession, bizarrely juxtaposing these themes on narrative and stylistic levels.

Von Trier's philosophical and aesthetic interest in religious themes as well as the dramatic and stylistic mode of the film are highly influenced by the work of the earlier Danish director Carl Theodor Dreyer (b.1889–d.1968), especially by his *La Passion de Jeanne d'Arc/The Passion of Joan of Arc* (1928) and *Ordet/The Word* (1955). *Breaking the Waves* negotiates among different belief systems – the church as a form of institutionalized religion, the law, medical science, feminism – and contrary concepts of virtue. While it is not allowed for women to talk inside the church, Bess creates her own space inside as well as beyond the church, speaking to God herself and translating the church's values through her own intuitive faith in love. She struggles between her community's ethics and her changed understanding of what is good and right derived

Denmark

Award:

European Film Award for Best Film 1996

from her marriage to, and her love for, Jan. Her understanding and practice of goodness is redefined such that it is incompatible with the patriarchal community that uses religion as power over women. Bess represents a feminist perspective in opposition to the male, misogynist elders but, at the same time, accepts what she understands as dictates from God without question.

Counterintuitive to this melodramatic and sentimental story of miracles and the supernatural, the film's aesthetic style is primarily naturalistic in tone, similar to von Trier's former work about ghosts in a hospital in the Danish television series *Riget/The Kingdom* (1994). A constant panning and shaky handheld camera, the use of natural lights and a harsh editing style with disorienting jump cuts give *Breaking the Waves* a documentary feeling. In order to underscore this quality, the film was transferred to video and then digitally edited to produce a washed out, dissolving and granulated image before being transferred back to film. In this regard, *Breaking the Waves* became an inspiration for the later well-received avant-garde film-making movement 'Dogme95', initiated by von Trier, together with the other Danish directors Thomas Vinterberg, Søren Kragh-Jacobsen and Kristian Levring.

Shot on location, the rugged and bleak Scottish landscape becomes a crucial element in von Trier's film. Waves crash upon the shore at the same time that Bess is howling and acting hysterically. The harsh, changeable Scottish weather, with frequent heavy rainfalls and biting winds, corresponds to the mood of the story. The Scottish Hebrides offers a romantic and beautiful *mise-en-scène*, yet the film de-emphasizes this setting with the inclusion of just a few static and fixed long shots. Against the expectation of a picturesque landscape, sparse and claustrophobic indoor scenes dominate the film. This becomes even more powerful through von Trier's directorial approach, emphasizing the actor's ability to improvise in movement, intonation and expression – most notably so in the self-reflexive gesture involving Bess looking directly at the camera and breaking the fourth wall.

Natural landscape shows up most prominently in eight computer-generated panoramas, created by Danish artist Per Kirkeby. These moving picture-postcard interludes, illuminated by artificial light sources and underscored by 1970s rock music, serve as title plates to the seven chapters and the epilogue of the film, introducing the content of each subsequent chapter. Old-fashioned like a picture-book fable or a classical English novel, their aesthetic style is visually sensual and colourful, in contrast with that of the narrative in general. Except for the ringing bells at the end, these sequences provide the only locus of music in the film, giving them greater impact as a result. Struggles between different belief systems within the narrative are echoed via stylistic contrasts. Leaving interpretations about the motivation, sincerity or irony of the film's religious subject wide open, critics embraced *Breaking the Waves* as a masterpiece, and the film has become a huge critical as well as a healthy economic success.

Stefan Udelhofen

Brigadoon

Country of Origin:
USA
Language:
English
Studio/Production Company:
Metro-Goldwyn-Mayer
Director:
Vincente Minnelli
Producer:
Arthur Freed

Synopsis

Two men from New York become lost in the highlands of Scotland while hunting. Upon the clearing of the mists they discover a town in the midst of preparations for a wedding celebration. Cynic Jeff Douglas and dreamer Tommy Albright realize that the idiosyncrasies of the town are more than quaint and isolated peasant life. They learn of the 'miracle' of Brigadoon which dislocated the town in time such that one century passes outside for every night within. The only condition is that should anyone ever leave the whole town would vanish forever. Jeff becomes increasingly incredulous throughout the town's preparations for the evening's marriage ceremony while Tommy becomes enchanted with both Brigadoon and the bride's elder sister Fiona Campbell. A jealous rival of the groom declares that he will destroy the miracle for all by leaving the town, resulting

Brigadoon (1954), British Film Institute Collection

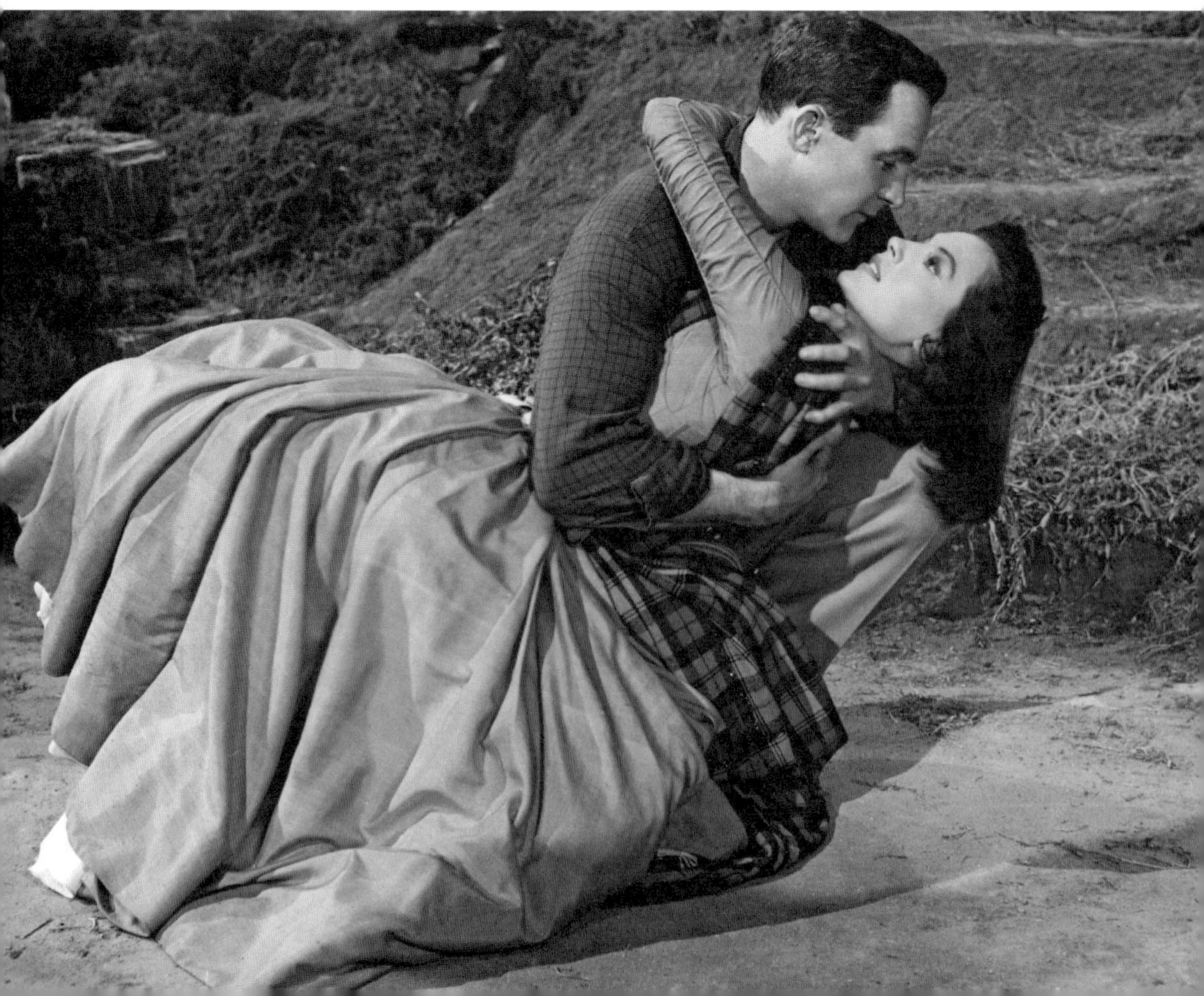

Screenwriters:

Arthur Jay Lerner, from the musical by Arthur Jay Lerner (book and lyrics)
Frederick Loewe (music)

Cinematographer:

Joseph Ruttenberg

Art Directors:

Cedric Gibbons
Preston Ames

Choreographer:

Gene Kelly

Composers:

Conrad Salinger
Frederic Loewe
Alan Jay Lerner

Editor:

Albert Askt

Duration:

108 minutes

Genre:

Musical
Romance
Fantasy

Cast:

Gene Kelly
Van Johnson
Cyd Charise

Year:

1954

Filming Location:

Metro-Goldwyn-Mayer Studios, Culver City, California, USA

in a chase which ends in the death of the young man. The two Americans leave the town as night falls. Tommy finds his normal life in New York increasingly dissatisfying and returns to Scotland to find the bridge to Brigadoon once again open to him because of the power of his love.

Critique

Brigadoon may be categorized as a standard Hollywood musical-romance developed from a tested Broadway success but the film moves far beyond a simple adaptation of the stage musical for a cinematic production. The film utilizes nearly every technique at its disposal in its project of creating its thoroughly cohesive and autonomous cinematic world. Carefully interwoven aspects of song, dance, score, set design and camera movement actively participate in the total schema of the film's creation, a *Gesamptkunstwerk* or 'total artwork' in the sense of a wholly integrated fusion of the literary, plastic and performing arts. In many sequences dance is as important to narrative exposition as dialogue, colour design is as important as on-screen action and music is as important as plot or character. Abstract and impersonal aspects of film-making take on considerably more dynamic and participatory roles in the progression of the story than typical of the genre. Formal qualities of the film itself merge to the point of indistinction with those of the narrative content.

The story itself has been criticized for exploiting stereotypes of a quaint and exotic Scotland towards the ends of forcing a standard romantic production-of-the-couple storyline; a world-weary modern American has his eyes opened to pure and innocent love by a naive and beautiful woman from an idyllic pastoral Scottish community. The presumption that an isolated mountain village gives privileged access to a more direct and authentic way of life can be seen as an opportunistic fantasy sustainable only from a position of superiority. While this position is an understandable criticism, it fails to pay adequate attention to the varied ways in which the fictional town of Brigadoon is self-consciously constructed by the film as a 'dream' or 'fairy tale'. Brigadoon, in its own cinematic lens, is already presented as caught up in the problematics of fantasy opposed to reality, of tangible material experience opposed to its ideal spectral supplement. The question *Brigadoon* is framing is the quintessentially cinematic one of the nature and status of a 'world' such that it is 'belief' that necessarily constitutes it.

What emerges in the opposition of Jeff/Tommy is the antagonism between the cynical-realist and the optimist-idealist worldview. Jeff discounts and dismisses anything that he cannot understand and consequently 'touch, taste, hear, see, smell and swallow'. Tommy, on the other hand, holds reservations about such determinate judgments and even wistfully ponders (prior to his encounter with Fiona) whether anyone is capable of loving anymore. While Jeff must mask his disbelief in irony and sarcasm, Tommy suspends his disbelief with the happy result of a romantic interlude with Fiona. By the time the film reveals the details of the Brigadoon 'miracle' at roughly the middle of the film, Tommy and Jeff have already taken diametrical stances as to whatever explanation may be offered. Jeff dismisses Brigadoon as 'dream stuff [...] all made up out of broomsticks and wishing wells' while Tommy has begun to imagine a future for himself in the town. The film plays on the tension between a series of dualities raised by the experiential reality of an unreal place – the oppositions between dream and reality, belief and explanation, faith and perception and fundamentally, idea and world.

The most dramatic example of this last conflict erupts during the climactic scene of the hunt for Harry Beaton, the young man who resents being trapped and who declares the end of Brigadoon by announcing his intention to break its enchantment by leaving. What this remarkable sequence enacts is the necessary intolerance by any world for whatever element which would violate the rules of its existence. The logic not just of Brigadoon but of meaning in the most general sense demands that Harry be stopped – what allows for the consistency of Brigadoon's world qua world is its exclusion of any explicit denial of the idea of Brigadoon. While Jeff's sarcasm can be shrugged off as harmless and reasonable doubt, Harry's equation of the town's boundaries with the dimensions of a prison must be treated as an existential threat due to the fact that Harry acts as an element of Brigadoon itself. Until this point it may be possible to view Brigadoon as merely a dream vision or fantasy world, but Tommy's participation in the manhunt makes this world real in a deeper sense – far from simply believing in Brigadoon, he acts on behalf of the town because of his belief in it. The passage from belief as proposition to belief in belief itself as engaged commitment always depends upon some such reflexive material supplement (*Žižek* 2006: 353–54).

To view Harry's death as a necessary blood sacrifice serves to further explain an otherwise incongruous detail. When the wedding party turns to manhunt, many shirts inexplicably vanish in the space of a match cut. Dancing wedding guests suddenly become half-dressed hunters. The significance of bare-chested men becomes clear with an understanding of the gleeful brutality and primordial lust of the moment. On the one hand there is no plausible reason for anyone to remove their shirt, but on the other the affective response to Harry's becoming inimical is an equal and instantaneous becoming barbarous. Brigadoon requires the elimination of Harry not only for its continued existence but also for Tommy's inclusion in it. The closure of worlds demands exactly such symbolic exchanges. The cost of belief is always of some type of irrevocable investment. At the end of the sequence, Tommy and Fiona meet and express passionate relief at the salvation of Fiona's 'whole world'. The tension of the scene lies in the distinction that for Tommy this world is the town Brigadoon, feared lost to Harry's revocation of the enchantment. For Fiona the world is feared lost for the reason that Tommy had left it. The insider who doubts has been replaced by the outsider who really believes. Brigadoon endures to the same extent that Tommy becomes a world. No longer New York or Scotland but a bastard third term that simultaneously comprises both and neither, Brigadoon marks a world as disjunction. Not without parentage but neither in possession of legitimate pedigree, Brigadoon thus constituted renders sensible the concept of another world (Deleuze 1990: 111).

Minnelli's accomplishment in *Brigadoon* is to bring to the cinematic form a singular work which provides a dramatic formulation of the procedure so central to the modern cinematic project: the creation of other possible worlds. The enduring value of the film is its enactment of precisely what is 'other' about another world at the same time as its demonstration of the material force of possibility. Neither absolutely counterfactual nor simply different, entirely latent nor precisely manifest, the titular world is accessible only on the condition of authentic divergence. Jeff lives a full day in the town and lives it as no more than a dreamt reality while Tommy returns to New York and finds that Brigadoon persists in erupting and overwhelming lived reality. The official motto of the film should thus be inverted. It is not the case that 'love makes anything possible' so much as that the possible as such is structured much like love – inherent within this world yet opening onto another.

Alex F Brown

References

Deleuze, Gilles (1990) *The Logic of Sense*, New York: Columbia University Press.

Žižek, Slavoj (2006) *The Parallax View*, Cambridge/London: MIT Press.

The Brothers

Country of Origin:
UK

Language:
English

Studio/Production Company:
Sydney Box Productions

Director:
David MacDonald

Producer:
Sydney Box

Screenwriters:
Muriel Box
Sydney Box
Paul Vincent Carroll
David MacDonald

Cinematographer:
Stephen Dade

Art Director:
George Provis

Synopsis

Mary Lawson is a young, Scottish orphan consigned to serve the Macrae family on the remote Isle of Skye. As time progresses, she finds herself positioned at the centre of a bitter rivalry between the Macraes and the MacFarishes. Her service to the Macraes is troubled when she is caught seeing Willy, one of the MacFarish boys. External conflict with the MacFarishes adds to an increasing internal conflict between the two Macrae boys, John and Fergus, as John fails in his attempt to court Mary while she falls in love with Fergus. As a result of a physically demanding competition between the Macraes and the MacFarishes, Hector Macrae, father to the brothers and head of the family, dies of heart problems and leaves charge of the family and farm to John, the older brother. John, after giving Mary an ultimatum – which she refuses – conspires to murder her out on a boat in the fog. But, on the morning of the planned murder, he manipulates Fergus's gullibility and convinces his younger brother to do the deed. Fergus kills Mary, but then kills himself as well out of shame for what he has done. After a few days, the men of the village come looking for Mary and Fergus, and they end up executing John after it is revealed that he planned the two lovers' deaths.

Critique

In the chilling last scene of *The Brothers* during which the men interrogate John as to the location of Mary and Fergus, John asks

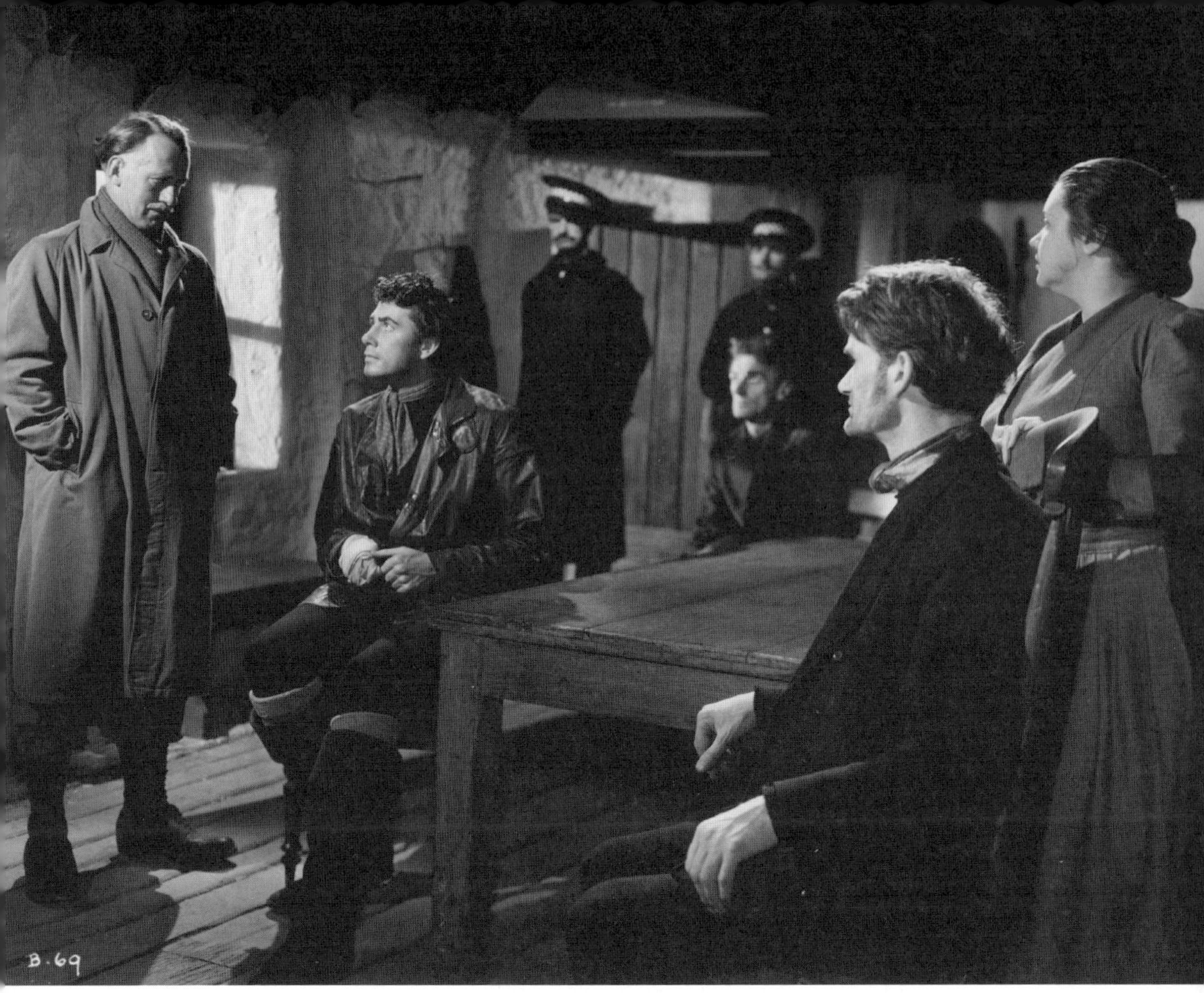

The Brothers (1947), British Film Institute Collection

Composer:

Cedric Thorpe Davis

Editor:

Vladimir Sagovsky

Duration:

98 minutes

Genre:

Romance
Melodrama
Social/Psychological Drama

Cast:

Patricia Roc
Duncan Macrae
Maxwell Reed

Year:

1947

them the paradigmatically bad question 'Am I my brother's keeper?' As we should well know from Genesis 4:9, it would seem that there is no way to ask this question and avoid trouble. But the beautiful thing about that question is that we know very well what the correct answer is, but the meaning of the question nevertheless remains elusive. Clearly, judging by the fates of Cain and John, the answer is 'yes', but the question becomes nebulous when we ask: what of Mary? Is John Mary's keeper also? Just who exactly is 'my brother' in this situation? And what does it mean to be 'my brother's keeper'?

This Old Testament question seems to foreshadow the New Testament where the question will be formulated in a different way. If we look to Matthew 22:39 we encounter the admonition that 'you shall love your neighbour as yourself', which means the question changes into 'who is my neighbour?' This exact question is the inspiration for a book by the Danish philosopher Søren Kierkegaard entitled *Works of Love* (2009 [1847]), and his reflections on the topic will illuminate our understanding of *The Brothers*. More precisely, Kierkegaard's reflection allows us to reflect on some of the more

Filming Locations:

Gaumont-British Studios, Lime Grove, Shepherd's Bush, London, UK
Isle of Skye, The Highlands, Scotland, UK

interesting moral situations presented in the film. We will discuss two points: first, the distinction between love of family and romantic love as well as the related problem of conflict in devotion between these two objects of love, along with, second, how this distinction and conflict reflects on the love shared between Fergus and Mary. In doing this, we arrive at a Kierkegaardian answer to the question 'am I my brother's keeper?' and we show how erotic love can become corrupt.

Turning our attention to point one, we could first look at the tragedy of the film, the murdering of Mary by Fergus, as being caused by the conflict between romantic love and familial love, in that John and Fergus are pushed to extreme behaviours due to the pressure coming from both the memory of their deceased father and their loves for Mary. This conflict of passions becomes a moral conflict when we ask: to whom are Fergus and John more devoted, their father or Mary; to their family, or to the object of their romantic passion and desire? The film foregrounds the theme of family as we watch the island clans feud in the name of familial tradition and ancestral glorification. But *The Brothers* questions the boundary between loved ones 'inside' and 'outside' of 'the family'. Mary works, eats and sleeps with the family, as a kind of de facto family member, but is at the same time only tenuously included 'within the family', while her uncertain status, neither clearly 'inside' nor 'outside' remains a persistent problem for 'the family' over the course of virtually the entire duration of the film.

Yet, does the lack of blood relation really matter – and should it? If one loved another, like they loved a blood relative, does such a distinction persist as a significantly meaningful one? Kierkegaard would agree that the distinction is still meaningful, yet he would also suggest that it may be transcended. In his work, Kierkegaard distinguishes between love that is tied to the eternal versus love that is not tied to the eternal – otherwise distinguished as Christian love versus erotic love, or agape versus eros. The eternal is what defines Christian love by tying loving passion to God's grand command 'you *shall* love your neighbour'. This kind of command-centred love, due to its universal application to all people, makes no temporal, or worldly, distinctions between people. 'It allows all distinctions to stand, but it teaches the equality of the eternal. It teaches that everyone shall lift himself above earthly distinctions' (Kierkegaard 2009 [1847]: 83).

This is how a love that is inspired by and tied to the eternal would understand worldly distinctions, like who is and who is not family. But, it would not be limited to these worldly distinctions because, regardless of distinctions that separate one person from another, the command still exists: 'you shall love'. John was able to deceive Fergus because he convinced him that Mary was essentially and inevitably other – and, as such, that she was a threat. In response Fergus acts not out of love to his family, but instead out of servitude. From a Kierkegaardian perspective, a commitment of love – one where love becomes a duty – cannot lead one to murder one who is other because this duty transcends the idea of a clear and steadfast distinction between same and other. 'One's neighbor is not the beloved, for whom you have passionate preference

[…] for with your neighbor you have before God the equality of humanity' (Kierkegaard 2009 [1847]: 72).

Thus, in response to John's question 'am I my brother's keeper?', we can say that eternal love makes it one's duty to be one's brother's keeper, and that in light of the eternal, distinctions between family and other become worldly and arbitrary. In this way, your brother becomes your neighbour and your neighbour is everyone. Such a reflection leads us to the interesting idea that John's punishment is not really an act of revenge by Willy and the other town-folk; it is instead a response from the eternal, as the village neighbours flood into John's house as a reminder of one's duty to all others. This is why the mob does not respond to him when he asks them his question because they are the answer; they represent the equality and universality of the eternal in that crimes committed against any one person (two in this case) become crimes committed against the whole.

Seeing now that Fergus's actions were not inspired by an eternal love, we can see how erotic love can become murderous. Kierkegaard suggests there are two kinds of love, and that erotic love can become murderous not by a confused predication but by its very nature as erotic love. What is missing from erotic love is an unchanging integrity, and because of that it can become any number of things, from hatred to jealousy to torment.

This becomes the case for Fergus, whose love is so spontaneous – to the point of arising from a moment of anger and turning into passionate love right on the beach—that it could just as well result in these other emotions (including hate) as it could love. Kierkegaard compares spontaneous love to a fermenting liquid that has yet to be changed by the eternal and separated from the poison brewing inside of it. If Fergus had acted according to love inspired by the eternal, then there would be no miasma from it to coax. But, evidenced by his murder of Mary, we see that Fergus was filled with a dangerous and volatile erotic love lacking in the integrity of the eternal.

The advantage to understanding the film in this way is that it portrays Fergus's motives as complex and his psyche as conflicted yet sincere. At first glance, he appears as a simple character with little motivation other than to obey orders and to seek fulfilment in response to an active sexual drive. That would be sufficient to explain Fergus if we assume that he didn't actually love Mary and that his feelings towards her had nothing to do with love. Instead, a Kierkegaardian reading presents him as a genuine character that loves in a volatile and dangerous way.

Nathaniel Taylor

Reference

Kierkegaard, Søren (2009 [1847]) *Works of Love* (trans. Howard and Edna Hong), New York: First Harper Perennial.

Culloden

Country of Origin:
UK
Languages:
English
Scottish Gaelic
Studio/Production Company:
BBC
Director:
Peter Watkins
Producer:
Peter Watkins
Screenwriter:
Peter Watkins
Cinematographer:
Dick Bush
Production Designers:
Anne Davey
Colin MacLeod
Brendon Woods
Editor:
Michael Bradsell
Duration:
69 minutes
Genre:
Simulated Documentary
Historical Fiction
Social Critique
Cast:
Olivier Espitalier-Noel
George McBean
Robert Oates
Year:
1964
Filming Location:
Inverness and Culloden Moor, Scotland, UK

Synopsis

Wednesday 16 April 1746: somehow, a modern television news crew is on hand to confront viewers with, in the words of *Culloden*'s opening credits, 'an account of one of the most mishandled and brutal battles ever fought in Britain'. Immediately before and after they engage in bloody combat, soldiers and commanders on both sides (Jacobite, Hanoverian) at the Battle of Culloden explain, through a series of talking head-style interviews, many of the social and political causes that sparked the last civil war ever fought on British soil as well as many of the logistical reasons why that conflict ended in such a resounding defeat for the Jacobite forces commanded by Prince Charles Edward Stuart (popularly known as Bonnie Prince Charlie). After documenting the one-sided carnage of the titular battle itself, *Culloden* proceeds to put on record what the film's unseen journalist-narrator terms 'the worst atrocities in the history of the British Army'. The murderous 'pacification' of the Scottish Highlands after the final routing of Prince Charles's troops is presented as an extended and deliberate act of state-sponsored genocide, in which English and Lowland Scottish societies 'destroyed a race of people' in the Scottish Gaeltacht (i.e. Gaelic-speaking region) in order to cement the free mercantile and imperialist unitary British political project and identity associated with the 1707 Act of Union between the English and Scottish parliaments.

Critique

Culloden is a film predicated upon two central, and quite deliberately engineered, paradoxes. First, writer/director Peter Watkins's celebrated 1964 docudrama mixes painstaking historical accuracy (at times, charting the Battle of Culloden's progress on a minute-by-minute basis) with glaring anachronism (the structuring conceit that TV cameras were present to record an event that unfolded some two centuries before the birth of television). Second, the film strives to turn its forensic anatomization of the grisly end of one historically and culturally specific military conflict into a less time-bound parable that underscores the futility and hypocrisy of all wars. The result is a work that systematically demythologizes one of the most deliriously romanticized events in the entire course of Scottish history. As well as being a formally and thematically accomplished work in its own right, *Culloden* acts as a suggestive counterpoint to the traditional conflation of Jacobitism and a noble, but historically and politically unsustainable, Scottish national identity per se, as is evident within mainstream commercial feature films such as *Bonnie Prince Charlie* (Anthony Kimmins, 1948), *Rob Roy* (Michael Caton-Jones, 1995), *Chasing the Deer* (Graham Holloway,1994), and innumerable small- and silver-screen adaptations of Robert Louis Stevenson's 1886 novel *Kidnapped*.

Culloden derives much of its impact as a coruscating corrective to the sentimentality of a great deal of popular Jacobite mythology and historiography from the unsparing detail in which the film charts the causes and course of the battle that lies at its heart. Granted, the movie's sympathies clearly lie with the ordinary Highlanders who associate (or, in most cases, who are forcibly associated by others) with the Jacobite cause. *Culloden*'s opening shot, for instance, is of Hanoverian troops marching towards camera, thus momentarily placing viewers in the unenviable position of Charles Edward Stuart's hungry, exhausted, ill-equipped and hopelessly outnumbered troops. But on the other hand, the film is also at pains to make clear the fact that the two sociopolitical systems represented on the battlefield at Culloden Moor were both predicated on principles of systematic and wholesale socio-economic inequality and exploitation. *Culloden*'s unseen narrator more than once describes the traditional Highland clan system as 'ruthless', a mode of social organization that reduced most of its adherents to the semi-human status of tradable chattels. He also emphasizes at various junctures the intrinsic social complexity and divisiveness of what was, essentially, a pan-British civil war, rather than a military conflict waged between England and Scotland.

Culloden (1964), British Film Institute Collection

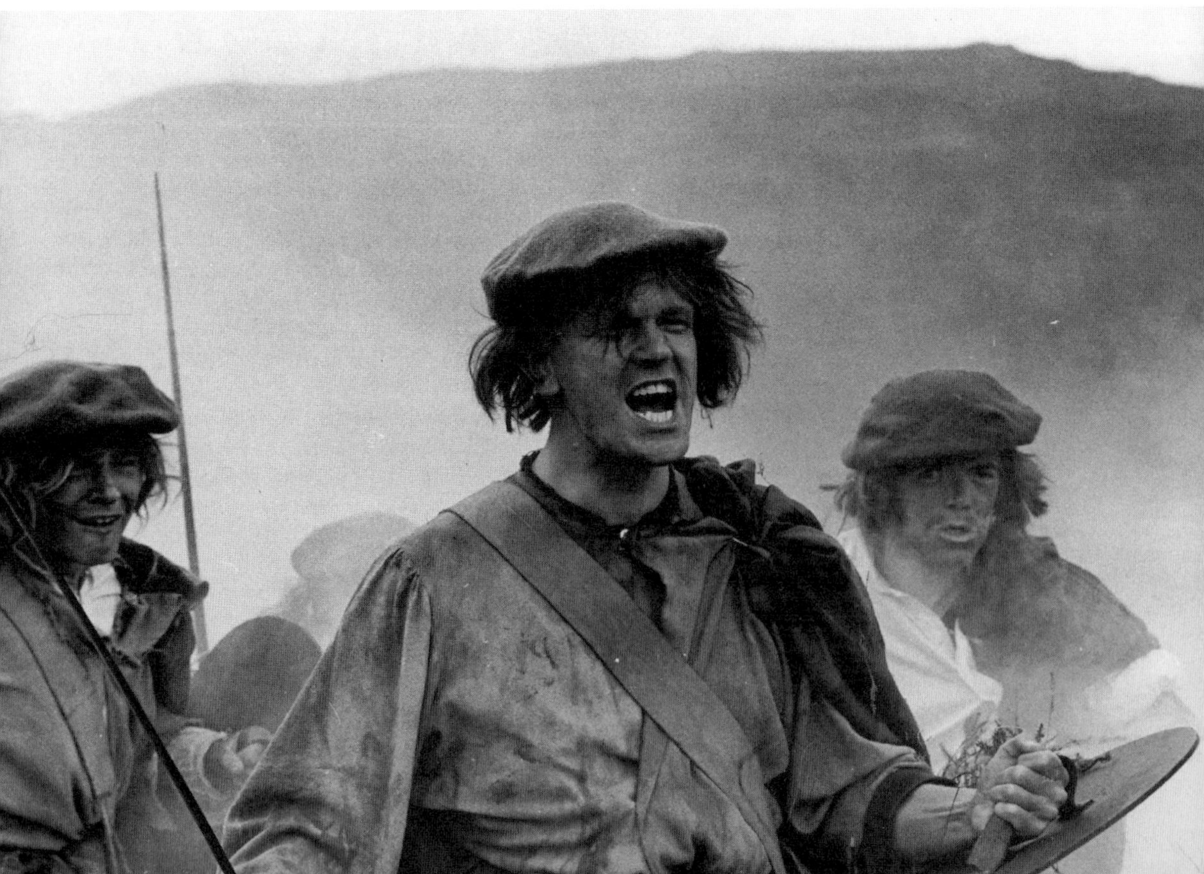

Despite the frequent popular cultural association of Highland Jacobitism with Scottish national identity, the narrator reminds his audience of the inconvenient historical truth that Prince Charles faced 'more Scots in arms against him than for him' when his troops made their last stand at Culloden.

Yet to present *Culloden* solely as a piece of passionate and precise historical revisionism would be to do the film a critical disservice. Nearly fifty years after it was made, and some 270 since the events that it depicts unfolded, Peter Watkins's work still possesses a remarkable degree of contemporary relevance and resonance. This is because *Culloden* frames itself as a movie about, to quote the World War I English poet Wilfred Owen, the pity of war per se, as well as that of one war in particular. It is, perhaps, no accident in this regard that the film's running time (69 minutes) exactly matches that of the blood-soaked battle which it records: viewers are thus confronted by the fact that thousands of human lives can be snuffed out in the time that it takes to watch a single television programme. Similarly pointed is the fact that the narrator's final, despairing words ('they have created a desert and called it peace') are drawn from the historian Tacitus's 98AD biography of Agricola. The latter was a Roman general who, like the Hanoverian commander the Duke of Cumberland in 1746, prosecuted a brutal campaign of colonial subjugation in the northern regions of Scotland. Elsewhere, the recurring visual motif of human faces disfigured by sword and shot recalls the iconic as well as horrific image of an elderly woman's shattered visage that forms part of the celebrated Odessa Steps sequence of Soviet director Sergei Eisenstein's *Battleship Potemkin* (1925), another great film about the brutality of failed revolution and civil war. Finally, we should also note the links that Peter Watkins himself drew between the historical events of the period that his film depicts and those of the period during which that film was made. The director has argued that, 'this was the 1960s, and the US army was "pacifying" the Vietnam highlands. I wanted to draw a parallel between these events and what had happened in our own UK Highlands two centuries earlier' (Watkins 1964). Although *Culloden* is possibly the most intellectually challenging and complex cinematic examination of an especially traumatic and important period within Scottish history, there are many other good reasons for studying Peter Watkins's film than simply that.

Jonathan Murray

Reference

Watkins, Peter (1964) '*Culloden*', http://pwatkins.mnsi.net/culloden.htm, Accessed 18 April 2014.

The Edge of the World

Country of Origin:
UK
Language:
English
Studio/Production Company:
Joe Rock Productions
Director:
Michael Powell
Producer:
Joe Rock
Screenwriter:
Michael Powell
Cinematographers:
Monty Berman
Skeets Kelly
Ernest Palmer
Art Director:
Gerry Blattner
Composer:
Lambert Williamson
Editor:
Derek N Twist
Duration:
75 minutes
Genre:
Romance
Melodrama
Social Drama
Cast:
John Laurie
Belle Chrystall
Eric Berry
Kitty Kirwan
Finlay Currie
Niall MacGinnis
Year:
1937
Filming Locations:
Foula, Shetland Islands, Scotland, UK

Synopsis

A yachtsman, yachtswoman, and Andrew Gray make their way to a desolate Scottish island. When they arrive, they explore the cliffs and find a grave marker that reads 'Peter Manson, Gone Over'. Andrew tells the tale of the marker, as it concerns the families Gray and Manson and the doomed way of life on the island. Ten years earlier, Andrew Gray and Ruth Manson fell in love while the patriarchs of the island discussed the fishing trawlers threatening the Islanders' livelihoods. Andrew and Ruth's brother, Robbie, argue over whether to stay or leave for the mainland. This dispute is settled by a race to the top of a cliff. Should Robbie win, the Islanders will emigrate; if Andrew wins, they stay. The race ends tragically with Robbie's death. Though a rift between the Grays and Mansons grows after the accident, Andrew and Ruth carry on a forbidden romance. After Andrew leaves to work on the fishing ships, Ruth gives birth to their son, unbeknownst to him. The baby heals the divide between the families, but when the child falls ill during a storm, it becomes imperative that the Islanders make contact with Andrew. Only he can bring a ship to the island to save the baby. As the Islanders rally to save the child, they realize that their isolation from the rest of the world is unsustainable in an era of mechanized fishing and modern medicine. But not everyone will leave the island and the old ways.

Critique

In a DVD commentary on *The Edge of the World*, Thelma Schoonmaker (acclaimed film editor and Michael Powell's widow) states that the film is 'a poem about an island'. If *The Edge of the World* is a poem, then it is an elegy, portraying the beautiful and unforgiving features of the island and the difficult yet pastorally communal ways of its inhabitants. The film has roots in the British documentary tradition of the 1930s, evoking films such as *Drifters* (John Grierson, 1929), and it also reveals Powell's love for both the Scottish Islands and melodramatic storytelling. Produced just before Powell's collaboration with Emeric Pressburger and their formation of the film company The Archers, *The Edge of the World* is an early triumph of a master film-maker and his team working under extremely difficult conditions.

The Edge of the World was Michael Powell's first independent production, and it was his first film-making adventure in the Scottish Islands. According to the aforementioned DVD commentary, the idea for the story was inspired by the real-life 1930 evacuation of the Island of St Kilda. Historically, the rise of industrialized fishing and the proliferation of large fishing trawlers made traditional Scottish Islander rowboat fishing obsolete. As many of the islands were owned by lairds who required that the islands' fishing business be profitable, many Islanders found themselves unable to remain on the islands when their main source of revenue decreased. Powell, who was raised on a farm, was touched by the stories of the displaced people severed from their close connection to the

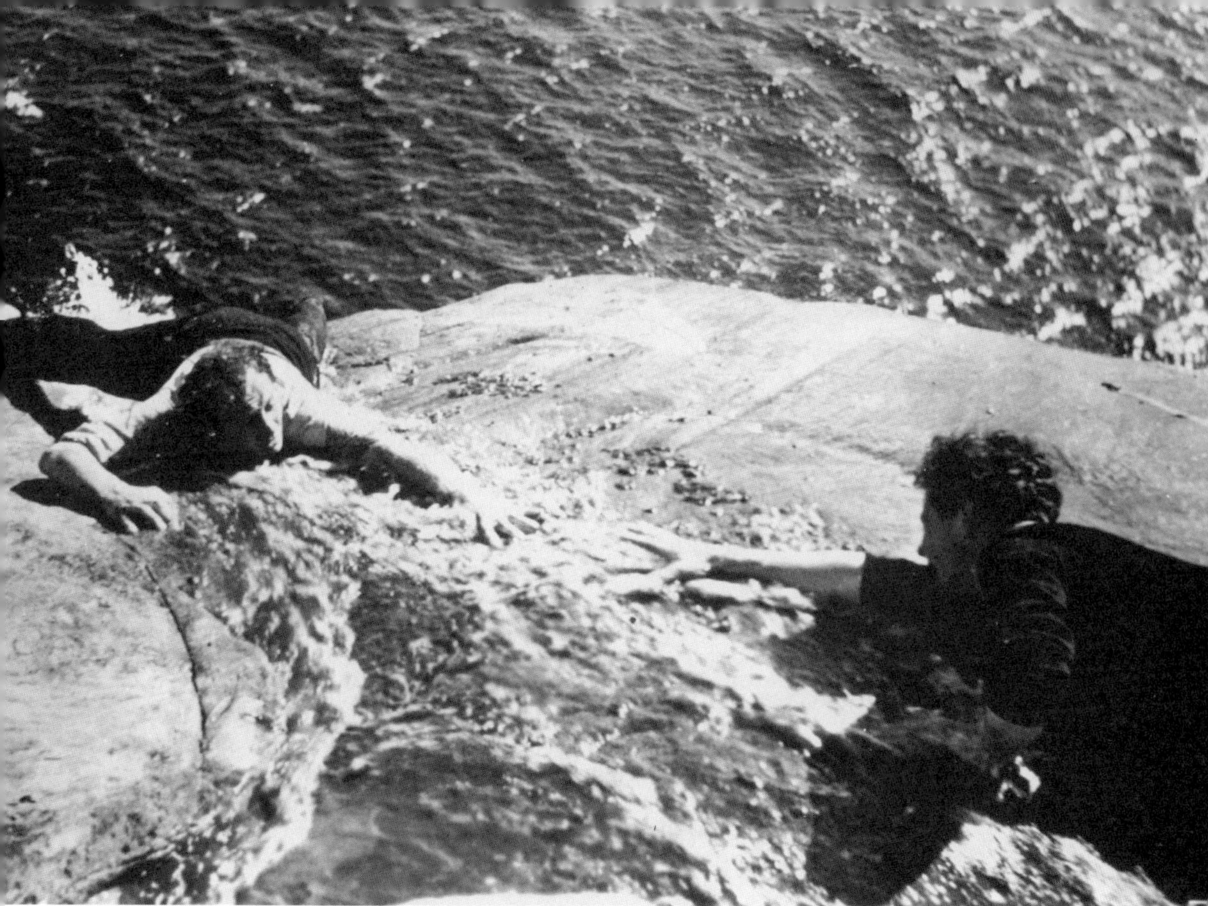

The Edge of the World (1937),
British Film Institute Collection

islands. The opening titles of the film state: 'The slow shadow of death is falling on the outer isles of Scotland. This is the story of one of them – and of all of them'. Powell laboured for seven years on 'quota quickies' (films produced to fulfil a government-mandated minimum percentage of British films screened in the United Kingdom), learning his craft, but he was eager to make a film from his heart. He finally received the chance with *The Edge of the World*, but it was a challenge.

In this age of computer-generated imagery and advanced special effects, it is worth noting how difficult the location shooting for *The Edge of the World* was. As Duncan Petrie (2000) states, the film was shot almost entirely on the Island of 'Foula in the Shetlands after permission to film on St Kilda had been denied by the Ministry of Defence' (37). Much of the filming took place between (or during) several bouts of terrible weather, including a stretch in which a gale prevented supplies from arriving for more than ten days. Because of the weather and isolation, Powell's band of 25 cast and crew members relied heavily on the support of the local people.

In spite of these conditions, the film-makers were able to capture many remarkable images and moments. There are several shots from the tops of steep cliffs, shots in which the camera seems to hang over the cliffs, and moments in which the actors risked life and limb by climbing and performing their own stunts. Today, many of these shots would be accomplished by means of computer-generated imagery and stunt doubles. Several more subtle visual effects were achieved with a kind of precision that foreshadows Powell's later work in *Black Narcissus* (1947) and *A Matter of Life and Death* (1946). Numerous superimpositions reveal characters' thoughts, memories and internal states through layered images. As Schoonmaker points out, these effects had to be accomplished 'in camera' due to the remoteness of the shoot. To do this, Powell and his cameramen shot one image at 50 per cent exposure, cranked the film backwards in the camera, and then shot another image at 50 per cent exposure in order to achieve the desired effect. This method requires amazing precision and blocking of the actors in order to work properly. It is all the more impressive to note that Powell was unable to view dailies in order to see if it had worked, so the crew was, in many instances, shooting 'blind'. These are just a few of the examples of the difficulties involved with the filming of *The Edge of the World*.

The challenges in making *The Edge of the World* included isolation, a very limited budget and harsh weather. These seem to mirror many of the challenges faced by the film's island characters. However, the film is more than a simple nature versus civilization melodrama. Even though the viewer sees that modern fishing ships threaten the livelihood of the Islanders, it is a modern ship that is able to travel in the storm to the island, allowing the baby to receive medical attention. Additionally, though life on the island is shown as communal and tight-knit, a good portion of the film's tension is a result of a conflict between the island's two main families. Perhaps it is not nature versus civilization, or the communal versus the individual at the heart of *The Edge of the World*, but rather the coming to terms with endings and uncertain new beginnings. In the film, Robbie is eager to leave the island for a more lucrative life on the mainland; his father, Peter, and Andrew wish to stay; the women and children are not allowed to contribute to the decision. Though their way of life may be unsustainable, all seem aware that, if they leave, then they abandon a way of life that will never return. It will only be preserved in memory (Powell repeatedly shows us how important memories are to the characters through superimpositions) and, in this case, on celluloid. The camera often lingers on the natural features of the island: its beauty as well as its harshness, and the people engaged in day-to-day work and other activities (seen as both pastoral and laborious) – as if to get one last look at this place and this lifestyle. These shots maintain documentary and ethnographic qualities, but their placement within the broader melodrama conveys a poignant sense of the permanent loss of both a place and a communal way of life. The sense of loss is powerful, yet it is tempered in the narrative by the reconstitution of the young family. *The Edge of the World*'s ability to capture a specific time and place, including its utopian and dystopian aspects, and to simultaneously draw from and challenge the might of the documentary in 1930s British cinema by embracing melodrama, make this film the chief accomplishment of Michael Powell's early career.

Zach Finch

References

Powell, Michael (2003 [1937]) *The Edge of the World* [DVD], Chatsworth, CA: Image Entertainment.
Petrie, Duncan (2000) *Screening Scotland*, London: BFI.

Floodtide

Country of Origin:
UK
Language:
English
Studio/Production Companies:
Aquila Film
Pinewood Studios
Director:
Frederick Wilson
Producer:
Donald P Wilson
Screenwriters:
George Blake
Donald P Wilson
Frederick Wilson
Cinematographer:
George Stretten
Production Designer:
Douglas Daniels
Technical Supervisor:
LE Overton
Editor:
Peter Bezencenet
Composer:
Robert Irving
Technical Consultant:
David Rawnsley
Duration:
86 minutes

Synopsis

David Shields longs to leave the Shields' ancestral farm to make ships in Glasgow. David's Uncle Joe and his grandmother help persuade David's sceptical father to allow David to do so. David then travels twenty miles to the big city to start work as a riveter and a plater at a shipyard where Uncle Joe maintains connections. Tim Brogan is assigned to teach David the ropes and also becomes David's roommate at a tenement lodging where shipyard workers commonly live. Tim also initiates David into Glasgow nightlife, as the two venture to the Barrowlands dancehall, where they meet Rosie, who Tim strikes up with, and Judy, who becomes David's girlfriend. David, however, is restless to become a ship designer and not just a yard worker. His curiosity leads him to run into the boss's daughter, Mary Ansruther, who is storing a small yacht she has designed at her father's shipyard. Not knowing who she is, David criticizes the design of Mary's yacht, which attracts Mary's interest in David. At the same time, David's restlessness is frustrating his immediate boss at his work station, Charlie Campbell, who nonetheless recognizes David's talent and drive. Soon, Ansruther calls David into his office to offer David a chance to study at the technical college and move up in the firm, beginning as a draughtsman. Due to his change in status within the firm, David moves to more posh lodgings, which are run by Mrs MacRae, a friend of the firm's chief designer, Mr Pursey. David initially gets off on the wrong foot with both by hosting a party in Mrs MacRae's drawing room with old friends Tim, Rosie and Judy that Mrs MacRae and Mr Pursey walk in on, returning from church and condemn as scandalously inappropriate. But David continues to devote himself to study and work, soon breaking with Judy because he no longer has time for or interest in her. Meanwhile, David's relationship with Mary blossoms; David visits her at her father's luxurious house on the edge of the city numerous times, and he goes sailing on the nearby loch with her, where he first declares his love for her. Time passes rapidly, and after David has completed his studies not only with distinction but also by earning an award for outstanding performance in naval architecture, Ansruther convinces his board of

Genre:

Historical Romance
Melodrama

Cast:

Gordon Jackson
Rona Anderson
John Laurie
Jimmy Logan
Jack Lambert
Janet Brown
Elizabeth Sellars

Year:

1949

Filming Locations:

Glasgow, Clydeside (Scotland, UK) (Shipyard scenes courtesy of John Brown & Company, Ltd, Clydebank)
Pinewood Studios, Iver Heath, Buckinghamshire, England, UK

directors to grant David instead of Pursey the opportunity to take charge of designing a new ship for an especially prestigious and lucrative contract. David's design is unorthodox, but it passes all tests, including simulation of gale conditions in the experimental test tank. Pursey ultimately congratulates David, with whom he has to that point maintained a tense relationship. At this time Tim shows up to announce his engagement to Rosie, and to invite David to an engagement party. When Mary subsequently invites David to a party with his new ship's buyer, and other bigwigs, David declines because of his prior commitment to Tim and Rosie. David's refusal to get out of the latter commitment by 'telling a polite lie' creates a temporary break in David and Mary's relationship. At Tim and Rosie's party, while David is giving an invited speech in honour of the couple, Judy walks in, uninvited, and before long tempts David, already having drunk too much, to follow her from the party, engage in amorous activity in a nearby alley and come back with her to her apartment. A storm that night threatens the safety of David's ship, ready for launch the next day, and Mary, assisted by Tim, hunts down David to bring him to dockside to save his ship. Mary and David remain tense afterward, and David doesn't show up at his ship's launch. Ansruther convinces Mary that she is responsible for tracking David down and setting him right, which she does, finding him on a hillside near Ansruther's estate. The film ends as the two walk off hand in hand into the horizon.

Critique

Floodtide is based on a novel by the prolific author of Glasgow and Clydeside-based stories of urban working-class life, George Blake, most famous for *The Shipbuilders*, widely regarded as a Scottish literary classic, and the basis for another, earlier film of the same title. Unlike *The Shipbuilders*, this film focuses far less on hardship and struggle as it does on celebrating shipbuilding and especially life centred on the industry, in an early post-World War II peak of resurgent optimism and prosperity. As many critics and reviewers have noted, the film is most impressive for its ability to convey striking images of a vibrant working-class culture, notably at play as well as at work, which has since disappeared. At the time the film was made, these images struck many contemporary audiences as freshly compelling, given how rarely commercial entertainment cinema had represented contemporary working-class Scottish life, centred on Scotland's largest city and its most famous industry. Feature-length fictional films engaged with Scotland had long preferred romantic images, most often from the distant past, of a virtually pre-modern rural life in the Highlands and the Islands – or gothic and macabre tales set in late-eighteenth- to early-nineteenth-century Edinburgh. *Floodtide* accentuates this difference by casting leading Scottish actors of the day speaking with authentic accents, here featured at the dramatic centre of the narrative, rather than included merely to provide local colour or comic relief. The film is briskly edited, not lingering on any particular scene, or plot development, while smoothly encompassing over three year's story time in less than an hour-and-a-half of screen time. And *Floodtide* offers sufficient detail concerning the technical dimensions of ship design and ship construction to compel audiences with an engineering interest, without allowing that focus to become predominant and deflect from the film's greater emphasis on romantic drama. What's more, the film's characterization of Tim Brogan has ultimately proven more compelling, for most critics and reviewers, than that of David Shields, because Tim Brogan epitomizes a type of working-class character relatively rarely found in commercial entertainment cinema: a skilled worker comfortably content with his station at his workplace, yet who does not allow what he does (or does not do) at work to overwhelm the rest of his life. Tim is persistently playful, fun-loving and high-spirited; a sharp dresser as well as a talented dancer and pianist; and an honest and loyal friend – and boyfriend. And Tim, while feisty enough as circumstances demand, is far from inclined toward any kind of criminal behaviour, and he suffers no apparent signs of substance abuse or embittered alienation on account of relative socio-economic deprivation.

Nevertheless, Floodtide is David Shields's story, and this is of a classic Scottish 'lad o' the pairts' – in American terms, a Horatio Alger-style rags to riches illustration of the ready opportunity for upward mobility available seemingly to any lad willing to work hard, and who brings to bear the drive and talent legitimately to earn such advancement. Repeatedly, members of the firm for which David works declare to him that this company always supports young men with talent and drive in working their way up the ladder. Ansruther himself appears to be a prime example of one who made it to the top, by and large 'through his own steam', after starting as a plater and a riveter just like David. Critics such as Colin McArthur (1982) and Duncan Petrie (2000) have aptly critiqued the film's portrayal of shipbuilding as a highly consensualist enterprise, with every employee working for the firm, at every level, all pulling together for the common good; we encounter no sign of class or sectarian conflict in Floodtide, contrary to the actual historical experience of life in places like the shipyard run by John Brown & Company, Ltd, Clydebank, which provides the source of the authentic shipyard scenes included in Floodtide. McArthur appreciates the film's divergence from Tartanry and the Kailyard yet critiques the film for its adherence to the conventional logic of classic Hollywood-style narrative realism, which inhibits critical analysis and reflection, by focusing instead on individual psychology and interpersonal relationships abstracted from larger social-historical conditions of possibility and forces of determination. As McArthur suggests, at several points Floodtide mocks a stuffy, sanctimonious and disingenuous petit-bourgeois milieu by directly contrasting this with a relaxed, jovial and bantering working-class milieu, yet the film resolves hints of class tension suggested in this contrast by working to 'valorise the men of the Clyde irrespective of class' (1982: 54). And, indeed, the film is dedicated to 'all the skilled and devoted men in whose hands the proud tradition of the Clyde is in safe keeping', which, according to the logic of the film, unites figures from Brogan to Ansruther, and even Board of Directors

Chairman Sir John, as all equal partners in a singular proud tradition. As McArthur adds, 'The class tensions are dissolved in the ideology of the film in which it is made clear that David, though on his way up, "doesn't forget his friends"' (54). What's more, McArthur continues, to mask the class basis of David's rejection of Judy, she is transformed, when reintroduced, into a 'slatternly virago' (54), who is bad by way of the seemingly intrinsic nature of her individual character. This characterization of Judy, McArthur suggests, enables David's rejection of her to mystify his distance from his working-class roots, and to make his reunion with the boss's daughter seem natural and desirable, especially in the final scene that unites 'the Scotland of beautiful hills and lochs and the Scotland of dynamic industrial activity' (54–55).

Even while identifying *Floodtide* as a quintessential example of the problematic myth of 'Clydesidism', Petrie interprets the film's narrative trajectory in slightly more positive terms than McArthur, pointing out that despite David's 'meteoric' rise, and despite his otherwise primarily individualistic focus of ambition, 'Davie's communitarian instincts remain largely intact, remaining good friends with Tim and being prepared to stand up a social engagement at the Ansruthers' in order to attend his friend's engagement party' (2000: 85). Thus, the film retains its emphasis on 'working-class camaraderie and energy' (217) even as David melodramatically bridges the gap between the classes, and between his past and present positions within the firm, by saving his ship from the flood tide through his own heroic manual labour, assisted by Tim, Mary and others from disparate positions across the company, while ultimately reuniting with Mary. Petrie also commends *Floodtide* for 'dispelling the traditional-modern, masculine–feminine dichotomy applied to leisure in *The Shipbuilders*' (85), championing the pleasures of the dancehall as well as the pub, and thereby valorizing 'a sphere of (feminised) consumption rather than (masculinised) production' so as to offer, especially via the character of Tim Brogan, 'a rather different and more progressive image of working-class masculinity than Danny Shields of *The Shipbuilders*' (86). Yet, as Petrie adds, in this film the relationship between men and women, like in *The Shipbuilders*, 'is clearly addressed as a potential site of tension and anxiety' (91), that is reflective, perhaps, of larger societal tensions and anxieties concerned with changing relative positions of men and women, in the immediate post-World War II era, with the transition to a peacetime economy and the advent of a new social democracy. Mary is a self-confident character, yet from the vantage point of the film her ambition to design her own boat is comical because she is, in doing so, obviously attempting to do something that only men can do well, and otherwise the film often portrays her as naive and spoiled. The film does even worse by Judy, forcing her to serve as the repository of the ultimately jettisoned tensions and conflicts the film wipes away at its climax, in the process abruptly transforming her from a character earlier akin to Rosie to one later akin to a femme fatale. Clearly, *Floodtide* endorses women staying in their 'proper traditional places', fulfilling their 'proper traditional roles', and recognizing that a 'good woman' follows her man's lead, supporting and assisting him in the pursuit of his dreams and ambitions, while a 'bad woman' 'selfishly' attempts to put her own desires and needs ahead, or even on equal par with, those of her man.

Floodtide is a notable example of the Rank independent frame process used at Pinewood Studios at the time – an effort to introduce a form of scientific management, in the interests of cost-saving efficiency, to the production of feature-length films. In the case of *Floodtide*, David Rawnsley's pioneering work with back projection plays a particularly central role, allowing for extensive and relatively quite impressive, for the time, fusion of images of the lead actors acting in the studio with moving images of Glasgow and Clydeside locations. In addition, the original music composed for the film by Robert Irving, and performed by the London Symphony Orchestra, led by George Stratton, provides a lively and frequently stirring accompaniment to the drama, underscoring the dominant mood within and across particular scenes, while remaining understated, eschewing sentimental or bombastic excess, unlike, for example, the score for *The Brothers*, a 1947 Scottish film directed by David MacDonald set on the Isle of Skye, released together with *Floodtide* on DVD by Park Circus in 2011.

Finally, however, *Floodtide*, although pleasant enough on its own terms, and interesting as an historical artefact, as a representation of life centred around shipbuilding in Glasgow and the Clydeside at a peak period in the late 1940s, does not fully live up to the promise its title proffers: although a literal flood tide threatens David's ship near the end of the film, in a figurative sense we experience little of a flood tide anywhere in this movie. David's success is, from the beginning, quite predictable, while none of the obstacles he faces are depicted as particularly substantial, and this rise is, simultaneously, depicted as nothing out of the ordinary within the shipbuilding industry. No growing, developing or unfolding of any kind of powerful surge promises, or threatens, to transform anything about what, according to *Floodtide*, is working just fine as it is. David follows in Ansruther's footsteps as the firm continues to be a company where everyone working for it is proud and content, and where any young man with talent, ambition and a willingness to work can, so it seems, follow David in turn.

Bob Nowlan

References

Baxter, John (1944) *The Shipbuilders*, British National Films.

Blake, George (1935) *The Shipbuilders*, Philadelphia: JB Lippincott Company.

McArthur, Colin (ed.) (1982) *Scotch Reels: Scotland in Cinema and Television*, London: BFI.

Petrie, Duncan (2000) *Screening Scotland*, London: BFI.

I Know Where I'm Going!

Country of Origin:

UK

Languages:

English
Scottish Gaelic

Studio/Production Company:

The Archers

Directors:

Michael Powell
Emeric Pressburger

Producers:

Michael Powell
Emeric Pressburger
George R Busby

Screenwriters:

Michael Powell
Emeric Pressburger

Cinematographer:

Erwin Hillier

Art Director:

Alfred Junge

Composer:

Allan Gray

Editor:

John Seabourne

Duration:

91 minutes

Genre:

Romance
Melodrama

Cast:

Wendy Hiller
Roger Livesey
Pamela Brown
Finlay Currie

Year:

1945

Filming Locations:

Carsaig pier, Mull, Argyll and Bute, Scotland, UK

Synopsis

Joan Webster is a young and materialistic professional woman working for Consolidated Chemical Industries. After informing her father of her impending wedding to the owner of the company, Sir Robert Bellinger, she leaves Manchester with the intent of marrying her fiancé on the Scottish Island of Kiloran. Inclement weather prevents her from completing the journey, however, and she is forced to stay at nearby Port Erraig on Mull. There she meets a number of colourful Scottish characters, including Catriona MacLaine, and the handsome naval officer, Torquil MacNeil. In their time together, Torquil reveals himself to be the cursed Laird of Kiloran, forced to lease the island to Bellinger for income. Joan, in spite of, or because of, her growing attraction to Torquil and life in the Scottish Islands, insists on crossing to Kiloran to reach her fiancé despite the warnings of the locals of the Corryvreckan whirlpool. Joan, Torquil and Kenny the boatman attempt to brave the crossing. In this act, Joan risks all of their lives and everything she ever wanted only to find that she does not exactly know where she is going.

Critique

I Know Where I'm Going! was produced at the height of The Archers's (Michael Powell and Emeric Pressburger) creative powers, yet, as Pam Cook points out, the film was 'a detour in The Archers' itinerary, an unscheduled stop between *A Canterbury Tale* (1944) and *A Matter of Life and Death* (1946)' (2002: 8). Like Joan's detour in Port Erraig, the film proved to be a surprising success. The film has also seen renewed praise in the last fifteen years by critics and scholars such as Duncan Petrie, Pam Cook, Ian Christie and director Martin Scorsese. Indeed, for many years, *I Know Where I'm Going!* was discussed less than other Powell and Pressburger masterpieces such as the aforementioned *A Matter of Life and Death*, *The Life and Death of Colonel Blimp* (1943), *Black Narcissus* (1947), *The Red Shoes* (1948) and Michael Powell's infamous *Peeping Tom* (1960). One possible reason for this is the film's seemingly straightforward romantic and mythic elements. Regardless of its evolving critical status, the film has remained popular with audiences.

The detour that became *I Know Where I'm Going!* began after mediocre responses from the box office and critics to *A Canterbury Tale* (Cook 2002: 9). Forsyth Hardy, citing Michael Powell's autobiography, recounts how Emeric Pressburger approached Powell with an idea for a film about a woman who wants to get to an island, 'but a storm stops her from getting there, and by the time the storm has died down she no longer wants to go there, because her life has changed quite suddenly the way that girls' lives do' (1990: 61). Pressburger wrote the story in five days while Powell went on the hunt for island locations (Hardy 1990: 61). Powell loved Scotland, and he had a 'fondness for romantic mysticism', so it should come as no surprise, then, that his quest led him to the Scottish Islands, and the setting for the next Archers film was discovered (Petrie 2000: 35). *I Know Where I'm Going!* was Powell's third filmic venture to the

I Know Where I'm Going! (1945), British Film Institute Collection

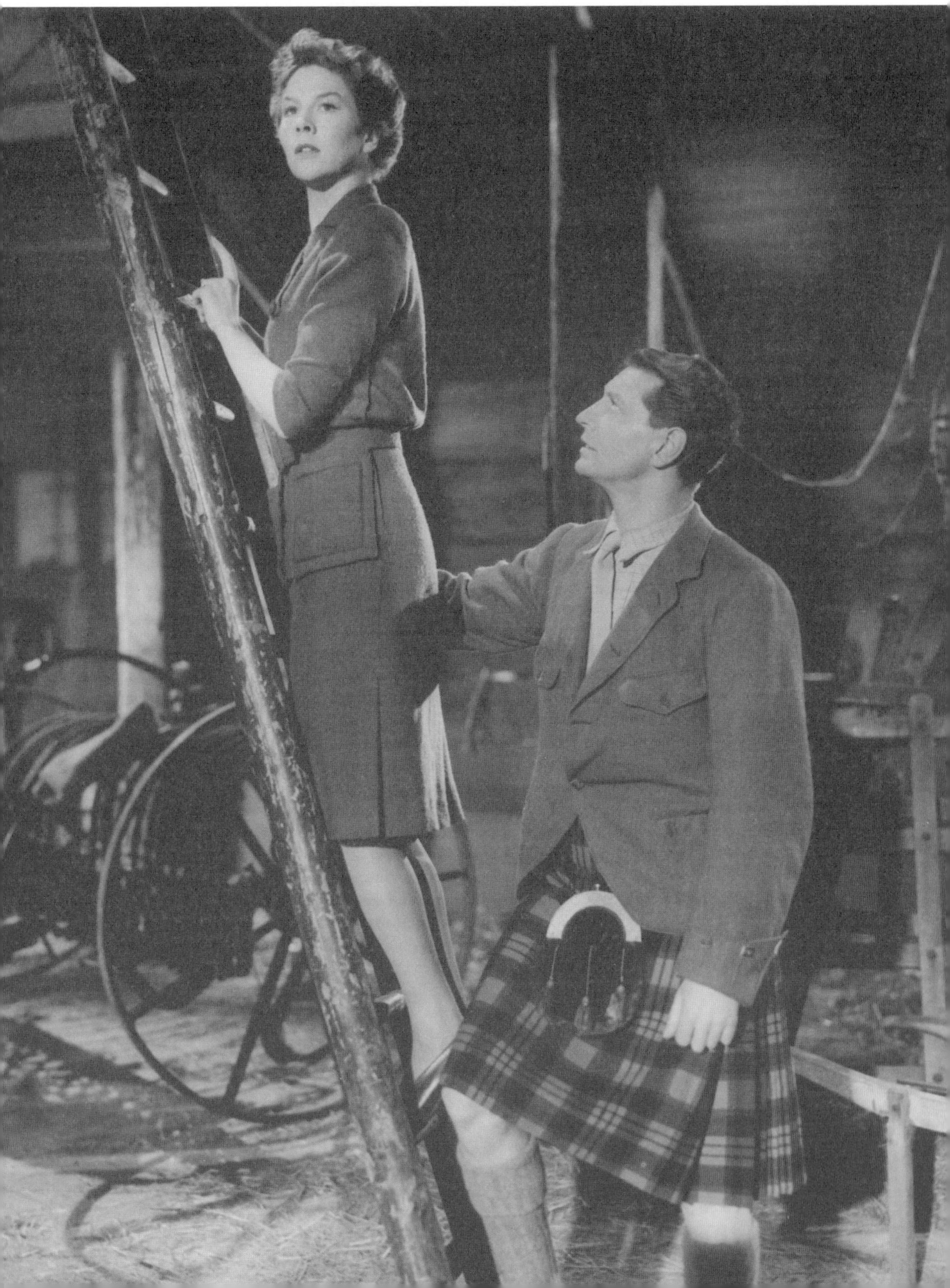

Denham Studios, Denham, Buckinghamshire, England, UK
Duart Bay, Mull, Argyll and Bute, Scotland, UK
Duart Castle, Mull, Argyll and Bute, Scotland, UK
Gulf of Corryvreckan, Argyll and Bute, Scotland, UK
House of Carsaig, Mull, Argyll and Bute, Scotland, UK
Jura, Argyll and Bute, Scotland, UK
Lochbuie, Mull, Argyll and Bute, Scotland, UK
Oban, Argyll and Bute, Scotland, UK
Scarba, Argyll and Bute, Scotland, UK
Sound Of Mull, Mull, Argyll and Bute, Scotland, UK
Tobermory, Mull, Argyll and Bute, Scotland, UK
Torosay Castle, Mull, Argyll and Bute, Scotland, UK
Western Isles Hotel, Tobermory, Mull, Argyll and Bute, Scotland, UK

Scottish Islands; the previous were *The Edge of the World* (1937) and *The Spy in Black* (1939). Acclaimed stage actress Wendy Hiller was cast as Joan, and Roger Livesey played Torquil MacNeil when James Mason dropped out just weeks before shooting commenced (Cook 2002: 35). In addition to Powell and Pressburger, The Archers film-making team consisted of cinematographer Erwin Hillier, composer Allan Gray, and production designer Alfred Junge. Except for Powell, all had worked for the renowned German production company UFA in the 1920s, which 'produced technically innovative and aesthetically ambitious films that were the envy of the world' (Cook 2002: 15–16). The influences of UFA, German expressionism and the talents of the émigrés from Weimar Germany on the productions of The Archers cannot be overstated. Indeed, their style and artistry can be seen throughout *I Know Where I'm Going!* in its shadowy and Gothic interiors and exteriors, visual effects and layers of sounds and images. Their employment of these elements remains expressive and engaging to this day.

Though produced during a short shooting schedule, the film's level of visual and aural complexity is as rich as any other production by The Archers. The production itself featured a mix of studio and location shooting. Roger Livesey was unable to go on location due to a theatre commitment, and a double was required for all location shots. The integration of the stand-in with the genuine actor is quite seamless (Cook 2002: 35). Deep focus, rear projection cinematography was used for the scenes involving the Corryvreckan whirlpool, and the film utilizes a number of 'trick' shots and superimpositions to convey Joan's dreams, interior states and the drama on the Island of Mull. For example, during her dream on the northbound train from Manchester, Joan envisions 'marrying' Consolidated Chemical Industries. This scene features a number of layered images and sounds: the minister (played by the same actor who plays her father), industrial gears and equipment, wedding bells, coins and pound notes. This series of layered images and sounds convey that Joan is not in love with a person, but with material wealth and status (she hears the words 'Lady Bellinger' in the dream, as well). This point is further reinforced by the fact that the audience never sees her fiancé, Sir Robert Bellinger, in the film. The closest he comes to anything like a human presence is his disembodied voice through the radio during the storm. The voice of Bellinger puts down the Scottish locals and reveals his aloof disdain for Torquil and his ilk. Like many of the other films directed by Powell and Pressburger, *I Know Where I'm Going!* requires repeated viewings to unpack the information contained in many of the scenes.

It is worthwhile to note how *I Know Where I'm Going!* prefigures *Brigadoon* (Vicente Minnelli, 1954) with its fantastical Scotland and a critique of modern materialism. In both films, Scotland is represented as a rural realm from a mythic past. Curses and old-fashioned communities remain, and the landscape is untamed and even dangerous. Mull, like Brigadoon, is set against the soulless materialism of the modern world as seen in Manchester (and New York in *Brigadoon*). On Mull and in Brigadoon, love can be found, even when it is unlooked for or initially unwanted, yet not without some risk to life and limb. The risk involved to attain love is presented as preferable to a loveless, but materially rich life in modern society. *I Know Where I'm Going!* repeatedly makes strong statements against materialism and rampant consumerism, as when Torquil says to Joan that the local people are 'not poor, they just haven't got any money'. Duncan Petrie argues that this stance is largely rooted in the British historical context at the end of World War II, which was marked by the support for impending policies of 'nationalization and the heavy taxation of the rich' (such as those who profited from the war, which would include chemical moguls like Bellinger) (2002: 39). This attitude and these policies reflected a sentiment that rejected post-war materialism, in favour of a coming-together rather than every-man-for-himself. *I Know Where I'm Going!*, like *Brigadoon*, proposes that a solution for, or escape from, the capitalist mandate to keep-up-with-the-Joneses is a retreat into a mythic past. However, these mythic places do not exist, nor did they ever exist as conceived in films such as *I Know Where I'm Going!* and *Brigadoon*. Even within the films' diegeses, some questions remain. What are Joan and Torquil going to do now that they seemingly finally do know at least something of where they are going? Likewise, in *Brigadoon*, we never learn what happens after Tommy and Fiona remain in the enchanted town. Yet, the appeal of both films endures. Perhaps this is because of their hopefulness and the ultimate triumph of love over the impersonal materialism that all too often seems to direct life in contemporary, capitalist society.

Zach Finch

References

Cook, Pam (2002) *I Know Where I'm Going!*, London: BFI.
Hardy, Forsyth (1990) *Scotland in Film*, Edinburgh: EUP.
Petrie, Duncan (2000) *Screening Scotland*. London: BFI.
Powell, Michael and Pressburger, Emeric (2002 [1945]) *I Know Where I'm Going!* [DVD], New York: Criterion.

Just A Boys' Game

Country of Origin:
UK
Language:
English (urban Scottish dialect)
Studio/Production Company:
BBC

Synopsis

Jake McQuillan is a man with a reputation as a fighter, the kind of individual someone who is trying to make a name for himself would seek to take on, despite the fact that Jake has supposedly 'hung up his guns years ago'. Like John McNeill in *Just Another Saturday* – writer Peter McDougall's previous collaboration with director John Mackenzie, Jake comes from a dysfunctional family. His mother has abandoned him and he lives with his grandmother, most of whose life is spent looking after her deeply unpleasant husband who has also had a history of gang fighting; indeed, it seems his son, Jake's father, was executed for murder after a fight in which both

Director:
John Mackenzie
Producer:
Richard Eyre
Screenwriter:
Peter McDougall
Cinematographer:
Elmer Cossey
Art Director:
Tim Harvey
Composer:
Frankie Miller
Editor:
Graham Walker
Duration:
75 minutes
Genre:
Social Realism/Naturalism
Social/Psychological Drama
Gangster
Cast:
Frankie Miller
Ken Hutchison
Gregor Fisher
Jean Taylor Smith
Year:
1979
Filming Location:
Greenock, Scotland, UK

grandfather and father were involved some years previously.

The action of the film begins with a ferocious battle in a pub, in which the police studiously avoid becoming involved, and then moves on to a Friday when Jake's friend, Dancer, persuades him to abandon his work at the Greenock container terminal and go on a drinking spree with Dancer and, later in the day, their other friend, Tanza. It is a pretty squalid day and it ends with a fight on the dockside in which a gang, whose leader has a grudge to settle with Jake, chases Dancer to his death as he runs into a steel hawser. 'That's how it goes. That's the game', says Jake afterwards. 'Aye, that's your game,' replies a distraught Tanza. The film ends with Jake's dying grandfather telling him that he was never fond of him, and 'when I was younger I could have taken you any time'.

Critique

Peter McDougall was brought up in Greenock, as was Alan Sharp who forsook a career as a Scottish novelist in favour of one as a Hollywood scriptwriter; among the latter's films are *The Hired Hand* (Peter Fonda,1971) and *Ulzana's Raid* (Robert Aldrich,1972). McDougall appears to share with Sharp an affinity for Westerns, and the dialogue of *Just a Boys' Game* is replete with references to them. Although John Ford's films are specifically mentioned, the action in *Just a Boy's Game*, with its emphasis on macho violence, owes more to Sam Peckinpah than to Ford.

The world of macho males and urban squalor – boarded-up houses, graffiti, etc. – is well caught in the filming, much of the action taking place in interior and exterior gloom which heightens the grim mood. It is difficult to warm to Jake, let alone his dreadful grandfather, although his long-suffering grandmother is a much more sympathetic character. Dancer's wife is more willing to indulge her husband and he is a far more appealing character than Jake – witty, for all his fecklessness, and affectionate to his children. Having him, rather than Jake, murdered heightens the sense of waste in the lives of so many of the characters in the film.

BBC London commissioned the film, but the morning after transmission BBC Scotland staged a radio discussion involving McDougall, the Provost of Inverclyde, where Greenock is located, and the present writer. Unsurprisingly, the Provost was much exercised about the impression of Greenock which the film created but had difficulty in rebutting the defence that this was a story based on all too real aspects of life in the west of Scotland. It is doubtful whether *Sweet Sixteen* (2002), Ken Loach's more widely famous film made over twenty years later, which is set in the same town and is focused on teenagers selling drugs to make money, would have cheered the Provost up. In retrospect, few critics today would disagree with John R Cook's comment that McDougall 'probably remains the most significant dedicated television playwright to have emerged from Scotland' (Cook 2008: 112).

David Hutchison

Reference

Cook, John R (2008) 'Three Ring Circus: Television Drama about, by and for Scotland', in Neil Blain and David Hutchison (eds), *The Media in Scotland*, Edinburgh: EUP, pp. 107–22.

Just Another Saturday

Country of Origin:
UK

Language:
English (urban Scottish dialect)

Studio/Production Company:
BBC

Director:
John Mackenzie

Producer:
Graeme McDonald

Screenwriter:
Peter McDougall

Cinematographer:
Phil Meheux

Art Director:
Austin Spriggs

Editor:
Peter Evans

Duration:
77 minutes

Genre:
Social Realism/Naturalism
Social/Psychological Drama

Cast:
John Morrison
Eileen McCallum
Bill Henderson
Ken Hutchison
Billy Connolly

Year:
1975

Synopsis

John McNeill's family is a dysfunctional one: he shares a bedroom – although not a bed – with his mother, and his father is an amiable drunk. John's role with his flute band is, however, to be macebearer, a role in which he is succored by his mother's pride, although his father clearly maintains reservations about the organization, and about his son's involvement in it.

What starts as a jolly, if clearly sectarian, event – an Orange Order celebration and parade in Glasgow – degenerates for some of the participants into drunkenness and then into violence, which is directed against the residents of a mainly Catholic street, some of whom retaliate. Subsequently, when John is drinking with Catholic friends in a pub, he himself is threatened and has to run for his life. At the end of the day he concludes that life in the Orange Order is not for him. His father tells him that such organizations keep working-class people apart from each other when they should be seeking solidarity 'to fight for something better'. 'Don't let yourself get trapped' is his father's advice. In response to this admonition, John announces that he will leave home and the city, much to his mother's distress.

Critique

Just Another Saturday depicts events in one day of the life of John McNeill, as he moves from relative innocence, and naive pride in belonging, toward alienation from the Orange Order as well as from his home city and nation. The Orange Order is known for its Loyalist orientation in Northern Ireland, but since the nineteenth century it has attracted a strong following among working-class Protestants in central Scotland and is renowned for its hostility to Catholicism, a hostility which can boil over into drunkenness and disorder. Although this film is set in Scotland, it was made by BBC London and it appears that the Corporation's Scottish drama department was less than overjoyed at its appearance. That may have been because of unhappiness about how Scotland – and Glasgow in particular, where the action is clearly set – are depicted. But there was also anxiety in London, which hesitated before commissioning the production, since the Troubles in Northern Ireland were at their height, and there was genuine concern that such a film might exacerbate the sectarianism that it sets out to examine. Surprising as it might seem, some of the

Filming Locations:

Glasgow and Edinburgh, Scotland, UK

scenes were shot with the cooperation of the Orange Order at one it its own parades, and in *Just Another Saturday* the fictionally dramatized events are skillfully interwoven with actual events. After transmission, the Orange Order, which is thanked in the final credits for 'its help in the making of this film', complained that it had been misled by the producers. It is hard to believe, however, that the Order would have agreed to cooperate if it had really known how the film would turn out.

John Mackenzie's direction offers a documentary feel, not least in its depiction of the rundown housing estate in which John lives, and in the fast cutting and jerky camera movements that characterize much of the film. Yet neither writer Peter McDougall nor director Mackenzie is at his best with the more reflective scenes which have an artificial feel; they are much more comfortable on the streets and with men in a pub telling each other stories and jokes rather than with exploring characters in depth. Nevertheless, *Just Another Saturday* is a powerful, if depressing, film, for the life of the segment of the Scottish working class which is depicted is a grimly unfulfilled one, from which many people would want to escape as soon as possible, as McDougall himself did.

Just Another Saturday won the Prix Italia Drama Award in the year of its transmission. Yet critical discussion of television film and drama has often been hindered by the lack of videotapes and DVDs. McDougall's plays for television only became available on DVD 30 years after transmission. The result has been that the kind of sustained discussion, which can accrue around feature films, has mostly been absent for work such as McDougall's. However Duncan Petrie has given considerable attention to this writer's output (Petrie 2000, 2004) and has emphasized the importance of its filmic elements – editing, lighting and settings – and of the contributions of his directors and cameramen to the successful realization of McDougall's dramatic ideas.

David Hutchison

References

Petrie, Duncan (2000) *Screening Scotland*, London: BFI.

__________ (2004) *Contemporary Scottish Fictions*, Edinburgh: EUP.

The Last King of Scotland

Countries of Origin:

UK
USA
Germany

Synopsis

Faced with the prospect of a quiet life in rural Scotland, medical school graduate Nicholas Garrigan spins a globe and resolves to move to the first country his finger lands on. After this turns out to be Canada, Garrigan spins again and this time lands on Uganda, for which he almost immediately departs. Upon arriving in Uganda and taking up his position at a rural clinic, Garrigan attends a rally for the new president Idi Amin who has just overthrown the previous president in a coup. A twist of fate has Garrigan called to

Studio/Production Companies:

DNA Films
Film4
Fox Searchlight
Cowboy Films
Slate Films
Tatfilm

Director:

Kevin Macdonald

Producers:

Lisa Bryer
Andrea Calderwood
Charles Steele

Screenwriters:

Peter Morgan
Jeremy Brock

Cinematographer:

Anthony Dod Mantle

Art Director:

Margaret Horspool

Composer:

Alex Heffes

Editor:

Justine Wright

Duration:

121 minutes

Genre:

Historical Drama
Social/Psychological Drama
Thriller

Cast:

Forest Whitaker
James McAvoy
Gillian Anderson

Year:

2006

Filming Locations:

Loch Lomond, Scotland, UK
Kampala, Uganda

the scene of a car accident that Amin was involved in. Impressed by Garrigan's manner of handling his injuries and influenced by an odd fascination with Scotland, the dictator goes on to offer Garrigan a role in his administration. In this position, Garrigan gradually begins to see that Amin is not the jovial, charismatic figure he initially takes him for and is drawn into complicity with the dictator's brutal regime. Garrigan's unhappiness with his situation leads him to an affair with one of Amin's wives, a tryst that ultimately has tragic consequences. Desperate for a way out of Uganda, Garrigan accepts the assistance of a British secret agent who offers the doctor passage home providing he in turn helps to assassinate the dictator.

Critique

For most filmgoers, *The Last King of Scotland* is famous as the film that won Forest Whitaker an Oscar for his dynamic and multifaceted portrayal of Idi Amin, one of the twentieth century's greatest monsters. As deserved as Whitaker's accolades for this role surely are, there is much more to *Last King* than this one great performance.

Based on Giles Foden's prize-winning novel of the same name, *Last King* tells the story of the Amin years through the eyes of a naive Scottish doctor. Breaking from Foden's meticulously detailed chronicle of the Amin years, the film's screenwriters turn to the genre of the political thriller and compress the many events of the novel (and the Amin years) into a two-hour timeframe. The results are a bit dizzying and misleading – the Entebbe hostage crisis, for instance, takes place seemingly weeks after Amin's expulsion of South Asian Ugandans when in fact the events took place four years apart – but they also lend an engrossing and visceral dimension to Foden's methodical and introspective narrative.

This is not to say, however, that the genre aspects of the film are always successful. Garrigan's decision to run off and sleep with Kay Amin (Kerry Washington) at a party at Amin's home is farfetched to put it mildly, and the film's ending is as unconvincing as it is gory. That said, Macdonald's direction gives the film a gritty realist feel that offsets some of its more melodramatic moments. At this point in his career, Macdonald was primarily known for his work in documentary and this experience is palpable in the approach to camera style and sound design in particular.

As many critics have noted (including Lesley Marx most stridently), *Last King* does not do much to challenge western stereotypes about Africa. The film's Uganda is one of exoticized and brutally violent people. Amin is amongst the worst examples of despotic African leaders who gained power under the auspices of anti-imperialism, only to use his power to enrich himself and murder thousands of his people. Though the film does offer a more nuanced and humanized version of the larger than life Amin, the film also revels in one of Africa's lowest post-independence moments.

Crucially, these views of Uganda come to the viewer through the lens of Garrigan and we are thus seeing Africa through the eyes of a deeply flawed character. This observation allows us to begin to see what is perhaps the film's greatest strength as a work of Scottish cinema: its critical examination of Scotland's role in the colonial and neo-colonial project. Garrigan is an allegorical figure par excellence, showing that despite its own claims of victimization by and difference from the English, Scotland has played a major role in enabling monsters such as Amin, a monster whom the film shows to be very much of the west's making. It was the United States and the United Kingdom, the film suggests, that helped to install Amin in the first place and it was the Scottish commanders of the notorious King's African Rifles regiment that gave him his tutelage in violence and brutality. These commanders later inspired Amin's love for all things Scottish, and when we see him in the film dressed in tartan, listening to bagpipes with Garrigan at his side, we are given powerful reminders of the complicity of Scotland in the sufferings of the Ugandan people and by implication many other countries who still cope with the legacies of imperialism and neo-imperialism.

Christopher Meir

Reference

Marx, Lesley (2011) '*The Last King of Scotland* and the Politics of Adaptation', *Black Camera: An International Film Journal*, 3: 1, pp. 54–74.

Mrs Brown

Her Majesty, Mrs Brown (US title)

Countries of Origin:

UK
Ireland
USA

Language:

English

Studio/Production Companies:

BBC Scotland
Ecosse Films
Irish Screen
WGBH Boston

Director:

John Madden

Producer:

Sarah Curtis

Screenwriter:

Jeremy Brock

Synopsis

Queen Victoria is in a protracted state of mourning for her late husband, Prince Albert, when her butler sends for John Brown, the royal couple's ghillie at their estate in Balmoral. Upon his arrival in the Queen's household, Brown is shocked at the state that Victoria has let herself lapse into. He resolves to shake her out of her stupor by refusing to bow to royal protocol and to speak to the Queen frankly about her condition. Initially horrified by her servant's impertinence, the Queen comes to be charmed by the Scotsman and soon finds herself trusting only in Brown. A close emotional bond develops between the two and the question if anything romantic develops is left deliberately open. Gossip soon spreads amongst the household and the realm at large as the Queen is dubbed 'Mrs Brown' by the tabloid media of the day. Brown, for his part, grows more and more ambitious as he gets closer to the Queen, earning him the resentment of all of the household and the Queen's immediate family. When the Republican movement starts to gain momentum in parliament, opportunist Prime Minister Benjamin Disraeli manipulates Brown into convincing the Queen to return to her public duties. The Queen does so, but feels betrayed by her confidant and the two fall out completely until Brown falls ill and the Queen comes to his bedside to apologize for her mistreatment of her dedicated servant.

Cinematographer:
Richard Greatrex
Art Director:
Charlotte Watts
Composer:
Stephen Warbeck
Editor:
Robin Sales
Duration:
105 minutes
Genre:
Historical Romance
Cast:
Judi Dench
Billy Connolly
Gerard Butler

Critique

Mrs Brown was one of the most high-profile Scottish films of the 1990s. The film was nominated for two Oscars and numerous other awards, received a warm reception from the critical press, and did very well at the box office in the United Kingdom and abroad. This success is not surprising considering its skilful manipulation of the so-called 'heritage' genre, its star performances and its somewhat unfortunate topicality as a critique of media pressures on the royal family.

In many ways, *Mrs Brown* is a prototypical 1990s British costume drama, fitting easily into the mould of the 'heritage' cycle of costume dramas that dominated 1980s and 1990s British cinema. Not only do we have the typical historical, royal setting and the meticulously detailed costumes and sets to go along with that setting, but we also see in the film an assured use of the camera style and editing conventions made famous by films such as *A Room With a View* (James Ivory, 1985) and *Howards End* (James Ivory, 1992). Director John Madden does show some stylistic savvy by utilizing these heritage conventions exclusively in connection

Mrs Brown (1997), British Film Institute Collection

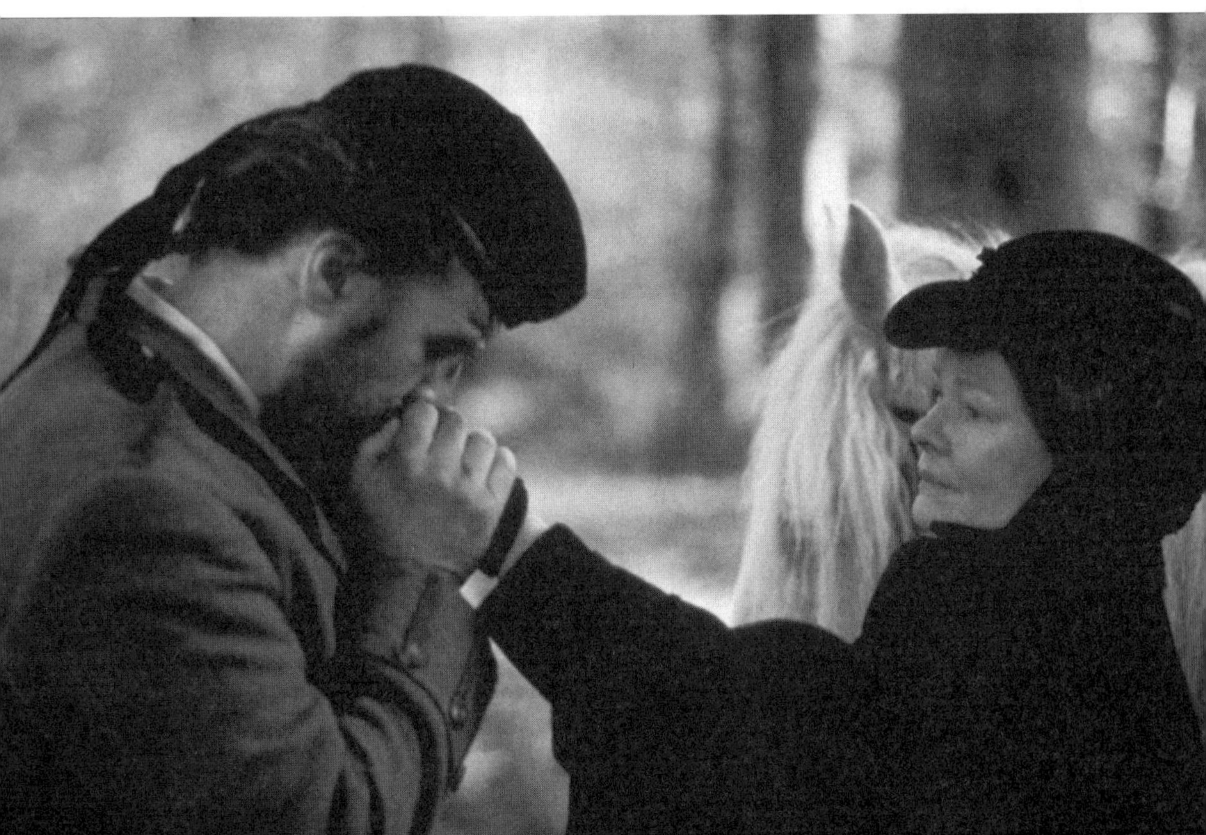

Year:

1997

Filming Locations:

Ardverikie Estate, Highland, Scotland, UK
Duns Castle, Duns, Scottish Borders, Scotland, UK
Luton Hoo Estate, Luton, Bedfordshire, England, UK
Osterley Park House, Isleworth, Middlesex, England, UK
Wilton House, Wilton, Salisbury, Wiltshire, England, UK
River Pattack, Scotland, UK
Lochan na h-Earba, Scotland, UK
St. Augustine's Church. Kilburn Park Road, Greater London, England, UK
Loch Laggan, The Highlands, Scotland, UK
Osborne, Isle of Wight, England, UK
Taymouth Castle, Kenmore, the Highlands, Scotland, UK

with upper-class English characters. Brown, in contrast, is associated with a visual dynamism (handheld cameras, frenetic editing and so on) that marks him as not fitting into the 'heritage' world of the Queen. The film draws this contrast most clearly when we see separate scenes in which the Queen and Brown are swimming. While the Queen and her maids, in head-to-toe bathing suits, gently lower themselves into a placid lake, Brown and his brother Archie (Gerard Butler) recklessly throw themselves against the crashing waves of the sea, wearing little but their beards.

As befits a 'quality' British costume drama, the acting is impeccable, but Dench and Connolly are particularly engaging as the odd couple at the film's heart. Dench plays Victoria as a haughty and formidable woman who is also lonely, vulnerable and desperate to make a real human connection in a world of scheming politicians and obsequious servants. That she does this with a figure as familiar as Victoria is a further testament to her abilities. Connolly, meanwhile, deftly imports his persona as a foul-mouthed, straight-talking, working-class Scot into a nineteenth-century character. This produces many memorable scenes in which Brown thumbs his nose at convention, but perhaps more interesting are the moments in which Connolly shows a sensitivity and restraint that belies his uncouth persona. His heartfelt apology to the Queen for having to drag her back into public life late in the film, for example, resonates more powerfully than many of his insults and rebukes directed at members of the royal household.

While the film was in some senses an explicit attempt to criticize the hounding of the royals by the British media, the death of Princess Diana shortly after the film's domestic release added a sombre gravity to this theme. These timely reminders of the human side of the British monarchy, however, should not overshadow the film's commentary on the Scottish aspects of British history. Brown is a figure lost in most historical accounts of Victoria's life and the film does well to try to reacquaint history with this famous Scotsman. While Diana's death may be the event most remembered when one thinks of the film's context, another was the ongoing break up of Great Britain. It is a powerful reflection of the film's devolutionary context – preceding, as it did, the 1997 devolution referendum – that a Scotsman should play a crucial role in keeping the monarchy intact at a moment when public sentiment seemed turned fatefully against it. Within such a context, Victoria's apology to the Scotsman whom she had ignored for so long despite his loyal service approaches allegory when considered against the backdrop of Scottish devolution and resurgent Scottish nationalism.

Christopher Meir

Nina's Heavenly Delights

Country of Origin:
UK
Language:
English
Studio/Production Companies:
Here! Films
Fortissimo Films
Scion Films Scottish Screen
Kali Films Priority Pictures
Director:
Pratibha Parmar
Producers:
Chris Atkins
Claire Chapman
Screenwriters:
Andrea Gibb
Pratibha Parmar
Cinematographer:
Simon Dennis
Art Director:
Margaret Horspool
Composer:
Steve Isles
Editor:
Mary Finlay
Duration:
94 Minutes
Genre:
Musical
Romance
Romantic Comedy
Social Drama
Melodrama
Cast:
Laura Fraser
Shelley Conn
Ronny Jhutti
Art Malik
Veena Sood

Synopsis

A young woman named Nina returns to Scotland following the death of her father, causing her to confront longstanding issues with her family and to come to terms with her sexuality. Although raised in Scotland by her Indian parents, Nina fled to London for years to escape an arranged marriage to a man whom she had no feelings for. Upon her return to Glasgow she becomes determined to honour the memory of her father by winning the 'Best of the West' curry cooking competition that he had entered his restaurant into just before his death. She is aided in this endeavour by a young chef named Lisa, whom Nina begins to find herself falling for, despite Nina's fear of coming out. Tensions culminate, and are ultimately resolved, in the dramatic cooking competition where Nina discovers that her father's motto of 'Always follow your heart' may have more truth to it than she had ever expected.

Critique

The decision to make one of the central messages of the film 'Always follow your heart' may seem quite cliché at first glance. However, despite the unoriginality of the saying, the motto holds a large amount of significance for the way in which the film communicates concerning lesbian-gay-bisexual-transgender-queer issues. Many of the characters represented in the film, including Nina, repress their feelings about love and hide them from those around them. With the exception of Nina, however, it does not seem as though they are ashamed about their desires; they are actually quite proud of who they are despite keeping their actions and feelings a secret from most of those around them. Everyone in her family obeys the motto of the father and follows what their heart tells them to do, regardless of the possible ramifications that may arise if other family members were to find out. A fear of rejection by their mother is what keeps Nina's siblings from revealing their own secrets to those around them, but Nina cannot bring herself to confide in any other family member or even her closest friends about her sexuality. The fears of rejection and becoming ostracized are common issues dealt with in films that revolve around a character coming out, but *Nina's Heavenly Delights* provides an unusual perspective on this trope where many of the characters have something else that they cannot bring themselves to come out about. The only exception to this is Nina's best friend, Bobbi (Ronny Jhutti), a flamboyant cross-dressing gay man who is much more openly proud about who he is than any of the other major characters. Despite being arguably the most out-there of any of the characters, Bobbi's pride allows the film to portray him as a role model for the others to reveal whatever secrets they may have to those around them. Although 'Always follow your heart' provides the characters with a motto to live by and repeat, the film emphasizes the power of taking pride in who you are and what you like regardless of what others may think.

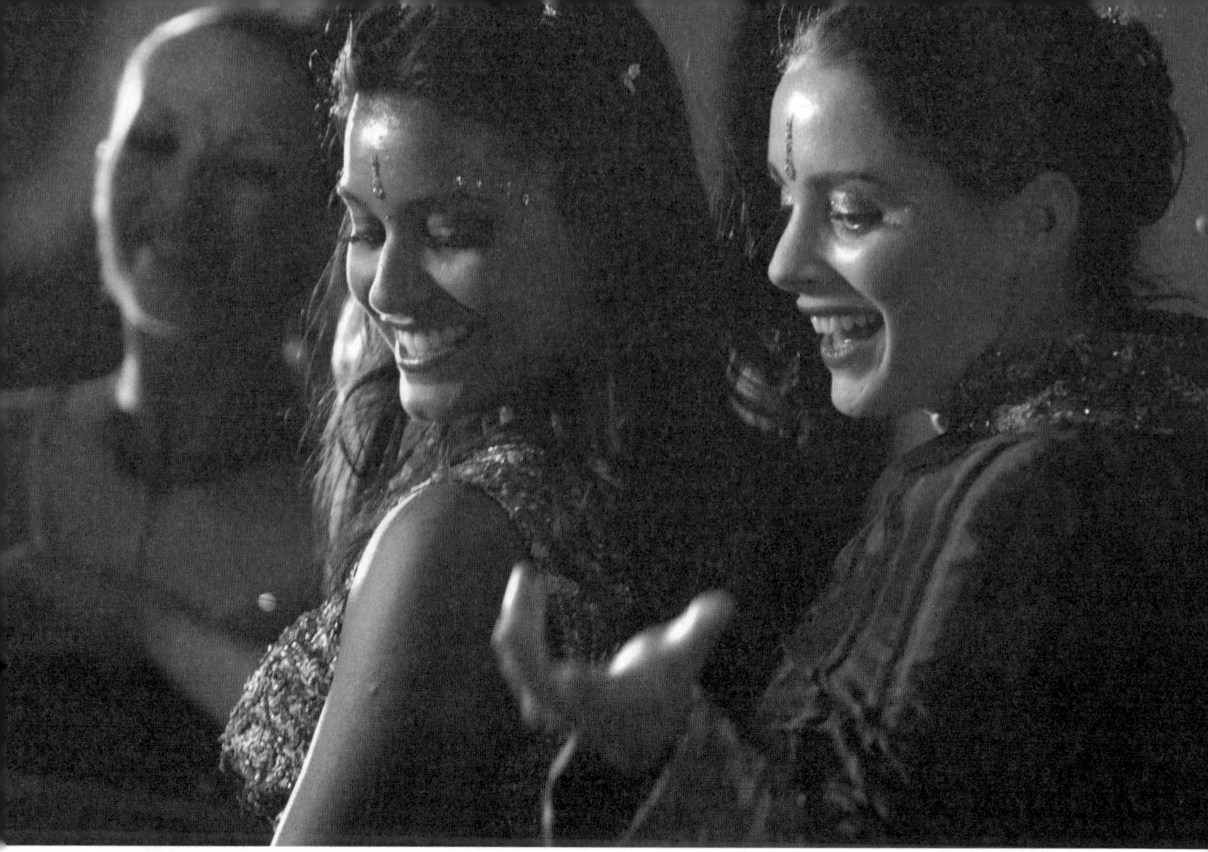

Nina's Heavenly Delights (2006), British Film Institute Collection

Year:
2006
Filming Location:
Glasgow, Strathclyde, Scotland, UK

Another striking dimension of *Nina's Heavenly Delights* is the way it provides an image of a different type of Scottishness than what is commonly portrayed in many other Scottish films. The film employs actors and actresses using clearly Scottish accents, includes scenes with traditional Scottish music and dance, and frequently cuts between close shot scenes to show aerial views of Glasgow that firmly remind viewers that the film takes place exclusively in Scotland's largest city. At the same time, the film displays elements of Bollywood cinema by using extravagant song and dance sequences involving all of the characters and by introducing fantastic elements such as the appearance of Nina's father's ghost. *Nina's Heavenly Delights* is more than just a movie about forbidden love and Indian cooking; it is a movie that attempts to accentuate contemporary Scottish multiculturalism. *Nina's Heavenly Delights* celebrates diversity and promotes a fusion between traditional Scottish and traditional Indian cultures. Both traditionally Scottish and traditionally Indian music are seamlessly woven into the film's soundtrack and both flow alongside contemporary pop music as well. The background music frequently transitions from one type to another, creating a sense that multiple forms of music and culture are interconnected within popular culture in contemporary Scotland. Although *Nina's Heavenly Delights* is first and foremost a coming out story, it is unusual in providing audiences with images of Scottish multiculturalism not commonly seen in other Scottish films.

Jason Burke

The Prime of Miss Jean Brodie

Country of Origin:

UK

Languages:

English
Latin
French
Italian

Studio/Production Company:

Twentieth Century Fox

Director:

Ronald Neame

Producer:

Robert Freyer

Screenwriter:

Jay Presson Allen

Cinematographer:

Ted Moore

Art Director:

Brian Herbert

Composer:

Rod McKuen

Editor:

Norman Savage

Duration:

116 minutes

Genre:

Social/Psychological Drama

Cast:

Maggie Smith
Robert Stephens
Gordon Jackson

Year:

1969

Synopsis

The film focuses on a rather eccentric and heterodox teacher, Miss Jean Brodie, at an all-girls school in Edinburgh. Miss Brodie's pedagogical modus operandi is defined by her disavowal of conventional teaching practices and disciplines in favour of the primacy of 'goodness, truth, and beauty' in the classroom. Miss Brodie, believing herself to be in her prime – her utmost potential for greatness – takes on a small group of girls hence known as 'the Brodie set' in an effort to help them reach their fullest potential. The film moves through the girls' school years as they progress from a young latent stage into a more mature, sexually curious adulthood. As the girls mature, they become involved in the personal and romantic affairs of Miss Jean Brodie, at a time in which Miss Brodie's love life begins to fall apart and the security of her job is put in question. Her time at the school ends when a member of her set, Sandy, betrays her by turning to the headmistress and board of governors to have Miss Brodie removed from her position in response to the death of one of the set, Mary McGregor, after Mary is convinced by Miss Brodie to travel to Spain and fight for Franco.

Critique

What ultimately fascinates about this film is not only what we take out of it, the lessons we may learn or the experience we may have enjoyed, but also what we find ourselves putting into it – the emotional connections we make with the characters. What is especially of interest is the audiences' emotional investment in Miss Brodie, considering how the film frames her as both hero and villain. The question with which we find ourselves captivated is not so much why does the film make Miss Brodie seem both ethical and unethical, but instead *how* do the ethical and the unethical come to resemble each other. How, in other words, does the fascist attitude that Miss Brodie expresses *mimic* an ethical attitude?

The film works well in leaving the viewer with two views of Miss Brodie: as both conniving and righteous. The two views result from the way the narrative is developed, both sutured to the view of the audience and to that of the girls Miss Brodie teaches. In this way, we are privy to two perspectives: our own perspective as an independent observer of Miss Brodie, critical of her fascist sympathy, and that of the girls who see her as revolutionary and ethical. This framing permits us to observe the fascist attitude from our early twenty-first century, post-European fascist perspective, and from a naively romantically idealist perspective prior to the widespread antipathy concerning anything even resembling fascism

Filming Locations:

Barnbougle Castle, Dalmeny, Edinburgh, Scotland, UK
Cramond, Edinburgh, Scotland, UK
Dalmeny House, Dalmeny, Edinburgh, Scotland, UK
Donaldson's School for the Deaf, Henderson Row, Edinburgh, Scotland, UK

following from World War II. By combining these two views, the viewer is able to see the fascist attitude from two different moral vantage points, and thus is left unable easily to reconcile the apparent contradiction between Miss Brodie's cruel and authoritarian behaviours versus her caring and fostering (as well as charismatic and inspiring) role as a teacher.

Mr Lloyd's comment about there being no contradiction in being both ridiculous and magnificent stands true, in Miss Brodie's case, for the ideas of the ethical and the unethical. The contradictory elements of Miss Brodie's behaviour can best be explained by

The Prime of Miss Jean Brodie (1969), British Film Institute Collection

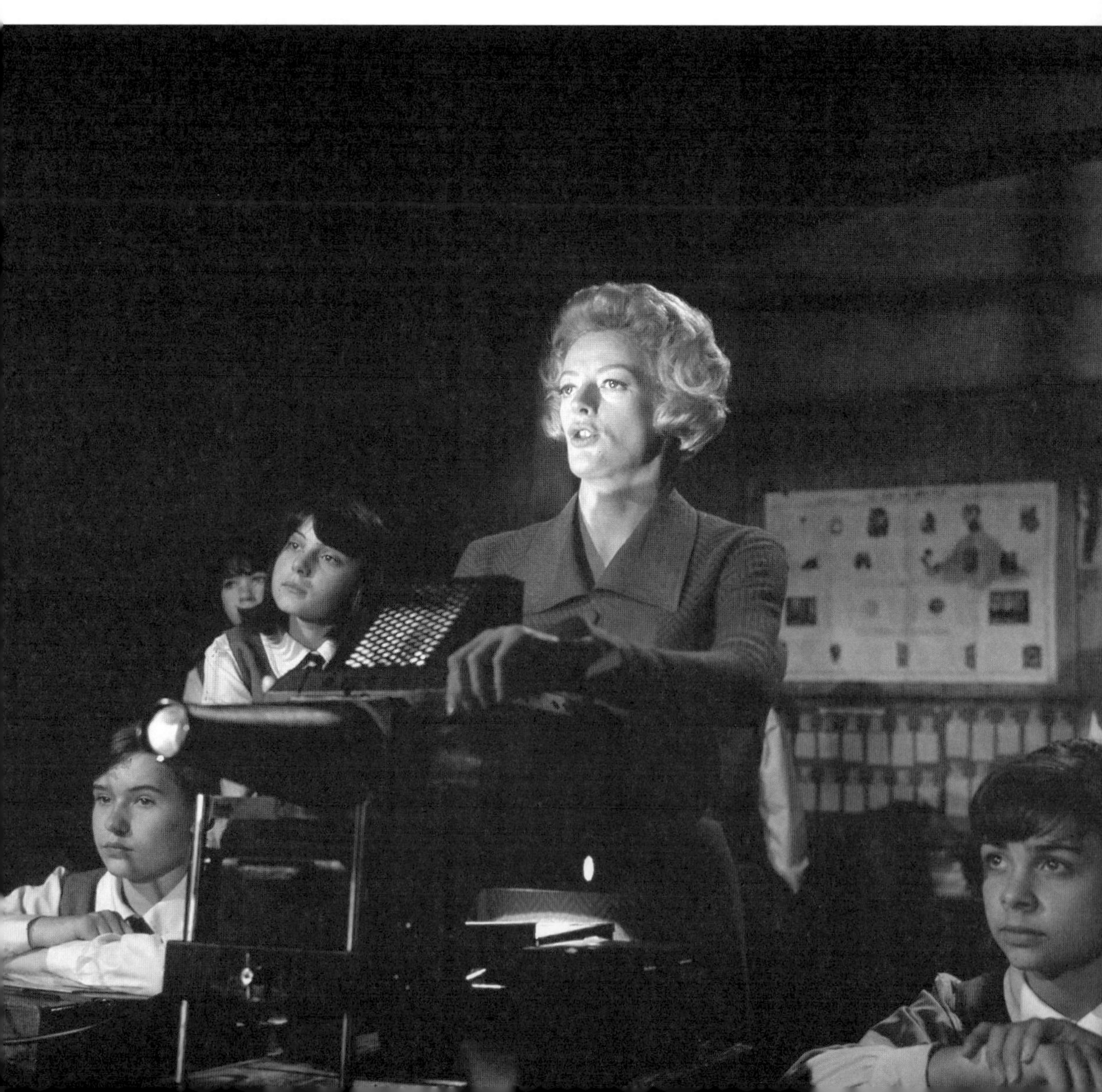

Greyfriars Churchyard, Edinburgh, Scotland, UK
Grim's Dyke House, Old Redding, Harrow Weald, Middlesex, England, UK
Pinewood Studios, Iver Heath, Buckinghamshire, England, UK
The Vennel, Grassmarket, Edinburgh, Scotland, UK

understanding her ethical and unethical behaviour as structurally interconnected. When understood dialectically, ethical and unethical are not opposing and independent ideas, but are instead oppositional whilst also sharing a unifying structural relationship. In the case of Miss Brodie, many of her behaviours that we would first understand as being contradictory (e.g. her feminism and fascist sympathies) can be understood as sharing a structural commonality in how they are performed.

Her dedication to her students, though appearing to be ethical in its fidelity, is an expression of her dedication to abstract ideals of goodness, truth and beauty. Dedication to these idealities and fascist sympathizing go hand-in-hand in that they seek a singularly totalized and ultimately final good. Fascism functions through the totalizing of ideal concepts like goodness, beauty, purity, nationality and kinship. These idealities, totalized in their scope of making subjects of all humans without any temporally contingent consideration (i.e. parading as eternal verities), first appear as notions worthy of dedication, yet, upon closer inspection, reveal their oppressive nature. Instead of contributing to more freedom for the individual, becoming subject to these idealities proves corrupt and enslaving. Because these idealities remain obscure notions instead of concrete features, they must be decided and defined by someone with charismatic power in order to be comprehensible. In this way, the subjective knowledge of one person or group of people can be elevated to an eternal law and, as situational exigencies spring up and subjective needs require new methods of fulfillment, these eternal laws become all the more oppressive and destructive. What seems to be a revolutionary devotion to an ethical principle becomes just another form of servitude to a destructive authority.

Miss Brodie's pseudo-feminism is a fine example of how the unethical can appear as radically ethical. Instead of being dedicated to women's liberation from oppression and degradation, she teaches her female students to subject themselves to totalized ideals and concepts that are equally as unrelenting, essentializing and uncompromising as any proffered by patriarchal authority. Within the situation of a patriarchal society, essentializing and determinist powers are already present in excessive amounts, so a truly radical and ethical dedication would be to what is lacking from that same situation. Miss Brodie's dedication to fascist idealities does not challenge the excesses of patriarchal society – it embraces them. In this way, her actions and teaching first appear as radical and revolutionary – just as the German and Italian fascist movements appear as radical by identifying with revolutionary socialist movements – yet are subverted by an unethical dedication to the excesses within existing capitalist, imperialist and patriarchal society.

Nathaniel Taylor

Rob Roy

Countries of Origin:

USA
UK

Language:

English

Studio/Production Companies:

United Artists
Talisman Productions

Director:

Michael Caton-Jones

Producers:

Peter Broghan
Michael Caton-Jones
Larry DeWaay
Richard Jackson

Screenwriter:

Alan Sharp

Cinematographer:

Karl Walter Lindenlaub

Art Directors:

John Ralph
Alan Tomkins

Composer:

Carter Burwell

Editor:

Peter Honess

Duration:

139 minutes

Genre:

Historical Romance

Cast:

Liam Neeson
Jessica Lange
John Hurt
Tim Roth

Year:

1995

Filming Location:

Glen Tarbert, Highland, Scotland, UK
Rannoch Moor, Highland, Scotland, UK

Synopsis

The 1995 United Artists film *Rob Roy* focuses on a violent dispute between Rob Roy, the McGregor Clan and the Duke of Argyll against the Duke of Montrose, his debt collector Killearn and his enforcer Cunningham. The catalyst for much of the film's plot occurs when Rob Roy puts up all of the land belonging to the McGregor clan as collateral on a loan given by the Duke of Montrose. Killearn gives the loan from Montrose to the McGregors as promised, but then Cunningham conspires with Killearn to murder the McGregor handler and keep the money themselves. Montrose calls in his debt from Rob Roy, but when he insists the money is stolen and will not give up his land he is declared an enemy of the Crown and hunted down by the English soldiers under the direction of Cunningham. These events create a violent back and forth between the McGregors, on the one side, and the Duke of Montrose and his royal troops, on the other side.

Critique

Rob Roy uses many of the same characters and themes found in the 1953 Disney film directed by Harold French, but the crux of the action focuses around money and honour instead of the general freedom that the Highland Clans were trying to win from the English in Rob Roy's earlier life as depicted in *Highland Rogue*. In *Rob Roy* all of the English characters that we encounter for any extended period of time are unabashedly evil. The principal villain, Cunningham, is depicted as a sexual deviant, and not-so-subtly coded as bi-sexual – which, again, according to the logic of this film, is a clearly suspect quality. Cunningham's initial entrance into the film introduces him to the audience and to Argyll's not-so-subtly coded macho warriors as an effete and foppish nobleman. Cunningham defies our expectations, however, when he proves to be extremely adept at swordplay. Of course, with the film-makers hoping to tap into the viewer's prejudices they will be hard pressed to view an effeminate man as capable of outfighting big and burly Highland warriors, so Cunningham's prowess is a key problem the film sets up early on as demanding a solution. Cunningham's questionable heterosexual credentials are intended to make viewers fear and mistrust him as the horrid villain the film will show him to be. As the film progresses Cunningham proves to be ruthless, vindictive and willing to do anything to hurt Rob Roy and his family. The film-makers appear to be playing to the notion that a man willing to have a sexual relationship with another man is capable of anything (rape, murder and general dishonourable conduct).

The film is hardly subtle in showing which characters the audience should sympathize with.

> Rob Roy is a hero not simply because he is tall, good and strong, but because he will sacrifice his life rather than compromise his word. And the film's villains are magnificent because they are so smart, cunning and smarmy: Not content with merely being despicable, they work at it. (Ebert 1995)

Caig Falls Bridge, Loch Arkaig, Highland, Scotland, UK
Castle Tioram, Moidart, Highland, Scotland, UK
Crichton Castle, Crichton, Midlothian, Scotland, UK
Drummond Castle, Crieff, Perth and Kinross, Scotland, UK
Eilean Donan Castle, Kyle of Lochalsh, Highland, Scotland, UK
Glen Coe, Highland, Scotland, UK
Glen Nevis, Fort William, Highland, Scotland, UK
Loch Earn, Stirling, Scotland, UK
Loch Leven, Onich, Highland, Scotland, UK
Loch Morar, Highland, Scotland, UK
Megginch Castle, Errol, Perth and Kinross, Scotland, UK

The 'good guys' in the film are willing to do anything possible to maintain their honour and that of their family, while the 'bad guys' are willing to do anything to bring dishonour to others.

The sexual and gender politics of this film become even more troubling when the only the major female character in the film, Mary McGregor (Jessica Lange), is sexually assaulted on camera by Cunningham as the audience and Killearn watch, horrified. Mary wisely attempts to keep this information from Rob Roy, knowing that sharing it would only incite her husband to act rashly. But her temper cannot be kept under control, either (she is a McGregor after all); she later physically attacks Killearn after he is captured by Rob Roy. Yet she is primarily depicted as a supportive, even peripheral figure, and, at best, a feisty victim. The only other female character we spend any time with is a household servant, Becky (Vicki Mason), who is impregnated and abandoned by Cunningham. His cruel treatment becomes too much for her to bear and she eventually commits suicide after telling Mary what has happened to her. These women have little agency in comparison with the male characters in the film, and are allowed little even by the ones who love them. Mary's decision to not tell Rob Roy of her assault is treated as a foolish mistake by her husband, who feels far more concerned that his honour has been taken away (even by this brutal attack) than he is concerned with Mary's honour – or her well-being.

As an epic action picture, *Rob Roy* certainly has enough set pieces to keep its target-audience happy. Our hero's daring escape from Cunningham is lifted from the 1953 Disney film *Rob Roy: The Highland Rogue*, but the violence carries more weight in this version. The audience definitely feels the brutal consequences of all of this death and violence in contrast to how it was euphemistically portrayed in the 1950s Walt Disney production. The world Rob Roy lives, struggles and fights in here is certainly darker and more graphically violent. The final swordfight between Rob Roy and Cunningham is one of the highlights of the film, as the audience gets a relatively authentic idea of what an actual swordfight would have been like. This is no elegant display of pretend swordsmanship, but instead two men struggling desperately to stay alive.

Vengeance being served and honour being preserved replace the typically over-the-top happy ending that *Rob Roy*'s earlier, classical Hollywood counterpart provides. But, this Scottish folk hero (ironically played by an Irish actor in a film released the same year as *Braveheart* [Mel Gibson, 1995] where another Scottish hero is played by an Australian actor) definitely has his opportunities to show off his swordplay, get the girl and put the bad guys in their place. Perhaps this film is more indebted to Walt Disney than it may initially seem.

Terry Hobgood

Reference

Ebert, Roger (1995) 'Review of *Rob Roy*', *Rogerebert.com*, 7 April, http://www.rogerebert.com/reviews/rob-roy-1995. Accessed 20 March 2013.

Rob Roy: The Highland Rogue

Countries of Origin:
USA
UK

Languages:
English
Scottish Gaelic

Studio/Production Company:
Walt Disney Productions
RKO Radio Pictures

Director:
Harold French

Producers:
Perce Pearce
Walt Disney

Screenwriter:
Lawrence Edward Watkin

Cinematographer:
Guy Green

Art Director:
Geoffrey Drake

Composer:
Cedric Thorpe Davie

Editor:
Geoffrey Foote

Duration:
81 minutes

Genre:
Historical Romance

Cast:
Richard Todd
Glynis Johns
James Robertson Justice

Year:
1953

Filming Location:
Glasgow, Scotland, UK
Argyll and Sutherland, Scotland, UK

Synopsis

Walt Disney's 1953 release of *Rob Roy: The Highland Rogue* focuses on the rebellion of the Scottish Highlanders against King George I, and the titular hero of this uprising. Rob Roy McGregor spends much of the film escaping capture from the royal troops who are attempting to punish him for his role as the leader of this rebel band of Scots. Throughout the film our hero is captured and pursued by the English troops after he is declared a traitor by George I. Eventually he becomes such a folk hero and celebrity that he is summoned to meet the King and Queen in person. In the midst of all this circuitous pursuit and capture, Rob Roy leads his clan against the English, gets married and does his best to protect his home and family. Like Michael Caton-Jones's 1995 version of the same story (*Rob Roy*), this film is based on the 1817 novel of Rob Roy's life by Sir Walter Scott. *Highland Rogue* brings this source to our attention as it shows the King having Scott's book read to him.

Critique

Rob Roy: The Highland Rogue certainly encourages its audience to identify with the Highlanders, whose motives for rebellion are never questioned. Rob Roy's persona as a 'Highland Rogue' means that he is portrayed as consistently courageous, lovable and intelligent. He enters the film in a march to battle where he is eventually captured when the Highlanders are routed by the larger English force. Every few scenes after this he is depicted either outsmarting the English with a daring escape, or managing to show up at just the right moment to save his wife Helen Mary (Glynis Johns) or another member of his clan.

Helen Mary and Rob Roy's mother Lady Margaret (Jean Taylor Smith) serve as the moral anchors of the film. Whenever Rob Roy gets carried away with his righteous mission, one of these two women conveniently makes their way into the scene to talk him down. Even after Lady Margaret is shot by an English soldier, her last message to Rob Roy is to bring peace. In typical Disney (and Classic Hollywood) fashion these women are also portrayed as domestically oriented, yet irascible and fearless. They do not show pain in front of their son/husband, and prove to be nearly as adept with swords and firearms as our hero. Of course, this does not preclude Rob Roy from showing up in the nick of time to save the damsels in distress as they are being attacked by the villainous English.

After Rob Roy and the McGregor clan receive the ultimate insult, having the McGregor name outlawed due to treason against the British Crown, they decide to exact vengeance on the English soldiers by storming and laying siege to a Highland fort. In these scenes the English soldiers prove to be mostly inept and dishonourable. They are outsmarted by the rag-tag Highland force, and when Rob Roy comes forward with terms for a truce,

Trossach and Aberfoyle, Scotland, UK
London, England, UK

the English commander decides to open fire while Rob Roy stands under a white flag. Some contemporary reviews found these battle scenes and the location shooting especially memorable:

> The battle scenes have a vividness of their own and the stamp of realism is appreciated when it is known that Highland forces were loaned for these scenes. The misty highlands have been effectively photographed and the overall background provides the right touch of atmosphere. (Anon. 1952)

There is little doubt that the film-makers intend for us to treat the English soldiers as the villains, but the short running time of the film never lets us see these troops as much more than a thinly sketched group of bumbling and ill-prepared antagonists. Even though they lose many of the filmed battles, the Highland troops seem the most 'warrior-like' while actually conveying discernible personalities. The deaths in the film are allowed little time to sink in before we move on to the next set piece, as any darker implications of death have no place in this mostly upbeat film. And this quality accounted for the film's contemporary appeal. Bosley Crowther's *New York Times* review, for instance, was mostly positive, generally praising the performances and not worrying too much about the historical veracity:

> What you can look for, however, is a fine lot of fighting among the hills, shooting of rifles, banging of claymores, skirling of pipes and buzzing of burrs, filmed and recorded in color on the actual Scottish countryside. And while Mr. Todd is not precisely the Rob Roy that history records, he is indeed a satisfactory fabrication until a better Rob Roy comes along. (Crowther 1954)

At the end of the film, viewers gain access to a meta-commentary on Rob Roy's place in popular culture and British folklore as King George I anachronistically reads the Sir Walter Scott novel, originally published nearly a century later, concerning Rob Roy's exploits. Doing so inspires the King to issue a pardon after inviting this same Rogue to his Court so that they can meet. While George I is portrayed as an almost childlike monarch, he is dubbed by Rob Roy himself as a great King as the music swells at this moment of reconciliation. All seems to be forgiven by Rob Roy – whose name, land and titles were revoked just a few scenes earlier. As the hero returns to his clan in the Scottish Highlands, all is right with the world and the audience can go home happy.

Terry Hobgood

References

Anon. (1952) 'Review of *Rob Roy: The Highland Rogue*', *Variety*, 31 December, . http://variety.com/1952/film/reviews/rob-roy-1200417433/, Accessed 21 April 2014.

Crowther, Bosley (1954) 'Rob Roy Opens at Criterion; Walt Disney Drama Moves in Angry Pursuits Among the Misty Scottish Hills', *The New York Times*, 4 February, http://www.nytimes.com/movie/review?res=9D0DEFD7143CE43ABC4C53DFB466838F649EDE, Accessed 21 April 2014.

Seachd: The Inaccessible Pinnacle

Country of Origin:
UK

Languages:
Scottish Gaelic
English

Studio/Production Company:
Young Films

Director:
Simon Miller

Producers:
Ishbel Maclennan
Carole Sheridan
Christopher Young

Screenwriters:
Simon Miller
Iseabail NicDhomhnaill
Aonghas Macneacail
Iain Finlay MacLeod
Joanne Cockwell

Cinematographer:
Ian Dodds

Art Director:
Ali Milligan

Composer:
Jim Sutherland

Editor:
Angus Mackay

Duration:
100 minutes

Genre:
Folklore

Synopsis

Seachd: The Inaccessible Pinnacle marks the first time that a feature Scottish cinematic narrative was produced in Scottish Gaelic. The film follows Aonghas as, after a trip to visit his dying grandfather, he recalls the loss of his parents at the tender age of seven and the stories told by his grandfather (stories steeped in both history and the fantastic) at moments when Aonghas and his siblings most needed moral guidance. As we watch the young Aonghas navigate the loss of his parents, his grandmother and the impending loss of his grandfather, we find ourselves led to the final act that he must complete in order to find the truths he has been seeking: a climb atop the 'inaccessible pinnacle' that took his parents thirteen years before.

Critique

Through the grandfather's stories, spectators are introduced to a set of magical figures, images and narratives that strongly resonate with the romance of Scottish Gaelic history. Scottish Gaelic folklore, much like *Aesop's Fables*, has been used for centuries as a mechanism to instill important moral lessons to children that are tied specifically to everyday conditions of existence in Highland and Island homelands. It is not uncommon to find stories that include magical ability, including powerful curses, as well as mythological creatures such as kelpies. The story of the kelpie retold by Aonghas's grandfather is of a water horse that entices those who come upon it to ride its back. Once in place, the horse takes its victim down a watery grave. Such stories find their historical counterparts in such moments as the Roman invasion, when the Romans came by sea to invade both England and Scotland. Here, the kelpie stands as an allegory, warning children of beguiling strangers. In the case of *Seachd*, the tale is told after the man who had guided Aonghas's parents up the pinnacle comes in order to explain to the family the events leading up to their deaths. The grandfather's tales consistently correlate to events either immediately leading to or following the telling.

Genre placement is difficult when approaching *Seachd*, as it is not quite a coming-of-age film or a drama, as typically understood. It is better to make sense of the film through its fantastical elements, and, in so doing, Tzvetan Todorov's notion of the *fantastique* proves useful. Todorov tells us that a sub-genre of the fantastic, the fantastic-marvellous, includes those 'narratives that are presented as fantastic and that end with an acceptance of the

Story-Telling
Myth and Legend
Coming of Age
Fantasy

Cast:

Aonghas Padruig Caimbeul
Padruig Moireasdan
Coll Domhnallach

Year:

2007

Filming Locations:

Eilean Iarmain, Sleat, Kilt Rock and Elgol – Skye (Highland, Scotland, UK)
Fort William and Glen Coe (Highland, Scotland, UK)

supernatural' (1973: 52). In *Seachd*, the grandfather's tales function this way. In regard to Aonghas's story, the film ends in such a way that what we've perceived as being the realistic anchor of the film takes on its own supernatural twists that allow spectators to view the film in its entirety in much the same way that the grandfather utilized his smaller tales with the children.

Although the use of the film as an allegory certainly depends on the national location of the spectator, the single fact that *Seachd* is the first feature film produced domestically in Scotland in Scottish Gaelic means that no spectator can resist the film's national reference. 'Cinema in any national frame cannot be viewed beyond its historical and political contexts' (Maingard 2007: 2). First, the use of Scottish Gaelic reinforces the film's use of Scottish folklore, pointing at all times back through the history of the nation. Second, Aonghas's story, structured by the losses of his parents and grandparents, in conjunction with the use of Scottish Gaelic and Scottish folklore, highlights the notion of a greater traumatic loss – of a people and of a culture. At the same time, *Seachd* can be seen as a response and resistance to the inevitability, and to the inevitable trauma, of these losses.

Adam Lowenstein confronts such national losses and the cinema's representation of them by defining 'the allegorical moment as a shocking collision of film, spectator, and history where registers of bodily space and historical time are disrupted, confronted, and intertwined' (2005: 2). In the case of *Seachd*, the grandfather's stories stand as markers of a history that he wishes to highlight, particularly in those moments when his grandchildren are confronted with traumatic loss. Spectators can view the film and its representation of loss as an allegory for those they have experienced in their own lives. Viewers maintaining an even rudimentary familiarity with Scottish history will recognize the ways these collisions occur simultaneously at personal, cinematic and national levels.

Jeremy Magnan

References

Lowenstein, Adam (2005) *Shocking Representation: Historical Trauma, National Cinema, and the Modern Horror Film*, New York: Columbia University Press.

Maingard, Jacqueline (2007) *South African National Cinema*, London: Routledge.

Todorov, Tzvetan (1973) *The Fantastic: A Structural Approach to a Literary Genre*, Cleveland: Case Western Reserve University Press.

Stone of Destiny

Countries of Origin:

Canada
UK

Language:

English

Studio/Production Companies:

Infinity Features Entertainment
The Mob Film Company
Alliance Films
Téléfilm Canada
Scottish Screen National Lottery Fund
The Harold Greenberg Fund

Director:

Charles Martin Smith

Producers:

Andrew Boswell
Alan Martin
Rob Merilees

Screenwriters:

Charles Martin Smith
Ian Hamilton

Cinematographer:

Glen Winter

Art Director:

Andy Thomson

Composer:

Mychael Danna

Editor:

Fredrik Thorsen

Duration:

96 minutes

Genre:

Caper
Historical Romance
Comedy
Social Drama

Cast:

Charlie Cox
Kate Mara
Stephen McCole

Synopsis

Based on a true story, *Stone of Destiny* narrates the tale of a daring heist jointly fuelled by the audacity of young minds and the tenacity of old mindsets. Ian Hamilton is a Glasgow University student at the start of the 1950s. Drawn increasingly into the political movement for Scottish Home Rule, a campaign led by the University's charismatic Rector, John MacCormick, Ian concludes that a grand symbolic gesture is required to precipitate a significant constitutional change to what he sees as Scotland's subordinate place within the wider United Kingdom. With the help of a small group of student friends – Bill, Kay, Gavin and Alan – he hatches a plan to repatriate the Stone of Destiny, the ceremonial rock upon which Scottish monarchs were once anointed, from its place underneath the Coronation Chair at Westminster Abbey in London. The Stone was forcibly removed from Scotland to that location by the English King Edward I in 1296 in an act intended to support his claim that English monarchs possessed the inalienable right to exercise superiority over their Scottish counterparts. After a series of mishaps, mistakes and miscommunications, Ian and his comrades manage to steal the Stone from Westminster on Christmas Day, first hiding it in a remote part of the English countryside and later placing it on the altar of Arbroath Abbey in north-east Scotland. Spontaneous popular celebrations in Scotland greet the students' actions. As Ian and the others are arrested at Arbroath, he triumphantly informs a journalist that he and his companions are 'the children of Scotland'. Closing intertitles inform viewers that the students were never prosecuted for their actions and that (in 1996) the British government eventually returned the Stone to Scotland 'on loan'.

Critique

Despite its ostensible appearance as an unapologetically mainstream and upbeat would-be international crowd-pleaser, *Stone of Destiny* in fact struggles painfully to chart a safe course between opposing poles of apolitical sentiment and ideologically complex and contentious matters of Scottish history and contemporary politics. Granted, director Charles Martin Smith's movie is conspicuously full-throated in its conscious celebration of 1950s Scottish nationalist students' youthful ardour and idealism. But, even in this sense, the film approaches the Stone of Destiny's story, and what that narrative symbolizes within the specific national and political contexts of the British Islands, less as an end in and of itself and more as a vehicle for something else entirely. Strip away the Scottish accents and agitation for self-determination and one is left with a series of heart-warming platitudes – 'our children are the future', 'the old accept the world as it is, the young imagine the world as it could be' – which have populated innumerable feel-good movies set within countless different national territories. Thus, while Ian's voice-over accompanying *Stone of Destiny*'s opening scene remembers how 'I was young and full of passion for my country', we might plausibly suggest that the movie is far more

Billy Boyd
Robert Carlyle

Year:

2008

Filming Locations:

Arbroath and Glasgow (Scotland, UK)
London, England, UK
Vancouver, Canada

attracted to, and sure-footed in, its engagement with the universal theme of 'young passion' than it is with the accompanying, and more culturally specific, one of 'country'.

Of course, it must be admitted that this is not how *Stone of Destiny* appears on the surface. Set at the start of the 1950s, the movie freely borrows a range of motifs from what was one of the most prominent and popular British cinematic cycles of the decade in question, the World War II movie. In the case of this modern-day film, however, it is British officials and the British state that assume the role of repressive antagonists, while Scottish students are the indomitable guerrilla fighters for freedom from colonial-cum-dictatorial rule. A number of sequences carefully foreground this subversive act of reverse cinematic quotation. An early montage of Ian and Bill plotting the Stone's liberation sees them manoeuvring toy soldiers around a map of Westminster Abbey, in what starts to feel like a remake of *The Colditz Story* (Guy Hamilton, 1955) starring an inanimate central protagonist. More pointedly yet, Ian's closing voice-over quotes from the 1320 Declaration of Arbroath, an incredibly important and enduringly influential historical document in which the original Scottish signatories rejected the 'domination of the English', and proclaimed that 'we fight [...] only and alone for freedom, which no good man surrenders but with his life'. If 1950s British war movies typically portray a heroically principled struggle for freedom conducted from the United Kingdom, *Stone of Destiny* instead frames itself as the story of a similar struggle being waged *between* elements within the United Kingdom's two largest constituent nations at the start of the decade in question.

Ultimately, however, the 'British war movie' parallel also underscores the extent to which *Stone of Destiny* is less confident in the inarguable rightness of its protagonists' nationalist cause than, say, *The Dam Busters* (Michael Anderson, 1953) or *Carve Her Name with Pride* (Lewis Gilbert, 1958) were in their depictions of patriotic British resistance to Continental fascist tyranny. At times, Ian's ardour is presented as innocuous/incongruous: more than one individual is bemused/amused by the carefully coded phone calls that the young man makes back to Scotland while working undercover in the enemy capital of London. In other instances, however, *Stone of Destiny* seems to concede that Scottish nationalism is a political discourse that might conceivably be afflicted by potentially dangerous hyper-masculine, and even militaristic, tendencies – despite the fact that Ian at one point invokes Ghandi's peaceful protests against British colonial rule in India as a point of reference for what he and he colleagues hope to achieve in/for Scotland. Thus, female protagonists are consistently deployed as supporting players who conveniently constrain and/or channel the fissile physical, emotional and ideological energies of Scottish men. The idea to repatriate the Stone of Destiny comes to Ian after he sees a press-cutting photograph of the famous early-twentieth-century Scottish nationalist Wendy Wood protesting in support of that cause. Ian's mother patiently mediates between him and his authoritarian father, a man who says that 'nobody could be prouder of Scotland than I am', but who appears to have been emotionally embittered by his acceptance of the Unionist constitutional settlement. John MacCormick ruefully notes that, despite his national prominence and power, his female housekeeper 'has been with the family since I was a boy – and still treats me like one'; it is she who counsels him to reverse his original decision not to support Ian's plan. Alan inspires his temporarily dispirited colleagues by recounting the famous story of the (female) spider that, legend has it, inspired Robert the Bruce in his struggle for Scottish independence in the early fourteenth century: 'six times he watched her spin that web [...] she never gave up'. Finally, and most obviously of all, Kay consistently punctures Ian's self-importance, telling him at one point that, 'you're not the great high and mighty, you're just another boy with grand ideas'.

In these and other ways, *Stone of Destiny* strives to pre-emptively rehabilitate an ideological discourse and political cause that the film ostensibly eulogizes as something self-evidently just and true, a phenomenon that does not require any significant form of qualification or reformation whatsoever. Ironically, however, one potential effect of the movie's covert caveats to, and suggested corrections of, the worldview articulated by Ian is to exacerbate, rather than ameliorate, anxieties about the perilous potential of nationalist political discourses and popular movements within a twentieth- or post-twentieth-century European context. For instance, Ian's climactic self-description of himself and his comrades as 'the children of Scotland' and Kay's earlier description of herself a Scottish mother/Mother Scotland, a young woman who looks forward to spending her life 'working with children and helping them find their way in the world' are both statements that could sit easily with the characteristic rhetoric of the far-right-wing, anti-democratic nationalisms that helped to precipitate World War II. *Stone of Destiny*'s lack of significant commercial success – and also, perhaps, the air of the student jape that continues to cling to the Westminster Abbey heist more than half-a-century on from that event – have entailed that this film has to date not received sustained attention from critics of Scottish cinema. But with regard to the enduring potency of the national historical events and icons that the movie invokes, and also to its associated experimentation with a binaristic them vs us form of nationalist politics, it might usefully be compared to one of the most exhaustively (and, sometimes, exhaustingly) discussed of all Scottish-themed movies, Mel Gibson's *Braveheart* (1995).

Jonathan Murray

Tunes of Glory

Country of Origin:

UK

Language:

English

Synopsis

Jock Sinclair, commanding officer of a post-war Highland regiment, is known for his heroic leadership in World War II, his gruff demeanour and his raucous distaste for formality. At a celebratory dinner amongst the regiment's officers, Sinclair announces that it is his last evening as commanding officer of the regiment, and that the new lieutenant colonel will arrive in the morning. Later in the

Studio/Production Company:
Knightsbridge Films
Director:
Ronald Neame
Producers:
Albert Fennell
Colin Lesslie
Screenwriter:
James Kennaway
Cinematographer:
Arthur Ibbetson
Art Director:
Martin Atkinson
Composer:
Malcolm Arnold

evening, and much to the surprise and chagrin of Sinclair, the new lieutenant colonel, Basil Barrow, arrives early to have a look at the facilities. They discuss their military honours, share in a tensely curt conversation and bid each other a good evening. From the next day onward, Sinclair and Barrow conflict with each other as Barrow tries to institute more formalized and proper fraternization within the regiment, especially in the form of their traditional dance. Meanwhile, Sinclair tries to retain his loyalty from the other officers and continue regimental practices he fostered. Their conflict comes to climax when Sinclair, after discovering that a young piper from the regiment was seeing his daughter, Morag, strikes the young piper. Barrow is troubled over how to deal with this incident, as it constitutes grounds for a court-martial, yet Barrow does not want to lose the loyalty of the other officers by having their old commander and friend removed. Barrow ultimately decides not to go forth with the court-martial, but then learns that the regiment is convinced Sinclair is still calling the shots. Seeing that he has failed to command the respect of the regiment like his forefathers had, he

Tunes of Glory (1960), British Film Institute Collection

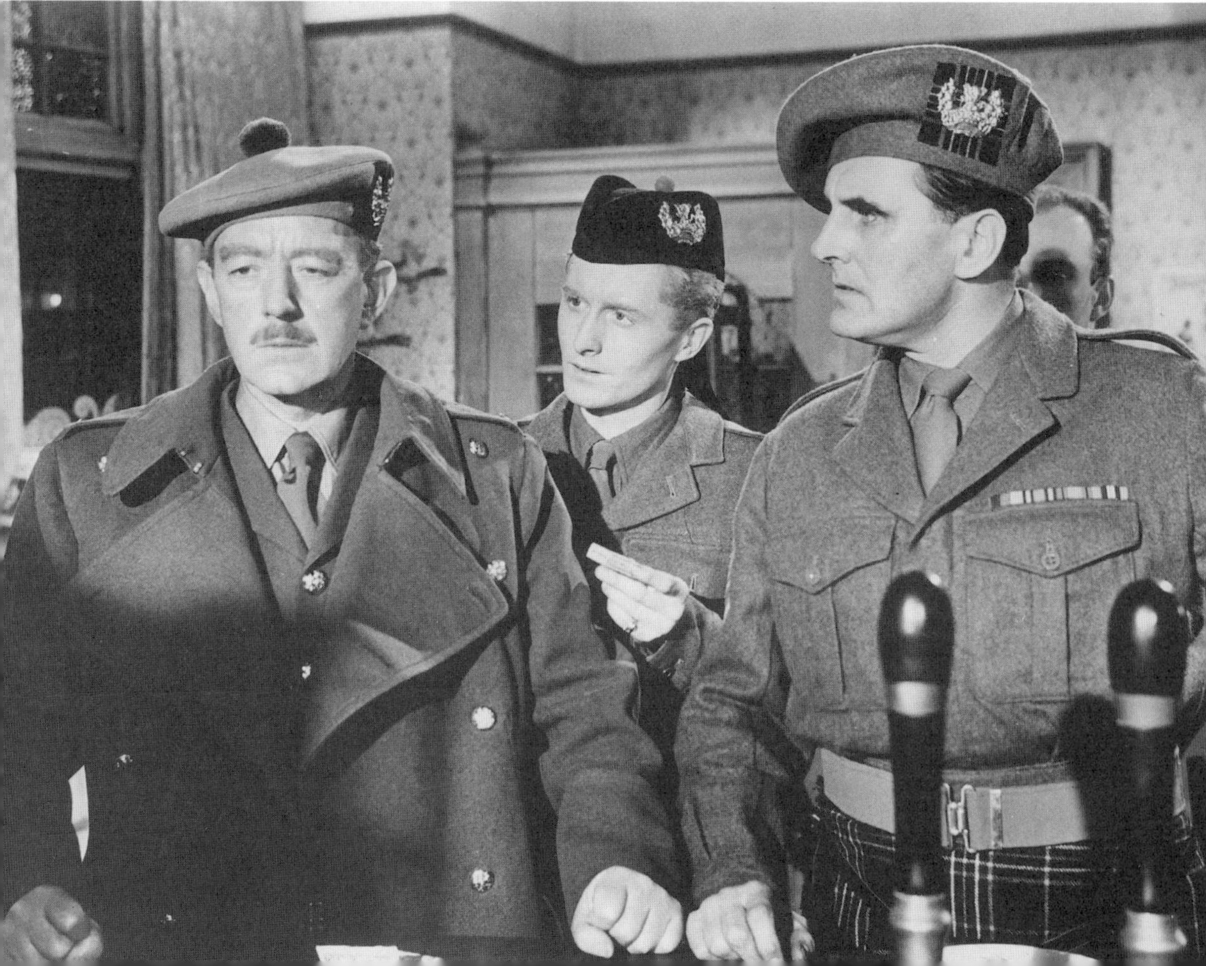

Editor:

Anne V Coates

Duration:

107 minutes

Genre:

Historical Romance
Social/Psychological Drama

Cast:

Alec Guinness
John Mills
Dennis Price

Year:

1960

Filming Location:

Shepperton Studios, Shepperton, Surrey, England, UK
Stirling Castle, Stirling, Scotland, UK

steals away to the bathroom and commits suicide. Sinclair, returning to his post as commanding officer, orders a military march and burial for Barrow, but is interrupted during his speech as he breaks down, falling against the wall and crying into his beret.

Critique

Tunes of Glory has been a challenging film for critics because of the ambivalence of, and the motivational ambiguity contained within, the ending scene. The mystery of this film seems to lie in the almost predetermined nature of Sinclair and Barrow's conflict. From their first face-to-face interaction there is a palpable tension between the two characters, ending with Sinclair tossing his whisky into the fireplace, creating a burst of sparks indicative of the coming explosive confrontation. Nearly everything about these two characters seems to be in conflict – from their class, ethnicity and demeanour down to Sinclair's fiery red hair versus Barrow's stern brown hair.

One reading of what happens is as follows. The impending trajectory of their conflict and its concluding consequences seem to provide a necessary resolution or reconciliation of their alterity. Their conflict is of two egos filling the same space such that the death of either Sinclair or Barrow is necessary for the other's continuance in the position. Thus, the problem does not arise from Barrow taking power from Sinclair and using it incorrectly, but instead both men occupy the same space of power. Upon the resolution of this conflict, Sinclair synthesizes their two personalities, even taking on Barrow's mannerisms. For instance, as Sinclair gives his orders concerning the burial and funeral march for Barrow, he demands to be called 'colonel' instead of 'Jock'. This new air of formality synthesizes their two modes of commanding. It is not the case that Sinclair merely replaces Barrow, but instead internalizes and incorporates Barrow's features to supplement and compliment his own.

Yet the problem with this reading is that it neutralizes the alterity of the Other. Were it the case that Sinclair could, in this dialectical conflict, fully synthesize the characteristics of Barrow, then he would be able to absorb – and thus resolve – Barrow's alterity and incorporate Barrow's mannerisms into his own – i.e. incorporate the Other into the Same. But Sinclair's breakdown can be read as the side effect of an attempted synthesis where he is able to assimilate the external mannerisms of Barrow, but ultimately unable to fully synthesize the essential being of Barrow. This essence that he cannot synthesize is not a spiritual or mystical thing like a Platonic essence, but is instead the final kernel of the Other that cannot be the Same – the alterity that cannot be reconciled or signified.

The foundation of the conflict between Barrow and Sinclair is not a conflict of essential qualities, whereby they are *fundamentally* determined to battle. Instead, their conflict is founded in their *symbolic* determination. The planes upon which they conflict – demeanour, traditions, class and ethnicity – are all discursive in their foundation. So, it is not the case that Sinclair qua essence and Barrow qua essence are determined to combat; instead they are bound to combat according to the network of signification that attempts to communicate their alterity.

Language is that which, by its constitution, is able to be internalized or assimilated from the Other into the Same. Thus, language is a function that helps to bridge the gap between two beings. Sinclair and Barrow meet at this level of linguistic signification by way of their shared social network: the military. Even more efficiently than other social networks, the military is able to communicate the alterity of the Other through categories of rank and honours, linguistically unifying a large group in conventional signification and conventional goals. But, regardless of how efficient a signifying network is, it can never fully unify separate beings into one, and it is this last non-signifiable unit of alterity that constitutes the individual – and ethical action towards the individual.

It is from this point of view that Sinclair sees himself as Barrow's murderer. Though their conflict is on the plane of signification, it led to the ultimate destruction of Barrow, in all his horrifying alterity. What sought resolution were the conflicts between different discursive significations, yet what ultimately gets resolved – i.e., consumed or destroyed – is not just these signifiers, but also the person they are connected to. The experience of the Other implicitly carries a kind of moral code, whereby the Other is so unfathomably different that it places the one who experiences the Other in a state of awe: do we dare destroy that which we cannot know?

After Barrow's death, Sinclair realizes the full depth and breadth of Barrow's alterity, and in realizing thereby the full extent of the consequences of his actions against Barrow, leading to Barrow's eventual suicide, Sinclair collapses from the weight of the revelation. He is a murderer because he exerted power over that which he did not have power. Sinclair was able to struggle against Barrow because their alterity was hidden, uniterated, by the social signifiers that defined them. However, after Barrow's death and after his signification becomes notably arbitrary (how much do honours matter to the dead?), Sinclair is confronted with the victim of his actions, unsymbolized and exposed.

Nathaniel Taylor

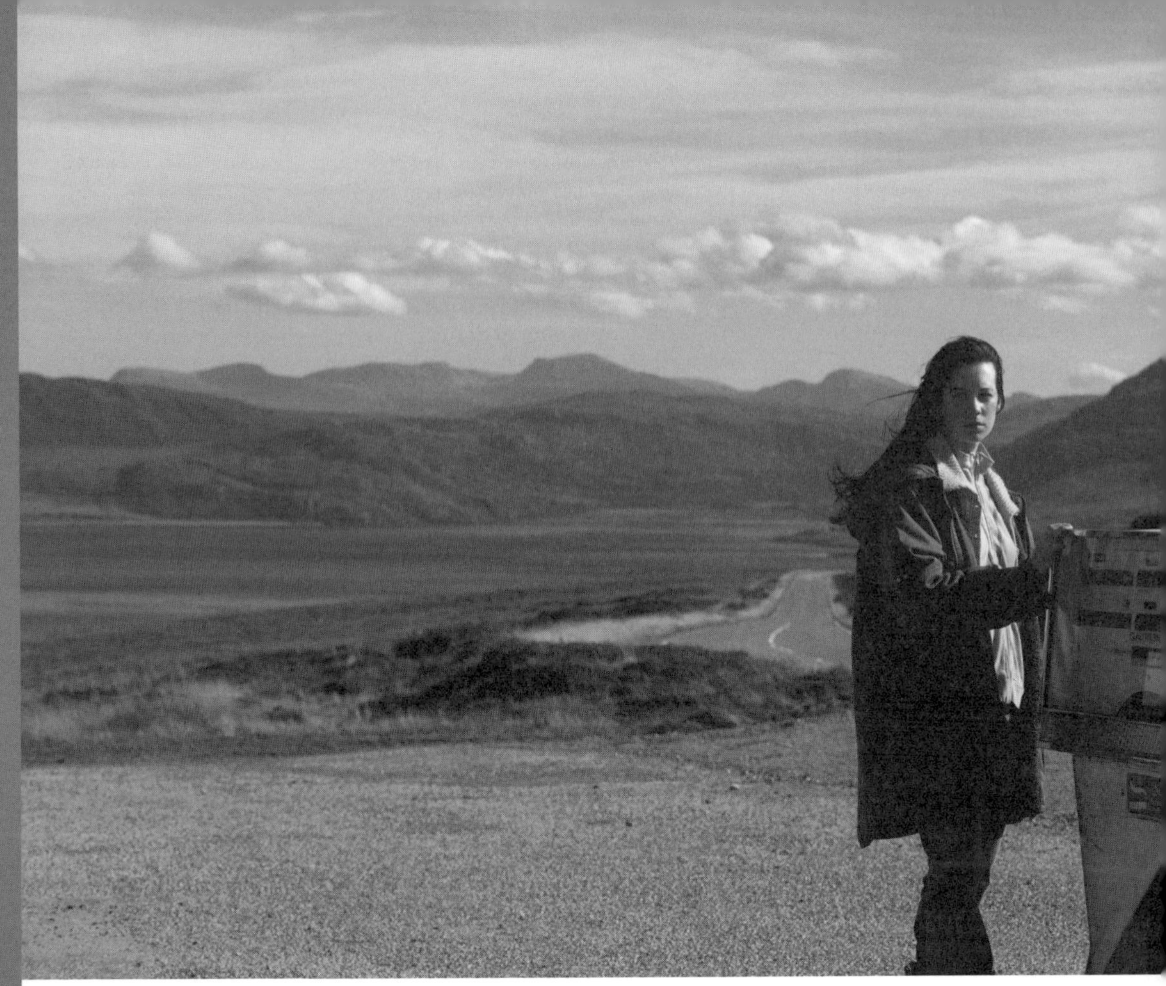

Shell (2012), British Film Institute Collection

From Social Realism to Social Art Cinema and Beyond

A commonly shared perception of the history of Scottish cinema describes a long period in which the primary kind of films made by Scottish film-makers inside Scotland were documentaries whereas the dominant fictional feature film images of Scotland, Scots and Scottishness in cinema were being made largely by non-Scots and often outside of Scotland. At the same time, Scottish audiences enthusiastically embraced the cinema from the 1890s onward, demonstrating considerable potential for more extensive and varied film production from within Scotland, if sufficient financial support could be secured. Aided by expansion and enhancement of available avenues of financial support, starting slowly in the 1970s, gradually picking up speed in the 1980s, and coming into its own in the 1990s, Scotland became a nation not only supporting a significant amount of fictional film production by Scots working within their own country, engaging with Scottish stories and characters, and with Scottish themes and issues, but also one in which these same 'New' Scottish film-makers produced quality films skilfully exploring issues connecting the local, the regional, the national and the international as well as demonstrating considerable artistic panache. For example, in *Screening Scotland* (2000), Duncan Petrie opens his book by recounting how, by the mid-1990s, Scotland had achieved 'an unprecedented profile in the realms of international cinema' (1) such that 'suddenly, Scottish films were the flavour of the month' (1). In *The Scot Pack: The Further Adventures of the Trainspotters and Their Fellow Travellers* (2000) Brian Pendreich offers a similar account, proclaiming that by the mid-1980s and accelerating throughout the 1990s Scots appeared to be everywhere in film-making, and as a direct result Scotland was perceived a hotbed of talent while Scotland, Scots and Scottishness were all now widely perceived as 'cool'. In *Contemporary Scottish Fictions: Film, Television and the Novel* (2004), Petrie integrates discussion of this new dynamism in Scottish film-making with parallel developments in Scottish literature and television production. As Petrie writes, the preceding twenty years represented a period of unprecedented flourishing of cultural activity and expression in Scotland, 'evidence of a new-found cultural confidence' and 'a vibrant and meaningful assertion of national difference' (1). This process of 'cultural devolution' Petrie credits as preparing the way for political devolution and restoration of the Scottish national parliament. Scotland, Petrie proclaims, was in the midst of a 'cultural renaissance' (1) with work in Scottish cinema making a significant contribution to this cultural rebirth. Nearing the end of the 2000s, writing as a contributor to *Scottish Cinema Now* (2009) Petrie tempers his optimism somewhat in recognizing the considerable challenges that continue to confront Scottish film-makers in gaining sufficient financial support to make their films, especially artistically and politically challenging films that don't readily promise significant immediate to short-term commercial return upon investment, and where these film-makers are not themselves representative of the kind of business-savvy entrepreneurs that the ethos of 'creative industries' often seems primarily concerned to nurture and assist. Nevertheless, Petrie ends this same article ('*Screening Scotland*: a Reassessment') optimistically once again. Petrie praises New Scottish cinema for contributing valuably to

> the reawakening of a sense of national self-awareness and cultural confidence. The predominant screen images of the nation have been transformed: a rural or remote setting for romantic or unsettling encounters has given way to a greater focus on an urban post-industrial environment framing narratives concerned with various aspects of contemporary existence and social change. Rural depictions are still in evidence, but these tend to eschew romance in favour of darker, more unsettling preoccupations [...] [And] many Scottish films continue to posit a critical engagement with the negative aspects and limitations of contemporary society and identity [...] [Scottish cinema today comprises] an important component of a national conversation that weaves together tradition and innovation, past and present, inside and outside, local and global. The permeability of categories is particularly important. (Petrie 2009: 167)

And even though sustaining the cinema of a small nation remains a major challenge, collaboration with Scandinavian film-makers, 'Dogme 95' style film-making, new digital technology and micro-budget/DIY production approaches all suggest the possibility for resilient productivity even as Scottish film-makers continue to require stronger sources of base funding, with enhanced funding for development and start-up especially crucial. Scottish cinema has achieved a breakthrough, and established a presence, over the course of the past 30+ years, but this continues to be highly precarious, with considerable anxiety and argument continually focused upon the need to obtain greater public funding support for all aspects of Scottish film production, as well as upon how this best should be allocated, according to what criteria, toward what range of kinds of projects, with what ends in mind, through what processes, by whom, with what degree of accountability and with what degree of participation by film-makers themselves. Yet, not only does Scotland continue to serve as a location for large-budget films not concerned with directly addressing 'Scottish issues' (for example, *Cloud Atlas* [Tom Tykwer, Andy Wachowski, and Lana Wachowski, 2012], *The Dark Knight Rises* [Christopher Nolan, 2012], *Skyfall* [Sam Mendes, 2012], *Snow White and the Huntsman* [Rupert Sanders, 2012] and *World War Z* [Marc Forster, 2013]), but also notable fictional feature films representative of the substantial involvement of Scottish film-makers, and engaging directly with Scottish characters and stories, and Scottish themes and issues, continue to be produced as well (for example, *The Angels' Share* [Ken Loach, 2012], *Shell* [Scott Graham, 2012], *The Railway Man* [Jonathan Teplitzky, 2013], *Under the Skin* [Jonathan Glazer, 2013], *Sunshine on Leith* [Dexter Fletcher, 2013], *Filth* [Jon S. Baird, 2013] and *For Those in Peril* [Paul Wright, 2013]).

Although the preceding short summary portrait of the history of Scottish cinema inevitably oversimplifies, it is nonetheless today a broadly consensual one. Yet Scottish film-making, from the emergence of what Petrie has identified as 'the New Scottish Cinema' onward, along with its most important close antecedents, is difficult to describe as a singularly coherent 'movement', sharing a common aesthetic and/or a common social-political affiliation and outlook. However, a recurrent point of emphasis in scholarly discussion has been the extent to which many of the most notable Scottish fictional feature films of the past 40 years have engaged with 'social realism', with which 'British cinema', especially from the 1950s through the 2000s, has been closely associated – or, perhaps, better put, which has often been touted as the mode of film-making in which British cinema has seen its greatest accomplishments, at least in terms of 'serious drama', during this same extended period of time. What is interesting, in this context, about the most notable and acclaimed Scottish films of recent decades is how often these depart from what might be identified as classic, or, more crudely, 'straightforward', social realism. Frequently scholars and critics point out how many of these Scottish films demonstrate European art cinema influences, notably those of expressionism and surrealism, and how often these films move beyond social realism and naturalism to encompass, and even to emphasize, poetic realism and magic realism.

Social realism is one of many, continually changing, conceptions and practices of realism, dating back to nineteenth-century literary origins. According to Samantha Lay, social realism is a form of 'critical realism' that is not merely focused on verisimilitude but rather assumes an interested position and deliberately intervenes in an ongoing argument concerning what is the 'truth' of the real (2002: 8). Social realism tends to focus on characters generally ignored or marginalized by mainstream productions, especially those who literally 'inhabit the margins of society' (14), and in particular working-class characters 'at moments of economic and social change' (14). A key aim of social realism is to help 'redress social and representational inequalities in relation to class' (15). According to Gill Branston and Roy Stafford, social realist cinema (especially British social realist cinema) maintains the following principal features: (1) 'recognisable authentic locations, usually industrial cities'; (2) 'authentic regional dialects and cultural references'; (3) 'non-professional actors (although often other kinds of performers such as comedians) or actors who are associated primarily with this kind of work'; (4) 'narratives based on the hardships of social disadvantage'; (5) 'lead characters who are "ordinary" and working class'; (6) '"observational", "documentary" style of camerawork'; (7) a '"spontaneous" naturalistic acting style'; and (8) showing characters walking in and out of the frame as well as overlapping each other in dialogue (2003: 453). To this compendium of principal characteristics, Lay adds that British social realist films tend to be independent productions, conceived and executed in an artisanal manner, and that British social realist film-makers deliberately reject many of the dominant conventions and points of emphasis in 'Hollywood realism': Hollywood films tend to be too distant from life as it really is, and too classist, without acknowledging this to be the case. British social realist film-makers are inspired by strong reforming and sometimes revolutionary impulses, while maintaining a pre-eminent interest in contemporary working-class life (especially white male working-class life) beyond London, particularly in the north of England. These film-makers prefer working with regionally authentic casts in regionally authentic locations so as to emphasize how character and place are intrinsically interconnected and that environmental factors are often decisive in relation to 'characters' fates and fortunes' (Lay 2002: 12).

The British documentary movement, emergent at the end of the 1920s and continuing through the 1960s, provided a significant influence upon fictional feature kinds of British social realist film-making. John Grierson, principal founder and leader of this movement, was a Scot, who maintained a strong interest in, and involvement with, documentary film-making in Scotland, even while living and working for long stretches of time in London – and Canada. Grierson, Forsyth Hardy indicates, functioned as 'a kind of conscience' for documentary film-making conducted under the auspices of the Films of Scotland Committees and served as 'the motivating force and the guiding light' throughout work on the 1938 Empire Exhibition series (quoted in McArthur 1982b: 78). In *I Remember, I Remember* (James Sutherland and John Grierson, Scottish Television, 1968), Grierson recounts the history of his work in documentary film-making as well as some of his chief inspirations and major emphases. Grierson was fascinated with modern industry – and modern agriculture and fishing, making use of the latest scientific and technological advances – and wanted to show this as a 'splendid adventure', equivalent in 'romantic' appeal to the heroic legends long associated with rural Highland Scotland. Throughout

I Remember, I Remember Grierson emphasizes documentary as an artistic rendering of the everyday, maintaining a particular imperative to reveal the 'dramatic' qualities inherent within the world of modern work. Frequently he enthuses over images of motion, and of workplaces as complex organisms involving a tightly integrated interconnection of highly rhythmic lines, and patterns, of movement. Films are created by selecting and assembling shots, as well as by accompanying these with music and voice-over commentary, that accentuate these aesthetic qualities. For Grierson, documentary is far from simply presenting a transparent 'window onto the world', but rather is concerned with conveying the 'magical' 'beauty' of 'the ordinary world'. Thus, Grierson's influence continued to prove significant even upon those who strongly reacted versus (what they saw as) Griersonian documentary realism – and this includes, for instance British Free Cinema Movement film-makers who rejected Grierson's 'patrician tendencies and elitist assumptions' (Lay 2002: 41). Both Grierson and Free Cinema film-makers shared a common conviction that cinematic realism required a creative interpretation of reality.

Yet the British documentary movement has often been criticized as propaganda, even though the film-makers themselves stressed their role was not to serve as mouthpieces for their sponsors, but rather as providing 'education and clarification' (Lay 2002: 46). Nevertheless, these documentaries tended to depict the state as a disinterested force working for the general (or the greater) public good, and they can be justly criticized as well for patronizing representations of the working class, portraying the latter in a de-subjectivized manner, as virtual cogs integrated into an artificially organic and harmonious structure, or machine, where their distinct class interests – as opposed to the owners of and the managers at their workplaces – are mystified. 'Social cohesion', Duncan Petrie writes, is a prime value championed by Grierson, and Griersonian cinema (2000: 22), meaning that Griersonian films are willing to support moderate social reform but nothing further. In his *Scotch Reels* interview (McArthur 1982b) Hardy admits that Grierson was never much motivated by any interest in promoting social change, but rather much more in projecting a country, showing – and celebrating – it for what it is. According to Neil Blain, the constraints of sponsorship negatively impacted the films made under the auspices of both Films of Scotland Committees, resulting in a highly 'selective vision' (1990: 58), while the Griersonian aesthetic, with its persistent 'tension between realist commitment and poeticism of style' (59) led to a 'formalist' conception of beauty, harmony, continuity and progress:

> An absorption with the shapes of materials, components and part-completed vessels, a general intension to eulogise and mysticise, and a script disposed to personification and hyperbole combine to emphasise tradition, timelessness and destiny over the specificities of work history and class structure. (Blain 1990: 65)

At the same time, as films such as *The Heart of Scotland* (Laurence Henson,1965) illustrate, this tendency toward abstraction results in an overemphasis on supposedly timeless and transcendent elements, as well as all-too-familiar associations of Scotland with 'vastness, emptiness, turbulence and bloodiness' (Blain 1990: 67).

Nevertheless, as Hardy points out in his interview (1982b) for *Scotch Reels*, both the first and second Films of Scotland Committees deliberately aimed to show a diametrically different portrait versus all-too-common portrayals of Scots in film as subsidiary comic figures. As Hardy sees it, the Empire Exhibition series, product of the first Films of Scotland Committee, might have inaugurated a major new direction in Scottish film-making, fictional as well as non-fictional, short and feature length, if not for World War II, and this new direction would have foregrounded a modern, optimistic, confident Scotland. Hardy admits that the (second) Films of Scotland Committee, which he headed, faced many challenges and difficulties, especially in securing sponsors, and in insuring that the sponsored films could make money through exhibition. And although Hardy does contend that sponsors did not in general interfere with how these films were made, he also admits the Films of Scotland Committee could only make films that sponsors wanted to sponsor. As Hardy recounts in *Scotland in Film* (1990), despite the enormous challenges this kind of film-making entailed, the (second) Films of Scotland Committee ended up making 150 films:

> at the end of twenty years [...] the sheer volume of film-making about Scotland was prodigious. Most of the films would not have been made but for the focus created by the Committee. The toil and trouble had been worthwhile and 150 films were there to prove it. (Hardy 1990: 129)

The Films of Scotland Committee under Forsyth Hardy's leadership provided significant training and employment to many future fiction film-makers, and as Petrie sums it up,

> the documentary provided a crucial continuity of indigenous film-making, facilitating a small but sustainable production sector in Scotland. Despite the creative limitations sponsored film-making entailed, ambitious film-makers now had an opportunity to learn and practice their craft in Scotland. This in turn provided the impetus for ambition to be nurtured, leading some to move beyond the confines of documentary towards the world of fiction and the possibility of a new Scottish cinema. (Petrie 2000: 119)

Grierson's emphasis on a 'poetic' rendering of the 'drama of everyday life', anticipates what Samantha Lay (2002) describes as a productive tension, within British social realist fictional film-making, between sociological and poetic forms of realism, beginning with the Free Cinema and New Wave film-makers of the 1950s. Certainly, Free Cinema and New Wave emphasis on taking working-class life seriously and foregrounding it as central drew upon a documentary imperative – seeking, as Hardy has described Grierson's aim, to show modern life as and for what it is. Initially, Lay suggests, British social realist fictional film-making also tended, again akin to Griersonian documentary, toward a more collaborative/collective/unit style, with less emphasis on the supposed 'signature' of individual film-maker(s), yet over time British social realism came to be increasingly strongly identified with auteurist film-making. Likewise, again at least partially akin to Griersonian documentary, British social realist fictional film-making, again especially early on, tended to emphasize collective protagonists, and collective antagonists, and to situate individuals within larger social groups of which these individuals' action and behaviour was depicted as symptomatic. Nevertheless, even 'classic' British social realist fictional film-making differed from Griersonian documentary in tending toward cyclical and episodic versus linear-sequential patterns of elaboration and development, in eschewing the suggestion of mechanical relations between clear-cut causes and effects, and in resisting neat resolutions along with happy endings. Despite the 'poetic' inclination of Griersonian documentary, these differences became more pronounced as British social realism evolved into British 'social art cinema'. Christopher Williams is responsible for the influential argument that by the early 1980s British (fictional) social realist cinema merged with (European) art cinema to create the 'new formation' of 'social art cinema' (1996: 200). According to Williams, social art cinema combines distinct qualities of art cinema – emphasis on 'individual identity, sexuality, psychological complexity, anomie, episodicness, interiority, ambiguity, style' (198) – with an equally strong emphasis on examining these issues in relation to the social group, the social context and a diffuse yet nonetheless insistent sense of the overarching sociality forming, constituting, defining and delimiting all individual, inter-individual, subjective, psychological, somatic, spiritual and aesthetic focuses of concern. As Williams earlier suggests, in the same article, 'an almost frenzied curiosity about social life and its systems' (1996: 191) has long been a distinct feature of British film (and British culture); as a result, exploring and investigating the social 'is what British cinema has been and is good at doing' (192), and, in relation to the British contribution to the first 100 years of the history of cinema, it is clear that 'the main British tradition is social' (193). Convergence with art cinema, however, means that greater credit is advanced toward films that focus on interior subjectivity, character over plot, alienation and anomie, ambiguity and undecidability, open-endedness and lack of decisive closure, and on a visual (and audio-visual) style that deliberately calls attention to itself and to the story-world as artificial constructs.

As David Martin-Jones (2009) indicates, Scotland does not maintain a distinct social realist tradition, unlike in England, other than that passed on by the history of Griersonian-style documentary film-making in Scotland. This may well account for how readily 'New Scottish Cinema' has embraced the kind of blending of social realism and art cinema that Christopher Williams (1996) identifies as social art cinema. Simon Brown (2011) has recently argued that this embrace, especially on the part of scholars and critics, has been overemphasized, marginalizing popular 'genre' film-making in Scotland in favour of the work of supposed 'new Scottish auteurs' such as Lynne Ramsay, Peter Mullan, David Mackenzie and Richard Jobson. According to Brown, too exclusive an emphasis on European art cinema influences has rendered it difficult to appreciate the significance not only of influences from other kinds of cinema, but also the ways late-twentieth and early-twenty-first-century Scottish films engage the intersection of the universal and the particular, while exploring local, regional, national *and* international resonances of contemporary lived experience. Brown here opens up a productive line of inquiry that parallels David Martin-Jones's work, in terms both of Martin-Jones's concentration on (popular) Scottish 'genre' films, and on examining the way these 'Scottish' films engage identities beyond the national, narrowly conceived, including 'ethnic, sexual, gendered, diasporic, transnational, global/local, [and] regional' (Martin-Jones 2009: 19). Nevertheless, whether entirely deserved or not, Scottish cinema studies scholarship has to date given priority critical attention to New Scottish social art films and film-makers, and it is important to consider how and why so.

Bill Douglas is widely regarded as the pre-eminent Scottish art film-maker, and indeed as a major figure within twentieth-century European art cinema. In particular in the case of his *Trilogy* – *My Childhood* (1972), *My Ain Folk* (1973) and *My Way Home* (1978) – yet also for his later, and still underappreciated, *Comrades* (1986), Douglas created powerful works of 'poetic realism' that have, if anything, steadily increased in influence and appeal since the 1970s. According to Martin-Jones (2009), Bill Douglas's work, and especially his *Trilogy*, exemplify qualities conventionally accepted as definitive of art cinema: characters without clearly defined goals or desires, as well as who are psychologically complex and contradictory; an emphasis on interior subjectivity as well as, often, on introspection, memory, fantasy and dream; a drifting, episodic quality to the elaboration of the central narrative; documentary realist filming techniques employed in self-reflexive ways, aiding a deliberate exploration of complicated relations between reality and illusion (or reality and perception of reality); and a pronounced foregrounding of the presence of director as auteur (218–19). Andrew Noble (1990) praises Douglas as a Dostoyevsky of cinema, cites Douglas's own acknowledgment of the influence of Beckett and Pinter, and, as many others have done as well, compares

Douglas's films with silent cinema – in Noble's case, with the work of Alexander Dovzhenko. Douglas, Noble indicates, maintained the 'belief that cinema should be about the arousal of sympathetic intelligence' (1990: 138), with a considerable stress on 'intelligence'. As Noble points out, Douglas deliberately holds back from directly spelling out what can much more artfully be indirectly suggested, allowing images, arrangements within images and sequences of images to speak for themselves, thereby insisting on communication between the film and the audience by way of what is shown as opposed to what is told. Douglas, moreover, as many scholars have commented, is characteristically, especially in his *Trilogy*, meticulously precise, and concise, in the ways he renders even the exceedingly complex. Douglas's editing is likewise frequently praised for its skillful achievement of a contrapuntal quality, with Douglas, in Noble's words, deliberately emphasizing 'the creative fusion of contraries' (140). Douglas's ability to draw considerable intellectual as well as emotional resonance from even the slightest of expressions, gestures and movements; from faces and postures; and from silence and stasis are yet further qualities of Douglas's artistry that have also been widely praised. What is not always as readily recognized, or appreciated, however, is Douglas's considerable wit and his keen historical insight: as Noble interprets the *Trilogy*, Douglas here offers an elliptical yet incisive series of critical reflections on both romantic Scotland and the decline of the British Empire (according to Noble, Jamie, the protagonist of the *Trilogy*, represents the antithesis of Peter Pan, whereas the *Trilogy* itself represents the antithesis of Kailyard). In making sense of the question of 'realism' in relation to Douglas's work, Noble draws upon James Agee in proposing that Douglas's achievement involves 'collaboration with reality'; this amounts to a considerable talent at defamiliarization, with Douglas enabling, even 'teaching', his audiences to see, hear and feel what they otherwise are habitually inclined to miss – or mistake. In sum, Noble declares, Douglas' film-making 'has the feel of documentary realism and yet every frame seems perfectly composed' (140).

In *Contemporary Scottish Fictions* (2004) Duncan Petrie indicates, contrary to an earlier relative neglect within Scotland, 'it is now possible to posit Douglas as ultimately a more influential figure than [Bill] Forsyth, as the father of a new Scottish art cinema and its apparent obsession with issues of autobiography, memory and the figure of the child' (164). David Martin-Jones (2009) likewise proposes, as instances of Scottish (social) art cinema, the films not only of Lynne Ramsay and Peter Mullan but also of David Mackenzie, along with Andrea Arnold's *Red Road* (2006) all clearly reflect the influence of Douglas, and the same is true of a Ahost of other films as well – including *Play Me Something* (Timothy Neat, 1989), *Silent Scream* (David Hayman, 1990), *Blue Black Permanent* (Margaret Tait, 1992), *As An Eilean* (Mike Alexander, 1993), *Small Faces* (Gillies MacKinnon, 1996), *Regeneration* (Gillies MacKinnon, 1997), *Stella Does Tricks* (Coky Giedroyc, 1996), *The Winter Guest* (Alan Rickman, 1997), *Carla's Song* (Ken Loach, 1997), *My Name is Joe* (Ken Loach, 1998), *Sweet Sixteen* (Ken Loach, 2002), *Ae Fond Kiss* (Ken Loach, 2004), *16 Years of Alcohol* (Richard Jobson, 2003), *A Woman in Winter* (Richard Jobson, 2005) and *Seachd: The Inaccessible Pinnacle* (Simon Miller, 2007).

Although not Scottish himself, Ken Loach has made five feature-length fictional films set in Scotland, in particular in Glasgow, as well as focused on a series of Glasgow Celtic football fans in his contribution to the portmanteau film *Tickets* (2005), co-directed with Abbas Kiarostami and Ermanno Olmi. Loach has worked with the Scot Paul Laverty as screenwriter on twelve films, from *Carla's Song* through *The Angels' Share*, along with fellow Scot Rebecca O'Brien as producer, and co-founder of Sixteen Films, on twelve feature films and multiple additional short and documentary films, while he has also played a pivotal role in launching the successful film careers of many Scottish actors, dating back to Robert Carlyle as the protagonist – a Scottish construction worker in London – of *Riff-Raff* (1991) (Worth noting as well, in this connection, is that the Glaswegian Bill Jesse wrote the screenplay for *Riff-Raff*). As Loach writes in the book-length edition of Laverty's screenplay for *The Angels' Share*, he finds Glasgow compelling for multiple reasons: the city is

> powerful in the culture of the people there, in the sense of humour, the attitudes that people have to life, and the history that's produced there. It's a very collective, not an individualist culture, and yet people have as hard a time there as anywhere you could imagine. (Laverty 2012: 177)

John Hill (2009) likewise explains the appeal of Scotland, and in particular Glasgow, to Loach, as traceable to the nation's, and the city's, strong opposition to Thatcherism, continued wide support for social democracy and persistent 'attachment to collective values that often found expression in the language of class identity and politics' (89). As Hill suggests, Loach appreciates qualities within Scottish history and culture that encourage Scots to continue to identify as working class, even though Loach upholds an internationalist outlook, supportive of the position that working-class people maintain an ultimately much more fundamental commonality of interest with people in the same class position across national lines than they do with members of bourgeois and petit-bourgeois classes in their own countries.

Ever since he first started in the mid-1960s, Ken Loach has made films focused on sharply confronting social inequality and social injustice. And even though his approach to film-making has changed over this course of time (as Jacob Leigh, for instance, details in *The Cinema of Ken Loach: Art in the Service of the People* [2002]), what ultimately stands out for most scholars discussing Loach's work is a strong continuity in Loach's conception of and approach to film-making. Loach, in short, is widely acclaimed as *the* exemplary British social realist auteur. Among persistent common elements in Loach's film-making, which many have cited, are the following: location shooting, use of non-professional actors, visible emphasis on the characters and their interactions with each other and their environment rather than on the camera/the apparatus or on the choices involved with/the processes of editing, preference for natural lighting and for medium to long shots as well as for eye-level camera heights and straight-on camera angles, and, as Leigh elaborates, 'the use of a long lens for close shots and long shots' as well as 'panning and re-focusing between framings', which in turn 'flattens space and minimises perspective', resulting in 'often a shallow depth-of-field in Loach's films, with only one plane in focus' (Leigh 2002: 60–61). Loach is also famous for the exhaustive amount of research he and his team do in the course of preparing to make a film, striving always for maximal 'authenticity', with this same priority emphasis on authenticity including a rigorous casting process, where actors are frequently cast because they can draw upon direct connections between their own life-experience and that of the fictional characters they will play, where they are expected to speak in an 'authentic dialect' and to use 'authentic accents', and where, in order to achieve a 'naturalistic' 'spontaneity', actors are only provided small portions of the script at a time, usually just enough for a day's shoot, even just enough for a single scene – and even sometimes just recounting their own lines and movements, allowing actors to demonstrate the same kind of surprise in response to other characters' lines and actions as would be the case with the characters they are playing. Loach's actors, moreover, typically perform many takes on the same scene with Loach selecting the most spontaneously natural-seeming performances from among the accumulated series. Loach emphasizes space, place and environment in ways that are deliberately designed to convey as closely as possible what it is like to live the lives his characters do, in the conditions and circumstances they do, because he strongly believes in the decisive impact of social environment, especially in relation to quality of life-experience.

Loach is especially concerned with the destructive impact of unemployment and underemployment, resulting in the squandering of the considerable talents and abilities, as well as the very lives, of so many members of the working class and the poor. Often enough, Loach also targets the inadequacy of social services, and of other leading social institutions, for failing working-class and poor people struggling with considerable hardships in their lives, such as homelessness, domestic violence, drug and alcohol addiction, and the temptations along with the pressures of both independent and organized crime. In relation to the impact of Thatcherism, New Labour and the more recent Con-Dem (Conservative-Liberal Democrat) coalition's attempted naturalization of austerity, Loach's films remind audiences of the devastating cost of these policies, not only in economic terms but also in terms of a decline in social morality, in erosion of community and in an eclipse of communitarian ideals. Yet, even in his bleakest films, Loach reminds us of how often working-class and poor people, as well as others down and out and on the edge, do reach out to help each other, do demonstrate an altruistic concern for and appreciation of other people, and do look beyond an egocentric self-concern. These efforts are not always sufficient to prevent tragic consequences, but they are rarely altogether absent from Loach's films. And, in one tendency that has especially divided critics, Loach frequently includes characters in his films articulating, often passionately and at length, direct statements of these films' major arguments versus the systemic forces and the privileged interests his films sharply critique.

A major argument Jacob Leigh advances in his book on Loach's cinema is that the latter's films are often, in fact, 'melodramas of protest'. Loach is

> not a realist film-maker if one takes that phrase to evoke a film-maker who presents the action of his films from an 'objective' viewpoint; on the contrary, his films usually direct our attention to events on screen from a sharply defined perspective. (Leigh 2002: 18)

Loach employs conventions of melodrama – strong encouragement toward emotional identification and sympathy with his principal characters – in an effort to get audiences to 'observe and to understand these characters as well as to empathize with them, 'to feel close to, and emotionally engaged with' them – to share their 'epistemic and emotional perspective' (Leigh 2002: 19). As Leigh interprets this strategic conception, 'The melodrama of protest attempts to rouse the audience, to activate a sense of outrage at the injustices or atrocities of the authorities against an innocent protagonist' (22). What's more, Loach's films often, again even those ending the most bleakly, employ considerable humour, usually accentuated enough so as to fracture any illusion of *cinéma-vérité*.

Yet, as John Hill (2009) contends, despite the comedy and humour that show up in even these especially bleak films, *My Name is Joe* and *Sweet Sixteen* 'remain overwhelmingly pessimistic in tone', while 'the pessimism and discourse of failure' here reinforces long-standing tendencies within Scottish cinema, and Scottish culture, to overemphasize 'an elegiac tone and sense of national loss' (98) – recalling the massacre of Glencoe, the devastation at Culloden and in the aftermath of that defeat, as well as the Highland Clearances and the decline and end of shipbuilding and other once-prominent forms of heavy industry as dominant centres of the Scottish economy at a time when Scotland acted as, in TM Devine's (2012) words, 'the world's workshop' (249). Nevertheless, as Hill admits, despite this potential to reinforce bitter and nostalgic tendencies in Scottish popular cultural discourse, the success of Loach's films have helped raised the profile for film-making in Scotland, especially in Glasgow (and, in a further irony, Loach's Scottish films have benefitted significantly from lottery funding, despite Loach's reservation that the lottery constitutes a de facto tax on the poor). Hill also raises a partial criticism of Loach's and Laverty's films for focusing too much on 'the impact of unemployment and poverty upon traditional forms of working-class masculinity' (2009: 96). According to Hill, Loach and Laverty tend to neglect the new kinds of manual labour jobs that continue to provide the primary means of employment for working-class men – and women – today, and charges Loach and Laverty with the same neglect versus how workers today make sense of and relate to these new kinds of jobs within a contemporary nexus of significant lines of social identity:

> Loach and Laverty's Scottish films have provided powerful images of working-class decline and deprivation but have been rather less successful in capturing the changing character of working-class employment and the variety of ways in which the politics of class, gender, ethnicity and nationality overlap and interweave in present-day Scotland. (Hill 2009: 102)

Yet, Hill acknowledges that Loach's and Laverty's depiction of the harshness of men's situation (dealing with chronic unemployment or underemployment) is complemented by a simultaneous depiction of women's inability or refusal to provide traditional forms of compensatory comfort: even as these men crave love and support, these women can't and won't give it to them on the terms the men all too often expect, and even, too often, continue to demand. So Loach's and Laverty's films do comment perceptively on significant changes in working-class women's traditional roles, especially versus men. In addition, Hill commends Loach's emphasis, in his 'West Central Scotland trilogy' (*My Name is Joe*, *Sweet Sixteen* and *Ae Fond Kiss*) on a 'demythologizing impulse towards romantic and touristic views of the Scottish countryside' (91). And, despite Loach's manifest scepticism and pessimism across the films constituting this 'trilogy' concerning prospects for progressive social change, his films nonetheless 'provide vivid reminders of those who have lost out in the transition from an industrial to a services-led economy' as well as valuably 'insist upon the centrality of economic factors in accounting for the problems that the characters face' (95).

Both Hill and Duncan Petrie (in *Contemporary Scottish Fictions* [2004]) contrast Loach's films, especially *My Name is Joe* and *Sweet Sixteen*, with *Trainspotting* (Danny Boyle, 1996). As Hill puts it, 'In Loach's universe [...] heroin use is divested of rock culture associations and much more firmly linked to class disadvantage and material hardship' than is the case with *Trainspotting* (2009: 95). No fantastical escape, or new direction, or alternative pathway is available for boys and men at the bottom in Loach's post-industrial Scotland, while drug use and drug dealing are portrayed as false avenues of attempted escape, resulting in ultimately destructive dead ends. Although Petrie interprets *Sweet Sixteen*'s tracing of youthful protagonist Liam's own (self-)destructive tendencies and the brutal surrounding environment that eventually overwhelms him, including his positive, caring and creative side, as 'ultimately little more than another tragic study in Scottish male self-destructiveness' (Petrie 2004: 172), Takako Seino sees the film as at the same time a riposte to the concurrent celebration of a new youthful 'Cool Britannia' (2012: 33). In turn, many scholars discuss *Ae Fond Kiss* as a deliberate response to the impact of 9/11 in accentuating racial/ethnic/national and religious tensions, while also noting how Loach here explores the significance of cultural and religious divisions as well as those of class. At the same time, however, as is typical with Loach, in Seino's words, *Ae Fond Kiss* 'displays that personal relationships always reflect the politics of the society to which they belong' (35). In sum, as Seino puts it, Loach is consistently critical of a 'society that deprives people of choice to have better lives' (35), and, as Leigh writes, despite changes in technique over the course of his film-making career, Loach remains consistent in aiming to create 'art in the service of the people' (2002: 178).

No other single film has been more frequently identified with 'New Scottish Cinema', nor has any other exerted a greater impact upon changing perceptions of Scotland in cinema, than *Trainspotting*. As Brian Pendreich writes, 'If *Braveheart* gave Scotland its belief in itself, *Trainspotting* made the country positively cool' (2002: 84). According to Pendreich, *Trainspotting* 'tapped into the Zeitgeist of Scottish life and literary renaissance' while 'the story of Mark Renton was the antithesis of the story of William Wallace' (2000: 14) – '*Trainspotting* proved films made in Scotland with Scottish actors could be international hits without the need for tartan and misty glens' and *Trainspotting* carried the spirit of 'the new Scottish literature' of the 1980s and 1990s into film (15). As Pendreich sees it, *Trainspotting* dismantles the Scottish myths that *Braveheart* endorses, while *Trainspotting* is a Scottish film whereas *Braveheart* is a Hollywood film. Despite the fact that *Trainspotting* is directed by an Englishman, Danny Boyle, Pendreich proclaims that (otherwise) *Trainspotting* 'was made by Scots, with Scots in virtually all the leading roles. It launched or boosted a couple of dozen [Scots'] film careers, in front and behind the camera' (2002: 82).

A striking dimension of the considerable popular and critical success of *Trainspotting* has to do with how far this film departs from conventional associations with cinematic 'realism', including social realism. As Pendreich notes (2002, 2000), *Trainspotting* foregrounds the surreal and the absurd in ways that mark a refreshing contrast with social realism. In *Screening Scotland* Duncan Petrie describes *Trainspotting* as a 'neo-expressionist' portrait of 'a mythic Edinburgh environment' (2000: 195), strongly suggestive of Quentin Tarantino, while in *Contemporary Scottish Fictions* (2004) Petrie identifies *Trainspotting*'s style as French *nouvelle vague* refracted through Dick Lester's British films (*The Beatles: A Hard Day's Night* [1964], *Help!* [1965] and *The Knack […] and How to Get It* [1965]) as well as, once again, 'the New Hollywood' of Martin Scorcese and Tarantino (102). Murray Smith, in a characterization that many subsequent scholars have found compelling, identifies *Trainspotting* as a defining instance of 'Black Magic Realism' (2002: 75). Black magic realism transforms conventional associations with and expectations of realism through farce, grotesquerie, comic absurdity and, especially, black humour, while in the case of *Trainspotting* drawing heavily upon effervescent rhythms of pop culture and especially popular music as well as upon fantastical and marvellous elements from non-naturalistic modes of film-making and comparable varieties of literature. According to Smith, *Trainspotting* redeems material impoverishment through aesthetic transformation – drawing forth vitality from grinding poverty, and showing that destitution does not necessarily stifle imagination, talent, will, ambition, pride or defiance. Smith argues *Trainspotting*'s reliance upon black magic realism enables the film successfully to 'depict both the reality of heroin use (its causes and possible effects, good and ill) while also representing the spirit of resistance […] and desire for transformation, which inspires its use in the first place' (86). For Smith, audiences, especially youthful audiences, identify with Renton not literally but rather figuratively – as an embodiment of a symbolic spirit of resistance to the aesthetic, emotional and spiritual emptiness of the cultural mainstream and of social normativity.

Much scholarly debate concerning *Trainspotting* focuses on how to interpret, and evaluate, the politics of the film. According to Richard Zumkhawala-Cook, *Trainspotting*'s cultural critique is 'so trapped by its own cynicism that in the end it affirms the hero of global culture: the young freewheeling upwardly mobile male corporate punk' (2008: 163–64), the one who can work the system to serve his own manifestly selfish ends. Zumkhawala-Cook reads the film as symptomatic of a frequent tendency within punk culture to move from rejection to cooptation by way of cynicism – suggesting that an only temporary period of rebellion ultimately prepares the erstwhile punk all the more successfully to exploit the system for selfish personal ends: 'The move of *Trainspotting*'s hero from self-destructive junkie to greedy self-serving market cowboy certainly parallels the historical transformation of the punk aesthetic itself' (171). Renton, Zumkhawala-Cook argues, ultimately aligns his erstwhile rebelliousness with Thatcherite values, and all the more insidiously so in seeming ironically to wink at and mock these values at the same time as he embraces them: 'Renton's "hope" is built on the fact that he is a fully autonomous subject free from responsibility to others' (170); Renton is 'a contemporary subject who subscribes to the neo-liberal logic of perpetual self-renewal through capitalist accumulation and dramatic material displays of "individuality"' (170). Moreover, Zumkhawala-Cook adds, just like in *Braveheart* (Mel Gibson, 1995) and *Rob Roy* (Michael Caton-Jones, 1995), the protagonist of *Trainspotting* is another leader within a group of men, who, as the ultimate hero, demonstrates that he is both one of and also not one of this same group: his individual distinctiveness and his ability to separate himself from the group is what makes him the most successful. From this vantage point, Renton is a contemporary masculine hero much more akin to past masculine heroes like Rob Roy and William Wallace than many might recognize. After all, Zumkhawala-Cook points out, *Trainspotting* is yet another in a long line of films involving a traumatic loss to a woman who disappears from the rest of the story while women are otherwise relegated to largely subsidiary roles. As Zumkhawala-Cook sums up his critique, *Trainspotting* disappoints because Scotland needs films that move beyond 'male fantasies of individualist heroism' (2008: 174).

Zumkhawala-Cook also criticizes Renton's famous tirade that begins with 'it's shite being Scottish' for promoting the idea that being colonized is a matter of choice on the part of the colonized, as well as for implicitly accepting that colonization is all right, depending upon who is the colonizer. As Zumkhawala-Cook interprets it, Renton's rant substitutes fatalism, despair and self-loathing for historical complexity. What's more, Zumkhawala-Cook adds, it is noteworthy that Renton finds a satisfying direction for his life, beyond taking heroin and communing with his friends in doing so, in England, not in Scotland, which reinforces traditional notions of Scotland's relative backwardness. As Renton increasingly separates himself from Scotland and his friends, 'The hero's greed, isolation, and self-interest are justified as the best outcome of a situation where both he and the sensibilities of his professional London life are victimized by passé Scottish affiliations' (172). Yet as Ellen-Raïssa Jackson argues, critics have often misinterpreted Renton's negative comments on what it means to be Scottish by reading these too literally, not recognizing that this statement comes from a character, like most of the others in both the book and the film, who is hardly an entirely reliable narrator and who is strongly invested in self-justification; what is interesting here, according to Jackson, is the way Renton suggests, in a moment of 'rupture' with 'the introspective and self-obsessed junkie narrative', the possibility of a 'direct relationship between individual consciousness and the political status of the nation' (2004: 116). In other words, it is necessary to examine what Renton says more carefully, not reading this merely as indicative of his 'shame' about being Scottish, but rather as indicative of a culturally semi-unconscious foregrounding of the need, however tentatively and confusedly articulated, to strike back at widely perceived, long-standing Scottish proclivities toward shame and guilt, 'inferiorism' and a 'crisis of (self-) confidence', and complicity with their own relative marginalization and subjection.

As Murray Smith observes, *Trainspotting* is indicative that British 'youth culture had entered a moment of exceptional disillusionment and diminished expectation, and had turned its back on conventional forms of political protest as on mainstream existence' (2002: 12). Thus the film's engagement with issues of laddishness, male sexual inadequacy and football and music obsessiveness is quite acutely sensitive to a dominant ethos within mid- to late-1990s British youth culture, as is the film's celebration of 'the slacker, the loser, Generation X, and, most pertinently here, "the chemical generation" – a new youth counterculture revolving around clubbing, raves, and Ecstacy' (12). Smith declares *Trainspotting* 'provides an articulate, authentic voice for a world not often represented, and a voice that speaks to a large audience, in spite of its idiosyncracies' (86). Renton, Smith argues, is a complex character, with many appealing qualities, that Smith finds more persuasively representative of an at least incipiently radical social critique as opposed to an ultimately cynical social conformity. What's more, Smith suggests, although the film draws upon American popular culture as a considerable source of reference and appeal, it does so without endorsing any overtly 'American' way of life or set of values. Likewise, as Smith points out, the film mocks, and even scorns, traditional 'heritage' icons of Scottishness, but also knowingly smirks at and makes fun of the same in relation to London, including traditional London icons of 'heritage' Englishness. By the end of the film it may well be, Smith adds, that *Trainspotting* foregrounds expression of the transgressive over expression of social responsibility, but by ending in a morally and politically ambiguous manner, the film prompts subsequent audience reflection concerning what kinds of lives people aspire to live and why so, according to what values, in conformity with or in opposition to what kinds of ends and interests – including consideration of what does (or what might) it mean to lead a socially 'responsible' as opposed to a socially 'transgressive' life.

Small Faces imaginatively re-examines Glasgow gangland subculture and the classic figure of the 'hard man' through the mediation of painting, drawing and artistic imagination and embellishment. The film also foregrounds complicated passages from childhood to adulthood, along with the extensive overlapping and tenuous boundaries distinguishing child from adult; family and extended family life; sibling relations; and the subjective vantage point of a precocious adolescent protagonist. *Small Faces* incorporates ample expressionist stylization of scene and action as well as strikingly surreal symbolic passages, again suggestive of a fusion of European art cinema and British social realism. Sandra-Elisabeth Haider (2002) finds the film a refreshing re-examination of the hard man image and role, showing the vitality and complexity of a working-class family life as well as of relations between gang violence and other, especially creative and artistic, pursuits, while frankly acknowledging the considerable costs involved in an all-too-common romantic mythologization of gang violence and refusing to excuse those caught up in so doing, no matter how youthfully naive or otherwise well-intended they might be. Duncan Petrie also praises *Small Faces* for the film's demythologization of gangland violence, its sensitive portrayal of family relations and growing up, and its arresting visual images of gang violence, tower blocks and especially Tongland depicted as a 'highly stylised dystopia' (2000: 204). Petrie further notes that Lex is, for Scottish cinema, an unusual character – a precociously self-confident, volubly articulate youthful protagonist, who functions as a direct commentator and guide, a virtual 'mini-adult' (2004: 171). As such, the fallible nature of Lex's commentary and guidance only adds to the compelling complexity of the film's enunciation.

Stella Does Tricks also skilfully blends a gritty, disturbing story of a precocious yet abused, troubled and increasingly desperate young female protagonist with pronounced expressionist elements, suggestive of complex interrelations between fact and fantasy. As a number of scholars have observed, *Stella Does Tricks* is an intricately layered film, in its engagement with complicated connections between past and present, interior and exterior and hopeful/resilient and bitter/despairing dimensions of Stella's experience, while the film offers a welcome contribution to New Scottish Cinema as a sensitive representation of female experience from a female subjective vantage point. *Red Road* sutures its audience in even closer alignment with the visual and auditory – the perceptual – perspective of its female protagonist, Jackie, yet at the same time, until late in the film Jackie's interior consciousness remains largely opaque. Again, this film combines pronounced elements of social realism and expressionism in crafting a suspenseful noir thriller that also engages issues concerning vengeance and retribution, compensation and forgiveness, suspicion and manipulation, repression and denial, problematics of female sexual agency, omnipresence of CCTV surveillance, and what it is like to live in tower block-dominated working-class housing estates at the periphery of the city. *Shell* yet again impressively fuses elements of intense naturalism with overtly poetic and resonantly symbolic qualities, suggestive of the influence of Bill Douglas, Lukas Moodyson and Andrei Tarkovsky, among other European 'art' film-makers. Once again, this film centres upon the perspective of a young female protagonist, the eponymous Shell, not only as she interacts with her sick, depressed and desperately lonely father, Pete, along with several frequent and novel visitors to their remote North-west Highlands petrol station and garage, but also, and ultimately even more powerfully, as Shell interacts with this very location, and with its distinct array of attendant 'natural' sights and sounds, including as these change with the weather and the seasons. The film depicts Shell's interior consciousness only indirectly, by physical suggestion, but nonetheless the film meticulously traces a subtle yet nonetheless substantial evolution in self-consciousness, outlook and ambition.

Wilbur Wants to Kill Himself (Lone Scherfig, 2002) once more depicts a superficially naturalistic-seeming series of events, centred around one small family, and especially two brothers, a bookstore, a health clinic and a hospital, which is shot precisely and economically so as not to call overt attention to the camera/apparatus, nor to the process of editing or the accompanying musical soundtrack. Yet *Wilbur Wants to Kill Himself* not only is replete with dark comedy and black humour, but also incorporates manifest elements of the surreal and the absurd, especially at pivotal moments, while tracing what amounts to a (post)modern fable, strongly resonant of elements of the magical and the marvellous, concerning matters of death and life, sickness and health, fate and loss, love and sacrifice, need and desire, and transience and renewal. *Aberdeen* (Hans Petter Moland, 2000), like *Wilbur Wants to Kill Himself* and *Red Road* the result of a collaboration between Scottish and Scandinavian film-makers, once more initially appears a highly naturalistic film, recounting a long and fraught journey – both physical and emotional – of two highly troubled characters, a young woman and her estranged father. Each, in his or her own way, is socially alienated and suffers from acute addiction. Yet the way the film circumscribes its depiction of the surrounding spaces through which Kaisa and Tomas travel so that these serve principally to reinforce and amplify, not to mention reflect and refract, the two principal characters' own tensions and struggles, as well as their own fragile strengths and profound weaknesses, demonstrates that *Aberdeen* as well draws substantially upon characteristic preoccupations and emphases of European art cinema. *Aberdeen*, which literally follows a considerably difficult yet ultimately surprisingly transformational journey from Norway to Scotland, is also noteworthy as an early example of a significant trend in twenty-first century 'Scottish' film-making which David Martin-Jones highlights in his 2009 book *Scotland: Global Cinema*, and that is making use of films set in Scotland or otherwise involving Scottish characters 'to try to understand globalization, its deterritorialized flows of people, and the new, potentially transnational, identities it generates' (63).

Donkeys (Morag McKinnon, 2010), the second film in the Advanced Party Initiative, involving collaboration between Glasgow-based Sigma Films and Denmark-based Zentropa Entertainments, is far less successful than the first, *Red Road*. Undoubtedly, this is in large part due to the many difficulties the film-makers faced in completing the work, and ending up with a much shorter film than envisioned, yet it does feature an often challenging straddling of the serious and the comic, while forthrightly addressing issues of incest and assisted suicide. *Dear Frankie* (Shona Auerbach, 2004) has been largely ignored, and, even when acknowledged, not especially well regarded by film scholars, yet Simon Brown (2011) argues this is unfortunate, because the film offers a much more interesting, and significant, achievement than commonly recognized. Brown stresses the fact that *Dear Frankie* is deliberately conceived by its makers as a 'fable', as a 'fairy-tale couched in life', and as 'a warmer [...] slice of realism', and suggests, because it is neither a Loachian social realist film nor an example of overt 'art cinema' like *Young Adam* (David Mackenzie, 2003), too many critics have judged it according to standards that don't fit the kind of film it is designed to be.

Among Scottish cinema studies scholars probably the two most frequently acclaimed Scottish film-makers since the late 1990s are Lynne Ramsay and Peter Mullan. Both Ramsay and Mullan are frequently touted as social art cinema auteurs. As Duncan Petrie writes, for example, Ramsay's aesthetics suggest a clear kinship with European art film-makers such as Robert Bresson, Bill Douglas and Terence Davies (2004: 104). Ramsay's films (most notably her three feature films – *Ratcatcher* [1999]; *Morvern Callar* [2002]; and *We Need to Talk About Kevin* [2011]) scholars often praise for their poetic, painterly and aleatory qualities, and for their acute sensitivity to nuance and detail. Her films present astute explorations of stasis and mobility, escape and entrapment, and distance and proximity; traumatic and post-traumatic states of individual consciousness and social being; and challenging dimensions along with disturbing varieties of parent–child and other conventionally intimate forms of social relations. Ramsay demonstrates particular skill in depicting objective uncertainty, subjective inscrutability and moral ambiguity. Peter Mullan's films (again, most notably his feature films – *Orphans* [1998]; *The Magdalene Sisters* [2002]; and *Neds* [2010]) likewise have been highly acclaimed by film scholars, not only as powerful critical commentaries on leading social institutions, including family, church and school, as well as on social problems of exploitation and abuse pursued along lines of class and gender, but also for synthesizing social realism with elements of expressionism, surrealism, absurdism, the carnivalesque, black humour and magic realism. *Orphans* offers not only a powerful rendering of the experience of bereavement concerning the loss of a literal mother but also an ambitious allegory concerning the Scottish nation at the turn of the century coming to grips with and finding a way forward vis-à-vis the still painfully recent losses of a series of figuratively protective and reassuring 'mothers' – Mother Industry, Mother City, Mother Church, Mother Welfare and Mother Britain. *The Magdalene Sisters* exposes the scandalous long-term practice in Ireland whereby many poor and working-class girls and young women demonstrating sufficient independent spirit to 'cause trouble' by challenging extremely repressive social, and especially sexual, norms for 'correct moral behaviour' were effectively enslaved by the Roman Catholic Church as 'punishment', often enough for the rest of their lives, working in church-run laundries. *Neds* critiques the social forces responsible for transforming working-class boys with intelligence, talent and creative potential into 'Non-Educated Delinquents' – and these forces include a brutally authoritarian educational system run by the Roman Catholic Church; alcoholism, domestic abuse and extreme emotional alienation within the family; vicious class prejudice and strict class segregation; the hegemony of destructive models of violent male masculinity; and the huge void left by way of a lack of substantial alternatives to gang affiliation as available avenues in which to invest youthful energy.

Beyond Lynne Ramsay and Peter Mullan the two most recent Scottish film-makers increasingly frequently discussed in 'auteurist' terms, and, yet again, praised for their considerable talent in moving beyond 'classic' varieties of British social realism, by drawing on a range of non- and post-naturalistic aesthetic styles, are David Mackenzie and Richard Jobson. In '*Screening Scotland*: a Reassessment' (2009) Duncan Petrie singles out Mackenzie and Jobson in particular as offering reason to be hopeful about the present and near-future state of Scottish cinema at the end of the first decade of the twenty-first century. According to Petrie, both demonstrate 'a profound engagement with certain thematic preoccupations that have defined Scottish cultural expression, most notably the Calvinist-inspired obsession with fear, personal responsibility and the machinations of fate' (2009: 161). By late 2013 David Mackenzie has now directed eight feature films: *The Last Great Wilderness* (2002), *Young Adam*, *Asylum* (2007), *Hallam Foe* (2007), *Spread* (2009), *Perfect Sense* (2011), *Tonight You're Mine* (2011) and *Starred Up* (2013). Among these films the two upon which Scottish cinema studies scholars have focused the greatest attention to date are *Young Adam* and *Hallam Foe*. The first was deliberately conceived and promoted as an 'art film' and is an ambitious adaptation of one of the most famous novels by the Scottish avant-garde writer Alexander Trocchi. Although the film features many impressive moments in capturing the look and feel of post-World War II Glasgow; in the performances of Ewan MacGregor, Tilda Swinton and Peter Mullan as the three central characters; and in conveying tension and suspense – all the while exploring challenging existential issues concerning freedom and responsibility, sexuality and desire, and individuality and community – many find the film uneven, and ultimately more a testimony to Mackenzie's considerable potential than to his successful accomplishment. *Hallam Foe* is generally regarded as realizing this potential. The film manages to win considerable sympathy for the eponymous, precocious yet troubled, protagonist, despite Hallam's mania, obsessiveness, voyeurism, stalking and difficulty transitioning from adolescence to adulthood, as the film explores, by way of form and style as well as content, complex issues concerning relations between looking and seeing, perceiving and knowing, thinking and understanding, identification and desire, recklessness and vulnerability, performance and authenticity – and of intricate interrelations between sexuality, sociality and identity.

Richard Jobson is a proudly Edinburgh-based and Edinburgh-focused film-maker; his most notable feature films to date–*16 Years of Alcohol*, *A Woman in Winter* and *New Town Killers* (2008) – all feature the capital city as a major presence in its own right, strikingly in three films conceived in dramatically different generic terms. Other feature films that Jobson, former frontman for the punk band the Skids and a long-time television presenter, has directed, as of late 2013, are *The Purifiers* (2004), *The Skids Live* (2010), *The Somnambulists* (2012) and *Wayland's Song* (2013). *16 Years of Alcohol*, based on an earlier novella by Jobson of the same title, critics have often discussed as an example of poetic realism, as opposed to social realism, and as, again, indebted to European art cinema, with its pronounced emphasis on introspection and reflection; its striking use of distanciation and ellipsis; and its expressionistic rendering of physical violence as well as of gang identification and internal gang rivalry. The film's investigation of a seemingly familiarly 'damaged' variety of Scottish urban working-class male masculinity focuses, less familiarly, on what that damage entails in relation to the interior consciousness of such a figure, in how it affects perceptions of and relations to both self and others, especially others from more privileged class backgrounds, and how it severely limits opportunities to overcome the past and pursue a different future. *New Town Killers* is an instance of social fantasy, as opposed to social realism, drawing upon comic book, video game, gothic macabre and film noir generic sources, as well as influences of Alfred Hitchcock, Stanley Kubrick and Michael Haneke, along with other prior films such as *The Most Dangerous Game* (Irving Pichel and Ernest B. Schoedsack, 1932) and *The Running Man* (Paul Michael Glaser,1987). Besides the appeal of a well-conceived and well-executed, frenetic chase thriller, the film also offers an incisive allegorical critique of ruthless practices pursued by ultra-elite banking and financial capitalists, as well as of amoral complacency and callous indifference among the middle classes.

New Scottish Cinema has addressed a persistent nexus of common issues, aside from frequently cited concerns over male masculinity in crisis, damaged male masculinity and changing conceptions and practices of male masculinity; concomitant changes as well as constancies in women's (and girls') social positions, roles and opportunities; and children in precarious straits, cut off, adrift, isolated, alone and orphaned either literally or figuratively. New Scottish Cinema repeatedly engages with the following nexus of issues: challenges and struggles in growing up and coming of age; the push and pull of family, friends and community; isolation and alienation, poverty and destitution, violence and crime, and exploitation and abuse; oppressive social institutions, and the impact, in particular, of social class, of social-class division and social-class conflict; and dreams of and efforts at escape, the possibilities and impossibilities of re-creation and re-invention, and opportunities as well as lack of opportunities for salvation and transcendence. New Scottish Cinema's readiness to forthrightly engage with difficult, disturbing, complex and challenging dimensions of life-experience, past and present, hardly suggests continuing Scottish inferiorism, insecurity or lack of self-confidence, but instead the opposite. What we find is a readiness to interrogate what is and what has been, *for what it is and for what it has been*, all the while strongly suggesting that what is and has been is not by any means the best that can or should be. This focus is symptomatic of a mature, confident, dynamic and progressive culture. As is Scottish film-makers' talent in bridging social realism and art cinema, in effectively redefining what cinematic realism can mean in late-twentieth-century and early-twenty-first-century terms. After all, if a film is judged to be 'realistic' this can mean that it enables us accurately and/or adequately to understand, and appreciate, some aspect or dimension of 'reality'. This aspect or dimension may not be something which is superficially apparent, something empirical that we directly perceive by way of our senses, but it may, nonetheless, at the same time, be very much real – it may be something of a different kind of level or quality of reality. Or it may represent an essence not just an appearance, or it may represent a collective category not just an individual instance, or it may represent an abstract dimension of the real as opposed to a concrete one. Indeed, New Scottish Cinema's exhibition of substantial qualities of poetic realism, magic realism, expressionism, surrealism, absurdism, gothic macabre and black humour may well represent insightful new kinds of engagements with as well as provide source and stimulus for productive new kinds of inquiries into diverse contemporary Scottish – and international – 'realities'.

Bob Nowlan

References

Bell, Eleanor and Miller, Gavin (ed.) (1994) *Scotland in Theory: Reflections on Culture & Literature*, Scottish Cultural Review of Language and Literature Volume 1, Amsterdam: Rodopi.

Blain, Neil (1990) 'A Scotland as Good as Any Other?: Documentary Film, 1937–82', in Eddie Dick (ed.), *From Limelight to Satellite: A Scottish Film Book*, Edinburgh: Scottish Film Council and British Film Institute, pp. 53–70.

Blain, Neil and Hutchison, David (ed.) (2008), *The Media in Scotland*, Edinburgh: EUP.

Branston, Gill and Stafford, Roy (2003) *The Media Student's Book*, London: Routledge.

Brown, Simon (2011)'"Anywhere but Scotland?" Transnationalism and New Scottish Cinema', *International Journal of Scottish Theatre and Screen*, 4: 1, http://journals.qmu.ac.uk/index.php/IJOSTS/article/view/109/pdf. Accessed 24 October 2013.

Devine, TM (2012) *The Scottish Nation: A Modern History*, London: Penguin.

Dick, Eddie (ed.) (1990) *From Limelight to Satellite: A Scottish Film Book* (ed. Eddie Dick), Edinburgh: Scottish Film Council and British Film Institute.

Haider, Sandra-Elisabeth (2002) *Scotland in feature film: The country's screen-image then and now, with focus on the city of Glasgow and the development of a Scottish film industry*, PhD thesis, University of Vienna, Hamburg: Diplomarbeit Agentur and the University of Vienna.

Hardy, Forsyth (1990) *Scotland in Film*, Edinburgh: EUP.

Hill, John (2009) '"Bonnie Scotland, eh?": Scottish Cinema, the Working Class and the Films of Ken Loach', in Jonathan Murray, Fidelma Farley and Rod Stoneman (eds), *Scottish Cinema Now*, Newcastle upon Tyne: Cambridge Scholars Publishing, pp. 88–104.

Jackson, Ellen-Raïssa (2004) 'Dislocating the Nation: Political Devolution and Cultural Identity on Stage and Screen', in Eleanor Bell and Gavin Miller (eds), *Scotland in Theory*, Scottish Cultural Review of Language and Literature, Volume 1, Amsterdam: Rodopi, pp. 107–19.

Laverty, Paul et al. (2012) *The Angels' Share* [Screenplay with commentaries from Paul Laverty, Ken Loach, Rebecca O'Brien and others], Pontefract, UK: Route Publishing.

Lay, Samantha (2002) *British Social Realism: From Documentary to Brit Grit*, Short Cuts Introductions to Film Studies, London: Wallflower Press.

Leigh, Jacob (2002) *The Cinema of Ken Loach: Art in the Service of the People*, Directors' Cuts, London: Wallflower Press.

Martin-Jones, David (2009) *Scotland: Global Cinema – Genres, Modes and Identities*, Edinburgh: EUP.

McArthur, Colin (ed.) (1982a) *Scotch Reels: Scotland in Cinema and Television*, London: BFI.

_________ (ed.) (1982b) 'An Interview with Forsyth Hardy', *Scotch Reels: Scotland in Cinema and Television*, London: BFI, pp. 73–92.

Murray, Jonathan, Farley, Fidelma and Stoneman, Rod (ed.) (2009) *Scottish Cinema Now*, Newcastle upon Tyne: Cambridge Scholars Publishing.

Noble, Andrew (1990) 'Bill Douglas's *Trilogy*', in Eddie Dick (ed.), *From Limelight to Satellite: A Scottish Film Book*, Edinburgh: Scottish Film Council and British Film Institute, pp. 133–50.

Pendreich, Brian (2002) *The Pocket Scottish Movie Book*, Edinburgh: Mainstream Publishing.

_________ (2000) *The Scot Pack: The Further Adventures of the Trainspotters and Their Fellow Travellers*, Edinburgh: Mainstream Publishing.

Petrie, Duncan (2004) *Contemporary Scottish Fictions: Film, Television and the Novel*, Edinburgh: EUP.

_________ (2000) *Screening Scotland*, London: BFI.

_________ (2009) '*Screening Scotland*: a Reassessment', in Jonathan Murray, Fidelma Farley and Rod Stoneman (eds), *Scottish Cinema Now*, Newcastle upon Tyne: Cambridge Scholars Publishing, pp. 153–70.

Seino, Takako (2012) *Realism and Representations of the Working Class in Contemporary British Cinema*, MPhil in Film Studies Thesis, De Montfort University, Leicester, England.

Smith, Murray (2002) *Trainspotting*, British Film Institute Modern Classics, London: BFI.

Williams, Christopher (1996) 'The Social Art Cinema: A Moment in the History of British Film and Television Culture', in Christopher Williams (ed.), *Cinema: The Beginnings and the Future – Essays Marking the Centenary of the First Film Show Projected to a Paying Audience in Britain*, London: University of Westminster Press, pp. 190–200.

Zumkhawala-Cook, Richard (2008) *Scotland as We Know It: Representations of National Identity in Literature, Film and Popular Culture*, Jefferson, NC: McFarland.

16 Years of Alcohol

Country of Origin:
UK
Language:
English
Studio/Production Company:
Tartan Works Ltd
Director:
Richard Jobson
Producers:
Hamish McAlpine
Richard Jobson
Mark Burton
Executive Producers:
Steve McIntyre
Wouter Barendrecht
Michael J Werner
Screenwriter:
Richard Jobson
Cinematographer:
John Rhodes
Art Director:
Mike McLoughlin
Composer:
Keith Atack
Editor:
Ioannis Chalkiadakis
Duration:
96 minutes
Genre:
Social Art Cinema
Poetic Realism
Social/Psychological Drama
Gangster
Cast:
Kevin McKidd
Laura Fraser
Susan Lynch
Year:
2003

Synopsis

As a child, Frankie idolized his parents, until he discovered his father was a philanderer, and his mother left. In the first phase of the film, we see Frankie experiment with alcohol. He also always appears to be on the outside of the community, looking in. By the second phase of the film, Frankie is seemingly submerged in a violent skinhead subculture. But again, he often appears to be slightly removed from the group. It is during this stage of the film that Frankie meets middle-class Helen, an art student, and his outlook on life changes. This becomes Frankie's first foray into a different world – one where love and respect are openly given and accepted, and alcohol and violence are not prime ingredients of life. Helen and Frankie's relationship fails due to Frankie's inability to let go of his past, and to believe that he can actually love and be loved. Although not returning to his previous peer group, Frankie does return to his alcohol-infused life. Soon after a violent run-in with an old gang member, Frankie meets Mary – a gentle, loving, softly spoken Irish woman. He joins Alcoholics Anonymous and a drama club, and begins to turn his life around. Finally Frankie has a real chance of allowing himself to be on the inside of a loving relationship. However, again, his emotional skeletons come to the fore as Frankie suspects that Mary has been seeing another man. Unable to find the strength and courage to confront the issue, Frankie rejects Mary. The film begins and ends at the point of Frankie's death, and his realization that in fact he had found what he no longer thought he could have – love.

Critique

16 Years of Alcohol is Richard Jobson's award-winning debut film adaptation of his 1987 novella of the same name. It provides insights both into Jobson's individual perspective as an artist and an analysis of the social position and background from which he came.

Set in Edinburgh, *16 Years of Alcohol* (hereafter *16 Years*) portrays urban working-class Frankie through three time periods of his life: young child, teenager and latterly in his thirties. The time span of this film runs from the 1960s onwards, and it is partly narrated through the music soundtrack. This is particularly evident in the era of Frankie's (Kevin McKidd) and Helen's (Laura Fraser) relationship, which features Roxy Music's 'Love is a Drug' (1975) as contemporary, and Frankie's personal taste in music, sardonically referred to by Helen as 'retro' – for example, his love of Symarip's 'Skinhead Moonstomp' (1969).

Jonathan Murray (2007: 88–90) argues that within contemporary Scottish cinema, the presence of a Scottish *voice* should not reduce understandings of narratives to that of a national allegory. Accordingly, despite the title and Jobson's Scottish national identity, *16 Years* is neither a contribution to the long-standing social realism tradition of film-making in Scotland, nor a film intended to provide a moral discourse on a supposed Scottish culture of alcohol abuse.

Filming Location:

Edinburgh (Old Town), Scotland, UK

Funding:

Scottish Screen
Fortissimo Film Sales
Metro-Tartan

Budget:

£420,000

Awards:

2003 British Independent Film Awards: Richard Jobson – Douglas Hickox Award for directorial debut; Susan Lynch – Best Supporting Actor/Actress Award
2003 Dinard British Film Festival: John Rhodes – Kodak Award for Best Cinematography; 2004 Irish Film and Television Awards: Susan Lynch – Best Supporting Actress in Film/TV

At the time of *16 Years*'s production, Jobson was one of a number of Scottish low-budget film-makers beginning to experiment with High Definition digital video for cinema. Jobson's film is noteworthy for its eschewal of social realism, its innovative testing of HD digital video's ability, and its European film-making style. The auteur and aesthetic approach of the film was secured, in Jobson's (25 June 2010 interview) view, due to initial funding having been secured from the Netherlands-based multinational film-production company Fortissimo.

Critical responses to *16 Years* have seemed to depend upon the ideological position of the reviewer, ranging from praise for a fresh approach to a Scottish fictional narrative, to criticism of the first-person narration of the protagonist. However, even at the more positive end of this spectrum, the film has tended to be pigeonholed as a new and exciting cinematographic approach to portraying a well-worn 'Scottish' narrative – one of alcohol and damaged masculinity. Although set in Edinburgh, this, however, is not a narrative only with applicability within Scotland's borders. It is the story of a young working-class boy brought up, within a particular era, surrounded by social images of what men are and how they should behave, who grows up with tightly circumscribed perceptions of what masculinity 'is'. To be 'a man' is to be respected by others through being tough, a fighter, a drinker and a quick thinker. *16 Years* tells the story of Frankie's struggle to understand that he can be different and to break away from the perceived expectations of his social group.

16 Years contributes to a discourse on the dichotomy of class identity which arguably is lived not just in Scotland but across the United Kingdom, in the United States and beyond. By drawing on already distinct perceptions of class in Scotland, it would have been easy to reproduce binary understandings and provide reassuring images of a 'Scottish class identity' within the film. However, Jobson, who was encouraged by Wong Kar-Wai to retain the lyrical first-person narration (Macnab 2004), makes the point that intelligence and poetry are not the reserves of the middle classes.

Alcohol abuse and sectarian violence remain rhetorical tropes reproduced by some British politicians and journalists as defining cultural-identity markers of the Scots. Within *16 Years* there are certainly numerous images of both: on three occasions we see the pre-teen Frankie drinking what appears to be whisky; there are iconic symbols of Celtic and Hibernian (Hibs) football teams; and there is, clearly, violence. Yet, unlike many representations of Scotland, these three are not necessarily connected. The film does not depict wholesale alcohol abuse amongst its characters; and there is nothing to suggest that the majority of characters have more than a moderate, social attitude towards alcohol. Frankie, by his own admission in the film, can be a violent man without alcohol. And despite the references to the Catholic-originated football teams mentioned above, there is no reference to sectarianism within Jobson's film. Instead there is a complex mixture of identities and relationships within this film which challenge many taken-for-granted assumptions about life in Scotland. For example, Jobson was keen to portray the strength of women throughout the film (Jobson 25 June 2010 interview). A key illustration of this occurs through Elaine C Smith's character (female speaker at the Alcoholics Anonymous meeting Frankie attends) who, in contrast to Frankie's self-reflective lyricism, has the ability to draw on a profound sense of humour, distinguishing her as independent and in control.

Jacqui Cochrane

References

Blandford, Steven (2007) *Film, Drama and the Break-Up of Britain*, Bristol: Intellect.

Dougan, Andy (2004) '*16 Years of Alcohol* (18): Drowning in a Sea of Pretension', *Glasgow Evening Times*, 29 July, p. 2.

Jobson, Richard (2010) Interview with Jacqui Cochrane, Edinburgh, Scotland, 25 June.

Macnab, Geoffrey (2004) 'Lyrical Lads', *Sight and Sound*, 14: 8, pp. 27–29.

Murray, Jonathan (2007) 'Scotland', in Mette Hjort and Duncan Petrie (eds), *The Cinema of Small Nations*, Edinburgh: EUP, pp. 76–92.

Aberdeen

Country of Origin:
Norway

Language:
English

Studio/Production Company:
Norsk Film

Director:
Hans Petter Moland

Producers:
Tom Remlov
Petter J Borgli

Screenwriters:
Hans Petter Moland
Kristin Amundsen

Cinematographer:
Philip Øgaard

Art Director:
Mike Gunn

Composer:
Zbigniew Preisner

Synopsis

A young woman named Kaisa travels to Norway to bring her father, Tomas, back to Aberdeen at her mother's request. What should be a relatively simple trip is hindered at every turn by Tomas's persistent drunkenness and Kaisa's fiery temper. It becomes apparent that the trip will be a challenge for them both, but they have no choice but to try and make it to Aberdeen once they discover that Kaisa's mother is dying of cancer. They both have to attempt to set aside the bitterness they feel towards each other in order to get to Aberdeen before Kaisa's mom passes away, but this proves to be a difficult and complicated process.

Critique

Aberdeen provides viewers with startlingly convincing characters who change dramatically throughout the course of the film. Powerful performances by both Skarsgård and Headey are especially moving. Neither Kaisa nor Tomas can accept what the other has become since they had last seen each other, and both of them frequently reminisce about the past in an attempt to reconcile their current dissatisfaction with what the other has become. They both resent each other, yet each is a reflection of the other in ways they refuse to accept. Kaisa's dependence upon cocaine mirrors Tomas's alcoholism, but their mutual addictions serve distinct purposes. Tomas's addiction to alcohol is the only distinguishably stable aspect of his life, a life that seems to have fallen apart after separation from

Editor:

Sophie Hesselberg

Duration:

106 minutes

Genre:

Social Art Cinema
Social/Psychological Drama

Cast:

Stellan Skarsgård
Lena Headey
Charlotte Rampling
Ian Hart

Year:

2000

Filming Locations:

Bergen, Hordaland, Norway
Glasgow, Strathclyde, Scotland, UK
Glencoe, the Highlands, Scotland, UK
Oslo, Norway
Saltcoats, North Ayrshire, Scotland, UK

his wife and daughter. We learn that he was at one point employed as an oil rig worker, a highly regimented lifestyle, but he has lost that life as well. While Tomas's alcoholism seems to be the only stable aspect of his life, Kaisa's dependencies destabilize her life. Cocaine and sex without emotional investment fuel her, and allow her to distance herself from her everyday routine as a lawyer. Their differences in personality are also striking, with Kaisa's aggression and dominant attitude contrasting sharply with Tomas's defensive, cowering demeanour. Tomas seems in many ways ashamed of his alcoholism and his failings as a father, whereas Kaisa does not appear to regret any of her personal decisions. Viewers may initially pity Kaisa for having to deal with Tomas's wretchedness, but as the film goes on she becomes more and more hopeless as well, while Tomas gains more of a sense of dependability. This shift challenges viewers to re-evaluate how they choose to identify, with whom, and why so. *Aberdeen*'s detailed and dynamic characterizations make the film stand out as a pinnacle achievement.

Aberdeen is, at its core, a film primarily interested in the relationship between father and daughter, and what happens when that relationship becomes monumentally strained. Throughout much of the movie the roles of the father and daughter are reversed. Tomas is essentially dependent upon Kaisa to move through the world; it is almost as if he is the child and she is the parent watching over him. Furthermore, rather than being a loving daughter who looks up to her father, Kaisa bullies him emotionally and physically humiliates him as well, assuming the role conventionally associated with an abusive parent. She manipulates Tomas, using his alcoholism as a tool to get him to do as she wishes, and frequently reminds him of his failings as a father. Their relationship as father and daughter degrades so far over the course of time that Kaisa does not hesitate to pull open the shower curtain, violating her father's privacy and exposing his nakedness. Tomas is so ashamed of his failings as a father that he does not even attempt to assume any sort of paternal authority until Kaisa propositions to him that they could be lovers. Even with the knowledge that she may not be his biological daughter, this is too much of an affront to Tomas's sensibilities to be ignored and he gets angry with her. It is this show of disrespect that finally forces Tomas to reverse the roles that have been played throughout the movie, and he begins to guide his daughter towards becoming a more stable person. These reversals in the film's central father–daughter relationship further a critique concerning gender norms. Kaisa's masculine traits and her aggressive demeanour towards her father may seem as surprising to many viewers as they initially did to Tomas, but the film manages to remain credible due to its strong script and powerful direction as well as acting performances.

Jason Burke

Ae Fond Kiss

Countries of Origin:

UK
Italy
Germany
Spain

Languages:

English
Punjabi

Studio/Production Companies:

Sixteen Films
Cinéart
Matador Pictures
Glasgow Film Fund
Scottish Screen
Tornasol Films

Director:

Ken Loach

Synopsis

Ae Fond Kiss follows the drama of an interracial couple as impacted by the spectre of British postcolonialism. Casim Khan, a young second-generation Pakistani Muslim man who lives with his family in Glasgow, falls in love with Roisin Hanlon, an Irish music teacher from his sister's Catholic school. As their relationship develops, struggles follow between two conflicting religious ideologies. On one side is Casim's traditional Muslim family that plans an arranged marriage for him. On the other side is the Catholic school board that questions Roisin's moral integrity when she starts her relationship with Casim. The meanderings of the couple constitute the plotline as the film examines religious fundamentalisms on both sides with relatively equal attention.

Critique

Casim and Roisin's bond grows along with a shared passion for music. The scenes when Roisin plays the piano are moments of romantic and aesthetic fascination. They are some of the few apolitical moments in a film replete with tensions of all sorts – cultural, religious and ideological. The film endorses the language

Ae Fond Kiss (2004),
British Film Institute Collection

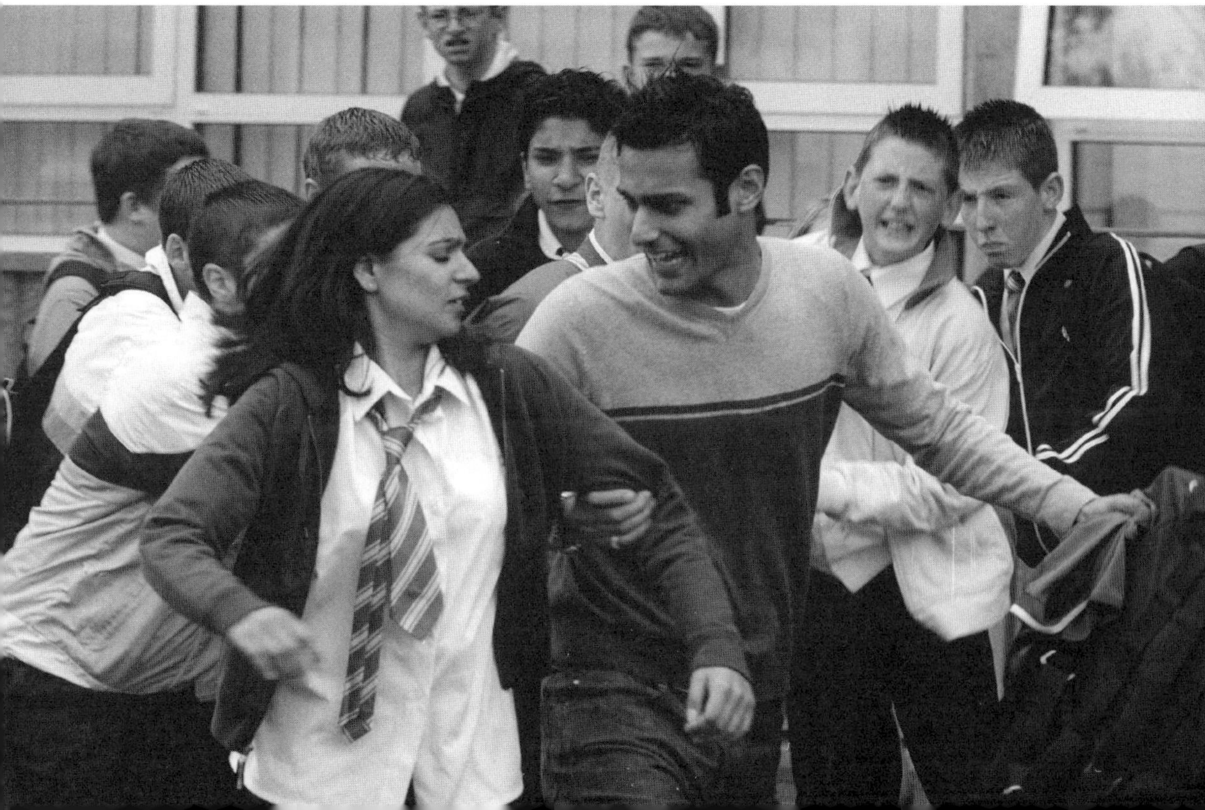

Producer:
Rebecca O'Brien
Screenwriter:
Paul Laverty
Cinematographer:
Barry Ackroyd
Art Directors:
Ursula Cleary
Fergus Clegg
Composer:
George Fenton
Editor:
Jonathan Morris
Duration:
104 minutes
Genre:
Social Realism
Social Drama
Romance
Melodrama
Cast:
Atta Yaqub
Eva Birthistle
Ahmad Riaz
Shabana Akthar Bakhsh
Year:
2004
Filming Location:
Glasgow, Strathclyde, Scotland, UK
Nerja, Málaga, Andalucía, Spain

of emotions shared through music and affection as a compromise for ideological tensions on both sides. These moments, however, are rare, which suggests that they are far from offering a facile romantic solution to real interracial tensions.

Casim's father has a dream/nightmare that momentarily detours the plot into the traumatic history of the partition of British India that led to the loss of his twin brother. Casim is named after the lost brother. When he resists the family tradition of arranged marriages, it feels like another partition, resurfacing his father's childhood trauma. This episode reveals the political unconscious that shapes the plotline. When Casim shows Roisin old pictures of the twin brothers together before the partition, we contemplate one especially explicit illustration of the film's desire to evoke and document a traumatic political history and its remote echoes in the present.

The film ultimately seems more invested in its postcolonial and cultural agenda than in its plot. This emphasis is set from the opening scenes when Tahara, Casim's sister, delivers a speech that critiques stereotypical western simplification of Muslim diversity. She illustrates her position with a concise picture of her layered identity: second-generation Pakistani teenaged woman of Muslim descent who is a student in a Catholic school. When she adds to the list the fact that she is a supporter of Glasgow Rangers and unbuttons her school shirt to show her fan T-shirt to the audience, she enters into a territory of local pride and conflict. A group of boys snatch her Glasgow Rangers T-shirt and call Casim, who came to school to pick Tahara up, a 'blackie'. On this occasion, Casim meets Roisin, an encounter that allows for other facets of interracial tensions to emerge, opening up the pathway the film will follow from this point forward.

Oana Chivoiu

The Bill Douglas Trilogy

Country of Origin:
UK
Language:
English
Studio/Production Company:
BFI

Synopsis

Jamie and Tommy are effectively orphaned siblings, their mother committed to an asylum and their respective fathers absent, who live with their ailing maternal grandmother in almost unimaginable penury in a Scottish mining village during World War II and in the years immediately after. Jamie, the *Trilogy*'s central character, is profoundly scarred by the dehumanizing conditions in which he does not so much live as exist. In particular, a chronic lack of secure and sustaining emotional relationships with parent figures, biological or surrogate, appears to be the central source of a long-term distress so deep that it threatens to render its sufferer near-catatonic. The

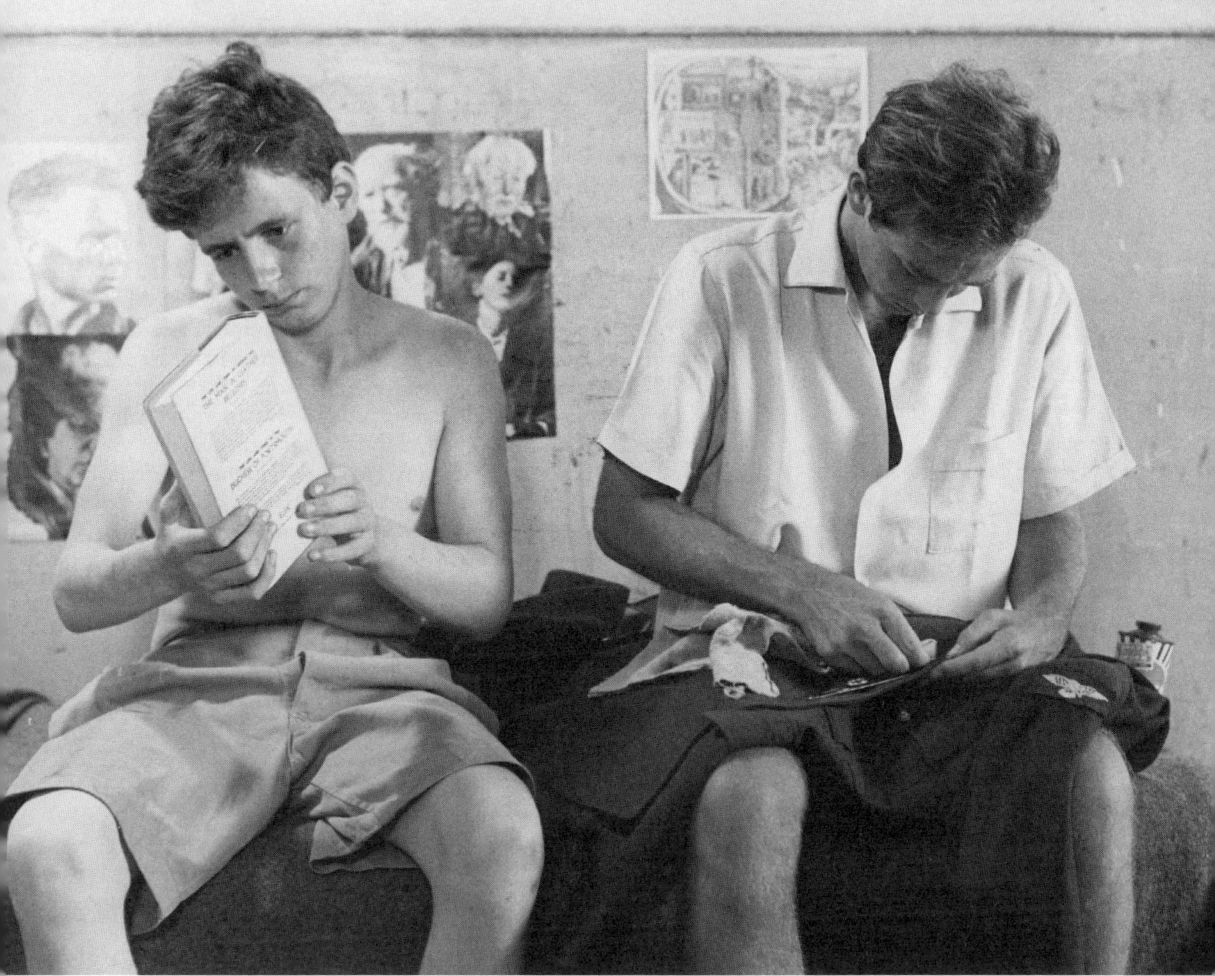

My Way Home (1978),
British Film Institute Collection

Director:
Bill Douglas
Producers:
Tony Bicât
Judy Cottam
Richard Craven
Geoffrey Evans
Nick Nascht
Charles Rees
Screenwriter:
Bill Douglas
Cinematographers:
Mick Campbell
Ray Orton
Gale Tattersall

Trilogy follows Jamie through a succession of awful or abortive domestic arrangements, before he at last finds a sustaining physical and psychological place in the world. Life with Tommy and Granny is replaced after the latter's death with grudging adoption by Jamie's father and paternal grandmother. The fecklessness of the former and psychosis of the latter eventually drives Jamie into a state home for orphaned and abused children. Although the gaping wounds left by a wretched childhood seem to have destined him for either a life of vagrancy or an early suicide, personal salvation arrives in the shape of a period of National Service in the British Army during the 1950s. Posted to a military base in Egypt, Jamie there meets Robert, an educated and thoughtful young middle-class Englishman. Despite Jamie's painful scars, and the two men's markedly different personal backgrounds, they form an intense and unqualified friendship. The *Trilogy* ends with their demobilization, and Robert's offer to extend his home to incorporate Jamie.

Art Directors:

Oliver Bouchier
Elsie Restorick

Editors:

Mick Audsley
Brand Thumim
Peter West

Duration:

172 minutes

Genre:

Poetic Realism
Social Art Cinema
Social/Psychological Drama
Coming of Age

Cast:

Stephen Archibald
Hughie Restorick
Jean Taylor Smith
Helena Gloag
Karl Fieseler
Joseph Blatchley

Years:

1972; 1973; 1978

Filming Locations:

Newcraighall, Edinburgh, UK
Cairo, Egypt

Critique

It is fitting that Bill Douglas's *Trilogy* is studded from the very outset with images concerned with the idea of elevation. As well as proving suggestive in any attempt to explore the complexity and power of the films' formal and emotional structures, this motif also echoes the terms of Douglas's critical reputation some two decades on from his death in 1991. Much scholarship constructs the *Trilogy* as Scottish cinema's advent and apotheosis, starting point and high point alike. Douglas is held up as an enduringly seminal figure to succeeding generations of artists for a number of reasons. He produced the films that made his international reputation despite facing wholly unpropitious industrial film-making circumstances in his native country. He overcame the glaring lack of distinctive and developed indigenous traditions of fiction film-making by synthesizing an innovative and individual directorial style from his own cosmopolitan awareness of, and enthusiasm for, key movements in twentieth-century European and American cinemas. He transfigured the stuff of an unedifying and unremarkable post-World War II Scottish childhood into art of great emotional and visual power. He established the importance of autobiography as a creative guiding principle for many Scottish film-makers of the succeeding three decades. For these and other reasons, the *Trilogy* remains a vital achievement within the context of Scottish cinema history: an accomplished work of art in its own right, but also a notably influential point of reference for many other native writers and directors throughout the remainder of the twentieth century and beyond.

Some brief examination of the elevation motif's place within the *Trilogy* may help explain why these films remain so critically admired today. For one thing, this recurring device symbolizes not simply physical and cultural isolation, but also extraordinary personal responsiveness on the part of Douglas and Jamie, his narrative surrogate. Take, for example, our introduction to the latter, some three-and-a-half minutes into *My Childhood*, alone and scavenging scraps of coal at the summit of an immense slag heap. As a siren sounds to end a shift at the local mine, children dash excitedly to meet fathers returning home from work. The spectator briefly shares Jamie's hilltop view of this daily reunion, before the camera cuts to document the same event at close quarters on ground level. On one hand, our fleeting access to Jamie's all-encompassing physical perspective stems directly from his glaring emotional lack: he crouches, exposed and alone, high above his fellow children because they have parents and he does not. But at the same time, the central protagonist's pain bestows upon him something that his seemingly more fortunate counterparts do not possess, namely, a preternaturally heightened capacity for social and emotional perception. Right from its opening moments, the impact of Douglas's *Trilogy* relies equally on the content and colour of its maker's life experiences and the personal qualities these inculcated within him, ones that contributed to the development of a formidable artistic talent. Or, to put matters another way, while Jamie's situation at the start of *My Childhood* may be a physically and psychologically chilling one, it also affords the possibility of an unusually clear and comprehensive oversight of the world that this lonely child inhabits.

The sense that the perspective on post-World War II Scottish society and culture which the *Trilogy* offers is consistently elevated in figurative terms, even if only intermittently so in a literal equivalent, is stressed yet more emphatically by the opening of *My Ain Folk*. Here, Jamie's brother Tommy cries cathartic tears in the local cinema while watching Technicolor footage, from the Hollywood movie *Lassie Come Home* (Fred Wilcox, 1943), of the eponymous canine performer standing alone on a rocky promontory, a breathtaking natural landscape visible below her in the background. This moment of extraordinary private transcendence is immediately contrasted with an everyday one of collective entombment: adopting the unenviable position of miners crammed into a pit lift at the beginning of their shift, the camera shows the local agricultural landscape above ground giving way to undifferentiated blackness as the men are transported below the surface. Douglas's point here is not that cinema allows artists and their audiences the opportunity to draw a clear-cut distinction between certain orders of image and human experience that could or should be acknowledged as transcendent (the idealized anthropomorphism of a 1940s mainstream American film) and others (the relentless physical grind of a mid-century Scottish working-class community's daily life and culture) that emphatically can or should not. Rather, he argues through example that the artistic medium he works within offers anyone who creates and/or consumes it with sufficient care the possibility of finding copious reserves of emotional and cultural meaning within apparently mundane narrative materials. In the sequence under consideration here, for example, Douglas recuperates two things at once. The *Lassie* footage is shown to represent something more than just a laughable excess of aesthetic and emotional stimulation; at the same time, the miners' daily toil is rescued – but not romanticized – through the assertion that it represents more than simply an absolute absence of such qualities.

The ending of *My Way Home*, the *Trilogy*'s final instalment, once again uses the motif of elevation to emphasize the sheer distinctiveness and power of its maker's thematic concerns and formal style. These might be described, however counter-intuitively, as acts of measured transfiguration – frequently euphoric in impact, but rarely – if ever – excessive in intention or execution. The gradually amplified sound of aircraft engines accompanies a cut from the previous scene of Jamie's and Robert's demobilization. This creates the fleeting illusion, for ten seconds or so, that the near-featureless, bleached landscape seen passing right to left before the camera might be the Egyptian desert far below the two young men returning to Britain. Of course, Douglas swiftly reveals that what is really seen at this point are the paperless walls of Jamie's now-abandoned first home, the domicile that viewers witnessed the boy living in (and through) at the *Trilogy*'s outset. Yet despite being orientated, logically speaking, on a horizontal axis rather than a vertical one, and being positioned a metre or so from, rather than thousands of feet above, where and what the camera records, a marked sense of elevation in the figurative sense persists. This is so not least because in closing the *Trilogy*, its creator seems to figure his eventual escape from a wretchedly unhappy childhood as a release that emanated from an artistic willingness to audaciously re-imagine, and thus re-evaluate, his individual history and native culture. Re-creation of such things in an ostensibly straightforward documentary manner with a view to clear-cut, wholesale rejection of them is precisely what Douglas seeks to avoid. Instead, the *Trilogy* works unsparing social interrogation and bravura creative imagination into mutually sustaining processes and ends. Above all else, it is perhaps this remarkable artistic achievement and ability that makes Bill Douglas such an enduring significant point of reference for the students, critics and makers of Scottish cinema who have followed in his footsteps.

Jonathan Murray

Carla's Song

Countries of Origin:

Scotland
Nicaragua

Languages:

English
Spanish

Studio/Production Companies:

Alta Films
Channel Four Films
Degeto Film
Filmstiftung Nordrhein-Westfalen
Institute of Culture
Parallax Pictures
Road Movies Dritte Produktionen
Televisión Española (TVE)
The Glasgow Film Fund
Tornasol Films

Director:

Ken Loach

Producers:

Sally Hibbin
Gerardo Herrero
Ulrich Felsberg

Synopsis:

George, a Glasgow bus driver, has not so much a flagrant disregard for rules but a compulsion to test the limits of those around him, particularly figures of authority. Carla, a Nicaraguan refugee, first catches his eye when she skips his fare, and he is only too happy to let this slip. However, Inspector McGurk boards the bus of his least favourite employee and, appalled by such rule breaking, nearly reports Carla to the police. George then steps in and facilitates Carla's escape. George eventually follows Carla to Nicaragua after he encourages her to return so that she can confront her demons. The film is set in 1987 and Carla, fighting in the Nicaraguan Revolution, has witnessed the torture of Antonio, her lover and the father of her child. The couple used to be part of a troupe, promoting the Sandinista cause and 'Nicaragua Libre'. This explains how she ends up in Glasgow, dancing marimba on the busy shopping streets. George only first learns about the civil war in Nicaragua through Carla's medical notes. His is a state of blissful ignorance and his journey to Nicaragua is a culture shock. Bradley, a humanitarian worker for Witness for Peace, whom the pair first meet on Nicaraguan soil, is far better educated and privy to a great deal more information than George, information that will turn out to be crucial as the film proceeds towards its dramatic climax.

Critique

In Glasgow, posters outside Carla's refuge shout: 'Smash the Tories poll tax!' – a system that was based on the number of occupants in a house as opposed to its value and, as such, heavily taxed the poor. UK Prime Minister Margaret Thatcher's dismantling of the welfare state is also alluded to once inside the women's refuge.

Screenwriter:

Paul Laverty

Cinematographer:

Barry Ackroyd

Art Directors:

Fergus Clegg
Lloren Cleggde

Composer:

George Fenton

Editor:

Jonathan Morris

Duration:

127 minutes

Genre:

Social Realism
Social Drama
Romance
Melodrama

Cast:

Robert Carlisle
Oyanka Cabezas
Scott Glen
Gary Lewis

Year:

1997

Filming Locations:

Glasgow, Scotland, UK
Conic Hill, Scotland, UK
Estelí, Nicaragua

When the social worker asks George to justify his presence in Carla's room, he quips that he is Carla's 'spiritual advisor', prompting her to snap back: 'Corporation supplying them nowadays are they?'

Carla's Song is a film of sharp contrasts, with the unlikely relationship between George and Carla providing an opportunity to explore differences between the First and Third worlds and the conflicts between left- and right-wing ideologies therein. A striking example occurs in comparing the calm of the Glasgow National Health Service hospital, where an attendant buffers the floors of the empty corridor, with the absolute chaos wrought on a Nicaraguan hospital by a Contra attack. In the latter instance the staff are overwhelmed but everyone pitches in: George and Carla give blood, a mural on the wall depicts a mother nursing her baby and carrying a rifle, and teenage girls in khakis abound. It is apparent that everyone is involved in this revolution.

Another key scene occurs when George and Carla hitch a lift with a group of farmers. Excited by the presence of a foreigner, the farmers want him to understand their situation. They show him the title deeds for their cooperative and explain that 40 families now live on the land previously occupied by one Somocista owner. Emphasis is achieved through translation: as Carla explains the revolution to George in English, she repeats emotive words in Spanish, such as blood, before giving the translation. This is further underlined by subtitles and punctuated by George's 'vernacular' translation: 'What happens if the rich bastard comes back?' Through tears Carla tells him, 'Revolution is new and the gringos don't come back here [...] Now everybody defends this revolution because it is for all people'. George, in contrast, cannot even tell them what crops are grown in Scotland, apart from whisky.

The film met a lukewarm reception on its release. Complaints about the film's earnest approach ranged as far as scathing criticism such as: 'It's propaganda for a war that's already over. Using atrocities as the hook for a love story makes the love story immaterial and the atrocities a gimmick' (Busack 2012). However, the real love story in the film is not between George and Carla but between Carla and her homeland. George, if anything, is little but a plot device – the average Joe who has his eyes opened to the suffering of a Third World country overthrowing a dictatorship. And is not this response of the outsider accurately representative of a great number of 'outsiders' who only hear what is filtered through mass media – is such a response not worth interrogating?

George is nevertheless arguably the least realistic character, with his swagger, 'Glasgae patter' (lots of swearing), and a clichéd 'working-class good guy' persona. When George fixes a leaking petrol tank with soap he nods to Bradley: 'That's what a good university education does for ye, ye knaw'. He also draws caricatures, one of McGurk and one of Bradley, which seem only intended to prove that he has artistic ability and an innate sense of anarchy. Carla's interest in George is limited. George's approach to bus driving is very similar to his approach to life: forge on, regardless of obstacles. The tepid attentions of a beautiful stranger are enough to encourage him to make grand gestures – dumping his fiancée and diverting 'his' bus to Loch Lomond. In return for his efforts, Carla gives him a hand-painted picture of Nicaragua after the bus ticket incident, toasts Nicaragua Libre and Antonio when he takes her to Loch Lomond, and offers her the unusual response, when he arranges for her to live with (a reluctant) Sammy, of reminding him of where she comes from. When she wakes up in hospital, George makes sure that the first thing she sees is her poster of the mountains of her homeland.

Carla is suffering from post-traumatic stress and George wants to look after her. But the reality is that George 'can't take the killing', in Nicaragua. But then, he has that option. When confronted with the scars on Carla's back, or the death of the man to whom he gave his smiley City of Glasgow T-shirt, it is too much for George to bear. Despite the animosity that quickly emerges between them, Bradley wants to make clear to George what is actually happening. George wants to understand the Contra attacks as the behaviour of 'animals'. Bradley explains: 'you think they make this up as they go along, kid? Grow up. It all came out from Langley [...] The CIA kid runs this whole show [...] There is no Contras, there is no war without them'.

Bradley himself, we discover, previously worked for the CIA in Honduras. Earlier in the film he is heard berating other members of the charity for sentimentalizing their reports rather than giving hard facts. He wants 'Witness for Peace, not War and Peace'. Apparently, director Loach and screenwriter Laverty aim to make the same distinction in their approach to *Carla's Song*. If anything, the second part of the film is a staged documentary, as a real co-op, Ulises Rodriguez, is listed in the credits.

Susan Robinson

Reference

Busack, Richard von (1998) 'Managua Trois', *MetroActive*, 10 September, http://www.metroactive.com/papers/cruz/09.10.98/carlas-song-9836.html. Accessed 29 September 2013.

Dear Frankie

Country of Origin:

UK

Language:

English

Studio/Production Company:

Scorpio Films

Director:

Shona Auerbach

Synopsis

Every few months Lizzie moves her son Frankie and mother Nell to a new home in an effort to evade Frankie's abusive father, whom she left when Frankie was just a toddler. To shield her son from the truth, Lizzie has told Frankie that his dad works at sea on the HMS Accra and she writes to him posing as his father. To Lizzie, the letters are not only intended to protect Frankie, but are also a means through which she can communicate with her reserved, yet highly observant, deaf son. One day Frankie learns from a classmate that the HMS Accra is due to dock in their new home of Greenock, on the outskirts of Glasgow, and he is eager to meet his 'father'. Panicked, Lizzie takes the advice of her new friend and

Producer:
Caroline Wood
Screenwriter:
Andrea Gibb
Cinematographer:
Shona Auerbach
Art Director:
Margaret Horspool
Composer:
Alex Heffes
Editor:
Oral Norrie Ottey
Duration:
105 minutes
Genre:
Urban Fable
Melodrama
Cast:
Emily Mortimer
Gerard Butler
Sharon Small
Jack McElhone
Mary Riggans
Sean Brown
Year:
2004
Filming Location:
Greenock, Scotland, UK
Distribution:
UK Box office: £132,541;
Distributor: Pathé
US Box office: $1.3 million;
Distributor: Miramax

boss, Marie, and hires a handsome stranger to play Frankie's dad for the day. Frankie quickly bonds with the man and it is not long before romance begins to flourish between the stranger and Lizzie. However, when Frankie's biological father dies after a long illness Lizzie decides to tell Frankie of his father's death, without revealing his true identity. In a letter sent after the death of his father, Frankie reveals he has always known that the stranger was not his dad and writes that he hopes to see him again in the future.

Critique

Scholarly engagement with *Dear Frankie* has been remarkably thin. Simon Brown (2011) attributes its exclusion from critical debate to the film's mainstream qualities. The narrative trajectory of *Dear Frankie* largely follows that of a romantic drama, placing emphasis on the romantic relationship between Lizzie and Frankie's 'father'. However, the film differs from romantic dramas in the conventional sense by employing aesthetics associated with the realist tradition, most prominently, as Brown (2011) notes, by shooting on location, featuring regional accents (some of which were dubbed for the film's North American release) and through setting the film within a working-class environment.

The film is set, and was filmed, in writer Andrea Gibb's hometown of Greenock, which lies on the River Clyde. This location has featured on-screen several times to date, including most notably Ken Loach's *Sweet Sixteen* (2002), which premiered just two years prior to *Dear Frankie.* The Greenock seen in the latter film however is quite different from that in the former. In keeping with Loach's oeuvre, *Sweet Sixteen* foregrounds Greenock's decaying post-industrial landscape and while this is not entirely absent from *Dear Frankie*, it certainly is not emphasized (Brown 2011). This can largely be explained by the film's focus on the romantic and family dynamics, which are at the thrust of its narrative, rather than wider social or political concerns (Brown 2011).

The universality of the film's themes and its focus on the romantic relationship between Lizzie and Frankie's 'father' perhaps account for its relative success in North America, a lucrative market for any film looking to generate a profit. Miramax acquired the North American rights to *Dear Frankie* and upon its release the film grossed a total of $1.3 million in this market – a respectable sum when considered in relation to other Scottish-based productions with similar funding structures (Hutcheson 2012). The casting of Gerard Butler, who at this time was gaining mainstream awareness through roles in films including *Lara Croft Tomb Raider: The Cradle of Life* (Jan de Bont, 2003) and *The Phantom of the Opera* (Joel Schumacher, 2004) – the latter released just months before *Dear Frankie* – would in all likelihood have enhanced its box office takings. The film was also included in the Un Certain Regard section at the Cannes Film Festival, a notable accomplishment for any debuting director. However, these successes were marred by the film's frosty reception in its home territory. *Dear Frankie* was met with disdain by several British critics, some of whom walked out of the film's press screening at Cannes, and it took just £132,514 at the UK box office.

Many reviewers criticized the improbability of the story, the worst describing it as completely unconvincing. Revealingly, Brown notes that those involved in its production envisioned the film as having a fairy-tale or fable quality and he quotes Butler as describing *Dear Frankie* as 'fairy-tale couched in the reality of everyday life' (2011: 9). The film's upbeat tone and engagement with the romantic-drama genre differentiates it from many other Scottish-set productions. Unfortunately, neither Gibb nor director Shona Auerbach has gone on to extensive careers within the film industry. Gibb has since penned *Nina's Heavenly Delights* (Pratibha Parmar, 2006), an interracial romance between two young Glaswegian women with a similarly optimistic outlook. At the time of writing (June 2013), Auerbach's second feature, *Rudy* is currently in production.

Linda Hutcheson

References

Brown, Simon (2011) '"Anywhere but Scotland?" Transnationalism and New Scottish Cinema', *International Journal of Scottish Theatre and Screen*, 4: 1, http://journals.qmu.ac.uk/index.php/IJOSTS/article/view/109. Accessed 27 August 2012.

Hutcheson, Linda (2012) 'Completion and Distribution of Scottish Screen-Funded Films', *International Journal of Scottish Theatre and Screen*, 5: 1, http://journals.qmu.ac.uk/index.php/IJOSTS/article/view/149. Accessed 8 June 2013.

Donkeys

Countries of Origin:
UK
Denmark
Language:
English
Studio/Production Companies:
Sigma Films
Zentropa Entertainments
Director:
Morag McKinnon
Producers:
Anna Duffield
Gillian Berrie
Screenwriter:
Colin McLaren
Cinematographer:
Lol Crawley

Synopsis

Alfred and Brian are two sixty-something men with little to show for their lives. They dream of retiring to Spain; however, several obstacles stand in their way. These include Brian's fear of flying and Alfred's ill health. Before they leave, Alfred would also like to make amends with his daughter, Jackie, with whom he has been estranged following the death of her husband. Alfred's attempts to rekindle his relationship with Jackie and granddaughter, Bronwyn, coincide with the arrival of Stevie, who has recently been released from prison and returned to Glasgow to visit his dying mother. A chance encounter at the hospital leads Alfred to realize that he is Stevie's father, a fact that Alfred wishes to remain unknown to everyone else. That is until Bronwyn inadvertently reveals that Jackie and Stevie are out on a date and Alfred is forced to reveal the truth, leaving yet more disaster in his wake. When Alfred learns that he has a terminal illness and at best a year left to live, he concludes that the only way of making things right with his daughter is by ensuring she is the beneficiary of his life insurance policy. Upon realizing that she will be entitled to more money if he dies within the month, he enlists Brian's help to bring about an end to his life.

Art Director:

Louise Lyons

Composer:

Magnus Fiennes

Editors:

Colin Monie
Jake Roberts

Duration:

78 minutes

Genre:

Social Drama
Social Art Cinema

Cast:

James Cosmo
Brian Pettifer
Kate Dickie
Martin Compston
Natalie Press
Natasha Watson
Tony Curran
Carolyn Calder
John Comerford

Year:

2010

Filming Location:

Glasgow, Strathclyde, Scotland, UK

Critique

The film's seven-year journey to the silver screen – or perhaps it would be more accurate to say Scottish silver screen as theatrical screenings were predominantly confined to this area – was less than ideal. The project encountered challenges at every stage of its supply chain, although, as will become apparent, some of these were by design.

Donkeys was the second film to be produced under the Advance Party Initiative, a rule-governed project spearheaded by Sigma Films (Scotland) and Zentropa (Denmark) that takes its lead from the influential Dogme 95 movement. Inspired by the Dogme philosophy of enhancing creativity through constraints, the central Advance Party idea, dreamed up by Dogme frontman Lars von Trier, involved challenging three first-time directors to each make a low-budget feature using the same group of characters. These characters were to appear in all three films with the same actors remaining in their respective roles (although the interpersonal relationship between the characters was permitted to change). Frequent Zentropa collaborators Lone Scherfig and Anders Thomas Jensen created seven characters and together the three Advance Party directors were allowed to add two more to the pool. Two Advance Party films have been completed, Andrea Arnold's *Red Road* (2006) and Morag McKinnon's *Donkeys*, while the third, Mikkel Norgaard's *The Old Firm*, looks unlikely to materialize.

When presented with the core group of characters, McKinnon wrote a treatment for a black comedy focusing on the character of Alfred, a 64-year-old man described in the Advance Party brief as, amongst other things, a compulsive liar. In Arnold's film Alfred is a secondary character played by Andy Armour; however when he appears as the lead in *Donkeys*, he is portrayed by the more high-profile actor James Cosmo: *Braveheart* (Mel Gibson, 1995), *Trainspotting* (Danny Boyle, 1996) and *Troy* (Wolfgang Petersen, 2004). Although this recasting led to speculation that the production was trying to increase its commercial appeal, it was also motivated, in part at least, by Armour's ill health. The character of Bronwyn was also recast (perhaps inevitable given the young age of the character and the gap between films) and a new principal character, Brian, created, unique to *Donkeys*. These alterations and additions essentially diminish the on-screen relationship between the two Advance Party films. This connection, however, does not disappear entirely as the characters of Stevie and Jackie have prominent parts in both productions. Yet, with only two of the nine characters reoccurring with recognizable character traits – Clyde and April, both important characters in *Red Road*, make just fleeting appearances in *Donkeys* – this link is perhaps more confusing to an audience familiar with Arnold's *Red Road* than it is enticing. As no reference is made to the Advance Party Initiative in the advertising materials created for *Donkeys*, the ambiguous relationship between the two films is further enhanced.

Writer Colin McLaren (24 July 2012 interview) has conveyed the difficulty he and McKinnon experienced when trying to find a role for all nine Advance Party characters. Initially it was intended that surplus characters would be placed as feuding stallholders at Glasgow's infamous market, 'The Barras', where Alfred works. Early scripts had as much as 50 per cent of the narrative set in this location. However, the final film contains very little of this setting, in part because the feuding stallholders lumbered the film with too many plot strands. After McKinnon was given permission from von Trier for unwanted characters to 'go by on a bus', many of The Barras scenes were cut, and ultimately one of the Advance Party characters, Avery, does not make even a brief appearance in the film. Problems experienced whilst filming at this location, namely at the hands of a resourceful member of the public that set off a drill every time action was called in an attempt to coerce money from the film-makers, also limited its presence in the final film. The reduced use of this location and its related storylines results in an increased emphasis on action elsewhere, namely that centring on the family dynamic and Alfred's relationship with best friend, Brian.

In keeping with the work of McKinnon and McLaren to date, *Donkeys* engages with controversial subject matter – in this instance incest and assisted suicide – that many film-makers shy away from. This has not always made the duo popular with funding agencies and many of their projects remain unmade (Hutcheson 2012). Following the success of their short *Home*, which won a British Academy of Film and Television Arts Award in 1999, the pair attempted to transition into features; however, a ten-year gap passed between *Home* and the release of *Donkeys*, their first feature. Both McKinnon and McLaren have expressed some dissatisfaction with their debut film. In particular, McLaren (24 July 2012 interview) singles out its at times uneasy transition in tone. This problem became apparent during post-production and two rounds of editing took place in an attempt to correct this problem (resulting in a two-year delay between principal photography and release). Despite this effort, the end product does not exhibit the intertwining of comedy and tragedy that their short proved they are capable of. This is particularly evident in the closing scenes during which the potential tragedy of Alfred's death is overshadowed by the film's hurried tying together of its disparate plot strands. The light-hearted way in which this is done does not allow the audience, or the characters, to reflect on Alfred's decision to take his own life or carefully consider the implications of his actions. Nevertheless, even with its flaws, *Donkeys* makes for an interesting viewing experience and its bold intentions, although never fully realized, must be praised.

Linda Hutcheson

References

Hutcheson, Linda (2012) 'Completion and distribution of Scottish screen-funded films', *International Journal of Scottish Theatre and Screen*, 5: 1, http://journals.qmu.ac.uk/index.php/IJOSTS/article/view/149. Accessed 8 June 2013.

McLaren, Colin (2012) 'Question and Answer Session', Interview by Linda Hutcheson [in person], MacRobert Cinema, Stirling, Scotland, 4 July.

_________ (2012) 'Follow-Up Interview', Interview by Linda Hutcheson [via email], 24 July.

Hallam Foe

Country of Origin:

UK

Language:

English

Studio/Production Companies:

Sigma Films
Film4
Glasgow Film Finance
Independent Film Sales
Ingenious Film Partners
Lunar Films
Scottish Screen

Director:

David Mackenzie

Producer:

Gillian Berrie

Screenwriters:

Peter Jinks
David Mackenzie
Ed Whitmore

Cinematographer:

Giles Nuttgens

Art Director:

Caroline Grebbell

Editor:

Colin Monie

Duration:

95 minutes

Genre:

Social/Psychological Drama
Social Art Cinema
Coming of Age

Cast:

Jamie Bell
Sophia Myles
Ciarán Hinds
Claire Forlani

Year:

2007

Synopsis

Hallam Foe's titular anti-hero is a teenage boy profoundly traumatized by his late mother's death by drowning. He has retreated, literally and figuratively, to a solitary life spent spying on others and living in his childhood tree house. Hallam's ongoing emotional pain and confusion stem in significant part from his refusal to accept the official verdict that his mother died by her own hand (she was severely depressed); instead, he believes that she was murdered by Verity, the woman who has subsequently married his father. When an angry confrontation with his stepmother ends in a bout of fierce, anguished copulation between the two, Hallam flees the family home and seeks to begin a new life in the Scottish capital city of Edinburgh. Once there, he accidentally espies Kate, a young woman who bears an uncanny physical resemblance to his late mother. Hallam follows Kate to her place of work, a prestigious city-centre hotel, and persuades her to give him a job there. His new position comes with an added bonus: the building's iconic clock tower offers an urban successor to the elevated voyeuristic vantage point previously provided by Hallam's old tree house. He uses this to spy obsessively on Kate, and even finds a way to ascend to the roof of the apartment block in which she lives, so that he can observe her daily comings and goings at close quarters. Hallam and Kate begin a relationship after he confesses the painful source of his fascination with her. The bond between the pair is fractured, however, by Kate's discovery that Hallam has previously spied on her, and also by the unexpected arrival in Edinburgh of his father and Verity, who require Hallam's signature in order to begin the redevelopment of some land left by his mother in her will. Enraged, Hallam briefly returns home and almost drowns Verity in the same loch where his mother died. This near-disastrous confrontation provokes a much-needed catharsis. Hallam and his father are reconciled, and the former accepts that his mother was not murdered by anyone. Back in Edinburgh, Hallam parts amicably from Kate, and the pair loosely agree to meet again in several years' time.

Critique

It feels fitting that *Hallam Foe* won the Hitchcock d'Or award for Best Film at the 2007 Festival Du Film Britannique in Dinard, France: co-writer/director David Mackenzie's fourth feature offers viewers a sense of what several of Hitchcock's best-known films might have looked and felt like if shot and set in present-day Scotland. Elements of Hitchcock's *Rear Window* (1954), *Vertigo* (1958) and *Psycho* (1960) are knowingly contained and combined within *Hallam Foe*'s narrative. The film's hero is, after all, a troubled young man who (1) cross-dresses as part of his refusal to properly

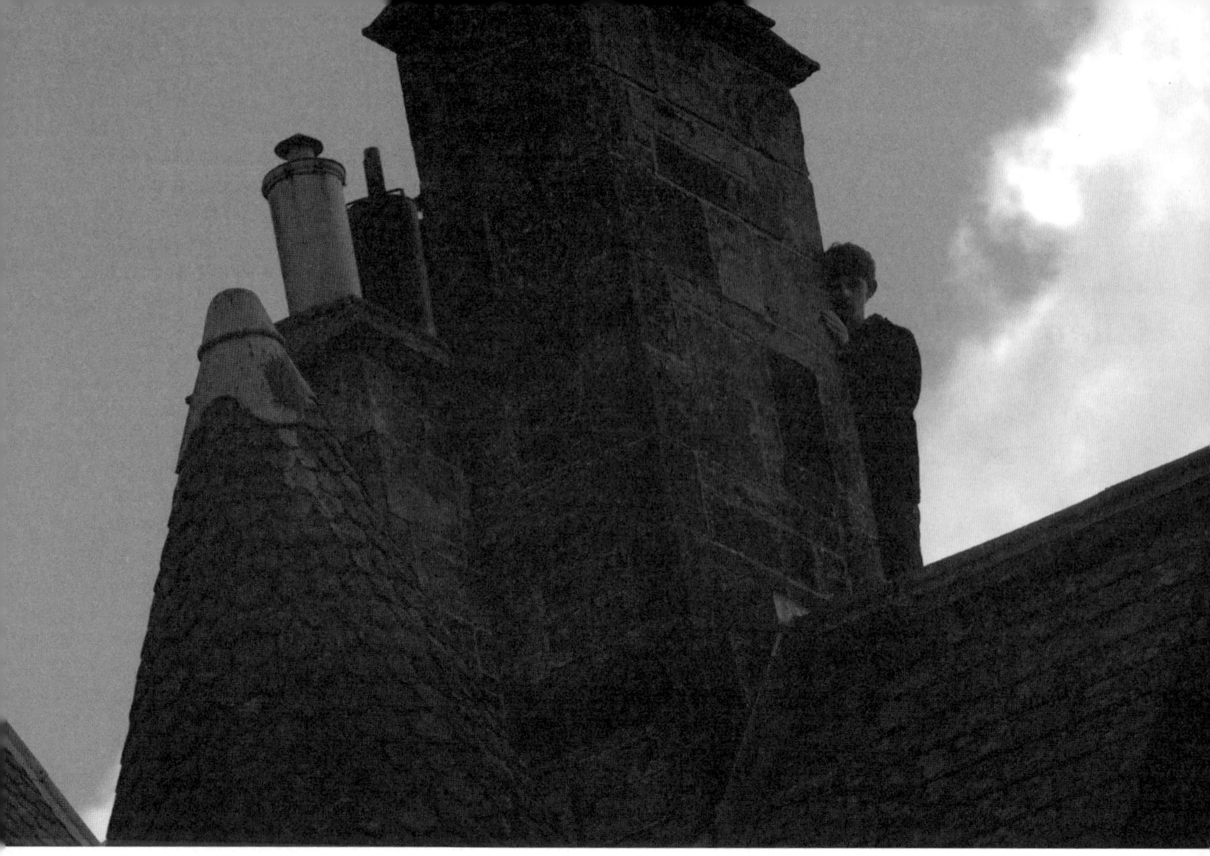

Hallam Foe (2007), British Film Institute Collection

Filming Locations:

Edinburgh, Glasgow and Innerleithen, Scotland, UK

acknowledge his mother's death and works in a hotel; (2) repeatedly traverses city rooftops and is obsessed with a blonde woman who is the uncanny double of his deceased beloved; and (3) is an obsessive voyeur who treats the countless lit windows of a major urban settlement as if they were the screens of a giant open-air multiplex cinema. To complete matters, *Hallam Foe* even comes with its own bona fide MacGuffin, the seemingly suspicious, but actually innocuous, hole that Hallam finds early on in the boat within which his mother drowned.

Ultimately, however, *Hallam Foe* is not so much an exercise in postmodern period pastiche as it is an emotionally sympathetic study of the psychological trauma that attends the uncertain transition between male adolescence and adulthood. While Hallam's personal circumstances and behaviour are unusually lurid in nature, the rite of passage that he undergoes during the months immediately before and after his eighteenth birthday will be familiar to many viewers who have led far more physically and psychologically sheltered lives than he has. Consider, for instance, the cumulative effect of the series of avian metaphors – Hallam spends much of his time living and moving far above ground, while Verity tells him near the movie's opening that 'it's time to fly the nest' – found throughout *Hallam Foe*'s narrative. Ultimately, these downplay the film's elements of proto-Hitchcockian tension (Hallam as the dangerous cuckoo in the nest of unsuspecting girlfriend Kate's personal and professional lives) and prioritize instead the idea of an emotionally gentler and more generous character portrait of adulthood successfully attained (Hallam as the bereaved little sparrow who eventually learns how to fly and fend for himself). A crucial difference between the two nest-like environments that Hallam is seen inhabiting (his childhood tree house, the hotel clock tower) also appears to support this reading of the movie. On one hand, the tree house is a space within which Hallam attempts to make time stand still (creating a shrine to his dead parent, regressing to prepubescent rituals and pastimes). But on the other, the clock tower is an edifice dedicated to the public acknowledgement of time's ceaseless passing. The people and events that Hallam witnesses from that vantage point help to propel him beyond the clutches of childhood grief.

Hallam Foe's examination of the vulnerability and pain that frequently characterize pre-adult life places the movie foursquare within a major tradition of Scottish film-making. From the days of pioneering works such as Bill Douglas's *Trilogy* (1972–78) and Bill Forsyth's *That Sinking Feeling* (1980), Scottish film-makers have repeatedly been drawn to themes of childhood and adolescent experience. At the same time, however, Hallam's privileged socio-economic background (his family owns a rambling country estate) distinguishes him from the working-class urban protagonists found within most Scottish childhood films. This fact is perhaps reflected in, and undoubtedly underscored by, the fact that much of *Hallam Foe*'s narrative unfolds within the aesthetically breathtaking and financially opulent environs of Edinburgh's historic city centre. Indeed, a significantly under-acknowledged trend within twenty-first-century Scottish cinema involves the increasing prominence of the country's capital city as a key physical and cultural setting for many Scottish film-makers' work. In a range of different ways, movies such as Annie Griffin's *Festival* (2005), Richard Jobson's *A Woman In Winter* (2005) and *New Town Killers* (2008), and Sylvain Chomet's *The Illusionist* (2010) introduce audiences to a local cultural milieu that is clearly distinct from the west coast urban industrial and rural Highland settings which dominated Scotland's cinematic representation throughout the twentieth century. For that reason, we could say that *Hallam Foe* reflects one important aspect of contemporary Scottish film culture's ongoing maturation, as well as telling a story within which a young Scotsman learns how to grow up.

Jonathan Murray

Morvern Callar

Countries of Origin:
UK
Canada
Language:
English
Studio/Production Companies:
BBC Films
Alliance Atlantis
Scottish Screen
Glasgow Film Fund
Company Pictures
BBC Scotland
H20 Motion Pictures
Director:
Lynne Ramsay
Producers:
Leonard Crooks
Andras Hamori
Barbara McKissack
Seaton McLean
David M Thompson
Screenwriters:
Lynne Ramsay
Liana Dognini
Alan Warner
Cinematographer:
Alwin H Huchler
Art Directors:
Philip Barber
James David Goldmark
Editor:
Lucia Zucchetti
Duration:
97 minutes
Genre:
Social/Psychological Drama
Social Art Cinema
Cast:
Samantha Morton
Kathleen McDermott
Paul Popplewell
Ruby Milton
Dolly Wells
Dan Cadan

Synopsis

Morvern Callar is a young English woman living in Oban in the Scottish Highlands and working in a supermarket. When her boyfriend commits suicide at Christmas time, she assumes authorship of his completed novel, which he intended to be sent to a publisher after his death. After a few days, Morvern decides to dispose of his body, cutting it up and burying the parts in the Highland countryside. She then uses the money for his funeral to go on a Spanish holiday with her friend Lanna. There, Morvern moves from the hedonism of the clubs and beaches to an attempt to find peace in the Spanish countryside, leaving Lanna alone in the process. The publishers she contacted arrive and offer her £100,000 as an advance on her dead boyfriend's manuscript. Morvern accepts the offer, and returns to Oban to pack up the rest of her life, before reappearing in a nondescript club, with no clear indication of her next step.

Critique

While director Lynne Ramsay emerged as part of the New Scottish Cinema movement of the 1990s, and won acclaim for her grim fable *Ratcatcher* (1999), her second feature Morvern Callar resists definition as a Scottish film. Although adapted from a bestselling Scottish novel by Alan Warner, and funded in part by the Glasgow Screen Fund, the BBC, Scottish Screen and Canada's Alliance Atlas, *Morvern Callar* functions more as a European art film with a poetic, impressionistic sensibility than an example of Scottish national cinema.

Morvern Callar explores the inscrutability of its lead character as she deals with a shocking event through a series of physical escapes. The film also intersperses moments of grisly off-screen violence with hypnotic dance and travelling sequences, which are set to an eclectic mixtape that includes music by Aphex Twin and The Velvet Underground. Such scenes situate *Morvern Callar* within the broader context of post-devolution Scotland, as well as of European and global migration.

Morvern and Lanna enjoy the mobility created by Morvern's newfound wealth while on holiday in Spain, but become increasingly disillusioned. As Lanna points out when Morvern circles back to the West Highlands, 'it's the same crap everywhere so stop dreaming'. Morvern's journey is consequently framed less by the strong sense of place and history that informed Ramsay's *Ratcatcher*, itself dealing with grief and loss, than by a consistent alienation across international borders.

Perhaps *Morvern Callar*'s greatest achievement, however, comes through Ramsay and actress Samantha Morton's presentation of Morvern as a character without either clear identification or motivation for her actions. Ramsay avoids a voice-over, or even scenes of direct exposition, to contextualize Morvern's actions and mindset. Instead, Ramsay focuses on Morvern's physical and verbal transformation as a sign of her fluid identity, from fragile grieving figure to a sensual and violent force of nature while in Spain.

Year:

2002

Filming Locations:

Almeria, Andalucia, Spain
Oban, Argyll and Bute, Scotland, UK

Ramsay's juxtaposition of Morvern's matter-of-fact body disposal, or her stumbling through the Spanish countryside, with flashes of ethereal pop and dance music that emerge from her headphones, further contribute to the film's dispassionate distance and raw emotional intensity. However, *Morvern Callar* is not simply an exercise in stylish detachment, with Ramsay occasionally pushing inwards as Morvern is fascinated by insects crawling in the mud of the Highlands, or when a fellow clubber in Spain opens up to Morvern over a death in his family.

With *Morvern Callar*, Ramsay secured her reputation as a film-maker who, despite launching her career off the back of the New Scottish Cinema of the 1990s, had committed to working within the broader canvas of the European art film in the 2000s.

Gareth James

My Name is Joe

Countries of Origin:

Spain
Italy
France
UK
Germany

Language:

English

Studio/Production Companies:

Channel Four Films
Parallax Pictures
Scottish Arts Council Lottery Fund
The Glasgow Film Fund

Director:

Ken Loach

Producers:

Ulrich Felsberg
Rebecca O'Brien

Screenwriter:

Paul Laverty

Cinematographer:

Barry Ackroyd

Art Director:

Fergus Clegg

Synopsis

Joe Kavanagh is an unemployed, recovering alcoholic in his late thirties; a man forced, like many of his neighbours, to live an emotionally and economically exposed existence in a dilapidated, drug-ridden public housing scheme in present-day Glasgow. Aided by his best friend, Shanks, Joe seeks to sustain his own self-worth and dignity by helping others to recover their own: he plays a volubly passionate part in local Alcoholics Anonymous meetings and coaches an amateur football team made up of former heroin addicts. Joe's life seems about to change yet further when he meets and then begins a relationship with Sarah, a local health worker involved in the state-sponsored support (but also surveillance) of Liam and Sabine, a young couple attempting to raise a child and stay off drugs. Ultimately, however, hard economic realities strangle heartfelt emotional aspirations. Joe learns that Liam and Sabine are being targeted by McGowan, a local criminal to whom the pair owes money. With no other way to avert impending physical violence – McGowan threatens either to break Liam's legs or make Sabine work as a prostitute – Joe reluctantly agrees to take a temporary job as the gangster's drugs courier. When Sarah discovers this, she immediately disowns him. Heartbroken and enraged, Joe resorts to suicidal measures, publicly assaulting McGowan and his goons and then embarking on an alcohol binge. Liam saves Joe's life by sacrificing his own, hanging himself in order to salve McGowan's wrath. The film then ends on a purposefully ambiguous note: Joe and Sarah are reunited at Liam's funeral, but the future – if any – of their romantic relationship remains unclear.

Critique

Right from its very first moments, *My Name is Joe* explores the often strained links between human solidarity and human empathy. The titular character's opening monologue, delivered to an

Composer:
George Fenton
Editor:
Jonathan Morris
Duration:
105 minutes
Genre:
Social Realism/Naturalism
Social Drama
Crime
Cast:
Peter Mullan
Louise Goodall
Gary Lewis
Year:
1998

audience of fellow addicts attending an Alcoholics Anonymous meeting, describes a damascene moment in which self-recognition and self-projection are predicated upon each other. Joe explains that the potentially liberating ability to acknowledge his own alcoholism stemmed from revelatory exposure to the dignified but unsparing testimony of a fellow sufferer: 'I looked at this woman and thought, "You're me."' In this way, Ken Loach and Paul Laverty's second feature film collaboration establishes – and simultaneously seeks to justify – the precise manner in which it represents and analyses the systemic socio-economic deprivation that scars the face of present-day urban Scottish society. On one hand, it is perfectly possible to see the narrative's pronouncedly emotional and melodramatic qualities as a distraction from, or dilution of, *My Name is Joe*'s ideological concerns. But on the other, the film argues right from its opening scene that one cannot truly stand with other people unless one first sees oneself in them, too; Loach and Laverty frame emotional involvement as the necessary precondition for any meaningful political equivalent.

My Name is Joe (1998), British Film Institute Collection

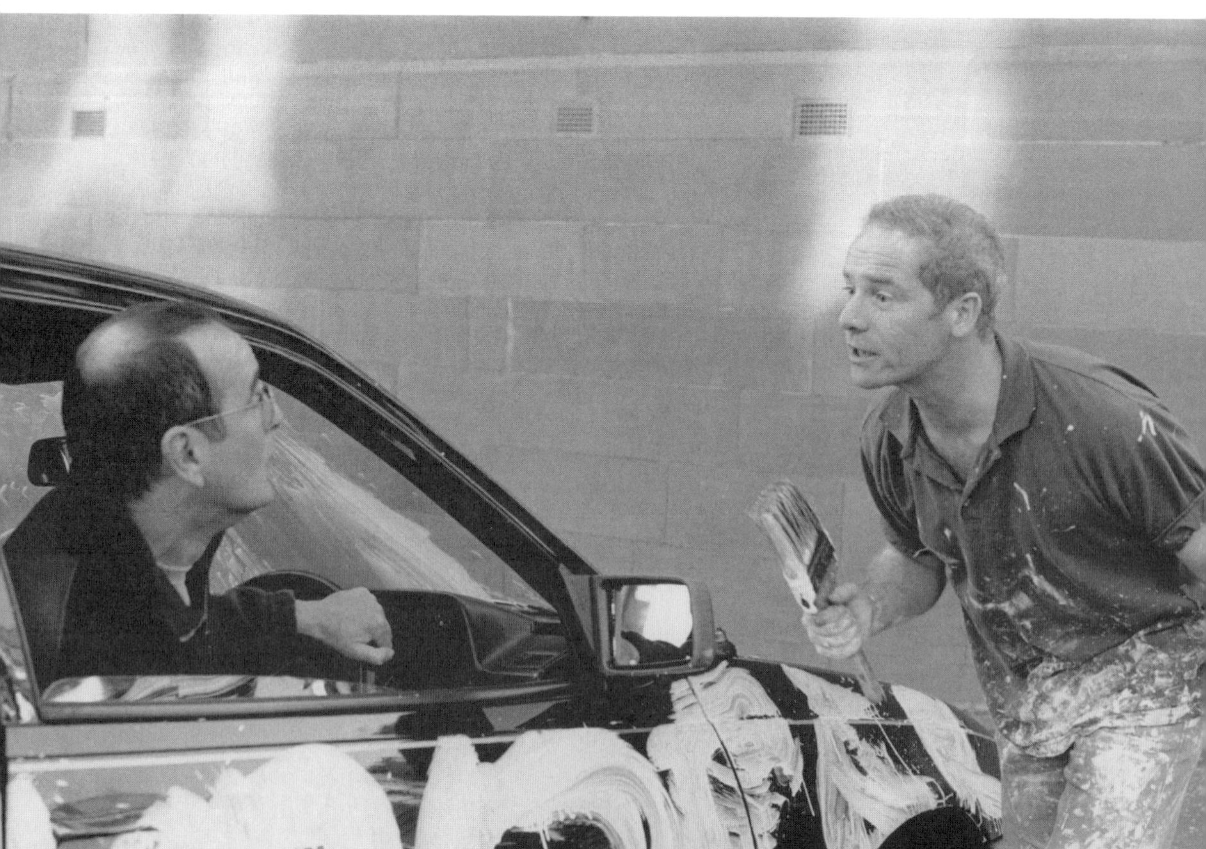

Filming Locations:
Glasgow and Inveraray, Scotland, UK

Because of this fact, *My Name is Joe* also travels a long way towards equating solidarity with class-based support of effectively anarchist values. As in several other post-1990 Loach movies (1994's *Ladybird, Ladybird*, for example), individual middle-class representatives of the welfare state harm the dispossessed human objects of their attentions at least as much as they help them. It is no accident that health visitor Sarah is first seen with the back of her car overflowing with rolls of wallpaper. While this is on one level a clever comic/romantic plot device – Joe and Sarah's romance begins after he offers to decorate her flat – it also works to make a much more disquieting ideological point. As the narrative progresses, viewers see how Sarah's well-intentioned social democratic values and actions merely paper over the gaping social cracks opened up by rampant economic inequality, and thus perpetuate rampant social dysfunction rather than challenging it. Her relatively privileged class and economic statuses prevent her from truly understanding, and thus entering into, the world of those that she seeks to help on a daily basis. Most obviously of all, Sarah cannot (or will not) understand Joe's anguished decision to temporarily courier drugs in order to save Liam and Sabine: her personal good fortune in life renders her incapable of comprehending the fact that, in Joe's words, 'some people don't have a choice'. For Sarah, moral choices and money exist as separate concerns; but as Joe and others who languish at the bottom of the social heap know only too well, the compromised nature of the former are often dictated by a crippling lack of the latter.

Little wonder, then, that self-help is the only real kind of social and spiritual sustenance on offer within *My Name is Joe*'s ultimately bleak worldview. Unlike the local medical centre and employment office, Alcoholics Anonymous and the recovering addicts' football team function as non-hierarchical entities within which the disenfranchized and demonized help each other without judgement being passed upon them from above. If the replica West German football strips in which Joe's junkies take to the field of play are in one sense a laughing matter (the team are anything but world-beaters), they also work to make a deadly serious point: Loach and Laverty present modern Scotland as a starkly divided society, all the more so because the walls that divide communities and entire social classes from each other are not always immediately visible to the naked eye. In its highly sophisticated attempt to marry expert emotional manipulation with a project of highly engaged political agitation, *My Name is Joe* created one of the biggest international critical and commercial successes to emerge from 1990s Scotland. More importantly yet, the film also established a dramaturgical and ideological template that structured all of its creators' subsequent Scottish-set movies.

Jonathan Murray

Neds

Countries of Origin:
UK
France
Italy

Language:
English

Studio/Production Companies:
Blue Light
Fidélité Films
StudioUrania

Director:
Peter Mullan

Producers:
Olivier Delbosc
Alain de la Mata
Marc Missonnier

Synopsis

Neds tells a tale of good boy gone bad. John McGill is an intellectually gifted, working-class, Roman Catholic schoolboy in early-1970s Glasgow. But he finds that the road to academic success and social mobility is anything but easy, not least due to a lack of positive male role models in his life. John's father is an emotionally abusive alcoholic and his older brother, Benny, is an especially feared member of one of Glasgow's many feral, and therefore feared, teenage gangs. To add insult to injury, John's class background sees him rejected by the family of a middle-class boy with whom he strikes up a much-needed masculine bond. Fatally wounded by this rejection, John falls in with a local gang and swiftly becomes one of the notorious Neds (non-educated delinquents) of the film's title. His status within local gang culture is cemented by the discovery of a previously untapped taste for physical violence. Ultimately, however, John's inability to contain or control his psychotic tendencies sees him isolated from all those around him. He nearly kills a fellow teenager, Canta, and then single-handedly takes on a rival gang in what looks very much like an unsuccessful suicide attempt. The film ends on a note of ambiguous biblical

Neds (2010), British Film Institute Collection

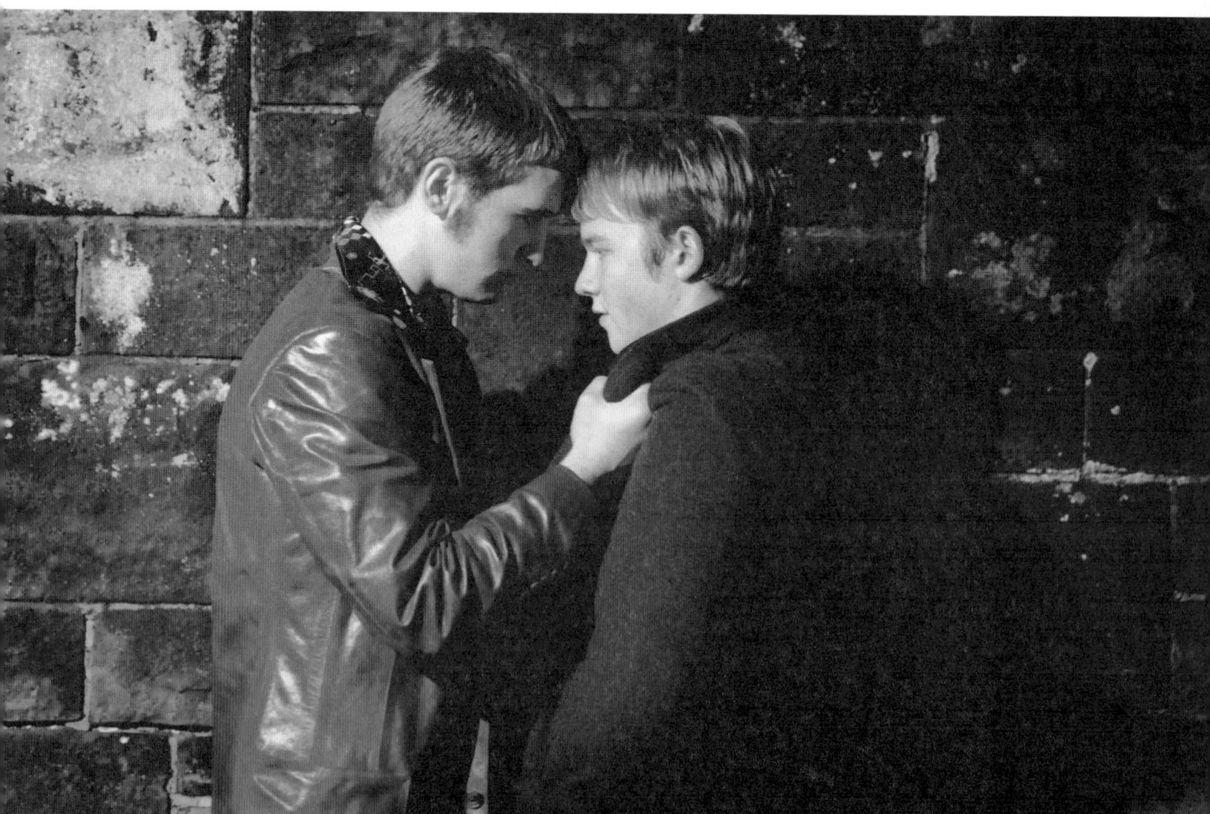

Screenwriter:
Peter Mullan
Cinematographer:
Roman Osin
Art Director:
Caroline Grebbell
Composer:
Craig Armstrong
Editor:
Colin Monie
Duration:
124 minutes
Genre:
Social/Psychological Drama
Social Art Cinema
Crime
Coming of Age
Cast:
Conor McCarron
Greg Forrest
Joe Szula
Year:
2011
Filming Location:
Glasgow, Strathclyde, Scotland, UK

symbolism: when a school van transporting John, Canta and other delinquent school pupils through a local safari park breaks down, the two boys abscond, wandering away from camera through a field of grazing lions.

Critique

Neds highlights writer/director Peter Mullan's prominent, but also complex, place within contemporary Scottish and British cinemas. On one hand, this artist's prolific acting and directorial careers in the decade-and-a-half since his starring role in Ken Loach's *My Name is Joe* (1998) might seem to align him closely with local traditions of social realist film-making. Many of the feature projects to which Mullan contributed during this period are marked by many of the characteristics that critics typically discern within the work of indigenous social realist film-makers: contemporary (often working-class urban) setting and stories; sociopolitical topicality (and often, controversy); and a left-wing ideological analysis of the allegedly iniquitous structure and functioning of contemporary Scottish and British societies. But at the same time, however, Mullan has consistently articulated strong reservations about what he sees as the aesthetic and ideological lack of imagination that much British social realist cinema displays. In one promotional interview supporting *Neds*, for instance, he complained that: 'I get bored with naturalism and social realism [...] I get restless with it. If one has an imagination, one should use it – in my book'. True to this logic, *Neds* is nothing if not an exuberantly imaginative take on the early-1970s working-class Glaswegian milieu within which the director grew up. To take but one illustrative example, the series of vicious knife fights in which central character John becomes embroiled reaches a surreal climax when Jesus Christ descends from the Cross erected outside the boy's local Roman Catholic church in order to claim a piece of the violent action. In sequences such as this, Mullan clearly flags his interest in exploring psychologically aberrant ideas and experiences alongside socially and historically accurate counterparts.

Yet *Neds* frequently feels closer in tone and approach to the classic Scottish/British social realist film-making practices than Mullan is perhaps willing to acknowledge. For one thing, the film is as unremittingly deterministic as any of Ken Loach's Scottish projects in its insistence that ordinary working-class individuals are rarely able to escape or transcend the deprived (and thus, dehumanizing) social circumstances into which they are born. After clearly establishing John's unusually pronounced academic ambition and ability, the plotline of *Neds* then employs a series of increasingly melodramatic coincidences and reversals in order to ensure that its central character never has the chance to fulfil his dreams of social mobility and personal fulfilment. In this regard, many viewers might find themselves sympathizing with the confusion of John's Latin teacher at school, who at one stage protests that, 'I find it hard to believe that in the space of six weeks you have suddenly degenerated into idiocy'. Yet because the dramatic and thematic logic of *Neds* seems classically social realist in its overarching insistence upon the impermeable nature of the class boundaries that John attempts to navigate, this unlikely personal regression is just what has to occur.

More positively, it might also be said that many of the most imaginative narrative moments and details within *Neds* do indeed demonstrate the validity of a key point that Mullan wishes to make through his work as a writer and director, namely, that Scottish and British traditions of cinematic realism do not represent the only way in which local film-makers can express and explore the complex realities of their native sociocultural histories and milieus. At one point in the narrative, for instance, John whiles away the morning hours of the school summer holidays by watching a television broadcast of a 1960s French TV adaption of *Robinson Crusoe*. On one hand, the snippet of quoted footage that viewers see here represents a painstakingly accurate (to the point of seeming arcane) social realist detail. But on the other, Mullan introduces the detail in question not as a quasi-documentary end in itself, but as raw material that can then be developed into a telling (because expressively and imaginatively executed) thematic motif. Ultimately, the film's narrative suggests that John is a Crusoe figure in reverse: the overbearing presence, not absence, of other people (bickering family, sadistic teachers, out-of-control gang members) is what represents the cause of his ever-escalating unhappiness and alienation.

Neds can be located within a wider Scottish cinematic context in several different ways. On one hand, the film can be seen as a representative example of Peter Mullan's small, but internationally lauded, oeuvre as writer/director to date. A range of key thematic preoccupations and storytelling approaches visible within Mullan's first two features, *Orphans* (1999) and *The Magdalene Sisters* (2001), resurface in his third: profoundly damaged and/or self-destructive models of masculinity, the repressive nature of institutionalized Catholicism, and a systematically engineered collision between elements of the absurd and the everyday, the scabrous and the serious, all spring to mind here. More generally, it might also be productive to contextualize *Neds* with regard to what many critics have identified as two of the most prominent (and frequently overlapping) strains of film-making within Scottish cinema from the 1970s onwards. These are a series of movies that explore experiences of childhood and/or adolescence and a local tradition of auteurist works marked by a profoundly autobiographical bent. To take two illustrative examples, Gillies MacKinnon's *Small Faces* (1996) and Richard Jobson's *16 Years of Alcohol* (2003) are films that share much in common with *Neds*. All three movies are set within broadly the same time period and local cultural milieu (late-1960s/early-1970s working-class urban Scotland); all three draw heavily upon their respective makers' personal memories of living in that place and time; all three acknowledge, but also critique, the seductive and destructive aspects of local gang cultures of the era; all three present education as a possible means of escape, both socially and spiritually speaking, from the dehumanizing effects of endemic social deprivation and inequality. Viewed in this light, perhaps the most disturbing aspect of the character John's near-total isolation and alienation by the conclusion of *Neds* is the fact that many native film-makers have to date presented that state as socially widespread across modern Scottish society.

Jonathan Murray

Reference

Matheou, Demetrios (2011) 'Peter Mullan: Glasgow belongs to me', *Sight and Sound*, February, http://old.bfi.org.uk/sightandsound/feature/49688, Accessed 22 April 2014.

New Town Killers

Country of Origin:
UK
Language:
English
Studio/Production Company:
Independent
Director/Screenwriter:
Richard Jobson
Producers:
Luc Roeg
Richard Jobson
Cinematographer:
Simon Dennis
Art Director:
Andy Drummond
Production Designer:
James Lapsley
Composer:
Stephen Hilton
Editor:
Steven Sander
Duration:
100 minutes
Genre:
Thriller
Suspense

Synopsis

Sean, a poor working-class young man in his early twenties, is struggling to get by and take care of his troubled older sister, Alice, who lives with him in their cramped council estate flat. Both their parents are gone – their mother recently dead after a history of severe drug abuse and their father disappeared when Sean was an infant. When Alice informs Sean that she is £10,000 in debt to loan sharks, has been threatened if she does not pay this back immediately, and has no resources to even begin to do so, Sean is angry with her but mostly desperate to find a way to help. Sean makes a futile attempt to follow the path of his graphic artist and disc-jockey friend, Sam, who has fled to Edinburgh from London and lives as a squatter, by attempting to turn a trick as a rent boy, but Sean freaks out and runs off right as his first potential client begins to touch him. While working as a men's toilet room attendant at a luxury restaurant in an elite city centre hotel, Sean is approached by two imposing, mysterious men, Alistair and Jamie, with the leader of the two, Alistair, offering Sean £10,000 if he will play a game with them, where Sean will agree to let them hunt him over the course of twelve hours one night. If Alistair and Jamie catch him, they win, but if Sean eludes them, he wins – and wins the money. Soon thereafter we learn that Alistair has manipulated Alice into debt, in order to play the game he wants with Sean, and we also learn soon thereafter as well that Alistair has already planned to get Sean fired from his job so that Sean is all the more readily inclined to accept Alistair's offer. When Sean does accept, the chase is on. Sean quickly learns how much power Alistair maintains – as he has many people working for him, effectively undercover, prepared to report Sean's whereabouts and to help block Sean's exit from the city. Sean likewise quickly leans how deeply malevolent Alistair is, as Alistair shortly makes clear he is hunting Sean in order to kill him. As the film proceeds, we, the film's audience, learn that Alistair has played this game many times previously, and has always won. As the chase proceeds, Sean manages a number of narrow escapes, but becomes savvier as time moves on, including recognizing that the killers have planted a tracking device on his clothing. Sean

Chase
Social Drama
Social Fantasy
Noir

Cast:

Dougray Scott
Alastair Mackenzie
James Anthony Pearson
Liz White
Charles Mnene

Year:

2008

Filming Locations:

Innocent Railway Tunnel, Edinburgh
Edinburgh Eastern Cemetery, Edinburgh, Scotland, UK
Guthrie Street, Old Town, Edinburgh, Scotland, UK
Heriot Row, Edinburgh, Scotland, UK
Leith, Edinburgh, Scotland, UK
Muirhouse, Edinburgh, Scotland, UK
Regent Road, Edinburgh, Scotland, UK
St John's Hospital, Livingston, West Lothian, Scotland, UK
West Register Street, Edinburgh, Scotland, UK

faces several difficult betrayals – first of a young woman in a bus terminal who initially seems friendly and helpful but turns out to be one of Alistair's spies, later in a hospital where he is being treated for an injured leg after jumping out of an upper-story window as he finds out the doctor in charge on the night shift is Jamie's wife, and, especially disappointingly, by his friend, Sam, who is deceived about the nature of the game and thereby alerts Alistair and Jamie to Sean's whereabouts in return for cash. Doing so doesn't turn out well for Sam who is viciously beaten by Alistair and dangled out a window screaming. Sam is just one of multiple ancillary victims in Alistair's game during the course of the night – others include a young gang member who doesn't recognize who the gang is dealing with when they confront Alistair, a dog Alistair shoots dead in a tunnel passageway, and the young man at a heavy metal gig with whom Sean trades his bugged jacket. Culminating this series of violent attacks on others, in their pursuit of Sean, Alistair and Jamie show up in Sean and Alice's flat, catching Alice by surprise, where Alistair mocks Alice as thoroughly worthless, deserving to die, throws boiling water at her face and kicks her in her pregnant abdomen. By this point, Jamie, who has been growing more troubled by Alistair's behaviour, intervenes to stop Alistair from abusing Alice further, but doesn't help her beyond that. Shortly after the two leave Sean and Alice's flat, Alistair, now tired of Jamie, shoots Jamie point blank in the head, and leaves him dead in the Maserati, walking off home. After Sean finds out what Alistair has done to Alice, Sean changes course – no longer seeking to elude Alistair, but rather pursuing Alistair in order to confront him over what he has done. Eventually, working with clues available in the abandoned Maserati, Sean tracks Alistair down to his luxury residence in the New Town, and engages in a final clash with Alistair, who has anticipated Sean crashing his home, and is enjoying this as a yet further part of the game. Sean manages to break free from Alistair right at the point when he is going to be killed, smashing Alistair in the face with the lucky pebble on his necklace. Sean ultimately triumphs when he manages to send copies of the files on Alistair's computer documenting the history of Alistair's manhunts to everyone on Alistair's contact list. Afterward, leaving Alistair's New Town residence, Sean is bloodied and limping, but makes it to the train station locker where Alistair promised he would leave the money if Sean won the game. His friend Sam has already been there, and was tempted to take the money, but instead stays to give it to Sean. The two friends reunite, with Sean forgiving Sam for his earlier betrayal. As they walk off together the film closes with a sepia-tinged panoramic sweep of the Old Town of Edinburgh, which director Jobson suggests represents an antithesis in moral values versus the New Town from which the killers hail.

Critique

New Town Killers aptly demonstrates Jobson's considerable talent as a highly creative micro-budget film-maker, able to compellingly synthesize a fast-paced comic book and video game-derived chase thriller with incisive social commentary and critique. The third in Jobson's Edinburgh triptych, following *16 Years of Alcohol* (2003) and *A Woman in Winter* (2006), *New Town Killers* bears little resemblance to either of the two preceding films other than casting the city of Edinburgh as a feature presence in its own right. In the case of *New Town Killers*, Jobson takes advantage of the Scottish capital's long-standing association with the gothic macabre, as well as with duality and antithesis, along with an astute selection and use of multiple atmospheric locations across the city centre, in order to craft a twenty-first century Edinburgh film noir, that, like the best of classic noir, focuses on sharp contrasts, and on points of striking juxtaposition and violent confrontation, not only between light and dark, but also in terms of wealth and power.

Unfortunately, a number of popular newspaper and magazine reviewers failed to grasp that *New Town Killers* is social fantasy, not social realism, and therefore failed adequately to appreciate what Jobson, cast and crew have realized with *New Town Killers*. Jobson himself has cited graphic novels and video games; multiple action/adventure and chase thrillers; classic film noir and more recent neo-noir; the work of Hitchcock and Kubrick; Michael Haneke's *Funny Games* (1997); and Edinburgh's own rich history of association with a multiplicity of notable true and fictional crimes, as principal influences upon *New Town Killers*, while reviewers have often cited *The Most Dangerous Game* (Irving Pichel and Ernest B Schoedsack,1932) and *The Running Man* (Carol Reed,1987) as enacting comparable plots. But *New Town Killers* also bears a noteworthy resemblance – at least in terms of pace, tone and mood – to a film like *Run Lola Run* (Tom Tykwer, 1998). Ultimately, however, the most important source for *New Town Killers* is likely Jobson's work with the philanthropic organization, Circle, in the Muirhouse area of Edinburgh, where Jobson helped out and interacted extensively with kids whose parents were alcoholics and junkies. Jobson credits this experience with inspiring him to write the script for *New Town Killers*: Jobson argues these young people maintain ample intelligence and talent that is far too often either ignored or denigrated. Sean, as the film's hero, is one who ultimately triumphs versus an exceedingly crafty and malevolent opponent in Alistair, and clearly exemplifies these qualities that Jobson asserts, while both Alice and Sam are depicted sympathetically as well.

New Town Killers conveys a considerable number of interconnected social critiques. Most prominently, the film develops the destructive implications of 'predatory lender' to a logically literal conclusion, through the character of Alistair, Chief Executive Officer of a Financial Investment powerhouse that Alistair has mockingly named Ethical Finances. The conceit is not subtle, yet there is no reason it need be, given the damage companies like Ethical Finances have in fact done in exploiting the misplaced hopes and dreams of the working class and the poor, by manipulating them into borrowing on credit, at levels and rates that are unsustainable. Jobson critiques not only specific companies that bombard young people with messages suggesting that happiness and success is equivalent with buying and consuming, and with acquiring and accumulating, but also with a larger culture that has complacently accepted and at least tacitly endorsed the seeming veracity of these kinds of messages. In this light, it is important to grasp the distinction the film marks out quite clearly between Alistair and Jamie: Alistair is a member of the ultra-elite, a super-rich and super-powerful capitalist entrepreneur, one of those who effectively, yet largely invisibly, controls the economy, whereas Jamie is representative of the aspiring petit-bourgeoisie, one who is willing to go along with Alistair's 'game', and even to play a crucial role in its success, right up to the point where it is impossible to further deny the amoral and nihilistic ramifications of the same game. Right before shooting him, Alistair mocks Jamie: 'you're so fucking middle class'. And, throughout *New Town Killers* Jamie, as well as multiple other representatives of the same middle class, exhibit what Jobson, in his DVD feature-length commentary, argues is an all-too-common 'anestheticized' response to the exploitation and deprivation that surrounds them, and which thereby renders those on the social margins effectively invisible. The latter remain so other than when their coexistence within the same urban community is conjured as a threat to petit-bourgeois comfort and security. In the same DVD commentary Jobson indicates that *New Town Killers* turns the common middle-class phobia concerning 'barbarians at the gates' on its head by showing the true barbarians are those with wealth and privilege, and that it is they who in fact represent a dangerous source of violence directed against the socially vulnerable and dispossessed. Alistair's wealth and power enables him to thrive as a serial mass murderer – and he is the kind of figure who can readily command, and, as necessary buy, extensive cooperation from many others in doing so, while those who assist him remain blithely ignorant of, or indifferent to, what Alistair is actually doing. Class prejudice is a prominent theme across *New Town Killers*; one notable example occurs in contrasting the way the same two cops, who earlier in the film brusquely warned Sean and Sam to move along while they were just hanging out talking, later obsequiously defer to Sean when he is dressed up in a suit and tie and driving a Maserati in the New Town district (even though Sean has Jamie's dead body in the boot of the car). A final major line of critique *New Town Killers* advances is of a larger cultural affinity toward the kind of cynicism and nihilism that Alistair epitomizes; Sean's loyalty to his sister, his forgiveness of his best friend for betraying him, and his lack of interest in material acquisition and conspicuous consumption all draw a sharp contrast with Alistair, and therefore it is unfortunate that a number of popular reviewers conflated the outlook of the film, and its director, with that of Alistair, who is clearly the film's villain.

New Town Killers is effectively designed and executed to suit the nature of the kind of film Jobson has conceived. The overall colour palette is limited and dark, with use of blood red a singular departure; dim, backlit sequences predominate; most of the film is shot (on High Definition Video) using handheld cameras, often rapidly swivelling, with plenty of zooming at varying speeds; cutting is persistently fast, frequently jumping, with shots across the bulk of the film lasting only three seconds or less; and the soundtrack, both that designed by composer Stephen Hilton as well as the eight songs from local Edinburgh bands, including the opening and closing versions of the title theme and two others from Isa and the Filthy Tongues, all fit smoothly within the film, effectively augmenting mood and underscoring theme. The work of cast and crew is additionally impressive on a film shot in four weeks, largely at night, during the winter, involving a great deal of physical stunt work – leaping, climbing and fighting – of a kind that would involve much greater time and proceed through many more takes in a Hollywood film. Art design is likewise impressive, including in contrasting the huge, enormously expensive artwork from major figures displayed on the walls throughout Alistair's residence (Alistair 'treats himself' to a new piece of art after every successful manhunt) versus the guerilla-style, graffiti-covered artwork in Sam's squat. Likewise, the contributions of Nik Taylor and Iain Gardiner, bringing to bear their considerable experience with video games in designing the opening and closing title sequences, add to the credibility of the film's deliberate appeal to gamers. Props are aptly chosen and effectively integrated into the plot – from the Maserati Quattroporte Alistair and Jamie drive to the pebble from the beach in the rural seaside village where Sean was born that he wears on a leather chain around his neck and which he ultimately uses against Alistair, directly alluding to David's defeat of Goliath. The photo of a young woman and child on Alistair's desk, which he earlier pretends in conversation with Jamie is of his own wife and child who were raped and then burnt to death by young hooligans, is eventually revealed to be a fake, ripped from a magazine, with, ironically enough, an ad for life insurance on the back; Alistair's manipulation of sentiment for his own amusement well befits a man who, akin to his namesake from *Crime and Punishment*, commits murder 'because he could'. Unlike Dostoevsky's Raskolnikov, however, Alistair experiences no subsequent anguish as a result. This change suits the critical stance of *New Town Killers* in proposing that people like Alistair are indeed often enough entirely shameless. Although Jobson could not have anticipated the financial meltdown that would unfold as his film was being released, the film nevertheless offers a prescient critique of the very same forces and tendencies that resulted in this crash, the Great Recession and ongoing global economic crisis, and the emergence of draconian forms of 'austerity' cutbacks in government spending as the new political orthodoxy across the supposedly 'advanced' capitalist 'First World', following in line with what much of the supposedly 'developing' 'Third World' had been forced to undergo for decades beforehand, including throughout the 'overheated' 'boom' years of the 1990s and the early 2000s. Edinburgh, a leading centre of banking and financial investment capitalism, and Edinburgh's New Town, the principal location for the concentration of this kind of capitalist enterprise, as well as a location where many wealthy bankers and investment executives do maintain their residences, provide appropriate locations in which to situate Jobson's social fantasy.

Bob Nowlan

Reference

Jobson, Richard (2009) Feature-length DVD audio commentary, *New Town Killers* [DVD], Pinewood Studios, Iver Heath, England:High Fliers Films.

Orphans

Country of Origin:
UK
Language:
English
Studio/Production Company:
Antonine Green Bridge
Director/Screenwriter:
Peter Mullan
Producer:
Francis Higson
Executive Producer:
Paddy Higson
Cinematographer:
Grant Scott Cameron
Production Designer:
Campbell Gordon
Art Director:
Frances Connell
Composer:
Craig Armstrong
Editor:
Colin Monie
Duration:
100 minutes
Genre:
Social Drama
Social Art Cinema
Cast:
Douglas Henshall
Gary Lewis
Rosemarie Stevenson
Stephen McCole
Year:
1998
Filming Location:
Glasgow, Scotland, UK

Synopsis

Rose Flynn, mother of Thomas, Michael, Sheila and John, has just died. The four siblings have gathered at their mother's residence to say goodbye to their mother, in her coffin. Thomas proposes they each cut off a piece of hair to place in the coffin, to signify their continuing connection with their mother. Sheila, who suffers from cerebral palsy, asks to kiss her mother goodbye so her brothers lift her out of her wheelchair to do so. A flashback recalls a scene approximately 25 years earlier, when all four siblings are gathered on their mother's bed, during a storm, as she comforts them, urging them not to worry as the storm will pass. The scene transitions to a karaoke lounge bar. Thomas gets up on stage to sing 'The Air That I Breathe', which he dedicates to his mother. Michael becomes increasingly agitated as he notices Duncan and friends laughing while Thomas is breaking down with grief, increasingly unable to proceed with the song. Michael rushes Duncan, a fight ensues, and after Duncan and a number of others are thrown out of the bar, we learn that Duncan stabbed Michael in the abdomen. John helps Michael out as they seek to go to an infirmary, but are refused passage in a cab by a driver who says he cannot afford Michael bleeding on his seats. Michael suggests visiting a friend, a nurse who is working at a nearby massage parlour, to have her bandage him up. While waiting outside, John becomes furious as a car drives through a puddle that splashes all over him, and then by a group of adolescent boys who taunt him for taking out his fury on the older man driving the car. When John stops to pick up his soaked jacket that he had brandished at the driver, he nearly runs into a bus, and then engages in an angry exchange with the bus driver – and the bus. After Michael returns, John is further upset that Michael doesn't intend to retaliate against Duncan but instead plans to pretend his injury happened at work so that he can obtain compensation. Michael leaves the scene determined to kill Duncan. Meanwhile, Thomas and Sheila proceed from the lounge bar to the church where their mother's funeral will take place the next morning. Thomas is determined to stay all night, keeping vigil with his mother's body, but Sheila wants to go home. Venting her frustration, Sheila bumps into Thomas who falls forward and knocks over a large statue of the Virgin Mary, which shatters to pieces. Sheila then departs alone while Thomas seeks to repair the statue. Sheila becomes stuck in a back alley and is befriended by an adolescent girl, Carole, who, with help from three local girls selling *The Daily Record*, pushes Sheila to Carole's house where Carole has invited the dumfounded Sheila to attend her father's surprise birthday party. Michael briefly visits his two young children, living with his ex-wife, who is out attending her regular Alcoholics Anonymous meeting. After helping his son who has wet his bed, Michael and his ex-wife, Alice, talk uncomfortably for a few minutes when she returns and before Michael leaves. John, meanwhile, has sought help from his friend Tanga, who delivers Chinese take-out, in getting a gun. John goes along with Tanga

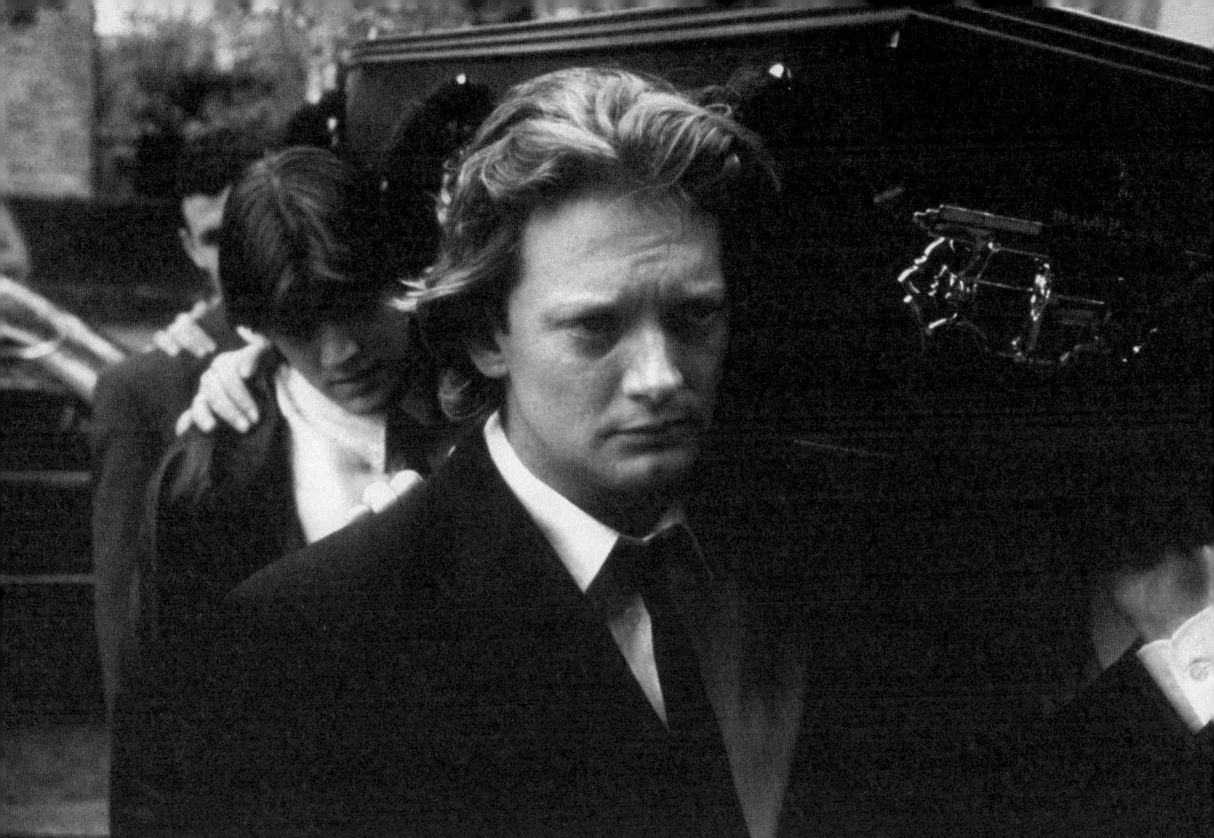

Orphans (1998), British Film Institute Collection

as he delivers to regular customers, the Bells, who Tanga resents because of their wealth and the man's dismissive attitude toward him. At a carnival Tanga obtains a gun, and gives it to John, while Tanga negotiates payment. John meets the boys who had taunted him earlier, and they continue to do so. When the boys get on the Cyber Sid Spyder ride, John reveals to them the gun he has concealed behind his jacket and pretends to threaten them with it. After that, Tanga is determined to seek his own revenge and returns to the Bells, where, atop John's shoulders, he spies on Mr Bell who is masturbating to pornography. When Tanga pokes Mr Bell in the behind with the gun, Mr Bell turns around and ejaculates in Tanga's face. Tanga, furious, enters the house and threatens to carry Mrs Bell upstairs to rape her before John intervenes. Meanwhile Michael has stopped at a pub for a pint, where he runs into a publican, Hanson, who throws customers who annoy him into a 'jail', a locked backroom storage area. Michael is thrown in and meets three others; together, they devise a plan to trick Hanson to open the door, and they then tie him up and enact their revenge. After a testy exchange with Michael in the church, Thomas continues his repair work and vigil until a gale force wind blows the roof off the church. This also causes a local power outage, the effects of which we see with Sheila, Carole's family, and their grumpy, elderly nextdoor neighbour, Mrs Finch, who seeks refuge with them even though she routinely denounces them for using 'her ramp' in front. As day breaks, Michael, riding a subway train, is approached by a young boy, curious at the puddle of blood seeping from the leg of Michael's pants, before the boy's mother hurries him away. Carole's mom, Alison, agrees to help get Sheila ready to go to the church for her mother's funeral. Michael arrives at Fleming's, where he works, and attempts to convince a group of co-workers that his injury happened there before he collapses backwards onto a wooden pallet, which races down a set of rails and floats off along the river Clyde. After obtaining assistance from a young deaf boy, John has secured ammunition for the gun, but just as he is ready to shoot Duncan, Duncan turns to reveal a baby strapped to his chest, and Michael can't do it. Immediately thereafter, Duncan's brother retaliates against Tanga, who is severely injured in his van, while John and Duncan wrestle about on a median in the middle of a busy motorway, before John gets the better of Duncan and decides not to kill him despite having the chance to do so with Duncan's own knife. At church the mass is proceeding despite the loss of the roof, with Thomas reading. Michael and John reunite in the entranceway; once they enter and move toward the front Michael collapses and is assisted in being rushed to a hospital by family members and relatives, except Thomas, who continues on with the reading. Later at the cemetery Thomas wants to carry his mother on his back as her sole pallbearer, but can't do it. Transitioning to several weeks later, Thomas is attending to his parents' grave. His three siblings meet him there, Michael just out of the hospital, and invite Thomas to join them for a curry. At first Thomas is reluctant to do so, citing the work he needs to do at the grave, but soon agrees to join them, and the siblings are reunited.

Critique

Peter Mullan's feature-length directorial debut was quickly embraced by a scholarly consensus as one of the most impressive and important films of 'the New Scottish Cinema' emerging in the mid to late 1990s. In his introduction to the published screenplay, Irvine Welsh, evincing a perspective shared by many others, writes 'I consider it one of the finest films ever to come out of Britain' (vii). Many scholars have found *Orphans* especially noteworthy because of the innovative way the film combines magic realism with social realism, and expressionism with naturalism, in a dark comedy that draws upon a considerable range of European art cinema influences. At the same time, the film is precisely rooted in Glasgow working-class community and culture, while alluding to sociological and psychological issues that maintain an international, and even a transnational, provenance. Mullan himself has suggested that his film is at least in part allegorical, with the loss of the literal mother here representing the loss of a series of figurative mothers – such as Mother Industry, Mother City, Mother Church, Mother Welfare and Mother Britain (see Martin-Jones, McCracken and Murray). And

Orphans is continuous with a recurrent significant focus of late-twentieth-century Scottish cinema on representations of children, especially children struggling in coming of age, that might well be read as indicative of a persistent anxiety about the future of the Scottish nation, and even, in Carol Craig's terms, as exemplary of long-standing, distinctly Scottish, difficulties with self-esteem. But, at the same time, as Jonathan Murray has suggested, *Orphans* departs from a previous Scottish cinematic tradition of national allegory focusing on loss by moving beyond elegy and nostalgia, and, as David Martin-Jones has suggested, Mullan's film argues 'the need for considered, cognitive reimaginings of community in contemporary Scotland at the turn of the twenty-first century' rather than resting content in appealing 'to audience emotions without addressing any "real" solutions to bleak social circumstances' (2009: 181). Rose Flynn's four children are anguished, bewildered, obsessed and confused, in the immediate aftermath of her death, yet the film ultimately emphasizes their need to work through their grief to push forward in making the best of the life they face ahead with the resources they can muster, now without their mother, yet, at least ultimately, reunited together once again, as siblings. At the end, Michael rebukes Thomas, when Thomas tells Michael, Sheila and John that he's there for them, arguing that Thomas isn't actually there for his siblings, those who are living, because he is devoting his attention and interest to a grave, in a cemetery full of dead people, where he doesn't belong. In response Thomas finally makes his peace with his mother's passing, effectively ending his long vigil, and leaving the cemetery to join his siblings. As Duncan Petrie writes, 'Mullan's resolution offers hope and redemption in the reintegration of the family by their mother's grave site, a scene shot in bright sunlight' (215).

Certainly *Orphans* respects the devastation that their mother's loss entails for Thomas, Michael, Sheila and John (it is worth noting that Mullan dedicates the film to the memory of his late mother, Patricia). Throughout the bulk of the film all four flail about awkwardly in response to the grief they feel; through the course of a single hellish night, the siblings pursue separate, yet overlapping, quests for satisfaction that turn out far differently in each case than initially imagined. As Welsh writes, 'The power of the film lies in how the script handles the universal but almost taboo issue of bereavement, with its attendant overwhelming feelings of guilt, anger, resentment and denial, all set in a working-class Scottish cultural context', effectively representing 'the (hopefully temporary) insanity that is bereavement' in a way that is 'harrowing and uplifting at the same time' while reaching 'the horrendous yet paradoxically people-affirming realization [...] that there can be no compensation' (viii) (Michael, chasing after compensation for much of the film, eventually realizes he never really wanted it, as all he actually wanted was his 'mammy', and, in a brief scene near the end of the film, Michael's co-workers at Fleming's discover the bandages he brought with him to the worksite, indicating his story has been thoroughly discredited, and he definitely won't get the compensation he earlier sought). For each sibling, in the face of the immediate trauma resulting from the death of the mother, it is disturbingly unclear who one fundamentally is, what the basis for meaningful existence is, what the source for purposeful action and behaviour is, and how to satisfyingly relate inner and outer experience, as well relations with self and with others. It is especially unclear what kind of family is left, not only as refuge and haven but also as source of strength and endurance. Strikingly, the three male siblings suffer this trauma especially acutely, in a film many critics have touted for its refreshing portrayal of Scottish urban working-class male masculinity, effectively imploding tropes commonly associated with the stereotypical Glasgow Hard Man. At the same time, the film deliberately de-glamourizes the kinds of physical and emotional violence likewise long associated with 'hard men', as this violence is here depicted, variously, as crude, ugly, pathetic, futile, inauthentic and absurd.

Orphans is replete with memorable moments, triumphant achievements in black humour, with the humour arising from bizarre and indeed surreal dimensions of the situation, the event, the expression or the exchange. Notable examples include John's over-the-top reaction to getting soaked; the ready availability of guns versus the limited availability of ammo; the apt syncing of the first line we hear from Billy Connolly on the tape in Tanga's van, 'Those are the rejects, you know', with John and Tanga in quest of violent revenge; Carole inviting Sheila to her dad's birthday party, accompanied by her mangy dog, while wearing her silly hat and playing the mouth organ, pushing Sheila, assisted by the paper girls singing along, across the playground; the funfair scene where John's 'revenge' versus the boys who had taunted him syncs up with the canned voice from their ride: 'Are You Ready to Scream?' and 'I Will Kill You'; Carole's mom commenting, 'Most kids bring home stray dogs, but you…'; Mrs Finch's possessiveness about 'her ramp'; the whole idea of a mad publican who keeps a jail for customers who bother him, the revenge his 'prisoners' concoct, and how the other prisoners react to Michael's recommendation of what to do with Hanson; Frank, from the lounge bar, exuberant over the birth of his child preaching 'Every cunt should love every cunt!' and later showing up in the middle of the storm just as cheerfully oblivious as he was many hours previously; Michael's perpetual bleeding throughout the film; the shattering of the statue of the Virgin Mary, and, of course, the roof blowing off the church; John and Duncan darting in and out of traffic and then fighting in the middle of a busy motorway, while Duncan's brother holds his baby and watches; Michael collapsing on the pallet and floating down the Clyde; and Thomas declaring, in all seriousness, 'she ain't heavy […] she's my mother' before collapsing under the weight of the casket and then being left to recover as the rest of the funeral party moves on to the grave site. Fittingly, the actors play their roles consistently straight, and their dead seriousness, even in the most farcical of circumstances, is what leaves the film's audience, as Mullan himself has indicated he deliberately intended, feeling uncertain whether to laugh or cry, and, often enough, inclined to do both.

Mullan wrote the script over the course of twelve months, concluding in December of 1996, and *Orphans* was filmed over the course of six weeks in April through May of 1997. Mullan invested a great deal of time and effort in casting, including requiring half-hour long auditions. Locations were carefully and deliberately chosen. And even though marking his debut as a director of a feature-length film, Mullan maintained considerable experience over the course of the preceding two decades acting (in theatre, film and television) and in directing a number of short films, including *Close* (1994), *Good Day for the Bad Guys* (1995) and *Fridge* (1995), with the same production company run by Paddy Higson – Antonine Green Bridge. Aside from the quality of the script, the acting and the direction, the cinematography and editing are also worthy of particular praise in a film that relies extensively on cross-cutting through most of its duration. *Orphans* won four awards at the Venice Film Festival in 1998, and prizes that same year at the Gijón International Film Festival and the British Independent Film Awards. It won the Grand Prix at the 1999 Festival du Film de Paris and won Mullan the Best Newcomer award at the 2000 Evening Standard British Film Awards. *Orphans* continues to provide rich territory for interpretation and reflection, given its skilful engagement with dualities of temperament, oscillations in emotion, and striking discrepancies as well as direct antitheses among multiple dimensions of subjectivity. In relation to the film's commentary on family dynamics and family bonds, reading 'family' both literally and figuratively, Minnie, in Hanson's bar, may well offer an apt summing up of *Orphans*' message: 'Canny choose yer family. Whit ye're born wi' is what ye get'.

Bob Nowlan

References

Craig, Carol (2011) *The Scots' Crisis of Confidence*, 2nd edn, Glendarual/Argyll, Scotland: Argyll Publishing.

Martin-Jones, David (2004) '*Orphans*: A work of Minor Cinema from Post-Devolutionary Scotland', *Journal of British Cinema and Television*, 1: 2, pp. 226–41.

_________ (2009) *Scotland: Global Cinema – Genres, Modes and Identities*, Edinburgh: EUP.

McCracken, Michael (2008) 'Lowest of the Low: Scenes of Shame and Self-Deprecation in Contemporary Scottish Cinema', MA thesis, University of North Texas.

Murray, Jonathan (2001) 'Contemporary Scottish Film', *Irish Review* 28, pp. 75–88.

Petrie, Duncan (2000), *Screening Scotland*, London: BFI.

Welsh, Irving (1999) 'Introduction', *Orphans: an original screenplay by Peter Mullan*, Suffolk, England: Castle Street Books, 1999, pp. vii-viii.

Ratcatcher

Country of Origin:

UK

Language:

English

Studio/Production Companies:

Pathé Pictures International
BBC Films
Arts Council of England
Les Productions Lazennec
Canal+
Holy Cow Films

Director:

Lynne Ramsay

Producers:

Gavin Emerson
Andrea Calderwood
Barbara McKissack
Sarah Radclyffe
Peter Gallagher
Betrand Faivre

Screenwriter:

Lynne Ramsay

Cinematographer:

Alwin H Kuchler

Art Director:

Robina Nicholson

Composer:

Rachel Portman

Editor:

Lucia Zucchetti

Duration:

94 minutes

Genre:

Social Realism/Naturalism
Social Art Cinema
Social/Psychological Drama

Cast:

Tommy Flanagan
Mandy Matthews
William Eadie

Year:

1999

Synopsis

Lynne Ramsay's *Ratcatcher* centres on the life of a boy, James Gillespie aged twelve, making sense of his world in 1970s Glasgow during a garbage dustmen's strike where garbage goes uncollected and piles up in the streets. At the beginning of the film, James pushes a boy, Ryan Quinn, into the polluted canal that runs behind the tenements where they live. Ryan drowns and no one but James is aware of his role in Ryan's death. *Ratcatcher* follows James after this event as he bounces between his family, his peers and his dreams. His family struggles under the care of James's father who is both unemployed and a drunk. His mother works to keep her children happy and clean, while his older sister sneaks away and his younger sister competes with him for affection from their parents. James's peers are a group of older adolescent boys who bully his friend Kenny, a mentally disabled boy, and take sexual advantage of a Margaret, aged 14 and middle class, who becomes a love interest and a person of comfort for James. As James moves into and out of situations familiar to many coming-of-age stories, he also dreams of a different world, represented by a suburban home under construction that James visits and breaks into at the end of the bus line. James believes the government is going to give his family this home so they can leave their impoverished situation. The movie is an examination of James's reality within the larger historical and political period as it conflicts with his belief, desire and search for a better life for him and his family.

Critique

The dustmen's strike that is the backdrop to this film was a precursor to the 'Winter of Discontent' that 'killed off the postwar liberal political consensus in England and led directly to the election of conservative Prime Minister Margaret Thatcher' (Cardullo 2002: 640). Thus, *Ratcatcher* fits Jonathan Murray's discussion, where more recent Scottish cinema has tended 'to interrogate discourses of nation and identity by giving voice to a plurality of social identities and experiences which are emphatically not reducible to, or subsumable by, the national dimension of the society they inhabit' (Murray 2001: 86). Through the images and narrative of the film, Ramsay presents this approach as a necessary means of subverting and complicating traditional nationalist narratives.

Two-thirds of the way through *Ratcatcher*, James's father is woken from a drunken slumber to save a neighbour's son from drowning in the canal behind the tenements where they live. As James returns to the apartment, he finds his father asleep in his underwear, covered in dirt. There is a knock on the door. Voices ask the boy if his parents are in. The strangers announce they are from the council and they ask to come in. James believes they are the people who will give his family a new house. He shakes his dad, 'It's the new house people!' As James's father opens his eyes the council people are looking at him. He is startled: 'Who the fuck are you?' They respond, 'We've come to inspect the condition of your property,

Filming Locations:
Govan and Glasgow, Strathclyde, Scotland, UK

and to assess your standard of living'. The man from the council holds his clipboard, and the woman's distaste is evidenced by her facial expression. Letting the government in is not a good thing; the government perceives poverty as inevitable, and this is their assessment of it.

James longs to move to a house far away on the border of everything he knows. He trusts in authority: he lets them inside as his dad lies asleep, hung-over and covered in mud. James's father attempts to stand with confidence, but struggles when confronted by the council's judgment as he looks for trousers. He tries to explain how he jumped in the canal to save a boy, but the council people pay no attention. The government enters with entitlement but little permission in order to 'assess' his life. However, while James's father literally wears the dirt of the canal from saving a life, it is only the dirt the council can see, not the act of rescue. The government's assessment is predetermined.

At the end of the film, the television news announces that the dustmen and the government have reached an agreement: the streets of Glasgow are being cleaned. As the dustmen clean the

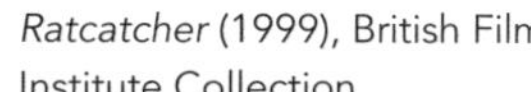

Ratcatcher (1999), British Film Institute Collection

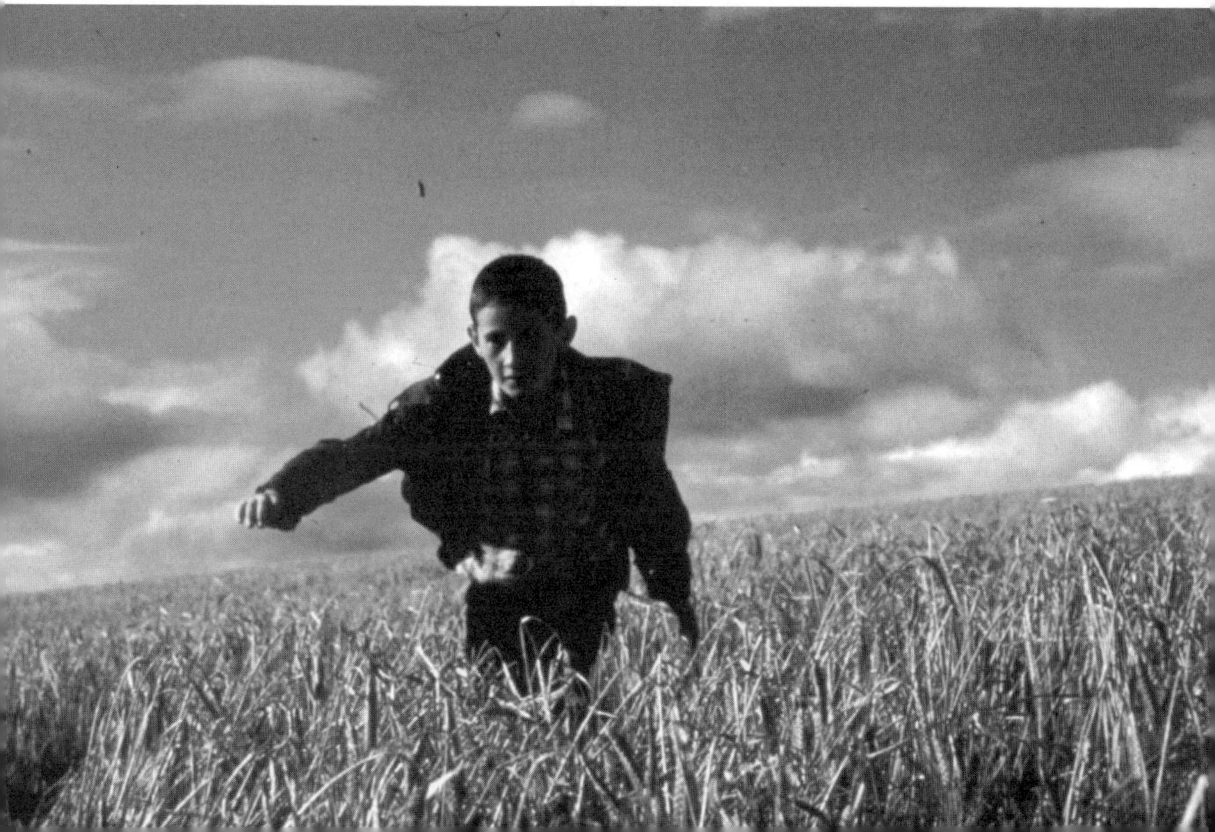

garbage they wear masks to protect them from hazardous waste while the children play free of masks. Earlier, James's mother cleans the lice from his head and he later repeats this ritual with his girlfriend. The cleaning of the city is presented in contrast to James and his girlfriend sitting in towels, deloused and bathed. Cleaning lice is an act of love and caring, done with bare hands; cleaning the garbage is an act of publicity and employment, requiring protection.

The government's cleaning is only surface level. Afterwards their absence is even more evident. As James walks through the clean streets we see what the garbage had covered: boarded windows, crumbling bricks and plaster, and a live rats' nest in a hidden nook. Discussing the historical setting of the film, Lynne Ramsay said, 'Well, I grew up then. I think it's an interesting time because the family unit began to split up. In *Ratcatcher*, people still stuck together' (Andrew 2002). In the interview, Ramsay alludes to the changes in national politics happening at this time in relation to the place of the state in people's lives. However, she also suggests a much more significant political act that takes place within the community that she grew up in: the act of looking out for collective well being, of caring for each other. At the end of the film, James draws his sister close. He gets up and tries to fix his mother's torn stockings as she sleeps. He does not escape poverty, but pulls those who care for him and for whom he cares close.

At the end of the film, James commits suicide by jumping into the canal. In this sense, *Ratcatcher* can be described as 'less a coming-of-age than a coming-to-ruin story' (Cardullo 2002: 643). However, '[Ramsay] wants, through the creation of sometimes strangely insinuating images that go beyond realism, to give *Ratcatcher* a kind of cumulative poetic impact which somehow compensates for its threadbare and dispiriting story' (Cardullo 2002: 643). If James's drowning is read as 'beyond realism', it is nevertheless reflective of the conditions of his growing up, as he literally and purposefully submerses himself in the poverty, pollution and danger of the place in which he lives. *Ratcatcher* suggests that the lives viewed by the state and national politics as impoverished, are in a much more complicated condition than merely devoid of wealth, labour or education. *Ratcatcher* thus presents an ambiguous portrait of poverty and national identity in 1970s Scotland, where a child's memory highlights a situatedness in the materiality of a particular place and time that acts as a model for anti-colonial action. Rather than make a political statement about national systems that do or do not have answers to social ills, Ramsay focuses on how individuals, in a society focused so intently on saving itself and of running from the deaths of people both apart and a part of its actions, might save each other by growing out of themselves and into the realities of the places they inhabit.

Aaron RM Hokanson

References

Andrew, Geoff (2002) 'Lynne Ramsay' [Interview], *The Guardian*, 28 October, http://www.guardian.co.uk/film/2002/oct/28/features. Accessed 18 April, 2011.

Cardullo, Bert (2002) 'Women and Children First', *The Hudson Review*, 54: 4, pp. 635–44.

Murray, Jonathan (2001) 'Contemporary Scottish Film', *Irish Review*, 28, pp. 75–88.

Red Road

Countries of Origin:
UK
Denmark

Language:
English

Studio/Production Companies:
Sigma Films
Zentropa Entertainments

Director:
Andrea Arnold

Producer:
Carrie Comerford

Screenwriter:
Andrea Arnold

Cinematographer:
Robbie Ryan

Editor:
Nicolas Chaudeurge

Duration:
113 minutes

Genre:
Social/Psychological Drama
Mystery
Suspense
Noir
Social Realism/Naturalism
Social Art Cinema

Cast:
Kate Dickie
Tony Curran
Martin Compston
Natalie Press
Paul Higgins

Synopsis

Jackie is a closed-circuit television operator who watches over the streets of Glasgow. During one of her shifts, she eyes a potentially dangerous situation unfolding on one of her many monitors: a man pursuing a woman behind a building and into a derelict waste ground. It quickly transpires that the two in fact know each other and as they hastily have sex, Jackie continues to watch, clearly enthralled by the situation. As her breathing sharpens and she clutches the joystick that operates her cameras, she exudes voyeuristic desire. However, as the man turns his face towards her camera, Jackie's desire turns to shock; she clearly recognizes him. How Jackie knows the man, who later becomes known to the audience as Clyde, is withheld from the viewer, and Clyde himself, until the climax of the film. Her relentless pursuit of Clyde drives the narrative and leads Jackie on a dangerous, emotional and sexual quest into Glasgow's notorious Red Road housing estate.

Critique

Andrea Arnold's bold debut feature film secured many accolades upon its release and confirmed the writer/director's place amongst Britain's great film-makers. The film's blending of realism and expressionism within the narrative trajectory of the thriller genre creates a tense, gritty world that Arnold uses to explore the emotional and sexual desires of lead character Jackie, who has withdrawn from the world following the death of her husband and child some years previously.

The film takes its title from Glasgow's notorious Red Road housing estate where much of the film was shot and set. As Jackie's obsession with Clyde grows, she leaves the confines of her control booth and begins tracking him on foot into the Red Road flats, where Clyde lives. The estate, comprised of eight tower blocks, the tallest of which is 31 stories, offers a visually imposing landscape for Jackie to traverse. The littered streets and graffiti-strewn buildings radiate almost a dystopian quality. Yet although the viewer is prompted to feel a sense of unease – the eerie soundtrack and withholding narrative adding to the tension suggested by this setting and situation – Jackie assimilates into the landscape relatively effortlessly. Her reserved nature and troubled

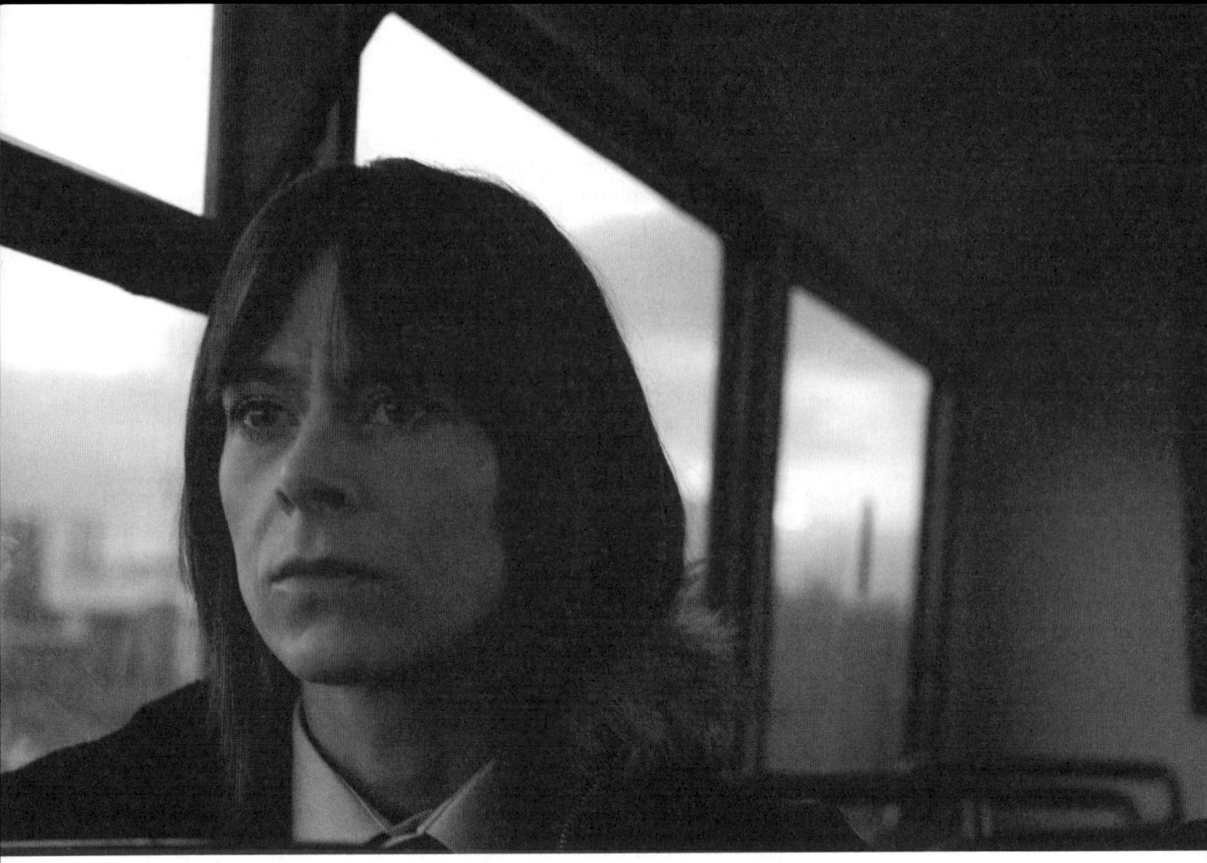

Red Road (2006), British Film Institute Collection

Andy Armour
Carolyn Calder
John Comerford
Jessica Angus

Year:

2006

Filming Location:

Glasgow, Strathclyde, Scotland, UK

past are not out of place amongst those living on the fringe of society.

The film's title also relates to the journey towards emotional recovery and sexual fulfilment on which the lead character is spurred. The exact nature of the relationship between Jackie and Clyde is withheld from the audience until the climax of the film. For much of the narrative, she appears both attracted to, and repulsed by the man. This is foregrounded during their first direct encounter, which does not come until 45 minutes into the film. After overhearing Clyde and a flirtatious waitress discuss a party he is throwing that Saturday night, Jackie decides to attend. In his living room, flooded with red lighting (a colour that is used throughout the film), Jackie sights Clyde; the difference on this occasion is that for the first time he returns her gaze. While his reaction conveys mild curiosity mixed with potential desire, in keeping with Kate Dickie's minimalist performance up until this point, Jackie's emotions remain guarded. As Clyde pulls her towards him, they embrace, and at first it seems tender and suggestively erotic; however after several moments she pulls away, fleeing the flat. Once in the elevator their encounter causes Jackie to physically retch.

The film defies any straightforward configuring of gender roles. While the victim of the thriller genre is traditionally female and the predator male (consider, for instance, the films of Alfred Hitchcock) Arnold plays with this convention without offering a straightforward reversal. Much of the danger surrounding Clyde arises from his unknown past; the audience is made aware that he was in prison, but the nature of his offence is withheld. Yet it is Jackie that stalks him, and without fear. The film's renegotiation of gender roles is perhaps most apparent in the film's daring sex scene, which although sexually explicit, is emotionally obscured. After achieving orgasm as a result of cunnilingus – Jackie is shown at prior points in the narrative in an unfulfilling sexual relationship with a married man – they engage in vigorous sex that is significantly devoid of mouth-to-mouth contact. Immediately afterwards, Jackie gathers her clothes and rushes from the room, leaving a dismayed Clyde to ask, 'Was it just a fuck you wanted then?' In the bathroom she fabricates evidence of rape and upon exiting the building gives a deliberate look to a closed-circuit television camera overhead. While Jackie's sexual release is made clear to the audience, it later transpires that her actions are also linked to a wider plan to exact revenge on Clyde who killed her husband and daughter whilst driving under the influence of drugs; Clyde was sentenced to ten years behind bars, but was released early for good behaviour. The film remains ambiguous as to the extent to which Jackie's desire for sexual fulfilment is linked to her need to return her family's killer to prison. It is only after Jackie observes, on camera, Clyde's estranged daughter visiting his empty flat that she drops the rape allegations. During a showdown between Jackie and Clyde, she finally reveals her identity to him (it transpires he had been unable to look at her in court). With this comes some element of closure and Jackie is finally able to part with the ashes of her husband and child. The final shots show Jackie walking down a street she frequently watches over on her monitors, accompanied by 'Love Will Tear Us Apart' performed by Honeyroot. Arnold's complex portrayal of female sexuality and retribution marks the film as distinct, in both a Scottish context and that of cinema more generally.

The production circumstances surrounding *Red Road* were also unusual. The film was the first to be released under the Advance Party Initiative, a project spearheaded by Glasgow-based Sigma Films and Denmark's Zentropa. The scheme, conceived by the provocative director Lars von Trier, was intended to produce three low-budget feature films centring on the challenge of putting the same group of characters, played by the same actors, into three films each by a different director. To date only two films have been completed: Arnold's *Red Road* and Morag McKinnon's *Donkeys* (2010). The third film, Mikkel Norgaard's *The Old Firm*, has yet to materialize.

Linda Hutcheson

Shell

Country of Origin:
UK
Language:
English
Studio/Production Company:
Brocken Spectre
Director:
Scott Graham
Producers:
Margaret Matheson
David Smith
Screenwriter:
Scott Graham
Cinematographer:
Yolisa Gärtig
Production Designer:
James Lapsley
Art Director:
Laurel Wear
Sound Designer:
Douglas MacDougall
Editor:
Rachel Tunnard
Duration:
91 minutes
Genre:
Social Realism/Naturalism
Social Art Cinema
Social/Psychological Drama
Cast:
Chloe Pirrie
Joseph Mawle
Year:
2012
Filming Location:
Dundonnell, Western Highlands, Scotland, UK

Synopsis

Shell, who is somewhere between 16 and 17 years old, lives with and helps out her father, Pete, run a petrol station and garage in a remote rural area in the North-west Highlands. Pete, originally from Yorkshire, moved to this area and built this station and garage for Shell's mother, who left Pete, and Shell, when Shell was only 4 years old. Although briefly educated in a nearby village, Pete has primarily home-schooled Shell, and the two have lived and worked together, in relative isolation, for many years. Pete suffers from periodic seizures, suggestive of epilepsy, with which Shell is highly familiar by now; Shell takes care of Pete when these come on, as she does in multiple other ways as well. Shell attends to the petrol pumps and the store in front, while Pete attends to the garage in back; they typically don't see much of each other during the day, after breakfast, while their conversation, even when together, is sparse, as by this point in their relationship they are able to communicate with little need for reliance upon many words. Only two regular visitors stop by the station, and both turn, each awkwardly, to Shell, for comfort and support: Hugh, a divorced middle-aged man, estranged from his two boys, and Adam, a boy approximately Shell's age, from the nearby village, who works for a lumber company. Yet several others who end up visiting the station also play a key role in the film. A couple, Claire and Robert, from Edinburgh, vacationing in the Highlands, hit a deer and wreck their car late one night. When Pete finishes off the deer to end its misery and then later skins and cuts it up, saving the meat as food to cook at home and to sell in the petrol station store, Shell is upset because she has formed a strong sense of spiritual kinship with the local deer. Claire shows kindness to Shell, giving her a copy of Carson McCullers's *The Heart Is a Lonely Hunter* as a present when she and Robert leave. Later, a young mother and her daughter stop by the station but inadvertently leave the girl's doll behind. Shell chases after the car, down the long highway running past the station, until she is able to give the doll back to the girl. Shell then takes some time to rest and look about along the road before returning to the station. Shell has also, around this same point in time, gone off with Adam to have clumsy sex, clearly not fulfilling to her, in his car, as well as brought back Adam to her house to meet Pete. And she has been pressing Pete to allow her to sleep with him, as well as started to show him affection in ways that verge upon those of a lover and not just a daughter. Pete is afraid to lose Shell, due both to his great dependence on her as well as his extreme loneliness, yet he recognizes he won't be able to keep her with him for much longer, and is frightened when he himself confuses her with his wife, who Shell now clearly resembles. Pete throws himself in front of a truck to commit suicide. Although initially devastated, Shell is ultimately ready to move on and move away, rejecting the strongly implicit offer by Adam that he move in and take Pete's place, instead accepting a lift from a truck driver who has just stopped at the station, leaving everything behind from her previous life and beginning a new journey as the film ends and the credits roll.

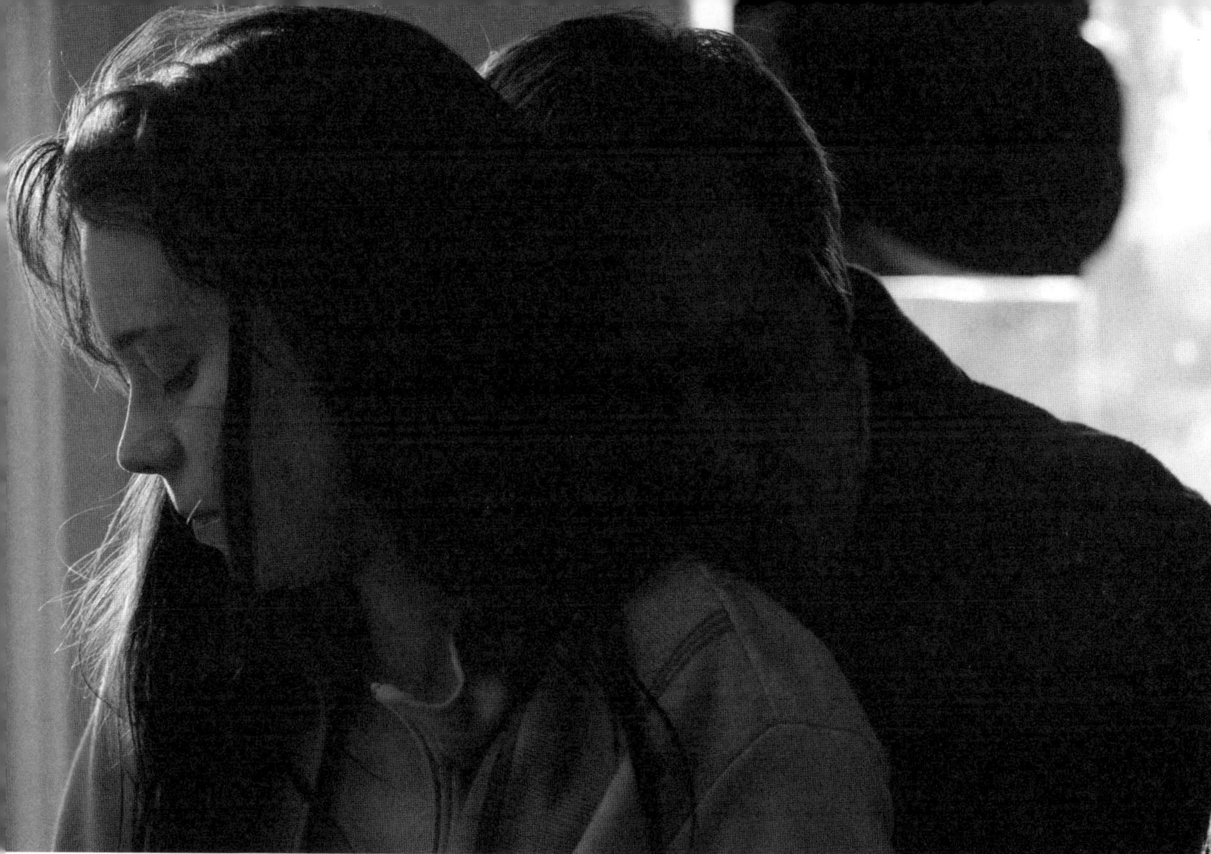

Shell (2012), British Film Institute Collection

Critique

Scott Graham's debut feature-length film is an impressive, powerful instance of poetic realism that befits a film-maker who cites the work of Bill Douglas, Lukas Moodyson, Bon Iver and, especially, Andrei Tarkovsky as chief influences. The idea for the film came to Graham while driving from Fraserburgh in Aberdeenshire, where he grew up, to Glasgow, where he currently lives. In doing so Graham passed many rundown garages and roadside petrol stations that prompted him to imagine what it might be like to live, work and, especially, grow up at such a place. As a result, with *Shell* Graham creates what he describes as a 'roadside movie' instead of the more familiar 'road' movie, focusing on the lives of characters who we usually pass by in road movies, the people who don't travel but rather who stay in place. In making this feature-length film Graham has substantially reworked and considerably expanded an earlier short of the same title, from five years earlier, changing the dynamic between the principal characters, as well as the predominant point of view, and working with an entirely new cast. As Graham has indicated, the idea that this might prove a feature film emerged when the previous short of the same title was being edited, with Graham then recognizing possible narrative and dramatic trajectories he had not previously envisioned. Now, with the feature film, Graham centres attention upon the eponymous character's own vantage point versus what she experiences. Shell is at a crossroads, as she is developing needs that cannot be fulfilled by continuing her life where it is at. At the same time, she is giving more to those around her than she is receiving from them. As Graham has attested, in multiple interviews, when the truck driver asks her, in the final scene, if she minds the music on the radio, this is a crucial development, even if it seems inconsequential, because the people in Shell's life have rarely asked her about what she would like.

Graham depicts Shell, Pete and the other characters we meet as complex, as multiply ambiguous, and as experiencing contradictory motivations of which they are not fully conscious. Shell is reasonably comfortable with her familiar life even as she is increasingly inclined to want to escape it, while she is tied to Pete as one to whom she experiences a strong sense of loyalty and responsibility on the one hand as well as an undeniable degree of attraction and desire on the other hand. (Graham does not shrink from representing the incestuous tendencies within their relationship honestly, while also depicting these sympathetically.) Shell's life, although seemingly overwhelmingly empty, is one that is, for her, nonetheless rich in sensation. Director of photography Yolisa Gärtig and sound designer Douglas MacDougall work with Graham to bring the sights and sounds of the location to the forefront of the audience's attention, so that we see and hear these quite emphatically, along with Shell. The film crew built a petrol shop, house and garage at a scenic lookout to take advantage of the opportunities that location provided for the many wide angle, fixed position, protracted duration, long and extreme long shots of the surrounding Highlands setting – in doing so successfully emphasizing a pronounced sense of both the bleak and the beautiful, and of the vastly expansive as well as the claustrophobically confining. The soundscape of the film persistently highlights the omnipresent fierce wind, and the frequent driving rain, as well as the sounds of the wind and the rain rattling the exterior surfaces of the station, house and garage. In few fictional feature films are these kinds of sounds so acutely foregrounded. As many reviewers have aptly suggested, the landscape becomes a third principal character in *Shell*.

Graham wrote the script for *Shell* in Amsterdam at the Binger Filmlab over the course of six months, where, he attests, the intensity of his near exclusive concentration on this task, in a foreign city, often leaving him feeling isolated and lonely, accentuating his sensitivity to these key themes – along with entrapment, claustrophobia, yearning, desire, survival, care of others versus care of the self, and needs of subsistence and well-being that exceed those of survival alone – that he deliberately incorporated into his screenplay. After finding the location for the shoot, and constructing the petrol station, house and garage on the site, actors Chloe Pirrie and Joseph Mawle spent two weeks, prior to the shoot, living together in the area, so that they could become familiar enough with each other ahead of time and thereby readily able to respond to each other without using words, as well as better to familiarize these two London-based actors with what it felt like to live at such a remote outpost. Subsequently, Graham, Pirrie, Mawle and the rest of the cast and crew shot the film over the course of four weeks, working 10–12 hour shifts, often shooting at night, on digital video. As Graham attests, despite support from multiple Scottish, British and Dutch sources, the budget for *Shell* was tight and the film needed to be precisely performed, so the actors did not improvise, but rather adhered to his script all the way through, including his specific instructions concerning exactly what the emotional resonances should be in each shot sequence within each scene. This approach has proven its value; critical responses to the film have been highly positive, ever since it debuted at the 2012 San Sebastian Film Festival.

The limited backstory included within the film succeeds in compelling audiences to pay close and careful attention to everything they see and hear, and to develop their own interpretations of what preceded. Likewise, the highly visual approach toward storytelling in *Shell* accentuates this requirement of close and careful attention. Graham, Gärtig, Pirrie and Mawle effectively convey what remains unspoken yet is communicated clearly and strongly nonetheless. Deliberately shooting Shell and Pete most often outside of the same frame visually dramatizes the isolation and loneliness they both feel, despite – and even to a significant degree on account of – their having each other, while also adding significantly to the impact of shots where the two are captured together within the same frame. As Graham has explained, in an interview with Samuel Wrigley (2013) for the British Film Institute, 'I think that intensifies the [sense of] loneliness and isolation. Although they have each other, they lead separate lives'. In addition, Graham's decision severely to limit the use of music (entirely eschewing the non-diegetic) enables us, he explains as part of the same interview, 'to feel as close to Shell's world as possible. She feels the silence'. The film-makers imbue this silence with tension and dread not only by means of a vague feeling of an inevitably transformative forward momentum that pervades the slow unfolding of the plot, despite the otherwise overriding sense of stasis that seems superficially most evident, but also due to the quality of the camera work. As Fionnuala Halligan (2012) writes in a review of *Shell* for *Screen Daily*, 'it's a completely unexpected take on the Scottish highlands and often brilliantly so [...] the pale blues and icy moonlight are cut through with moments of flashing scrub to make *Shell* seem otherworldly, not even Scottish'.

Yet, contrary to Halligan's last point, perhaps what *Shell* accomplishes is to reveal a cinematic dimension of the Scottish Highlands that has rarely been depicted, yet which is much closer, even much truer, to the felt experience of everyday life for many so-called 'ordinary people' living their lives in the Highlands – much closer, that is, than the tourist, heritage and romantically idealized portraits of the same region that are much more commonplace. The latter tend to be commonplace even in 'social realist' films, when urban-based Scottish characters venture, usually relatively briefly, into the Highlands, and where their perceptions of the Highlands are just as much filtered through the discourses of Tartanry and Kailyardism as is the case with many who come from much farther away briefly to visit the same territory. *Shell* offers a respectfully appreciative portrait but one that is far from either sentimental or nostalgic; even though the images deliberately enough approximate the dimensions of postcards, these are 'anti-postcards', as the image so captured in each case is the antithesis of a suggested 'essence' rendered tranquil and tame by way of such photographic framing, recording and processing. Graham has suggested he is consciously aware of the value of making films set in rural Scotland, including the Highlands and the Islands, as most of the British, and especially Scottish, feature-length film-making that has attracted wide critical and popular attention in recent decades has been focused on urban settings and urban stories. And his film's refusal of an easy, conventional resolution means, despite concluding with a tentative sense of hope, of a new beginning, for Shell, that sensory details of the atmosphere, and near frozen moments in the narrative, are what linger the most intensely. In this regard, Graham's portrayal of the deer maintaining a symbolic potency, and a special kinship with Shell, is, typically, both suggestive and elusive – the film makes no effort to interpret this symbol for us. Likewise, Shell's name, which she explains, once, is 'like the beautiful thing you get in the sea', opens up multiple avenues for possible interpretation without directing these in a singular way. And the same happens with the incorporation of *The Heart Is a Lonely Hunter*; yes, superficial resemblances concerning situations and experiences confronting the youthful female protagonists in that novel and in Graham's film are ample, but those connections are less profoundly resonant than more elliptically suggestive ones.

Perhaps what Graham, cast and crew have accomplished with *Shell* is to offer a both familiar yet distinctive reflection on Scottishness. In an interview with *The Skinny* (Bett 2013), Graham proposes that a prominent emphasis, in much Scottish art and culture (including literature, music and film) on what many have identified as the melancholy and the miserable, without this necessarily seeming to creators themselves to be entirely or simply equivalent with the melancholy and the miserable alone, 'probably goes to the heart of what it means to be Scottish'. As Graham suggests, Scots have often tended to perceive light, to experience hope, and to find truth by directly confronting and honestly engaging with what can readily seem considerably melancholic and miserable, but which can also seem simply what is right and necessary in order to do justice to the felt experience of many Scots in many locations and many situations across Scotland, past and present.

Bob Nowlan

References

24 Frames Per Second (2013) 'Interview: *Shell* director Scott Graham', 14 March, http://24framepersecond.wordpress.com/2013/03/14/interview-shell-director-scott-graham/. Accessed 17 April 2013.

Bett, Alan (2013) 'Role Play: Scott Graham on *Shell*', *The Skinny*, 4 March, http://www.theskinny.co.uk/film/features/304152-role_play_scott_graham_shell. Accessed 17 April 2013.

Halligan, Fionnuala (2012) '*Shell*: Review', *Screen Daily*, 26 September, http://www.screendaily.com/reviews/the-latest/-shell/5047043.article. Accessed 17 April 2013.

Lisitsina, Dasha (2012) 'The ties that bind: Scott Graham on *Shell*', *British Film Institute*, 19 November, http://www.bfi.org.uk/news/ties-bind-scott-graham-shell. Accessed 17 April 2013.

Wilkinson, Amber (2013) 'Inside *Shell*: Scott Graham on his dad/daughter drama', *Eye for Film*, 14 March, http://www.eyeforfilm.co.uk/feature/2013-03-14-scott-graham-interview-about-shell-feature-story-by-amber-wilkinson. Accessed 17 April 2013.

Wrigley, Samuel (2013) 'Life's a gas station: Scott Graham on *Shell*', *British Film Institute*, 15 March, http://www.bfi.org.uk/news-opinion/news-bfi/interviews/life-s-gas-station-scott-graham-shell. Accessed 17 April 2013.

Small Faces

Country of Origin:
UK

Language:
English

Studio/Production Companies:
Billy MacKinnon
BBC Films
Skyline
Glasgow Film Fund

Director:
Gillies MacKinnon

Producers:
Steve Clark-Hall
Billy MacKinnon

Screenwriters:
Gillies MacKinnon
Billy MacKinnon

Cinematographer:
John de Borman

Art Director:
Pat Campbell

Composer:
John Keane

Synopsis

Alan, Bobby and Lex are three teenage brothers growing up in late-1960s Glasgow. Each young man has a very different relationship to the notoriously violent youth gang culture that influenced the city during this period. Bobby, the eldest of the siblings, is at once both the most dangerous and endangered of the three in this regard. An emotionally scarred, illiterate school drop-out, he has found a tenuous measure of identity and self-respect through acting as second-in-command of the Glen, the teenage gang associated with the part of Glasgow in which the brothers live. Middle brother Alan, by contrast, is a studious, sensitive and creatively gifted scholar bound for an undergraduate place at the city's prestigious Art School. Lex, the youngest of the trio, bridges the two poles that his brothers personify, possessing something of Alan's artistic curiosity and talent but also prone to the kind of violent unpredictability that afflicts Bobby. When Lex inadvertently starts a feud with a neighbouring gang (an air pistol round that the boy fires hits that group's leader in the face), the consequences for the siblings vary markedly. Bobby is stabbed and killed by members of the rival gang; Alan is compelled to act temporarily as a kind of war artist for the Glen, but manages to extricate himself unscathed and so begin his art school studies; Lex appears to learn the error of his ways and readies himself to devote the remainder of his adolescence to the honing of his nascent artistic talents.

Critique

It is no accident that *Small Faces* begins and ends with scenes of Lex, the film's central character, hard at work drawing. Siblings

Editor:
Scott Thomas
Duration:
108 minutes
Genre:
Crime
Coming of Age
Social/Psychological Drama
Social Art Cinema
Cast:
Iain Robertson
Joe McFadden
Steven Duffy
Year:
1996
Filming Location:
Glasgow, Strathclyde, Scotland, UK

Gillies and Billy MacKinnon's autobiographical account of growing up on and around the mean streets of gang-ridden late-1960s Glasgow frames itself as a study of the ways in which acts of artistic creation possess the capacity to simultaneously record *and* reconfigure lived moments within individual and collective human experience. Moreover, despite the film's strong element of autobiography, *Small Faces* posits an understanding of art's social origins and impact within which the idea of reconfiguration seems to be of more importance than that of record. While the movie's opening credits unfold over a vivid portrait of a particular place as it existed at a particular time (Lex's felt-tip-pen portrait of Glasgow's gangland boundaries circa 1968), the first thing that viewers actually see is the young man's hand manoeuvring the instrument with which he creates that image. The consequent argument that works of art show the world not as it objectively, actually is, but rather as it appears once radically mediated and manipulated by the resources of individual imagination, is exemplified as much by the entire audio-visual structure of the MacKinnon brothers' movie as it is by the colourful introductory spectacle of Lex's map within the film itself. On one hand, the wildly skewed physical perspective

Small Faces (1996), British Film Institute Collection

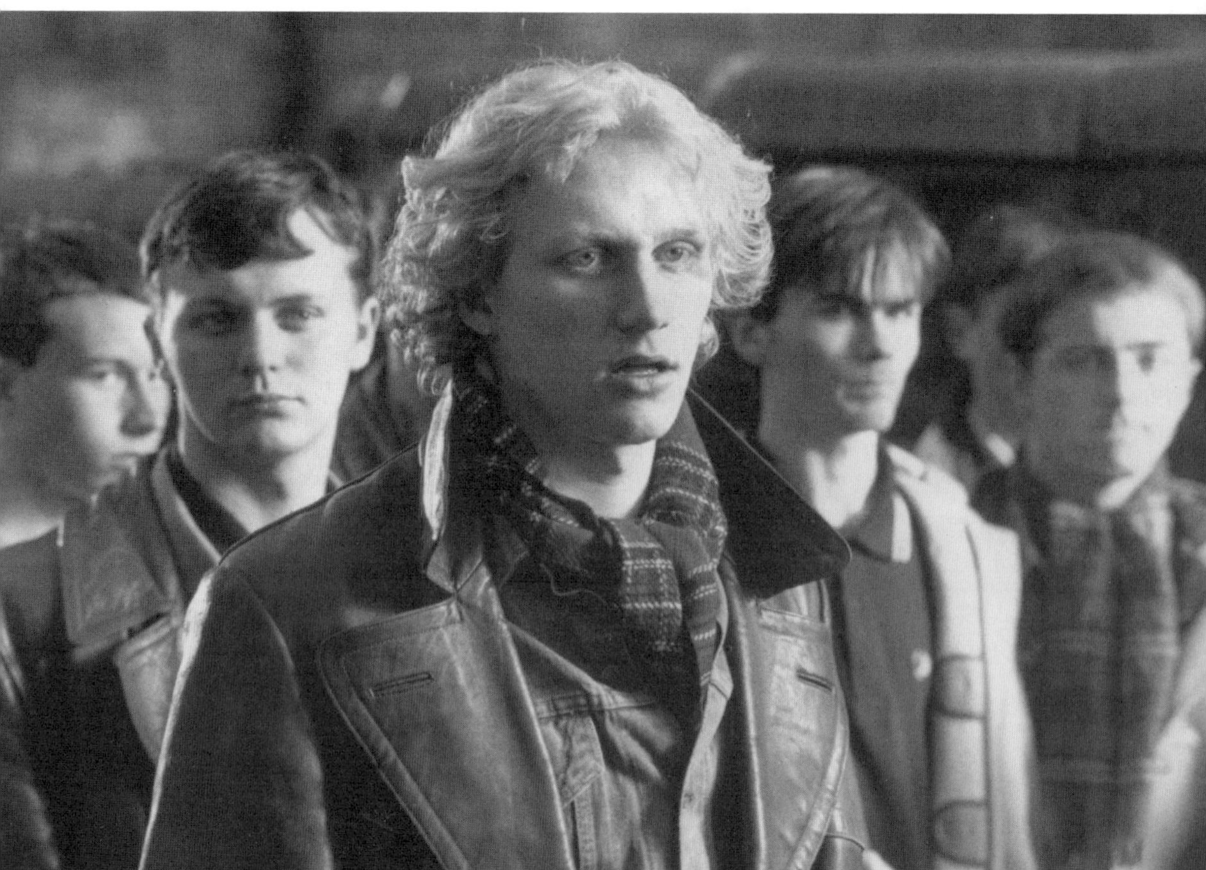

that characterizes the boy's drawing might potentially be explained away as an adolescent inability to master the demands of formal technique. But on the other, the subsequent preponderance of quasi-expressionist camera angles and bravura *trompe l'œil*-style perspectival illusions that pepper *Small Faces* stem from an abundance of technical mastery, not naivety, on the film-makers' part. Within a wider Scottish cinematic context, *Small Faces* thus lies closer to European art cinema-inspired works such as Lynne Ramsay's *Ratcatcher* (1999) or Peter Mullan's *Orphans* (1998) than it does to the more classically social realist portraits of urban deprivation and violence essayed by writers and directors such as Paul Laverty, Ken Loach and Peter McDougall.

Like his subsequent Scottish-set and part-funded feature project, the World War I drama *Regeneration* (1997), *Small Faces* testifies to Gillies MacKinnon's considerable directorial talent and ambition. Yet, to date, critics of Scottish cinema have largely overlooked his work. This fact seems doubly strange when one considers that MacKinnon was by far and away the most prolific Scottish film-maker of the 1990s, directing five theatrical features and a further three films for television during the period in question. Part of the explanation for Scottish film scholars' comparative neglect of such an extensive oeuvre perhaps lies in its pronouncedly cosmopolitan character. The latter involves both the production backgrounds to, and narrative settings of, many of the movies that MacKinnon has made. *Hideous Kinky* (1998), for example, is a British-French co-production with a story that for the most part unfolds in early-1970s Morocco, while *A Simple Twist of Fate* (1994) was a Hollywood studio-funded, American-set remake of George Eliot's nineteenth-century novel *Silas Marner*. The lack of critical attention paid to such works highlights a general issue to do with the very particular terms of reference and definition that Scottish cinema scholars have traditionally adopted within their work. For most critical writers, the canon of works taken to constitute the field of Scottish cinema is defined with primary reference to issues of narrative setting and content, rather than the national/cultural background of a given film-maker or makers. For this reason, Bill Douglas's *Trilogy* (1972–78) has been examined extensively within Scottish cinema studies, while his only other feature, 1986's *Comrades*, a project set in southern England and Australia, has not. Similarly, Bill Forsyth's first four Scottish-set features have been explored far more extensively than the trilogy of American-set and funded movies that the director produced during the late 1980s and early 1990s.

Between the 1970s and the end of the 1990s, the period during which figures like Douglas, Forsyth and MacKinnon were most active, it was possible to rationalize critical neglect of their non-Scottish output by arguing that such international careers and oeuvres were glaring exceptions, rather than the general rule, within an infant, tentatively expanding Scottish production sector. But that position is far harder to justify in the twenty-first century: today, a larger and more diverse local industry routinely attracts non-Scottish film-makers to shoot movies in Scotland on one hand, while also allowing many native writers and directors the opportunity to establish critical and commercial reputations that create chances to work within a range of different film industries around the globe on the other. Some contemporary scholarly work, such as David Martin-Jones's 2009 book *Scotland: Global Cinema*, has begun to respond positively to this phenomena, not least by arguing that the evaluative criteria by which we might choose to define a particular film and/or film-maker as 'Scottish' are not self-evident and static, but multiple and mutable in nature. One way in which that critical process could be usefully developed in future would involve far more sustained amounts of attention being paid to peripatetic Scottish film-making careers such as that of Gillies MacKinnon.

Jonathan Murray

Reference

Martin-Jones, David (2009) *Scotland: Global Cinema – Genres, Modes and Identities*, Edinburgh: EUP.

Stella Does Tricks

Country of Origin:

UK

Language:

English

Studio/Production Companies:

Compulsive Films
Sidewalk Productions
Scottish Arts Council Lottery Fund
Scottish Film Production Fund

Director:

Coky Giedroyc

Producers:

Adam Barker
Angus Lamont

Screenwriter:

AL Kennedy

Cinematographer:

Barry Ackroyd

Art Director:

Tim Ellis

Synopsis

The heroine of *Stella Does Tricks* is a multiply marginalized central protagonist. Sexually abused as a child by her alcoholic, failed stand-up comedian father, Stella has run away from her native Glasgow to London. There, however, she falls into the clutches of Mr Peters, an utterly amoral middle-aged pimp who baulks at nothing in order to exert complete physical and psychological control over his unhappy stable of young female victims. But Stella bravely attempts to leave Peters and forge a new life for herself, relying on two forms of personal support and strength as she does so. The first of these is internal in nature and relates to one possible meaning of the 'tricks' foregrounded within the film's title. A series of fantasy and/or memory sequences that punctuate the narrative demonstrate Stella's remarkable capacity, through the resources of her fecund imagination, to repeatedly confront the tragedies of her past and temporarily circumvent those of her present. Second, she also draws significant succour from the romantic relationship she begins with Eddie, a young drug addict making a living on the fringes of the capital's squalid sex trade. Ultimately, however, Stella's lover becomes yet another man whose personal weakness leads him to betray and abuse her. After Eddie allows her to be raped by a housemate in order to finance his addiction, Stella overdoses – whether accidentally or not remains unclear – on pills and alcohol. A final fantasy sequence, in which she dons one of her father's gaudy stage outfits in order to perform an onstage monologue in front of a small theatre audience, sees Stella conclude that 'some men have penis extensions and some men *are* penis extensions'. The implication is that this unedifying truth represents the cause of her premature demise.

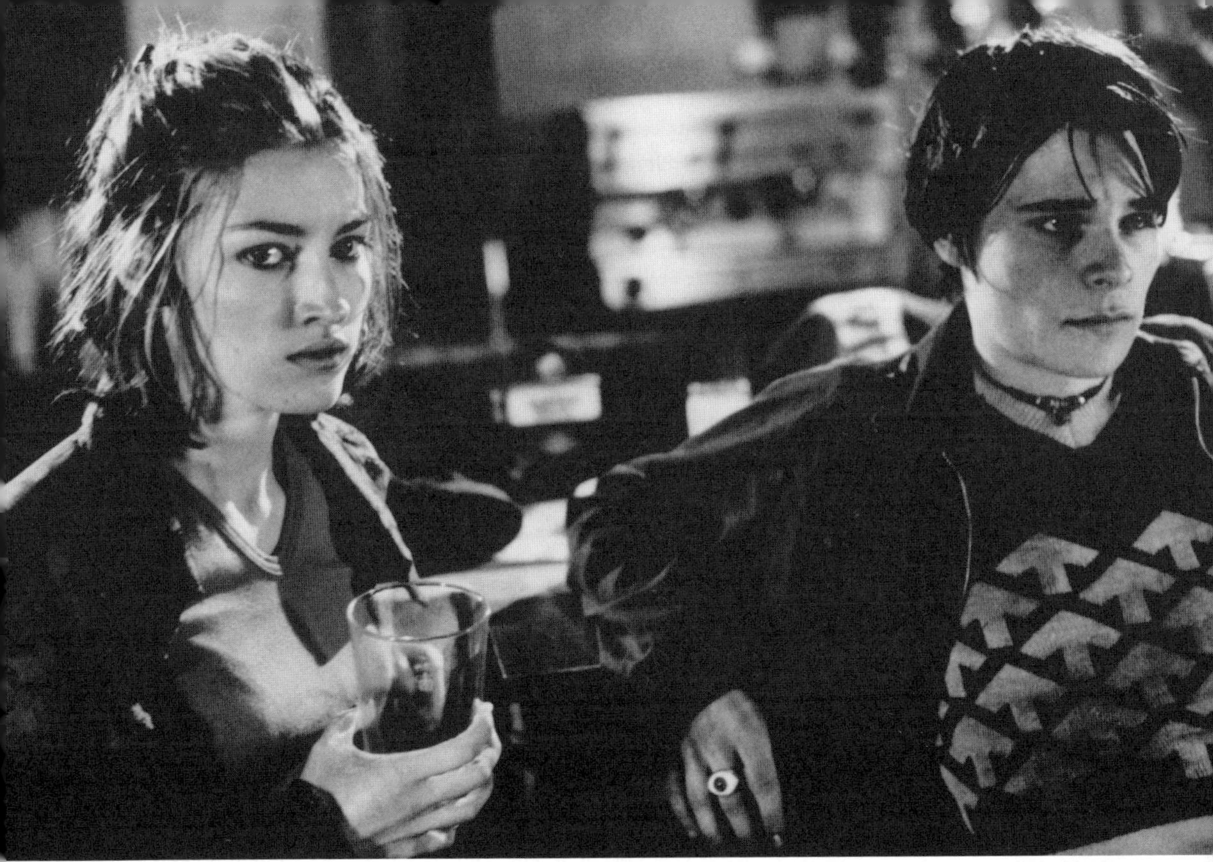

Stella Does Tricks (1996), British Film Institute Collection

Composer:

Nick Bicât

Editor:

Budge Tremlett

Duration:

99 minutes

Genre:

Crime
Coming of Age
Social/Psychological Drama
Social Art Cinema

Cast:

Kelly Macdonald
James Bolam
Hans Matheson

Year:

1996

Critique

Although not nearly as widely seen or discussed as the near-contemporaneous variations on Scottish and/or British social realist cinematic traditions essayed by film-makers such as Peter Mullan and Ken Loach, *Stella Does Tricks* is a notably ambitious and accomplished work. Writer Al Kennedy and director Coky Giedroyc offer viewers an unsparing documentary portrait of a bestially exploited late-twentieth-century British female underclass on one hand *and* an expressionistic exploration of the complex capacities and consequences of the human imagination on the other. From outset to end, constant and calculated shifts in narrative register (reality versus fantasy), timeframe (present versus past) and location (London versus Glasgow) clearly distance the movie from the more classically naturalistic modus operandi that structures much contemporary social realist cinema emanating from Scotland and the rest of the United Kingdom.

On closer viewing, however, *Stella Does Tricks* posits the idea that the factual and the fantastic have never been mutually incompatible narrative approaches within native cinematic and literary traditions of depicting the struggle for survival at the bottom of the British

Filming Locations:

Glasgow, Scotland, UK
London, England, UK

capital city's teeming social heap. Indeed, Kennedy and Giedroyc advance that argument right from their work's very opening, a profoundly disturbing first scene in which Sodom and Gomorrah comes to seem uncomfortably close to Kensington and Chelsea. As Mr Peters, Stella's repulsive middle-aged pimp, instructs his teenage slave to masturbate him while both sit on a public park bench in broad daylight, he simultaneously compels her to (re) play a grotesque fiction which parodies the sentimental ideal of the paterfamilias. During this performance, Peters becomes, in Stella's obedient words, 'the nice man who took me in [...] like in numerous of the works of Dickens'. Fact and fantasy are here figured as interdependent means through which individuals understand the world, and consequently come to act within it in very particular ways. The reality of wholesale sexual exploitation as an everyday component of modern-day British urban life is presented as a lamentable social phenomenon partially dependent upon the inability and/or refusal of both abuser and abused to accurately recognize and verbalize the true nature of their respective situations and motivations.

The swiftly established Dickensian literary reference point is also vital to *Stella Does Tricks* for several other reasons. Perhaps most obviously, it allows the film to stress the extent to which many of the glaring social inequalities and inequities depicted within much nineteenth-century British fiction still persist within British metropolitan life some 150 years later. Inhuman exploitation of children and the decimation of large swathes of London's poorest citizens through narcotic abuse stalk the images of *Stella Does Tricks* as surely as they do the pages of *Oliver Twist*. More complexly, however, such depressing artistic and social parallels also allow Giedroyc and Kennedy to contend that Scottish and/ or British social realist traditions of fiction (cinematic or otherwise) have been distorted by a historic predominance of male artistic voices and perspectives at the expense of female alternatives. For example, while their film exploits a range of motifs and plotlines familiar from Dickens's novels, it also refuses utterly to conform to the profoundly and wilfully sentimental ideal of gender identities and relations which surfaces repeatedly within that author's oeuvre. With regard to both her ultimate unhappy fate and the courageous agency with which she seeks to evade it, Stella is anything but a contemporary reincarnation of Little Nell, the impossibly virtuous cipher at the heart of *The Old Curiosity Shop*, or any subsequent indigenous fictional paragon of demurely helpless feminine purity and vulnerability. As she herself puts matters to Eddie, 'I'm not your girl, I'm nobody's girl'.

For such reasons, the idea that a truly just (and justly depicted) society would be one that acknowledged and encouraged feminine imaginative depictions of individual and collective experience as a necessary corrective to the traditional dominance of masculine equivalents permeates the narrative of *Stella Does Tricks*. The film's heroine is a born storyteller, a highly creative young woman who proudly and justifiably boasts to a group of fellow prostitutes that 'I can picture any fucking scene: I have the technology, it's my thing'. Indeed, one way of reading the work's narrative is to see it as a charting of Stella's struggle to re-imagine – and thus, to reclaim – her own identity and destiny after a lifetime of submitting to such things being misrepresented and maligned within the self-serving imaginations of a series of pathetic, but nonetheless profoundly dangerous, men. She admits as much to Eddie at one point, noting that 'I want to be like me – I've never been like me for years'.

In addition to forming a representative articulation of the gender politics of *Stella Does Tricks*, the assertion by the film's heroine that she 'can picture any fucking scene' also possesses considerable resonance and importance when considering the cultural development and diversity of Scottish cinema more generally. Remarkably, *Stella Does Tricks*, released in British cinemas in 1998, was at that point in time only the second Scottish-themed and Scottish-financed fiction feature ever directed by a woman, following in the footsteps of Margaret Tait's *Blue Black Permanent* (1992). Thankfully, Scottish film-making since the turn of the millennium has witnessed an increasing number of female-authored and/or female-centred works, including films such as *Blinded* (Eleanor Yule, 2003), *Donkeys* (Morag McKinnon, 2010), *Morvern Callar* (Lynne Ramsay, 2002), *One Life Stand* (May Miles Thomas, 2000) and *Red Road* (Andrea Arnold, 2006). While that phenomenon has not yet been properly acknowledged and explored by film scholars, *Stella Does Tricks* undoubtedly represented an important pioneering step in its long-overdue development.

Jonathan Murray

Sweet Sixteen

Countries of Origin:

UK
Germany
Spain

Language:

English

Studio/Production Companies:

Alta Films
BBC
Road Movies Filmproduktion
Scottish Screen
Sixteen Films
Tornasol Films

Director:

Ken Loach

Producers:

Rebecca O'Brien

Synopsis

Fifteen-year-old Liam may be a boy, but he is also a seasoned businessman. The grim socio-economic realities of childhood years spent on a workless, drug-ravaged public housing scheme in the Scottish Central Belt coastal town of Greenock have rendered his self-reliance and ingenuity as sharp as the knives he refuses to carry for protection on the local streets. While running a number of money-making schemes with his best friend, Pinball, Liam awaits the imminent release of his mother, recovering drug addict Jean, from prison. Desperate to wrest back his absent parent from the clutches of her manipulative partner, small-time pusher Stan, Liam starts selling heroin, aiming thus to buy Jean a fresh start, in the shape of a trailer home with stunning sea views, once she leaves jail. Initially, matters seem to go well: success in his latest business venture provides a substantial down-payment for the trailer home and attracts the admiring notice of a major local drug dealer, who makes Liam an offer of permanent employment. Ultimately, however, Liam's hopes, and the new abode that houses them, are turned to ashes. Pinball, fearful that his friend's success will destroy their relationship, burns down the trailer home. Jean, meanwhile, swaps one state of incarceration for another, returning to Stan

Michael André
Ulrich Felsberg
Gerardo Herrero
Screenwriter:
Paul Laverty
Cinematographer:
Barry Ackroyd
Art Director:
Fergus Clegg
Composer:
George Fenton
Editor:
Jonathan Morris
Duration:
106 minutes
Genre:
Social Realism/Naturalism
Social Drama

immediately after exiting prison. Enraged and bewildered by the failure of money to secure his happiness and that of those closest to him, Liam confronts and stabs Stan. *Sweet Sixteen* ends with its central character wandering alone along a local beach on his sixteenth birthday, the prospect of arrest and imprisonment marking the start – and, perhaps, simultaneous end – of his adult life.

Critique

Sweet Sixteen is the most dramatically and thematically accomplished of all the Scottish-set features made by director Ken Loach and screenwriter Paul Laverty in the two decades or so since their first collaboration, *Carla's Song* (1996). Right from the outset, Liam's actions and aspirations possess a degree of psychological and political complexity that exceeds those of his counterparts elsewhere in Loach's and Laverty's Scottish oeuvre. Unlike similarly deprived compatriots such as Joe – *My Name is Joe* (1998) – or Robbie – *The Angels' Share* (2012) – Liam is figured as both victim *and* villain within the Thatcherite-cum-Blairite socio-economic model that forms the central narrative backdrop to, and ideological target of, his co-creators' collaborative work. Like

Sweet Sixteen (2002), British Film Institute Collection

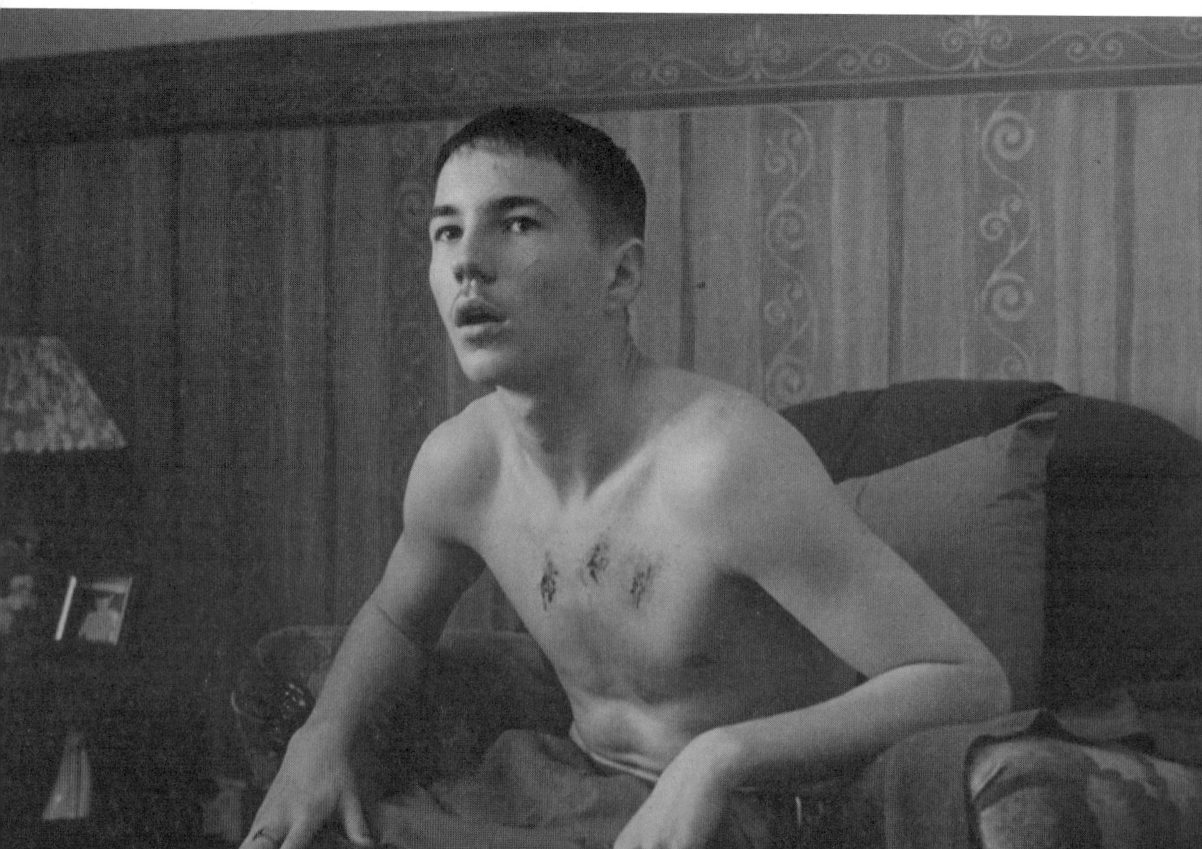

Melodrama
Crime
Coming of Age

Cast:

Martin Compston
William Ruane
Annmarie Fulton

Year:

2002

Filming Locations:

Greenock and Glasgow, Strathclyde, Scotland, UK

Joe and Robbie, Liam's personal circumstances demonstrate the frightening extent to which Free Market ideologies bring about the systematic economic dispossession of whole swathes of society. But unlike those characters, Liam also personifies that political creed's power to impoverish its victims in moral, as well as material, terms, thus rendering them as semi-/un-conscious agents of their own oppression. As such, he possesses the potential to provoke a degree of emotional care and political questioning unmatched by any other protagonist within Loach's and Laverty's Scottish work.

For a representative sense of just how involved and inquisitive a viewer response that Liam and *Sweet Sixteen* invite, one need look no further than the film's opening scene, a sequence as explicitly beautiful but implicitly disturbing as anything Loach and Laverty have created together. On a starlit night on the hills above Greenock, Liam and Pinball charge an enraptured crowd of local children 25 pence a time for the opportunity to gaze at the planet Saturn through Liam's telescope. The most immediately obvious overtones of the scene seem highly pleasurable and positive in nature: the small-scale innocence of the kids' enjoyment and their guides' entrepreneurialism; the telescope's functioning as a symbol of Liam's intrinsically attractive imaginative ability to seek out worlds other than the deprived one into which he has been born. More fundamentally, however, the sequence also presages the disquieting fact that who and what viewers see as *Sweet Sixteen* unfolds – Liam, Pinball and the society they inhabit – constitute rigorously monetized entities that are built upon the repression and perversion of human potential. After all, even in the movie's opening moments, the immensity of space is as much a commodity to be sold as it is a pleasure to be shared, while the seemingly harmless fantasy that Liam sells – you can escape to wherever and whatever you want, so long as you are able to pay for the privilege – is also one that he will be seen to buy into, with disastrous consequences for himself and those around him. Though Liam ardently believes that he can build an atomized life of nuclear familial security, both economic and emotional, on the addictions of others, that self-centred aspiration is shown to be as practicably inaccessible as the celestial body that viewers first see him charging children for a fleeting glimpse of.

Sweet Sixteen's introductory suggestion that Free Market socio-economic models commoditize all forms of emotional instinct and aspiration finds numerous echoes as the film progresses. Stan encourages Liam to kiss Jean during a prison visit, not out of respect for parent/child ties, but because this act offers a method to smuggle drugs into the jail for Jean to sell to other inmates. The appearance of the trailer home that Liam sets his heart upon buying – erected slightly apart from others in the caravan park, decorated with a miniature white picket fence, and set against an uninhabited backdrop of sky, sea and hillside – offers an elegant implication of the boy's belief that personal security lies in an escape from, rather than embrace of, collectivist social practices and values. And, perhaps most pointedly of all, there is the bitterly ironic counterpoint between the sight of Liam and Pinball selling smack to their fellow youths on the Greenock streets and the sound – not to mention, sentiment – of The Pretenders' song 'I'll Stand by You', a personal favourite of Jean's that Liam sends his mother a recording of in order to sustain her spirits during the final stretch of her prison term.

In the final analysis, then, Liam is a strikingly complex and thought-provoking protagonist. If we assume the narrative present tense of *Sweet Sixteen* to be 2002, the year of the film's international theatrical release, then he is quite literally, to coin a much-used phrase from British sociopolitical discourse, one of 'Thatcher's Children'. Born in 1987, Liam's actions and aspirations a decade-and-a-half later represent a wholesale internalization of the former Prime Minister's notorious assertion, in a press interview given in the aftermath of her third UK General Election victory that same year, that: 'There is no such thing as society. There are individual men and women, and there are families [...] people must look to themselves first'. Yet, while Loach and Laverty use Liam's journey as a narrative vehicle through which to emphatically refute the validity of that ideological principle, they never reduce their creation to the level of dramatic cipher or bogeyman. Liam's personal attributes and class background are not exploited as convenient fodder for wholesale idealization or demonization, exculpation or condemnation. Instead, the painstaking construction of Liam's character and personal journey work as a nuanced exploration of the fraught (because ultimately one-sided) interplay between individual agency/aspiration and socio-economic determinism that, in Loach's and Laverty's view, confronts significant sections of contemporary Scottish society. As such, they also show his creators' collaborative skills operating at a notable creative peak.

Jonathan Murray

Trainspotting

Country of Origin:

UK

Language:

English

Studio/Production Companies:

Channel Four Films
Figment Films
The Noel Gay Motion Picture Production Company

Director:

Danny Boyle

Producer:

Andrew Macdonald

Screenwriter:

John Hodge

Synopsis

Heroin addict Mark Renton decides to clean up and get his life in order, as do his close friends Spud and Sick Boy. The pressures of everyday life, however, soon begin to weigh on the friends, culminating in one particularly disastrous night for Spud, Renton and their friend Tommy. Spud, Renton and Sick Boy return to using heroin shortly thereafter and Tommy – heartbroken by the end of his sexual relationship – soon tries the drug himself and becomes addicted. The crimes the group commits to feed their habit ultimately lead to the arrest of Spud and Renton. Renton receives a light sentence for his offence while Spud is jailed. Renton's guilt over his luck in escaping jail while his friend is not so lucky leads him to overdose. While he is recovering from this near-death experience, Renton's parents nurse him to health and force him to quit using altogether. Renton then moves to London to start a new life only for his violent, thuggish friend Francis Begbie to track him down, followed quickly by Sick Boy. Returning to Edinburgh for the funeral of Tommy, who died from complications related to AIDS, the friends unite with Spud and decide to assist Sick Boy in the

Cinematographer:
Brian Tufano
Art Director:
Tracey Gallacher
Editor:
Masahiro Hirakubo
Duration:
90 minutes
Genre:
Black Magic Realism
Crime
Caper
Cast:
Ewan McGregor
Kevin McKidd
Johnny Lee Miller
Ewen Bremner
Robert Carlyle

sale of a large chunk of heroin to a London dealer. After the deal is complete, Renton steals the proceeds from his friends and embarks on a new life.

Critique

Trainspotting is the single most important film to have emerged from Scotland as well as one of the most important British films ever made. Its critical and commercial success is unparalleled in Scottish film history and it launched and/or permanently altered the careers of its entire cast and creative team. The names involved with the film are now a 'who's who' of British cinema, beginning with director Danny Boyle and lead actor Ewan McGregor and extending to Kelly Macdonald, Kevin McKidd, Robert Carlyle and Johnny Lee Miller, as well as Andrew Macdonald, who went on to found DNA Films and remains one of the nation's most influential producers.

The film's popularity at the time of its release can be partly attributed to the innovative marketing campaigns rolled out by Polygram and Miramax films, campaigns which made novelist Irvine Welsh – heretofore a writer with a cult following – an international celebrity and which also sold millions of copies of the film's original

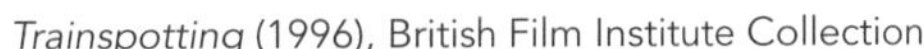

Trainspotting (1996), British Film Institute Collection

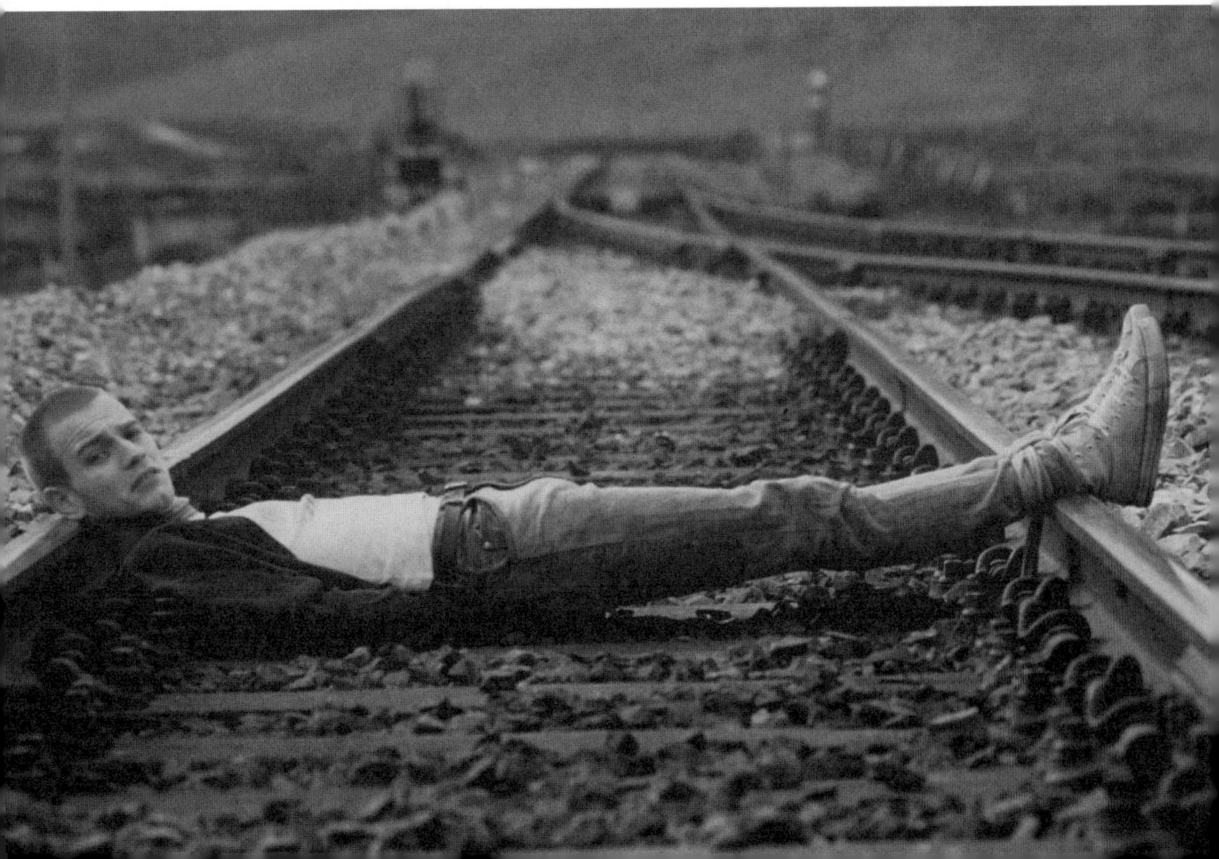

Kelly Macdonald

Year:

1996

Filming Locations:

78A Talgarth Road, West Kensington, London, England, UK
Calton Road, Edinburgh, Scotland, UK
Crosslands - 182 Queen Margaret Drive, Glasgow, Strathclyde, Scotland, UK
Azad Video, Dumbarton Road, Glasgow, Strathclyde, Scotland, UK
Big Ben, Houses of Parliament, Westminster, London, England, UK
Cafe D'Jaconelli - 570 Maryhill Road, North Kelvinside, Glasgow, Strathclyde, Scotland, UK
Canniesburn Hospital, Glasgow, Strathclyde, Scotland, UK
Carnaby Street, Soho, London, England, UK
Corrour Station, the Highlands, Scotland, UK
George Hotel - 235 Buchanan Street, Glasgow, Strathclyde, Scotland, UK
Hanover Street, Edinburgh, Scotland, UK
Jordanhill School - 45 Chamberlain Road, Jordanhill, Glasgow, Strathclyde, Scotland, UK
Lloyd's Building, Lime Street, Broadgate, London, England, UK
NatWest Tower, Old Broad Street, London, England, UK
Oxford Street, London, England, UK
Piccadilly Circus, Piccadilly, London, England, UK
Possilpark, Glasgow, Strathclyde, Scotland, UK
Princes Street, Edinburgh, Scotland, UK
Regent Street, London,

soundtrack, which featured a number of popular hit songs. The campaigns also heavily promoted the film's cast, with McGregor in particular being catapulted to international fame.

But it was not just a hip soundtrack, a counterculture novel or an emerging superstar lead that made *Trainspotting* the international phenomenon that it became. The film's rebellious pose, beginning with the now famous anti-bourgeois 'Choose Life' monologue, struck a note within international youth culture and made the film into a generational statement. Although themes of alienation, disillusionment and social rebellion are to be found in Welsh's novel, screenwriter John Hodge distilled the essence of these and amplified their volume in his adaptation. As such, the film presents heroin addiction as an act of social and political protest, a thematic conceit that often runs the risk of glamourizing or at least romanticizing a very real social problem for Scotland in the 1990s.

Although already apparent in the earlier *Shallow Grave* (1994), Boyle's frenetic audio-visual style reached new levels of emotional intensity and narrative integration in *Trainspotting*. Choreographing the film's opening police chase of Renton and Spud through the streets of Edinburgh with Iggy Pop's 'Lust for Life' created a particularly exhilarating bit of hyperactive editing. Similarly, techno music is used throughout the film to build tension and evoke Renton's subjectivity, with the sequence depicting his nightmarish withdrawal from heroin and the pulsing beat of 'Born Slippy', which accompanies his climactic theft of the drug profits from the arms of the sleeping Begbie, being two particularly vivid examples of this strategy. Finally, Boyle evokes pointed tonal contrasts when he pairs Lou Reed's 'Perfect Day' with Renton's overdose and when he counterpoints images of Renton digging through his own feces for morphine suppositories with music from the opera *Carmen*.

The film's style also combines magic realism, playful postmodern techniques and shock tactics to create some of its most celebrated scenes. Perhaps the most typical sequence in this regard is the aforementioned toilet bowl sequence, which begins with a playful addition of the words 'The worst...in Scotland' to a sign for the toilet Renton enters in a state of distress. The subsequent toilet diving moment is equal parts fantastic and revolting, much like later sequences including Renton's haunting by Allyson's dead baby. Other sequences such as Spud's pelting of his girlfriend's family with feces or the crosscutting between Renton's climax and Archie Gemmill's famous goal against Holland also show the mixing of shock, humour and stylistic experimentation that made the film feel so unique within the context of late-twentieth-century British cinema, dominated as it was in the 1990s by tasteful costume drama and gritty social realism.

Despite, or more likely because of, the film's attack on Scottishness in the form of Renton's now famous 'It's shite being Scottish' rant, *Trainspotting* is a defining film within the Scottish canon. One book (Smith 2002) and many, many articles have been written about the film and it remains one of the most talked about British films within academic and critical circles. Numerous films have attempted to emulate the formula of *Trainspotting*, with Guy

England, UK
Rouken Glen Park, Thornliebank, Glasgow, Strathclyde, Scotland, UK
Royal Eagle Hotel - 26-30 Craven Road, Bayswater, London, England, UK
St. Paul's Cathedral, Ludgate Hill, London, England, UK
The Firhill Complex - Hopehill Road, Glasgow, Strathclyde, Scotland, UK
Tower Bridge, London, England, UK
Tower of London, Whitechapel, London, England, UK
Trafalgar Square, St James's, London, England, UK
Volanco - 15 Banalder Street, Glasgow, Strathclyde, Scotland, UK
W.D. & H.O. Wills Tobacco Factory - 368 Alexandra Parade, Glasgow, Strathclyde, Scotland, UK
Waterloo Bridge, River Thames, London, England, UK
Wellington Arch, London, England, UK

Ritchie's cockney gangster films and the Welsh rave film *Human Traffic* (Justin Kerrigan, 1999) being just some of the many British films that borrowed from the tone and style of Boyle's film. Within Scottish cinema, *Trainspotting* had the pleasant legacy of showing that Scottish films could once again be economically viable but also at the same time set a stylistic and economic paradigm that few other films could successfully emulate. The '*Trainspotting* effect' can be observed shaping films as diverse as *The Acid House* (Paul McGuigan, 1999), the works of Richard Jobson, Lynne Ramsay's *Morvern Callar* (2002) and David Mackenzie's *Young Adam* (2002) and *Hallam Foe* (2007).

Christopher Meir

Reference

Smith, Murray (2002) *Trainspotting*, London: BFI.

We Need to Talk About Kevin

Countries of Origin:
UK
USA
Language:
English
Studio/Production Companies:
BBC Films
UK Film Council
Footprint Investments LLP
Piccadilly Pictures

Synopsis

Eva Khatchadourian is a woman who gives life to a child and sees her own life taken from her as a result. Once a highly successful, New York-based travel writer, viewers first see Eva as a socially ostracized, alcohol-and-anti-depressant-dependent wreck. *We Need to Talk About Kevin* then oscillates between narrative present and past tenses in order to gradually reveal the reasons for her present-day unhappiness and isolation. On one hand, some part of Eva's present-day unhappiness seems traceable to the endless frustrations and restrictions imposed by heterosexual maternal responsibility as conventionally defined and practised. Her husband, Franklin, blithely assumes that his wife will assume all domestic responsibilities and accept physical relocation from the city to sterile suburbia once their first child, Kevin, is born. One way of reading Lynne Ramsay's film therefore involves viewing it as the story of a woman whose confinement is inaugurated, rather than ended, by the successful delivery of her progeny. More obviously

Lipsync Productions
Independent
Artina Films
Rockinghorse Films
Caemhan
Panaramic
Beryl Betty
Atlantic Swiss Productions

Director:

Lynne Ramsay

Producers:

Jennifer Fox
Luc Roeg
Robert Salerno

Screenwriters:

Lynne Ramsay
Rory Stewart Kinnear
Lionel Shriver

Cinematographer:

Seamus McGarvey

Art Director:

Charles Kulsziski

Composer:

Jonny Greenwood

Editor:

Joe Bini

Duration:

112 minutes

Genre:

Social/Psychological Drama
Social Art Cinema
Crime

Cast:

Tilda Swinton
John C Reilly
Ezra Miller

Year:

2011

Filming Locations:

Buñol, Valencia, Spain
New York City, Norwalk, and Stamford, USA

and immediately troubling than Eva's identity as a mother, however, is Kevin's as a son. From infancy to adolescence, he wastes no opportunity to aggravate and alienate his increasingly bewildered and bruised female parent, all the while artfully concealing this campaign of emotional and psychological warfare from his unsuspecting father. Thus, while Eva fears for – and, eventually, just plain fears – the state of Kevin's mental health, Franklin increasingly doubts that of his wife. In the end, it is she who is proved right in the most awful way possible. Just before he turns sixteen (the age at which he would become legally accountable as an adult), Kevin cold-bloodedly kills his younger sister, Celia, and Franklin before proceeding to calmly massacre many of his fellow pupils at the local high school. The film ends by locating its narrative present some two years after the crimes that Kevin committed. Despite the unimaginable pain he has inflicted upon her, Eva continues to visit her son in prison; he, however, is unable (or unwilling) to reveal the reasons for his terrible actions.

Critique

The first stage in any assessment of *We Need to Talk About Kevin* involves deciding exactly who/what it is that the film's title entreats us to discuss. The most literal (and lurid) reading of all, for instance, is to see this movie as a contemporary secular rebooting of the 'demon child' horror template so expertly established and exploited in earlier works such as *Rosemary's Baby* (Roman Polanski, 1968) and *The Omen* (Richard Donner, 1976). Viewed in this way, director Lynne Ramsay's long-awaited third feature turns out to be little more than a superior potboiler purveying the unlikely story of a blameless parent driven mad by the birth of a child who is irredeemably bad. Indeed, should one choose to understand *We Need to Talk About Kevin* in this manner then it might even be said that the movie narrates more than one over-familiar cinematic horror story at once: Ramsay becomes the latest in a very long line of talented European arthouse directors who finds that a career move stateside significantly compromises the integrity and agency of their creative voice and vision.

But there are other ways in which to interpret the subject of *We Need to Talk About Kevin*'s title – and, by extension, the thematic agenda and success of the whole movie itself. We could, for example, set Ramsay's film alongside works such as Gus Van Sant's *Elephant* (2003) or Michael Moore's *Bowling for Columbine* (2002), two similar high-profile twenty-first-century filmic attempts to understand the mentality and motives of the small number of American schoolchildren who have in recent years achieved notoriety by murdering large numbers of their unsuspecting fellow pupils. Alternatively, we might see Kevin as a less sympathetic or less salvageable version of the angst-ridden male adolescent protagonists familiar from much recent American independent cinema. Like *Donnie Darko* (Richard Kelly, 2001) or *Thumbsucker* (Mike Mills, 2005), *We Need to Talk About Kevin* could be understood as an uneasy study of a dysfunction understood to be societal – the emotional pain and perversion inflicted by the values of middle-class suburban conformity – rather than individual in both scope and impact. The numerous similarities that the film suggests between Kevin and Eva (it hardly seems accidental, for instance, that shots of her operating an office photocopier are intercut with brief flashback images of his conception and gestation) would certainly support such a reading. Or we could adopt a different critical approach yet again, and consider 'Kevin' as a synecdoche for the feminine frustration, self-flagellation, and lack of fulfilment that are systematically fostered by the iniquities of a patriarchal social order. While the vituperative communal view that Eva is somehow responsible for her son's crimes is obviously and flagrantly unreasonable, Franklin's earlier assumption that his wife would/should give up her professional and psychological independence in order to raise their family while he continues his working life exactly as before is, arguably, no less myopic or unkind.

Finally, it is also possible to interpret *We Need to Talk About Kevin* through primary recourse to the name of the film's creator, rather than that of its titular character. After all, Lynne Ramsay's third feature is marked by a number of suggestive similarities to the director's first two. The opening image of a gauze curtain that functions as a presentiment of death links *We Need to Talk About Kevin* to *Ratcatcher* (1999), Ramsay's critically acclaimed debut feature. Both movies explore intimate experiences of crippling guilt and self-censure: James, the central protagonist of *Ratcatcher*, blames himself for the accidental death of a child, much as Eva cannot free herself of the conviction that Kevin's crimes are somehow really her own. Alternatively (or as well), *We Need to Talk About Kevin* could also be seen as a companion piece to Ramsay's second film, *Morvern Callar* (2002). The main connection here has to do with the director's interest in the precious – but precarious – nature of personal freedom and self-realization for many modern-day women: both Eva and Morvern are, for example, shown to be most fully alive and fulfilled when travelling alone in Spain, free from the expectations and obligations routinely foisted upon them within their respective domestic habitats. As the discussion above hopefully indicates, in addition to suggesting to its audience that we need to talk, Lynne Ramsay's third feature provides no shortage of potential subjects for us to talk about.

Jonathan Murray

Wilbur Wants to Kill Himself

Language:

English

Synopsis

Wilbur, a young man depressed by childhood trauma, is overtly determined to take his own life. However, his continued and somewhat ineffective suicide-attempts are futile, not least due to the caring intervention of his elder brother Harbour. Besides looking after the suicidal Wilbur, who continues to go in and out of hospital where his is treated by the dispassionate psychiatrist Horst,

Studio/Production Companies:
Zentropa Entertainment6 (DK)
Danish Film Institute (DK)
TV2/Danmark (DK)
Nordisk Film
Biografdistribution (DK)
Scottish Screen (SK)
Glasgow Film Fund (SK)
Sveriges, Television (SE)
Les Films du Losange (FR)
Nordic Film & TV Fund (NO)

Director:
Lone Scherfig

Producer:
Sisse Graum Jørgensen

Screenwriters:
Lone Scherfig
Anders Thomas Jensen

Cinematographer:
Jørgen Johansson

Art Director:
Jette Lehman

Composer:
Joachim Holbek

Sound:
Rune Palving

Editor:
Gerd Tjur

Duration:
105 minutes

Genre:
Social Art Cinema
Social/Psychological Drama
Dark Comedy

Cast:
James Sieves
Adrian Rawlins
Shirley Henderson
Lisa McKinlay
Mads Mikkelsen
Julia Davis
Susan Vidler

Year:
2002

Filming Locations:
Glasgow, Strathclyde, Scotland, UK

Harbour is managing the old bookstore they inherited from their departed father. Unfortunately, the good-hearted Harbour buys more books then he sells and a closure is impending if things do not change. When Wilbur tries to hang himself in the bookstore, the ill-fated and lonely-single mom, Alice, a frequent visitor to the bookstore, intervenes and Wilbur is hospitalized once again. Wilbur's suicide attempt in the bookstore brings Harbour and Alice together and they fall in love. Soon Alice and her daughter Mary become new members of the family and subsequently co-owners of the bookstore. Life seems to be turning for the better for the four and even Wilbur seems to have lost his suicidal tendencies, now that Alice and Mary have become the centre of attention for the brothers. Wilbur starts working again and even tries to find a girlfriend. Although he has no trouble attracting women he instead starts fancying Alice, who soon reciprocates. As the cruel twist of fate will have it, Harbour is diagnosed with incurable cancer. Meanwhile, the romantic relationship between Wilbur and Alice develops and, when Harbour is hospitalized, Wilbur slowly but increasingly confidently steps in to take over his brother's place.

Critique

This thematically dramatic, low-key, dark comedy is the fourth feature film created by Danish director Lone Scherfig, and the follow-up to her international success, the Dogma movie *Italian for Beginners* (2000). *Wilbur Wants to Kill Himself is* Scherfig's initial venture into English-language film-making. Scherfig co-wrote the script with prolific Danish screenwriter and director Anders Thomas Jensen, and the general storyline and all around dark humour of the film mark a direct continuation with a range of Danish popular black comedies created by Anders Thomas Jensen in the early to mid-2000s. However, in this case the story is set in Glasgow and deals with the ill-fated lives of some of the local Glaswegians.

Love and death, and life and loneliness. These pairs encapsulate the overall thematic structure guiding the narrative thread throughout the film, most obviously embodied in the ongoing tragicomic suicide attempts of Wilbur. *Wilbur Wants to Kill Himself* offers multiple rich examples of tragicomically situational humour, where otherwise highly serious character interactions and life situations are topped off by comic relief. *Wilbur Wants to Kill Himself*, moreover, manages to exceed a mere dramatization of the overarching message that life is ultimately unjustly absurd. Rather than being plot-driven, the film focuses on its characters and emphasizes their emotional development. The nuanced and emphatic portrayals of the central characters, whether these are less likeable as in the case of the initially selfish and pugnacious Wilbur or more likable as in the case of the initially introverted and love-yearning Alice, or the persistently kind and selfless Harbour, are deftly portrayed by the film's actors and Scherfig shows an actively engaged interest in and a sensitively attuned understanding of character development. As a result, *Wilbur Wants to Kill Himself* makes it difficult not to care for these ordinary people and their daily struggles. This impact is further

Filmbyen, Avedøre, Sjælland, Denmark

underscored by the composition of a limited and restricted, yet naturalistically convincing everyday milieu, where the desaturated world that Wilbur, Harbour and the other characters inhabit mirrors their outwardly bleak and colourless lives. The thorough focus on character development, and the empathic portrayal of everyday people, has now become a benchmark of Scherfig's directorial style, which began to develop during Scherfig's early involvement in the Dogma movement. In the end *Wilbur Wants to Kill Himself* manages to balance elegantly between deadpan humour and an engaging portrayal of its characters, while dealing with some of life's largest issues. This allows the bittersweet tone of the film to come off not as cynical but rather as authentic and humane.

Nis Grøn

Young Adam

Countries of Origin:

UK
France

Language:

English

Studio/Production Companies:

Recorded Picture Company
Scottish Screen
UK Film Council
Studio Canal
Future Films
HanWay Films
Sigma Films
Sveno Media

Director:

David Mackenzie

Producer:

Jeremy Thomas

Screenwriter:

David Mackenzie

Cinematographer:

Giles Nuttgens

Art Director:

Stuart Rose

Composer:

David Byrne

Synopsis

Joe and Les spend their days manning a barge with Les's wife Ella and child in the impoverished Scotland of the early 1950s. After the two find the corpse of a young woman floating in the Clyde, speculation over the girl's identity and reasons for ending up in the river fills their time. Seemingly growing weary of all the gossip, Joe impetuously begins an affair with Ella, while flashbacks show his stormy romance with Cathie. The flashbacks also reveal Joe to be an aspiring writer caught between the creative pressures of his profession on one hand and the economic pressures of his life with Cathie on the other. These ultimately lead to the couple splitting acrimoniously only for Cathie to return later and confront Joe with the news that she is pregnant with his child. As they argue, Cathie falls into the Clyde and drowns, becoming the corpse that Joe and Les discovered earlier in the film. Les discovers the affair between Ella and Joe and leaves the barge, which is owned by Ella. Joe quickly begins to feel entrapped in his life with Ella while another man is wrongly charged with Cathie's murder.

Critique

While it was in production, Ewan McGregor dominated the news surrounding *Young Adam*. The film was a homecoming of sorts for the actor, who had not made a Scottish film since the breakthrough successes of Danny Boyle's *Shallow Grave* (1994) and *Trainspotting* (1996). McGregor himself had stolen even more headlines when he publicly attacked the UK Film Council over their failure to assist when financial difficulties threatened to derail the project. Finally, the actor was once again on the attack in the media when the Motion Picture Association of America (MPAA) threatened to give the film an NC-17 rating in the United States – a rating which would have ended the film's commercial ambitions before it was even released – over scenes of full-frontal nudity involving the actor.

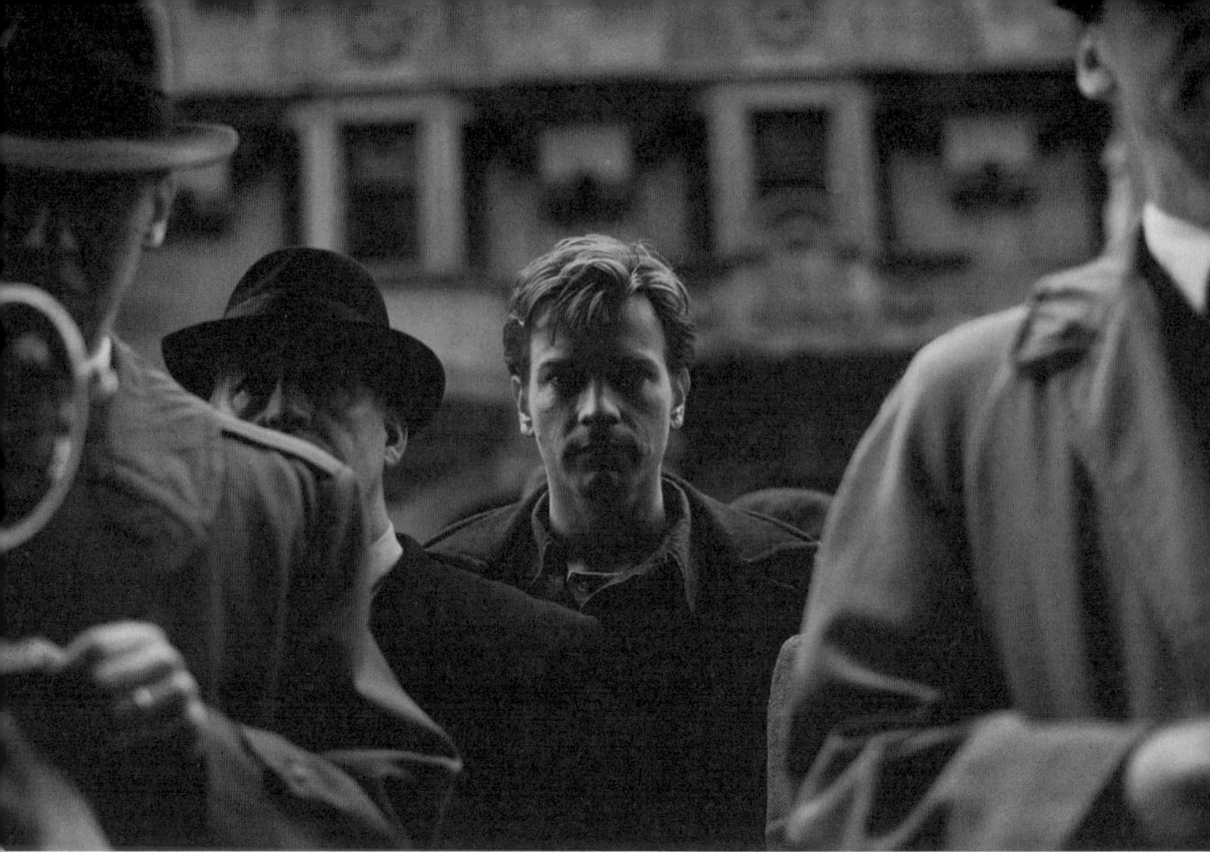

Young Adam (2002), British Film Institute Collection

Editor:

Colin Monie

Duration:

98 minutes

Genre:

Social/Psychological Drama
Social Art Cinema
Crime

Cast:

Ewan McGregor
Tilda Swinton
Emily Mortimer
Peter Mullan

Year:

2002

Filming Location:

Clydebank, West Dunbartonshire, Scotland, UK
Dumbarton, West

While all of these controversies helped to raise the film's profile, they have also overshadowed the film itself. The film was the second feature from David Mackenzie, an emerging writer/director of great promise who was now adapting a cult novel by Scottish Beat novelist Alex Trocchi and who had partnered with legendary independent producer Jeremy Thomas. Thomas would be instrumental in arranging the complex financial package for the film, assembling an elite team of actors and technicians, and guiding the marketing and promotion of the film.

This creative team helped Mackenzie to create a film that is at times mesmerizing and intriguing before losing momentum and fizzling out. Mackenzie's script utilizes unmarked flashbacks to initially misdirect the audience and to conceal the identity of the body in the river, creating no small amount of intrigue about the outcome of the investigation and the motives of Joe himself. McGregor is at his best in the film in these opening scenes, playing the brooding Joe as a conflicted loner who clearly has something to hide. Swinton is particularly memorable as the hard-edged and deeply lonely Ella while Mullan offers one of his many variations on wounded Clydeside masculinity. The cinematography and production design vividly brings to life the bleak world of post-war Scotland and infuses it with beauty and mystery. David Byrne's score

Dunbartonshire, Scotland, UK
Forth and Clyde Canal, Scotland, UK
Glasgow, Strathclyde, Scotland, UK
Grangemouth, Falkirk, West Lothian, Scotland, UK
Perth, Perth and Kinross, Scotland, UK
Renton, West Dunbartonshire, Scotland, UK
River Clyde, Glasgow, Strathclyde, Scotland, UK
Union Canal, Scotland, UK

is haunting and foreboding and works well in tandem with the film's pacing and cinematography.

As the film proceeds, however, it loses its way somewhat. Mortimer and McGregor fail to strike up the chemistry required of their volatile lovers. Without this, Joe and Cathie are not particularly compelling. The film's (in)famous custard scene – in which Joe assaults Cathie with all sorts of household items and the two make violent love – lacks the passion or transgressive intensity of cinematic precursors such as the violent sex scenes in *Last Tango in Paris* (Bernardo Bertolucci, 1972) or *9 1/2 Weeks* (Adrian Lyne, 1986). Joe's obsessive pursuit of sex following Cathie's death becomes almost comical as he makes love to Ella's indifferent sister at one point and half-heartedly falls into bed with his landlord's wife in a later scene. The film's strategy of making Joe an unlikeable anti-hero works too well and there is little in the film's final scenes for the audience to care about as Joe watches helplessly as the wrong man is sentenced to death for Cathie's murder.

Despite its flaws, *Young Adam* was able to make a splash in the international art cinema market, due largely to the casting of McGregor and the expert marketing and promotional work of Thomas, whose company HanWay Films worked as international sales agent. While the film does not ultimately succeed in realizing the existentialist vision that guided Trocchi or indeed which guides most art cinema, its moments of brilliance – such as Joe's initial flirtation with Ella at the dinner table or the nearly hypnotic scenes of Clydeside labour as Joe and Les graft out a living on the barge – are worthwhile and speak to Mackenzie's great potential as a film-maker. Mackenzie's work subsequent to *Young Adam* continues to be uneven in similar ways, and one hopes that he will eventually put together a film that lives up to the abilities seen in glimpses in *Young Adam*.

Christopher Meir

COMEDY
FANTASY AND
HORROR

Comfort and Joy (1984),
British Film Institute Collection

As David Martin-Jones argues, analyses of genres and genre films in studies of Scottish cinema have been relatively neglected compared with discussions of auteur-driven and international art films (2009: 22). Part of the reason for this, he contends, is that in arguing for a national cinema tradition and its significant films, it is natural to focus on the works of select, important film-makers and influential films that have resonated with critics and international audiences. As a result, many films that belong to 'lesser' generic categories, such as comedy, fantasy and horror, are given less attention. Certainly, some Scottish genre films have received ample attention, and respected Scottish film-makers have made important genre films. But a bias remains in favour of the art film over the genre film. Ignoring genre films, and film-makers who have made genre films, does a disservice to the study of any national cinema; as Martin-Jones indicates, these films represent Scotland's 'numerous forgotten traditions' (22).

This essay addresses three of those 'forgotten traditions' of Scottish cinema: comedy, fantasy and horror, although representative films incorporate characteristics of multiple genres. As Rick Altman (1999) has pointed out, genre mixing was common even in Hollywood's 'Golden Age'; genres have never been pure and they are constantly evolving. However, thinking in terms of the characteristic features of a particular genre can be useful; identifying the general semantics (to use Altman's term) of films in terms of generic categorization may be productive in order to engage with the themes and concerns raised in the specific films. For instance, horror films have long been acknowledged to often feature a 'return of the repressed'. For a discussion of horror in the context of Scottish cinema, then, questions such as 'What is returning that has been repressed?' are useful when thinking about broader concerns of Scottish history and culture.

Films labelled as 'genre films' also serve several industrial functions. Genre films often travel well, finding broad audiences in a way idiosyncratic or art films may not. For instance, horror film fans are more likely to seek out horror films regardless of their national origin. Steve Neale argues that genres are, in part, a set of expectations, and a major concern for audiences is that their expectations are satisfied (1980: 19). Though genre films reflect and respond to specific national, cultural and industrial contexts, generic tropes and expectations are one way for films to achieve a wider appeal.

Genre film analysis is also a way to discover and appreciate film-makers who have not received much attention to date. As Martin-Jones writes, 'popular genres can provide the necessary generic frameworks within which filmmakers can cut their teeth' (2009: 9). Many directors, such as Robert Wise in the case of *The Body Snatcher* (1945) and Danny Boyle with *Shallow Grave* (1994), worked on low-budget, genre projects in order to gain a foothold within the film-making profession and industry. Several native Scottish film-makers achieved their start by making genre films. Notable examples include Bill Forsyth, and, more recently, Colm McCarthy whose feature debut, the 2010 horror film *Outcast*, was produced after directing shorts and television episodes. Viewed in this way, genre films are an important training ground for new film-making talent within Scotland and beyond.

COMEDY

The Ealing comedies of the 1940s and 1950s provided the first of the major feature comedies set in Scotland with Scottish subjects. The two most prominent of these films are Alexander Mackendrick's *Whisky Galore!* (1949) and *The Maggie* (1954). These films used Scotland as a setting for madcap happenings portraying local Scottish residents as quirky, yet clever characters, able to fool English and American outsiders. Although portrayed stereotypically, viewers of these films are encouraged to identify with, and root for, the locals and to laugh at the obtuse authority figures. The second era of Scottish comedies is more recent, beginning with the emergence of Bill Forsyth and his directorial debut, *That Sinking Feeling* (1980). Forsyth is widely considered to be one of, if not the most important of Scottish directors, and it is worth acknowledging that his earliest and, some argue, his best works were comedic genre films that used the format to address larger social and cultural issues. This tactic proved influential as later Scottish comedies such as *American Cousins* (Don Coutts, 2003), addressed issues of Scottish identity within a gangster comedy format.

The Ealing tradition and legacy has played an important role in British film history. Adrian Garvey writes that the Ealing comedy 'has become a touchstone for British film, emerged in the mid-1940s and continued to produce films for a decade' (2012: 107). Many comedies were made at the Ealing Studios, and, as Garvey attests, their narratives were often celebratory of 'eccentric forms of rebellion or collective action' (108). This can be seen in films such as *The Lavender Hill Mob* (Charles Crichton, 1951), but perhaps most prominently in *Whisky Galore!*. The film tells the story of a town of Scottish Islanders deprived of the most essential of necessities, whisky. When a nearby stranded ship is discovered with 50,000 cases of the liquid, the locals acquire the whisky and engage in elaborate ruses to keep the authorities at bay. The film appears to engage in propagating Kailyardism. For instance, in this volume Gareth James contends that '*Whisky Galore!*'s eccentric small community can be viewed as a clear example of Kailyardism, a romantic stereotype of a primitively pre-modern Scottish working-class life that fails to connect with twentieth-century social realities'. Yet Duncan Petrie argues the film pokes fun at the English, personified by Captain Waggett (Basil Radford), as arrogant and ignorant of the local customs and languages (2000: 44). Petrie also proposes that the film parodies Griersonian-style documentary film-making during its opening sequence, as the voice-of-authority narration tells the audience that the Islanders are 'happy people with simple pleasures' (44). The film then reveals how inaccurate this ethnographic assessment of the Islanders is, further mocking the English air of superiority. The film's complex stance toward the Kailyard myth invites far more debate and critical engagement with the myth than would normally be attributed to a simple comedy.

Decades later, Scottish film-makers used comedies to address social realities such as a lack of employment and opportunity for youth, and problems in housing and education. Bill Forsyth was among the first to do so, directing several important Scottish comedies such as *That Sinking Feeling*, *Gregory's Girl* (1981), *Local Hero* (1983) and *Gregory's Two Girls* (1998). Forsyth has rightly been acclaimed as one of Scotland's most important indigenous film-makers, and he has largely done so working within the framework of the genre film, particularly the comedy. This fact should not diminish his contributions to, and influence upon, Scottish national cinema. Forsyth's feature-length debut, *That Sinking Feeling*, is a low-budget comedy about a group of unemployed young men who attempt to put their untapped abilities and ambitions to use in a heist. The film makes use of a variety of comedic strategies, including slapstick and black humour, epitomized by the line: 'There has to be more to life than suicide'. The film's sink heist and the problems executing it serve as plot devices to explore the lack of opportunity for young men in Thatcher-era Glasgow. In order to alleviate their boredom and depression, the boys attempt to steal a load of stainless steel sinks in order to sell them for quick cash. Problems abound, of course, but the boys' untapped resourcefulness is on full display. *Gregory's Girl* similarly explores the boredom of youth and the inadequacies of the educational system, as Gregory works his way through the new town of Cumbernauld (a town outside of Glasgow created specifically to alleviate the housing-shortage crisis within the city) and towards romance in the early 1980s. David Martin-Jones argues that in its sequel, *Gregory's Two Girls*, 'it is the identity of the nation, in particular as a site of resistance to the hegemony of corporate globalization, which is ultimately at question' (2009: 34). Thus, social and local issues are an important element in many Scottish comedies.

It can be seen in these very limited examples that Scottish comedies engage with social problems and questions of local and national identities. Even comedic scenes in Scottish films not commonly identified as strictly comedies often serve to address social problems. Examples such as *Trainspotting*'s (Danny Boyle, 1996) famous 'worst toilet in Scotland' scene, reveal the depths of Renton's addiction and the squalor of the Edinburgh underbelly. Scottish comedies and comedic moments in Scottish films often contain elements of social or cultural critique, and they are rarely superficial.

FANTASY

As Katherine A Fowkes writes in her analysis of the fantasy film, the term 'fantasy' is difficult to pin down. One commonality that has been generally agreed to characterize fantasy is the 'ontological rupture', or 'fundamental break with our sense of reality'. Fantasy in most films is thought of as '"fantastic" story elements that are integral to a film's story-world' (2010: 2, 5). In the context of Scottish cinema, those fantastic elements might include the sudden transformation of a character into a housefly (as in *The Acid House* [Paul McGuigan, 1998]), or a plague that robs people of their senses, one by one (*Perfect Sense* [David Mackenzie, 2011]). In fantasy films, 'fantastic phenomena are understood to really exist *within* the story world – an existence as real as the reference world from which they break' (Fowkes 2010: 5). According to Fowkes, these elements must be integral to the story – slapstick comedy's unlikely circumstances or singular moments of weirdness do not make a fantasy film. Though fantasy may contain scary moments, its overarching goal is not to frighten, as it is the horror film's (6).

In Scottish films, fantasy and fantastic elements often work to defamiliarize the familiar in order to make larger social and philosophical arguments. The Russian Formalist Viktor Shklovsky defined the concept of defamiliarization as a way to breathe new life into things that have become mundane or cliché. This can be accomplished by asking 'what if?' and looking at things from a new point of view. He wrote in his essay 'Art as Technique' that 'the purpose of art is to impart the sensation of things as they are perceived and not as they are known' (1965 [1917]: 12). This might be accomplished by an ontological rupture, forcing the reader or viewer, for example, to confront the strangeness and cruelty of a practice such as corporal punishment by adopting the point of view of a whipped horse, as Shklovsky noted from Tolstoy's story *Shame*. *The Acid House* adapts three Irvine Welsh short stories, each of which contain elements of fantasy. In the first story, 'The Granton Star Cause', Boab (Stephen McCole) has a terrible day in which he loses his job, his girlfriend, and his parents kick him out of the house. As a 'reward' for his self-pity, God (Maurice Roeves) transforms him into a housefly in order to change his perspective. In this form, he is able to take some measure of revenge against those who have wronged him and to look at the world in a new way. This fantastic transformation enables the defamiliarization of everyday institutions such as family, work and romantic relationships, revealing the unexpected and unseen aspects of those institutions, such as Boab's parents' desire to engage in sadomasochistic sexual practices.

Perfect Sense also defamiliarizes through its use of a fictional, global plague that robs humans of their senses. As the characters gradually lose their senses, questions such as 'what does it mean to be human?' and 'how do society and its institutions react under the extreme pressure of imminent collapse?' are explored. Though reviewers have acknowledged that the plague itself is fairly ridiculous, it is its fantastic nature that allows for such extreme scenarios and deep questions to be brought to the foreground.

The animated film, *The Illusionist* (Sylvain Chomet, 2010), explores questions of technological progress, belief and magic. It tells the story of a Parisian magician, circa 1959, whose act is no longer able to entertain audiences more enthralled with rock and roll and television. Travelling to the Island of Iona, he finds an inn where the patrons still appreciate his talents and he befriends a young woman, Alice, who believes he possesses real magical powers. They develop a deep friendship, and the magician attempts to maintain the illusion that he does indeed possess genuine magical abilities. However, he comes to realize that Alice is growing up, and she will soon no longer need or want him and his tricks. The role of childhood and magic amidst a changing social milieu drives this story of how innocence gives way to experience, and the film contemplates what might be lost in a world in which, as the magician later writes to Alice, 'Magicians do not exist'.

Scottish fantasy cinema engages with myth (as has been written about elsewhere in this volume), the fantastic, and it defamiliarizes the everyday in order to make broader social and cultural commentaries.

HORROR

Scottish horror films may be divided broadly into two groups. The first group includes films that primarily take place in cities, most notably Edinburgh and Glasgow. Examples of such films include the numerous incarnations and derivatives of the bodysnatching Burke and Hare. The second group of films is set in the Highlands and the Islands, where the wild landscape and strange customs dominate. Horror films with settings in the rural Highlands and Islands include *The Wicker Man* (Robin Hardy, 1973), *Dog Soldiers* (Neil Marshall, 2002) and *Wild Country* (Craig Strachan, 2006). Scholars have argued that horror films often reflect a society's fears and anxieties, and in this reflection one may see a nation's collective nightmares. For several Scottish horror films, these nightmares take the forms of the dark side of urban life, and the return of repressed peoples and cultures in remote locations.

The city as a site for horror films, and in particular the body snatching horror films analysed in this volume, reflects some of the anxieties created by the rapid increase in urbanization in Scotland during and after the Industrial Revolution. As Duncan Petrie writes, horror films set in the city, particularly Edinburgh, contemplate 'the city as dualistic site of light and dark, respectability and criminality, science and superstition' (2000: 79). In the modern urban environment, the possibility of human monsters mingling amongst a dense population of strangers is very real. The Burke and Hare films based on the real-life murderers present viewers with the unsettling horrors of urban violence. Among films portraying the resurrection men or variations of their story are the aforementioned *The Body Snatcher*, *The Flesh and the Fiends* (John Gilling, 1960), *The Doctor and the Devils* (Freddie Francis, 1985), *Burke and Hare* (Vernon Sewell, 1972) and *Burke and Hare* (John Landis, 2010). Petrie has further argued that these films offer a counterpoint to representations of Edinburgh as 'a bourgeois city of art, culture and beautiful architecture' as seen in films such as *Happy Go Lovely* (Bruce Humberstone, 1951) (75). The horror of the Burke and Hare films lies as much in the anonymity and isolation one might feel in a city (in the films the victims are often stalked alone and at night) that could lead to potential victimhood, as the acts of murder themselves.

The other major settings for Scottish horror films are the Highlands and the Islands. In these films, it can be argued that there is a return of repressed, ancient religions and cultures that have been almost entirely snuffed out by modernity. Yet, as Freud writes in his examination of the uncanny, that which is repressed is only buried, not destroyed, and it inevitably returns. In some Scottish horror films, the return of the repressed takes the form of Islanders or Highlanders with 'strange' customs that are potentially dangerous or deadly to outsiders, and monsters, such as werewolves, who lurk in remote regions.

The Highlands and Islands have long been part of a 'British myth of Scotland as wilderness (the myth of Tartanry), that emerged after the Highland clearances' (Martin-Jones 2009: 90). In *The Wicker Man*, a devoutly Christian policeman investigates the case of a missing girl on the remote, fictional Scottish Island of Summerisle, and discovers a people who believe in an ancient pagan religion. From his point of view, their customs are offensive and impious. His attempts to impose what he feels is good Christian law and order upon the residents of Summerisle reveal his ignorance and prove to be fatal. The inherent righteousness and authority of the Mainland/Christian figure is questioned (and thus the entire Mainland/Christian establishment) by an unexpected encounter with customs and a religion long thought extinct because of the influences of Christian evangelism and the forces of modernization, industrialization and colonization.

In *Wild Country*, the Highlands are the site where the main character, Kelly Ann (Samantha Shields), a teenager who has been forced to give her baby up for adoption, is able to, as Martin-Jones writes, connect with 'the myth of wild, cannibalistic Scotland in order to break free of religious doctrine and be part of a family' (2009: 132). However, in this film, the family she becomes a part of is a werewolf clan. Werewolves in literature and film have been thought to represent the primal (or the fear of the primal) within all people, especially those coming from bourgeois society. In Scottish horror films, the Highlands are the location for that primal nature to (re)emerge. In *Wild Country*, fantastic creatures such as werewolves exist side by side with the legend of Sawney Bean and his clan of cannibals. Martin-Jones contends that Kelly Ann's rejection of Father Steve's (Peter Capaldi) Christian teachings also indicate a 'wilder expression of youthful sexual freedom' (132). Kelly Ann's position as the protagonist of the film invites viewers to sympathize with her rejection of organized religion and modern society, and embrace of a more primal (and supernatural) existence in the wilderness of the Highlands with the werewolf clan.

In sum, Scottish horror films depict the Highlands and Islands as remote, wild sites where Celtic and pagan religions and customs clash with modern British ones. They are also places where there may be a primal return to nature, which questions the mainstream social structures, customs and assumptions.

Zach Finch

References

Altman, Rick (1999) *Film/Genre*, London: BFI.

Fowkes, Katherine A (2010) *The Fantasy Film*, Chichester,West Sussex: Wiley-Blackwell.

Freud, Sigmund (2003 [1919]) *The Uncanny* (trans. D McClintock), London: Penguin.

Garvey, Adrian (2012) 'Comedy', in E Bell and N Mitchell (eds), *Directory of World Cinema: Britain*, Bristol: Intellect, pp. 106–09.

Martin-Jones, David (2009) *Scotland: Global Cinema – Genres, Modes and Identities*, Edinburgh: EUP.

Neale, Steve (1980) *Genre*, London: BFI.

Petrie, Duncan (2000) *Screening Scotland*, London: BFI.

Shklovsky, Viktor (1965 [1917]) 'Art as Technique', in Lee T Lemon and Marion J Reis (eds and trans.), *Russian Formalist Criticism: Four Essays*, Lincoln: University of Nebraska, pp. 3–25.

The Acid House

Country of Origin:
UK
Language:
English
Studio/Production Companies:
Film4
Zeitgeist Films
Director:
Paul McGuigan
Producers:
David Muir
Alex Usborne
Screenwriter:
Irvine Welsh
Cinematographer:
Alasdair Walker
Art Directors:
Rohan Banyard
Jean Kerr
Composer:
Dan Mudford
Editor:
Andrew Hulme
Duration:
111 minutes
Genre:
Fantasy
Cast:
Stephen McCole
Maurice Roeves
Garry Sweeney
Simon Weir
Jenny McCrindle
Irvine Welsh
Alex Howden
Ann Louise Ross
Kevin McKidd
Michelle Gomez
Gary McCormack
Alison Peebles
Ewen Bremner
Martin Clune
Jemma Redgrave

Synopsis

The Acid House consists of three segments. In 'The Granton Star Cause', unlucky Boab gets kicked out of his football club, dumped by his girlfriend, kicked out of his house by his parents, fired from his job and arrested for defacing a phone booth. While drowning his sorrows at a pub, he is approached by God, who scolds him for being a pushover. God transforms Boab into a fly. Boab takes advantage of his new body by putting feces into the food of his ex-girlfriend and her new lover and by placing rat poison into his boss's sandwich. While spying on his parents as they have sex, his mom smashes him with a rolled up paper, thus killing him. In 'A Soft Touch', nice-guy Johnny is approached by his sullen ex-wife Catriona Doyle, prompting him to recall the end of their relationship. Although warned by his mother and friends that the Doyles were a 'bad sort', the two were married and had a child together. However, soon after their daughter arrives, Catriona begins ignoring Johnny, drinking excessively and prostituting herself behind his back. Things boil over when neighbour Larry moves in and begins an aggressive affair with Catriona, prompting several confrontations and Johnny's eventual flight. The segment comes full circle as Catriona discovers Larry's philandering and loss of interest in her, at which point she seeks out Johnny. Johnny and Catriona tentatively reconcile over a quiet drink. In 'The Acid House', raver Coco tries to appease his anxieties over his engagement to Kirsty by taking a hit of acid. Meanwhile, pregnant Jemma and her husband Rory are picked up by an ambulance as she goes into labour. A bolt of lightning strikes the ambulance at the moment Jemma gives birth, prompting nearby Coco (who is tripping) to switch bodies with their newborn baby. Coco's body goes into a kind of vegetative state, while his developed mind takes the place of the baby's. Kirsty slowly nurses Coco's adult body back to health, while Coco-as-baby reveals his intelligence to his new mother Jemma. The baby convinces Jemma to bring them to a downtown pub, which happens to be where Kirsty and Coco's body are sitting. Coco's mind and body are once again united.

Critique

The Acid House accentuates the overtly surreal aspects of Irvine Welsh's writing. Although only adapting three of the stories from his short story collection, the selections showcase several congruences that give the movie some degree of cohesion. Each of the segments features an emasculated male protagonist who is forced out of his comfortable, yet ultimately doomed, circumstances. Each contrasts their drab urban settings with the possibly liberating potential of some fantastic alternative (for Boab, the possibility of flight; for Coco, the removal of mind from body; and, less dramatically, Johnny's realization that he can remove himself from Larry's and Catriona's self-destructive orbit, as he temporarily turns his eyes towards one of his co-workers). Finally, each segment walks a fine line, at once suggesting that the events depicted belong to the quotidian world while at the same time making clear that these are exceptional days-in-the-life.

Arlene Cockburn
Jane Stabler

Year:

1998

Filming Locations:

Edinburgh and Glasgow, Scotland, UK

The film clearly owes a stylistic debt to Danny Boyle's *Trainspotting* (1996), whose combination of drugs, electronica and swagger proved an international smash. Paul McGuigan has since established himself as a successful director in his own right, but *The Acid House* sometimes seems like the work of a man who was learning and inventing on the hoof. In 'The Granton Star Cause', McGuigan chooses lots of handheld set-ups (the industry shortcut toward ersatz realism), cuts action to music and suggests Boab's tenuous psychological state through filters and lighting effects. To his credit, McGuigan evokes a different tenor for 'A Soft Touch', which eschews any of the pyrotechnics of the first segment, instead playing out like an extended riff on the now ubiquitous social realist style pioneered by Ken Loach: naturalistic lighting, extensive location work in gritty urban environments and dialogue delivered with all the inarticulate flaws that are true to life. In each segment, Welsh's dialogue is maintained where appropriate (he adapted his own screenplay), but aspects of each scenario are extended as needed. For example, Johnny's torment at Larry and Catriona's spontaneous affair is drawn out, and his decision to seek his mother's advice more pronounced than in Welsh's story.

The primary set piece is the titular segment, the most outwardly fantastic and in some senses the most hit-or-miss of the three. It is clearly a chance for Ewen Bremner to once again resume his role from *Trainspotting* as the ultimate Edinburgh thrill seeker. 'The Acid House' foregrounds issues of class in a more explicit way than the other two segments, the actions of which take place in wholly working-class worlds. Here, Jemma and Rory immediately affect posh credentials, and we perceive their clean and orderly apartment visually at odds with the dark, derelict and littered playground where Coco does his acid trip. The mind/body switch is a chance not only to explore the type of altered states that appeal to a character like Coco, but also an attempt at telling a fish-out-of-water story. Once Coco begins to speak to Jemma through the baby's body, he questions her locution, her choice of food, her relationship with her husband and her sense of fun. Jemma, in turn, questions Coco's coarseness (not to mention the incredible fact that he thinks and speaks like a grown man, albeit a slightly childish one). McGuigan and his collaborators chose to make an animatronic baby, meaning that the lip movements synch reasonably well to Ewen Bremner's voice, yet ensuring that viewers are plunged deep into the uncanny. Appearing less a real child and more as an homage to the monstrous brood in Larry Cohen's *It's Alive* (1973), this creepy baby forecloses on the possibility of any viewer sympathy.

Taken together, the segments in the film feel like an extended meditation on masculinity. In each case, the male protagonists fail to achieve financial, personal or moral successes, and are instead belittled by their peers, punished for fighting back or doomed to stay in their cycles of self-resentment. McGuigan's film is adventuresome, but not especially hopeful or essential.

Kevin M Flanagan

Reference

Welsh, Irvine (1995) *The Acid House*, New York: Norton.

American Cousins

Country of Origin:

UK

Language:

English

Studio/Production Companies:

Scottish Screen
Little Wing Films
Bard Entertainments

Director:

Don Coutts

Producer:

Margaret Matheson

Screenwriter:

Sergio Casci

Cinematographer:

Jerry Kelly

Art Director:

Frances Connell

Composer:

Donald Shaw

Editor:

Lindy Cameron

Duration:

89 minutes

Genre:

Comedy
Gangster

Cast:

Gerald Lepkowski
Danny Nucci
Shirley Henderson
Dan Hedaya
Russell Hunter

Year:

2003

Synopsis

Roberto's job is not a glamorous one. As manager of the Cafe del Rio, a family run fish-and-chip shop in Glasgow, the only sources of excitement in his life are stamp collecting and Alice, a pretty employee that he harbours untold feelings for. Fate, however, is sending him a surprise – two distant cousins that he has never met before. New Jersey gangsters by trade, Gino and Settimo come to Scotland seeking refuge after a deal in Eastern Europe takes a turn for the worst. With Gino quickly taking a shine to Alice, and the shop soon coming under attack from mobsters and loan sharks alike, Roberto comes to realize that if he wants to improve his life, he will have to take a stand.

Critique

The principal focus of interest in this film is the relationship, and especially the contrast, between Roberto and Gino.There is no real reason why cousins Roberto and Gino should be living such disparate lives. Each of them is a young, good looking, third-generation Italian immigrant from the same family – the only thing separating their backgrounds is a matter of location, with Roberto having been raised in Glasgow and Gino in New Jersey. Yet, somehow, the pair seem worlds apart. Roberto is tied to his work, introverted and unable to express himself. Gino, on the other hand, is sharply dressed, confident and not afraid to say what he thinks. Probably the easiest way to separate the two would be to test their response to one simple, and perhaps rather Scottish, enquiry: 'fish and chips, or ice cream?' Asked this question at Glasgow Airport's immigration control as a way of assessing his career plans in the country, Italian American Gino immediately takes offence: 'it's mostly organized crime where I come from', he answers bluntly. Yet when he repeats the question to Roberto as they meet for the first time, his Scots Italian cousin simply smiles, proud that he can do both.

This distinction between the relative simplicity of Roberto's life and the extravagant nature of Gino's is implied from the outset. With an introductory montage that cuts between shots of two rooms – one a white background dotted with thick red liquid, the other filmed with an unworldly green tint – Roberto is introduced midway through the making of a strawberry sundae, whilst Gino stands in a murky warehouse where several men will soon be dead. As Roberto will later relate, the whole story stems from a coin toss made by their grandfathers when they still lived in Italy; one of them would move to Scotland, the other to America. 'And my grandfather won', Gino reflects, 'I could have ended up in Glasgow'. Yet, as Roberto wryly replies, Gino's adventurousness has only seen him 'end up' in Glasgow anyway, the perceived dreariness of his cousin's life

Filming Location:

Glasgow, Strathclyde, Scotland, UK

providing much needed shelter from the danger of his own.

By placing emphasis on these opposing traits – Roberto's apparent placidity and Gino's surface-level bravado – the film creates an intriguing dichotomy within the men's shared identity as Italian immigrants. Gino's country of birth may often be described as the world's greatest melting pot, but with America remaining a relatively young nation, cultural background can mean everything. Indeed, though US population figures may be vast, the very structure of terms such as 'Italian American' suggest that many inhabitants would identify with their heritage first and their citizenship second. For Gino, then, Italian identity is a badge that should be worn with pride – and what line of work values familial ties more so than that of the mob? Roberto's answer would be obvious: the restaurant business. His life may be quieter than Gino's, but every shift Roberto works at Cafe del Rio is an acknowledgement of his roots. Fish and chips may seem a quintessentially British notion, but for Roberto, there is pride in the knowledge that the Italians do it best.

Yet where Gino's Italian American identity establishes his ancestry with a sense of priority, for the Scots Italian Roberto heritage is somewhat suppressed by assimilation. Choosing to identify outwardly as Scottish, Roberto's passion for his Italian lineage is channelled entirely into his work, allowing the tasks of frying fish and preparing ice cream to take on a sense of honour few would understand. The result is that whilst Gino wields his exoticism with confidence, Roberto's demeanour is closer to the sort of mild-mannered character Hugh Grant would play in a Richard Curtis film, the strengths of his heritage struggling to be seen anywhere outside of the kitchen. 'Remember who you are', his grandfather, Nonno, tells him, 'our family, from a tough place – a place where a man could not survive unless he had a lot of toughness inside him'. But Roberto needs a catalyst. With his cousin's arrival eventually threatening not only his pride, but also his livelihood, the film's climax sees him dealing with gun-toting hit men like he has been doing it all his life. Gino, on the other hand, is terrible at frying fish.

Patrick Harley

The Anatomist

Country of Origin:

UK

Language:

English

Studio/Production Companies:

Associated Rediffusion Television
Dola Films
Towers of London Productions

Synopsis

Walter, in love with Mary Belle, puts his career and marriage plans on hold in order to continue his 'important' work assisting the famed Dr Knox, an Edinburgh anatomist whose knowledge of the human body has inaugurated unprecedented medical breakthroughs. However, their work demands cadavers for experiments and visual lessons. With a dwindling supply of available bodies, failed grave robbers Burke and Hare are approached to procure a fresh corpse. They drunkenly murder Mary Peterson, niece to one of Knox's assistants, and continue to kill over

Director:

Dennis Vance

Producers:

Dennis Vance
Harry Alan Towers (billed as Vincent Johnston)

Screenwriter:

Denis Webb (from the play by James Bridie)

Art Director:

Duncan Sutherland

Editor:

Ben Hipkins

Duration:

82 minutes

Genre:

Horror

Cast:

Alastair Sim
George Cole
Diarmuird Kelly
Michael Ripper
Jill Bennett
Margaret Gordon
Adrienne Corri

Year:

1956 (TV broadcast)
1961 (Theatrical release)

Filming Locations:

National Studios, Elstree, Hertfordshire, England, UK

the next six months. Once found out, Burke is hanged, Hare exiled and the angry Edinburgh citizenry demands that Knox be brought to justice. He is pursued, but protected by his loyal medical students. Walter and Mary Belle reconcile, and medical lectures are held in the Bishop residence to an appreciative audience.

Critique

Although most tellings of the crimes, culture and trial of the Burke and Hare murders focus on the personalities of those two men, this ITV play mainly dramatizes the complicity of the rich and respected men who needed the bodies in the first place. *The Anatomist* is all about the cult of personality around Dr Robert Knox, an affable but occasionally sinister genius. Alastair Sim's performance enhances this man's eccentricities (an unhappily married man, he pursues Amelia and suggestively plays flute accompaniment to her piano), yet leaves an undercurrent of rage. The film eventually exonerates Knox – his students and the 'respectable' members of Edinburgh society side with him – but not without showing his capacity for violence. Knox contrasts with Walter, a contentious coward who is physically assaulted by Knox, and who agonizes over their crimes for months before Knox even acknowledges them. The film's surprisingly upbeat ending (a dispersed crowd and a return to Knox's teaching) runs counter to the historical Knox's eventual path: he was eventually shunned by Edinburgh and, after the death of his wife, worked in London in relative obscurity.

Much of the film revolves around the romantic relationships that orbit the death of Mary Peterson. Walter meets her after quarreling with Mary Belle and Dr Knox. Though drunk when they meet, he later recognizes her corpse as it is delivered by Burke and Hare. The last act of the film is framed around the various characters reconciling after Burke's execution. The facile happiness engendered by the Walter/Mary Belle reconciliation and Knox's temporary salvation suggests the popular stage's compulsion for happy endings.

Both Diarmuird Kelly and Michael Ripper shine, and their relatively restricted screen time is regrettable. In this telling of their crimes, Burke and Hare are almost officially sanctioned by the medical establishment. The fact that *The Anatomist* does not show their turn to murder as an act of desperation and poverty suggests the morally bankrupt nature of these institutions. Since the killing of Mary Peterson happens off-camera (as does the implicit violence of the bloodthirsty mob), the nuances of the characterizations have to 'sell' the gruesome outcomes. In their relatively short sequences, Kelly and Ripper project the oddball grotesqueries necessary to frighten viewers.

While this now reads as an old-fashioned stage-to-screen adaptation of a middling play, the presence of Jill Bennett and Adrienne Corri makes it a transitional document. Both were to play important roles in the more contentious, experimental and physically confrontational films of the next decade. This was also one of the first projects overseen by prolific producer Harry Alan Towers, who was responsible for over a hundred film and TV works over five decades.

Kevin M Flanagan

Reference
Knight, Alanna (2007) *Burke & Hare*, Kew, Surrey, UK: National Archives Publishing.

The Body Snatcher

Robert Louis Stevenson's The Body Snatcher

Country of Origin:
USA
Language:
English
Studio/Production Company:
RKO Radio Pictures
Director:
Robert Wise
Producers:
Val Lewton
Jack J Gross
Screenwriters:
Val Lewton (as Carlos Keith)
Philip MacDonald
Cinematographer:
Robert DeGrasse
Art Directors:
Albert S D'Agostino
Walter E. Keller
Composer:
Roy Webb
Editor:
JR Wittredge
Genre:
Horror
Duration:
77 minutes
Cast:
Henry Daniell
Boris Karloff
Bela Lugosi
Edith Atwater
Russell Wade

Synopsis

Based on Robert Louis Stevenson's 1884 short story of the same title, the 1945 film is set in Edinburgh, circa 1831. Donald Fettes is the prize medical student of the brilliant surgeon and anatomist, Dr Wolfe 'Toddy' MacFarlane. Fettes attempts to convince his reluctant mentor to help a young girl who has lost the use of her legs. MacFarlane makes it clear that he is more interested in anatomical science than in helping the ill and afflicted. However, his foremost passions for teaching and research demand more cadavers than the police are legally able to provide. Enter the villainous cabman, John Gray, who moonlights as a grave robber. Though MacFarlane eventually agrees to perform the surgery and it proves to be a success, his research and teaching demand more and more bodies. MacFarlane thus becomes dependent upon Gray's willingness to commit murder in addition to grave robbing. Meanwhile, Fettes learns that his teacher was once the top pupil of Dr Knox, the employer of the infamous grave robbers and murderers, Burke and Hare. In true Gothic fashion, the relationship between Knox and Burke and Hare returns in the form of MacFarlane's arrangement with John Gray. Determined to break this cycle and be rid of Gray, MacFarlane murders the resurrection man, whose blackmailing and shared past with Dr Knox make him a dangerous enemy. The death of Gray, though, does not end the horror for MacFarlane's conscience, as he hears Gray in his mind, insisting that MacFarlane will 'Never get rid of me!'

Critique

The Body Snatcher was the eighth and final team-up of Karloff and Lugosi, and while those actors had established themselves as the premier horror stars of the era, Robert Wise's career as a director was just beginning. Audiences know Wise best for his later work and his success as the director of the science fiction film *The Day the Earth Stood Still* (1951), and the musicals *West Side Story* (1961) and *The Sound of Music* (1965). However, Wise made a few notable horror films, including his directorial debut for producer Val Lewton and RKO, 1944's *The Curse of the Cat People*, and, later, *The Haunting* (1963). As Duncan Petrie points out, *The Body Snatcher* was one of a series of 'atmospheric low-budget horror films' produced by RKO in the 1940s (2000: 76). Other notable entries in this cycle of RKO horror films are Jacques Tourneur's *Cat People* (1942), *I Walked with a Zombie* (1943) and *Night of the Demon* (1958). *The Body Snatcher* proved to be a solid contribution to the RKO horror corpus of that era. It was well-received at the time of its release, and it remains a favourite among classical horror film aficionados.

The film debuted in New York City on 25 May 1945, just over two

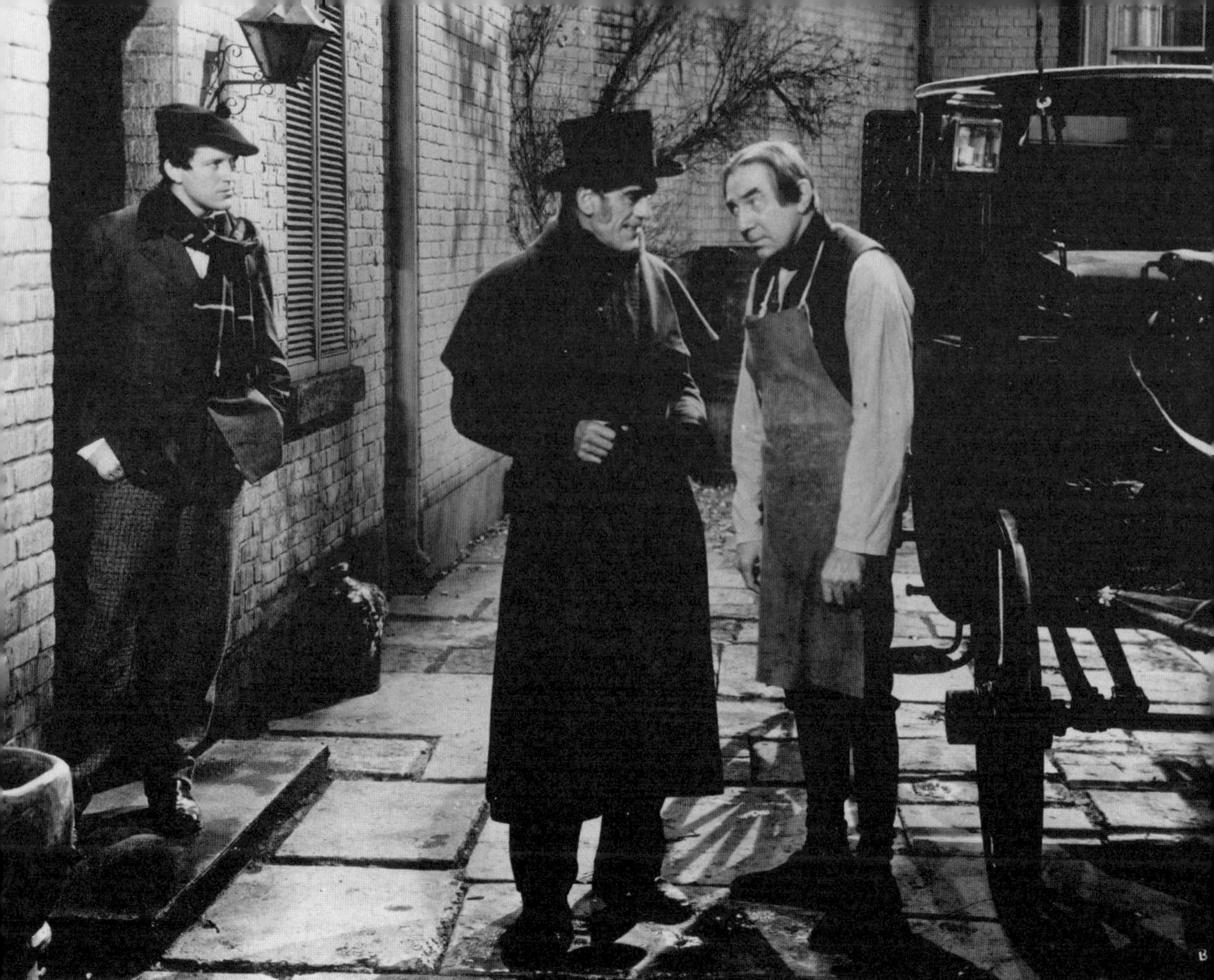

The Body Snatcher (1945), British Film Institute Collection

Year:

1945

Filming Locations:

RKO Ranch, San Fernando Valley, Los Angeles, California, USA
RKO Studios, Hollywood, Los Angeles, California, USA

weeks after its Hollywood premiere. Film critic Bosley Crowther wrote in the next day's *New York Times* that the film 'has enough suspense and atmospheric terror to make it one of the better of its genre', and he went on to praise Karloff's performance, calling it played with 'ghoulish delight' (1945). According to Steve Haberman on the DVD commentary track, the *Hollywood Reporter* praised the performances of Karloff and Henry Daniell, and called the film 'a veritable orgy of killing and grave robbing' (2005). The film has been recently re-released on DVD, along with many other Val Lewton and RKO horror films. Among these releases is a 2005, five-disc, nine-film collection from Turner Home Entertainment.

Robert Louis Stevenson described 'The Body Snatcher' in a letter to the editor of the publication in which it appeared, *The Pall Mall Gazette*, as 'blood-curdling enough – and ugly enough – to chill the blood of a grenadier' (1884). The 1945 film version is different in many respects, but on the whole it remains true to the spirit, and especially the atmosphere, of Stevenson's tale. Among the film's departures from the short story is the film's chronological narration. Most of the short story is told in a framed flashback by an unnamed narrator who has pieced together the story of Fettes and MacFarlane, both of whom were students of Dr Knox. The film version features no flashback, and Fettes is MacFarlane's pupil, rather than his peer. A number of characters were created or significantly altered in the film version, as well. Joseph (Bela Lugosi), Meg (Edith Atwater), Mrs Marsh (Rita Corday), Georgina Marsh (Sharyn Moffett) and the Street Singer (Donna Lee) were created for the film. Steve Haberman also points out that John Gray was expanded specifically for Boris Karloff to share a lead billing in the film (2005). Karloff's version of Gray contains elements of the short story's Fettes, Burke and Hare, and he is the main antagonist of the film rather than MacFarlane, who is the main antagonist of the short story. The endings differ significantly, too. In the short story, both Fettes and MacFarlane perceive the body that they have snatched is the murdered Gray, rather than the woman whom they dug from the fresh grave. Both flee in terror and are haunted by their grave robbing guilt. In the film, the blame is firmly on MacFarlane as the murderer of Gray. The ghostly appearance of Gray's body is explicitly shown to be a product of MacFarlane's conscience, leading to his death in the climactic carriage crash. The short story ends somewhat more ambiguously, but both Fettes and MacFarlane survive to be haunted by Gray in their dreams.

Though there are many differences between the two, the film takes on the short story's themes of guilt and the costs of scientific progress, though the film takes a clearer stance on these issues by contending in its final, on-screen quote by Hippocrates that the horrors of body snatching are collateral damage in the process of knowledge creation. The film is especially faithful to the atmosphere of the short story, adding to the visual iconography of Edinburgh as a fitting setting for dark and macabre tales. In particular, a few key scenes are magnificently shot and executed. Gray's murder of the street singer as she walks into the foggy darkness; Gray's 'Burke-ing' of Joseph in a dingy, candlelit room; and the final, carriage crash sequence are all filled with shadows and clever sound design. The singer's strangled voice, and Gray's repeated 'Never get rid of me!' in the mind of MacFarlane convey the terror of these scenes through sound and vocal performance. Because of its expressive *mise-en-scéne* and striking acting performances, the film stands as a classic of the RKO horror cycle and one of the best entries among the many films inspired by the Burke and Hare tale.

Zach Finch

References

Crowther, Bosley (1945) 'The Body Snatcher', http://www.nytimes.com/movie/review. Accessed 1 September 2013.

Haberman, Steve (2005) Audio commentary, in Robert Wise, dir. (1945), *The Body Snatcher* [DVD], Atlanta, GA:Turner Home Entertainment.

Petrie, Duncan (2000) *Screening Scotland*, London: BFI.
Stevenson, Robert Louis (1884) 'The Body Snatcher', http://gaslight.mtroyal.ca/body.htm. Accessed 30 September 2013.

Burke and Hare aka Horrors of Burke and Hare aka The Bodysnatchers

Country of Origin:
UK

Language:
English

Studio/Production Companies:
Armitage
Kenneth Shipman Productions

Director:
Vernon Sewell

Producer:
Guido Coen

Screenwriter:
Ernle Bradford

Cinematographer:
Desmond Dickinson

Art Director:
Scott MacGregor

Composer:
Roger Webb

Editor:
John Colville

Duration:
91 minutes

Genre:
Horror

Cast:
Derren Nesbitt
Glynn Edwards
Harry Andrews
Yootha Joyce

Synopsis

William Burke and Tom Hare live in a decrepit lodging house with their wives. Despite trying their hands at grave robbery, Burke principally helps the group survive thanks to piecework and shoe mending. When one of their lodgers falls ill, Hare persuades Burke to help him sell the cadaver to one of the anatomists in Surgeon's Square, the seat of Edinburgh's medical community. They somewhat ineptly bring the body to the eminent Dr Knox, who urges them to bring more specimens. Meanwhile, recent student arrival James, a quiet and timid youth pursuing a medical degree, gets introduced to the vices of the city. His cohort brings him to Madame Thompson's brothel, a lavish establishment where he meets, and falls in love with Marie. Burke and Hare resort to murder in order to supply Knox with bodies, while Marie and James start a steady courtship (despite her continued employment as a prostitute). Madame Thompson's brothel is destroyed in a fire, causing a downtrodden Janet and Marie to seek lodgings elsewhere. Burke, who recently murdered local figure Daft Jamie in a night of drunken revelry, plies the two women with drink and offers to let them stay at his lodgings in Westport. After an erotic frolic, both women are killed, and their corpses sold to Knox. James' recognition of Marie's body during an anatomy lesson, coupled with Jamie's disappearance, causes James (and the authorities) to track Burke and Hare to their home, where they are hosting a wild party, complete with their most recent victim stuffed in the cupboard. The two are discovered, thus ending their exploits and the career of Dr Knox.

Critique

Veteran director Vernon Sewell (this was his final film, after a long career dating back to the early sound era) helms the most uneven telling of the Burke and Hare story, one whose excesses are clearly guided by the increasingly lackadaisical standards of the British Board of Film Censors. While neither as violent nor as sinister as *The Flesh and the Fiends* (John Gilling, 1960), this *Burke and Hare* awkwardly merges a mostly historically faithful version of the sordid Burke and Hare murders with extensive nods to the nascent sex farce genre. Clearly inspired by the successful template of *Tom Jones* (Tony Richardson, 1963), this film tempers its disparate tendencies – its equal investments in the traditions of historical costume drama and low comedy – with some contemporary rock music and attitudes that have more in common with a 1960s Soho than with early-nineteenth-century Edinburgh. The film's theme song, written by Norman Newell and performed by The Scaffold, plays over the opening credits, which are accompanied by sketches that are meant to invoke the movie's historical milieu. This uneasy tension between

Dee Shenderey
Francoise Pascal
Yutte Stensgaard
Madame Thompson
Daft Jamie
James Arbuthnot

Year:

1972

Filming Location:

Twickenham Film Studios, St Margarets, Twickenham, Middlesex, England, UK

old and new is sustained throughout the film. Sewell's static, boxy staging and largely studio-bound interiors feel old hat as they show the kinky sex fantasies of the clients of Madame Thompson's bawdy house. The saturated colours certainly enliven the proceedings and highlight the period costumes, although in retrospect it all feels like a synthetic confection that panders to its contemporary audiences.

This clash of old and new suggests a further tonal contrast between the inflexible, crusading morality of Dr Knox and the opportunistic excesses of Burke and Hare. Although both are complicit with one another, Knox steadfastly ties his willingness to breach ethical grey areas to his faith in scientific research, while Burke and Hare go 'off the rails' to such a vast degree that they would surely have been incarcerated for something else had they not been discovered as murderers.

This telling of these famous crimes gives the least screen time to Knox, who is reduced to a few brief defences of his work and a sex joke or two. Harry Andrews, who specializes in eccentric authority figures, and played them to perfection in *Entertaining Mr. Sloane* (Douglas Hickox, 1970) and *The Ruling Class* (Peter Medak, 1972) is given very little to do, and therefore hardly matches the gravitas of Peter Cushing's Knox from *The Flesh and the Fiends* nor the inspired (yet surprisingly tolerated) madness of Alastair Sim from *The Anatomist* (Dennis Vance, 1956/1961). William Burke begins with some scruples, but is quickly goaded into a life of crime by Hare. Derren Nesbitt's take on Burke is generally clumsy, making his eventual *ménage à trois* all the more unbelievable. Glynn Edwards's Hare (here given the first name Tom instead of William) is more monstrous, emerging as the film's only sustained antagonist. Sadly, the film gives women an extremely limited set of roles, either as prostitutes or, in the case of Ms Burke and Ms Hare, as hags.

Kevin M Flanagan

Burke and Hare

Country of Origin:

UK

Language:

English

Studio/Production Companies:

Ealing Studios
Fragile Films

Director:

John Landis

Screenwriters:

Piers Ashworth
Nick Moorcroft

Synopsis

Hucksters William Burke and William Hare seemingly move from one business idea to the next. When one of Hare's elderly lodgers suddenly dies, the two find that they can turn a profit selling corpses to Dr Knox, an esteemed surgeon with an insatiable appetite for dissection. Thanks to a recent crackdown on grave robbery by Edinburgh militia leader Tom McLintock, Burke and Hare set their sights on 'helping along' the poor, elderly and nearly dead, a task they undertake both with zeal (one victim is scared to death, another driven off a cliff) and relative ease (Hare and his wife, Lucky, own a boarding house, which attracts some targets). With his newfound wealth, Burke meets and falls in love with the reformed prostitute Ginny, an aspiring thespian who needs backing for an all female production of Macbeth. Meanwhile, local criminals McTavish and Fergus convince Burke and Hare to give them a cut of their now immensely profitable business. A royal medical contest prompts an

Cinematographer:
John Mathieson
Art Directors:
Bill Crutcher
Nick Dent
Composer:
Joby Talbot
Editor:
Mark Everson
Duration:
91 minutes
Genre:
Horror
Cast:
Simon Pegg
Andy Serkis
Tom Wilkinson
Isla Fisher
Tim Curry
Bill Bailey
Jessica Hynes
David Hayman
David Schofield
Ronnie Corbett
Allan Corduner
Year:
2010
Filming Location:
Knole, Sevenoaks, Kent, England, UK
Luton Hoo Estate, Luton, Bedfordshire, England, UK
Stirling Castle, Stirling, Scotland, UK
Edinburgh, Scotland, UK
Dashwood Mausoleum, West Wycombe, Buckinghamshire, England, UK
Ealing Studios, Ealing, London, England, UK

intensified rivalry between the old fashioned Dr Munro and Knox, who is collaborating with the photographer Niecpe on a visual atlas of the human body (it contains images of dissected corpses, all of which were supplied by Burke and Hare). Burke and Hare manage to break free from McTavish (they kill him) and see through the production of Ginny's play (it is a regional success), but they are arrested thanks to McLintock's discovery of the source of Dr Knox's subjects. In a conveniently selfless gesture, Burke agrees to take the blame for the murders, claiming to Ginny that he is sacrificing himself in the name of love. This gesture allows Ginny, Lucky and William Hare to go free. The film ends with Burke's execution and a postscript on the cultural afterlives of these characters.

Critique

This is an, at-once, exuberant and audacious reimagining of the crimes of Burke and Hare. Helmed by American horror director John Landis, the film makes excellent use of its period costumes, genuine Edinburgh locations and its internationally renowned cast (a mixture of British film industry standouts like Pegg, Hynes and Serkis; Scots like Fisher and Corbett; and fun cameos, ranging from Ray Harryhausen to Costa-Gavras to Christopher Lee). What is astonishing is how much this film questions the ethical implications behind Burke and Hare's decision to murder for profit. In all other cinematic tellings of their exploits, the two emerge as villains whose actions cannot be rationalized or explained away, despite their economic destitution, the difficulties of being Irish-Catholic in Protestant Scotland or the unbridgeable barriers between social classes. What Landis's *Burke and Hare* does, to the contrary, is justify the Burke and Hare murders thanks to Burke's love for Ginny, his occasional guilt over killing the innocent and his desire to help his close friends. This justification is somewhat acceptable to audiences – mainly because of Pegg's and Serkis's likeability, their quick wits and their familiarity to audiences as morally questioning protagonists – but ultimately side-steps a possibly depressing conclusion thanks to Burke's rebirth as a kind of messiah figure who (in a moment of knowing cliché) sacrifices all for love.

This blackest of comedies walks the fine line between laughing at death and laughing with it. Although not especially gory, the film does show many deaths, most of which are memorable for their slapstick delivery. In particular, the moment where Burke and Hare scare an obese man into a heart attack stands out as typical. The scene is set up in such a way as to show how Burke and Hare made a premeditated attempt at accosting the man (he walks through a dark, narrow passageway, alone and at night), but takes equal pains to show that neither Burke nor Hare physically assaulted him. Rather, Hare startles the man and he collapses from fear. This, in turn, keeps the two away from a direct sense of blame, and proves acceptable to Dr Knox, who prefers a generally unmarked corpse.

Burke and Hare leavens its dark subject-matter with extensively self-referential nods to its own status in history. While generally a period costume drama, it uses its historical moment (1828 Edinburgh) as the springboard for a series of recurring gags. Some of these are built into characterizations: the film connects the birth of photography (Niecpe) to Knox's scientific rationality, showing how their conceptions of visibility occupy a similar philosophical sensibility, despite the fact that the Frenchman is constantly denigrated for his foppish attitudes and stands in stark contrast to the almost humourless Knox. Most significantly, the film showcases a number of sequences that trace contemporary institutions to improvised ideas delivered as if they will one day be significant. For example, one sequence shows Lucky and William Burke making love, with Lucky warning William that they will soon run out of product. She advises that they open up a business where people will pay them to properly dispose of corpses. Over the course of a few lines of dialogue, the two iron out the essential components of the funeral parlour. In another moment, McTavish and Fergus attempt to extort money from Burke and Hare. They have trouble articulating the significance of their demands: a percentage in exchange for no trouble and the right to continue working. Burke sees it for what it really is: the makings of a protection racket. Later (on his own), Fergus is described as a successful life insurance salesman.

Yet, while the film's playful sense of intertextuality (it also uses *Macbeth* in parallel to its own narrative) sets it apart from other tellings of the Burke and Hare story, its actual relationship to the historical record is dubious at best. The film might better be understood not as an historical comedy, but rather as a comic fantasia on history. It takes the evocative milieu of Edinburgh during the early stages of the Industrial Revolution and invests it with the wishes of the twenty-first century.

Kevin M Flanagan

Comfort and Joy

Country of Origin:

UK

Language:

English

Studio/Production Companies:

Thorn EMI
Kings Road Entertainment
Scottish Television

Director:

Bill Forsyth

Producers:

Davina Belling

Synopsis

When Glasgow radio DJ Alan 'Dickie' Bird is suddenly left by his girlfriend shortly before Christmas, he finds himself trying to find new purpose in life. Deciding to follow a pretty young woman he spots in the back of an ice-cream van one evening, he witnesses the vehicle being attacked and destroyed by masked men. Eager to get to the bottom of the crime, Alan soon finds himself in the midst of an underground feud, not between mobsters, but between two warring ice-cream companies.

Critique

Writer-director Bill Forsyth's fifth feature film revolves around a seemingly absurd notion: that of grown adults getting physically angry over ice cream. Bizarre as the idea may seem, however, the story in fact takes it cues from the Glasgow Ice Cream Wars, real-life events that saw competing vendors of refrigerated treats collide in a series of violent crimes during the early 1980s. Yet whilst those

Clive Parsons
Paddy Higson

Screenwriter:

Bill Forsyth

Cinematographer:

Chris Menges

Art Director:

Andy Harris

Composer:

Mark Knopfler

Editor:

Michael Ellis

Duration:

106 minutes

Genre:

Comedy

Cast:

Bill Paterson
Eleanor David
Clare Grogan
Alex Norton
Patrick Malahide
Rikki Fulton

Year:

1984

Filming Location:

Glasgow, Strathclyde, Scotland, UK

conflicts (rumoured to be over the sale of stolen goods and drugs, rather than just confectionary) eventually escalated to the deaths of six people via arson, Forsyth's script strips the matter back to its more farcical central concept. It is a wise decision, and one that makes for an amusing film.

Bill Paterson excels as the sardonic lead, a middle-aged man left without focus or identity when his kleptomaniac girlfriend, Maddy, walks out on him, taking four years worth of acquired goods with her. Ever sensible, Alan tells her early in the film that 'if you're going to steal things, at least be practical: we needed onions, we did not need more Christmas lights'. Unfortunately he fails to realize until after Maddy's departure that her impulsive thievery was responsible for the entire contents of his flat. Asked by a friend if he ever bought anything himself, Alan can only reply: 'The mortgage. That's mine'.

Alan's innate need for companionship is made clear by his profession. As a radio host, he is consistently either talking, or surrounded by the voices of others. Unaccustomed to being alone, he soon becomes so desperate for company that he gives chase to a 'Mr Bunny' ice-cream van when a pretty girl smiles at him from inside. As he follows his target through a tunnel and into an unfamiliar part of town, the film undergoes its *Alice in Wonderland* moment – the protagonist having followed the rabbit through its hole. What happens on the other side introduces Alan to a new world, one where balaclava-clad thugs launch an assault on an ice-cream van until the vehicle limps away in tatters, with its jingle – now a distorted dirge – still emanating from inside. In the morning, Alan will find his own car seats riddled with ice-cream-cone bullets, an accompanying note warning him to keep his mouth shut.

Yet it is these very absurdities that keep *Comfort and Joy* firmly anchored to the world we are all familiar with. At the heart of Forsyth's script lays a keenly observed truth, namely that many of us do peculiar things when it comes to making a living. As preposterous as it seems to Alan that ice-cream men should be talking of forbidden territory and unwritten laws, he is quickly reminded of his own 'big contribution to humanity', working at a radio station where pre-recorded jingles are used to convey everything – whether it is his breakfast show's slogan, 'the early worm catches the bird', or the rather less catchy 'sit tight and we'll bring you the traffic situation right now in your car'. When the warring dessert factions meet for a suitably daft battle involving crossbows and oversized mallets towards the film's end, the message is clear: modern man is an inherently strange concept and fighting each other does nothing but accentuate this strangeness.

Patrick Harley

The Doctor and the Devils

Country of Origin:

UK

Language:

English

Studio/Production Companies:

Brooks Films
Twentieth Century Fox

Director:

Freddie Francis

Producer:

Jonathan Sanger

Screenwriter:

Ronald Harwood, based on an original screenplay by Dylan Thomas

Cinematographer:

Gerry Turpin

Art Director:

Brian Ackland-Snow

Composer:

John Morris

Editor:

Laurence Mery-Clark

Duration:

93 minutes

Genre:

Horror

Cast:

Timothy Dalton
Jonathan Pryce
Stephen Rea
Twiggy
Julian Sands
Phyllis Logan
Sian Phillips
Philip Davis
Patrick Stewart
Beryl Reid
Nichola McAuliffe

Year:

1985

Synopsis

Thomas Rock is a brash anatomist at odds with the Edinburgh medical establishment. Equal parts dreamer and humanist, he takes to his lectures with gusto and even acts as a surgeon to the city's poor. However, he complains that his allotment of cadavers – which, by law, can only be supplied from the bodies of executed criminals – is too small to sustain his work. He buys corpses from grave robbers, but soon becomes blindly accustomed to buying fresher specimens from Robert Fallon and Timothy Broom, alcoholic itinerant labourers who soon turn to murder in exchange for steady income. Although Fallon and Broom's first sale is of an intercepted corpse exhumed by long-time 'resurrection men', the duo abuses their ownership of a lodging house for the old and destitute, killing the sick and preying upon the lonely. However, Fallon betrays himself to idealistic Dr Murray by killing Alice, friend to Murray's love Jenny. Murray confronts Fallon just before he kills Jenny. Broom gets off by betraying Fallon, who is hanged. The scandal ends Dr Rock's career in Edinburgh, exiling him from the city.

Critique

Fronting an all-star cast, this late production from Hammer and Amicus favourite Freddie Francis somberly adapts Dylan Thomas's screenplay of *The Doctor and the Devils* (initially published 1953), a lightly fictionalized re-imagining of the Burke and Hare murders. According to Francis, the Ronald Harwood script was extensively re-written during production in order to restore more of Thomas's original content (1991: 18). The narrative orbits around the struggles of Dr Rock (the Dr Knox character), played to earnest perfection by Timothy Dalton, a suave young actor who was to controversially re-vitalize the James Bond franchise only two years later. In fact, for a director and cinematographer like Francis (whose work is usually celebrated for its compositions, spatial depth and technical polish), *The Doctor and the Devils* is squarely an actor's game. Despite two gorgeous location shots of Edinburgh that bookend the film (one shows Rock's arrival at, and contemplation of, the city; the other shows him leave, a dejected failure), the bulk of the movie was made in the studio. While the myriad street scenes are reasonably dynamic in their successful relating of the hustle, bustle and grim realities of the lumpen Edinburgh of the nineteenth century, this ambiance takes a backseat to the film's singular characterizations.

Most memorable is Jonathan Pryce's portrayal of Fallon (the William Burke character), a man at once mentally unstable (because of his dependence on alcohol) and physically combative (because of his calculating opportunism and spontaneously sudden movements). In a key scene, Fallon defends himself against partner Broom's accusations that his sadistic pleasure in killing has ruined their lucrative business. As Broom (the William Hare equivalent), Stephen Rea offers a behavioural alternative to Fallon's uncontrollable channeling of the id. More low-key and suspicious, Rea plays Broom with patience. This rift causes Fallon to go on a

Filming Location:

Lee International Studios, Shepperton, Surrey, England, UK

final spree (which ends with his attempted rape/murder of Jenny). After Fallon is hanged, Broom defends his caution: despite his attachment to the murders, he remains a free (if despondent) man.

The rest of the plot threads dramatize material that is common to other versions of the Burke and Hare story. Almost all of these subplots feature a binary set of comparisons that suggest incompatible world views. Although Francis goes out of his way to show Rock as a compassionate doctor and a loving husband (his saving of Billy Bedlam sees to that), his desires for unbridled research are challenged by a hostile medical faculty, who are most directly embodied by the washed-up Professor Macklin (Patrick Stewart). For Rock, the real tragedy of the tale isn't the needless death, but rather the intractable conservatism of the scientific community. Rock's protégé Dr Murray (Julian Sands) falls for well-known prostitute Jenny (Twiggy). While their story is adrift in clichés (Jenny, as the 'hooker with a heart of gold', displays equal parts street smarts and a lovely singing voice; Murray attempts to 'reform' Jenny through his respectability and the possibility of a stable life), their class tension underscores the latent struggles of the rest of the movie.

The Doctor and the Devils compares favourably to other filmic renderings of the Burke and Hare story, and is a swan song to the kind of movie that Francis specialized in during the 1960s.

Kevin M Flanagan

Reference

Winston Dixon, Wheeler (1991) *The Films of Freddie Francis*, Metuchen, NJ: Scarecrow Press.

Dog Soldiers

Countries of Origin:

UK
Luxembourg

Language:

English

Studio/Production Companies:

Kismet Entertainment Group
The Noel Gay Motion Picture Company

Director:

Neil Marshall

Producers:

Christopher Figg
Tom Reeve
David E Allen

Synopsis

Hikers in the Scottish Highlands have been going missing, leaving only shreds of clothes and a few scraps of flesh. Cooper, a promising soldier, has failed the selection process for Special Forces, despite performing well, by refusing to shoot a dog at the command of the sadistic Captain Ryan. Four weeks later, Cooper and the rest of his squad are on a routine training mission against Special Forces in the Highlands under the command of Sergeant Wells, a mouthy but respected leader.

When the soldiers come across the steaming entrails of the apparently 'crack' Special Forces squad and a cowering, gibbering Ryan, it becomes clear that this routine mission is in fact a step into the complete unknown. But even the unknown or the supernatural can be understood through worn-out stereotypes and leaden one-liners. Wells's diatribe 'if Little Red Riding Hood should turn up with a bazooka and a bad attitude, I expect you to chin the bitch' is representative of how possibilities for the uncanny are precluded by solecisms such as 'you women, same old shite' and references to 'that time of the month'.

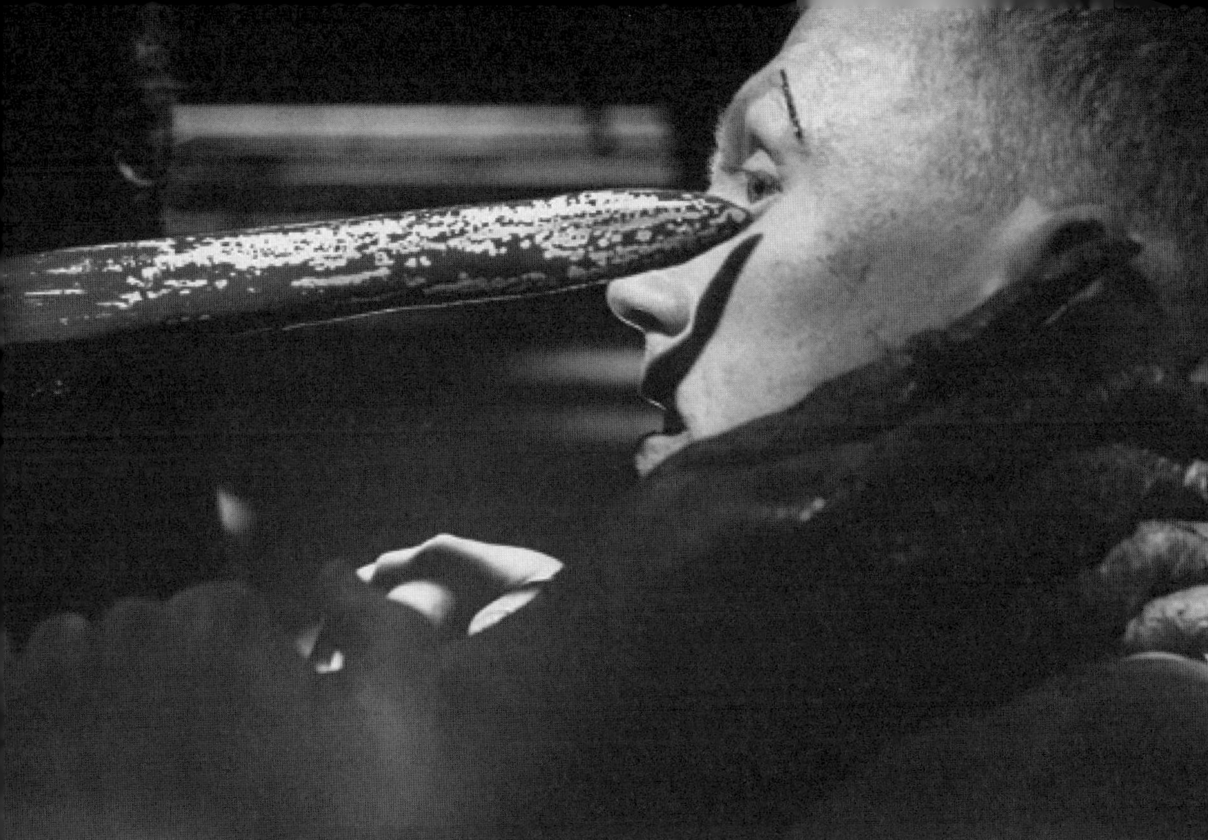

Dog Soldiers (2002), British Film Institute Collection

Screenwriter:
Neil Marshall
Cinematographer:
Sam McCurdy
Art Director:
Christina Schaffer
Composer:
Mark Thomas
Editor:
Neil Marshall
Duration:
105 minutes
Genre:
Horror
Cast:
Sean Pertwee
Kevin McKidd
Emma Cleasby

When the dog soldiers, or rather, the roaming pack of wolves, next go in for the kill, Megan, in her guise as a strong woman and rough terrain driver, arrives to whisk the men away to the apparent safety of an abandoned cottage. Megan claims to have known the family; she is a zoologist and lives in the 'house in the next glen'.

Critique

The soldiers may break and enter the three bears' house, blow off the roof and scare the dog, but this is no moralistic fable. Fairy-tale references are of limited significance and the real tensions lie in the areas of sex and class. This sort of interpretation is invited when the men discuss their fears by the campfire. Spoony opts for castration while Cooper burrs, 'spiders, and wimmin, and … spiderwimmin'. Megan, the only female cast member, is a conglomeration of types: strong woman, honeypot, femme fatale, bitch, 'posh bird' … it's a long list. Her shape shifting, not just from woman to wolf but from cipher to cipher is sudden and she acts more as a vehicle for the next plot twist rather than lending the film any psychological depth.

In comparison, the wolves are rather appealing: lithe-limbed, taut and ready to pounce. Most of all, they maintain a dignified silence. The only occasional use of the wolves' perspective seems a missed

Liam Cunningham

Year:

2002

Filming Locations:

Luxembourg, The Grand Duchy of Luxembourg
Glen Affric, Scotland, UK

opportunity. From it, the viewer can only gain a sense of their speed and that they see in monochrome. Greater emphasis on this might have given the film more complexity, rather than simply using it to depict a series of unfortunate and gory events. While the adrenaline and chemistry from the actors is at times palpable, the integrity of their performances and the film's genuine visual, visceral thrills are marred by glib quips that reinforce tired stereotypes. That said, a climactic scene where the men are fending off the big bad wolves from the house, causing a highly-strung Terry to vomit on the head of a wounded Captain Ryan, is a surprisingly adept instance of comic relief.

Also impressive are the pyrotechnics, the seemingly infinite creativity of the squad in devising explosions, as the effects involved are expertly executed and edited. The pace, moreover, will leave even cynics stuttering and deaf to the inadequacies of the script. The blood and guts, nevertheless, are safely constrained to budget-horror movie territory. Wells finds something very similar to a steak covered in BBQ sauce among the remains of Special Forces and there is a good portion of what looks like Cumberland sausages covered in the same red goo. At one point, Wells, mid-agony, grabs his abdomen and declares: 'Sausages!' Joke-shop props are forgivable when the narrative is sufficiently gratifying, but gags such as 'you seem to know [Wells] inside out by now' exceed the balance.

The film offers not so much a multiplicity of interpretations when it comes to the wolves but rather some very vague thrusts at plausible explanations. Women and lunar cycles aside, the antagonism between Cooper and Ryan, and Cooper's inability to 'make the grade', is couched in terms of a class divide. Just before Ryan's transformation, Cooper spits out a reference to 'toffy-nosed twats' and how he'd 'take the underdogs any time'. Ryan goads him, 'monkey see, monkey do', implying that Cooper's social background acts as a brake to his progression in the army.

Linnie Blake suggests,

> The over-preoccupation with the military world of men without women visible in British horror under New Labour (in films such as *The Bunker*, *Deathwatch* and *Dog Soldiers* in particular) clearly indicated a certain discomfort with Britain's imperial past and the reluctance on the behalf of contemporary men to identify unquestioningly with the hypermasculine ethos that underpins nationalistic war. (Blake 2012: 85)

She goes on to argue that these films exhibit an awareness of the need to reconceptualize traditional models of masculinity, owing to the sea change in male experience in recent decades.

The other lads make references to 'balls of British steel' and scream 'come and have a go if you think yer hard enough!' Reference is made to the Battle of Rorke's Drift, where British and colonial troops held off Zulu warriors despite being vastly outnumbered, but only in terms of courage against the odds. This reference does little to reformulate British masculinity, and since these characters are promptly devoured, it is necessary to look to Cooper, the sole survivor, for meaningful possibilities. Early in the film, Ryan fails Cooper on the grounds that he is a 'man of conscience'; Cooper argues that he would shoot the dog, but not without reason. He is superstitious, keeps a lucky rabbit's foot and he doesn't outright dismiss Megan's supernatural explanation.

There's also the question of what all this has to do with Scotland. Scenery plays a part, although much of the special effects were filmed in a studio in Luxembourg. Cooper is Scottish and little is made of this, although it may be that Cooper is less willing to concede to his 'superior', the RP-speaking Captain Ryan, because he is a comparative outsider to English class divisions. The rest of the men are English and sport a variety of regional accents. Megan also snarls at him: 'No point being nice to women, Cooper. Being nice to me will get you killed.'

So Cooper, open to the unknown, kind to women and unwilling to prop up the British class system, emerges from the cottage sweaty, bloodstained, but alive. He may well be intended to represent a development in the British male psyche. That, or he simply has the home advantage in the ample 'Scotch mist', while the Highlands provide a landscape sufficiently isolated to allow the less pleasant aspects of human behaviour to play out to their logical end.

Susan Robinson

Reference

Blake, Linnie (2012) 'New Labour, New Horrors: Genetic Mutation, Generic Hybridity and Gender Crisis in British Horror of the New Millennium', in Patricia Allmer, David Huxley and Emily Brick (eds), *European Nightmares: Horror Cinema in Europe Since 1945*, New York: Columbia University Press, pp. 77-87.

The Flesh and the Fiends aka Mania, The Fiendish Ghouls

Country of Origin:
UK
Language:
English
Studio/Production Company:
Triad Productions
Director:
John Gilling

Synopsis

Eminent Doctor Robert Knox commands a central position in the Edinburgh medical scene for his rational lectures and unmatched knowledge of human anatomy. His assistants, including conscientious Geoffrey Mitchell and the wayward Chris Jackson (whose new relationship with Mary Patterson has derailed his studies) assist him in preparing cadavers for autopsy. At a party, Knox is put on the spot by prominent members of the medical profession and the clergy for his single-minded pursuit of knowledge, thus exposing his severity. Knox responds with an eloquent defense of his work, and sets about dissecting with greater zeal. He begins an unquestioning acquisition of corpses from William Burke and William Hare, two itinerant Irish labourers who, having failed at consistent grave robbery, turn to murder. At first Knox and his cohort are pleased with the fresh, fine bodies they are given. However, the increasingly prolific Burke and Hare soon overstep the unspoken bounds of their power, as they kill not just the old and sick, but prominent local figures (Daft Jamie) and young women (Mary, Chris's tempestuous lover). Mary's murder sets the

Producers:

Robert S Baker
Monty Berman

Screenwriters:

Leon Griffiths
John Gilling

Cinematographer:

Monty Berman

Art Director:

John Elphick

Composer:

Stanley Black

Editor:

Jack Slade

Duration:

97 minutes (*Mania* cut runs 91 minutes)

Genre:

Horror

Cast:

Peter Cushing
June Laverick
Donald Pleasance
George Rose
Billie Whitelaw
Renee Houston
Dermot Walsh
John Cairney
Melvyn Hayes

Year:

1960

Filming Location:

Shepperton Studios, Shepperton, Surrey, England, UK

Edinburgh mob onto Burke and Hare, who are captured and sent to trial. The trial brings to light the relationship between the two and Knox, who (now disgraced) attempts to maintain his dignity and the respect of his students. Hare pins all of the duo's blame onto Burke, who is publicly hanged. Although released, Hare is attacked and blinded. Finally, Knox resumes his career as a lecturer, despite the permanent damage to his reputation.

Critique

This is the first fully 'cinematic' telling of the Burke and Hare story. Although largely confined to studio sets, the production features crisp black-and-white cinematography from Monty Berman that is occasionally suggestive of American film noir (the street scenes, in particular, feature that common mixture of psychologically evocative play of light and shadow that has trickled down from the German Expressionist cinema of the 1920s, combined with the familiarity of the haunted, empty spaces of the city). This production also owes a bit to *The Greed of William Hart* (also known as *Horror Maniacs* [Oswald Mitchell, 1948]), whose writer (John Gilling) here serves as both director and co-writer. In some senses, then, this film remakes the Burke and Hare story to fit with the genres (heritage horror) and social concerns (the sudden discourse of sexual 'permissiveness') of the day, all while staying conscious of the visual legacy of this famous set of crimes.

The most obvious point of comparison is between *The Flesh and the Fiends* and the recently renowned work of Hammer studios, whose use of Cushing in horror-inflected historical costume dramas (usually as an authority figure, leisured gentleman or aristocrat of some stripe or another) would typify one of the most recognizable areas of the British film industry for the following two decades. Cushing does not disappoint in this role. He plays a driven, if sinister and over-committed, anatomist whose genuine desire to improve the world through science has divorced him from the sensible bounds of ethical behaviour. This pervasive theme (the failure and latent violence of professional men with institutional power) becomes a favoured story of the left and youth countercultures in the 1960s. However, despite the film's questioning of Knox, it ultimately ends with his quizzical re-establishment as a lecturer (the historical Knox was eventually driven to London, where he laboured in obscurity as a doctor for the poor).

However, the film also interfaces with some of the concerns of the nascent British New Wave. Like celebrated adaptations such as *Room at the Top* (Jack Clayton, 1957) and *Look Back in Anger* (Tony Richardson, 1958), *The Flesh and the Fiends* contains anxieties about class mobility. One of the central dramas of the film is between Mary, who aspires for bourgeois respectability and stability, and Chris, whose love for Mary suggests his willingness to breach the proprieties of his social class and professional life in pursuit of love. This gambit, however, is doomed: Mary rejects Chris in a bout of drunken resentment, and is that night nearly raped and then murdered by the opportunistic Hare.

Pleasance plays William Hare with unsettling ambiguity. While earlier screen versions of this story mark him as a one-dimensional villain from this first, *The Flesh and the Fiends* shows how he grows into the exploitative man of legend. Pleasance exhibits a laconic, wise-aleck sense of humour that undercuts his violent temperament. His crazed physicality (especially with his attempted rape of Mary) far exceeds the off-screen implications of previous historical horror films.

The Flesh and the Fiends is direct and graphic, showing corpses (old and new) with great detail, lingering on stabbings and strangulations, and (in the 'Continental Version' spiced up for export to more permissive markets), highlighting scenes of frontal nudity that would not look out of place in a bawdier Hogarth print.

Kevin M Flanagan

Gregory's Girl

Country of Origin:

UK

Language:

English

Studio/Production Companies:

Lake Films
Scottish Television (STV)
National Film Finance Corporation (NFFC)

Director:

Bill Forsyth

Producers:

Davina Belling
Clive Parsons

Screenwriter:

Bill Forsyth

Cinematographer:

Michael Coulter

Art Director:

Adrienne Atkinson

Composer:

Colin Tully

Editor:

John Gow

Duration:

87 minutes

Synopsis

Set in the Scottish new town Cumbernauld, teenage Gregory loses his lead position in the school's unsuccessful football team when the much more talented Dorothy joins in. Now playing goalkeeper, Gregory falls in love with his gorgeous new teammate. He follows the advice of his friends and his younger sister Madeleine, asking Dorothy out for a date. To Gregory's surprise, she accepts and wants to meet him later. While Gregory waits for Dorothy, her friend Carol arrives and tells the confused Gregory that Dorothy won't show up. Instead, she asks him for a walk to the city centre. There, Carol hands Gregory off to Margo who takes Gregory for a walk to another place, where they finally meet Susan. Susan confesses that her friends arranged all this because she wants to meet Gregory and get to know him better. Gregory is delighted, and they spend the rest of the day together in the park. Afterwards, they go home together and eventually kiss in front of Gregory's house. Meanwhile, Gregory tells his sister about the events of the day, while two of his friends try unsuccessfully to hitchhike to Caracas, because they believe women greatly outnumber men there.

Critique

With his second feature film, director Bill Forsyth made his breakthrough as one of the most innovative and original Scottish film-makers. This coming-of-age romantic comedy was critically acclaimed and is still one of the best remembered and most popular Scottish films of all time. Financed partly by the commercial broadcaster Scottish Television, it anticipates a successful financing model for Scottish and British feature films that became important from the 1980s onwards, especially due to the engagement of Channel 4 which also financed the sequel *Gregory's Two Girls* (1998). Primarily aimed at a local audience, the film also prepared the ground for an indigenous, mostly low-budget Scottish cinema,

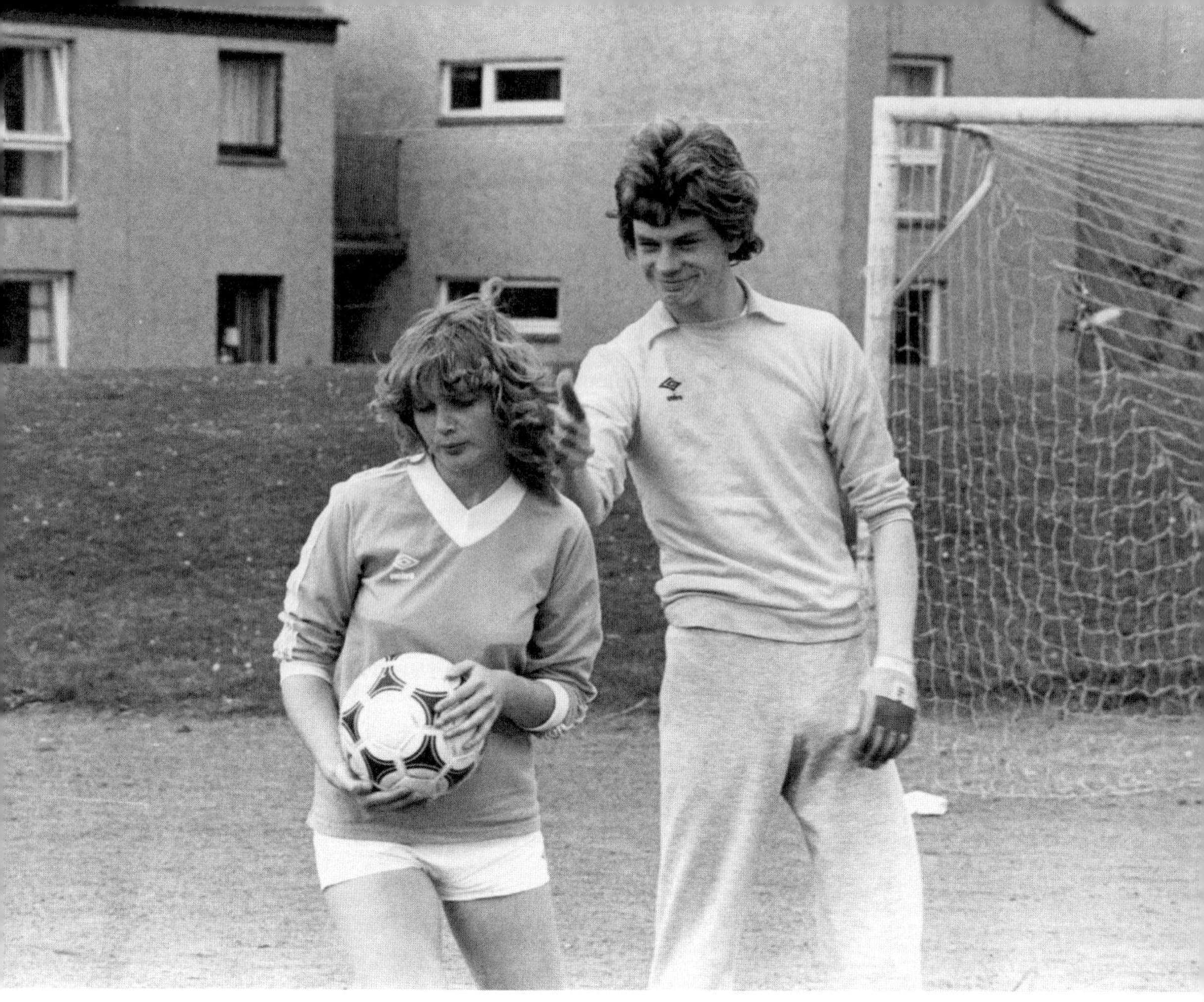

Gregory's Girl (1981), British Film Institute Collectior

Genre:

Comedy

Cast:

Gordon John Sinclair
Dee Hephurn
Jake D'Arcy
Clare Grogan
Robert Buchanan
Allison Forster
Billy Greenless
Allan Love

Year:

1981

Filming Locations:

Cumbernauld, Scotland, UK

while Forsyth earned the opportunity to make films with higher budgets like his next film, *Local Hero* (1983).

Gregory's Girl reveals a more authentic national cinema, contrary to patriotic British films released around the same time, like *Chariots of Fire* (Hugh Hudson, 1981) or *Gandhi* (Richard Attenborough, 1982). The narrative setting of the new town Cumbernauld plays a crucial role for the film as a representation of modern-day urban Scotland. The film shows a Scottish landscape that avoids conventionally predominant representations of Scotland in popular culture. The completely new, planned town is seen as an ambitious example of high modern architecture, and it presents a progressive and innovative vision of contemporary Scottish society. With its many outdoor scenes, the film makes constant use of Cumbernauld's significant pedestrian footpath network, and its bridges and underpasses that separate pedestrians and vehicles from each other. It is shown as a friendly and safe place, where schoolgirls can run through the park at night without fear.

Award:

BAFTA Award for Best Screenplay 1982

Corresponding with its presentation of the playfulness of new Scottish urban life, *Gregory's Girl* is also well aware of the classical narrative conventions of cinema and how to break them. The film leaves many questions open and several problems unsolved. For instance, it is unclear if the miserable situation of the school's football team decisively changed after Dorothy became the new star. Instead of a purposeful narration, the film's plot follows an episodic development, and is most interested in sometimes absurd or otherwise seemingly unimportant details that also create comic relief. Forsyth shows a comprehensive picture of the school, where a lot of things can happen, even if they are not relevant to the problems introduced at the beginning of the film. Besides the main two plots of an unsuccessful football team and an infatuated schoolboy, *Gregory's Girl* is well aware that many other stories take place at the same time and could be told instead. For example, no one questions the appearance of a pupil dressed up like a penguin. Also, the fact that the mostly overlooked Susan becomes the final love interest for Gregory is surprising but consequential – as the film suggests her story prior to this point could well have been an equally interesting focus of attention. The film is nevertheless stylistically consistent by developing two supporting roles at the end of the film to make an unambiguous statement about the significance of repetition in providing structuring meaning to everyday adolescent life. At the end, Dorothy is shown again, running through Cumbernauld like she did in the beginning of the film.

Its lack of forward motion not only reveals the film's central motif of adolescence but also its progressive gender politics. None of the characters undergo significant evolution at the same time as the film breaks free of conventional gender identities. Most obviously it does so by means of a reversal of stereotypical gender roles. The male characters of the film act eccentrically and reveal their lack of control over their bodies. This is one source of visual comedy in the film, but it also reveals they are stuck somewhere between childhood and adulthood. Contrary to this, almost all of the girls are portrayed as mature, rational and cooperative individuals who are superior to their male counterparts in every instance. They are highly poised and show tremendous bodily coordination. This depiction suggests a precociously early arrival at the cusp of adulthood with seemingly little further development required. These playful treatments of modern male and female adolescence, outlined with light humour and comic relief, explain *Gregory's Girl*'s enduring popularity.

Stefan Udelhofen

Gregory's Two Girls

Countries of Origin:

UK
Germany

Language:

English

Studio/Production Companies:

Young Lake
Channel Four Films
Scottish Arts Council Lottery Fund
Kinowelt Filmproduktion

Director:

Bill Forsyth

Producers:

Christopher Young
Alan J Wands

Screenwriter:

Bill Forsyth

Cinematographer:

John de Borman

Art Director:

Steven Wong

Composer:

Michael Gibbs

Editor:

John Gow

Duration:

112 minutes

Genre:

Comedy

Cast:

Gordon John Sinclair
Dougray Scott
Maria Doyle Kennedy
Carly McKinnon
Martin Schwab
Hugh McCue
Fiona Bell

Year:

1998

Synopsis

While cultivating an obvious anti-Americanism and passionately preaching about political and social activism during his lessons, the 34-year-old secondary school teacher Gregory Underwood is far from being an activist himself. His personal life lacks activity as well. While dreaming of seducing his under-age pupil, Frances, he avoids the advances of his work colleague, Bel. His life changes fundamentally when his pupils ask him for help to uncover the corrupt practices of the local company, Rowan Electronics, owned by Greg's former schoolfriend, Fraser Rowan. Besides being a huge employer and doing charity work, Fraser sells torture equipment to African despots. At first confused and unwilling to participate, Greg changes his mind when he meets his sister's boyfriend, Jon, and the former torture victim and political activist, Dimitri. Together with pupils Frances and Doug, Greg breaks into Rowan's factory where they find relevant evidence. Flushed with self-confidence afterwards, Greg starts to get serious with Bel. The next day, Greg and Frances try to get help from the Scottish Office in Edinburgh, without success. Once again, they must act alone. Greg and Frances follow a van with torture equipment to a ferry terminal. There, they steal the van and throw the equipment into the sea. Afterwards, Greg and Frances spend the night in the back of the van.

Critique

Bill Forsyth's eighth feature film is more far-reaching than merely a belated sequel to his earlier hit, *Gregory's Girl* (1981). While playing with numerous references to this predecessor, *Gregory's Two Girls* is more bittersweet, ironic and pessimistic. Revisiting the Scottish new town Cumbernauld nearly twenty years later, almost everything except the main protagonist has changed. Now in his mid-thirties and physically mature, Greg is still awkward, insecure and stuck in a state of seemingly perpetual adolescence. Yet he is now an English teacher at his old high school; he reads *New Internationalist* and he quotes Noam Chomsky during his lectures. Whereas *Gregory's Girl* was not at all interested in the progressive development of its characters, Greg now has to fully grow up whether he wants to or not. *Gregory's Two Girls* focuses mainly on Greg's challenges on his way to adulthood, but at the same time it questions the transformation of Scottish identity shaped by a global environment.

Like *Gregory's Girl*, the setting of Cumbernauld plays an important role in the narrative. This time, its hallmarks of interconnected underpasses, aerial walkways, alleys and traffic-free streets no longer reveal the town as a friendly space. Moreover, the film emphasizes surveillance and paranoia. These are underlined with comic effect due to the hilarious performance of Gordon John Sinclair. The unworldly Gregory feels watched by someone as he looks around on his way home from school and hides in his home from the drunken Bel. But this aspect becomes more serious, first with the introduction of Dimitri, and especially after Greg gets interrogated by the police twice, is seen on CCTV during the

Filming Locations:

Cumbernauld, Scotland, UK
Edinburgh, Scotland, UK
Stirling Castle, Scotland, UK
Dumbarton Castle, Scotland, UK

break-in and is tape recorded during his visit at the Scottish Office in Edinburgh. His old school friend, Fraser Rowan, is also closely associated with technologies of observation and communication, visually signified by Rowan's frequent use of mobile phones, headset microphones, binoculars and as he confronts Gregory with the recording.

Filtered through a pessimistic, yet still comedic undertone, the film deals with two highly provocative and serious topics. Greg's inappropriate sexual desire for one of his underage pupils ironically provides the starting point for his mature development and ultimately leads him into an appropriate adult relationship with his friend, Bel, as well as to his later involvement as a political activist when he intervenes in the trade of torture equipment. Both plots are not clearly distinguishable and they become closely intertwined in a controversial, but also necessary, resistance against convention. Significantly, like Forsyth's other films, *Gregory's Two Girls* is open-ended, leaving unclear the personal and legal consequences of the characters' actions as well as the possible benefits from them.

This combination of concerns marks the film as a politically informed critique that carefully analyses the effects of globalization on Scotland. Referring to the huge impact of the high-tech electronics and computing industries on Scottish labour in the late twentieth century, the film outlines the shaping effects of the global flows of capital and corporate hegemony, as well as American cultural hegemony. Against these de-territorial global powers, the film explores the meaningfulness of regional political action and localized resistance, similar to Forsyth's *Local Hero* (1983). In this regard, the new town Cumbernauld always holds 'something new', like the Chilean refugees Greg is introduced to. They are outlined as fluid in their Scottish identity, living there for decades, singing Spanish songs as well as the unofficial anthem, 'Flower of Scotland', and acting with global forces in their specific, local way to find a new home far from their origin. In contrast, the film's portrayal of the Scottish Office reveals an image of Scotland as a mostly powerless 'dead country' lost in the past. Tartan Scottish imagery associated with the nation and shown in Hollywood films like *Rob Roy* (Michael Canton-Jones, 1995) and *Braveheart* (Mel Gibson, 1995) is, Forsyth suggests, no longer a viable foundation for meaningful social and political change. Rather, Scottish identity at the turn of the twentieth century into the twenty-first century is shown as the effect of a seamless web of local, national and global tensions. Ultimately, the film suggests that grassroots activism is the best strategy in order to engage with this nexus so as to shape and define modern Scottish culture in opposition versus a hegemonic American economic and cultural (neo)imperialism.

Stefan Udelhofen

Horror Maniacs aka The Greed of William Hart

Country of Origin:

UK

Language:

English

Studio/Production Company:

Gilbert Church Productions

Director:

Oswald Mitchell

Producer:

Gilbert Church

Screenwriter:

John Gilling

Editor:

John F House

Duration:

79 minutes

Genre:

Horror

Cast:

Tod Slaughter
Henry Oscar
Aubrey Woods
Patrick Addison
Jenny Lynn
Winifred Melville
Mary Love
Ann Trego
Arnold Bell
Edward Malin

Year:

1948

Filming Locations:

Bushey Studios, Bushey, Hertsfordshire, England, UK

Synopsis

William Hart and his accomplice, Moore, murder helpless or incapacitated victims and sell the cadavers to Dr Cox, a respected surgeon in Edinburgh's medical community. After Hart and Moore murder Mary Patterson, her corpse is nearly identified by her uncle David Patterson, an assistant to Cox. Suspicious-yet-upstanding Hugh Alston and Janet monitor Hart and Moore, who continue their spree by killing 'Daft' Jamie and Meg. Despite being caught by the authorities (and Hart's last-minute attempt to pin the blame squarely on Moore), the number of missing persons causes the community to pursue Hart and Moore as a mob. The film ends as the two criminals are overwhelmed by this vengeful crowd.

Critique

This film is a vehicle for Slaughter, a cinematic holdover from the age of popular Victorian stage melodrama, a modality that was largely laid to rest by the popularization of technically reproducible media like film. While his films never achieved establishment recognition, they nonetheless proved popular with audiences who were in the market for lurid fare. As with his previous turn in *Sweeney Todd: The Demon Barber of Fleet Street* (George King, 1936), wherein Slaughter's character was implied to sell the bodies of his victims to a woman who baked them into meat pies, the grisly murders and bodily mutilation implied by the film's premise are largely left off-screen. The horrific implications of these serial murders are left more to details provided by dialogue and characterization than to on-screen violence.

Horror Maniacs was originally intended as a telling of the historical murders of William Burke and William Hare, a duo who posed as 'resurrection men' (procurers of corpses for medical experimentation, usually through grave robbing) but who were, in fact, murdering their victims and passing them off as found cadavers secured through increasingly incredulous circumstances. The British Board of Film Classification would not pass the film with the names of authentic murderers, so Burke and Hare became Hart and Moore, with Dr Robert Knox becoming Dr Cox and victim 'Daft' Jamie (who was widely known within the community for his mental impairment) retaining his name.

Despite being a recognizable horror film, *Horror Maniacs* might be more profitably regarded as a chamber melodrama. Because the limited budget and the studio-bound nature of the production (sets standing in for the popular historical memory of nineteenth-century Edinburgh), much of the action is limited to antechambers and confined sleeping quarters. The film effectively plays up class and region-based antagonisms, with Irish labourers Hart and Moore cracking jokes about their adopted Highland kinsmen while remaining suspicious of authority figures. As occasional unskilled workers caught in Edinburgh's vast network of poverty, Hart and

Moore are cast as opportunists, who use their victim's poverty, weakness for drink and inquisitiveness as excuses for personal profit. Of course, the 'moral' characters in the film – especially the almost priggish, righteous Alston – win the day. Although the real-life crimes of Burke and Hare were put to trial, Moore and Hart are given over to mob justice.

While workmanlike in its production and execution, *Horror Maniacs* represents the kind of historical horror film that would influence studios such as Hammer, Amicus and Tigon from the 1950s to the 1970s. Moreover, it showcases the British film industry's selective interest in the history of Scotland (even as it remains largely censorious of such stories).

Kevin M Flanagan

Reference

Chapman, James (2001) 'Tod Slaughter and the Cinema of Excess', in Jeffrey Richards (ed.), *The Unknown 1930s: An Alternative History of British Cinema, 1929–1939*, London: IB Tauris, pp. 139–60.

The Illusionist

L'Illusionniste

Countries of Origin:

UK
France

Languages:

English
French
Scottish Gaelic

Studio/Production Companies:

Pathé
Django Films
Ciné B
France 3 Cinéma

Director:

Sylvain Chomet

Producers:

Sally Chomet
Bob Last

Screenwriters:

Sylvain Chomet
Jacques Tati

Synopsis

Attempting to eke out a living with dogged, dignified determination at the tail-end of the 1950s, Tatischeff is an aging music hall magician confronted by the inexorable decline of audience-interest in the trade that he plies, due to the rise of rock and roll and other competing popular cultural distractions. The search for work forces the old man northwards away from his native Paris, first to London and then to the Western Isles of Scotland. In the latter place he meets Alice, a naive young local woman who is enraptured by Tatischeff's personal kindness and what she takes to be his genuine magical powers. For those reasons, she follows Tatischeff to Edinburgh, where the magician takes up a theatrical engagement and uses his wages to support Alice, indulging her increasingly extravagant – if innocent – demands for couture clothing and other luxuries. All-too-aware that this surrogate parent–child is both practically and psychologically unsustainable, Tatischeff eventually departs from Edinburgh without telling Alice, leaving her some money, a bouquet of flowers and a note saying that 'Magicians do not exist'.

Critique

According to conventional critical wisdom, French animator Sylvain Chomet's *The Illusionist* is a cinematic paean to Edinburgh, the city within which the film is largely set and from which it was largely made. But while Chomet's work may indeed constitute 'the most beautiful love letter ever written to [that] city on screen'

Art Director:
Bjarne Hansen
Composer:
Sylvain Chomet
Editor:
Sylvain Chomet
Duration:
80 minutes
Genre:
Fantasy
Animation
Year:
2010
Filming Location:
Edinburgh, Scotland, UK

(Gibbons 2010), *The Illusionist* does not celebrate classic cinematic stereotypes of Scotland as a ravishingly romantic pre- or semi-modern idyll, at least not as a self-sufficient end in and of itself. Rather, Chomet's movie uses certain familiar images of Scotland and Scottishness as a vehicle through which to develop a melancholic allegorical reading of cultural change within late-twentieth-century western society. Ultimately, *The Illusionist* argues that a range of quintessentially modern phenomena, such as post-Elvis pop music, television and mass consumerism, have deadened the imaginative and emotional sensibilities of contemporary audiences by destroying the late-nineteenth and early-twentieth-century traditions of popular entertainment that so enriched the lives and minds of earlier generations.

As part of that thematic project, *The Illusionist* freely acknowledges a glaring irony, namely, that the film itself is part of the very problem that Chomet goes to such extravagant, amusing and moving lengths to bemoan. Based on an unfilmed script by the great French director Jacques Tati, *The Illusionist* is, after all, a wistful cinematic account of the death of its central character's trade and secrets at the hands of cinema and a range of other related popular cultural traditions that first emerged at various points during the first half of the twentieth century. This much is clear already from the self-referential gag with which the movie introduces its viewers to Tatischeff and his act: the magician is

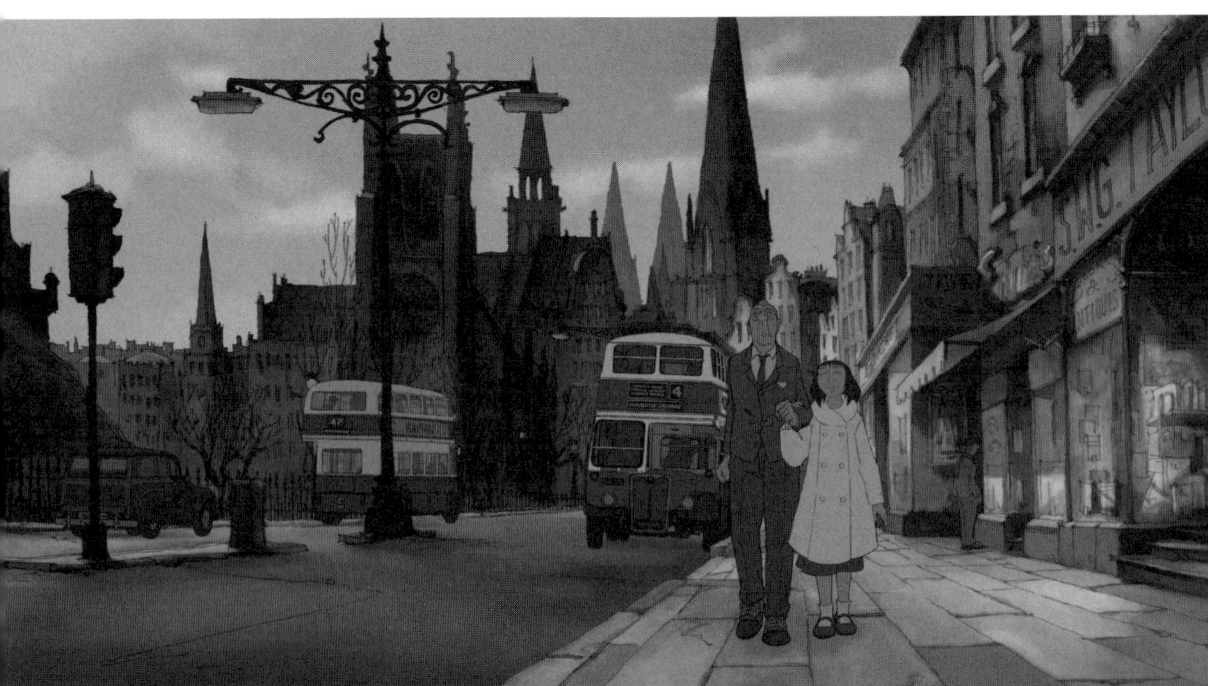

The Illusionist (2010), British Film Institute Collection

unexpectedly forced to fill time on a Parisian theatre stage when the projection equipment due to start screening a film – called, incidentally, *The Illusionist* – malfunctions at the last minute, leaving the paying audience with nothing to see. In arch moments such as these, Chomet traces the dying of the light in one sense – the sad, slow demise of Tatischeff's career and wider profession – to the coming of the light in another – mass electrification is the technological advance that enables TV, rock and roll and cinema to come into existence and then obliterate popular appreciation of, and demand for, the traditions of music hall theatre.

It is significant in this regard that the only two characters who display any discernible enthusiasm for Tatischeff's act are both Scottish: Alice and a bibulous Hebridean laird. However, Chomet does not ascribe the attractive credulity of those protagonists to some misty-eyed sense of Celtic ethnic origin. Rather, the director emphasizes the more prosaic fact of the physical remoteness of the island community from which Alice and the Laird hail: electricity arrives on it only at the same time that Tatischeff does. The gloomy inference is that the rural Islanders will in the long term prove no less resistant to the gaudy distractions of the electric age than the screaming London teenyboppers who viewers earlier see mobbing a fictitious local beat group, Billy Boy and the Britoons, during Tatischeff's unsuccessful engagement in the British capital. In this sense, while *The Illusionist* calculatedly exploits elements of the *Brigadoon* (Vincente Minnelli, 1954) myth of rural Scotland as an oasis within the wider cultural desert of the modern world, it cannot be said that the film straightforwardly endorses that stereotype. The uneven development and dissemination of technology, rather than any meaningful differences in cultural sensibility, is what distinguishes the movie's unspoilt Scottish settings from their metropolitan French and English counterparts.

Yet while *The Illusionist* is clearly aware of the dangers attendant upon acts of cultural stereotyping in one sense, it could be argued that the movie falls prey to these in another. Regardless of the degree to which one might sympathize with the aesthetic preferences and discernment manifest within Chomet's reading of recent popular cultural history, it ought also to be noted that the terms in which his movie critiques modern urban popular cultures and ways of living – as fundamentally inauthentic, emasculating and feminized to the point of mass hysteria – take their place within a long and ideologically questionable tradition within European thought and artistic practice. The exaggeratedly effeminate off-stage gait of the Britoons suggests the idea of cynical male homosexuals purveying ridiculous romantic scenarios to credulous heterosexual girls. Alice's insatiable demands for high-end fashion that Tatischeff cannot afford imply the idea of mass consumerism as an intrinsically feminine malaise. So, too, does the final indignity to which the aging magician submits. With no other means of supporting Alice, Tatischeff briefly accepts a degrading job publicizing the annual sales at Jenners, the iconic department store located on Edinburgh's famous Princes Street. Dressed, tellingly enough, in an unflattering and shocking pink outfit, he is forced to perform in a glass cage formed by the storefront windows, magically producing the time-worn accoutrements of feminine glamour – handbags, brassieres – from up his sleeves in an attempt to attract the attention of (mostly female) shoppers passing by outside.

Even the one ostensibly happy element of *The Illusionist*'s narrative resolution – Alice's induction into adult sexuality when she meets and then begins a relationship with a handsome young local man – seems troubling when viewed through the prism of the film's lop-sided gender politics. Rather than achieving personal independence from one father figure (Tatischeff), it seems that an essentially helpless ingénue merely passes into the waiting hands of a more virile successor. Like the magician, Alice's boyfriend also seems immune to the feminized seductions of modern consumer culture: if the older man is dedicated to fostering the life of the imagination, the younger man diligently pursues that of the mind. Alice first sees her lover-to-be reading intently while sitting at the window of a public library, and he later waits for her outside the door of the same building as she collects her belongings from Tatischeff's lodgings for the final time. If we were to figure Sylvain Chomet as the titular illusionist of his undeniably beautiful movie, then the expertly executed mirage with which he tantalizes his viewers is that of a nostalgically genteel social-cum-sexual Scottish Neverland in which it is a man's job to protect and a woman's to be protected.

Jonathan Murray

Reference

Gibbons, Fiachra (2010) 'North Berwick is like the Caribbean', *The Guardian*, 6 November, p. 5.

Local Hero

Country of Origin:

UK

Languages:

English
Russian
Japanese

Studio/Production Companies:

Goldcrest Films
Enigma Pictures

Director:

Bill Forsyth

Producer:

Davd Puttnam

Synopsis

Mac is sent by his employer, Knox Oil and Gas, to negotiate the purchase of all the land in the village of Ferness on the north coast of Scotland. Mac arrives in Aberdeen and is escorted to Ferness by Knox field representative Danny Oldsen. After being delayed by fog, the two arrive in Ferness to negotiate the deal with what they think will be a naive, unsuspecting group of villagers. The townsfolk, though, have gotten wind of the interest of the American company and have appointed local accountant Gordon Urquhart to lead the talks. As part of their negotiation strategy, the locals pretend not to be aware of the talks and do their best to charm the visitors and thereby drive up the price of their land. Initially stiff and business-oriented, Mac eventually succumbs to the charm of the apparently simple life of the village, falling in love with Urquhart's wife in the process. The negotiations hit a snag when it is discovered that the beach belongs to Ben, a local eccentric who lives in a dilapidated hut on the beach. Ben refuses to sell up, leading the villagers to consider

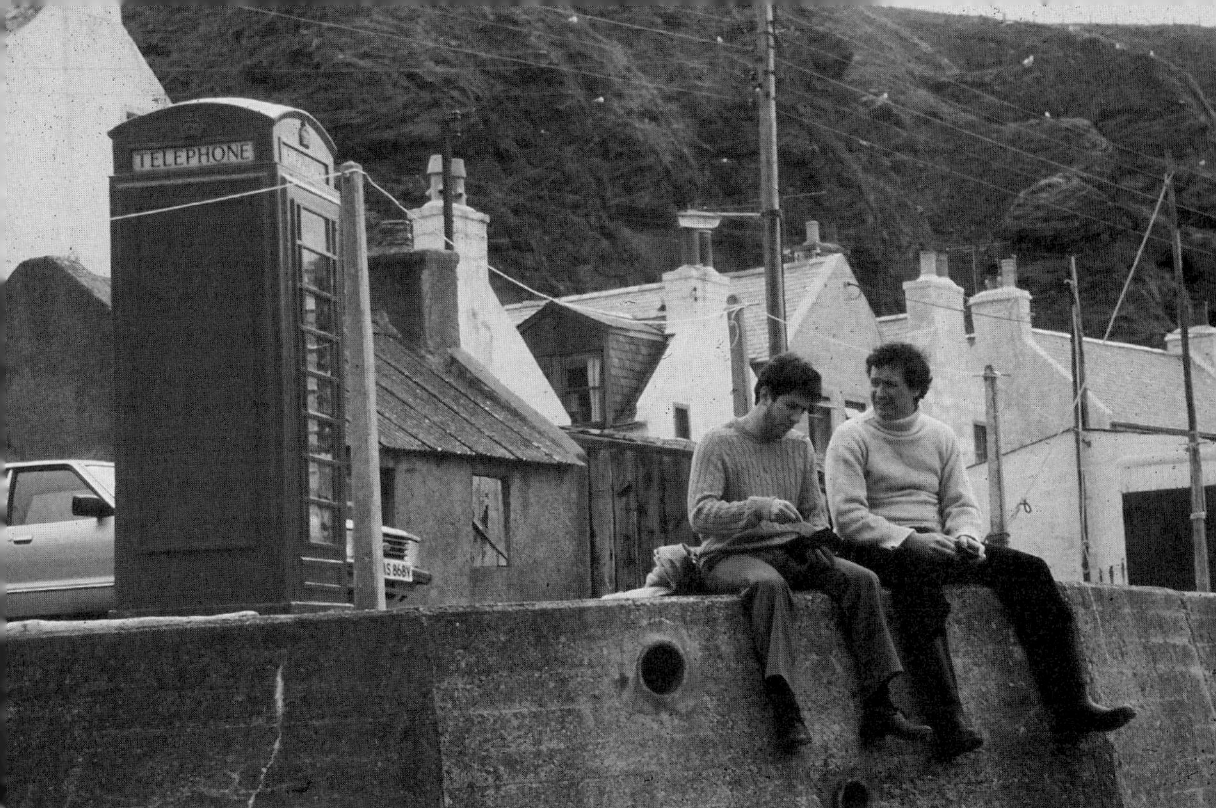

Local Hero (1983), British Film Institute Collection

Screenwriter:

Bill Forsyth

Cinematographer:

Chris Menges

Art Directors:

Adrienne Atkinson
Frank Walsh
Ian Watson

Composer:

Mark Knopfler

Editor:

Michael Bradsell

Duration:

111 minutes

Genre:

Comedy

Cast:

Peter Riegert

drastic measures. Felix Happer, the eccentric Chief Executive Officer of Knox, flies to Ferness to take over the talks and strikes up a rapport with Ben and decides on a whim to set up an observatory in the village and not a refinery. Though he has become entranced by life in Ferness, Mac is abruptly ordered back to Houston where he resumes a life he now finds empty and unrewarding.

Critique

When he set out to make *Local Hero*, Bill Forsyth was already the most popular indigenous film-maker Scotland had ever produced. After the micro-budget success of *That Sinking Feeling* (1980) and the runaway popularity of *Gregory's Girl* (1981), Forsyth's next project would see him collaborate with producer David Puttnam (who was himself coming off the runaway success of *Chariots of Fire* [Hugh Hudson, 1981]) and the English studio Goldcrest Pictures on a comedy that took as its inspiration the Ealing classic *Whisky Galore!* (Alexander Mackendrick, 1949).

Like all of Forsyth's best work, *Local Hero* is equal parts witty comedy and lyrical meditation on the human condition. Few films from the 1980s manage to both parody and probe the corporatized 'yuppie' lifestyle that dominated the decade with the wit and

Burt Lancaster
Dennis Lawson
Peter Capaldi
Fulton Mackay

Year:

1983

Filming Location:

Houston, Scotland, UK

insight that Forsyth does here. Mac and Danny epitomize this emerging class as does the noisome (and hilarious) self-help guru Moritz (Norman Chancer) whose therapeutic methods – including abusive prank phone calls and obscene signposting – are only a slight exaggeration of the many that were fashionable at the time. Happer's (Burt Lancaster) plight, as well as Mac's, as a man with only his wealth to keep him company, showcases Forsyth's Romantic take on the failings of the world of Reaganomics and Thatcherism. While Happer in the end is able to transcend the limitations of his world, Mac is forever entrapped by it, with the film's downbeat ending refusing to allow his return to the village.

These two American characters are in some senses contrasted with the supposedly naive and simple people of Ferness. But the majority of the villagers are actually more than willing to take the trappings of wealth over the 'simple life', an inversion that allows Forsyth to upend expectations of the Kailyardic tradition of Scottish representation. Other inversions show Ferness to be quite the worldly place with visitors from Africa and the USSR in addition to the Americans being fixtures in the village. Only the beachcomber Ben (Fulton Mackay) conforms to Kailyardic expectations as the holdout to the Americans and their offer to buy up the village. His character is the extreme Romantic in terms of putting the land ahead of his own wealth, but even in this he is far from a simpleton or caricature. He is instead presented as a wise, crafty environmentalist eccentric, every inch the foil of the much wealthier yet equally eccentric (and, ironically for an oil man, environmentalist) Happer.

The many jokes at the expense of Kailyardic expectation are accompanied by an equal number at the expense of tartan iconography. The seemingly clichéd 'Highland mists' are re-imagined by Forsyth as a banal fact of life in the region, one which can prove an irritation to travellers, particularly when one of the travellers is fond of showing off their mastery of languages. The much abused aerial shot of the Highland landscape likewise comes in for genial satire when Forsyth at one point cuts from a shot of the Aberdeen airport to what seems to be a bird's-eye view of the village, a shot which is revealed to actually be a plastic model of the village built by oil company geologists. Forsyth pokes fun at these clichés and many others, but never fully descends into parody, preferring instead to pastiche Tartanry and Kailyardism, a decision that has made the film more complex, entertaining and ultimately more durable than more harshly satirical films such as *Scotch Myths* (Murray Grigor, 1983).

Besides its interesting deployment of Scottish representational discourses, the film also features several wonderful performances, including an underrated turn by Peter Reigert who adds subtlety and nuance to what could have been a one-dimensional city-slicker character. There are also justly celebrated performances by Fulton Mackay, Burt Lancaster and Peter Capaldi, who made his acting debut in the film. The film also features one of the great scores of the 1980s. Mark Knopfler's soundtrack pastiches many of the conventions of Celtic music to create a score that is as moving and knowing as the film's script. The soundtrack would ultimately outsell the film itself and become a classic in its own right.

The film's reception amongst Scottish academic critics has been, until recently, negative in the extreme, with many seeing only the film's usage of Tartanry and Kailyardism as betrayals of Scottish culture by an indigenous artist all too eager to make it big abroad. Particularly strident in their critiques were intellectuals associated with the Scotch Reels event at the Edinburgh Film Festival in 1981 and subsequent published book. In recent years, however, a new generation of critics has sought to restore the film and its director to the place they deserve, which is at the forefront of Scottish film-making in the 1980s.

Christopher Meir

Outcast

Countries of Origin:

Scotland
Ireland

Language:

English

Studio/Production Companies:

Fantastic Films
Headgear Films
Makar Productions

Director:

Colm McCarthy

Producers:

Eddie Dick
Brendan McCarthy
John McDonnell

Screenwriters:

Colm and Tom McCarthy

Cinematographer:

Darran Tiernan

Art Director:

Fiona Gavin

Composer:

Giles Packham

Editor:

Helen Chapman

Duration:

98 minutes

Synopsis

Mary and Fergal have just arrived in Edinburgh and are offered a high-rise flat in one of the city's neglected and poverty-stricken housing estates. They are unusual tenants. On the first night Mary strips naked, makes a paintbrush from a lock of her own hair, slashes a shallow cut down her sternum and uses the blood to make a magic paint. This she then daubs on the walls in a series of strange and ominous symbols, ostensibly to protect Fergal, but it soon becomes clear that it is those around him who need protection most.

Cathal and Liam are also making the drive to Lothian, Edinburgh's surrounding region, to a travellers' settlement where Cathal consults 'the Laird' and has more of these runic symbols tattooed on his back. The pair then head to the city and kill a series of crows, hoping that reading their entrails will lead them to the location of Mary and Fergal.

Meanwhile, Fergal is getting to know the other residents of the housing scheme, much to his mother's apprehension. Petronella is the troubled girl-next-door. Her mother is an alcoholic, indicated by Jitta's consumption of Buckfast, a strong tonic wine that has become synonymous with social deprivation and petty crime in Scotland, at least in the media. This leaves Petronella the sole caretaker for her mentally disabled brother, Tomatsk.

A number of times Fergal is shown to be reading *Titus Alone*, and he sketches the face of Cathal on the inside cover. Like Titus of the *Gormenghast* books, mother and son seem outside the modern world. They are not just outcasts from society, consigned to a dilapidated housing scheme, but from the present. Their lives are bound by myth and ritual, as well as fear and the supernatural. The setting may be that of gritty realism, but the viewer is not prodded towards an explanation grounded in, for instance, a mother's unnatural fear of her son's sexual maturity, resulting in hallucinations of her son as a murderous beast. We are presented with the supernatural in familiar contexts and left to draw our own conclusions.

Genre:

Horror

Cast:

James Nesbitt
Kate Dickie
Niall Bruton
Hanna Stanbridge
Karen Gillan

Year:

2010

Filming Locations:

Edinburgh and surrounding area, Scotland, UK
Galway, Ireland

Critique

The film is based in Celtic mythology. Mary is a member of the ancient race of Sídhe and, according to Cathal, she seduced and 'trapped' him. Cathal is intent on killing Fergal because, as he remarks, 'then this beautiful skin I'm in will be mine'. This is to say nothing of Fergal's vicious tendencies once he is transformed into the beast – a greenish, clawed giant humanoid that enjoys the flesh of nubile women. Coming of age and teenage pregnancy are prominent themes. Mary was fifteen when she conceived Fergal, while Petronella, the Laird tells her when he finds her begging at the Mercat Cross, was only able to destroy Fergal because she was pregnant with his child.

Refreshingly, the film offers no distinct villain. Fergal may be bloodthirsty, but it is a curse that he was born with. We do not know Mary's motivations for trapping Cathal. Cathal, in turn, did not know the consequences of his actions. As the film suggests, family feuds are complex and often remain unresolved. Add to this the extreme

Outcast (2010), Courtesy of Creative Scotland

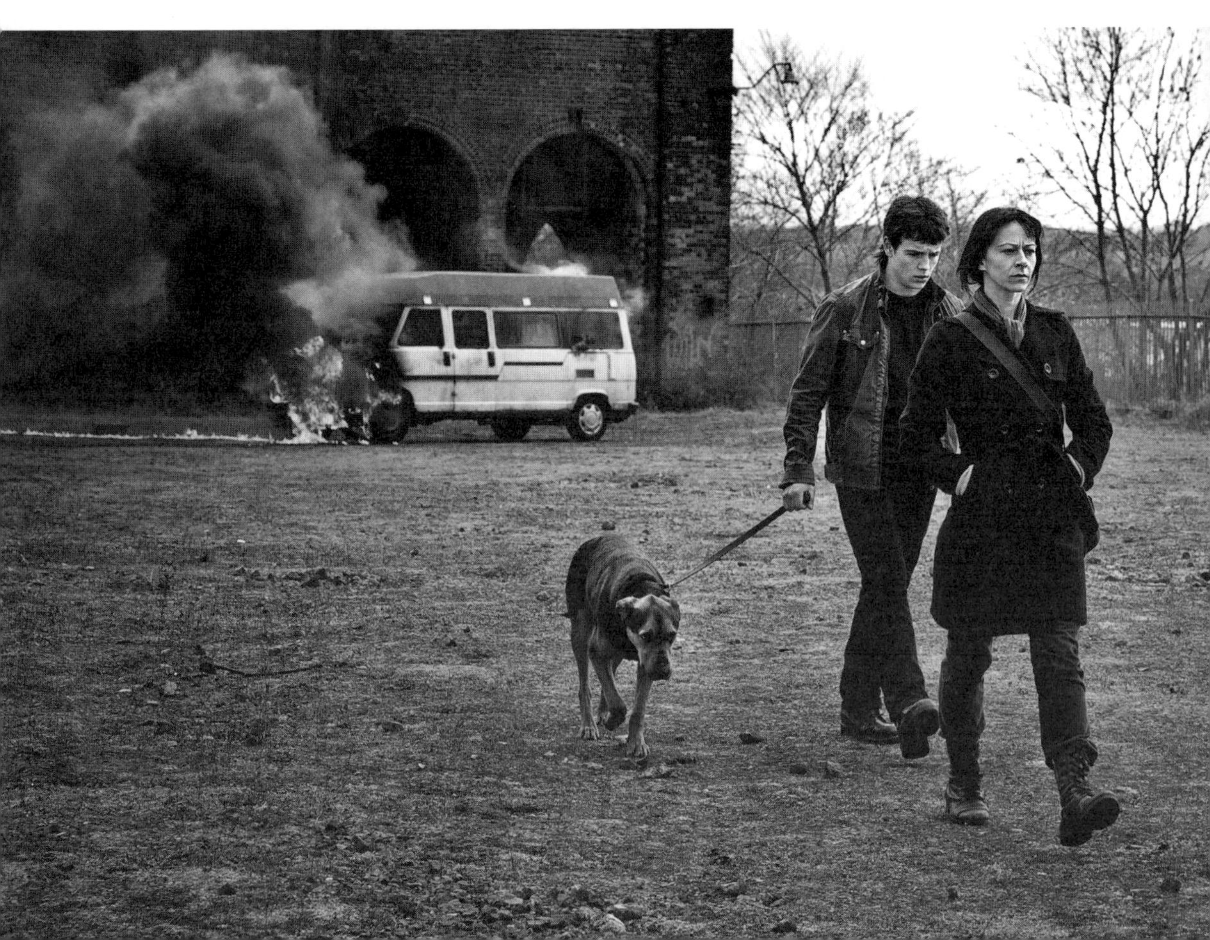

unease resulting from conflicts between mother and son that seem to be wrought with sexual tension. Still, the film happily avoids the inference of an Oedipus Complex (Cathal wants to kill Fergal to be free, not because of any passion for Mary, and Fergal desires to live and to love Petronella).

The film is well-made and it thus seems largely irrelevant to focus on slight discrepancies in regard to accents, expected behaviour and speech patterns. The one exception is the housing officer who, due to Mary's spell, is doomed to wander lost forever in the estate, or at least until she is consumed by the beast. She is much more a stereotype, an incarnation of the tenant's worst nightmares and prejudices – being formally dressed and in a position of authority – but less a reflection of the reality of those in this profession, while her fate does not particularly serve the plot. She seems a victim caught up in supernatural circumstances she has no hope of understanding.

Otherwise, the characters are credible. Mary is a worthy opponent of Cathal, and Petronella is far from a damsel. Fergal, despite his monstrosity, leaves the least impression. What is interesting about him is his alter ego appears to be a principled beast, attacking a boy who is about to beat Tomatsk and restraining himself from devouring Petronella. As such, we can even sympathize with and understand this ugly monster.

Similarly, the high-rises are artfully shot and at sunset are sombrely picturesque. Locations are also merged: for example, the estate in Sighthill has as its background the Scottish Mining Museum, situated some 12 miles away in the town of Newtongrange. These industrial buildings are perhaps a nod to Victorian and urban Gothic, representing the encroachment of modernity on the ancient and mysterious.

This is also the setting for an interrupted liaison between Petronella and Fergal; they are disturbed by commotion caused by Liam and Cathal down below, and flee unseen. Their relationship is only consummated, symbolically enough, in the tunnel of a children's play park. The event precipitates Fergal's final transformation, the death of Cathal and Petronella's slaying of the beast in the crumbling remains of the colliery.

The ending is ambiguous. Young women may now walk home free from fear of attack, or at least from supernatural assailants, but Petronella's pregnancy could be taken as indicative of another saga in the making. The Laird gives her a charm, a pipe in the form of an expectant mother, and wishes her well. Whether this is because Petronella will need luck as a destitute single mother, which is no doubt true, or due to the fact that the child she is carrying poses a threat, is left open to speculation. What can be concluded is that *Outcast* successfully uses Edinburgh as a diversely compelling setting – from its closes and pubs to its suburbs and precincts – for an original story, as opposed to simply relying on a scenic location to tell a story, or worse still, produce what is effectively a tourist brochure.

Susan Robinson

Perfect Sense

Countries of Origin:
UK
Sweden
Denmark
Ireland
Language:
English
Studio/Production Companies:
BBC Films
Zentropa Entertainments
Scottish Screen
Danish Film Institute
Film i Väst
Irish Film Board
Sigma Films
Subotica Entertainment
Director:
David Mackenzie
Producers:
Gillian Berrie
Tomas Eskilsson
Malte Grunert
Screenwriter:
Kim Fupz Aakeson
Cinematographer:
Giles Nuttgens
Art Director:
Andy Thomson
Composer:
Max Richter
Editor:
Jake Roberts
Duration:
92 minutes
Genre:
Fantasy
Cast:
Ewan McGregor
Eva Green
Year:
2011

Synopsis

Chef Michael and epidemiologist Susan are single, middle-class professionals living in opulent isolation in present-day Glasgow. Both are psychologically scarred by traumatic events in their respective personal pasts. A long-term eating disorder has left her infertile, while he is wracked by guilt caused by his failure to care for a terminally ill former lover. A chance meeting (the restaurant where Michael works abuts Susan's warehouse apartment) causes the pair to begin a tentative romance. The subsequent development of an increasingly intense emotional bond between the lovers is accelerated by the outbreak, and seemingly uncontrollable escalation of, a terrifying global pandemic; the latter's inexorable nature and progress is at intervals charted by an unseen omniscient narrator. For reasons unclear to medical science, humankind loses the power of several major senses – smell, taste, hearing and sight – one after the other. This catastrophe affects Michael's and Susan's private and professional lives in profound ways, as the glowering threat of species extinction overshadows their attempts to persevere with the social transactions of day-to-day life and a mutually sustaining relationship with each other.

Critique

What could a suitably ambitious film-maker not do if armed with a viral contagion capable of obliterating humankind? *Perfect Sense* reminds viewers that illness frequently functions, to paraphrase Susan Sontag (2001), as both malady and metaphor. The more aggressive and widespread a given medical affliction is, the greater its potential symbolic resonance becomes: confronting the manner in which our world ends appears to offer a chance to better comprehend the manner in which the world works. For this reason, mid-way through *Perfect Sense*'s narrative the film's unidentified omniscient narrator coolly itemizes several of the potential causes of the inexplicable disease that lie at the heart of the movie. In doing so, she invites viewers to employ their own personal preferences and beliefs as a way of adjudicating between such competing explanations. Thus, for a moment *Perfect Sense* seems to possess the capacity to become a parable for (variously): the Gaia-style revenge of an ecologically abused planet; a terrorist attack by the sworn enemies of western powers such as the United States and Britain; divine retribution exacted upon a fallen world; late capitalism's utterly amoral drive to stimulate and sustain constant consumption by any and all means possible.

What is most striking about director David Mackenzie's sixth feature, however, is the fact that the film conspicuously strives to avoid *all* ideologically inflected interpretations of its narrative premise and content. Instead, *Perfect Sense* seeks to work as a universalizing fable that explores, in the unseen narrator's words, the common human experience of 'the days as we know them – the world as we imagine the world'. For this reason, the movie

Filming Location:
Glasgow, Strathclyde, Scotland, UK

implants a cruelly ingenious irony within the metabolic-cum-metaphoric structure of its viral protagonist's relentless progress: the unstoppable physical degeneration of the human species is accompanied – for Michael, Susan and many others at least – by a parallel process of psychological purification. The loss of each sense is presaged by an excruciatingly intense moment of emotional catharsis, as individuals are forced to verbalize and exorcize their most deep-seated regrets and fears. Thus cleansed, the final point of collective death is marked, as the narrator frames matters, by the arrival of 'the shining moments [...] a profound appreciation of what it means to be alive: but most of all, a shared urge to reach out to one another'. At the film's climax, human extinction and perfection occur simultaneously.

It seems no accident in this regard that Mackenzie's work is structured by two recurring visual/narrative motifs. Viewers are confronted by repeated rapid-fire montages of global reactions, both quotidian and catastrophic, to the unchecked spread of a virus that deprives humanity of its vital bodily senses on one hand, and a preponderance of aquatic metaphors and locations on the other. The function of both devices is to posit *Perfect Sense*'s preferred philosophical axiom, namely, the existence of an intrinsic human identity and experience that transcends ethnic, racial and national boundaries. Digital footage of the planet's various peoples succumbing to (and striving to survive) incurable illness simultaneously stresses both the fragility of the human frame and the dignity of the human spirit, regardless of colour, creed, physical habitat or socio-economic status. The surfeit of water-based sights and sequences (for instance, Susan walking on a beach with her sister, Michael visiting a fish market to buy produce for his restaurant) work towards the same end: water is tasteless, colourless and odourless in its unadulterated state and is also the primary building block from which all human bodies are fashioned. Even Michael's and Susan's professional occupations, cordon bleu chef and epidemiologist respectively, are of significance here. At first sight, such specialized, highly remunerated jobs seems to align the story and themes of *Perfect Sense* with a very specific cultural milieu – an intensely urbanized, economically and technologically advanced and complacent First World society. Fundamentally, however, the highly specialized interests and expertise of both central protagonists gesture back towards the film's preferred vision of an all-encompassing human identity and destiny. In their different ways, after all, Michael and Susan are equally preoccupied with the way of all flesh: he with the things that human bodies consume, she with the things that consume human bodies.

Perfect Sense's resolute universalism might seem to fatally complicate any attempt to locate the film in relation to a contemporary Scottish cinematic context. It is, however, plausible to contextualize the film in just this fashion. On one hand, the movie's preoccupation with painfully heightened romantic and sexual experience links it to other works within director David Mackenzie's prolific oeuvre. Like *Perfect Sense*, *Young Adam* (2002) and *Hallam Foe* (2007) also build their narratives around markedly alienated and damaged central protagonists. Moreover, all three movies employ water as a metaphorical device that charts the emotional depths which their main characters plumb. *Young Adam*'s Joe accidentally kills his lover by pushing her into Glasgow's River Clyde, while *Hallam Foe*'s narrative is built around its titular teenage anti-hero's tortured response to his severely depressed mother's death by drowning. More generally, we might also note the fact that *Perfect Sense* was a co-production among director Mackenzie and producer Gillian Berrie's Glasgow-based independent production company Sigma Films, and a range of Nordic partners, including Denmark's Zentropa Entertainments. The 2000s witnessed a notable number of Scottish-Scandinavian co-productions, a long-term collaborative process initially cemented by Mackenzie, Berrie and Sigma's debut feature, *The Last Great Wilderness* (2002). A characteristic that links many movies within this co-production cycle – works such as director Lone Scherfig's *Wilbur Wants to Kill Himself* (2002) or writer/director Andrea Arnold's *Red Road* (2006) spring to mind in this connection – is their determination to prioritize the exploration of (allegedly) universal human experiences over the cultural specificities of their Scottish narrative settings. In this regard, *Perfect Sense*'s apocalyptic imagining of a world in which it is no longer possible to see, hear, taste or smell cultural heterogeneity represents a logical conclusion to a prominent cycle of avowedly internationalist film-making in Scotland during the twenty-first century's opening decade.

Jonathan Murray

Reference

Sontag, Susan (2001) *Illness as Metaphor and AIDS and Its Metaphors*, London: Picador.

Shallow Grave

Country of Origin:

United Kingdom

Language:

English

Studio/Production Companies:

Film4 International
Glasgow Film Fund

Director:

Danny Boyle

Producer:

Andrew MacDonald

Synopsis

Danny Boyle's theatrical feature debut is a film that brings together elements of the thriller and black comedy. The plot features three roommates: Alex, Juliet and David in search of a fourth roommate to share a spacious apartment. The potential candidate has to share the spirit of the three – cynical, mischievous and carefree. After a series of interviews, the fourth roommate, Hugo – equipped with a mix of confidence and mystery – simply shows up and occupies the room. His presence in the apartment triggers an avalanche of events that alters the space of the apartment, the relationship between the three roommates and challenges personal limits. When Hugo is found dead in his room along with a suitcase full of money, the plot unfolds in thriller format. The three decide to get rid of the body and retain the money. Their agreement almost instantly brings out the trickster in each of them.

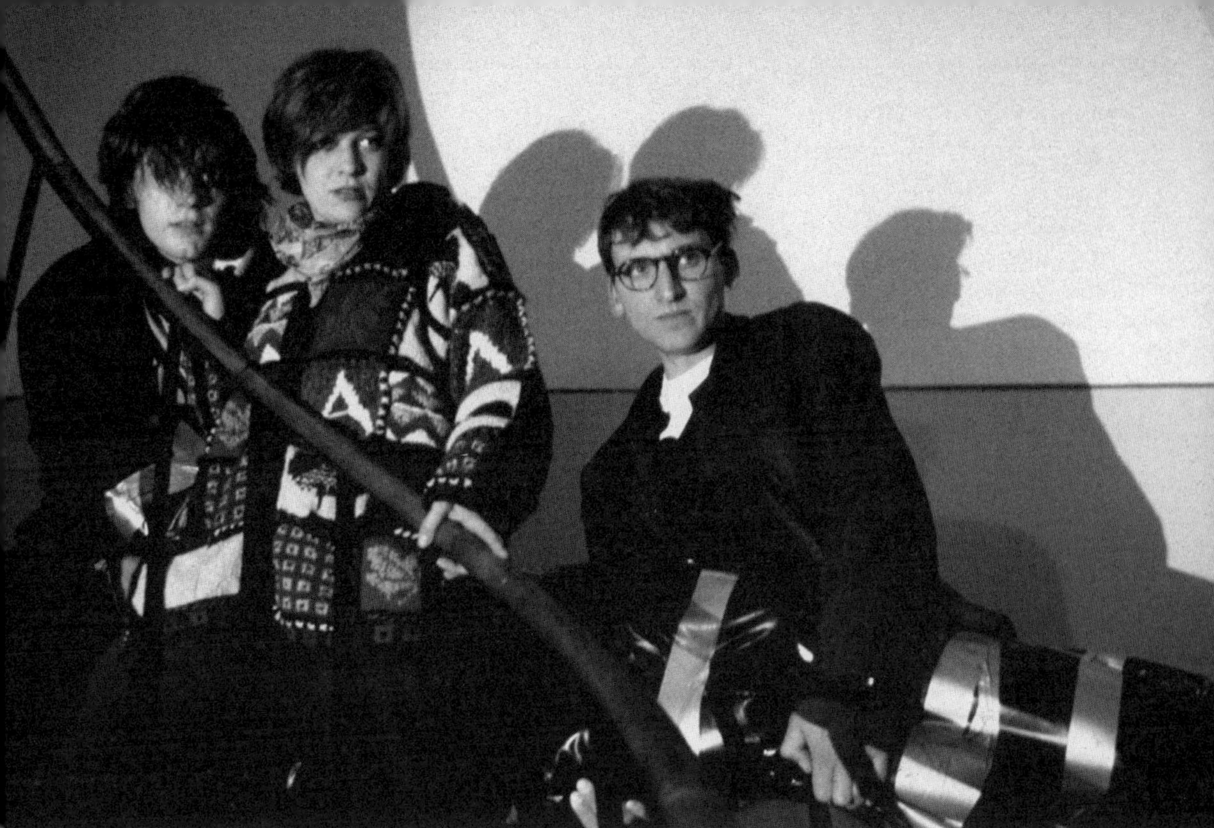

Shallow Grave (1994), British Film Institute Collection

Screenwriter:
John Hodge
Cinematographer:
Brian Tufano
Art Director:
Zoe MacLeod
Composer:
Simon Boswell
Editor:
Masahiro Hirakubo
Duration:
92 minutes
Genre:
Horror
Cast:
Christopher Eccleston
Kerry Fox
Ewan McGregor

Critique

The film explores a theme of rich psychological reflection: one's relationship with money and the web of implications upon personal relations. The power roles in the Alex–Juliet–David triangle shift and follow an interesting but not surprising trajectory, as all the characters remain victims of their own immaturity and *naïveté*. The film contains comic moments that are briefly interjected by the escalation of violence. Alex and Juliet readily agree to do whatever it takes to keep the money, without envisioning what consequences that might entail. David (who incidentally is an accountant) seems more reserved and hesitant in the beginning but ends up being the most actively involved in securing the money for himself. Juliet's interests gravitate around Alex's personality, David's tight grasp of the suitcase with money and finally the money itself, with which she hopes to secure her quasi-cinematic cliché of a carefree and anonymous life abroad.

The film opens with fast-paced techno music accompanying images of the main locations featured in the plot – the grim face of Glasgow bathed in glowing sunlight, a dark forest and a beautiful apartment where the camera and the music slow down. Of the three locations, the apartment is the most carefully constructed space

Year:

1994

Filming Locations:

6 North East Circus Place, New Town, Edinburgh, Scotland, UK
New Town, Edinburgh, Scotland, UK
North Bridge, Edinburgh, Scotland, UK
Royal Alexandra Hospital, Paisley, Renfrewshire, Scotland, UK
Townhouse Hotel - 54 West George Street, Glasgow, Strathclyde, Scotland, UK

as evidenced by correspondingly intricate camera work. The first frames in which the three roommates interview potential tenants feature the apartment as a theatrical setting. There are numerous compositions in which the camera focuses concomitantly on the characters and the space they occupy. Particular attention is paid to proportions, light and colour. With the escalation of violence, the characters seem to grow bigger under the close scrutiny of the camera. As an effect of this shift, the apartment loses its once-generous proportions. The accumulation of psychological tension between the three roommates renders the apartment literally too small. The pliability of space-character development is one of the most engaging dynamics in the film.

While violence in *Shallow Grave* serves to achieve and maintain some level of suspense, the psychological depth behind it is – to cite the title, shallow. This prevents the audience from fully grasping the characters and processing the mounting level of abjection. Instead, this lack of psychological depth is supplemented with dark humour. In the end, while Alex is oozing blood, he does not forget to smile for the camera, and rejoice the thought of having tricked Juliet. The final close-ups of Alex smiling in a bloodbath are moments of self-consciousness that illuminate the aesthetic engagement of the film with violence and humour. With the success of *Shallow Grave* followed shortly by that of *Trainspotting* (1996), Boyle's cinema is credited to have defined a new identity for the Scottish cinema of the mid-1990's, which fashions an international appeal while maintaining its national/local profile. The tone for this new identity is set at the beginning of *Shallow Grave* when the voice-over refutes the local character of the story to reinforce its universal dimensions: 'this could have been any city – they are all the same'.

Oana Chivoiu

That Sinking Feeling

Country of Origin:

UK

Language:

English

Studio/Production Company:

The Sinking Feeling Film Cooperative

Director:

Bill Forsyth

Producers:

Bill Forsyth

Synopsis

Young men of the city are out of work for reasons they cannot understand. Every day is a degrading struggle for food, lodging and self-respect. A chance encounter with a show window inspires the daring idea of committing a robbery of the local industrial plumbing warehouse. Targeted for plunder is the vast stockpile of stainless steel sinks. The boys assemble a crew and formulate a detailed itinerary for the heist. Each player in the conspiracy has their own important role and task to perform. Hurdles include the drugging of a van driver, the distraction of a night watchman and the fencing of unwieldy kitchen hardware. Against all odds the boys pull together, function like a well-organized business and are filled with entrepreneurial spirit. Reflecting upon their success, the team plans their next big job – pumping a tanker-truck full of the soft drink Irn Bru from the local factory and selling it down along the coastal beaches.

Paddy Higson
Screenwriter:
Bill Forsyth
Cinematographer:
Michael Coulter
Art Director:
Adrienne Atkinson
Composer:
Colin Tully
Editor:
John Gow
Duration:
87 minutes
Genre:
Comedy

Critique

Bill Forsyth's first feature film takes the form of a screwball comedy featuring an ensemble cast, location shooting and expert use of minimal resources. Neither movie stars nor lavish set-pieces embellish this movie – just cleverly chosen and skilfully filmed Glasgow landmarks, industrial parks and tower blocks. None of the major characters ever quite rise to the level of a lead with the reciprocal effect that not even the smallest role is reduced to that of a support. The young man (Ronnie) who originates the plan to steal sinks is no more important than the woman who chides him for trying to plot a robbery without money. The ultimate effect is that the film rises out of the 'town called GLASGOW' in the form of a subsuming collective smog of individual utterances and the productive fictionalizing of a time and place with a non-productive ambiance. *That Sinking Feeling* is thus a film whose star is its milieu, the 'fictitious town' of which the real Glasgow is the performer.

This humble meandering farce of unemployment and industrious burglary in a decrepit industrial wasteland is simultaneously the

That Sinking Feeling (1980), British Film Institute Collection

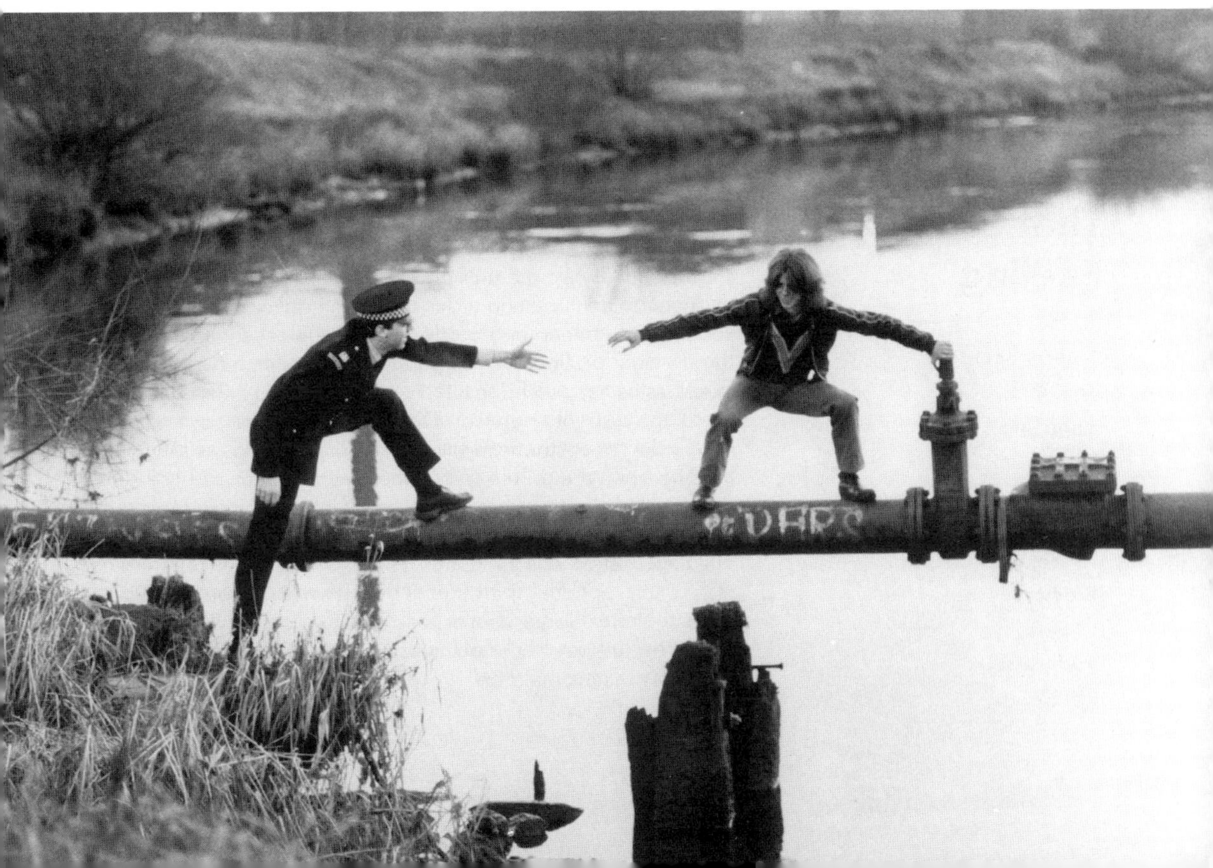

Cast:

Glasgow Youth Theatre
The Fictitious Town Called GLASGOW

Year:

1980

Filming Locations:

Glasgow, Strathclyde, Scotland, UK

static representation of an actual mode of living in the Glasgow of the late 1970s. The film subtly and perhaps unwittingly becomes the bearer of an intense political charge if the greatest proximity of art to politics is the production of a differential spectrum of thought and understanding of a given unity (Ranciere 2010: 140–41). A city – 'fictitious' or otherwise – forms the common site of differing sensibilities and contrary ideals which nevertheless combine and reconfigure the structure of possible material relationships. Against objections to the claim that the film is political (and not discounting Forsyth's own) it should be insisted that nothing is more politically relevant than the ideologies and aspirations which comprise and invest a social totality. The lads' inability to respond to their own charge that 'there's got to be something more to life than committing suicide' is the strongest insinuation of the truth that multiple forms of social deprivation characterize their local society.

The film's expositional strategy could be characterized as a series of missed communications, distorted perceptions and atomized relations. A conversation consists of the same statement repeated variously using different words and ending nowhere. Phrases are misunderstood and important messages are delivered to incorrect recipients, intercepted by interlopers and obstructed by overwhelming noises. Numbers lose all sense of reference – 45 pence prices one out of a meal while £60 for a sink inspires visions of opulence. The simple instruction to search 'the lavatory pan upstairs' leads to a warehouse floor stocked with an endless proliferation of toilets. Taking inventory is a process of listing all the things one has none of. In a police description of a stolen bakery van, 'no chocolate donuts' becomes a distinguishing feature worth repeating. A gnawing hunger and a giddy desperation infuse everything with the sense of constipated production and the signs of a metastasizing non-productivity. Wee Man apparently spends his days racing up and down a playground slide in the park and unattended children adorn the landscape like perambulating shrubberies.

Two complex plot elements – the warehouse robbery and a chemical formula for suspended animation – take on peculiarly inverted values. The potion looks like the work of 'a maniac … a psychopath', while the unlikely heist sparkles with the prospects of 'a goldmine'. The chemicals turn a van driver into a 'snoring zombie' who becomes a costly burden whereas the load of sinks turns a clear profit. Sold to a canny exhibitioner, a pile of stainless steel basins heaped haphazardly on the floor of an art gallery marks the disparity between production of real goods and the production of aesthetic ideology. The piece serves as a monument holding open the pure gap between manufacture and use – as an accidental or 'readymade' art object, 'Sink' genuinely reproduces the dynamic of the forces of which it is a product and an expression. The exploitation and alienation of which it serves as the material objectification take on a value of their own (Agamben 1999: 66–67). The exhibition buyer is correct to recognize in this random pile of useless metal the qualities of 'a very, very good piece […] absolutely as it should be'.

Forsyth's accomplishment in *That Sinking Feeling* is the aesthetic production of the ideology of the structurally unemployed. What is portrayed here is that there is a sustaining mood and a tonality to the inability to find work in a world that demands remunerative labour as the material signifier of social value. This 'sinking feeling' is not simply an inert sense of worthlessness but itself a dynamic pathos generative of both the impetus and justification of criminal activity as the secret obverse of more exalted entrepreneurial success. Much of the comedic tension derives from the displacement of the discourse of commerce and productivity onto a ragged band of upstart brigands in the act of planning and executing their robbery. Not only must the gang recruit only 'people with skill, courage and determination' but they also hold pep talks, training sessions and maintain an ordered and efficient division of labour. At one point the heist is pitched directly in terms of investment capital. In its attempt to subvert and exploit the local productive economy the gang merely ends up reproducing its mechanisms and values. Far from displaying the contradictory opposite of capitalist ideology, the budding criminals end up directly enacting its hidden support. Such reversals of transgression into conformity are the very signature of ideological manipulation at the same time as expressing the truth of the ruling-class consciousness (Jameson 1981: 286–90).

It remains to be asked whether such dialectical inversions can be accomplished without leaving their traces inscribed in some form of excremental remainder. If the subject of the film is read as the ideals and appearances that drive the grimy material reality of Glasgow's quotidian existence then something has to be suppressed which would otherwise threaten to rise up and stain the picture. The comatose van driver drugged into metabolic stasis and 'scheduled to wake up in the year 2068' will do so 'carrying the hopes, the dreams, the fears of all'. There is no clearer figure of working-class consciousness in the film. In order for the boys to inflect the active subjectivity of a stagnant and stultifying political economy, something must be squeezed out and left behind to hold the place of the occluded and repressed class struggle. The cost of the gang's sailing onward is that something unspoken remains dead in the water. It is all the more appropriate that this price be the very literal unconsciousness of class-consciousness.

Alex F Brown

References

Agamben, Giorgio (1999) *The Man Without Content*, Stanford: SUP.

Jameson, Frederic (1981) *The Political Unconscious: Narrative as a Socially Symbolic Act*, Ithaca: Cornell University Press.

Rancière, Jacues. (2010) *Dissensus: On Politics and Aesthetics*, London/New York: Continuum.

Whisky Galore!

Country of Origin:
UK
Languages:
English
Scottish Gaelic
Studio/Production Company:
Ealing Studios
Director:
Alexander Mackendrick
Producers:
Michael Balcon
Monja Danischewsky
Screenwriters:
Compton Mackenzie
Angus MacPhail
Cinematographer:
Gerald Gibbs
Art Director:
Jim Morahan
Composer:
Ernest Irving
Editor:
Joseph Sterling
Duration:
82 minutes
Genre:
Comedy
Cast:
Basil Radford
Joan Greenwood
Bruce Seton
Catherine Lacey
Wylie Watson
Year:
1949
Filming Location:
Barra, Scotland, UK

Synopsis

The year is 1943. The remote Scottish Island of Todday in the Outer Hebrides has been largely unaffected by World War II, until a whisky shortage threatens the small community's way of life. Meanwhile, the English Sergeant Odd and schoolteacher George Campbell romance Peggy and Catriona, daughters of the island's storekeeper Joseph Macroon. Odd has to adjust to the local customs of the island, while Campbell deals with his formidable mother's set ideas over his proper future. When a boat containing 50,000 crates of whisky sinks near the island, the Todday natives enter into an escalating duel of wits with Captain Paul Waggett, a pompous Home Guard official who wants to confiscate the whisky. Odd helps the Islanders as part of his marriage promise to Peggy and acceptance into island life, while Campbell proves his independence from his mother. The Islanders finally outwit a humiliated Waggett, and celebrate a double Macroon wedding with their newfound whisky.

Critique

Whisky Galore! works as both a typical Ealing comedy, and as an example of some of the problems associated with stereotypical representations of Scotland in post-World War II British cinema. The post-war Ealing comedies were distinguished by their gentle satire of wartime and middle-class life, producing a series of films that remain classics of British cinema. Aside from *Whisky Galore!*, other films produced from 1947 through 1955 include *Hue and Cry* (Charles Crichton, 1947), *Passport to Pimlico* (Henry Cornelius, 1949), *Kind Hearts and Coronets* (Robert Hamer, 1949), *The Lavender Hill Mob* (Charles Crichton, 1951) and Alexander Mackendrick's *The Man in the White Suit* (1951), *The Maggie* (1954) and *The Ladykillers* (1955).

Alexander Mackendrick, director of *Whisky Galore!*, *The Man in the White Suit*, *The Maggie* and *The Ladykillers*, brought a somewhat darker take to the playfully anti-authoritarian Ealing style. His films arguably provide more mischievous characters, blacker comedy and more penetrating satires of post-war Britain than other Ealing comedies of the time. *Whisky Galore!* was his first film for the studio, and adapted Compton Mackenzie's novel of wartime mischief in the Outer Hebrides, itself based on a real incident from 1941. The film shares many of the features of other Ealing comedies, most notably a nostalgia for a small community fighting against bureaucracy to preserve their way of life, and the use of on-location shooting for added realism.

Whisky Galore!'s remote Scottish setting intensifies these features, with the Gaelic-speaking Todday Islanders representing a resourceful group that ultimately humiliate Waggett, and pursue the hedonism of whisky as integral to island life. Efforts to balance out the rougher edges of Todday were eventually made by Ealing, with studio head Michael Balcon commissioning a re-edit before its successful release. The film went on to become Ealing's most

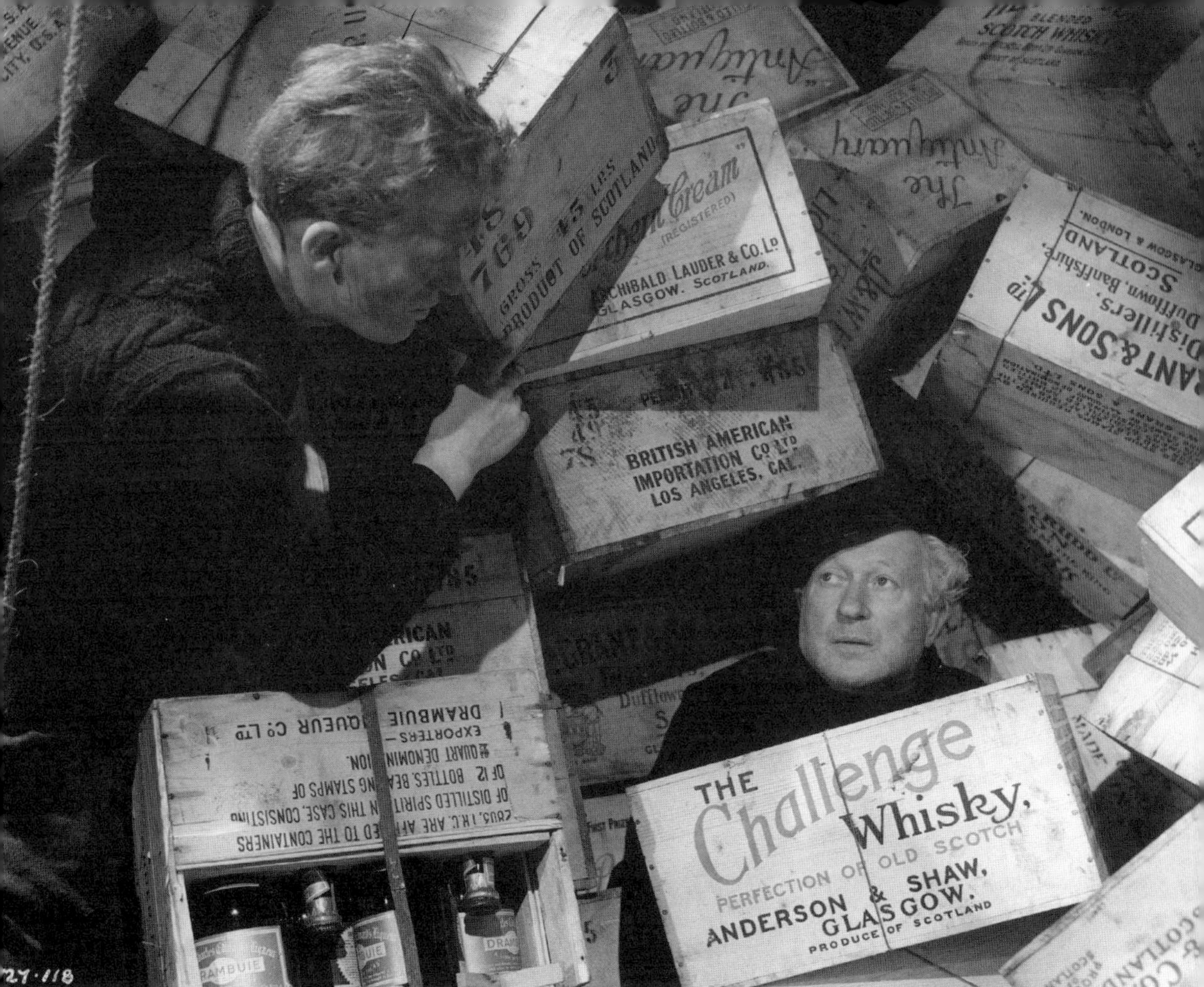

Whisky Galore! (1949), British Film Institute Collection

profitable production, and an influence on later Scottish-produced box office successes like Bill Forsyth's *Local Hero* (1983).

However, while gently subversive in its criticism of Waggett's bureaucracy, *Whisky Galore!* is reactionary in terms of its ruthless protection of and nostalgia for a traditional way of life. Women also become marginalized to preserve a patriarchal society, with the result arguably being a promotion of parochial values. The film's romantic representation of Scotland as a wild, untamed part of wartime Britain also reinforces cinematic and more general myths of Scottish life. *Whisky Galore!*'s eccentric small community can be viewed as a clear example of Kailyardism, a romantic stereotype of a primitively pre-modern Scottish working-class life that fails to connect with twentieth-century social realities.

The box office success of *Whisky Galore!* came during a period where films like *I Know Where I'm Going!* (Michael Powell and Emeric Pressburger, 1945) and *Brigadoon* (Vincente Minnelli, 1954) epitomized trends for a romantic vision of Scotland produced by English or American studios for worldwide consumption. Alexander

Mackendrick also contributed to this cycle a few years later with *The Maggie*, another comedy set around a sentimental and reactionary take on contemporary Scottish life. As a result, *Whisky Galore!* is both a much-loved comedy, and an example of some of the contemporary representational limits of depicting Scotland on-screen.

Gareth James

The Wicker Man

Country of Origin:

UK

Language:

English

Studio/Production Company:

British Lion Film Corporation

Director:

Robin Hardy

Producer:

Peter Snell

Screenwriters:

Anthony Shaffer (screenplay)
David Pinner (novel: Ritual)

Cinematographer:

Harry Waxman

Art Director:

Seamus Flannery

Composer:

Paul Giovanni

Editor:

Eric Boyd-Perkins

Duration:

88 minutes

Genre:

Horror

Cast:

Edward Woodward
Christopher Lee
Diane Cilento
Britt Ekland

Synopsis

When Sergeant Neil Howie of the West Highland Police is called to the remote Island of Summerisle in order to investigate the disappearance of young girl named Rowan Morrison, he is baffled to find that the inhabitants claim she does not exist. Discovering to his horror that the village is a practising Pagan community, Howie – a devout Christian – starts to suspect foul play. With the May Day festival soon approaching, the Sergeant begins to fear that the child will be offered as a sacrificial appeasement following the poor harvest of the previous year. Only at the film's climax does he learn the horrific truth: it is he who is to be killed, burnt alive whilst trapped within a giant wicker man.

Critique

Based around the plot of David Pinner's 1967 novel *Ritual*, the central concept of *The Wicker Man* is endlessly intriguing. Imagining a scenario in which a society completely different from our own exists within miles of the life we know so well, it asks how we would act when faced with a morality of which we have no comprehension. With the community of Summerisle, *The Wicker Man* does not just outline this possibility, but constructs it as a fully realized truth. Every aspect of village life is drawn before us, from the outdated medical practices that see toads placed in mouths, to the schoolhouse where children not only dance around maypoles, but are explicitly taught about their phallic significance. It may seem an unusual existence to us, but how can it be judged according to rules it has never acknowledged? With the issue proving just as interesting today as in 1973, it is not surprising that director Robin Hardy has recently chosen to revisit the themes with his companion piece *The Wicker Tree* (2011), and, even less so, that the film was the recipient of a remake in 2006.

What makes the collision of viewpoints in Hardy's original even more pronounced, though, are the staunch beliefs of the protagonist himself – the piously Christian police officer, Sergeant Howie. Curiously omitted in Neil LaBute's oft criticized reworking, Howie's own faith plays a pivotal role in the film, not only in explaining the reactionary nature of his response to Pagan ritual, but also in establishing him as the perfect carrier for the film's narrative themes. Considered an overly sober individual even in

Year:

1973

Filming Locations:

Anworth, Scotland, UK
Burrow Head, Scotland, UK
Gatehouse of Fleet, Scotland, UK
Castle Kennedy, Scotland, UK
Creetown, Scotland, UK
Culzean Castle, Scotland, UK
Isle of Skye, Scotland, UK
Kirkcudbright, Scotland, UK
Plockton, Scotland, UK
Port Logan, Scotland, UK
St Ninian's Cave, Physgill, Scotland, UK

his hometown, Howie's colleagues are shown joking about his involvement in a two-year sex-free romance, suggesting that his future wife will spend 'more time on her knees in church than she will on her back in bed'. To Howie, however, these matters are serious ones. A man cannot be good unless he is pure and to be pure means both abstaining from fornication, and attending church – a belief he makes clear when meeting with the Lord of Summerisle during his investigation. With the Lord insisting that Summerisle's inhabitants are 'a deeply religious people', the Sergeant responds incredulously: 'Religious – with ruined churches, no ministers, no priests?'.

Yet at this point in the film, it is possible to see Lord Summerisle's position as a reasonable one. After all, the customs of his island do not seem dangerous, so much as different – with one notable example being supplied by the film's distinctive soundtrack. Comprised of songs written by musician Paul Giovanni, and

The Wicker Man (1973), British Film Institute Collection

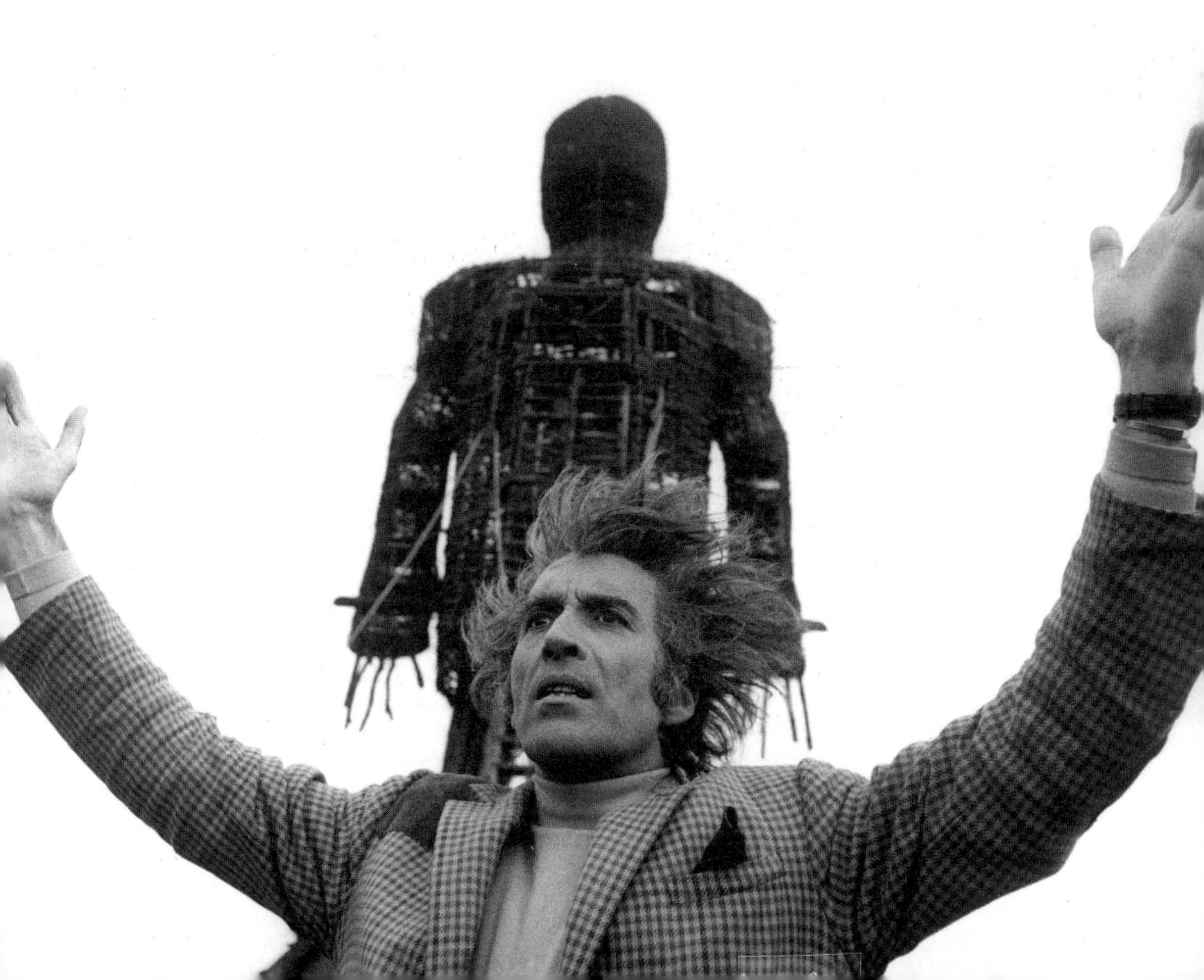

performed by the cast, the score provides the village with its own traditional folk hymns – the majority of which are unashamedly linked to the notions of sex and reproduction. Songs with titles such as 'Gently, Johnny' and 'The Landlord's Daughter' may seem bawdy and vulgar to Howie, but with the townspeople regularly copulating in public gardens and girls leaping naked through flames in hope of being impregnated by the gods, these well practised refrains are just part of a belief system based around the miracle of fertility. Indeed, having suggested to Howie that the Virgin Mary might be Christianity's own celebration of the same notion, Lord Summerisle admits: 'I am a heathen, conceivably, but not, I hope, an unenlightened one'.

Regardless of the peaceful images painted by the island leader, however, one matter bestows a constant sense of unease in both Howie and the viewer: the fate of Rowan Morrison. With the villagers seemingly united as one mind, they first claim that they have never seen the girl, before later suggesting that she has died, but that there is nothing left of her physical form. Discovering photos linking Rowan to the previous year's failed apple harvest, Howie begins to theorize that the girl may be alive, waiting to be revealed as a sacrifice during the upcoming May Day festival. Infiltrating the village parade, he soon finds out how wrong he has been. With the girl gleefully serving as bait, the locals capture Howie and begin to prepare him as the offering instead. The sacrifice of a child, Lord Summerisle explains, is nothing to that of 'the right kind of adult'. As a sexually chaste Christian, Howie's faith has doomed him. Dragged towards the cage of a looming wicker man, he implores his captors, 'in the name of God, think what you're doing', his words mirroring those of the crucified Christ, 'Father – forgive them, they know not what they do'. He speaks too late, his pleas soon turning to screams. Meanwhile, at the foot of the wicker man, Lord Summerisle and his followers simply smile. Joining hands, they commence another song.

Patrick Harley

Wild Country

Country of Origin:

Scotland

Language:

English

Studio/Production Companies:

Gabriel Films
Wild Film Partners

Director:

Craig Strachan

Synopsis

Kelly Ann recently gave birth to, and subsequently gave up for adoption, a baby boy. The meddling local priest, Father Steve, in words slathered with condescension tells her of the happy couple, the 'beautiful baby boy' and congratulates her: 'You made a family today'. Kelly's mother can only offer her sweets in consolation and looks on with an air of detachment, pronouncing, 'you don't want to make the same mistakes'. Six months later, Kelly Ann goes on an overnight 'Wild Country Hike' with the church youth club. Driving through the countryside, Father Steve informs them that they are deep in 'Sawney Bean country'. Sawney Bean being the head of an infamous family of cannibals said to reside in Ayrshire in the sixteenth century. He then drops them off, heading on to

Producers:

Catherine Aitken
Ros Borland
Angela Murray

Screenwriter:

Craig Strachan

Cinematographer:

Jan Pester

Art Director:

John Knight

Editor:

Colin Monie

Duration:

70 minutes

Genre:

Horror

Cast:

Samantha Shields
Martin Compston
Peter Capaldi
Alan McHugh
Nicola Muldoon
Kevin and Jamie Quinn

Year:

2006

Filming Locations:

Glasgow and surrounding area (Mugdock Country Park, Dunbartonshire), Scotland, UK

Budget:

US $1.5 million (approx.)

the pick-up point, a bed and breakfast 25 miles away. The group is later joined, much to Kelly Ann's distaste, by her ex-boyfriend Lee. Despite their quick-thinking and ingenuity, the teenagers are picked off one-by-one by a herd of four-legged beasts. By sunrise only Kelly Ann, Lee and an abandoned baby found by the couple, remain. Lee decides to take on the beast with his pocket knife, allowing Kelly to escape to the B&B where she then transforms into one of the beasts and devours Father Steve.

Critique

There is much to be admired in this film, especially given its small budget. Realism, from the mundane to the socially aware, is deftly balanced with the supernatural and drama is always followed up by a strong and welcome dose of humour. For instance, the farmer's response to his ravaged herd is the oblivious plea: 'Don't let it be foot-and-mouth. Anything but foot-and-mouth. Or mad cow disease'.

Capaldi and Compston give great comedic performances. Father Steve is a great depiction of a lascivious and hypocritical old fool. With gleeful malice, he jumps into his boxers, paunch wobbling, before 'counselling' Kelly on her incredible story, diagnosing her with postnatal depression and meeting his very sticky end. His trite speech is the utterance of someone who understands little of his lack of importance and as such underestimates the veracity of those around him: 'I've seen this before with birth mothers. I should have been more vigilant. I mean, I know you were depressed. I thought you were coping with it […] you stole this child, didn't you Kelly Ann?' And the line that truly damns him: 'How do you think his mother feels?'.

Compston's performance often verges on hammy, alternating between headlong panic and casual concern: 'The sheep-shagging pervert! His heid's up at the castle! Cut aff! […] And Kelly Ann found a baby'. It's an entertaining contrast to Kelly Ann's cool decisiveness which at times borders on suspect – will she expend everyone for the sake of keeping a substitute for the baby stolen from her? The plot allows for both interpretations: Kelly Ann as a strong and quick-witted maternal figure who was wrongfully denied her baby; or a wild, impulsive young girl. Indeed, she sees the beast almost as a human threat: 'You can't have him you ugly bitch!' With this in mind, Kelly's breastfeeding serves two functions; demonstrating that she is a nurturer, and as a plot device, allowing for her later transformation.

It is significant that matters of sex and sexuality are often punctuated with the supernatural. When it is revealed that the animosity between the couple is again the work of Father Steve, who told Lee that Kelly did not want to see him and that she was giving up the baby, Lee remarks: 'I was a bit pissed aff at first', swiftly earning himself his first 'boot in the balls'. Then, the first of many suspect noises is heard, but only by Kelly, who believes it is a baby crying.

When the group set up camp by a ruin, Kelly, responding to a different call of nature, goes into the bushes only to be upset by a crazy-eyed shepherd dressed in sheepskins. Lee volunteers to keep watch and the couple reconcile. At the exact moment Lee receives another assault for making a move on Kelly, she hears the cries again. Certain that they are coming from the ruins, the pair investigate – finding a baby boy surrounded by the fresh and bloody remains of the shepherd. This can be interpreted alongside instances such as David's reaction to Kelly's breastfeeding: 'You know I'm a little bit thirsty myself'. His awkward response, disguised as humour, to something entirely natural would not be considered unusual for many teenagers in the same circumstance. Also, in the ruins, the boys urinate to mark their territory and show the beast 'who's boss' but this isn't without concessions to civility: 'Watch what you're doing!' 'Sorry mate'.

Even in the most extraordinary circumstances manners and expected behaviour prevail. Kelly's transformation, and the final scene of the family of three beasts bounding into the sunset, is perhaps her emancipation from the stigma of teenage motherhood; the Father Steves, with their ideas of propriety and superficial piety. But this is rather bleak, only after such an extreme series of events has Kelly 'made a family' of her own.

Scotland's teenage pregnancy rate is notoriously high, at least in Europe, but it is not overemphasized that Kelly Ann is from one of Glasgow's poorer areas. She and the other teenagers are not presented as stereotypes, but rather as young people with emotional intelligence who look out for one another. The dialogue is natural, not a forced idea of Glaswegian speech, and the viewer is compelled to sympathize with them and not the adults. It could not be much more different from, to make a comparison, *Juno* (Jason Reitman, 2007) – where parents are supportive and a droll sense of humour can paper over most of the cracks.

This is an altogether darker tale that chooses not to side-step or gloss over the least appealing aspects of human nature: deceit, pretence and prejudice. The story of Sawney Bean is toyed with throughout the film but not fully developed. It perhaps serves a reminder that no matter how civilized we appear or attempt to be, more basic instincts will always run alongside and compel us to act in ways that are inexplicable or even despicable. In this sense, Scotland, like everywhere else, will always be a 'wild country'.

Susan Robinson

Glasgow 1980, directed by Oscar Mazaroli (1971)

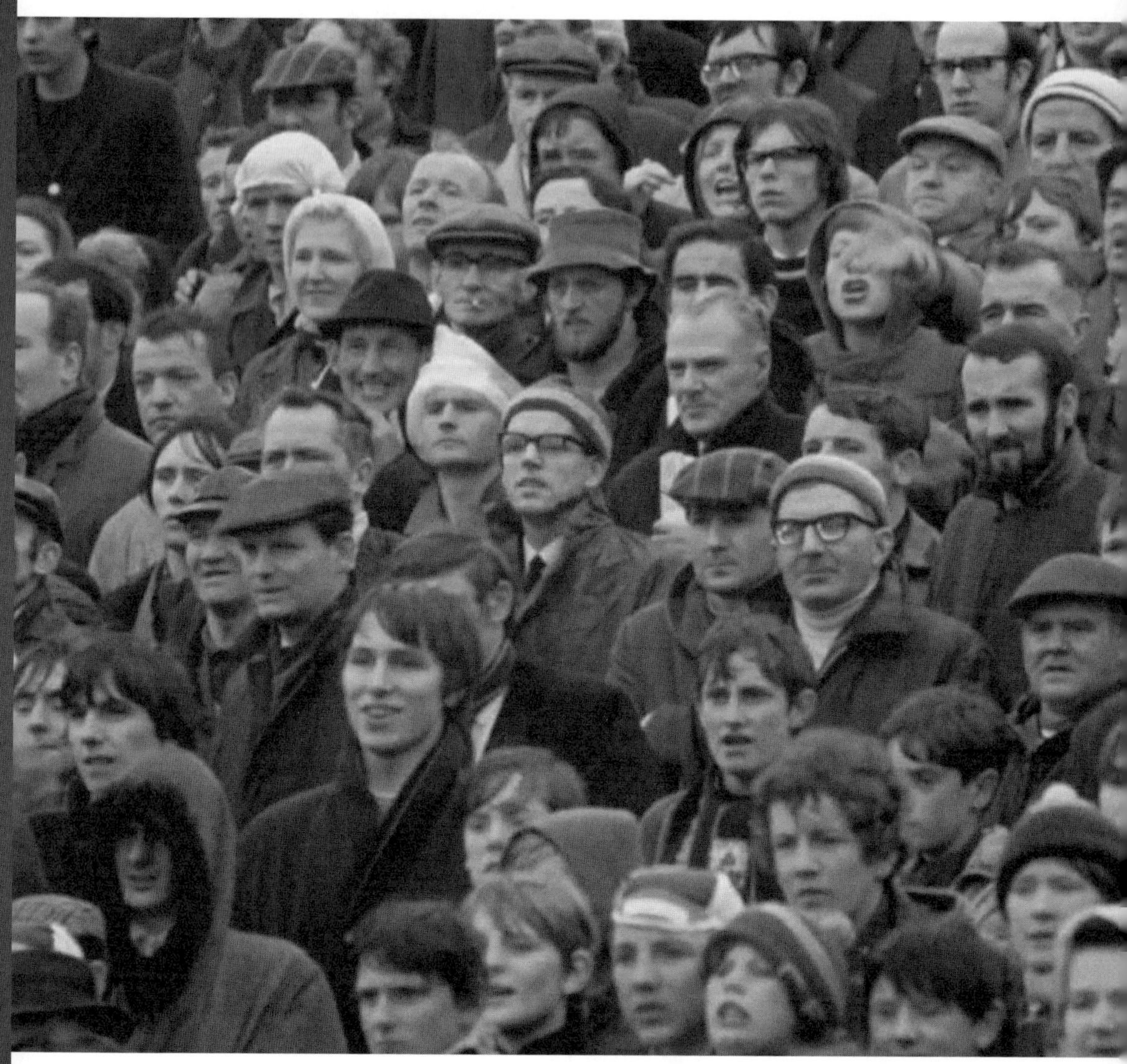

DOCUMENTA

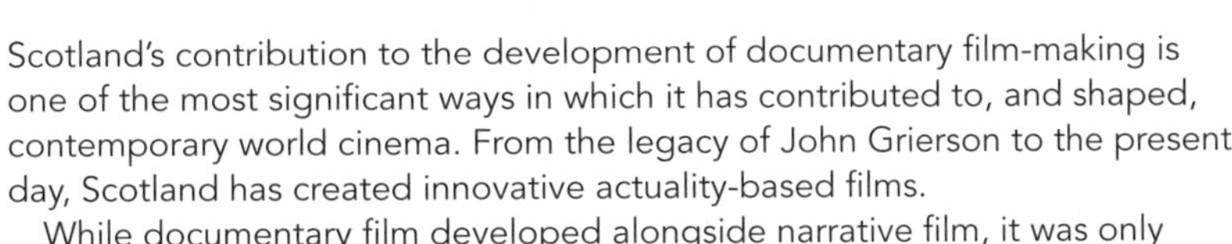

Scotland's contribution to the development of documentary film-making is one of the most significant ways in which it has contributed to, and shaped, contemporary world cinema. From the legacy of John Grierson to the present day, Scotland has created innovative actuality-based films.

While documentary film developed alongside narrative film, it was only during the late 1920s that film-makers began to realize the extent to which film could be used to 'document' communities and activities of interest.

Scotland's depiction on film can be traced from 1895, which saw the production of *The Execution of Mary Queen of Scots*, made by Thomas Edison. Although a re-enactment of an historical event, the film presaged an interest in royalty and 'official' subjects frequent in early documentary. Other stepping-stones toward the modern documentary include footage of X-ray experiments taken in 1896, filmed by Dr John MacIntyre at Glasgow Royal Infirmary, and *The Gordon Highlanders* (1899), in which a regiment is filmed leaving Aberdeen in preparation for the Boer War.

John Grierson first used the term 'documentary' to describe Canadian film-maker Robert Flaherty's film *Moana* in a review of the film that was published in the *New York Sun* on 8 February 1926. Actually a docufiction account of the daily life of a family in Polynesia, *Moana* prompted Grierson to articulate in a new word the importance of using film for anthropological purposes. Grierson saw the potential to use documentary for political purposes, such as raising awareness of the everyday conditions of existence, especially on the job, of the working class. Grierson's seminal essay, 'First Principles of Documentary Film' (1932), served as a manifesto in support of the development of documentary film and remains an influential text on the subject to this day. From the 1920s onwards, Grierson frequently collaborated on documentary projects with multiple directors, including Robert Flaherty, Paul Rotha, Stuart Legg and Basil Wright.

Between the 1920s and 1930s, Scottish film culture underwent an ideological and organizational shift marked by the creation of several film societies and libraries. These included the Film Society of Glasgow, which focused primarily on the production and study of educational films – many of which included documentary properties. From this source also sprung the creation of the Meteor Film Producing Society. This society became extremely influential in the formation of Scottish film-making collaborations, and its participants included historically significant figures such as Eddie McConnell and Stewart McAllister. It was due to their participation in Film Society activities that both film-makers first came to the attention of Grierson, whose influence rapidly extended beyond directing his own films, in a prolific career managing and producing the output of documentaries directed by many other film-makers.

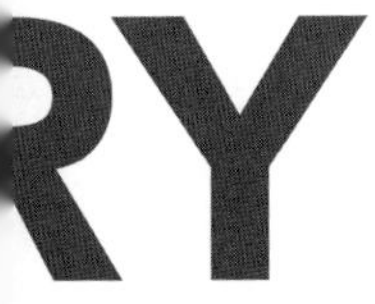

A preoccupation with manual work and the lives of the working classes are strong themes that run throughout the films of this period. Notable examples include *Drifters* (Grierson, 1929), which depicts the lives of North Sea herring fisherman, and *Night Mail* (Harry Watt and Basil Wright, 1936). Grierson invited McAllister to his newly established production company, the General Post Office Film Unit, which had produced *Night Mail* and which would go on to produce many further documentaries, including much of Humphrey Jennings's work.

In 1931, Jenny Gilbertson produced her first documentary, *A Crofter's Life in Shetland* (1931), which shows the lives of agricultural workers in Shetland. The work impressed Grierson so much that he purchased several of her films for the General Post Office Film Library. Gilbertson would become one of the best-established female documentary film-makers to come out of Scotland, and Grierson's support of her at this stage in her career is another indicator of his influential role as both a mentor and a teacher.

Scottish film-making's creative landscape was further enhanced by the establishment of the Scottish Film Council in 1934, and later by the Scottish Film Office, which was set up in 1938. These developments paved the way for a close relationship between Scottish film-making and the recently established British Film Institute. The Council emphasized films with a social message – of the four panels the Scottish Film Council comprised of, one was for 'education' and another for 'social service'. This gives further insight as to how Scottish documentary film-makers were able to flourish during the war years. The influence of McConnell, McAllister, Watt and Grierson was to be particularly crucial during World War II.

Another important film body that was established in this period was the Scottish Educational Film Association. The Scottish Educational Film Association was formed in 1935 as a merger of the Scottish Educational Cinema Society and the Scottish Educational Sight and Sound Association. It aimed to support the use of film as a medium of education, and nurtured educational films by working closely with the Scottish Film Council. The Scottish Film Council and the Scottish Educational Film Association worked to provide exciting initiatives, such as running mobile cinema shows in rural areas for evacuees. This cultural nurturing of documentary meant that until the beginning of World War II, indigenous Scottish cinema was almost all non-fiction and education based.

Grierson's General Post Office Film Unit made a significant mark in maintaining morale during the first few years of World War II. The Unit produced propaganda films including *London Can Take It!* (1940) and *The Front Line* (1940) – the overall purpose was to maintain British strength in the face of the German blitz. After 1940, the General Post Office Film Unit became the Crown Film Unit, which was managed by the British Government's Ministry of Information and served the propaganda purpose of producing short documentary films both for British citizens and foreign countries about life in Britain. Watt's *Christmas Under Fire* (1941), a portrait of British citizens over Christmas in 1940, was nominated for the Best Documentary Short Academy Award in 1941.

Post-war Scotland saw the country's development of new industry and exports increase, with many newly nationalized industries working to improve the British economy. The improvement of Scotland's industry was evident by increased production in many sectors, ranging from nylons and safety lamps to golf clubs. New factories sprung up around Glasgow, and the activity therein was recorded in numerous public information films. Many such films produced at the time were sponsored by public funding bodies, including the Central Office of Information, and showed this rapid industrialization and hive of activity in a positive light, which served, in turn, to promote a sense of Scottish nationalism.

Glasgow's transformation at this time is particularly well recognized in films of the period. As journalist Ian Jack wrote in the *Sunday Times*:

> Some marvelous [*sic*] and intriguing things have been happening in the city. Epidemics of stone cleaning and tree planting have transformed its former blackness into chequer works of salmon pink, yellow and green. Old buildings have been burnished and refitted. Museums, delicatessens and wine-bars have opened and thrive. New theatres occupy old churches. There are business centres, sports centres, heritage centres, arts centres. There are film-makers. There is even a nationally acknowledged novelist or two. Its new appearance persuades that it may become Britain's first major post-industrial success. (Jack, quoted in McKay 2004)

As much as the depiction of a new, vital Scotland was explored in educational films of the 1950s, anti-establishment cinema groups also challenged it. The left-wing Dawn Cine Group made films including *Let Glasgow Flourish* (1952/56), which challenged the 'rosy' view of the public-information films. *Let Glasgow Flourish*, although an amateur film, effectively undermined the 'official' view that had been illustrated by the Glasgow Corporation Housing Department. An indicator of the size of the underbelly of Glasgow life at the time, it shows the impact of Glasgow Council's attempt to sell council houses on the Merrylee estate, an action that triggered many protests from local residents. The film effectively highlights some of the problems overlooked by the council, namely overcrowding and extreme poverty. *Let Glasgow Flourish* continued the Griersonian focus on promoting progressive social change and today serves as an effective reminder of the economic difficulties of the era.

Economic depression often serves as a potent catalyst for radical change, not least in creative industries. The next period in Scottish history proved no exception. During the early 1960s, when the Scottish and indeed British economy started to glide towards recession, Glasgow School of Art and the Meteor Film Producing Society witnessed unprecedented creative output – not least amongst documentarists. Eddie McConnell's first documentary, made in 1957, depicted the lively creative artists at the Glasgow School of Art. Attending the School proved to be a critical part of McConnell's, and many others', formations as a film-maker. Shortly after graduation, McConnell's film *Faces* (1961) brought him to Grierson's attention and was shown at both the Edinburgh and London Film Festivals.

As well as acting as cameraman on a large number of other directors' films, McConnell's creative output was impressive for often blurring the boundaries between documentary and experimental genres. His many films included short and full-length documentaries that depict Scottish industries, such as *Topliner: The Manufacture of Industrial Refractories* (1968). McConnell did not lose touch with his roots, in 1973 directing the documentary *Benno Schotz: Sculptor and Modeller*, which presents the sculptor working at his studio in Glasgow. Narrated by Michael Elder, the film looks closely at Schotz's working methods and discusses his past as an engineer.

McConnell's later output indicates an increasing leaning towards films that may be termed 'experimental'. These include *Second Glance Hands* (1983) and the film *Pine Trees* 1974) which combines the classic Hans Christian Andersen story with visual representations of how a pine tree grows and changes throughout the seasons over the course of its lifespan. McConnell's last screened film was *Shell Shock* (1991).

Louise Gibson Annand was also a major contributor to Scottish documentary whose career flourished during this same period. Annand was influential not only as a film-maker – but also as a female film-maker in a largely male-dominated field, particularly so at the time she was actively working. Originally a teacher,

Annand started to direct films in the early 1950s, the first being *At the Museum* (1953), in which a small boy and his mother travel to the Kelvingrove Museum. It was made on behalf of the Scottish Educational Film Association.

As well as serving as the Chair of the Scottish Educational Film Association, over the course of her career Annand was Chair of the Glasgow Lady Artists Club Trust and twice President of the Society of Scottish Women Artists. One of her most significant films was a documentary about the life of Charles Rennie Mackintosh, which she co-directed in 1965 with William Thomson. The film provides unique insight into the life of this historic talent, both taking in his own home and some of the architectural feats he is responsible for creating, such as Cranston's Tea Rooms and the Glasgow School of Art building. This work gave insight into the rich tapestry of artistic life in Scotland. It also marked a departure from Grierson's 'cinema as a pulpit' ideology, as Annand's work reflects middle-class interests, tastes and endeavours not directly concerned with promoting either social cohesion or social change.

During the same period Murray Grigor first became active. Originally from Inverness, Grigor's documentaries show a clear thematic development beyond Grierson's model, even though Grigor's first film, *Mackintosh* (1968), was edited by Grierson collaborator Eddie McConnell. Between 1967 and 1972, Grigor was the director of the Edinburgh International Film Festival, and he would go on to become director of many other major bodies, including Channel 4. While some of Grigor's early work documented life in Edinburgh, one example being his depiction of a boarding school in *Fettes* (1970), Grigor's main passion was for architecture and many of his films have provided biographies of architects. These have ranged from Robert Adam to Carlo Scarpa. Grigor's *Portrait of the Artist: The Architecture of Frank Lloyd Wright* (1983) received several awards.

Partly as a reflection of the increasing success of the women's movement in the 1960s, Scotland also saw a proliferation of female film-makers and, in particular, female documentary makers. One such film-maker was Elizabeth Balneaves. In 1967, Balneaves successfully collaborated with Jenny Gilbertson on the documentary *People of Many Lands – Shetland* (1967), which was made for television and returned Gilbertson to her spiritual home of the Shetland Islands for production. Gilbertson's fascination with wild, isolated landscapes would continue to inspire her, and she made many more films about the Arctic that were broadcast both in the United Kingdom and internationally.

Whilst widely regarded as an experimental or art film-maker, Margaret Tait also contributed significantly to Scotland's documentary legacy. After she established Ancona Films with Peter Hollander in Edinburgh in 1956, Tait regularly recorded city life as it took place around her. She also organized the annual Rose Street Film Festival. Her return to her native Orkney also prompted documentation of that community. *The Drift Back* (1956), which depicts a journey of mainlanders to the Island of Orkney, is a particularly strong representation of the people of Orkney. Another of Tait's significant contributions to the documentary canon was the short *Hugh MacDiarmid: A Portrait* (1964), which George Mackay Brown touted as 'an original kind of tribute' to the famous Scottish poet.

In the twenty-first century, Scottish documentary film has continued to show exceptional creative innovation. One of the most influential contemporary documentary film-makers is Kevin Macdonald, who started his film-making career with a documentary about the biography of his grandfather, *The Life and Death of a Screenwriter* (1994). *One Day in September* (1999), an investigation into murders of eleven Israeli athletes during the 1972 Olympic Games, garnered an Oscar for Best Documentary Film in 2000. Macdonald has successfully crossed over into drama directing, with acclaimed features including *The Last King of Scotland* (2006), yet he retains his interest in inventive documentary. In 2011, he worked with Ridley Scott on the groundbreaking project *Life in a Day*, a crowd-sourced documentary in which Internet users submitted videos of their respective lives for inclusion in the project. The result involves 4,500 hours of footage from 192 nations, and premiered at Sundance in 2011.

The establishment of the Scottish Documentary Institute in 2004 ensures that Scotland's film-making talent continues to produce quality documentary films. A research and support centre for documentarists, it seeks to nurture and inspire development from or based in Scotland. In 2007, it set up Scottish Documentary Institute Productions in order to develop feature-length documentaries. Feature films supported by the Institute include *The Future My Love* (Maya Borg, 2012) and *Breathing* (2013). The Bridging the Gap initiative has also seen the successful production of a number of short documentaries including *Cutting Loose* (Finlay Prestell and Adrian McDowall, 2011). Further initiatives enhancing the international reputation of Scottish documentary include Edindocs, a documentary festival that regularly showcases emerging Scottish and Scotland-based documentarists.

As another grandfather of documentary, Werner Herzog, has declared: 'civilization is doomed or is going to die out like dinosaurs if it doesn't develop an adequate language for adequate images'. The democratization of video-making has had a knock-on effect as to the 'adequacy' of images – not least in the documentary form. Now, we are faced with abundance, and the glut is sometimes overwhelming. Scotland's cultural tendency towards invention and creativity – long seen in philosophy, economics and the sciences as well as the arts – might then benefit from continuing to develop the 'adequate language for adequate images'. With this in mind, Scotland's future as a documentary hub will be as assured as its past.

Lucy Brydon

References

Barnow, Erik (1976) *A History of Non-Fiction Film*, New York: Oxford University Press.

McKay, Johnston (2004) 'Modern Times: 1950s to the present day', *The Glasgow Story*, http://www.theglasgowstory.com/storyf.php. Accessed 15 August 2012.

Documentary is Never Neutral (2003) 'Quotes on documentary', Reel Life Stories: Documentary Film and Video Collections in the UC Berkeley Library's Media Resources Center, http://documentaryisneverneutral.com/ words/docquotes.html. Accessed 15 August 2012.

1938 Films of Scotland Committee-Sponsored Empire Exhibition Series

Bob Nowlan

The Face of Scotland

Country of Origin:
UK
Language:
English
Studio/Production Company:
Realist Film Unit
Director:
Basil Wright
Producer:
John Grierson
Cinematographer:
AE Jenkins
Composer:
Walter Leigh
Sound Recorder:
WF Elliott
Duration:
13 minutes
Genre:
Documentary
Voice-over Commentary:
Basil Wright
John Grierson (voice of John Knox)
Year:
1938

Synopsis

The last extensive peacetime public showcase of the prowess of the British Empire, the Empire Exhibition, was staged in Glasgow's Bellahouston Park and ran from May through October 1938. It attracted a total attendance of nearly 13 million, and featured 178 exhibitors as well as numerous restaurants, snack bars and live music performances, along with the largest amusement park in Britain. The only previous Empire Exhibition held in Britain took place at Wembley in 1924–25. Hosting the 1938 Empire Exhibition provided a welcome opportunity to celebrate Glasgow's and Scotland's contributions to industry, commerce, social and economic development, culture and the arts. Walter Elliot, Secretary of State for Scotland, working together with the Scottish Development Council, set up the first Films of Scotland Committee in 1937 with the express aim of producing a series of documentary films offering the millions of visitors to the Empire Exhibition a portrait of the modern Scottish nation, with each individual film to address a major dimension of contemporary Scottish life. The Films of Scotland Committee hired the native Scot, John Grierson, widely acclaimed for his pioneering work in documentary film production, to serve as the general supervisor of the project. Under Grierson's supervision, seven films were produced in time for the Empire Exhibition. *The Face of Scotland* offers a paean to the enduring strength of the Scottish character, from the time of tentative Roman incursions through the present day – praising of the Scots for remaining persistently resilient and resourceful. *Wealth of the Nation* likewise champions Scots' admirable resilience and resourcefulness in successfully overcoming a significant decline in the profitability of the great nineteenth-century industries of coal, iron and steel – as well as doing so in response to the devastating impact of the Great War and the Great Depression – by creating dynamic new industries, increasing the speed and ease of transportation and communication across the nation, and securing a healthier and more satisfying balance between labour and leisure. *Scotland for Fitness* exhorts Scots to take advantage of abundant opportunities available across Scotland for men and women to become and stay fit, especially in time available outside of work, such as by hiking and hill walking, training and playing for an amateur football squad, or participating in stay-fit classes involving a forerunner of late-twentieth to early-twenty-first-century aerobics. *They Made the Land* pays tribute to the triumph of the determined Scot in transforming a Scottish landscape, initially hostile to the development of a successful agricultural economy, into a richly abundant sector which, in modern times, is becoming all the more impressively productive through its extensive reliance on cutting edge scientific research. *Sea Food* parallels *They Made the Land* by demonstrating both the vibrancy of the Scottish fishing economy, for those who work multiple different jobs across the sector, and the pivotal contributions of the modern scientific research conducted under the auspices of the Scottish Fisheries Board. *The Children's Story* depicts a virtual revolution in educational theory and practice,

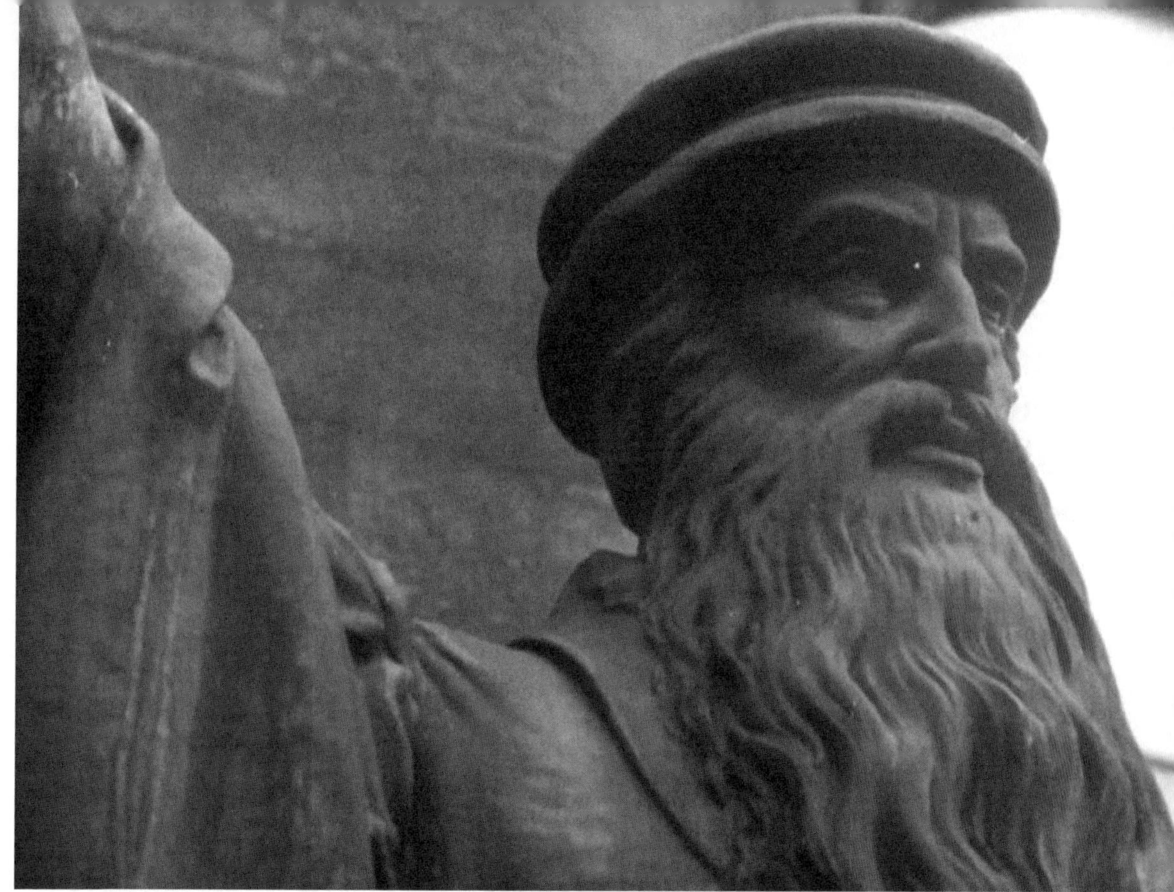

The Face of Scotland, directed by Basil Wright (1938)

Filming Locations:
Across Scotland

in a nation which was the first to provide universal public education, with a new emphasis on hands-on, interactive forms of learning; practical and vocational learning; the importance of training the body as well as the mind; and attending to children's health and needs for play to balance book learning, recitation, testing and examination. *Sport in Scotland* proclaims that 'sport in Scotland flourishes like the heather on the hills', a claim the film substantiates by depicting Scots participating in a wide array of different sports, from grouse hunting on the moor to rugby, association football, golf, tennis, yachting, bowling, mountaineering, hiking, fishing, swimming, shinty and the traditional Highland games – and by demonstrating Scotland's enthusiastic embrace of sports, as spectators, exemplified by Scottish support for the Scotland versus England football match at Wembley in 1938, won by Scotland.

Wealth of a Nation

Country of Origin:
UK
Language:
English
Studio/Production Company:
Scottish Films Productions
Director:
Donald Alexander
Assistant Director:
Bladon Peake

Critique

The 1938 Empire Exhibition series of films celebrates Scotland and its people with persistent enthusiasm. The series depicts Scotland as a single, united nation sharing a common national character, and

Producer:
Stuart Legg
Cinematographers:
Harry Rignold
Jo Jago
Duration:
17 minutes
Genre:
Documentary
Voice-over Commentary:
Harry Watt
Year:
1938
Filming Locations:
Across Scotland

committed toward a common national purpose: Scotland is 'on the move', drawing upon deep-rooted strengths and a long record of many past accomplishments not only successfully to overcome recent challenges but also successfully to create a progressive new society. The Scotland these films depict evinces little to no evidence of social division and conflict, or of competing interest and need. *Wealth of a Nation* does admit the tremendous impact of the Great Depression on the Scottish economy, as well as the accumulation of serious problems in traditional Scottish urban working-class tenement housing, but quickly counters that admission. According to *Wealth of a Nation*, both problems are being successfully alleviated, enabled by substantial state intervention. Likewise, the same film shows brief images of Scots at community meetings pressing government representatives to respond to their demands, while also suggesting, once again, that the state always responds positively to such popular pressure. A dramatically fabricated short sequence depicts government representatives briefly talking among themselves after one such meeting where these councilors, albeit somewhat reluctantly, agree that they must give in to their constituents' demands for more local playing fields.

These films' collective portrait of Scotland, and its people, embarked upon a progressive renaissance is, in retrospect, notably ironic given the outbreak of World War II less than a year later – and the corollary fact, not manifest in any of this series of films, that Scotland's industrial recovery had already been in part fuelled by rearmament in anticipation of the war soon to come. As Duncan Petrie has suggested, in *Screening Scotland* (2000), these films respond to considerable economic, social and political anxiety in Scotland at the time, with many Scots not only having been severely impacted by the Great Depression but also convinced that Scotland had suffered disproportionately in comparison with the rest of the United Kingdom. At the time these films were commissioned, the UK government in London had only recently created the Scottish Office, the Scottish Development Council and the Scottish Economic Committee to respond to Scottish concerns – and to head off both a prospective rise in nationalist sentiment as well as the prospect of increased support for more militantly oppositional movements in labour union and working-class politics. Both Walter Elliott and John Grierson strongly believed in the necessity of large-scale state intervention to ensure economic regeneration and social progress – and, not surprisingly therefore, the Empire Exhibition series of films depicts the state as performing a highly prominent and overwhelmingly benevolent role in providing necessary financial, administrative, organizational, logistical, intellectual, scientific and technical resources to the Scottish people. Periodically, this depiction becomes blatantly paternalistic, and not just because of the reliance, throughout the series of films, on an authoritative male 'voice of God' narrator. As David Bruce, former director of the Scottish Film Council, has commented on *Scotland for Fitness*:

> The documentary makers did not always get it right. The noble aim of *Scotland for Fitness* was 'the awakening in the minds of Scots men and women a pride in their bodily

Scotland for Fitness

Country of Origin:
UK
Language:
English
Studio/Production Company:
GB Instructional
Director:
Brian Salt
Associate Producer:
Stanley L Russell
Cinematographer:
GW Pocknall
Duration:
11 minutes
Genre:
Documentary
Voice-over Commentary:
Sir Iain Colquhoun
Year:
1938
Filming Locations:
Across Scotland

> activity'. A small, rather weedy, aristocrat sits behind a desk and tells us in a drawly voice the virtue of devoting our free time ('when the one o'clock gun sounds on a Saturday') to various leisure pursuits – walking and football for men, keep-fit classes for women. A fascinating record of the establishment attitude of the times – patronizing, condescending, chauvinist – and, delightfully, as unintentionally hilarious a ten minutes as ever hits the screen. (Bruce, quoted in Scottish Screen Archive 2003: 14)

As Richard Butt has written, these films need to be understood, moreover, as actively contributing toward the production of a shared national culture, a modern Scottish national culture – while the films likewise make signal contributions toward the production of the specific kinds of subjects, and subjectivities, required of this culture:

> The group of 1938 films are interesting precisely because they occur at this historical juncture, and indeed they can only be understood in terms of these shifting historical circumstances. Institutionally, they are located within two key developments: state intervention in public culture, and the structural transformation of the public sphere into a mass mediated public sphere. What is particularly striking is the extent to which these documentaries, despite their differences of subject, operate at a specifically national level [...] [and] rather than simply representing the nation, the documentaries play a more formative role whereby, as part of the public sphere, they are among the many indirect mechanisms that actually make the nation's existence, and the governance of its subjects, possible. (Butt 2013)

At the same time, however, that these documentaries assume this formative role within a new, modern nation, they seek ideological grounding for their articulation of national unity in an often highly mystifying account of Scottish history. *The Face of Scotland*, for instance, loosely refers to Scots, past and present, as a single race, sharing a common 'stock', whose distinctive character is rooted simultaneously in the rugged Scottish land as well as in the determined efforts of the Scots to tame and conquer this land. Although not as tendentiously emphasizing the same 'blood and soil' conception of national identity, *They Made the Land* nevertheless echoes this argument in suggesting that Scots' efforts, over multiple successive generations, at draining and reforesting as well as in experimenting with new tools and machinery, along with new crops and new livestock, have decisively impacted Scottish character: 'a land so bitter' that it 'only gave grudgingly' required Scots respond with enormous 'faith and courage' in order not to be beaten by the necessary source of their survival and subsistence. According to *They Made the Land*, Scots pulled together to meet this challenge; no mention is made of the massive social transformation involved with the Highland Clearances nor of the disproportionate concentration of the ownership of Scottish

They Made the Land

Country of Origin:
UK
Language:
English
Studio/Production Company:
GB Instructional
Director:
Mary Field
Cinematographer:
George Stevens
Duration:
20 minutes
Genre:
Documentary
Voice-over Commentary:
EV Emmett
Year:
1938
Filming Locations:
Across Scotland

Sea Food

Country of Origin:
UK
Language:
English
Studio/Production Company:
Pathé
Duration:
12 minutes
Genre:
Documentary
Year:
1938
Filming Locations:
Across Scotland

The Children's Story

Country of Origin:

UK

Language:

English

Studio/Production Company:

Strand Film Company

Director:

Alexander Shaw

Duration:

15 minutes

Genre:

Documentary

Year:

1938

Filming Locations:

Across Scotland

Sport in Scotland

Country of Origin:

UK

Language:

English

Studio/Production Company:

Scottish Film Productions

Director:

Stanley L Russell

Producers:

Basil Wright
John Grierson

Screenwriters:

Albert Mackie
James McKechnie

Cinematographers:

Henry Cooper
Graham Thomson

Duration:

11 minutes

Genre:

Documentary

farmlands in the hands of the wealthy few. Likewise, *Wealth of the Nation* largely ignores the issue of who in fact does own the total social wealth of the nation, in what relative (dis)proportion, while *The Children's Story* offers no explanation of why the changes in the educational practice it praises have occurred, when, where and as they have. In short, the latter film neglects how these institutional changes in turn respond to broader societal changes. *The Children's Story* represents educational reform as taking place in a vacuum, ignoring the impact of changes in the relative strength of opposing social forces, and ignoring the shifting needs of hegemonic versus counter-hegemonic interests, as these struggle against each other via the mediation of curricular structure and pedagogical practice. The only explanation the film suggests for why Scottish schooling is changing is that Scots have simply drawn upon their long-standing commitment to the premium value of educational attainment in order to devise beneficial new approaches.

Nevertheless, for as much as these films appear as embodiments of state propaganda, it is worth appreciating how widely popular and refreshingly novel they were at the time they were made and released. The series achieved 4,725 screenings in British cinemas, beyond screenings taking place at the Empire Cinema as part of the Empire Exhibition, reaching a total audience of over 22 million. As Butt (2013) has pointed out, *They Made the Land* was still in circulation seventeen years later when the second Films of Scotland Committee was established in 1955, and *The Face of Scotland* had by then only recently been withdrawn. What's more, the film-makers involved in working on the series deliberately aimed to depict a Scotland sharply at odds with classic cinematic images dependent upon the tropes of Tartanry and the Kailyard, where Scots were all too often depicted as simple, primitive, pre-modern figures, usually in subsidiary roles, offering little beyond comic relief and supplementary colour. Because of how radically the Empire Exhibition series set itself at odds with familiar cinematic images of Scotland and Scots, the British Council refused to include the films in its exhibition at the 1939 World Fair in New York City. Even though John Grierson made use of his connections to ensure the films were included in the American Social Sciences exhibition, as Forsyth Hardy has written,

> there was a great deal of resentment about the Council's decision. It was felt that an opportunity of showing a more genuine image of Scotland wasn't being taken and therefore there was a feeling that the Scottish experience was not going to get across over there. (Hardy 1982: 75)

As Hardy attests, it is also worth remembering that all seven of these films were made in a total of eighteen months, and the collective result is a remarkably ambitious effort at providing a comprehensive portrait of a nation at a single, present, moment in time. Emphasis on singling out Scotland as a nation, and insisting on its distinctive character and its intrinsic unity is most striking as well. Even though the Empire Exhibition series questions neither the propriety nor the efficacy of the British Union, of Scotland as a nation within a

Voice-over Commentary:
Albert Mackie
Jack House
Year:
1938
Filming Locations:
Across Scotland

united kingdom of nations, the films do not focus on what unites Scotland with England, Wales and Northern Ireland, but rather on what distinguishes Scotland – and the Scottish people. In addition, the films largely succeed in demonstrating the artistry involved in documentary film-making – a key point of emphasis for Grierson. The films typically move rapidly through a considerable series of distinct images, while carefully explaining those scenes that become the focus of relatively prolonged emphasis. The films well exemplify Grierson's signature emphasis on the motion picture as a way of observing the world in motion, of finding and showing the beauty in everyday life, and of aiming to make the ordinary business of life, especially at work, as dramatically splendid as possible. And, if temporarily extracted from consideration within more troubling or challenging social contexts, the fascination the films find in scientific research and technological innovation does prove usefully instructive.

References

Butt, Richard (2013) 'The Films of Scotland Documentaries', *Scran*, http://sites.scran.ac.uk/films_of_scotland/History/chapter02.htm. Accessed 20 February.

Grierson, John (1968) *I Remember, I Remember*, Films of Scotland Committee and Scottish Television.

Hardy, Forsyth (1982) 'An Interview with Forsyth Hardy', in Colin McArthur (ed.), *Scotch Reels: Scotland in Cinema and Television*, London: BFI pp. 73-92.

McArthur, Colin (ed.) (1982) *Scotch Reels: Scotland in Cinema and Television*, London: BFI.

Petrie, Duncan (2000) *Screening Scotland*, London: BFI.

Scottish Screen Archive (2013) http://ssa.nls.uk. Accessed 20 February.

________ (n.d.) *Films of Scotland: The Work of the Films of Scotland Committee*, Glasgow: Scottish Screen Archive.

________ (2003) *Scotland's Moving Image Collection*, Glasgow: Scottish Screen Archive.

Donald Cammell: The Ultimate Performance

Country of Origin:
UK
Language:
English

Synopsis

This film documents the life and career of rogue film-maker Donald Cammell, from his birth under Edinburgh's Camera Obscura to his self-inflicted death in the Hollywood hills. The story takes in Cammell's first career as society portrait painter, his successful collaboration with Nic Roeg on *Performance* (1970) and his fraught subsequent productions, often characterized by clashes with studios and producers.

Critique

Kevin Macdonald and collaborator Chris Rodley co-direct this captivating biography, using the only existing filmed interview of

Studio/Production Companies:

BBC
Total Performance Limited

Directors:

Chris Rodley
Kevin Macdonald

Producers:

Chris Rodley
Kevin Macdonald
Donald Cammell

Cinematographer:

David Scott

Composer:

David Sinclair

Editor:

Budge Tremlett

Duration:

75 minutes

Genre:

Documentary

Cast:

David Cammell
James Fox
Myriam Gibril
Mick Jagger
Elliott Kastner
China Kong
Frank Mazzola
Barbara Steele
Nicolas Roeg

Year:

1998

Filming Locations:

London, England, UK
Los Angeles, California, USA

Cammell, taken for Saskia Barron's two-part *Empire of the Censors* (1995), a history of the British Board of Film Censors (now the British Board of Film Classification). Macdonald and Rodley were able to talk to friends and collaborators among a diverse and flamboyant crowd, including Mick Jagger, Barbara Steele, Kenneth Anger, Nicolas Roeg and Cammell's brother David and last partner China Kong. Best of all is Frank Mazzola, editor of several Cammell projects, and a former LA gang member who became an actor and advisor on gang life for *Rebel Without a Cause* (Nicholas Ray, 1995). Macdonald, like his producer brother, is a robustly commercial and narrative-based film-maker, so it is interesting to see him engage with subject matter that flirts with the avant-garde. In fact, Macdonald's documentaries divide between meditative, character-based films like his portrait of his grandfather, screenwriter Emeric Pressburger, *The Making of an Englishman* (1995), and events-based narratives like his Oscar-winning *One Day in September* (1999). Working backwards from the event of Cammell's dramatic death, here he combines the strengths of both approaches. Rodley's background is in arts films for the BBC and Channel 4, where a particular interest in contemporary music, challenging modern art and edgy cinema make him a natural fit for exploring Cammell's oeuvre: as the maker of films on David Cronenberg, Andy Warhol, pornography and Johnny Cash, his overall body of work seems like a good identikit match for Cammell.

Cammell's life and art had many strange points of connection, and so the film-makers are able to draw from the style of his films, particularly his directorial debut (co-helmed with Roeg), the seminal *Performance*, and this never seems obtrusive. Indeed, the fragmented editing patterns, the striking use of music and the juxtaposition of contrasting worlds (organized crime and disorganized, drug-fuelled creativity) seem quite natural for a documentary mingling interviews and archival footage. In addition to the players named previously, the film-makers have enviable access to James Fox, who appeared in 1960s farrago *Duffy* (1968), from a Cammell script, before embodying psychopathic enforcer Chas in *Performance*. His experience on the film was rumoured to have driven him out of the acting profession for years, something he denies here, while nevertheless admitting his fragile state at the time and the challenging nature of the project and his collaborators. The mysterious Myriam Gibril, a teenage runaway adopted as lover by Cammell while she was still underage, and cast in the film as one of Mick Jagger's two mistresses, also makes a unique appearance, and both co-star Anita Pallenberg and fellow Rolling Stones ex Marianne Faithfull give their own testimony on the turbulent times of the film's shooting. The interest generated by the making of Cammell's one true classic (often attributed mainly to its co-director, Nicolas Roeg, even though Cammell originated the project and completed the edit while Roeg was making his follow-up film) is maintained even as the documentary explores Cammell's later, arguably lesser films *Demon Seed* (1977), *White of the Eye* (1987) and *Wild Side* (1985). What makes these stories compelling is the cast of storytellers. 'Tai-Pan', an abortive project that was to have starred Marlon Brando, is discussed by both down-to-earth movie mogul Elliott Kastner, repeatedly insisting on the project's virtues as a 'meat and potatoes' movie, and by experimental film-maker and magician Kenneth Anger. When Anger claims that Brando 'uses his power in a way that is Not Good', it is genuinely unclear if the power he is referring to is the late star's movie business clout or something most sinister and unearthly.

Macdonald is a master of the suspenseful yarn branch of documentary (as exemplified by *Touching the Void*, his 2003 hit, and carried on into his fiction features such as *The Last King of Scotland* [2006]), but he sometimes stumbles when it comes to more poetic aspects of cinema. In particular, his music choices can seem either crassly obvious or generic, recycling Philip Glass or period-redolent pop hits. The trance-like echoing of a Boney M track in *Touching the Void* was a rare imaginative triumph. But here, using the music composed for *Performance* by Jack Nietzsche along with an original score by David Sinclair, Macdonald and Rodley arrive at a mood complimentary to the subject: skewed, trippy, allusive and elusive. The same approach allows the film-makers to fully exploit the macabre connections between Cammell's suicide and the mob execution that concludes *Performance*. Are they guilty of glamourizing the film-maker's tragic demise? Possibly. But for storytellers and cinematic alchemists, the chance to show a portrait of Borges emerging from a bullet-hole must have been irresistible, and it is surely a temptation Cammell would have understood.

David Cairns

Everybody's Child

Country of Origin:
UK
Language:
English
Studio/Production Company:
Aconite Productions
Director:
Garry Fraser
Producer:
Aimara Reques
Executive Producer:
Ewan Angus
Screenwriters:
Garry Fraser

Synopsis

Garry Fraser is striving to transform his life. Fraser, a recovering drug addict and ex-convict, was the child of a violent family upbringing, full of abuse and neglect, living in poverty on the Muirhouse public housing estate in North Edinburgh. Fraser spent time in 36 different care homes in eight years starting at the age of eight; at age sixteen Fraser left care and became a drug dealer. After spending time in prison, after participating in a treatment program designed to help substance abusers find education and employment, and after obtaining a HND (Higher National Diploma) in filmmaking from Telford College, Fraser, now 34-years-old, is focused on making a new life for himself, and for his wife and three kids. Fraser is now working as a fledgling film-maker and as creative director of a social enterprise, Wideo Video, designed to provide an opportunity for young people in North Edinburgh, from the same kind of socio-economic background as Fraser, to channel their energy and talent into making poetry, plays and videos, rather than into drugs and crime. *Everybody's Child* is Fraser's first feature-length film, after previously making several critically acclaimed shorts. In this film Fraser revisits his past in an attempt to better understand why he turned out as he did – and also in an attempt, by facing up to

Lorna Hutcheon
Cinematographer:
Garry Torrance
Production Manager:
Su Bainbridge
Composer:
Stuart Jackson
Sound Designer:
John Cobban
Additional Original Music:
Adam Holmes
MOG
Editor:
Lee Archer
Duration:
75 minutes
Genre:
Documentary
Year:
2012
Filming Location:
Edinburgh and surrounding area, Scotland, UK

demons from his past, to be able to finally put this past behind him and move confidently into the future. Over the course of the duration of *Everybody's Child* we, the film's audience, follow along with Fraser as he revisits places and people from his past, and as he offers virtually continuous commentary on his life and times. We journey with Fraser as he walks about and drives around the Muirhouse housing estate. We journey with Fraser as he meets up and talks with surviving members of a family he knew well growing up, and who, like so many others from Muirhouse in the 1980s, suffered deaths within the family as a result of AIDS; a local social worker specializing in substance abuse, addiction and recovery; an after-adoption social worker, who discusses Fraser's more than 1,500 pages-long case file; and a woman with whom Fraser was temporarily close as a youth, who attempted to provide him a foster home, before Fraser was taken back from her custody. With Fraser we visit a local cemetery where so many people Fraser knew, growing up in Muirhouse, are now dead as a result of AIDS, that 'there's not enough flowers to go around'. With Fraser, we revisit the first children's home in which he was placed, where he was subjected to protracted sexual abuse by an older male, with no viable outlet to complain or escape. We also revisit the area in North Edinburgh where Fraser controlled heroin distribution across five streets, where he made a lot of money, and where he managed to escape the police by removing the locks from the back doors to the back greens on eight adjacent buildings. We spend time in the streets where he played as a child right near flats where he lived, and we travel to Gipsy Brae in Muirhouse, a tranquil beachfront Fraser recalls as the last place where he was actually innocent. We also observe Fraser interacting affectionately with his wife and kids at home, and inspiringly with the teenagers he is teaching and helping as part of Wideo Video. We even follow along with Fraser as he takes his HIV test (near the end of the film, we find out he is negative), and as he pauses for a haircut and a shave. Near the middle of the film we witness Fraser's failed attempt to stop taking drugs altogether, including a National Health Service prescription in response to his addiction, as he relapses into taking heroin once more – and we witness his subsequent remorse and shame about doing so. In some of the toughest sequences in the film we accompany Fraser out of Edinburgh to Midlothian as he first meets up and talks with his father, who was a physically abusive alcoholic when Fraser was a child, and then, we wait outside, as Fraser meets up and talks with his mother, who was, and who remains, callously indifferent and unloving, unwilling to take responsibility for any of what Fraser experienced, and who persists entirely uninterested, as she was when Fraser was a child, in anything other than a minimally necessary relationship with him. Right before the end of the film, however, we ride with Fraser to reconnect with his film-making instructor at Telford College, where the two discuss the considerable promise Fraser showed from early on as well as the steady yet increasingly rapid emergence Fraser has since demonstrated – as a talented film-maker. At the end of *Everybody's Child*, before the credits roll, Fraser declares that making film as he does, of the kind he does, in his way – with his heart on his sleeve and forthrightly confronting topics most others would refuse – is not a choice for him, but a necessity: it is necessary for him in order to maintain his life moving forward, for the well-being of his family, as a role model to kids from backgrounds and with experiences like he has had to show them what is possible, and as a moral responsibility to make up for what he lost in his past.

Critique

Everybody's Child is a powerfully moving account of resilience, determination and triumph (which premiered in a 60-minute version titled *My Lives and Times* on BBC2 television on Sunday, 22 of July 2012). Fraser's openness throughout the process is highly compelling, especially his openness in allowing his first feature-length film to chart his mental, emotional and indeed physical responses to revisiting past traumas. Fraser knows he cannot fully anticipate how he will respond in this journey, nor can he guarantee that he will be able to cope with what he rediscovers. What's more, Fraser does not even know whether he will be able to succeed in making his way successfully through the course of making this film. The film's riveting fusion of the intimately autobiographical with the searchingly sociological ultimately succeeds in superseding the generic characterization many have associated with the films he has made to date: 'urban realism'. *Everybody's Child* is willing to acknowledge questions where answers are neither simple nor easy, and where memory, reflection, witness and testimony prove more affecting, and more effective, than directly arguing a single, straightforward thesis. At the beginning, and before embarking on this journey, Fraser is clear about what he is seeking: to show why people in places like Muirhouse end up doing things like the younger Garry Fraser did. At the end, however, even though Fraser and the rest of those involved in making *Everybody's Child* have persistently explored exactly this territory, the explanation the film suggests, in response to this same question of 'why', is, strikingly, both complex and tenuous. Among factors identifiably responsible, we recognize all of the following: poverty; poorly designed and overcrowded housing; lack of opportunity to pursue meaningful and fulfilling alternatives to drugs and crime; parental abuse and neglect; instability and inadequacy seemingly rooted in the structural logic of the care system; as well as methadone therapy perpetuating addiction, dependency and victimization. Yet *Everybody's Child* offers no clear articulation of the relative weight of responsibility among these and other factors in shaping people like Garry Fraser – and this is especially the case in what the film leaves us as explanation for how and why Fraser has himself managed to overcome these obstacles (including lapsing into resuming heroin use during shooting, while a message near the end of the credits announces he has been drug free since the film was shot). *Everybody's Child* does strongly suggest that people like Fraser maintain much good to offer the greater society: that they are intelligent and talented, and that they can channel this intelligence and talent in myriad positive directions, given the right opportunity, the right assistance and the right encouragement. In this sense the film's title is apt: as Fraser himself has more than once declared, in relation to his film, 'everybody's child deserves the best chance in life'. At the same time, however, the film complicates this message by emphasizing the portrait of a man who clearly did not receive such a 'best chance', yet who, seemingly to a large degree through his own will and self-belief – his own dedication and commitment – has begun to succeed in making up for the chance not offered him as a child.

Fraser succeeds in his ambition to depict the 'truth behind *Trainspotting*' and to provide a critical counter to the made-for-television series *The Scheme* (Michael Friel and Julian Kean, 2010-11). Muirhouse is a principal location in *Trainspotting* (Danny Boyle, 1996), and this housing estate, as well as residential district of Scotland's capital city, was ground zero during the period in the 1980s when Edinburgh was often referred to as the 'AIDS capital of Europe'. At the same time, Fraser attempts to suggest, as brutal as conditions often were, growing up in Muirhouse in the 1980s, actual lived experiences tended to be more complex than many fictional portraits suggest: people did, often enough, struggle, and at least partially succeed, in carrying on their everyday, normal, ordinary lives – working, raising families and, yes, playing and having fun. And even when Muirhouse (and nearby Pilton) residents became heavily involved with drugs and crime, this did not eliminate their potential to be and do otherwise. In this respect, the film's complex treatment of its subject is illustrated in the sadness Fraser and the film periodically project about the fact that Muirhouse is no longer as full of people as when Fraser was a child. Despite the overcrowding, despite gang violence, despite rampant drug use, despite the AIDS epidemic and despite frequent domestic abuse and neglect, Muirhouse still felt like a community, indeed like home, to many who lived there. Frustrations with the many hardships they frequently faced are often enough intermixed, for Muirhouse and Pilton residents, with a persistent pride in who they are and where they come from. So, Fraser's film views ambivalently recent efforts of various government bodies, together with private entrepreneurs, to replace out-of-date boxed flats with a range of up-to-date models for multi-family housing, and to move many of those who suffered the worst at the apex of the epidemic out of the neighbourhood.

Everybody's Child succeeds in simultaneously centring on Fraser, in fact paying meticulously close attention to changes in affect, as displayed through posture, manner, gesture, tone of voice and, especially, facial expression, while at the same time giving voice, as Fraser has intended, to a much larger group of people who are most often unable to find adequate means through which to speak for themselves so as to be heard by those who need to hear them. Fraser takes on the charge of speaking as a typical representative of those all too often dismissed as an underclass. Editing smoothly balances close, tight shots of Fraser with shots that situate him as a key but far from singular figure in a larger environment – as well as with ample but relatively economically spare use of establishing, location shots in which Fraser is not directly present. Camera movement is primarily handheld as we walk and sit close to Fraser, while the camera is fixed and steady in shots taken as we drive – either with Fraser, or, briefly, separate from Fraser – around areas pivotal to Fraser's story. A small amount of archival footage from the 1980s is incorporated into the film, including as part of a brief yet nonetheless striking superimposition sequence of Muirhouse estate exteriors – from then and now. Framing and reframing remains consistently well-timed, smooth and precise without ever becoming either slick or distracting. Musical accompaniment is most often carefully understated and subtly minimal, frequently consisting of single notes or brief phrases, principally from cello, viola, guitar and synthesizer. The music accentuates the sombre, serious mood of the narrative, never interfering with or running counter to the dominant tone emphasized within the narrative. Much more aggressively prominent are the few rap sequences – especially the title rap, performed by MOG, over the closing credits – which well befit Garry Fraser's story, as Fraser is, himself, a prolific and accomplished rap poet.

Everybody's Child exemplifies an exciting potential direction in early twenty-first century Scottish film-making – as a new generation of film-makers, working with relatively low budgets and relatively limited resources, nevertheless confidently mine their own experience to tell stories, through cinematic means, that honestly and compellingly attest to what it is and has been like to live at a particular place and in a particular time, and, often enough, to undergo struggles and to confront difficulties that are simultaneously both wrenchingly personal and authentically representative. When this kind of commitment is animated with the powerful sense of moral responsibility so forcefully emphasized in *Everybody's Child*, and with the passionate commitment to film-making, as a way of life, that we find with Garry Fraser, then the promise is a most hopeful one, indeed.

Bob Nowlan

References

Aconite Productions (2012) *'Everybody's Child' Film* [Official website], http://www.everybodyschildfilm.com. Accessed 28 January 2013.

BBC2 (2012) *My Lives and Times*, http://www.bbc.co.uk/programmes/b01l5fvn. Accessed 28 January 2013.

Anon. (2012) 'Muirhouse', *Edinburgh Past and Present – The Edinburgh Website*, http://edinburghpastandpresent.com/#/muirhouse/4548925933. Accessed 28 January 2013.

Fraser, Garry (2013) Facebook page, http://www.facebook.com/wideo. Accessed 28 January 2013.

Miller, Phil (2012) 'Documentary Takes Candid Look at Exclusion', *Glasgow Herald*, 19 July.

Trueland, Jennifer (2012) 'From Drug Addict to Up and Coming Filmmaker', *Caledonian Mercury*, 6 February, http://caledonianmercury.com/2010/02/06/from-drug-addict-to-up-and-coming-filmmaker/001752, Accessed 28 April 2014.

Zambian Astronaut (2012) '*Everybody's Child*: The Soundtrack', http://www.zambianastronaut.com/everybodys-child-film-soundtrack/. Accessed 28 January 2013.

Night Mail

Country of Origin:
UK
Language:
English
Directors:
Harry Watt
Basil Wright
Producers:
Harry Watt
Basil Wright
Screenwriters:
Basil Wright
Harry Watt
John Grierson
Cinematographers:
H.E. Fowle (as Chick Fowle)
Jonah Jones
Sound Director:
Alberto Cavalcanti
Composers:
Benjamin Britten
WH Auden
Editors:
Basil Wright
Richard Q McNaughton
Duration:
24 minutes
Genre:
Documentary
Cast:
Pat Jackson (narrator)
John Grierson (commentary)
Stuart Legg (commentary)
Year:
1936

Synopsis

Night Mail is the story of a day in the life of a postal express train, which transports mail from the south of England to the north of Scotland. Roughly following the trajectory of a typical journey, *Night Mail* documents the logistical process that distributes the mail, showing how bundles are dropped off and sorted without stopping the train. This process allows for impressionistic meditations on the increasingly industrialized landscape, as well as the poetic capacity of machines.

Critique

An acknowledged classic of the John Grierson-founded wing of the British Documentary Movement of the 1930s, *Night Mail* is a short film about postal delivery that is as important in its production methods as it is in its claims about national identity. Although not filmed with the strictest eye for spatial verisimilitude or spontaneous action – many of the interactions are scripted, and a sequence supposedly showing men sorting mail on a train was actually recreated in a studio – the film does attempt to approximate the working conditions and challenges of the postal worker, all while demonstrating how their labour feeds into larger conceptions of national industry (Watt 2007: 7–8). *Night Mail* features real postal employees presumably engaged in their areas of expertise, though none of them are credited by name or profiled in an individualizing way. The General Post Office production unit (under the commissioning auspices of documentary film-making pioneer Grierson) worked in a collectively overlapping fashion, sharing many of the technical duties and complicating the process of ascribing intentional authorship to any one person.

The film highlights the central contradiction at the heart of Grierson's vision for documentary. On the one hand, it emphasizes public service values, explaining an issue of national importance to a presumably clueless (yet hopefully interested) audience. *Night Mail* achieves this splendidly in that it carefully shows the technological mechanisms that allow the postal train to function as it does. For example, the sequence where a recent trainee has to ready a postal parcel to be dropped off at the correct location makes masterful use of discontinuity editing, creating tension though constant cuts to a close up of his face, the face of his supervisor, a medium shot of another co-worker who is to lower the package and shots of the rapidly moving exterior of the train. Once the package is lowered, camera coverage cuts between shots from

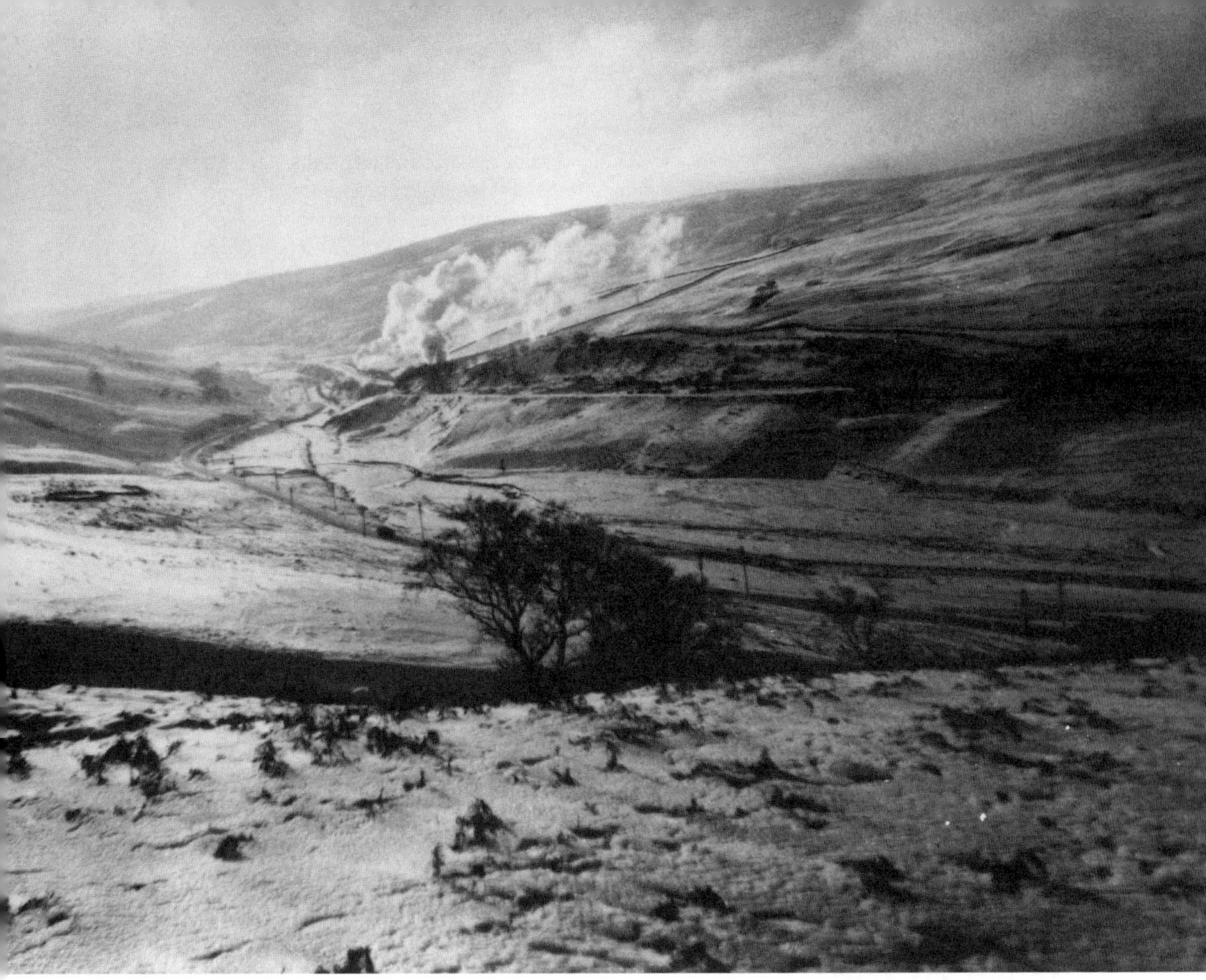

Night Mail, directed by Harry Watt and Basil Wright (1936), British Film Institute Collection

Filming Locations:

London, England to Glasgow, Scotland, UK

within the train and shots from outside that more fully highlight how the drop-off mechanism works. So, while *Night Mail* succeeds at showing the efficient process at the heart of the postal train's mission, it also does so by explicitly constructing a visual reality that exceeds the drabness of the workaday world. Thus, the other side to the contradiction underwriting Griersonian documentary is the need to embellish raw fact with poetic invention. This is clearly the impulse behind the collaboration between composer Benjamin Britten and poet WH Auden, whose poem 'Night Mail' remains at the heart of the film's most celebrated scene. In one of cinema's most concerted attempts to adapt poetic verse to screen, Britten's music accentuates Stuart Legg's delivery of the cadences of Auden's poem, a scattered account of the postal train, its function, its contents and the hopes and dreams it inspires. Simultaneous to this aural assault (chanted at breakneck speed) are images of the train, the countryside, the power lines above the tracks, the conductor and animals running at speeds comparable to the roaring engine. This sequence tests previously imagined limitations on the viable form for the still developing documentary genre.

Finally, *Night Mail* matters for its construction of regional identities. While it is very much a film about the united cultural character of England and Scotland (it is literally about the thing that connects the two), it also makes sure to parcel out demarcating lines. When the train makes its stop in Crewe, Cheshire (just south of Liverpool), the film makes the point of explaining that, along with the changeover in mail packages, the train will be adding its Scots workers to finish out the journey. This subtle detail draws out a wider claim: for all of *Night Mail*'s attempts at illustrating unity, there remain distinctive cultural allegiances. The sequences shot in Scotland accentuate the dual features that differentiate those landscapes from the south, focusing as much on the rolling Highland hills as on the heavily industrialized urban cityscapes of Glasgow.

Kevin M Flanagan

Reference

Watt, Henry (2007) 'Don't Look at the Camera' [DVD booklet], in Harry Watt and Basil Wright, dirs (1936), *Night Mail* [DVD], London: BFI, pp. 5–9.

Return to the Edge of the World

Country of Origin:

UK

Language:

English

Studio/Production Companies:

BBC
Poseidon Films
Pinewood Studios

Director:

Michael Powell

Producers:

Frixos Constantine
Michael Powell
Sydney Streeter

Screenwriter:

Michael Powell

Synopsis

Director Michael Powell and a few members of his original cast and crew return to the island where they filmed *Edge of the World* in 1937, to meet the locals and their relatives who assisted on the original film, and to relive their distant memories.

Critique

Lawrie Knight, a friend who had worked with Michael Powell in the 1940s, once told me that if you met the Scottish actor John Laurie, within twenty seconds he would tell you about his Hamlet. So it's a pleasure to me to see the moment in *Return to the Edge of the World* when the 81-year-old disembarks from a twin-engine plane on the remote Island of Foula, approaches the camera and recites his credits, featuring that long-ago Hamlet higher on the list than the role in *Dad's Army* (Jimmy Perry and David Croft, 1968-1977) he will always be remembered for. A consummate barnstormer, Laurie lets his eyes dart around in his skull like mad spies, alighting momentarily as if upon mirages of his past triumphs.

The film, a 23-minute long set of bookends designed to bracket Powell's 1937 *The Edge of the World*, his first hit, is a fascinating behind-the-scenes glimpse, made more poignant by its belatedness. It concentrates equally on the story of the film, which changed Powell's career, the spectacular scenery of the

Cinematographer:

Brian Mitchison

Composer:

Brian Easdale

Editor:

Peter Mayhew

Duration:

24 minutes

Genre:

Documentary

Cast:

Michael Powell
John Laurie
Frankie Reidy
Sydney Streeter
Grant Sutherland

Year:

1978

Filming Location:

Foula, the Shetland Isles, Scotland, UK

Scottish Islands and the story of the Islanders and the changing circumstances affecting their lifestyle.

Despite its short length and its placement very late in his career, the film is recognizably a Powell production: early on he cuts from a circling bird to an aeroplane, echoing a similar match cut in 1944's *A Canterbury Tale*. The alternating voice-overs by himself and Laurie recall the quirky use of narration in *A Matter of Life and Death* (1946) and *I Know Where I'm Going!* (With Emeric Pressburger, 1945), in which Laurie's voice whisper-sings to us during a dream sequence. Powell himself is an attractive host, striding across the cliff tops of Foula with the gait of a much younger man, and fixing the lens with eyes both steely and dreamy as his high, sharp voice recollects the circumstances in which he first heard about the story of another island, St Kilda, which was eventually evacuated by the government when the population shrank too much to be sustainable. 'Don't tell anyone: I'm a poet', says Powell, sitting on a cliff and unpacking a small camera reminiscent of the one used by Carl Boehm as the eponymous hero of *Peeping Tom* (1960). Disposing of the making-of part of his film quickly, he shuffles between nature photography and quick portraits of Islanders and film crew, with a potted history of island life since the film. Two of his actors and his chief of construction (now his producer) accompany Powell on the trip, leading to a roll call of the dead, cast, crew and Islanders – those who did not quite make it to the occasion of the film's 41st anniversary. The film's most affecting sequence, for all the theatricality of Laurie's delivery, this passage stands as a more compellingly central dimension of the film than either the sociological or film-historical aspects we encounter elsewhere: a tribute to fallen friends.

David Cairns

Seawards the Great Ships

Country of Origin:

UK

Language:

English

Studio/Production Companies:

Central Office of Information (COI)
Templar Film Studios
Films of Scotland
Clyde Shipbuilders Association

Director:

Hilary Harris

Synopsis

With a running time shorter than thirty minutes, this densely packed documentary provides a behind-the-scenes look at the world's leading shipbuilding industry along Scotland's River Clyde. After telling of the wide variety of vessels built in the area, the film then takes its audience through the manufacturing process – from drawing room conception to dockside launch – relating this story with admiration and pride. It takes monumental amounts of steel and hard work to create the largest moving objects made by man.

Critique

The first Scottish production to win an Academy Award, *Seawards the Great Ships* earned 1961's statuette for Best Short, Live Action Subject. Nominated in this category, rather than that of Best Documentary (Short Subject) it proved itself against works of truth and fiction alike in order to claim its title – a feat that is made to

Screenwriters:

John Grierson (treatment)
Clifford Hanley (commentary)

Cinematographer:

Hilary Harris

Composer:

Marcus Dods

Editor:

Hilary Harris

Duration:

28 minutes

Genre:

Documentary

Cast:

Bryden Murdoch (original version)
Kenneth Kendall (international release)

look effortless by a combination of captivating cinematography, sharp editing and extraordinary sound production.

Although the film's subject could seem somewhat dated to modern audiences, at a time when only a handful of functioning shipyards remain on the River Clyde (a figure diminished from a peak of between 30 and 40), it is in some ways more fascinating than ever: an enchanting snapshot of an industry gone by. In truth, by 1960 the Clyde's shipbuilding was already in decline following both the targeted attacks of the Luftwaffe in World War II and the rise of competition from other nations around the globe. But one would never assume this from the content of *Seawards the Great Ships*. 'Britain is an island nation', narrator Bryden Murdoch asserts in an authoritative Scottish brogue, 'a nation of islanders and shipbuilders. On its shores, generations of craftsmen have built great ships for the world, but nowhere in such profusion as on the River Clyde – in Scotland'.

Placing its focus on the immense scale of the construction process itself, the film portrays shipbuilding not only as an impressive industry, but also one maintaining a pronounced sense of majesty. Magnitude is conveyed from the film's very first shot – the camera lingering on the image of a hulking orange-brown hull, the background behind its half constructed chassis nothing but sky.

Seawards the Great Ships,
Directed by Hilary Harris (1961)

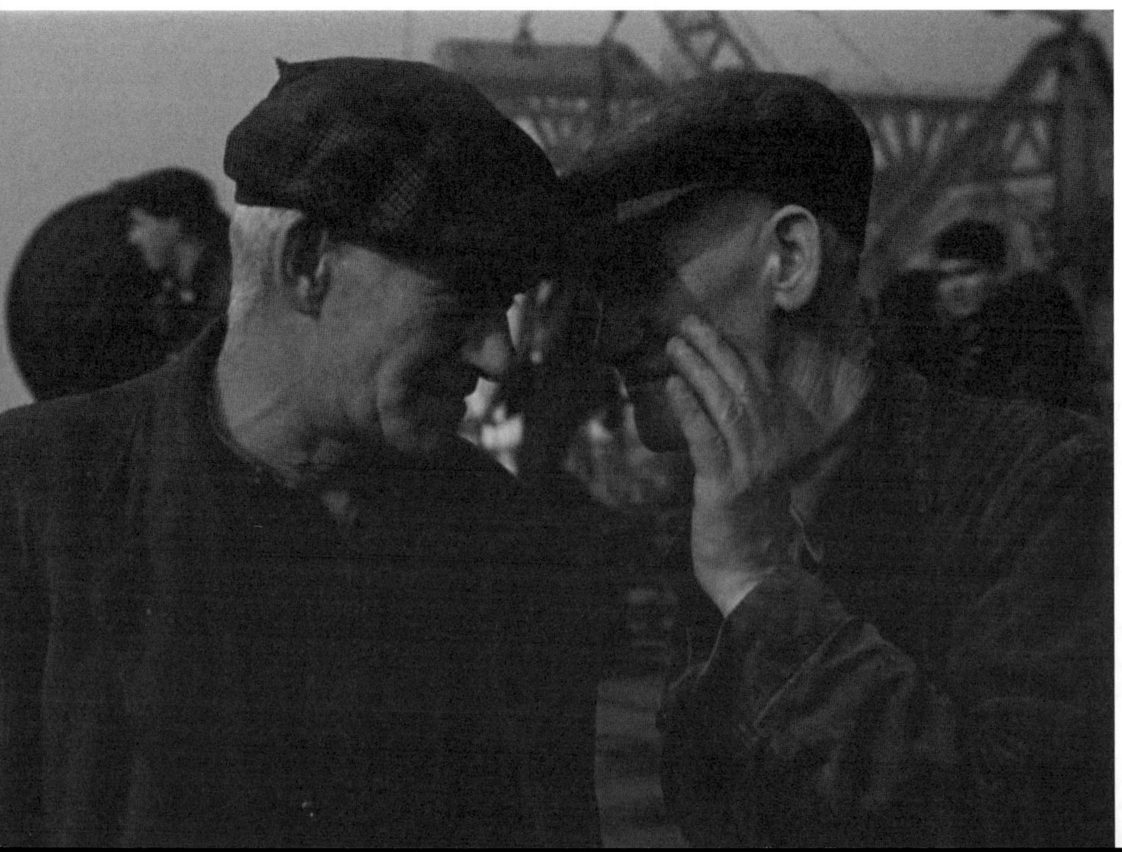

Year:
1961
Filming Location:
River Clyde, Scotland, UK

A crane arm passes overhead, scored only by the almighty rumbles of the shipyard, before the frame begins to pan downward toward the base of the ship's bow. Yet just as our eyes reach it, a match cut changes the view to the colossal wedge of a finished ship, cutting through the water as the camera retreats from its path. With the soundtrack now provided by a booming brass section, a seamless transition is made into a montage of ship launches, the voices of the women christening them overlapping as they ask God to bless the enormous vessels. The boats are considerable in number, each appearing on-screen for a matter of seconds – some in colour, some in black and white. In just a matter of moments, the film has established the vast turnover of a remarkable trade.

It is a powerful introduction, delivered at breakneck speed. And with director Hilary Harris utilizing the rest of the 28-minute runtime to showcase the shipbuilding process from start to finish, the film's pace rarely slows. Combining this rapid tempo with Murdoch's stirring reading of Clifford Hanley's almost poetic commentary, *Seawards the Great Ships* breathes vigorous drama into an unlikely subject. Facts and figures are delivered with a sense of awe ('It may take twenty men in a drawing office nine months to put a ship on paper. It will take thousands of men and hundreds of machines a year to turn it into steel'), whilst the near constant use of terms such as 'giant', 'monstrous' and even 'titanic' serve as constant reminders of the scale on show. Yet as the science behind shipbuilding is described as 'grimly serious' work, the film also leaves space for a lighter side, with the labourers of the shipyard given opportunity to show their sense of humour. In one segment we see doodles drawn on an unpainted ship (chalk outlines that turn portholes into fairground-style head-in-the-hole stands, a gruff workman's face taking position atop of a woman's body), whilst another segment allows the workers voices themselves to be heard, exchanging playful jibes over lunch. Word has it that Harris had to settle for scripted dialogue, however, as the real thing was found to be far too laden with expletives.

Yet, like a ship, Harris's film does not reach the peak of its splendour until the last stages of its construction. With the final act starting on an impressive crane-mounted shot, the camera traverses vertically through six levels of scaffolding before continuing high above the deck of a nearly complete vessel. As it reaches the summit of its climb, the angle rotates and slowly reveals the ship's full form stretching into the distance. Thus begins an immaculately filmed montage of winching, drilling, welding and riveting, the boat teaming with workmen, each with a part to play. The cacophonous noise generated would shred nerves, were it not for the undeniable spectacle visible on-screen. With another ship launch scene following shortly afterwards, the audience now approach this decisive moment in a new light. This is not just a boat sliding into the sea, but the birth of a new creation. As Murdoch puts it, 'she will never again be entirely still until she is no longer a ship'.

Patrick Harley

RECOMMENDED READING

Abrams, Lynn and Brown, Callum G (2010) *A History of Everyday Life in Twentieth-Century Scotland*, Edinburgh: EUP.

Aitken, Ian (1990) *Film and Reform: John Grierson and the Documentary Film Movement*, London: Routledge.

Aitken, Stuart (1991) 'A Transactional Geography of the Image-Event: The Films of Scottish Director, Bill Forsyth', *Transactions of the Institute of British Geographers*, 16: 1, pp. 105–18.

_________ (2007) 'Poetic Child Realism: Scottish Film and the Construction of Childhood', *Scottish Geographical Journal*, 123: 1, pp. 68–86.

Anderson, Lin (2005) *Braveheart: From Hollywood to Holyrood*, Edinburgh: Luath Press Ltd.

Ash, Marinell (1990) 'William Wallace and Robert the Bruce: The Life and Death of a National Myth', in Raphael Samuel and Paul Thompson (eds), *The Myths We Live By*, London: Routledge.

Balkind, Nicola (ed.) (2013) *World Film Locations: Glasgow*, Chicago: UCP.

Beattie, Bryan and Hassan, Gerry (ed.) (2011) *ImagiNation: Stories of Scotland's Future*, Drumderfit, Scotland: Big Sky Press.

Bell, Eleanor and Miller, Gavin (ed.) (1994) *Scotland in Theory: Reflections on Culture & Literature*, Scottish Cultural Review of Language and Literature, Volume 1, Amsterdam: Rodopi.

Bell, Emma and Mitchell, Neil (eds) (2012) *Directory of World Cinema: Britain*, Bristol: Intellect.

Beveridge, Craig and Turnbull, Ronald (1989) *The Eclipse of Scottish Culture: Inferiorism and the Intellectuals*, Edinburgh: Polygon.

NDED

Blain, Neil and Hutchison, David (ed.) (2008) *The Media in Scotland*, Edinburgh: EUP.

Blandford, Steven (2007) *Film, Drama and the Break-Up of Britain*, Bristol: Intellect.

Brown, Ian (ed.) (2010) *From Tartan to Tartanry: Scottish Culture, History and Myth*, Edinburgh: EUP.

Brown, John (1983), 'A Suitable Job for a Scot', *Sight and Sound*, 52: 3, pp. 157—162.

__________ (1983–84), 'Land Beyond Brigadoon', *Sight and Sound*, 53: 1, pp. 40—46.

Brown, Simon (2011) '"Anywhere but Scotland?" Transnationalism and New Scottish Cinema', *International Journal of Scottish Theatre and Screen*, 4: 1, http://journals.qmu.ac.uk/index.php/IJOSTS/article/view/109/pdf. Accessed 24 October 2013.

Bruce, David (1996) *Scotland the Movie*, Edinburgh: Polygon.

Bryan, Pauline and Kane, Tommy (eds) (2013) *Class, Nation and Socialism: The Red Paper on Scotland 2014*, Glasgow: Glasgow Caledonian University Archives.

Cabeleira, Helen, Martins, Catarina and Lawn, Martin (2011) 'Indisciplines of inquiry: The Scottish Children's Story, documentary film and the construction of the viewer', *Pedagogica Historica*, 47: 4., pp. 473-490.

Cardullo, Bert (2011) 'A Cinema of Social Conscience: An Interview with Ken Loach', *Minnesota Review*, 76: 1, pp. 81–96.

Caterer, James (2004) 'Playing the Lottery twice: The Dual Nationality of *Stella Does Tricks*', *Journal of Media Practice*, 5: 3, pp. 133–43.

Caughie, John (2007) '*Morvern Callar*, art cinema and the "monstrous archive"', *Scottish Studies Review*, 8: 1, pp. 101–15.

Cochrane, Jacqui (2011) '*16 Years of Alcohol*: An Allegory of a Nation?', *Participations*, 8: 2, pp. 308–26.

Cook, Pam (2002) *I Know Where I'm Going*, London: BFI.

Craig, Cairns (1996) *Out of History: Narrative Paradigms in Scottish and English Culture*, Edinburgh: Polygon.

__________ (2009) *Intending Scotland: Explorations in Scottish Culture Since the Enlightenment*, Edinburgh: EUP.

Craig, Carol (2011) *The Scots' Crisis of Confidence*, 2nd edn, Glendarual/Argyll, Scotland: Argyll Publishing.

Crawford, Robert (1997) 'Dedefining Scotland', in S Bassnett (ed.), *Studying British Culture: An Introduction*, London: Routledge, pp. 83–96.

Devine, TM (2003) *Scotland's Empire 1600–1815*, London: Penguin.

__________ (2008) *Scotland and the Union 1707–2007*, Edinburgh: EUP.

__________ (2011) *To the Ends of the Earth: Scotland's Global Diaspora 1750–2010*, London: Penguin.

__________ (2012) *The Scottish Nation: A Modern History*, London: Penguin.

Dick, Eddie (ed.) (1990) *From Limelight to Satellite: A Scottish Film Book* (ed. Eddie Dick), Edinburgh: Scottish Film Council and British Film Institute.

Dick, Eddie, Noble, Andrew and Petrie, Duncan (eds) (1993) *Bill Douglas: A Lanternist's Account*, London: BFI (in association with the Scottish Film Council).

Doll, Susan (ed.) (2008) *Bill Douglas: Bitter Memories, Brutal Realism*, Facets Cine-Notes. Chicago: Facets Multi-Media.

Ellis, John (2002) *John Grierson: Life, Contributions, Influence*, Illinois: Southern Illinois University Press.

Gardiner, Michael (2005) *Modern Scottish Culture*, Edinburgh: EUP.

Gold, John R and Gold, Margaret M (1995) *Imagining Scotland*, Aldershot: Scholar Press.

Goode, Ian (2005) 'Scottish cinema and Scottish imaginings: *Blue Black Permanent* and *Stella Does Tricks*', *Screen*, 36: 2, pp. 235–39.

__________ (2007) 'Different Trajectories: Europe and Scotland in Recent Scottish Cinema', *PORTAL Journal of Multidisciplinary International Studies*, 4: 2, pp. 1–11.

__________ (2011) 'Cinema in the country: The rural cinema scheme – Orkney (1946–1967)', *Post Script*, 30: 2, pp. 17-31.

Griffiths, Trevor (2013) *The Cinema and Cinema-Going in Scotland, 1896–1950*, Edinburgh: EUP.

Haider, Sandra-Elisabeth (2002) *Scotland in feature film: The country's screen-image then and now, with focus on the city of Glasgow and the development of a Scottish film industry*, PhD thesis, University of Vienna, Hamburg: Diplomarbeit Agentur and the University of Vienna.

Hames, Scott (ed.) (2012) *Unstated: Writers on Scottish Independence*, Edinburgh: Word Power Books.

Hardy, Forsyth (1979) *John Grierson: A Documentary Biography*, London: Faber & Faber.

__________ (1990) *Scotland in Film*, Edinburgh: EUP.

__________ (1992) *Slightly Mad and Full of Dangers: The Story of the Edinburgh Film Festival*, Edinburgh: Ramsay Head Press.

Harvie, Christopher T (1977) *Scotland and Nationalism*, London: Allen & Unwin.

Hassan, Gerry and Ilett, Rosie (eds) (2011) *Radical Scotland: Arguments for Self-Determination*, Edinburgh: Luath Press.

Hjort, Mette and Petrie, Duncan (eds) (2007) *The Cinema of Small Nations*, Edinburgh: EUP

Hobsbawm, Eric J and Ranger, Terence O (eds) (1992 [1983]) *The Invention of Tradition*, Cambridge, CUP.

Hydra Associates (1996) *Scotland on Screen: The Development of the Film and Television Industry in Scotland*, Glasgow: Scott Stern Associates.

Kemp, Philip (1991) *Lethal Innocence: The Cinema of Alexander Mackendrick*, London: Methuen.

Kennedy, Harlan (1996) 'Kiltspotting: Highland Reels', *Film Comment*, 32: 4, pp. 28–33.

Kinchin, Perilla and Kinchin, Juliet, with Neil Baxter (2001) *Glasgow's Great Exhibitions 1888 1901 1911 1938 1988*, Wendlebury: White Cockade Press.

Knight, Alanna (2007) *Burke & Hare*, Kew, Surrey, UK: National Archives Publishing.

Kuhn, Annette (2008) *Ratcatcher*, London: BFI.

Laverty, Paul et al. (2012) *The Angels' Share* [Screenplay with commentaries from Paul Laverty, Ken Loach, Rebecca O'Brien and others], Pontefract, UK: Route Publishing.

Lay, Samantha (2001) 'Bill Forsyth', in Yoram Allon, Dell Cullen, and Hannah Patterson (eds), *Contemporary British and Irish Film Directors: A Wallflower Critical Guide*, London: Wallflower Press.

__________ (2002) *British Social Realism: From Documentary to Brit Grit*, Short Cuts Introductions to Film Studies, London: Wallflower Press.

Leigh, Jacob (2002) *The Cinema of Ken Loach: Art in the Service of the People*, Directors' Cuts, London: Wallflower Press.

Leith, Murray Stewart and Soule, Daniel PJ (2011) *Political Discourse and National Identity in Scotland*, Edinburgh: EUP.

Lindsay, Maurice and Bruce, David (1990) *Edinburgh: Past and Present*, London: Robert Hale.

Lloyd, Matthew (2011) *How the Movie Brats Took Over Edinburgh: The Impact of Cinephilia on the Edinburgh Film Festival, 1968–1980*, Edinburgh: St Andrews Film Studies.

Loach, Ken (1998) *Loach on Loach* (ed. Graham Fuller), London: Faber & Faber.

Lynch, Michael (1992) *Scotland: A New History*, London: Pimlico.

Maan, Bashir (1992) *The New Scots*, Edinburgh: John Donald.

Macdonald, Kirsty A (2011) '"The Desolate and Appalling Landscape": The Journey North in Contemporary Scottish Gothic', *Gothic Studies*, 13: 2, pp. 37–48.

MacPherson, Robin (2012) (2012) 'Scottish cinema: Myth and reality from Hollywood to Holyrood', in Emma Bell and Neil Mitchell (eds), *Directory of World Cinema: Britain*, Bristol: Intellect, pp. 225–27.

Makarushka, Irena SM (2012) '*The Magdalene Sisters*: How to Solve the Problem of 'Bad' Girls', *Journal of Religion and Film*, 16: 2, pp. 1–42.

Malcolmson, Scott L (1985) 'Modernism comes to the cabbage patch: Bill Forsyth and the "Scottish Cinema"', *Film Quarterly*, 38: 3, pp. 16–21.

Martin, Andrew (2000) *Going to the Pictures: Scottish Memories of Cinema*, Edinburgh: NMS Publishing Ltd.

Martin-Jones, David (2005) *Deleuze, Cinema and National Identity*, Edinburgh: EUP.

__________ (2004) '*Orphans*: A work of minor cinema from post-devolutionary Scotland', *Journal of British Cinema and Television*, 1: 2, pp. 226–41.

__________ (2005) 'Sexual Healing: Representations of the English in Post-Devolutionary Scotland', *Screen*, 46: 2, pp. 227–33.

__________ (2009) *Scotland: Global Cinema – Genres, Modes and Identities*, Edinburgh: EUP.

Marx, Lesley (2011) '*The Last King of Scotland* and the politics of adaptation', *Black Camera: An International Film Journal*, 3: 1, pp. 54–74.

Matheou, Demetrios (2011) 'Peter Mullan: Glasgow belongs to me', *Sight and Sound*, http://old.bfi.org.u k/sightandsound/feature/49688. Accessed 28 April 2014.

McArthur, Colin (ed.) (1982) *Scotch Reels: Scotland in Cinema and Television*, London: BFI.

__________ (1993) 'In praise of a poor cinema', *Sight & Sound*, August, pp. 30–32.

__________ (2003) *Brigadoon, Braveheart, and the Scots: Distortions of Scotland in Hollywood Cinema*, London: IB Tauris.

__________ (2003) *Whisky Galore! and The Maggie: A British Film Guide*, London: IB Tauris.

McBain, Janet (1985) *Pictures Past: Scottish Cinemas Remembered*, Edinburgh: Moorfoot.

__________ (ed.) (1998) *Scotland in Silent Cinema: A Commemorative Catalogue to Accompany the Scottish Reels Programme at the Pordenone Silent Film Festival, Italy 1998*, Glasgow: Scottish Screen.

McCrone, David (1992) *Understanding Scotland: The Sociology of a Stateless Nation*, London: Routledge.

McCrone, David, Morris, Angela and Kiely, Richard (eds) (1995) *Scotland the Brand: The Making of Scottish Heritage*, Edinburgh: EUP.

McIntyre, Steve (1984) 'New iImages of Scotland', *Screen* , 25: 1, pp. 53–60.

Meir, Christopher (2004) 'Bill Forsyth', *Senses of cinema*, http://sensesofcinema.com/2004/great-directors/forsyth/, Accessed 28 April 2014.

Morace, Robert (2012) 'The devolutionary Jekyll and post-devolutionary Hyde of the two *Morvern Callars*', *Critique: Studies in Contemporary Fiction*, 53: 2, pp. 115–23.

Murphy, Robert (ed.) (2009) *The British Cinema Book 3rd Edition*, London: BFI.

Murray, Jonathan (2001) 'Contemporary Scottish Film', *Irish Review*, 28, pp. 75–88.

__________ (2004) *That Thinking Feeling: A Research Guide to Scottish Cinema 1938–2004*, Glasgow: Scottish Screen/Edinburgh College of Art.

__________ (2005) 'Kids in America?: Narratives of transatlantic influence in 1990s Scottish cinema', *Screen*, 46: 2, pp. 217–25.

__________ (2007) 'Scotland', in Mette Hjort and Duncan Petrie (eds), *The Cinema of Small Nations*, Edinburgh: EUP, pp. 76–92.

__________ (2011) *Discomfort and Joy: The Cinema of Bill Forsyth*, Berlin: Peter Lang.

__________ (2012) 'Blurring borders: Scottish cinema in the twenty-first century', in *Journal of British Cinema and Television*, 9:3, pp. 400–18.

__________ (in press) *The New Scottish Cinema*, London: IB Tauris, November 2014.

Murray, Jonathan, Stevenson, Lesley, Harper, Stephen and Franks, Benjamin (eds) (2005) *Constructing the Wicker Man*, Glasgow: University of Glasgow, Crichton Publications.

Murray, Jonathan, Farley, Fidelma and Stoneman, Rod (ed.) (2009) *Scottish Cinema Now*, Newcastle upon Tyne: Cambridge Scholars Publishing.

Nairn, Tom (1977) *The Break-up of Britain: Crisis and Neo-Nationalism*, London: New Left Books.

Nash, Andrew (2007) *Kailyard and Scottish Literature*, New York: Rodopi.

Neely, Sarah (2005) 'Scotland, Heritage and Devolving British Cinema', *Screen*, 26: 2, pp. 227–33.

__________ (2005) 'The Conquering Heritage of British Cinema Studies and the "Celtic Fringe"', in J Hill and K Rockett (eds), *Film History and National Cinema*, Dublin: Four Courts Press, pp. 159–83.

__________ (2008) 'Stalking the image: Margaret Tait and intimate filmmaking practices', *Screen*, 49: 2, pp. 216–21.

__________ (2009) '"Ploughing a lonely furrow': Margaret Tait and professional filmmaking practices in 1950s Scotland', in Ian Craven (ed.), *Movies on Home Ground: Explorations in Amateur Cinema*, Newcastle upon Tyne: Cambridge Scholars Publishing, pp. 301–26.

Pendreich, Brian (2002) *The Pocket Scottish Movie Book*, Edinburgh: Mainstream Publishing.

__________ (2000) *The Scot Pack: The Further Adventures of the Trainspotters and Their Fellow Travellers*, Edinburgh: Mainstream Publishing.

Peter, Bruce (1996) *100 Years of Glasgow's Amazing Cinemas*, Edinburgh: Polygon.

__________ (2011) *Scotland's Cinemas*, Ramsey, Isle of Man: Lily Publications.

Petrie, Duncan (2001) 'Devolving British Cinema: The New Scottish Cinema and the European Art Film', *Cineaste*, 26: 4, pp. 55–57.

__________ (2004) *Contemporary Scottish Fictions: Film, Television and the Novel*, Edinburgh: EUP.

__________ (2000) *Screening Scotland*, London: BFI.

__________ (2005) 'Scottish Cinema', *Screen*, 46: 2, pp. 213–16.

__________ (2012) 'From the *Rive Gauche* to the New Scottish Cinema: Alexander Trocchi, David Mackenzie, and *Young Adam*', *Critique: Studies in Contemporary Fiction*, 53: 2, pp. 124–34.

__________ (2013) 'Planting the Seeds of Ambition: Scottish Film in the 1960s', The *Scottish Sixties: Reading, Rebellion, Revolution?*, Eleanor Bell and Linda Gunn, eds., Amsterdam: Ropoi, 2013, pp. 242-259.

Pittock, Murray GH (1991) *The Invention of Scotland: The Stuart Myth and Scottish Identity, 1638 to the Present*, London: Routledge.

__________ (2001) *Scottish Nationality*, Basingstoke: Palgrave.

__________ (2014 [2008]) *The Road to Independence? Scotland Since the Sixties*, Contemporary Worlds, London: Reaktion Books.

Powell, Michael (1990) *Edge of the World: The Making of a Film*, London: Faber & Faber.

Prebble, John (1963) *The Highland Clearances*, London: Penguin.

Ray, Celeste (2001) *Highland Heritage: Scottish Americans in the American South*, Chapel Hill: University of North Carolina Press.

Riach, Alan (2005) *Representing Scotland in Literature, Popular Culture and Iconography: The Masks of the Modern Nation*, Basingstoke: Palgrave Macmillan.

Saeed, Amir, Blain, Neil and Forbes, Douglas (eds) (1999) 'New Ethnic and National Questions in Scotland', *Ethnic and Racial Social Studies*, 22: 5, pp. 821–44.

Scullion, Adrienne (1995) 'Feminine pleasures and masculine indignities: Gender and community in Scottish drama', in Christopher Whyte (ed.), *Gendering the Nation: Studies in Modern Scottish Literature*, Edinburgh: EUP, pp. 169–204.

Sherrington, Jo (1996) *'To Speak Its Pride': The Work of the Film of Scotland Committee*, Glasgow: SFC.

Smith, Murray (2002) *Trainspotting*, British Film Institute Modern Classics, London: BFI.

Smout, TC (1972) *A History of the Scottish People 1560–1830*, London: Fontana.

__________ (1986) *A History of the Scottish People 1830–1950*, London: Fontana.

Todd, Peter and Cook, Benjamin (2006) *Subjects and Sequences: A Margaret Tait Reader*, West Sussex: Wallflower Press.

Various (2005) 'Scottish Cinema Dossier', *Screen*, 46: 2, pp. 213–45.

Wightman, Andy (2011) *The Poor Had No Lawyers: Who Owns Scotland (And How They Got It)*, Edinburgh: Birlinn.

Williams, Christopher (ed.) (1980) *Realism and the Cinema*, London: Routledge and Kegan Paul.

__________ (ed.) (1996) *Cinema: The Beginnings and the Future – Essays Marking the Centenary of the First Film Show Projected to a Paying Audience in Britain*, London: University of Westminster Press

Womack, Peter (1989) *Improvement and Romance: Constructing the Myth of the Highlands*, London: Macmillan.

Young, James D (1979) *The Rousing of the Scottish Working Class*, London: Croom Helm.

Zumkhawala-Cook, Richard (2008) *Scotland as We Know It: Representations of National Identity in Literature, Film and Popular Culture*, Jefferson, NC: McFarland.

SCOTTISH CINEMA ONLINE

Aconite Productions
http://www.aconiteproductions.co.uk
Glasgow-based Aconite Productions produces documentaries concerned with topical issues, including from new writers and directors.

All Media Scotland
http://www.allmediascotland.com
All Media Scotland provides resources for journalists, broadcasters, communication professionals and media students to keep up with what is happening, as well as usefully to contribute, across a broad range of Scottish media.

Bill Douglas Centre
http://www.exeter.ac.uk/bdc/
The Bill Douglas Centre at the University of Exeter maintains a valuable collection of materials not only relevant to Bill Douglas's own work but also of interest concerning a more extensive history of cinema and the visual arts.

Black Camel Pictures
www.blackcamel.co.uk/home/
Black Camel Pictures is a Glasgow-based company focused on Scottish-based feature films and emerging new kinds of multi-platform productions.

British Academy of Film and Television Arts Scotland
http://www.bafta.org/scotland/
The British Academy of Film and Television Arts Scotland (BAFTA Scotland) provides charitable assistance in supporting the development and promotion of film, television and video game productions, including by way of the annual BAFTA Scotland and BAFTA Scotland New Talent Awards.

British Board of Film Classification
http://www.bbfc.co.uk
The British Board of Film Classification regulates ratings in terms of the age appropriateness of films, videos and video games released in the United Kingdom.

British Broadcasting Corporation Film Network
http://www.bbc.co.uk/filmnetwork/films/region/scotlandhttp://www.bbc.co.uk/filmnetwork/

The British Broadcasting Corporation Film Network provides online access to short films and videos, features on film events and resources for film-making and networking, in Scotland as well as across the rest of the United Kingdom.

British Council Film
http://film.britishcouncil.org

British Council Film connects Scottish and other United Kingdom films and film-makers with international audiences, helping promote UK films and film-makers beyond the United Kingdom as well as fostering creative exchanges between UK and international film-makers.

British Film Institute
www.bfi.org.uk

The British Film Institute maintains extensive film archives covering the entirety of the United Kingdom, as well as substantial research facilities and resources, while also hosting both daily and festival screenings along with publishing the film magazine *Sight and Sound*.

British Film Institute Mediatheque at Bridgeton Library, Glasgow
http://bfi.org.uk/archive-collections/introduction-bfi-collections/bfi-mediatheques/bfi-mediatheques-around-uk/mediatheque-bridgeton-library-glasgow

The BFI (British Film Institute) Mediatheque in Glasgow provides public access to a specially commissioned collection of diverse materials from Scottish film and television, titled 'Scottish Reels', culled via collections of the BFI National as well as Scottish Screen archives, and spanning more than a century of Scottish life and culture.

Cinematic Scotland
http://cinematicscotland.com

Cinematic Scotland provides a diverse range of information about the moving image in Scotland, past and present, including shooting locations, casts and crews, and cinema houses and other exhibition venues.

Creative Scotland
http://www.creativescotland.comhttp://www.scotland.org/creative-scotland/film

Creative Scotland is the principal quasi-autonomous non-governmental organization in Scotland providing assistance, especially in the form of financial investment, education and training, to support production, distribution and exhibition of film, along with providing comparable support for other forms of artistic and creative industry in Scotland.

Edinburgh Film Focus
http://www.edinfilm.com

Edinburgh Film Focus is the local film commission for Edinburgh, East Lothian and the Scottish Borders, helping promote and assist pre-production, production and post-production work in the region.

Edinburgh International Film Festival
http://www.edfilmfest.org.uk
Begun in 1947, the annual Edinburgh International Film Festival encompasses screenings of films as well as presentations and discussions of issues and directions in film-making on an international scale, while frequently including significant representation of Scottish and other UK films.

Fife Screen and Tay Screen Scotland
http://www.tayscreen.com
Fife Screen and Tay Screen Scotland is the local film commission for the Fife and Tay regions of Scotland, helping promote and assist pre-production, production and post-production work in these regions.

FilmG – The Gaelic Short Film Competition
http://www.filmg.co.uk/en/
FilmG – The Gaelic Short Film Competition provides promotion, training and support for Gaelic language short films and videos, culminating each year with a series of awards for impressive achievement in relation to a specific competition theme.

Film Bang
http://filmbang.com/home
Film Bang provides information and other resources for film and television production in Scotland, including contacts for production companies and personnel as well as for production workshops and facilities.

Film City Glasgow
http://www.filmcityglasgow.com
Film City Glasgow promotes and assists pre-production, production and post-production work in the city of Glasgow, and in the Greater Glasgow metropolitan region.

Glasgow Film Festival
http://www.glasgowfilm.org/festival
Begun in 2005, the annual Glasgow Film Festival, headquartered at the Glasgow Film Theatre, includes screenings, panel discussion, live performances and special events across the city, and is preceded, earlier in the year, by the Glasgow Youth Film Festival and the Glasgow Short Film Festival.

The Herald and the Sunday Herald, Arts and Entertainment – Film
http://www.heraldscotland.com/arts-ents/film
The Glasgow-based *Herald* newspaper's web source offers articles on films, film releases and film screenings, film-makers, film-making and film events.

Highlands of Scotland Film Commission (Comisean Fiolm Gáidhealtachd Na H-Alba)
http://scotfilm.org
The Highlands of Scotland Film Commission promotes and assists pre-production, production, and post-production work in the Scottish Highlands.

The Independent Cinema Office (Scotland)
http://www.independentcinemaoffice.org.uk/resources/cinemas/scotland
The Independent Cinema Office (Scotland) is the Scottish section of a UK-wide organization providing support for independent exhibitors of all kinds – including cinemas, film festivals and film societies.

The List – Film
http://film.list.co.uk
The List is a leading, Glasgow- and Edinburgh-based, monthly arts, culture and entertainment magazine, that provides significant coverage of film releases, screenings and events, especially in Scotland's two largest cities.

LUX Artists' Moving Image Collection – Margaret Tait
http://lux.org.uk/collection/artists/margaret-tait
LUX Artists' Moving Image Collection provides access for rental, purchase and download of film and video work by Margaret Tait and other artists working in experimental film, video art, installation art, performance art, personal documentary, essay film and animation.

National Library of Scotland
www.nls.uk
The National Library of Scotland is the world's leading centre for the study of Scotland and the Scots, encompassing a major research library and a variety of collections of world-class importance, and which also periodically sponsors exhibits and events related to Scottish cinema and cinema-going.

Park Circus
http://www.parkcircus.com
The Glasgow-based Park Circus provides restored versions of classic, cult and back catalogue films from a wide array of sources – including a significant number of Scottish and other British films.

Reel Scotland
http://www.reelscotland.com
Reel Scotland is an independent source for reviews, previews, features and interviews covering film and television in Scotland.

Scotland on Screen
www.scotlandonscreen.org.uk
Scotland on Screen provides access to educational films and videos, as well as related resources for use in the classroom by students and teachers.

Scotland the Movie Location Guide
www.scotlandthemovie.com
Scotland the Movie Location Guide provides information about films and television shows made in Scotland, organized according to region.

The Scotsman, Lifestyle – Film
http://www.scotsman.com/lifestyle/film
The Edinburgh-based *Scotsman* newspaper's web source offers articles on films, film releases and film screenings, film-makers, film-making and film events.

Scottish Cinemas and Theatres Project
http://www.scottishcinemas.org.uk
The Scottish Cinemas and Theatres Project provides information and additional resources concerning the social history of cinema-going and of purpose-built exhibition venues, particularly in Glasgow and Edinburgh.

Scottish Documentary Institute
http://www.scottishdocinstitute.com
The Scottish Documentary Institute is an Edinburgh-based documentary research centre, set up in 2004, that specializes in documentary training, production and distribution, and which has enabled the production of films that have screened at many international festivals.

Scottish Screen Archive
http://ssa.nls.uk
The Scottish Screen Archive is dedicated toward the preservation of the history of film and video production in Scotland, and maintains facilities for viewing along with additional resources for research, as well as providing materials for distribution and exhibition.

Scottish Television, Entertainment – Film
http://entertainment.stv.tv/film/
The web location maintained by Scottish Television (STV) offers information and other resources related to film and video screenings, releases and events.

Scran
http://www.scran.ac.uk
Scran provides educational access to digital materials representing material culture and history in Scotland and elsewhere in the United Kingdom.

Sigma Films
http://www.sigmafilms.com
Sigma Films is a Glasgow-based production company, established in 1997, that has been responsible for a number of the most critically acclaimed Scottish films made since that time, including those part of the Action Party scheme as well as films directed by David Mackenzie.

Sixteen Films
http://www.sixteenfilms.co.uk
Sixteen Films is the production company for the films Ken Loach directs, Paul Laverty writes and Rebecca O'Brien produces.

The Skinny – Film
http://www.theskinny.co.uk/film
The Skinny is a leading Edinburgh- and Glasgow-based independent and alternative music, arts and culture print and web magazine, which often includes significant coverage of film and video releases, screenings and events.

Bob Nowlan

TEST YOUR KNOWLED[...]

1. What is the setting of *Outcast*?
2. What film marks the first time that a feature Scottish cinematic narrative was produced in Scottish Gaelic?
3. What film released in 1996 was the second Scottish-themed and Scottish-financed fiction film ever directed by a woman?
4. At the end of *The Illusionist*, Tatischeff eventually departs from Edinburgh without telling Alice, leaving her some money, a bouquet of flowers, and a note saying what?
5. In *The Illusionist*, traditional music hall entertainment is eclipsed by television and what new genre of music?
6. Alfred Hitchcock's film *The 39 Steps* is based on a 1915 novel of the same name by whom?
7. Where is Gino from in the film *American Cousins*?
8. In what century is William Wallace shown as defending Scottish independence from British rule in *Braveheart*?
9. Who is the historical figure who was actually referred to as Braveheart?
10. What does 'the angels' share' refer to regarding the process of whisky making?
11. Garry Fraser's autobiographical film that was first shown on BBC in 2012 as *My Lives and Times* was later renamed what?
12. How many films were included in the 1938 Glasgow Empire Exhibition Series?
13. What year was the first British Empire Exhibition Series?
14. In the film *Floodtide*, what is the main character, David's, occupation?
15. The film *Floodtide* is based on the novel *The Shipbuilders* by what author?
16. The film *We Need to Talk About Kevin* was directed by whom?
17. What 1938 narrative does the film *New Town Killers* most closely resemble in plot structure?
18. The antagonist Alistair from *New Town Killers* is reminiscent of what Dostoyevsky character?
19. What 1998 Peter Mullan film won four awards at the Venice Film Festival and the Grand Prix at the 1999 Festival du Film de Paris?
20. In the film *Shell*, what business does the protagonist's father, Pete, own?
21. What region of Scotland is *Shell* set in?
22. Why was St Kilda evacuated?
23. This term is used to describe the low-brow, often misrepresented, elements of Scottish culture (including bagpipes, kilts, etc).
24. This book, edited by Colin McArthur and published in 1982, epitomizes the position that staunchly critiques cinematic representations of Scottish myths – and others like them – as stereotypes.
25. The term 'Kailyard' is also known as this.
26. Kailyard is often associated with this famous author, perhaps most well-known for his children's book *Peter Pan*.
27. What is the term used to describe the hyper-masculine male role model often promoted in traditional views of Scottish culture?
28. These films tended to be relentlessly positive in tone and to depict Scots as maintaining an overriding commonality of interest across class lines, and across other lines of actual social division.
29. What was the budget cut-off to be considered qualified as an instance of the 'poor Scottish cinema' advocated for by Colin McArthur?

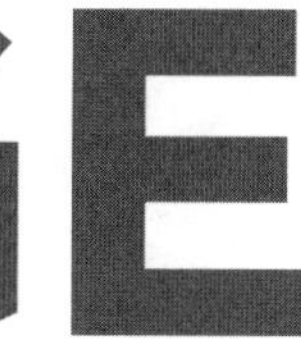

30. Critics who condemn the nostalgia of Scottish culture are sometimes referred to (by their own critics such as Cairns Craig) as what?
31. What movement took place in Scottish Presbyterianism that could be interpreted as a religious form of quasi-nationalism, involving a rejection of the right of authorities closely tied to the government in London to decide how Scottish religious affairs would be conducted at the local level?
32. This poet was the archetypal 'lad o' pairts', and was appreciated for his links to the seventeenth-century Covenanters, widely regarded as martyrs, as well as for his preservation of the ancient vernacular language.
33. The cult of this man suggested that the Scots had never been conquered.
34. What popular Scottish rebellion film has been criticized for lending itself to conservative politics and potentially encouraging fascism?
35. *Mrs Brown* is notable for recounting an historical episode, and in particular an historical relationship, otherwise not represented in film, and in recounting how a Scots ghillie played an important role in the private and public life of whom?
36. The film *Comfort and Joy* is based on the real-life wars that took place between what kind of vendors?
37. What is wrong with Alan 'Dickie' Bird's girlfriend in *Comfort and Joy*?
38. *Seawards the Great Ships* describes the shipbuilding industry along what Scottish river?
39. What award did *Seawards the Great Ships* win in 1961?
40. What is the goal for the human sacrifice that comes at the end of *The Wicker Man*?
41. What makes Howie an ideal candidate for the sacrifice at the end of *The Wicker Man?*
42. Connection to what event led to the ruin of the career of Dr Robert Knox, forcing him to relocate to London?
43. Prior to becoming murderers, Burke and Hare failed at what illegal profession?
44. What special skill does Bess McNeill poses in *Breaking the Waves*?
45. Why does Bess McNeill commit adultery at her husband's request?
46. What is the miracle of the town of Brigadoon?
47. How did Jeff Douglas and Tommy Albright find Brigadoon?
48. Who was the British monarch during the rebellion of Rob Roy?
49. *Rob Roy: The Highland Rogue* is based on the novel of the same name by what author?
50. In the film *I Know Where I'm Going!*, Joan dreams that she is marrying what corporation?
51. How long did it take to write the story for *I Know Where I'm Going!*?
52. In *Dog Soldiers*, why does Cooper not make the Special Forces?
53. Who plays Rob Roy in the 1995 film titled after its namesake?
54. In the 1995 film *Rob Roy*, the protagonist puts up land as collateral for a loan belonging to what clan?
55. The script for what abandoned film led to Lynne Ramsay taking a decade-long hiatus from her career as a film director?
56. What is the name of the select group of girls that Miss Brodie takes a special interest in?
57. What film studio produced the film *The Prime of Miss Jean Brodie*?
58. In *Tunes of Glory*, what is the eventual fate of Barrow?
59. The attempted assimilation of Barrow's personality into that of Sinclair's is signified at the end of *Tunes of Glory* when he insists on being called by what title as opposed to his usual nickname 'Jock'?
60. What famous philosopher wrote about the concept of love in a way that is highly useful for demystifying the plot and themes of *The Brothers*?

answers on next page

Answers

1. Edinburgh, Scotland
2. *Seachd: The Inaccessible Pinnacle*
3. *Stella Does Tricks*
4. Magicians do not exist
5. Rock and roll
6. John Buchan
7. New Jersey
8. Thirteenth century
9. Robert the Bruce
10. Spirit lost to evaporation
11. *Everybody's Child*
12. Seven
13. 1924–25
14. Ship designer
15. George Blake
16. Lynne Ramsay
17. *The Most Dangerous Game*
18. Raskolnikov
19. *Orphans*
20. Petrol station and garage
21. The Highlands
22. Unsustainable diminished population
23. Tartanry
24. *Scotch Reels: Scotland in Cinema and Television*
25. A cabbage patch
26. JM Barrie
27. The 'hard man'
28. Scotland on the Move
29. £300,000 or less
30. Nostophobes
31. The Great Disruption
32. Robert Burns
33. William Wallace
34. *Braveheart*
35. Queen Victoria
36. Ice-cream vendors
37. She's a kleptomaniac
38. The River Clyde
39. Academy Award for Best Short, Live Action Subject
40. A successful apple harvest
41. He is a sexually chaste Christian
42. The Burke and Hare body-snatching case
43. Grave robbing
44. She can speak to God
45. He is paralysed
46. Time passes more slowly there
47. They got lost while hunting
48. King George I
49. Sir Walter Scott
50. Consolidated Chemical Industries
51. Five days
52. He refuses to shoot a dog
53. Liam Neeson
54. The McGregor clan
55. *The Lovely Bones*
56. The Brodie set
57. Twentieth Century Fox
58. Suicide
59. Colonel
60. Søren Kierkegaard

Alex Long

NOTES ON CONTRIBUTORS

The Editors

Bob Nowlan is Professor of Critical Theory, Cinema Studies and Cultural Studies with the Department of English at the University of Wisconsin-Eau Claire. He is producer and host of the weekly radio show *Insurgence*, featuring contemporary indie rock, pop, folk and folk rock; classic post-punk and new wave; and music of protest and resistance. Besides work in Scottish studies he is currently working on a book tentatively titled *Ian Curtis: The Myth and the Music.*

Zach Finch is a PhD student in English with a concentration in Film, Media and Digital Studies at the University of Wisconsin-Milwaukee. He is a graduate of the University of Wisconsin-Eau Claire and North Carolina State University. His work on Scottish cinema continues with his forthcoming dissertation.

The Contributors

Kyle Barrett is a PhD student from the University of the West of Scotland. His PhD research addresses the issues of transnationalism and new paradigms in digital film-making. Kyle teaches practical-based modules including documentary and short film, and continues to create film projects as both research and practice.

Alex F Brown is a graduate of the Liberal Studies programme at the University of Wisconsin-Eau Claire who maintains an interest in the work of Heidegger, Lacan, Deleuze and Badiou as well as a diverse range of modern arts and cinemas from opera through science fiction.

Lucy Brydon is a writer and film-maker from Edinburgh. She has a BA in Literature and Creative Writing from the University of Warwick, and lived in Shanghai between 2005 and 2010. An alumna of the Columbia University Film Programme in New York, Lucy's film and multimedia work has been screened internationally. Lucy currently lives in London where she runs her own production company, Shy Child Productions.

Jason Burke is a student at the University of Wisconsin-Madison studying English. He is also heavily involved in the campus film committee, WUD (Wisconsin Union Directorate) Film, and he has contributed to the programming of a film series in the Summer of 2013 and as Associate Director for Alternative Film Programming in the 2013–14 academic year.

David Cairns is a critic and film-maker based in Scotland. He teaches at Edinburgh College of Art. His new film, *Natan* (2013), co-directed with Paul Duane, recently won Best Documentary Feature at Dallas Video Fest.

Jacqui Cochrane is a postgraduate doctoral researcher at Glasgow Caledonian University, Scotland. Having successfully completed her Masters in Research in 2010, she is currently undertaking for her doctoral research an investigation of the discourses which surround the production and reception of television drama fiction produced for and by Scottish-based broadcasters between 1990 and 2010.

Oana Chivoiu is finishing her dissertation in Theory and Cultural Studies at Purdue University. Her publications have appeared in *Short Film Studies*, *Film International*, *Many Cinemas*, the World Film Locations series (Paris, Las Vegas, Marseille and Prague) and the Directory of World Cinema series. Her latest article 'Childless Motherhood: The Geopolitics of Maternal Bliss in Fatih Akin's "The Edge of Heaven"' has been published in the collection *Disjointed Perspectives on Motherhood*, edited by Catalina Florina Florescu., through Lexington Books in October 2013.

Kevin M Flanagan is a PhD candidate in the Critical and Cultural Studies Program at the University of Pittsburgh. He is editor of *Ken Russell: Re-Viewing England's Last Mannerist* (Scarecrow Press, 2009) and has published essays in *Framework*, *Proteus: A Journal of Ideas* and *Media Fields Journal*. His dissertation focuses on representations of war in Britain during the 1960s and 1970s.

Nis Grøn has an MA degree in Film Studies from the University of Copenhagen, Denmark, and is currently completing a PhD at Lingnan University, Hong Kong, focusing on a comparative study of small national cinemas and the identification of problems that are shared and solutions that work within the context of small nations.

Patrick Harley is a freelance film journalist based in Glasgow. He has written reviews, news stories and features for websites such as *Best For Film*, *New Empress*, *HeyUGuys* and *Glasgow Film*.

Terry Hobgood is the Cultural Arts Director for the Town of Benson, NC, USA. He has a Master's in Library and Information Studies from UNC Greensboro, an MA in English from NC State University, and a BA in Film Studies from UNC Wilmington.

Aaron RM Hokanson has a PhD in Curriculum and Instruction from the University of Minnesota. He has worked with diverse populations in various settings in the United States and Australia. His work emerges from a belief in the revolutionary educative possibility in the diversity of everyday life and relationships.

Linda Hutcheson is a doctoral student at the University of Stirling. Her thesis examines contemporary Scottish cinema, focusing in particular on the Advance Party Initiative. Her research areas include Scottish and British cinema, with specific interests in national and transnational film theory, film marketing, and the process of film production.

David Hutchison has spent most of his career at Glasgow Caledonian University. Among his publications are *The Modern Scottish Theatre* (Moledinar Press and Richard Drew Publishing,1977) and *Media Policy* (Wiley-Blackwell,1999). With Neil Blain he co-edited *The Media in Scotland* (Edinburgh University Press, 2008). He became chair of Regional Screen Scotland in 2010.

Gareth James is a freelance film and television writer; he completed a PhD on the history of American cable network Home Box Office in 2011, and has published work on the BBC, American Independent Cinema, and the Western. His research interests include contemporary American and British cinema, television and marketing.

Alex Long is currently a graduate student at the University of Wisconsin-Eau Claire studying English Literature with an emphasis on critical theory. Throughout the completion of his Master's programme and the eventual pursuit of a PhD, Long intends to direct his research toward furthering the discourse related to social class antagonism and extreme poverty.

Robin MacPherson is Professor of Screen Media, Director of the Institute for Creative and Industries and Screen Academy Scotland at Edinburgh Napier University, and leads ENGAGE, an EU MEDIA-funded collaboration with the Irish, Estonian and Finnish film schools. A BAFTA nominated documentary and drama film and television producer, he joined Edinburgh Napier in 2002 from Scottish Screen where he was head of development. In 2010 he was appointed by the Scottish government to the Board of Creative Scotland and joined the Board of Creative Edinburgh in 2011. He is a Fellow of the Royal Society of Arts, and blogs at http://www.robinmacpherson.wordpress.com.

Jeremy Magnan is a professor of Cinema Studies at the College of Lake County and a doctoral student at the University of Wisconsin-Milwaukee where he specializes in international film and the horror genre. He dedicates his contribution to Kristen Cook.

David Martin-Jones is Professor of Film Studies at the University of Glasgow. He is the author or editor of six books, including *Scotland: Global Cinema* (Edinburgh University Press, 2009) and *Cinema at the Periphery* (Wayne State University Press, 2010), an anthology which contains his previous work on Gaelic film-making. He has published widely on various cinemas from around the world, including articles on cinema in Scotland in such journals as *Screen* and *Journal of British Cinema and Television*.

Colin McArthur is former Head of the Distribution Division of the British Film Institute. He has written extensively on Hollywood cinema, British television, and Scottish culture and lectured widely in the United Kingdom, other European countries and the Americas. His publications include *Underworld USA* (Merlin Secker and Warburg, 1972), *Television and History* (BFI, 1978), *Dialectic! Left Film Criticism from Tribune* (Key Texts, 1982), *The Casablanca File* (Half Brick Images 1992), *Whisky Galore! and The Maggie* (BFI, 2002) and *Brigadoon, Braveheart, and the Scots: Distortions of Scotland in Hollywood Cinema* (IB Tauris, 2003). He is now a trader in a London antiques market.

Christopher Meir is Lecturer in Film at the University of the West Indies, St Augustine. He has published a number of articles and book chapters on Scottish cinema and is the author of the forthcoming book *Scottish Cinema: Texts and Contexts* (Manchester University Press, 2014) as well as co-editor of a forthcoming anthology of essays on the producer entitled *Beyond the Bottom Line: The Producer in Film and Television Studies* (Continuum, July 2014).

Jonathan Murray lectures in Film and Visual Culture at Edinburgh College of Art. His books include *Discomfort and Joy: The Cinema of Bill Forsyth* (Peter Lang, 2011) and *The New Scottish Cinema* (IB Tauris, in press). He is also a contributing writer to *Cineaste* magazine.

Susan Robinson studied English Literature at the University of Edinburgh and has worked for the Edinburgh International Film Festival and Edinburgh UNESCO City of Literature. She has also contributed to the film website *Reel Scotland* and *World Film Locations: Glasgow* (Intellect, 2013). She takes lots of photos of Edinburgh.

Nathaniel Taylor is a McNair Fellow studying philosophy as well as critical studies in literature, film, and culture at the University of Wisconsin-Eau Claire. His research interests include ethics, philosophy of art and literature, and history of philosophy.

Stefan Udelhofen is a doctoral student in Media Studies at the a.r.t.e.s. Graduate School for the Humanities Cologne. He received his MA degree in Theatre, Film and Television Studies, Political Science and Psychology from the University of Cologne in 2011. His main research interests are media culture and media history, European, Indian and transnational cinema, and digital media.

Tom Wallis is the Assistant Director of North Carolina State University's Film Studies Program and the co-author of *Film: A Critical Introduction* (3rd edn, Lawrence King Publishing, 2011) with Maria Pramaggiore. He serves on the Programming Committee for Durham, NC's Full Frame Documentary Film Festival and dotes on his Scottish deerhound, Fergus.

FILMOGRA

16 Years of Alcohol (2003) **190**
The 39 Steps (1935) **116**
1938 Empire Exhibition Films of Scotland Committee Series of Documentary Films (1938) **328**
Aberdeen (2000) **201**
The Acid House (1998) **272**
Ae Fond Kiss (2004) **203**
American Cousins (2003) **274**
The Anatomist (1961) **275**
The Angels' Share (2012) **118**
The Bill Douglas Trilogy (1972, 1973, 1978) **204**
The Body Snatcher (1945) **267**
Bonnie Prince Charlie (1948) **124**
Brave (2012) **126**
Braveheart (1995) **129**
Breaking the Waves (1996) **131**
Brigadoon (1954) **134**
The Brothers (1947) **137**
Burke and Hare (1972) **280**
Burke and Hare (2010) **281**
Carla's Song (1997) **208**
Comfort and Joy (1984) **283**
Culloden (1964) **141**
Dear Frankie (2004) **210**
The Doctor and the Devils (1985) **285**
Dog Soldiers (2002) **286**
Donald Cammell: The Ultimate Performance (1998) **333**
Donkeys (2010) **212**
The Edge of the World (1937) **144**
Everybody's Child (2012) **335**
The Flesh and the Fiends (1960) **289**
Floodtide (1949) **147**
Gregory's Girl (1981) **291**
Gregory's Two Girls (1998) **294**
Hallam Foe (2007) **215**
Horror Maniacs (1948) **296**
I Know Where I'm Going! (1945) **152**
The Illusionist (2010) **297**

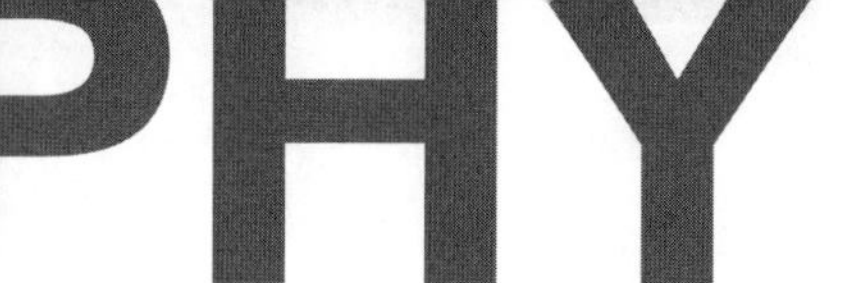

Just a Boys' Game (1979) **155**
Just Another Saturday (1975) **157**
The Last King of Scotland (2006) **158**
Local Hero (1983) **300**
Morvern Callar (2002) **218**
Mrs Brown (1997) **160**
My Name is Joe (1998) **219**
Neds (2010) **222**
New Town Killers (2008) **225**
Night Mail (1936) **340**
Nina's Heavenly Delights (2006) **163**
Orphans (1998) **230**
Outcast (2010) **303**
Perfect Sense (2011) **306**
The Prime of Miss Jean Brodie (1969) **165**
Ratcatcher (1999) **236**
Red Road (2006) **239**
Return to the Edge of the World (1978) **342**
Rob Roy (1995) **168**
Rob Roy: The Highland Rogue (1953) **170**
Seachd: The Inaccessible Pinnacle (2007) **172**
Seawards the Great Ships (1961) **343**
Shallow Grave (1994) **308**
Shell (2012) **242**
Small Faces (1996) **247**
Stella Does Tricks (1996) **250**
Stone of Destiny (2008) **174**
Sweet Sixteen (2002) **253**
That Sinking Feeling (1980) **310**
Trainspotting (1996) **256**
Tunes of Glory (1960) **176**
We Need to Talk About Kevin (2011) **259**
Whisky Galore! (1949) **314**
The Wicker Man (1973) **316**
Wilbur Wants to Kill Himself (2002) **261**
Wild Country (2006) **318**
Young Adam (2002) **263**